KU-567-033

Urban Design Reader

Edited by
Matthew Carmona and Steve Tiesdell

ELSEVIER

AMSTERDAM • BOSTON • HEIDELBERG • LONDON • NEW YORK • OXFORD
PARIS • SAN DIEGO • SAN FRANCISCO • SINGAPORE • SYDNEY • TOKYO
Architectural Press is an imprint of Elsevier

Architectural
Press

Architectural Press is an imprint of Elsevier
Linacre House, Jordan Hill, Oxford OX2 8DP, UK
30 Corporate Drive, Suite 400, Burlington, MA 01803, USA

First edition 2007

Copyright © 2007, Matthew Carmona and Steve Tiesdell.
Copyright of individual chapters is retained by copyright holders as detailed at the
end of each chapter. Published by Elsevier Ltd. All rights reserved

No part of this publication may be reproduced, stored in a retrieval system
or transmitted in any form or by any means electronic, mechanical, photocopying,
recording or otherwise without the prior written permission of the publisher

Permissions may be sought directly from Elsevier's Science & Technology Rights
Department in Oxford, UK: phone (+44) (0) 1865 843830; fax (+44) (0) 1865 853333;
email: permissions@elsevier.com. Alternatively you can submit your request online by
visiting the Elsevier website at http://elsevier.com/locate/permissions, and selecting
Obtaining permission to use Elsevier material

Notice
No responsibility is assumed by the publisher for any injury and/or damage to persons
or property as a matter of products liability, negligence or otherwise, or from any use
or operation of any methods, products, instructions or ideas contained in the material
herein. Because of rapid advances in the medical sciences, in particular, independent
verification of diagnoses and drug dosages should be made

British Library Cataloging in Publication Data
Urban design reader
1. City planning
I. Carmona, Matthew II. Tiesdell, Steven
711.4

Library of Congress Cataloging-in-Publication Data
A catalogue record for this book is available from the Library of Congress

ISBN-13: 978-0-7506-6531-5
ISBN-10: 0-7506-6531-9

For information on all Architectural Press publications
visit our website at www.architecturalpress.com

Typeset by Charon Tec Ltd (A Macmillan Company), Chennai, India
www.charontec.com

Printed and bound in Great Britain

07   08   09   10   11   11   10   9   8   7   6   5   4   3   2   1

Working together to grow
libraries in developing countries

www.elsevier.com | www.bookaid.org | www.sabre.org

ELSEVIER   BOOK AID
            International   Sabre Foundation

Contents

Introduction

An activity with ancient roots, but also one that has been rediscovered and reinvigorated in recent years, urban design has become a serious and significant area of academic endeavour, of public policy and of professional practice. This is reflected by the increasingly widespread recognition of its value across public and private sectors around the world. This change has been matched by increasing demand for urban design practitioners and, more generally, for urban design skills throughout the built environment and land and property professions, and by an increasing demand for urban design education at universities and in the workplace.

The new interest in urban design is as a form of – and contribution to – place-making. Carmona *et al.* (2003), for example, defined urban design as the making of places for people. More precisely and realistically, they saw it as *the process* of making *better* places for people *than would otherwise be produced*. A definition that asserted the importance of four themes – that urban design is for and about people; the significance of 'place'; that the field of opportunity for urban designers is typically constrained and bounded by economic (market) and political (regulatory) forces; and the importance of design as a process.

It is useful to acknowledge the difference between an understanding of urban design for analytical purposes (i.e. what is urban design?), by which all urban development may be considered to contribute to urban design, and a more normative understanding of urban design (i.e. what is 'good' urban design?), by which only some urban development might be considered to be urban design. Seen analytically, urban design is the process by which the urban environment comes about; seen normatively, it is – or should be – the process by which better urban environments come about. We must also be aware of the possibility and existence of implementation gaps between what urban design seeks to do and what it actually does do.

Urban design also refers to products or outcomes and to various processes. It is, for example, variously a product (the design of the created environment), interventions into a process (e.g. a land and property – or real estate – development process) and a process itself (i.e. the design process).

The notion of urban design as a process is a reoccurring theme in this book. Design is a creative, analytical and problem-solving activity through which objectives and constraints are weighed and balanced, the problem and possible solutions explored and optimal resolutions derived. The process of design should also add value to the individual component parts, so that the resulting whole is greater than the sum of the parts. In the final analysis the quality of the whole is what matters because it is this that we experience.

There are (very) few 'hard-and-fast' rules or absolutes in urban design – substantially because the process of design involves relating general (and generally desirable) principles to site and programme requirements, where the context and creative vision will always vary. Indeed there is a danger of generally desirable design principles being treated as inflexible dogma or of design being reduced to the simplistic application of a formula – practices that negate the active process of design. Design principles must always be used with the flexibility derived from a deeper understanding and appreciation of their basis, justifications and interrelations and the context to which they are to be applied. In any design process there are no perfect 'right' answers – there are only better and worse answers, the quality of which may, in turn, only be known over time.

Who then are the urban designers? A good answer is that urban designers are those who make decisions that affect the quality of the urban environment – only a (small) proportion of whom might actively claim to be urban designers. There is a continuum from 'knowing' to 'unknowing' urban designers (see Carmona *et al.*, 2003: 15–16). 'Knowing' urban designers are typically the professionals employed or retained on account of their urban design expertise (i.e. urban design practitioners). At the other end of the continuum are the 'unknowing' urban designers: those who make urban design decisions without appreciating that this is what they are doing. This is not a distinction that necessarily reflects on the quality of outcomes (i.e. the product) – the outcome of each can be 'good' or 'bad'. As Jonathan Barnett (1982: 9) has argued:

> Today's city is not an accident. Its form is usually unintentional, but it is not accidental. It is the product of decisions made for single, separate purposes, whose interrelationships and side effects have not been fully considered. The design of cities has been determined by engineers, surveyors, lawyers, and investors, each making individual, rational decisions for rational reasons.

But, without conscious recognition of the qualities and additional value of good urban design, the creation and production of urban environments often occurs by omission rather than explicit commission.

Urban design's current status is based on a large and growing body of theoretical writings that have their roots in critiques of post-1945 modernism and in the urban development of the past fifty years, and, in particular, in a set of classic texts dating from the very early 1960s from writers such as Kevin Lynch (1960), Jane Jacobs (1961) and Gordon Cullen (1961), and in another larger set dating from the late 1960s and 1970s including Ed Bacon (1967), Ian McHarg (1969), Christian Norberg-Schulz (1971), Robert Venturi *et al.* (1972), Jan Gehl (1971), Colin Rowe and Fred Koetter (1978), Christopher Alexander (Alexander *et al.*, 1977; Alexander, 1979) and William Whyte (1980). The ideas and observations of these writers and others have been debated, criticized, tested, developed and extended by a wide range of theorists, practitioners and policy makers in the period up to the current day. The resulting urban design literature is extensive and growing, and constitutes the foundation for contemporary urban design policy and practice.

An attempt to structure the urban design literature into a number of interrelated dimensions was made in our book *Public Places Urban Spaces: The dimensions of urban design*, co-authored with Tim Heath and Taner Oc (Carmona *et al.*, 2003). This book provided an exposition of the different, but intimately related, dimensions of urban design thought and practice. Synthesising and integrating ideas and theories from a wide range of sources, it derived from a comprehensive reading of existing literature and research. Taking a holistic approach, it neither focused on a limited checklist of urban design qualities nor – it was hoped – excluded important areas.

Drawing on the material that inspired the writing of *Public Places Urban Spaces*, the current book presents a selection of key texts in (substantially) their original form. While including a good range of contemporary texts/authors/figures in urban design, together with papers that are simply useful as distillations of key areas of urban design knowledge, the intention has been to produce a 'useful' reader that includes a good range of 'classic' or 'staple' texts – that is, those that are referred to again and again. In this respect, this reader presents papers from the classic urban design canon – for example, Kevin Lynch on legibility, Jane Jacobs on vitality, Gordon Cullen on townscape, and Edward Relph on meaning and sense-of-place. The reader does not seek to replace the 'classic' texts. Instead, it seeks to provide an introduction and a taste of them, while placing them in relation to each other. To see them in their 'whole' and in context, readers need to go to the original sources, something that is essential for an in-depth understanding. It is also noticeable how many of the later selections – Jarvis (1980) and Sternberg (2000), for example – refer back directly to these works.

By this means, we bring together key texts that provide foundations for the place-making view of urban design. This urban design canon has been followed by others who, for example, have argued that urban design is an important and necessary consideration in the land and property development process, either directly or indirectly – Tibbalds (1992), Rowley (1998) and Duany *et al.* (2000) – and those who have advocated urban design as a response to what are seen as the failings of contemporary development practice (e.g. Trancik, 1986; Loukaitou-Sideris, 1998). A selection of these texts has also been included.

Public Places Urban Spaces utilised a simple three-part structure:

- *The Context for Urban Design* consisting of three chapters – urban design today, urban change, the contexts for urban design.
- *The Dimensions of Urban Design* consisting of six chapters, each focusing on a particular dimension of urban design.

- *Implementing Urban Design* consisting of four chapters – the development process, the control process, the communication process and holistic urban design.

To allow easy cross-referencing between the two volumes, a simplified version of the same structure has been adopted here. This allows those readers of *Public Places Urban Spaces* seeking additional in-depth source material on a particular writer to find that material here. Similarly, readers of the present volume wishing to examine the broader context within which the ideas of a particular writer fit can turn to *Public Places Urban Spaces*.

This reader might also be viewed as a companion volume to Alexander Cuthbert's *Designing Cities, Critical Reading in Urban Design* (2003, Blackwell Publishing, Oxford). One of the first urban design readers, the selection of papers contained in *Designing Cities* was chosen to emphasise a particular paradigm – namely that urban design is best viewed as a branch of spatial political economy – and purposefully omitted many of the 'classic' urban design contributions that many scholars might expect to see. *Designing Cities* instead chose papers that are largely from outside the traditional urban design canon – Cuthbert's intention being to select articles that would help create a 'theory-of' urban design. By contrast, the present volume focuses on 'theory-in' urban design and, although emanating from the 'Making Places' tradition, is largely 'paradigm neutral'.

As well as being a companion volume to *Public Places Urban Spaces*, *Urban Design Reader* is a self-contained text in its own right, with its own internal logic and coherence. The main part of the book comprises original papers organised into eight sections. Each of the six 'dimensions' chapters from *Urban Spaces Public Places* is the subject of a section. These follow an initial group of papers dealing with definitions and understandings of urban design, and are followed by a final section dealing with implementing urban design. Each section begins with a brief introduction to the dimension and the contributions that the constituent papers make to it. The introduction contextualises the material and establishes links between constituent papers in each selection and between selections.

The papers are necessarily abridged. Shortening a paper or book chapter conceived as a whole inevitably involves tough choices. The approach taken has been to preserve the essence of the articles – that is, the substantive contribution they make to the field of knowledge. Inevitably the papers chosen attempt to contextualise their argument against other work in the same publication or elsewhere, or alternatively elucidate the argument through illustration and/or the use of case studies and examples. Where this is not key to the understanding of the central arguments in the papers, it has been omitted.

The individual papers must also be seen as contributions to a new whole – that is, to produce a coherent and reasonably comprehensive coverage of the field of urban design. It is, nonetheless, inevitable that when removed from their context the papers lose some of their meaning. It has also been necessary to select a balanced range of papers. Given the breadth of the urban design field, however, there are inevitably omissions and areas that we can only cover in passing. These include such areas as sustainability, telecommunications and other technological developments, the cultural dimensions of urbanism, gender dimensions of urban design, spatial and social segregation, and many others. Indeed, these areas could be the focus of readers in their own right. Equally others may select an entirely different group of papers to represent the place-making canon in urban design. In the final analysis, this is a personal selection and we make no claims for it beyond the fact that these are the papers which we have found most useful and stimulating in our own work. We can only hope that others will agree.

Matthew Carmona and Steve Tiesdell

Note:
References and Notes at chapter ends have been reproduced from the original sources. Some reference lists therefore include publications not cited in the present text and some reproduce discrepancies in publication dates that were evident in the original sources.

Section One

Understanding urban design

The term 'urban design' came into currency in North America in the late 1950s, replacing and superseding the more traditional, narrower and somewhat outmoded term 'civic design'. Typified by the City Beautiful Movement, the latter was associated with a highly artistic and physical (visual and spatial) approach to urban design, focusing on the siting and design of major civic buildings – city halls, opera houses, and museums – and their relationship to open spaces. Contemporary urban design is more expansive than this. It is primarily concerned with the quality of the public realm – both physical and socio-cultural – and the making (and managing) of meaningful 'places' for people to enjoy and use. More recently the quest for more sustainable urban form has become a more explicit component.

This section presents a set of six chapters exploring understandings of urban design and discussing its precise nature and purpose. Chapter 1 is **Francis Tibbalds'** 'Places matter most', from his 1992 book *Making People-Friendly Towns: Improving the public environment in towns and cities* (Longman, Harlow – now published by Spon Press). A founder of the UK-based Urban Design Group in 1978, Tibbalds' ideas and activism in the cause of urban design had been evolving throughout the 1980s. Their moment came when Tibbalds' term as president of the Royal Town Planning Institute (RTPI) in 1988–89 coincided with His Royal Highness Prince Charles publicly expressing his views about contemporary architectural – but, more implicitly, urban – design in the second half of the 1980s. The Prince subsequently offered a framework for what he saw as architectural design (although much of his framework was well within the remit of urban design). Firmly within the visual-artistic tradition, the Prince's ideas sparked an important debate. In response, Tibbalds offered a more sophisticated (and empathetically) urban design framework, comprising the following ten principles: places matter most; learn the lessons of the past; encourage the mixing of uses and activities; design on a human scale; encourage pedestrian freedom; provide access for all; build legible environments; build lasting environments; control change; and contribute to the greater whole. Each of these principles was the focus of a specific chapter in Tibbalds' book. The chapter selected here sets out what might be considered Tibbalds' 'golden rule' of urban design – 'places matter most' (i.e. that the creation of places through good design is more important than the design of the individual buildings of which they are composed).

Defining precisely what is meant by urban design is challenging (see Cowan, 2004) and many definitions based on spatial scales or disciplines are unduly limiting. In practice, little value arises from putting boundaries around urban design; it is more enriching and positive to identify, clarify and debate central beliefs and activities. This is the approach taken in Chapter 2 – **Ali Madanipour's** 'Ambiguities of urban design', originally published in the *Town Planning Review* in 1997 and subsequently a chapter in his book *Urban Design – A Socio-Spatial Enquiry* (John Wiley, London). Its principal value is its comprehensive discussion of ways of defining urban design by confronting the ambiguities about possible meanings. Madanipour identifies seven sources of ambiguity: the first three are concerned with the 'product' of urban design (i.e. urban space or the urban environment), the last three concern urban design as a 'process' and the product–process dilemma is the subject of the fourth ambiguity. Although his ambiguities are deliberately presented as oppositional and mutually exclusive, for most it is a case of 'and/both' rather than 'either/or'. Madanipour concludes that because urban design is a process through which we 'consciously shape and manage our built environments', urban designers are interested in, and engaged with, both the process and its product. In common with many commentators, Madanipour also sees contemporary urban design as a multidisciplinary field of activity rather than a discrete discipline or profession.

Chapter 3 is **Bob Jarvis's** 'Urban environments as visual art or as social settings?', originally published in the *Town Planning Review* in 1980. In this chapter, Jarvis argues that two broad traditions of urban design thought stem from different ways of appreciating design and the products of the design process – as aesthetic objects or 'displays' (i.e. for 'looking at') and as environments (i.e. for 'living in' or 'using'). This distinction is discussed in terms of a 'visual-artistic' tradition, emphasising visual form, and a 'social usage' tradition, primarily concerned with the public use and experience of urban environments. In doing so, Jarvis focuses on the 'classic' urban design canon and adds value to it by organising it into two traditions. While the social-usage understanding of urban space has continued to develop rapidly since Jarvis's article, the visual-aesthetic understanding has not. Thus, while the social-usage tradition is represented across the range of contributions in the social, perceptual, temporal, functional and morphology dimensions covered in this book, the visual-aesthetic tradition has developed little beyond Cullen and the townscape school of the 1960s (see Section Five). The exception to this is the environmental aesthetics literature and also in architectural circles, where aesthetics and expression continue to dominate much of the discourse.

Chapter 4 is **Ernest Sternberg's** 'An integrative theory of urban design', originally published in the *Journal of the American Planning Association* in 2000. Through a complex and sophisticated argument, Sternberg also provides an extremely valuable commentary on the classic urban design canon. By synthesising and extending the key content of those works, he argues that the ideas informing urban design usually coalesce around contending approaches, each associated with one or two leading writers. These principles include 'urban form' (Camillo Sitte), 'legibility' (Kevin Lynch), 'vitality' (Jane Jacobs) and 'meaning' (Christian Norberg-Schulz). Sternberg argues that, by implicitly acknowledging the 'non-commodifiability' of the human experience across property boundaries, the approaches share an intellectual foundation: '...*the view that good design seeks to reintegrate the human experience of urban form in the face of real estate markets that would treat land and buildings as discrete commodities.*' He then proposes that urban design's primary role is to reassert the 'cohesiveness of the urban experience' and identifies integrative principles by which urban environments can transcend commodification. This is a view of urban design as a process of joining-up – joining up a fragmented set of built environment professions and professionals; joining up a fragmented set of development processes; and joining up (or healing) fragmented environments (see Loukaitou-Sideris, 1996; Carmona, *et al.*, 2003: 14–15). Sternberg concludes by arguing that, without conscious concern for urban design as a process of restoring or giving qualities of coherence and continuity to individual, often inward-focused developments (i.e. ensuring that the whole is greater than the sum of the parts), the issue of overall quality will inevitably be neglected.

Chapter 5 is **Anastasia Loukaitou-Sideris and Tridib Banerjee's** 'Postmodern urban form', originally published in their 1998 book *Urban Design Downtown: Poetics and Politics of Form* (University of California Press, Berkeley). Complementing Jarvis's paper, Loukaitou-Sideris's paper highlights the changing nature of urban design practice – and, indeed, urban design generally – over the past 30–35 years through examples of plans in San Francisco and Los Angeles. This chapter reminds us that, in addition to traditions of thought and principles that spring from them, urban design involves a set of processes constituting a practice of urban design. It therefore provides a useful complement to Sternberg's contribution, reminding us that despite the 'integrative' aspirations of many theorists, the theory and practice of urban design and urban development generally in the contemporary age is often characterised by fraction, fragmentation, segregation and division.

The sixth and final chapter is **R. Varkki George's** 'A procedural explanation for contemporary urban design', originally published in the *Journal of Urban Design* in 1997. Its chief value lies in shaping (and developing) our understanding of the activity of urban designers. The chapter presents, in simple terms, a convincing argument that urban design is essentially a 'second-order' design activity (i.e. urban designers 'design' the decision-making environment of other development actors). The chapter first reviews what have been regarded in the literature and in practice as the 'tactics' used by contemporary urban designers. A case is then made for why the term *second-order design* is a good explanation for these tactics. The essence of the argument is that urban design articulates the way that the components of the urban environment are to be put together, but without itself designing those components in detail. Detailed design is the task of architects, highways engineers, landscape architects, etc. Rather than imbuing the creative task of designing urban places in the hands of a single 'all-knowing' designer, the argument assumes that it is shared among a range of actors. It also recognises that urban designers typically work within a context of multiple clients often with conflicting interests and objectives, developing as a consequence multiple solutions to a problem, rather than a single solution (see also discussions of the role of the urban designer within the development team in Section Eight).

Matthew Carmona and Steve Tiesdell

1

'Places' matter most

Francis Tibbalds
[1992]

Places matter much more than either individual buildings or vehicular traffic. Yet, all over the world, our planning endeavours seem to concentrate almost exclusively on the latter considerations. We seem to be losing the ability to stand back and look at what we are producing as a whole. Most of us can think of collections of roads and buildings that simply do not add up to anything at all. We need to stop worrying quite so much about individual buildings and other individual physical artifacts and think instead about places in their entirety. We need to forget the spaced-out buildings of the past few decades, separated from each other by highways and left-over tracts of land. These unthinking, tired solutions to development have not served us well. We must concentrate on attractive, intricate places related to the scale of people walking, not driving. We must exploit individuality, uniqueness and the differences between places. An attractive public realm is very important to a feeling of well-being or comfort. Traditionally, building craftsmanship was not just about buildings, but also spaces. This should still be the case. Collaboration between all the environmental professions will be essential to achieve this.

The inescapable reality for all of us is that people judge the activities of architects and planners, landscape architects, highway engineers and civil engineers by the quality – principally the physical quality – of what they see and experience around them. And rightly so. Because, at the end of the day, it is the *product* rather than the *process* that matters most to the users. For all manner of reasons and quite understandably, the judgement that they make is rarely a complimentary or favourable one – largely due to the legacy of several decades of Modernist planning.

There are signs of a new approach to architecture and planning – a fundamental change in approach from the days of ruthless Modernism. British architect Terry Farrell succinctly describes how in the Modernist approach the primary object was a building or some other physical artifact. It was often separated from its neighbours by large tracts of land and/or highways – the left-over public realm. Designs were open and non-urban in character. The modernists obsessively and rigorously applied concepts of the grid, simplistic hierarchies, tidiness, low densities, zoned separation, the international style, large-scale engineering, a severance with history and tradition, high technology construction and mechanization. They thought at the scale of a moving vehicle. Growth and comprehensive redevelopment were the norm. Unconstrained, green field or war-damaged sites were the ideal canvas.

The devastation that this approach has produced on the public realm can now be seen in virtually every town and city in the United Kingdom and in many other countries too. A strong rejection of this philosophy is now emerging. We are witnessing a return to the spirit of urbanism that characterized well-loved traditional towns and cities. The concern is once again for the scale of people walking, for attractive, intricate places and for complexity of uses and activities. The object has now become the public realm – the space between buildings – rather than the buildings themselves. The aim is to create urban areas with their own identities, rooted in a regional and/or historic context. The physical design of the public domain as an organic, colourful, human-scale, attractive environment is the overriding task of the urban designer.

On urban sites, then – both in town and city centers and in inner city and suburban areas – we need a proper *urban* solution, with an *urban* scale. We need a clear appreciation of the urban grain and built form – what is sometimes called the morphological context. We also need to understand fully the local architectural *typology* – related to the uses and functions of the particular buildings. New proposals – whether for a large piece of urban design or an individual building – must have a positive relationship to the existing morphology – by harmonizing with it, by adapting to it or, where there are clear reasons so to do, by contrasting with it. The important thing is to take a positive design stance not just an arbitrary one.

During the 1950s and 1960s many towns and cities around the world underwent change on an unprecedented scale in terms of built development and in terms of massive highway construction. This undoubtedly resulted in considerable commercial vitality and unique levels of accessibility for motor vehicles, but it is now fairly widely recognized that it also produced physical environments that fall a long way short of current public aspirations.

Much of the problem derives from the loss of urban scale or grain. Traditionally cities were composed of blocks of buildings with streets around them. The so-called *comprehensive redevelopment* schemes of the past twenty or thirty years have tended to destroy this familiar and successful urban form and the results have been largely unsatisfactory. They have rarely produced places which are now widely recognized as being attractive.

It is a useful exercise to compare the plan forms of towns over time. Most traditional towns and cities are compact and tightly organized with a simple block layout punctuated by hard and soft open spaces. In many places this clear structure was lost, or significantly eroded, during the middle part of the twentieth century. A combination of war damage and the desire for new roads, new shopping centres and various forms of mass housing has, in many instances, led to the loss of original street patterns.

We don't have to let this happen. As vacant sites are brought into use and obsolescent buildings are redeveloped, the opportunity must be seized to use the new buildings to create proper urban streets again, with proper frontages – to make a tight-knit urban fabric where public spaces and landscape are intended, rather than just being the left-over bits that were of no use to the architect or developer. Spaces left over after planning and development has taken place are not only visually unattractive and functionally useless: they are also awkward and expensive to maintain, with the all too frequent result that they become neglected and unkempt. There are thus functional and environmental advantages to the restoration of the street.

Of course, it is not only streets that are important. The places that make up the public realm come in many shapes, sizes and uses. They include streets, squares, public footpaths, parks and open spaces and extend, also, to riversides and seafronts. These places all belong to the wider community. It is important never to forget that they are there for their use, benefit and enjoyment. In designing and developing buildings and environments which interrelate with the public realm, it is therefore essential to ensure that this tremendous value of the public realm to the wider community is acknowledged, respected and enhanced.

One of the joys of towns and cities is their variety. Different areas have different characteristics – of activities, scale, uses and function. Some places are lively and busy. Others are quiet and secluded. There will be intricate, dense areas; open, monumental areas; soft areas; hard areas; old areas; new areas; areas of high building; areas of low building; shopping areas; commercial areas; entertainment areas; recreation areas; and so on and so on. We need to recognize this variety – to define areas of cohesive character. Often such areas will have blurred edges. They will overlap. This simply adds to the richness of the environmental character. But, great care is also required. As places, precincts or areas of special character are recognized, defined, created or developed, it is important to ensure that they are real and not contrived. It will not be an asset to the town or city if they take on a fake-believe or stage-set quality. Nor should such areas be allowed to develop simply as single-use enclaves.

All too often towns and cities simply continually re-adapt to accommodating more and more traffic and bigger and bigger buildings. What is desperately needed is a new approach to producing and looking after good urban spaces. We have actually got to address the re-structuring of our urban areas, over possibly quite long time scales, to reflect a new set of priorities in which the needs of people – as pedestrians, cyclists, the young, the old and the infirm, as well as the able-bodied – take precedence over the voracious demands of traffic and developers. The current fragmentation of urban areas in many ways mirrors the fragmentation and separation of the professions who are supposed to be looking after them – urban planners, traffic engineers, landscape architects, land surveyors and architects in particular.

Greater multi-professional collaboration would, I am convinced, produce better, more coherent places, because no one profession has all the answers to the complex task of designing livable cities.

Public places within a town belong to the people of that town – they do not belong to developers or investors, the police or traffic wardens. Their nature will be influenced by their scale, shape and size; the ways in which they are related one to another; the uses and activities which they contain, and the way in which traffic of all kinds is handled. The proper civilized use of places – streets, squares, alleys, promenades and so on – can be achieved visually, functionally and psychologically, through sensitive and imaginative design. If, for example, motorists feel like guests in a predominantly pedestrian area, hopefully they will behave like guests. Is this not infinitely to be preferred to a plethora of street signs and prohibitions backed up by tedious byelaws and penalties?

The same is true of buildings. New buildings are also guests in the existing urban environment and need to show due deference to their host and their companions. This is not to invite false modesty; nor is it to say that that there shouldn't be room for the occasional live wire or prima donna. What architects and clients need to accept, however, is that the greatest contribution that they can make to the built environment of the town or city is to construct good, backcloth buildings.

The challenge is clearly very great – finding ways of promoting the renaissance of the public realm in our towns and cities. But it is a potentially very rewarding and enjoyable one. It demands a new set of priorities in which, basically, *places* take precedence over buildings and traffic. This will be hard for the individual players to accept – be they architects, engineers or developers – if they maintain their professional separations. The more they learn to collaborate – to try to meet agreed, common objectives for the urban environment – the easier and more productive the process will become.

In the hope that it will be useful to readers, this chapter concludes with a short list of recommendations, related to the theme of the chapter, which can be used as a checklist by practitioners.

Recommendations/action checklist

1. The first priority is to agree what sort of public realm is appropriate in any particular area and then to agree the buildings, development and circulation system which are appropriate to it. Usually this is done the other way round, with devastating results for the urban fabric.
2. Places need to offer variety to their users. They need to be unique and different from one another – each rooted in their own particular historical, geographical, physical or cultural context.
3. In most instances, individual buildings will be subservient to the needs and the character of the place as a whole. If every building screams for individual attention, the result is likely to be discordant chaos. A few buildings can, quite legitimately, be soloists, but the majority need simply to be sound, reliable members of the chorus.
4. Many town centres are small enough to be considered as single places. In the larger towns and the central areas of cities, over time, areas of different character are probably discernible. These should be defined and developed, providing they are for real, rather than artificial bits of make-believe or urban theatre that will, in the long run, devalue reality.
5. Try not to view the organization or reorganization of towns and cities purely from the rather exclusive points of view of the motorist or the developer. It is of greater importance to consider the needs and aspirations of people as a whole – with priority being given to pedestrians, children and old people. This simple change or widening of priorities could, by itself, transform our urban environment and lifestyle.

Source and copyright

This chapter was published in its original form as:

Tibbalds, F. (1992), 'Places Matter Most', in Tibbalds, F. (1992), *Making People-Friendly Towns: Improving the public environment in towns and cities*, Longman, Harlow, 1–17.

Published by Taylor and Francis Group, an Academic Division of T&F Informa plc.

2

Ambiguities of urban design

Ali Madanipour
[1997]

Despite its frequent appearance in educational and professional literature, urban design is still an ambiguous term, used differently by different groups in different circumstances. Yet the growing attention to the subject and the rising number of academics and professionals who are engaged in urban design have brought to the surface a pressing need for a clearer definition. In this paper I will start by analysing those aspects of urban design which have caused such ambiguity and then look for a definition that addresses these uncertainties.

Urban design is a far from clear area of activity. Signs of the need for a clear definition of urban design can be seen in a variety of sources. The adequacy of the existing definitions is still in doubt, as evident in a recent conference on research and teaching in urban design (Billingham, 1995). This indicates why the search to find a satisfactory definition of urban design continues (Kindsvatter and von Grossmann, 1994; Rowley, 1994; Department of the Environment, 1995). A brief look at this search, however, shows how it is still at an early stage. An example is a recent attempt which, after reviewing a number of definitions of urban design, concludes that finding 'a short, clear definition . . . simply is not possible' (Rowley, 1994, 195). Instead, it was suggested we should focus on the substance, motives, methods and roles of urban design.

Do we need a short, clear definition for urban design? There are many ambiguities about some disciplines and professions as they inevitably overlap with each other. Controversy and never-ending discussions about what constitutes architecture, as distinct from buildings, can be taken as one example. It might be said that ambiguity offers a wider scope for innovation and development; once we have clearly defined

a subject we have denied it some flexibility. But how can we claim to be seriously engaged in urban design if we are not even able to define it? What we need is to remember to separate complexity from ambiguity. In our search for the meaning of urban design, we should be able to address complexity, but we should also do our best to clarify ambiguities.

We can see these ambiguities in a number of previous attempts to find a definition for urban design. For example, we can examine the list of definitions collected by the late Francis Tibbalds, a past president of the Royal Town Planning Institute and a passionate supporter of urban design (Tibbalds, 1988). These show a puzzling variety of views on urban design, including 'lots of architecture'; 'spaces between buildings'; 'a thoughtful municipal policy'; 'everything that you can see out of the window'; or 'the coming together of business, government, planning, and design' (Tibbalds, 1988, 12). The more plausible definitions include 'the interface between architecture, town planning, and related professions'; 'the three dimensional design of places for people . . . and their subsequent care and management'; 'a vital bridge, giving structure and reality to two dimensional master plans and abstract planning briefs, before detailed architectural or engineering design can take place'; 'the design of the built-up area at the local scale, including the grouping of buildings for different use, the movement systems and services associated with them, and the spaces and urban landscape between them'; and 'the creative activity by which the form and character of the urban environment at the local scale may be devised' (Tibbalds, 1988, 12). Here, as in other attempts to define urban design (Shirvani, 1985), we see a variety of foci: some are dealing with the domains of urban design, especially with its involvement with the physical fabric of the city; others have focused on its scale, its points of departure from, or congruence with, planning and architecture, its political and management aspects, or its place in the planning process.

To arrive at a definition for urban design, we will need to take into account these various attempts and to identify the elements which create confusion and ambiguity. We could be then on our way to a clearer conception of what urban design is about. In its search for a definition of urban design, this paper relies on three sources of information. First, the practitioners' approach to urban design: I have collected information from the British firms specialising in urban design, asking them to send examples of their work and to explain their approach to urban design. Second, the educators' approach: I have collected the brochures and documents from British and American universities in which urban design is taught as a postgraduate degree programme. Third, the published discussions on urban design, which have been produced by both professionals and academics. An analysis of these sets of information shows the extent of ambiguity in the usage of the term urban design and its application, as well as showing ways of overcoming these ambiguities. By reviewing these documents, I have come to identify seven areas of confusion and ambiguity:

1. the scale of urban fabric which urban design addresses;
2. the visual or the spatial emphases of urban design;
3. the spatial or the social emphases of urban design;
4. the relationship between process and product in the city design;
5. the relationship between different professionals and their activities;
6. the public or the private sector affiliation of urban design; and
7. the design as an objective-rational or an expressive-subjective process.

An examination of these arenas, I argue, will illuminate the range of issues and tensions within urban design and will show how a way can be sought to clarify the definition of urban design and its roles and areas of involvement. As with any such attempts, the aim here is to find some patterns in a complex reality. As my intention is to confront areas of ambiguity, I have presented my argument along a list of dualities. This, however, should not be taken as an attempt to simplify the complexities of urban design. I have used dualities merely for analytical clarity in the context of ambiguity. The duality often represents the two ends

of a spectrum, with the actual circumstances located somewhere in between.

The paper starts by addressing the ambiguities about the product of urban design, urban space, discussing the question of scale, visual, spatial, and social concerns. This leads to an analysis of the relationship between process and product, which is a central, overarching area of ambiguity. This will be a point of connection to the discussions of urban design as a process, which includes the professional activities of urban designers and their affiliations. A wider debate about the nature and scope of the urban design process will take us to the paper's conclusion, which offers a definition of urban design.

Macro- or micro-scale urban design?

A main area of confusion is in the scale of urban fabric in which urban design is engaged. Definitions of urban design refer both to the design of cities and settlements as a whole and to the design of some parts of urban areas. The range of issues and considerations addressed at these two macro- and micro-scales of urban design, however, are very different from each other. Whereas the design of cities and settlements has focused on the broad issues of organisation of space and functions, micro-urban design has concentrated on the public face of architecture, on public space in parts of the cities, and more detailed considerations of design at that scale. When observed simultaneously, as happens in the definitions of urban design, they could create a large degree of ambiguity.

Such ambiguity can be seen in a comparison between two sets of definitions. Francis Tibbalds's preferred definition is the one which describes urban design as 'the physical design of public realm' (Tibbalds, 1988, 12). The term public realm often refers to the space in the city which is not private, the space outside the private realm of buildings, the space between the buildings. But does this lead to a lack of attention to the private space which makes up the bulk of every city's space? If 'urban' is merely the public parts of the city, what should we call the totality of urban space with its both public and private dimensions? How do we compare this micro-scale urban design with Kevin Lynch's broader definitions? In one attempt he defined urban design as dealing with 'the form of possible urban environments' (Lynch, 1984). He offered an even broader definition elsewhere (Lynch, 1981, 290), as 'the art of creating possibilities for the use, management, and form of settlements or their significant parts'.

The latter is a definition of urban design which is very close to city planning, albeit with a particular interest in the physical fabric and its form. If we compare this with the Royal Town Planning Institute's definition of planning as being involved in the 'management of change in the built and natural environments' (Royal Town Planning Institute, 1991, 1), the similarity becomes evident. On the other side of the spectrum, however, where urban design is seen as designing small urban places, it becomes close to the aesthetic and spatial concerns of art and architecture.

The large and small scales of engagement are rooted in much deeper debates about the nature and concept of space. It was partly reflected in the modernist–postmodernist confrontations. The modernists concentrated on the design of an abstract but integrated space. The postmodern reaction to such abstraction was an attention to smaller scale urban places and their meaning. This shift of attention is reflecting a broad range of shifts and transformations in political, economic, and cultural circumstances of the time. Economically, there has been a reduction in the resources which could be spent on cities as a whole, leading to policies and projects which concentrate on some parts of the city. Culturally, there have been strong reactions to the blanket treatment which the comprehensive planning and large-scale urban development have imposed on individual and group differences. It is in relation to these fundamental changes that macro-urban design has been largely abandoned in areas confronting economic decline. Yet at the same time, where growth pressure has been on the rise, such as in the sunbelt cities of the United States and in the fast developing economies and their rapidly expanding cities, macro-urban design has remained a pressing need.

One solution is to acknowledge this divide and to maintain that there are two different types of urban design: a macro-urban design and a micro-urban design, with different concerns and foci. This division could offer an opportunity to develop specialisms in dealing with urban fabric and would lead to a deeper understanding of the processes and products involved at each level. Yet the two levels have so much in common and are so interrelated that we may see them as belonging to the same process of designing the urban space.

The degree of overlap and commonality between the two scales of urban design, could be convincingly treated within the same definition, to see urban design as 'an interdisciplinary approach to designing our built environment' (Vernez-Moudon, 1992, 331). By adopting a broad definition, we will have acknowledged the similarities and differences between the shaping of urban space and urban place making as two parts of the same process.

As urban design deals with all scales of urban space, it has caused ambiguity about its role and areas of involvement. Nevertheless, what links these different scales of involvement is the central feature that they all collectively make up the urban space and urban design is the activity which shapes the urban space. In this sense, it might be broken into different arenas in which different designers could concentrate. The timescale and issues involved in master planning for new settlements are inevitably different from those involved in details of street design.

It should be argued that an integrated concept of space is needed, one in which an open interpretation of place is adopted. Following this line of argument, we should stress that, although a degree of specialisation through the separation in scale of engagement can be useful, the nature of both processes should be seen as closely interrelated. Only in this way can we avoid a further divide in the scope of those dealing with urban space. To confront the ambiguity about scale, therefore, we must conclude that urban design deals with urban space at all its scales.

Urban design as visual or as spatial management?

Another source of ambiguity is the perception of urban design as dealing with visual qualities of the urban environment, which contradicts a broader view of urban design as addressing the organisation of urban space. This may be the main source of confusion about, and the main area of criticism against, urban design by its opponents, at least in Britain. To confront this confusion, we need to address two tendencies: one which sees urban design as an exercise in producing 'nice' images, and the other which sees urban design as only attending the aesthetics of the urban environment.

Urban design as nice images

At a recent conference on town centre management, Peter Hall asked for the traditional idea of urban design to be abandoned, 'The concept of urban design should not be taken in its old-fashioned sense—producing nice drawings to pin on the wall' (Hirst, 1995, 6). But why, we may wonder, should urban design be associated only with drawings and not with realities?

Attention to the social and economic problems of cities has often sidelined design activities as irrelevant, or at best as unaffordable luxuries. In the middle of economic decline, it was argued there was no need for design, as associated with new developments, at a time when no development was in sight.

For a project to be implemented, there may be several designs and designers involved, each producing drawings to communicate their ideas. These ideas, however, may never be implemented, as the money may run out or the decisions be changed. As they are about cities, and cities take a long time to evolve and change, these designs may be implemented but in a very long period of time, with inevitable changes and adjustments to take account of a changing political and economic context. But the abundance of beautiful images, which are produced without taking into account the mechanisms of implementation and/or which may lead to nowhere, especially at the time of economic difficulty, has a powerful impact on non-designers, who see design as merely images rather than ideas for spatial transformation. Even if they see these as ideas, the element of innovation and 'futurism' inherent in design may convince the viewers of the design's irrelevance to reality and its constraints.

This view of design, as an elitist, artistic enterprise which has no relationship to the real, daily problems of large sections of urban societies, has led to the reduction of urban design to a visual activity. This confusion has been especially strengthened by the way design communicates through visual, rather than verbal, means. Furthermore, designers' understanding of the social and economic issues of cities has not always been their major strong point.

The way out of this confusion is to realise that design is an activity proposing ideas for spatial transformation. If it communicates more through visual rather than verbal means, its content should not be equated with its means. In design, as in other forms of communication, form and content are very closely interrelated. But confusing the form and means of communication with the content of communication is an avoidable mistake. For example, can we mistake urban policy for just nice words?

Urban design as aesthetics of urban environment

This is a more profound problem. To see urban design as dealing with the visual rather than spatial aspects of the environment is a widespread tendency. This can be an understandable mistake, as when we want to understand space our first, and the most important,

encounter is a visual experience. We first see the objects in front of us and then begin to understand how they relate to each other. It is true that vision is the major channel through which we experience space. It is also true, as Porteous (1996, 33) stresses, that other senses make a major contribution to our spatial understanding. If our understanding is limited to a visual understanding, we only concentrate on shapes. If, however, we go beyond appearances, we start a spatial understanding, a three-dimensional experience. We can enter this space, rather than just seeing it. The same applies to the design of spaces. We do not create mere appearances but spaces which we can use for different purposes.

An example of treating urban design as a visual concern is Edward Relph who, following Barnett (1982), sees urban design as attending to the visual qualities of urban environments. For him, urban design focuses on 'the coherence of townscape, including heritage districts, the relationship between buildings both old and new, the forms of spaces, and small-scale improvements to streets' (Relph, 1987, 229). Another example is the policy guidance given to the planners on design in the planning process (Department of the Environment, 1992), which appears to treat design as mainly dealing with the appearance of the built environment.

The longstanding tradition of 'picturesque' in Britain, which pays special attention to the visual qualities of the environment, may be seen as a fundamental drive in this case. Even at the height of modernism, which promoted a more utilitarian aesthetics, picturesque tradition was strong in Britain, as exemplified by the postwar resentment against modernism and the name it was given in Britain, 'brutalism'.

The tendency to equate urban design with townscape management, however, also draws upon another major trend in the past two decades, what Boyer (1990) calls the return of aesthetics to city planning. This process, she argues, is part of the commodification of culture, through which 'eventually even city space and architectural forms become consumer items or packaged environments that support and promote the circulation of goods' (Boyer, 1990, 101). The return of capital to the city centres as the real estate investment is what lies behind the creation of specially designed environments and spectacles, leading to aestheticisation of everyday life.

Visual improvement of the cities has been used to market cities as a whole, as increasingly cities have to compete in the global markets to attract investment. The investment may be made by companies searching for better returns on their investment and a better quality of life for their employees. Investment may also be made by the employees and by middle classes returning to the cities looking for new lifestyles. As urban design emerged in the 1980s along these trends of urban marketing and middle class colonisation of parts of the cities, it has generated a critical reaction, reducing it to a merely aesthetic enterprise. Commentators have seen it as a type of new packaging for urban environment, hence its visual emphasis.

There are two mistakes that can be corrected. The first is that urban design is not merely dealing with visual qualities of the urban environment. The way out of this confusion is to realise that visual qualities are but one element among the spatial qualities of the built environment. To separate and emphasise the visual qualities of urban space is to ignore the major role of design as the generator of ideas for spatial change. The second correction is that urban design as spatial management is a tool. If it has been used to maximise investment return and exchange value, it is not the tool that should be blamed. This tool can be equally used to maximise use value, to be at the service of all citizens rather than only some sections of the urban society. In this case, I would suggest, the terms innovative, rather than fashionable, and spatial, rather than visual, can be used to define urban design.

Whatever the role of urban designers in this process, the aesthetic, visual qualities of the urban environment and the organisation of urban space are both qualities which are addressed by urban design, both dimensions of urban space and reflecting the circumstances of the people who produce and use it. As Harvey (1989, 66–67) puts it, 'How a city looks and how its spaces are organised forms a material base upon which a range of possible sensations and social practices can be thought about, evaluated, and achieved'. It will be a limited view to see urban design as dealing only with one of these aspects, as has been predominant in the 1980s, or to see it outside the social practices of which it is a part.

Urban design as social or as spatial management?

We argued that urban design deals with spatial, rather than merely visual aspects of the urban environment. But do we mean by this that there is no social dimension involved? Do we mean that urban design is all about transforming spatial arrangements and not dealing with aspects of use and management of those environments? Are there not more deeply seated social and cultural relations between society and space

that urban design addresses? Social and spatial are intertwined in our understanding of urban space (Madanipour, 1996a). The same applies to the transformation of urban space. When we are engaged in shaping the urban space, we are inevitably dealing with its social content.

The modernist design had the ambition of changing societies through space. This was a mechanistic view of how society and space are interrelated, which became known as environmental determinism and social engineering. This view is now widely discarded. But what is increasingly finding acceptance by social sciences as well as spatial arts and sciences, is that there is a strong interaction between space and the social processes.

There are, however, commentators who see urban design as merely spatial involvement without a social dimension. This is particularly the case when the visual element of urban design work is emphasised. What needs to be argued here is that spatial transformation will be both caused by and causing social change. This may happen at a variety of scales and degrees of impact. The correlation, however, is inevitable. This is especially felt when aspects of urban design such as the management of urban environments or change in land use are dealt with. More broadly, the social and psychological significance of the built environment is where the connection between the two can be observed.

The way society and space are interrelated is a main concern of urban design education. Policy makers have also shown interest in broadening the scope of urban design. After stating that a 'single common definition of urban design' is not available, the Department of the Environment's (1995) urban design campaign offers a definition which addresses several relationships

> [B]etween buildings and the streets, squares, parks and other open spaces which make up the public domain; the relationship of one part of a village, town or city with other parts; and the interplay between our evolving environment of buildings and the values, expectations and resources of people: in short, the complex interrelationship between all the various elements of built and unbuilt space, and those responsible for them. (Department of the Environment, 1995, 2)

Urban design therefore can be seen as the socio-spatial management of the urban environment using both visual and verbal means of communication and engaging in a variety of scales of urban socio-spatial phenomena. One aspect of the relationship between social and spatial dimensions of urban design has been formulated as the relationship between process and product.

Process or product?

The sources of ambiguity between the macro- or micro-scale of urban design and between urban design as visual or spatial management refer to urban design as dealing with its product, the urban space. This leads us to a fundamental source of potential confusion in defining urban design: whether the term refers to a process or a product. Architects have historically been interested in the product of their design and not in the administrative and urban development processes through which designs are implemented. On the other hand, planners have shifted from an interest in the physical fabric of the city to the policies and procedures of change in the environment (Dagenhart and Sawicki, 1992). As urban design stands between architecture and planning, it relates to the paradigms of both, which can create overlaps and reduce clarity of scope. Depending on the commentators' standpoint, they might have a tendency to one or the other of these paradigms, preferring to see urban design as only a product or a process. Yet urban design, as many urban designers have stressed, refers to both a process and a product 'it is defined by what urban designers do as much as it is by what they produce' (Kindsvatter and von Grossmann, 1994, 9).

But how can we say that urban design is both a process and a product? Surely, urban design is not a product, if by product we mean parts of urban space, as this statement appears to mean. Urban design is a process, whose product at the first instance is a set of ideas, policies, and images. Once implemented, they form a new or an altered part of urban space. Urban design, therefore, is a process that is interested in its product, the built environment. A more precise way of putting it may be: urban design is a process which deals with shaping urban space, and as such it is interested in both the process of this shaping and the spaces it helps shape.

In a sense this two-sided nature is reflected in the two component parts of the term, 'urban' and 'design', the former referring to the product and the latter to the process. The ambiguity of the scales of urban design refers to a more fundamental question: what is urban? What parts of the ever-increasing urban areas are addressed by urban design? The dominant trend in Britain seems to address the city

centres as the main urban space (Worpole, 1992), leaving the rest of the cities as mere peripheries where the lower densities of population and activities appear to make them less interesting.

In Britain, there has been a decline in large-scale urban redevelopment or development of new settlements. This explains, to a large degree, why urban design is generally concentrated on the micro-scale of urban space, preoccupied with place making. Large-scale urban development, however, is a major trend in many cities of the developing world, where population growth and higher densities encourage the rise of land prices and press for radical change (Madanipour, 1997, forthcoming). In the United States, where some areas have experienced phenomenal growth pressures, large-scale urban development, as reflected in the 'New Urbanism' movement, has also been a main feature. Parallel with the predominance of retailing in the city centres in Britain and in the national economy as a whole, urban design becomes pressed to concentrate on creating and supporting environments in which shopping, or consumption in general, is the main attraction to pull the crowds, leaving aside other uses and places as of secondary importance. The drive for regeneration of decayed inner-areas of the cities has also led to such concentration on the city centres, taking the attention away from the urban region as an integrated space.

The urban space, however, is more than the city centre. It includes the suburbs, where large numbers of the urban population live. As these suburbs have matured and new nuclei of services and employment have developed on the outskirts of the cities, any engagement with the city which disregards the suburbs is turning a blind eye to a substantial portion of urban space (Gottdiener, 1986). In the case of the larger cities in Britain, multinucleated urban regions have evolved either through development of new shopping and office centres in the suburbs, or have grown by engulfing the older, smaller settlements into the urban whole. The urban space with which design is engaged is therefore the space of an urban region, including the centre and its peripheries. Restricting urban design to the city centres would deprive urban design of a broader perspective, and the urban space from a potentially powerful tool for its transformation.

As for the definition of design, we come across a fairly wide range of meanings. For example, the dictionary definitions of the word refer separately to a sequence of distinguishable moments in a process: from when there is only an intention, to when the ideas are conceived in mind, to when preliminary sketches are prepared, to when they are formulated as a set of instructions for making something which leaves the details to be worked out, and to making plans and drawings necessary for the construction of a building which the workers have to follow (*Oxford English Dictionary; Longmans English Larousse*). Each of these definitions is given as an independent definition for design. And yet if we put them all together, they still mean design, or rather the design process.

Nevertheless, these definitions fail to inform us of all the moments in the sequence of the design process or of the process as a whole. On the other hand, the attempts which have been made to provide a more comprehensive definition of design have found an entirely different focus. For example, in his entry for the *Encyclopaedia Britannica*, Kevin Lynch (1984) offered a definition of design as 'the imaginative creation of possible form intended to achieve some human purpose: social, economic, aesthetic, or technical'. Elsewhere, he elaborates this definition of design as 'the playful creation and strict evaluation of the possible forms of something, including how it is to be made' (Lynch, 1981, 290). Here the focus is on an action, the creation of possible form, which is not mentioned in our dictionary definitions, with a reference to its mode, mechanisms, and areas of concern.

The relationship between process and product goes beyond this formal analysis, as they are closely interwined. To understand urban space, it should be argued, following Henri Lefebvre (1991), that we will need to look at the processes which produce the space. Urban design is a major component part of these processes and it is concerned with cities and with how to shape and manage them. However, there are many professionals who are involved in this process of shaping. Where do urban designers stand?

Professional divide

A major area of ambiguity seems to be where we expect a practical clarity to reign. Where should we look for definitions of urban design and find out what urban designers do?

The Urban Design Group is the main forum dealing with the subject in Britain, largely bringing together urban design professionals. To produce a manifesto for urban design, initiated in 1986, the Group proposed a seven-point agenda which was aimed at 'making explicit what urban designers do, or should do' (Billingham, 1994, 38). Urban design, as outlined in this agenda, is an interdisciplinary activity, occupying 'the central ground between the recognised environmental professionals'. It is 'concerned with the careful stewardship of the resources of the built environment' and with 'helping the users and not only the producers of the urban environment'. Therefore they 'must understand and interpret community needs and aspirations', as well as 'understanding and using political and financial processes'. In short, urban designers operate 'within the procedures of urban development to achieve community objectives'. Following this principle, 'Urban design education and research must be concerned with the dynamics of change in the urban environment and how it can be adapted to be responsive to the ways in which people's lives are lived' (Billingham, 1994, 34). A list of 'an irreducible minimum' of the criteria for the form of the 'good city' concludes the agenda (Billingham, 1994, 35). These criteria, derived from a variety of sources, include attention to variety, access, security and comfort, opportunity for personalisation, and clarity.

But are these concerns exclusive to urban designers? Can other environmental disciplines and professions not claim to have similar concerns? The first point in the Urban Design Group's agenda, however, explains more:

> Urban design has emerged as a discipline, primarily because it is able to consider the relationships between the physical form and function of adjacent sites, unlike the Architect who is constrained by site boundaries and client intentions and the Planner who has been reluctant to address issues appertaining to the physical design agenda. (Billingham, 1994, 34)

Does this principle imply that urban design is physical design for more than a site, for a group of adjacent sites? After all, interest in physical design was the first principal objective of the Urban Design Group as published in its first issue of *Urban Design Group News* in July 1979. The Group was being established, 'To provide a forum for those who believe that planning should be more concerned with improvement of the design of the physical environment and the quality of places and to encourage all the professions to combine to this end' (Linden and Billingham, 1994, 30).

A decade later in February 1995, the agenda was updated by the Group in a one-day conference. The new text is a marked improvement on the previous agenda. It has remained, however, 'an amalgam of the views expressed at the day's discussion' (Billingham, 1996, 38). It is rather loosely organised under the headings Objectives, Guiding Principles, Approaches, and Processes, the contents of which at times overlap. The strength of the agenda lies in its concern for the quality of places, as well as promoting creative thinking in dealing with cities. The Group shows continuity in its postmodernist concern for context, as it identifies itself as demonstrating 'practical alternatives to the type of design that pays no regard to context, and decision making which is driven by bureaucracy' (Billingham, 1996, 38). This critical edge, however, is not directed towards the economics of the urban development process, in which the emphasis on 'investment return' threatens the quality of environment. The agenda rightly stresses the need for accessibility, sustainability, and empowerment. As may be expected from a brief compilation, it falls short of spelling out how these ideas can be operationalised in the context of powerful processes which work against them. As such the agenda offers some ideals, which can influence and inspire practice. What needs to be done, however, is to work out the institutional processes which would enable the realisation of these ideals.

One of the components of such institutional processes, which the Urban Design Group also points out, is promoting a collaboration between various disciplines involved in shaping places. It is clear after all that urban design is an interdisciplinary activity. If professionals from different disciplines of the built, natural, and social environments work together in teams, they create an urban design process. Similarly, if urban space is to be shaped and managed by any professional, there will be a need for multi-disciplinary concerns and awareness. The key is to go beyond the narrow boundaries of professions and disciplines and approach urban space from an interdisciplinary, socio-spatial perspective.

A public or private sector activity?

Another area of confusion, which on the surface is in close connection with professional divides, is about the affiliation of urban design with the public or private sector. The question is: Which camp does it belong to? Who performs it? Who does it serve? Is it mainly performed by, or serving, the private developer or the city council? The confusion can therefore extend to urban design's political role, which potentially could be a conflicting duality.

If urban design is seen as visual management of the city centres only to maximise returns on private sector investment, then it is intended to serve a minority interest. Some criticisms of urban regeneration

undertakings in Britain have taken this view and have therefore associated urban design with the interests of private companies. As visual management is then seen as a luxury when more basic needs of health, education, and housing are at stake, urban design has been seen as reactionary or at best irrelevant. If, however, urban design is practised by the public sector, it is held to be at the service of the public at large, contributing to the improvement of the quality of the urban environment. The question is which side do we identify urban design with?

We may confront this ambiguity by stating that as a technical, social, and aesthetic process, urban design can be practised by any agency large enough to initiate or deal with urban development projects. Furthermore, with the increasing role of public–private partnerships in urban development and regeneration, it may be difficult to locate the camp to which urban design belongs. This can be illuminated in a discussion of the relationship between use value and exchange value in urban space production, leading to the notion that urban design is not necessarily bound to the public or private sectors. Each of these sectors may be engaged in urban design and, depending on who performs it, it may have different roles and serve different interests. Performed by whichever camp, urban design is the process which shapes and manages the urban space. Such urban space will inevitably reflect the values and aspirations of those who produced it.

Objective-rational or subjective-irrational?

We have looked at ambiguities about the aspects of the product with which urban design deals. We have come across ambiguities about its role as a professional activity and its association with different sectors of the political economy. We also need to be aware of ambiguities about the nature of the process. We need to know what kind of process urban design is. Is urban design objective and rational, or subjective and even irrational? This is partly referring to the confusions about how we understand space; between visual, spatial or social emphases. For those who see urban design as merely the visual management of the city, it can become mainly an aesthetic-expressive and, therefore, subjective process. On the other hand, for those who see urban design as dealing with spatial transformation and its social significance, urban design finds a more objective emphasis. There are obvious limits to each of these views, as we have witnessed in the process of urban change. To find a way out of this ambiguity, we need to see whether design is a rational process and if so, how? It is a broad understanding of rationality that will show us a way out of such narrow dualism.

René Descartes, who was 'the greatest rationalist ever' (Gellner, 1992, 1), had a firm belief in design as a rational endeavour. He mistrusted 'custom and example', and hence he saw the gradual growth of cities as a representation of the irrational custom and example. His rationalist principle was that, 'we ought never to allow ourselves to be persuaded of the truth of anything unless on the evidence of our reason' (Gellner, 1992, 1). For him, the best buildings, legal systems and opinions were those designed by a single author. On this basis, he held that, 'ancient cities . . . are usually but ill laid out compared with the regularly constructed towns which a professional architect has freely planned on an open plain' (quoted in Gellner, 1992, 4). This view of design as a rational undertaking was based on a classicist, individualist, and bourgeois notion of reason and rationality, which came under attack by later generations of empiricists and idealists. This rationalist view of design came to dominate the modernist thinking. Modernists promoted design as a rational process based on functionalism. However, this narrow definition of rationality has been criticised, as it was not paying enough attention to other dimensions of design and its impact on everyday lives. In Henri Lefebvre's (1991) terms, it was promoting an 'abstract space', and what was needed was a 'differential space' which accounts for diversity and everyday experiences.

A contemporary and more complex notion of rationality is offered by Jurgen Habermas's (1984) models of action and rationality. In his communicative action theory, Habermas attempts to broaden the scope of rationality by addressing, simultaneously, all three objective, social, and subjective dimensions of the social action. Rather than interpreting rationality as merely instrumental rationality, the social and psychological concerns of social actors are also brought into a definition of rational action. Despite the rigidities and limitations of this approach (Honneth, 1991), we may use these three moments of rationality to analyse design. The notions of action and rationality provide us with a tool to have insight into the dynamics of each action in the series of actions which constitute the urban design process. They focus on how individuals relate to their objective, subjective, and social contexts. Drawing upon the communicative action theory, we can analyse the urban design process as a combination of three distinctive

and yet interwoven threads: the stage when designers are interacting with the objective world through the application of science and technology; the stage when designers are involved with other individuals and institutions constituting their social setting which is somehow involved in the process; and the stage when designers are interacting with their own subjective world of ideas and images. Depending on the circumstances, however, these analytically distinctive stages are usually closely interlinked to constitute a single, complex process.

Urban design as a technical process

We can look at urban design as a purely technical process, in which specific skills from town planning, architecture, and engineering, among others, are employed to utilise resources in the production and management of space. Designers often need to ensure an effective use of the rules and resources in the preparation and implementation of the design. In doing so, a high level of technical competence is required: from understanding of the rules and regulations with which the design process deals, to analysing the circumstantial conditions, to developing alternative approaches, and to formulating a final solution for a specific task.

In the majority of design and development projects, the technical approach has been dominant. Entirely new settlements would be built as physical objects which are the product of a technical process. Especially in the periods of rapid economic expansion, the technical approach tends to predominate. The whole project of the modern movement in architecture was based on technological necessity, as the built environment was required to be made fit for the machine age.

The main concern in urban design has often been the transformation of physical space. In this technical process, an instrumental rationality is used to evaluate each segment of the action against its aims and context. Any action which is not corresponding to functional expectation, technological capability, or financial capacity has been regarded as irrational. Designers rely on knowledge and skills of their own and of other related professionals dealing with the built environment to utilise the available resources.

But there are limits to the rationality that can be employed. Any change in one of the structures, which may be largely out of the agency's influence, would turn the rationality of a decision into an irrationality. The introduction of a new technology, for example, would make a solution obsolete and in need of revision, whereas at the time of decision making, it would have been thoroughly rational. Other examples include changes in administrative organisations, a change in interest rate or a crisis of over-production can all render what looked rational into irrational.

Urban design as a social process

We can also look at the urban design process as a social process due to the involvement of a large number of actors with various roles and interests who interact in different stages of the process. Design is often prepared by a group of designers interacting with other professionals: the agencies who control resources and rules such as landowners, financiers, planning authorities and politicians. The interaction continues with the parties involved in the implementation phase, with the users of the space, and with those who would be affected by it.

According to instrumental rationality, the process would only be rational if it ends in the purpose that was expected from it. As distinct from that, the form of rationality used here is one which aims at consensus between the players involved, and is in general making reference to norms and values shared by them as a point of departure. However, the patterns of rationality in the process and its outcome are open to distortion due to the power relations involved. Any disruption in this dialogue would either end in the break up of the process or to a new level of practical discourse where consensus is sought. If, however, all levels of interaction are not open to rational discourse, then the distortions might put any potential consensus at risk.

An example of the absence of consensus between the players which has led to disastrous results is the postwar planning policy and implementation of slum clearance without consulting the communities. The modernist rejection of context can be seen as the manifestation of instrumental action, which has been a major feature of the scientific and technological age. On the other hand, its opponent, contextualism, can be seen as focusing on the social interaction, which employs norm-based rationality.

It can be argued that arriving at a consensus would not necessarily guarantee the rationality of the action. It seems that consensus in technical-rational action is more readily available since the point of departure in any discourse will be existing technology and scientific knowledge, even though scientific knowledge might be contestable or alternative technologies, at comparable costs, be available for any specific task.

Since the product of urban design is the manifestation of a set of policies or interests as solidified in physical space or its management, it becomes evident how the role of urban designers can be important. They would act as intermediary players in a complex interactive process. Their ability to convince others through all forms of presentation will have strong impacts on the process as a whole.

Urban design as an aesthetic-expressive process

There is also a third angle: to look at urban design as an aesthetic-expressive process, what Lynch (1981; 1984) called a playful and imaginative creation of possible form. In this process, designers are interacting with their own subjective world and, by employing their aesthetic understanding and graphic skills, express their spatial concepts in the form of an appropriate scheme.

Here, among the identifiable structures, with which the agency interacts, are the subjectivity of the designer and the medium of expression. The subjectivity of the designer has been developed through contacts with the outside world. It includes a 'library' of images and arrangements in the real world, which the designer sees as appropriate and beautiful. Designers often work by making frequent references to this library in the design process. Through a process of adaptation and adjustment, trial and error, designers set the stored images, or new combinations of them, against a concrete context and arrive at the required form.

Interacting with the medium of expression can have different layers. On the one hand, according to the requirements of the task at hand, appropriate forms of expression and presentation are chosen. Graphic and verbal techniques of communication are employed to convince the other agencies, and first of all the client, of the worth of the design. On the other hand, traditions in a design profession have their own normative powers as to what is acceptable. At this level, there is always an ongoing discourse between the members of a design profession, which not only involves the present members of the profession, but also embraces historical periods and their representatives. Through these interactions, conventions are developed, which become a source of influence on, and if needed suppression of, lay judgements.

Through a Habermasian viewpoint, the form of rationality here is the authenticity with which the ideas are being expressed. In the subjective realm, the authenticity of expression might produce a moment

University of Strathclyde
Dept. of Architecture and Building Science

of truthfulness, but it would hardly account for the plurality of such moments as produced by plurality of personalities and interests. It can be seen how expressive rationality can have an adverse effect on rational consensus. Any attempt to reach a consensus in expression might be threatened by attempting to standardise the richness of expression and experience that a combination and variety of individuals and periods can offer. Of course, this point can not be overstressed since there is an optimum level of variety that people can accept, beyond which there is a tendency to simplicity and homogeneity rather than plurality.

Many have tended to look at urban design from only one of these three angles that we analysed. Some tend to see it as only a technical process and therefore equated with 'big' architecture or 'big' engineering. Some see it as only a social interaction to reach new institutional arrangements, and so tend to focus on its management capacities rather than on production of space. Yet others tend to see it as an artistic activity which should be taken up only by talented designers. Such uni-dimensional foci would naturally lead to narrow definitions and viewpoints at the cost of undermining the reality of the process and its plurality of aspects.

It is quite obvious from this analysis that each segment in the urban design process can have at the same time an involvement of three forms of action and rationality, each having a direct impact on the other forms. Despite the limitations of such an attempt towards making a multi-directional approach to the analysis of the urban design process, it can provide a powerful analytical and normative tool in complex situations. It can contribute to gaining an insight into the urban design process and its component parts (Madanipour, 1996b). It can also be useful in the practical design processes by urging the designers to be constantly aware of the multiplicity of the dimensions of the process in which they play a significant part.

Conclusion

Urban design, as we have seen, still suffers from a lack of clarity in its definition, partly due to its coverage of a wide range of activities. We have also seen that a broad definition is what we need to deal with these ambiguities. Rather than being confined in the differences and minutiae of these activities, it is still possible to see it as a process through which we consciously shape and manage our built environment.

Urban designers are interested and engaged in this process and its product. By using this broad definition, we can avoid seeing urban design as merely engaged in the visual qualities of small urban places, or, on the other side of the spectrum, in the transformation of an abstract urban space. It is only through broad definitions that we can encompass the range of interests and involvements of urban design, in all its macro- and micro-scale, process and product, and visual and spatial aspects.

Urban design therefore can be defined as the multi-disciplinary activity of shaping and managing urban environments, interested in both the process of this shaping and the spaces it helps shape. Combining technical, social, and expressive concerns, urban designers use both visual and verbal means of communication, and engage in all scales of the urban socio-spatial continuum.

We have seen an emergence of interest in urban design. Its concern for making places and improving the quality of the urban environment has attracted support from unexpected quarters (Cuthbert, 1996). In a social world in which 'expert-systems' have found crucial importance (Beck, Giddens and Lash, 1994), urban design has emerged as a critique of those expert-systems involved in shaping urban environments. Even if this does not lead to the rise of a new discipline, a clearer understanding of urban design will help the development of the established disciplines of town planning and architecture, by singling out the directions to which they have not paid enough attention. As such its impact on these expert-systems will be 'reflexivity', offering a new dynamism and the possibility for change and improvement. In this context, helping to clarify the nature and scope of urban design becomes a pressing need. For those who are engaged in urban design, a clearer understanding will be beneficial in showing the directions in which both research and practice could develop. Self-awareness and confidence by those who are involved in shaping places will inevitably improve their capacity to make better places.

References

Barnett, J. (1982), *An Introduction to Urban Design*, New York, Harper and Row.

Beck, U., Giddens, A. and Lash, S. (1994), *Reflexive Modernisation: Politics, Traditions and Aesthetics in the Modern Social Order*, Cambridge, Polity Press.

Billingham, J. (ed.) (1994), *Urban Design Source Book 1994*, London, Urban Design Group.

Billingham, J. (1995), 'Urban designers facing research identity crisis', *Planning*, 19 May, 20–21.

Billingham, J. (ed.) (1996), *Urban Design Source Book 1996*, London, Urban Design Group.

Boyer, M. C. (1990), 'The return of aesthetics to city planning' in D. Crow (ed.), *Philosophical Streets: New Approaches to Urbanism*, Washington DC, Maisonneuve Press, 93–112.

Brunette, P. and Willis, D. (1994), 'The spatial arts: an interview with Jacques Derrida' in P. Brunette and D. Willis (eds), *Deconstruction and the Visual Arts: Art, Media, Architecture*, Cambridge, Cambridge University Press, 9–32.

Columbia University (1992), *Columbia University Bulletin 1992–94: Graduate School of Architecture Planning and Preservation*, New York, Columbia University.

Cuthbert, A. (1996), 'An interview with Manuel Castells', *Cities*, **13**, 3–19.

Dagenhart, R. and Sawicki, D. (1992), 'Architecture and planning: the divergence of two fields', *Journal of Planning Education and Research*, **21**, 1–16.

Department of the environment (1992), *Development Plans and Regional Planning Guidance* (Planning Policy Guidance Note 1), Department of the Environment, London, HMSO.

Department of the Environment (1995), *Quality in Town and Country: Urban Design Campaign*, London, Department of the Environment.

Gellner, E. (1992), *Reason and Culture: The Historic Role of Rationality and Rationalism*, Oxford, Blackwell.

Gottdiener, M. (1986), 'Recapturing the centre: a semiotic analysis of shopping malls', in M. Gottdiener and A. Lagopoulos (eds), *The City and the Sign: An Introduction to Urban Semiotics*, New York, Columbia University Press, 288–302.

Greene, S. (1992), 'Cityshape: communicating and evaluating community design', *Journal of the American Planning Association*, **58**, 177–89.

Habermas, J. (1984), *The Theory of Communicative Action: Vol. 1: Reason and the Rationalisation of Society*, Cambridge, MA, MIT Press.

Harvard University (1994), *The Official Register*, Cambridge, MA, Graduate School of Design, Harvard University.

Harvey, D. (1989), *The Condition of Postmodernity*, Oxford, Blackwell.

Hirst, C. (1995), ' "Urban design would halt decline of town centres' claims leading academic', *Planning Week*, 16 November, 6.

Hodge, B., Maitless, N., Newbury, S., Pollock, L., Rowe, P. and VERZONE, C. (eds) (1994), *Studio Works 2*, Cambridge, MA, Graduate School of Design, Harvard University.

Honneth, A. (ed.) (1991), *Communicative Action: Essays on Jurgen Habermas's Theory of Communicative Action*, Cambridge, Polity Press.

Kindsvatter, D. and Von Grossmann, G. (1994), 'What is urban design?', *Urban Design Quarterly*, Spring/Summer, 9.

Lefebvre, H. (1991), *The Production of Space*, Oxford, Blackwell.

Linden, A. and Billingham, J. (1994), 'History of the Urban Design Group' in J. Billingham (ed), *Urban Design Source Book 1994*, London, Urban Design Group, 30–33.

Lozano, E. (1990), *Community Design and the Culture of Cities: The Crossroads and The Wall*, Cambridge, Cambridge University Press.

Lynch, K. (1981), *Good City Form*, Cambridge MA, MIT Press.

Lynch, K. (1984), 'Urban Design', entry in *The New Encyclopedia Britannica, Macropaedia*, Volume 18, 15th edition.

Madanipour, A. (1996a), 'Urban Design and Dilemmas of Space', *Environment and Planning D, Society and Space*, **14**, 331–55.

Madanipour, A. (1996b), *Design of Urban Space: An Inquiry into a Socio-spatial Process*, Chichester, John Wiley.

Madanipour, A. (1997 forthcoming), *Tehran: The Making of a Metropolis* (Belhaven's World Cities Series), Chichester, John Wiley.

Porteous, J. D. (1996), *Environmental Aesthetics: Ideas, Politics, and Planning*, London, Routledge.

Relph, E. (1987), *The Modern Urban Landscape*, London, Croom Helm.

Rowley, A. (1994), 'Definition of urban design: the nature and concerns of urban design', *Planning Practice and Research*, **9**, 179–97.

Royal Town Planning Institute (1991), *The Education of Planners*, London, RTPI.

Shirvani, H. (1985), *The Urban Design Process*, New York, Van Nostrand Reinhold.

Tibbalds, F. (1988), 'Mind the gap', *The Planner*, March, 11–15.

Vernez-Moudon, A. (1992), 'A catholic approach to organising what urban designers should know', *Journal of Planning Literature*, **6**, 331–49.

Worpole, K. (1992), *Towns for People: Transforming Urban Life*, Buckingham, Open University Press.

Acknowledgements

I am grateful for the helpful comments of the participants in the Nottingham University conference, 'Challenges of the New Millennium', where an earlier version of this paper was presented in March 1996. These ideas are also presented in my book, *Design of Urban Space* (1996), in which the nature and scope of urban design are explored further.

Source and copyright

This chapter was published in its original form as:

Madanipour, A. (1997), 'Ambiguities of Urban Design', *Town Planning Review*, **68** (3), 363–383.

Published by Liverpool University Press.

3

Urban environments as visual art or as social settings? A review

R. K. Jarvis
[1980]

The working methods of the urban designer have been described as a mysterious and impenetrable 'black box', where the input (the need for detailed plans, the powers available, the detailed data) and the output (the schemes regularly reported in periodicals) are well and frequently described, but the working methods remain unexplored and undocumented.[1] Whereas architects will often describe the evolution of their designs, the complexities of urban design, which can involve a number of agencies over a long period of time, are rarely made public. In the absence of such information and an accompanying understanding, didactic programmes for urban design can at best provide only clues about the urban designers' concerns and working methods.

With the current emphasis in planning agencies on environmental enhancement and improvement programmes, small area approaches and design guidance, this absence of information is a serious problem. There is a risk that urban design will come to be regarded as nothing more than a stage in the building programme, a specification for architecture, instead of a clearly expressed and understood management of places to make them suitable for everyday use. If this outcome is to be avoided and urban design is to develop to meet current needs, then a better understanding of the 'black box' becomes an imperative.

As an initial step in opening the 'black box' it is suggested that both critical analysis of the products of design and the selection and manipulation of the inputs in the design process (working method) are

closely related to and specified by the underlying philosophies of those involved. Although this review relies on urban design theory and advice rather than case studies of the design process, the results are felt to provide support for this generalisation and to merit further and more comparative study. Two underlying approaches to urban design, each with very different emphases, can be discerned from a review of the relevant literature. Both can be seen in the work of Camillo Sitte. One emphasis is on visible form and is the approach that seems to dominate contemporary design advice; the other is primarily concerned with the public use and experience of urban environments. This latter approach is less developed than the artistic tradition, and it invites not only the application of findings from the rapidly developing field of man-environment relations but also public design participation.

Even the language of the two approaches differs. The visual artistic tradition speaks in aesthetic, abstract terms. Drawing on their personal experience authors often use familiar words in an unfamiliar way to convey effect. At the other end of the spectrum urban design analysis based on social usage may hardly include any reference to the appearance of a place at all; behavioural matters and their congruence or incongruence with the surroundings predominate.[2] The purpose of this review is not to deny the importance of visual matters in urban design, although it does demonstrate their dominance in urban design philosophy and method to the virtual exclusion of any other approach to urban environments. It is rather, through a classification of the differences between the artistic tradition and the social usage approaches, to provide a basis for discussion and to indicate how, in recent design theories and their potential for practice, the two approaches can be seen to draw into a closer, more positive relationship.

The review begins with a consideration of the essentials and standpoints of the artistic tradition with its visual emphasis as represented in the exemplary writing of leading authors and practising designers. It is a historical review, beginning with the influential ideas of Camillo Sitte at the end of the nineteenth century and Le Corbusier in the early decades of this century. It then considers the basis of early design advice from central government to local planning authorities after the Second World War as expressed by Thomas Sharp, Frederick Gibberd and William Holford in *Design in Town and Village*. The distinctive personal contribution of Gordon Cullen and his view of *Townscape* are then explored along with developments suggested by Roy Worskett.

The artistic tradition in urban design

Camillo Sitte

Camillo Sitte's *City Planning According to Artistic Principles*[3] acknowledged and discussed both approaches, but his aim to establish the principles for laying out a pattern of streets, plazas, monuments and buildings that would re-establish urban design as an artistic enterprise of the highest order laid emphasis on the visual experience of urban spaces. Sitte saw nineteenth century city planning as a rigid set of street systems without artistic merit. The achievement of all the beauties of art and attainments of the past, he claimed, would be attained through the careful organisation of urban spaces following certain principles derived from sensitive observation of ancient, mediaeval, renaissance and baroque examples.

The chapter headings in his book—'That the centre of plazas be kept free'; 'That public squares should be enclosed entities'; 'The size and shape of plazas'—indicated both comprehensive content and, at the same time, the limited viewpoint of these artistic principles. Although Sitte was aware of practical considerations of terrain and social custom, his writing stressed sensual, and overwhelmingly visual,

impressions; as when he described (p. 61) the mediaeval street—'the ideal street must form a completely enclosed unit. The more one's impressions are confined within it, the more perfect will be its tableau. One feels at ease in a space where the gaze cannot be lost in infinity.'

It would be wrong, however, to suggest that Sitte was unaware of the functional problems of day-to-day experiences. Nonetheless it was the deterministic view of city planning as artistic education for the masses, albeit in changed social conditions, that emerged from Sitte's work. Social change is observed in relation to urban space and activity. 'We cannot prevent the public fountains from being reduced to a merely ornamental role', he wrote 'the colourful, lively crowd stays away from them because modern plumbing carries water … into house and kitchen …'[4] But instead of examining the new locations that old activities occupy, or new uses for these plazas and porticoes, Sitte ultimately turned to edification to justify his principles in modern conditions: 'the forever edifying impression of artistic perfection cannot be dispensed with in our busy everyday life. One must keep in mind that city planning in particular must allow full and complete participation to art, because it is this type of artistic endeavour, above all, that affects formatively, every day and every hour the great mass of the population, whereas theatre and concerts are available only to the wealthier classes' (p. 111).

Le Corbusier

Le Corbusier was the aesthetic antithesis of Sitte, but the 'never departed from' principles that underlay his urban design were equally founded on visual and formal qualities. A complete volte-face from the humanistic principles sketched in *Vers une Architecture*[5] marked the superficial symbolism of *Urbanisme*[6] where civilisations and cities were described *en masse*, frequently in an affirmative and declamative style.

Sections of the early paragraphs of *Urbanisme* are characteristic—'A town is a tool … the lack of order to be found everywhere in them offends us; … A City! It is the grip of man upon nature … Geometry is the means, created by ourselves, whereby we perceive the external world and express the world within us … Geometry is the foundation … Machinery is the result of geometry. The age in which we live is therefore essentially a geometric one' (p. 1). But this is the geometry of regular lines, surfaces and solids deriving from the school exercise book.

Developing the principle of 'Order' Le Corbusier claimed that, if natural chaos is overcome, then free man can create cities of pure geometry. Once again superficial visual analogies were introduced to reinforce the point: a nomads' desert camp; a mediaeval town tight within its walls ('the sort of small town which so delights the town planner' p. 32) within which nomads take root; a massing of rectangular 30-storey buildings, before which circles a flying boat show that 'we are no longer nomads: we must build towns' (p. 32). Corbusier gave no indication that he appreciated that there may be orders other than pure geometry, orders which might have made either the nomad camp or the mediaeval equally well 'ordered' in relation to their social and physical settings.

Lacking a social dimension itself, visual analysis became determinism. Le Corbusier's discussion of the effect the city has 'with regard to fatigue and well-being, cheerfulness or depression, its capacity to enable or fill us with pride, indifference, disgust or revolt' led him in fact to a reiteration of geometric principles: 'Town Planning demands uniformity in detail and a sense of movement in general layout …' (pp. 61–78). Le Corbusier gave a generation or more of designers a mandate to interpret social needs directly into a symbolic geometry, in his case a geometry that was simple and rectangular, without any reference to social reality.

Design in Town and Village

Early post-war design advice in Britain, prepared for local authorities, differed in politic and aesthetic from Corbusier's modernist autocratic design planning, but visual criteria still predominated. The contributors to Design in Town and Village,[7] the first official advice on design, emphasised appearance and layout and gave little consideration to user needs. Thomas Sharp discussed the visually enclosed shapes of village streets and greens and offered suggestions for their extension and development, but gave only the briefest and most general reference to their social structure. Similarly, Frederick Gibberd emphasised the 'street picture' in his essay on residential area design and described the various compositional devices through which it might be built up: the relationship of house to paving; of form or character, of facade patterns and building lines; the organisation of spaces at corners, along roads or at right angles to them, and against more open landscapes.

Apart from some brief references to the untidy and confused scene of back gardens where 'the tenant can behave more or less as he likes … provided he is not a nuisance to his neighbours' (p. 64) there were no explicit references to people's activities in housing areas at all. The result of this approach was exemplified in the treatment of front gardens; instead of consideration of privacy, of trespass, of the individuality of house approaches, of the use of space, problems of pictorial composition predominated: so that 'if all the front walls and fences are swept away and the space between the pavement and the house designed as communal front lawn, the composition will be even more complete' (p. 31).

Gordon Cullen and *Townscape*

The contrast between Gordon Cullen's *Townscape* philosophy and the principles of Design in Town and Village too is one of aesthetic, of style rather than a fundamental difference of approach.[8] Conversational style and impressionistic sketches replace formal prose and precise drawings; complexity, contrast and, above all, serial vision, replace the rather sterile aesthetic of official design. But the emphasis is still visual: 'we turn to the faculty of sight for it is almost entirely through vision that the environment is apprehended' (p. 10). Urban design is not only for visual delight, it is also seen as an elite concern: 'although many of his problems may be large ones dealing with such matters as the siting of traffic arteries, their realisation depends on mere nuances of design, which perhaps among visual planners only architects perceive in all its meaning' (p. 123).

The essential value of Cullen's approach lies in its uninhibited, personal and expressive response to space. For instance, Cullen mingles aspects of spatial analysis with poetic evocation: 'the quality of Thereness which is lyrical in the sense that it is perpetually out of our reach, it is always There' (p. 34). But as a result it is Cullen's own values, based on visual composition that predominate. Landscapes are categorised in order to bring clarity of visible pattern without regard to function, and at a smaller scale the idea of *thisness* ('a thing being itself', p. 64) is propounded with carefully selected photographs and evocative captions.

This approach fails when Cullen does not consider other people's reactions to these same environments. Cullen places a sensitive observer at the perceptual centre of the townscape, but uses his own gifted interpretations from that position to stand for the rest of society. Cullen's role is that of an interpreter, going about places with the intention of seeking his own meanings and expressing his personal values; but other people, with other social roles, without the interests or values which derive from an artistic training, may not share them, or if they do, may not give them the same importance. Because interpretations and values are immediately transposed to stand for the material objects they describe the kind of plurality of meaning places and features might have is not appreciated. The basis of design becomes a limited aesthetic made up of serial vision, place, content and (superficial) function.

Roy Worskett

The influence of Cullen's writing, both in *Townscape* and in his occasional series for the *Architectural Review*, has been enormous and much British work on urban design can be related to the same visual principles.[9] Roy Worskett, for example, builds on Cullen's definitions to identify four 'design disciplines' as the basis for an urban design framework for conservation.[10] Again the emphasis is on spatial organisation and tends to exclude reference to other values in the environment. Thus, the *Town–Landscape Relationship*, even though it is intended to consider vantage points along routes of approach to a settlement to assess 'the appearance of town in its countryside setting' (p. 78), does not mention the navigational or functional values that such an appearance may have to those approaching or how such appearances might relate to the decisions the observer might have to make—getting his luggage ready or changing lanes on a motorway.

Although functional aspects of urban analysis had already been developed on a wider perceptual basis by Kevin Lynch and others, Worskett, while he recognises that this is the least objective part of the architect's work, nonetheless states that it is the architect alone who 'must get the feel of the townscape and communicate it to his colleagues' (p. 119).

A framework for comparative evaluation

Fundamental criticism of the values and standpoints embodied in the visual tradition is rare,[11] and, although Sitte himself showed some concern about the suitability of places to their use, the elements and working methods of an alternative approach to the design of urban environments have not received very much attention. Recent work, most particularly that of Kevin Lynch and Christopher Alexander, develops and re-affirms the validity of a social usage approach, which treats urban environments as social settings rather than works of three-dimensional art. The suggested framework for comparative evaluation is derived from Martin Kreiger's recent review of large-scale planning, in which he identifies three 'binds', that is, three sets of inescapable limitations of particular attitudes.[12]

Kreiger's three 'binds' applied

Kreiger's first bind is a consequence of the desire for a formal, general model which will provide a scientific foundation for planning analysis and proposals; it leads, unfortunately, to the exclusion of richly described personal viewpoints both of, and within, the (planning/design) process. Recent attempts to model visual effects in urban design have also met this limitation. Either there has been an explicit exclusion of the anecdotal (in terms of a connected narrative of events and incidents in context) in preference for a mathematical calculation of quantity[13] or the viewpoints have remained those of a highly-trained and gifted observer of the scene.

The second bind identified by Kreiger, which also has parallels in urban design, is that of the general omission of feeling persons, and the woodenness of their introduction when they are used. An extreme example of this limitation occurs when fictional 'representative' characters or places are used to exemplify interests and processes of change in order to represent aesthetic qualities of visual interest to a lay audience or readership.[14]

Kreiger's third bind is the 'aesthetic from nowhere', a disembodied critical modification of past practices, which is strikingly exemplified in urban design by the recent design guides. For instance, the earliest guide rejects the recent past as 'depressingly characterless and subtopian in appearance',[15] and proceeds to re-establish a new visual theory with little reference to its contemporary social and economic context, to the extent that the suburb is replaced either by 'new urban' or 'new rural' styles in the 'spectrum of settlement patterns'.

Kreiger's resolutions for these binds are especially interesting as he directs attention towards a newly established group of disciplines that attempt rationally and methodically to understand and explain everyday experiences of the world—the very element missing from *Townscape*—and which can provide orientations away from formal models. Among these (p. 161) for instance, are phenomenology (which 'tries to explain how the world comes to make sense to us in terms of how it is organised and structured, and how we organise and structure it, where the world studied is the ordinary everyday one'), language philosophy, and recent developments in linguistics (which 'indicate … the importance of particular situations which are richly described'), and ethnomethodology ('how we make up the categories we use in our social life, how we index the world').

Each of these studies is seen as variously emphasising the importance of the individual as part of wider social groupings, his interpretation of the world around and his contacts within it. Each lays an emphasis on the interpretation of the everyday world, an approach which is very different from those of either the established formal planning models or the architectural aesthetics of most urban design theory. A fundamental connection between the new group of studies lies in the attitude that regards the users of land not in some disembodied way (Krieger's criticism), but as motivated, perceiving and responsive persons for whom successful interaction with their environment is an essential prerequisite of 'land use'. The development of a design approach which, one way or another, is based upon these attitudes is traced in the following section.

The social usage approach to urban design

Kevin Lynch

Kevin Lynch's short book *The Image of the City*[16] is seminal among pioneers of the social usage approach. Its importance lies not so much in its limited application in practice,[17] but in the foundation for urban design it established by making apparent the perceptual basis of urban images. Lynch attempted to shift urban design's framework in two ways, and both are stated explicitly in the opening pages of his book.

The first shift is the realisation that, although the city may give pleasure and thereby relate to artistic creation, it is not a cultivated but a commonplace experience, shared by different people: in Lynch's words—'on different occasions and for different people, the sequences are reversed, interrupted, abandoned, cut across. It is seen in all lights and weathers' (p. 1). The city is experienced in the context of everyday events and associations, past and present and extending beyond the immediate present and its perception: 'Nothing is experienced by itself', writes Lynch 'but always in relation to its surroundings, the series of events leading up to it, the memory of past

experiences' (p. 1). To emphasise the personal orientation of this standpoint and to include more than architectural matters Lynch adds that 'we are not simply observers of this spectacle, but are ourselves a part of it, on the stage with the other participants' (p. 2).

The second major shift is in the object of study. Instead of examining the city itself, its physical and material form, Lynch states that it is people's perceptions of it that are to be examined: 'We must consider not just the city as a thing in itself but the city being perceived by its inhabitants' (p. 3). The implication here that there may be a *difference* between the city itself and the city that is being perceived is fundamental. It is an admission without parallel in urban design literature, and still seems difficult for many designers to conceive.

Despite being intended as a 'first word and not a last word, an attempt to capture ideas and suggest how they might be developed and tested' (p. 3), *The Image of the City* seems to have provided another jargon vocabulary for designers. Little use—or development in practice—of the techniques has been made and certainly the broader implications of the idea that it is individual perceptions and reactions that should be important features in urban design practice, complementary at least to traditional architectural emphasis, have generally been neglected.

Jane Jacobs

Jane Jacobs' *The Death and Life of Great American Cities*,[18] published just after *The Image of the City*, is well known for its aggressive criticism of the results of city planning, especially large scale redevelopments. However, the author points out, even in the first paragraph of the book, that her 'attack is not based on quibbles about rebuilding methods or hair splitting about fashions in design. It is an attack, rather, on the principles and aims that have shaped modern city planning' (p. 13). The attack on results has endured as the image of her book. Her methods—alternative principles for city design—have been neglected, but they are important indicators of an urban design based in real life social situations and use. They stand up well when viewed against Krieger's critique; they are based on richly described real life situations, whose credible individuals and incidents form the basis of an evaluative aesthetic derived from experience in the world.

The opening chapters of the book discuss the uses of urban elements, such as sidewalks and parks, in great detail. This approach she contrasts with visionary, utopian design, deriving equally from

Le Corbusier and the advocates of Garden Cities, visually beguiling, but 'as to how the city works it tells ... nothing but lies' (p. 33). This approach is carried through into her detailed design suggestions; the necessary design conditions for sidewalks, for instance, are all social ones, and their details are based on close observations of people's behaviour.

Typically, Jacobs is not in favour of purely visual arguments for city design. The criticism that diversity looks ugly and that homogeneity looks inherently better is quickly dismissed. Her suggestions for visual order are of a different nature. Arguing that the city can never be a work of art because art is made only by selection from life and a city is life at its most complex and intense, she suggests instead that the role of urban design should be 'a strategy of illuminating and clarifying life and helping to explain to use its meanings and order—in this case helping to illuminate, clarify and explain the order of cities' (p. 389).

Indicators of change

By the end of the 1960s there were several indications of the possibilities of a behaviourally based urban design, of something more than simply another aesthetic re-formulation. Ideas that environmental design is closely inter-related with the behaviour of people using the environment in everyday circumstances, that design study should focus on the behaviour, perception and expectations of the users in the context of their surroundings equally with the physical elements of surroundings, and that the eventual users of the urban areas being designed should be involved in the design process, had begun to gain acceptance.

Christopher Alexander

Christopher Alexander's work, more often referred to in the context of design methods, is crucial in this development. In *Notes on the Synthesis of Form*[19] and *A City is not a Tree*[20] Alexander points to failings in design philosophies that considered form without context, and to the dangers of approaching city design in a way that did not allow for a rich diversity of cross connections between activities and places. But it is in a short paper—*The Atoms of Environmental Structure*[21]—written with Barry Poyner, and actually dealing with a single element in a building, that Alexander for the first time deals explicity with the issue of including social and behavioural matters in design processes.

The basis of Alexander's new approach was the replacement of the idea of 'need' (a generalised and imprecise statement of the kind 'people need ...') with that of 'tendencies' (an observable pattern of behaviour). Conflicts between tendencies could, he argued, be resolved in one of two ways—either by suppression of one or more of the tendencies (a restriction on what people can or may do) or, more creatively, the environment can be adapted to allow the tendencies to continue unhindered. The identification of these conflicts, which may not be immediately apparent in the existing, less than ideal environment is a vital stage in the design process. The purpose of design is then seen as the resolution of these conflicts or to prevent them occurring.

The final stage in the Alexander/Poyner argument is that the features of the environment which prevent individual conflicts occurring are not so much the elements themselves, but the basic geometrical relationships between them and that defining these relationships is the key to design success. Social and environmental criteria could thus be positively identified and integrated into the design process.

Others sought to integrate human behaviour in a systematic way at a larger scale. In *The Dynamics of Behaviour-contingent Physical Systems,* Raymond Studer sought to define an all-embracing description of viable environmental design.[22] Practical indications of a socially based urban design also became apparent in the late 1960s. Donald Appleyard and Rai Okamoto indicated how a systematic approach to urban design derived from human behaviour could become a design tool based on transport systems.[23]

Towards a more comprehensive framework

Constance Perin

Attempts to develop a more comprehensive framework began to be published in the 1970s. Reviewing design methods and developments in psychology and the social sciences, especially Barker's *Ecological Psychology*[24] and criticisms of the results of conventional architectural design, Constance Perin[25] proposed procedural changes in design, for instance, the inclusion of researched user requirements in design briefs and extensive government-sponsored research into the effects of environmental change. Designer's analysis, she argues, should focus on human behaviour. Perin suggests the idea of a 'Behaviour Circuit', '... tracking people's behaviour through the fulfilment of their everyday purposes at the scale of the room, the house, the block, the neighbourhood, the city, in order to learn what resources—physical and human—are needed to support, facilitate or enable them' (p. 78).

David Thomas

Arguing from the basis of closely observed everyday activities David Thomas proposes 'Normal Usage' as the basis for a new approach to urban design.[26] Instead of concentrating upon the physical environment (those elements that can be owned, designed and individually made) designers should, he argues, concentrate on the realities that people realise during their everyday activities. Such an approach is implicit, but undeveloped, in the continuous, publicly accountable planning process which 'created opportunities for people to express their concern for the kind of realities that they considered important and did not necessarily own, or that no-one can own' (p. 5).

The separation of theory and practice

In recent years theory and research have developed apart from urban design practice. The opportunities and needs for the application of research, especially in environmental psychology have, however, been frequently stressed. David Canter sees patterns of behaviour activity and perception as fundamental to any description and design of 'place'.[27] Donald Appleyard[28] and Gary Moore[29] while more circumspect in their evaluation of the immediate applications, nonetheless emphasise the potential to be explored. Methods for incorporating user viewpoints and needs are widely published and discussed, even in non-specialist design courses.[30]

Such connections do not seem to have been taken up in the mainstream of urban design where the visual tradition, which translates idea to sketch to drawings to bill to works on site, almost automatically predominates. Recent new work by Kevin Lynch (*Managing the Sense of a Region*[31]) and Christopher Alexander (*A Pattern Language*[32]) suggest openings towards a new synthesis of theory and practice of use and design.

A new synthesis of theory and practice

Managing the sense of a region

Traditional urban design analyses and policies with their emphasis on vision alone among the senses,

on normal ('that is healthy, active, middle-class adults', p. 86) people, their focus on special designed places and spatial effects, and the separation of aesthetics from other aspects of urban life and experience, receive little attention in *Managing the Sense of a Region*. Lynch's principal emphasis is to propose an approach to design that deals explicitly with the environment in everyday life.

A consequence of the impoverished orthodoxy of much urban design theory is that fundamental questions of purpose are never asked; but Lynch begins his prescriptive analysis by asking 'what for?', identifying reasons and purposes which extend far beyond picturesque spatial effects. Fundamental to all his examples are human experience, use and activity; from them Lynch gives purpose and direction to urban design proposals, so that even the most obviously constructional elements are part of a programme embracing not only vision and aesthetics, but 'how the well being of persons and small groups arises as they directly interact with their settings, and not primarily from their role of passive observers' (p. 37).

Such purposes require new techniques and Lynch comments that 'most sensory studies restrict themselves to a field survey and in so doing they implicitly impose the professional values of their staff on the results and lose much of the inner meaning of the sensed world' (p. 61). In addition to reviewing techniques for the analysis of spatial and temporal form, sequences, visibility, ambient quality, ambience and information, natural features, from the perspective of ordinary use, Lynch describes techniques to analyse visible activity, spatial behaviour and the images people hold of places. Such integral analyses would systematically identify not only the placing of activity in time and space and how those activities relate to their surroundings, but also 'how they picture it to themselves, what they feel about it, what it means to them' for which 'our basic source of information, however, is direct dialogue with people, and this is an analysis that should never be neglected in any analysis of seemliness' (p. 111).

A pattern language

The genesis of *A Pattern Language* in the work of Christopher Alexander and the Centre for Environmental Structure has been traced elsewhere.[33] In the present review it is not so much the utopian philosophy behind the language ('towns and buildings will never be able to be come alive unless they are made by all the people in society and unless these people share a common pattern language', p. x) or the methodological implications of the language[34] that are important, so much as the way which physical, constructional and spatial elements are interwoven, embody and are founded on human behaviour and social experience in a series of 'patterns'—a view similar to the 'relationships' Alexander described with Barry Poyner.

The patterns themselves are not to be regarded as complete designs, but as a sketched minimum framework of essentials, a few basic instructions, a rough freehand sketch, to be shaped and refined not so much on the drawing board but in use and construction. They provide the designer with a useable, but not predetermined, series of relationships between everyday life and spaces. Even those patterns which are closest to the traditional spatial concerns of urban design—where, for instance, Sitte is frequently cited by Alexander—are either introduced, researched or expressed in terms that deal explicitly with people's use of places. There are, for example, *Small Public Squares*, based on evidence of density and intervisibility of personal facial expressions and *Public Outdoor Rooms*, providing opportunities for casual social interaction.

A Pattern Language and *Managing the Sense of a Region* provide clear evidence of the possibilities for an urban design that starts from and measures its success by use and activity in places rather than physical form alone. Such an approach seems to imply not only a change in attitude but also in procedure. Appleyard & Okamoto's proposals for explicit local social evaluations,* Thomas's empathetic user studies, Lynch's proposals for 'community liaison' and 'root consultancy' as an integral part of the design plan[35] and Alexander's decentralised utopianism, are far removed from current practice, where 'design' is the stage when planners retreat into their expert shells to 'implement' their plans.

Whether such a shift in the political and operational modes of the professional, 'expert' designer is possible in practice warrants further consideration. It is possible to envisage personal and intuitively derived approaches, bridging between the two approaches emerging in individual instances, establishing new design relationships which have not been documented. The traditional pictorial approach to design tends toward an esoteric and specialised view of environmental quality—the environment as fine art, to be appreciated. An alternative approach based on user experience and involvement not only gives scope for a richer and more relevant product, related to use and daily needs, but also, as a result of its explicit consideration of these social situations in the design and evaluation process, a far greater potential for a participatory urban design process in which users' and designers' experiences can be brought together creatively to make places better for everyday use and enjoyment.

Notes

1. McLoughlin, J. B., *Control and Urban Planning*, London, Faber, 1973, p. 134
2. The two approaches can be contrasted in analyses of Stockholm presented in Bacon, E., *The Design of Cities*, London, Thames and Hudson, 1967, pp. 271–272 and Lerup, L., 'Environmental and Behavioural Congruence as a Measure of Goodness in Public Space—The Case of Stockholm' in *Ekistics*, No. 204 (November 1972), pp. 341–358
3. Sitte, C., *City Planning According to Artistic Principles* (1889), translated by G. R. and C. C. Collins, London, Phaidon, 1965
4. Sitte, C., 1889, op. cit.
5. Le Corbusier, *Vers une Architecture* (1923), translated as *Towards a New Architecture* by F. Etchells, London, Architectural Press, 1946, p. 183
6. Le Corbusier, *Urbanisme* (1926), translated as *The City of Tomorrow and its Planning* by F. Etchells, London, Architectural Press, 1929, p. 1
7. Ministry of Housing and Local Government, *Design in Town and Village*, London, HMSO, 1953. The contributors are Thomas Sharp (The English Village), Frederick Gibberd (The Design of Residential Areas) and W. G. Holford (Design in Town Centres)
8. Cullen, G., *Townscape*, London, Architectural Press, 1961; a recent discussion of residential area design (Ward, C., 'The House that Jack Built' in *Bulletin of Environmental Education*, August/September 1978) links some of Cullen's admired examples back to Raymond Unwin, an obvious influence on the Ministry booklet
9. Whistler, W. and D. Read, *Townscape as a Philosophy of Urban Design* (Council of Planning Librarians Exchange Bibliography 1342), Monticello, Illinois, 1977
10. Worskett, R., *The Character of Towns: An Approach to Conservation*, London, Architectural Press, 1969
11. The most recent is Maxwell, R., 'An Eye for an I: The Failure of the Townscape Tradition' in *Architectural Design* (September 1976), from a standpoint of semiological and psychological theories; Kelly Smith, N., 'Man's Environment' in *Arena*, Vol. 83, No. 913 (June

---

* Appleyard's more recent suggestions on 'The Environment as a Social Symbol Within a Theory of Environmental Action and Perception'.[36]

1967) had pointed to the lack of any human base in planning other than visual conditioning

12. Kreiger, M. H., 'Some New Directions for Planning Theories', *Journal of the American Institute of Planners,* Vol. 40, No. 3 (May 1974), pp. 156–163

13. Urban Motorways Project Team, *Report of the Urban Motorways Project Team to the Urban Motorways Committee: Technical Paper No 4: Visual Effects Quantified Intrusion,* London, Department of the Environment, 1974, paras. 1.04 and 1.05

14. As, for instance, in the 'Muffingilders Hall' saga by Gordon Cullen, where an entire fictional history from mediaeval guilds to chance inheritance is used to present a background for a redevelopment scheme: Cullen, G., *Notation—The Layman's Code for his Environment,* London, Alcan, 1967, pp. 21–29

15. Essex County Council, *A Design Guide for Residential Areas,* Chelmsford, Essex CC, 1973

16. Lynch, Kevin, *The Image of the City,* Cambridge, Mass., The MIT Press, 1960

17. Goodey, B., *The Perception of the Environment* (Occasional Paper 17), Birmingham, Centre for Urban and Regional Studies, 1971, pp. 23–24; and Appleyard, D., 'The Major Published Works of Kevin Lynch: An Appraisal', *Town Planning Review,* Vol. 49, No. 4 (October 1978), pp. 551–557

18. Jacobs, J., *The Death and Life of Great American Cities: The Failure of Town Planning,* Harmondsworth, Middlesex, Penguin, 1964 (first published 1961)

19. Alexander, C., *Notes on the Synthesis of Form,* Cambridge, Mass., Harvard UP, 1964

20. Alexander, C., 'A City is Not a Tree' in *Design,* No. 206 (1965)

21. Alexander, C. and B. Poyner, 'The Atoms of Environmental Structure' (1967), republished in Moore, G. (Ed.), *Emerging Methods in Environmental Design and Planning,* Cambridge, Mass., The MIT Press, 1970

22. Studer, R. G., 'The Dynamics of Behaviour-Contingent Physical Systems', paper presented at the *Design Methods in Architecture* symposium, Portsmouth, 1967, and published in Broadbent, G. and A. Ward (Eds.), *Design Methods in Architecture* (Architectural Association Paper No. 4), London, Lund Humphries, 1969, p. 59

23. Appleyard, D. and R. Okamoto, 'Environmental Criteria for Ideal Transportation Systems' in Barton-Aschmann Associates, *Guidelines for New Transportation Systems,* Washington DC, US Department of Housing and Urban Development, 1968, pp. 137–190

24. Barker, R. G., *Ecological Psychology,* Stanford, Stanford UP, 1968

25. Perin, C., *With Man in Mind: An Interdisciplinary Prospectus for Environmental Design,* Cambridge, Mass., The MIT Press, 1970

26. Thomas, D. L., *Planning the Design of Settled Topographies,* Vol. 1, London, National Coal Board, 1970

27. Canter, D., *The Psychology of Place,* London, Architectural Press, 1977

28. Appleyard, D., 'A Planner's Guide to Environmental Psychology: A Review Essay', *Journal of the American Institute of Planners,* Vol. 43, No. 2 (April 1977), pp. 184–189

29. Moore, G. T., 'Knowing about Environmental Knowing: The Current State of Theory and Research on Environmental Cognition' in *Environment and Behaviour,* Vol. 11, No. 1 (March 1979)

30. See, for instance, Jones, J. C., *Design Methods: Seeds of Human Futures,* London, John Wiley, 1970, especially pp. 214–239; and The Open University, *Man Made Futures: Design and Technology,* Milton Keynes, The Open University Press, 1975, especially Units 13–16

31. Lynch, K., *Managing the Sense of a Region,* Cambridge, Mass., The MIT Press, 1976

32. Alexander, C., S. Ishikawa, M. Silverstein and others, *A Pattern Language: Towns, Building, Construction,* New York, Oxford UP, 1977

33. Ward, T., review of *A Pattern Language* in *Architectural Design* (1979), pp. 15–17

34. The theoretical basis, *A Timeless Way of Building,* is promised, but is unpublished at the time of writing

35. Appleyard, D., 'The Environment as a Social Symbol within a Theory of Environmental Action and Perception', *Journal of the American Planning Association,* Vol. 45, No. 2 (April 1979), pp. 143–153

36. Lynch, K., *Managing the Sense of a Region,* op. cit., pp. 55–68

Source and copyright

This chapter was published in its original form as:

Jarvis, R. (1980), 'Urban Environments as Visual Art or Social Setting', *Town Planning Review,* **51**, 50–66.

Published by Liverpool University Press.

4

An integrative theory of urban design

Ernest Sternberg
[2000]

Though urban design is the most traditional field of planning, it sorely lacks cohesive theoretical foundations. Much writing takes the form of guidebooks or manuals, which rely on rules of thumb, analytical techniques, and architectural ideas whose theoretical justifications are unclear. At best we have a number of contending approaches, such as Formalism and New Urbanism, which tend to operate in a theoretical vacuum, as if cut off from larger streams of planning thought, and to invite dogmatic adherence. This article examines the works of leading thinkers in urban design, in search of the theoretical foundations that underlie seemingly divergent approaches, to suggest that we could construct a more general theory, one that reflects principles that several of these approaches share.

To be sure, publications on physical planning (of which urban design can be considered a part) do sometimes address the theory of planning, but they are likely to refer to such matters as rationalism, incrementalism, participation, group process, and communication. Such concepts are properly a part of *procedural theory*, which is concerned with how we can know or decide—how intelligence can be exercised on behalf of the community. Practitioners should indeed be aware of these questions of process in planning, but they must also comprehend the substantive features of the object in question—they must be able to inquire into the distinctive principles underlying urban design as compared to those in other fields of planning. They need a complement to procedural theory: a *substantive* planning theory that sheds light on the specific concerns of the

urban designer (for precedent in distinguishing procedural from substantive theory, see Alexander, 1992, pp. 94–98).

What indeed is the urban designer's substantive concern? Especially for those inspired by architectural education, the urban designer's task is the shaping of human settlements' physical features at scales larger than a single building or a single plot of land. He or she does so through manipulation of the concrete elements of distance, material, scale, view, vegetation, land area, water features, road alignment, building style, and numerous other items that make up the natural landscape and the built environment. (For more views on the definition of urban design, see Mandanipour, 1997.) Urban design would therefore seem to be the profession that sets out to shape the spatial or physical environment.

But this definition is problematic, in part because it is too encompassing. Wellhead location and hurricane susceptibility, real estate development and brownfield reclamation, sewer systems and stadium location, land drainage and building codes—in the course of their work, urban designers might well have to become involved in any of these matters. But they would share this involvement with a variety of other practitioners, ranging from civil engineers to horticultural specialists, not to mention the neighboring branches of physical planning, and it would not be especially enlightening to label all their activities as urban design. To encompass all those professional activities that shape the built environment within one label would diminish the intellectual heritage that gives the field its distinctive perspective and enriches its practitioners' design capabilities.

In a better definition of the scope of urban design, we should focus on those matters to which the field brings a distinctive perspective. As we will see shortly when we review some of the classic writings, urban design comes into its own as the field that engages the human experience of the built environment: the sense of understandability, congeniality, playfulness, security, mystery, or awe that lands and built forms evoke.

Put in this way, urban design still has to be distinguished from architecture. Perhaps an urban designer, as compared to an architect, is concerned with objects of a larger scale. But *scale* is ambiguous in this context, since an urban designer might quite reasonably focus on a small item, say a curb cut or a street lamp, while an architect, even one unconcerned about urban design, might well deal with a larger object, such as a building complex. Urban design is better understood to have as its focus not large scale per se, but rather those features of the built environment that—for reasons into which this article will inquire—transcend the individual parcel or property or take place in the public realm. In brief, urban design inquires into *the human experience that the built environment evokes across private properties or in the public realm.*

In doing so, the urban designer confronts issues that are quite different from those of an architect working for a single client; the urban designer engages a physical world driven by the dynamics of private commerce and public affairs. After all, the openings or closings of business establishments, occupation and abandonment of houses, and juxtapositions of buildings are driven far more by the market process than by any designer's creative imagination. This is a world in which price mechanisms, power relations, and interest-group conflicts bring about urban form. The urban designer must contend with the multiple forces that generate the built environment, primarily those of the private real estate market and secondarily government regulations aimed at policy objectives that encompass not just urban form, but such additional matters as transportation efficiency and disaster mitigation. He or she must seek to affect the built environment through complex interactions with private investors, landowners, community members, interest groups, legislators, and funding agencies (see Barnett, 1974).

In light of these concerns, a theory of urban design faces a number of challenges. First, it should not simply advocate one set of design approaches but should rather reveal the principles that underlie several of them. Second, it should be a substantive (not just procedural) theory. Third, it should make us aware of the constituents of the human experience of built form. Fourth, it should recognize the sources of urban form in both markets and plans; it should answer to both the economic and architectural streams of planning thought. Fifth, and not least, the theory should be able to do what any good theory does: to direct our attention to pertinent features of reality—in this case, experiential features of space and built form—and thereby to help guide practice.

Commodification in the environment

Drawing on the work of Karl Polanyi and on the organic tradition in planning (Polanyi, 1957 [1944]; Sternberg, 1993), this article holds that such a theory is indeed possible. This theory is founded on the concept that the market economy cannot effectively extend to realms of human experience that are *noncommodifiable.*

To "commodify" an object is to make it tradeable and commensurable on markets (see Radin, 1996). Polanyi (1957) holds that for the market system to function, it must commodify the objects that people value. His view of commodification should be contrasted with that of Karl Marx, whose *Das Kapital* holds that market exchange "fetishizes" commodities, distorting their true use values. Polanyi believes that ordinary goods and services are quite properly understood as commodities and traded on markets; he explicitly divorces his idea of commodification from that of Marx. It is consistent with Polanyi's thought that market exchange in most ordinary commodities is highly desirable, since markets are efficient mechanisms for bridging supply and demand.

It is in his next step that Polanyi breaks with orthodox economic thinking and makes his critical contribution to planning thought: He makes clear that nature (or the natural and built environment in general) and humanity are resistant to commodification. They are, nonetheless, often commodified: The environment is turned into the land and building commodities, and the human being into the labor commodity. Doing so can falsify and degrade them, causing human suffering and environmental deterioration. For example, a forest encompasses multiple ecological interrelationships among plant and animal species and their territories. When we commodify forested land by subdividing it into discrete parcels with discrete rights to their use, each put up for purchase and sale by owners who make self-interested land use decisions mediated only by the market's price fluctuations, we risk subverting the many hydrological, botanical, and wildlife interrelationships that cross parcel boundaries. Humanity (family, body, community, morality) and its environment, including the built environment, cannot be efficiently traded through a pure market, except by degrading them. The attempt to turn a natural region into land units or a human being into labor units, each traded with a view to private property rights, degrades a larger whole of which it is a part. The very process of commodification undermines that environmental or human realm's *integrity* (Sternberg, 1996).

Fragmented among private owners, and divided among functional bureaucracies (whether governmental or private), urban land, too, has undergone such commodification. The resulting trade in land and buildings can have important economic benefits. But it also undermines the human experience of urban built form. As one moves across urban land, the beholder's experience resists this commodification, seeking coherence, understandability, security, and comfort. It is in creating, protecting, and restoring cohesive experiences of built form that urban design acquires its distinctive social role.

Polanyi sometimes referred to his brand of economics as "substantive" economics, in contrast to "formal" economics conventionally taught in academic departments of economics (Dalton, 1968). Building on the concept of noncommodifiability, we can formulate a planning theory that is "substantive" in two senses, as contrasted to "procedural" in procedural planning theory, and also as contrasted to "formal" in formal microeconomics. Applied to urban design, this theory would seek out the integrative principles underlying the human experience of built form across property boundaries.

The organicists and the economists

Though the idea of noncommodifiability may seem unfamiliar, it has important precedents in planning thought in the concept of the "organic," which pervaded the work of early 20th-century writers on planning, most notably Patrick Geddes and Lewis Mumford. The organicists observed that modern society (especially its central dynamic mechanism, the market) atomized community, nature, and city. Inspired by biological metaphors and philosophical concepts of vitalism, the organicists set out to reassert the natural growth and wholeness that a "mechanical" market society would tend to undermine. In keeping with the sentimental and unrigorous traditions of the 19th-century Romantic movement, the organicists promoted ideas that were nebulous and all encompassing. It sometimes seemed in their work as if everything was part of an organic whole, making it quite difficult to distinguish those realms in which planning was justified from those in which market-based allocation would be effective while public planning would be irrelevant or harmful. Oblivious to the 20th century's raging debates about economic systems and democracy, Geddes and Mumford also failed to situate their ideas in the prevalent streams of economic and social thought (and, hence, were widely dismissed as eccentrics). Specifically, even though the urban and regional phenomena they studied were driven by market forces, such as those of the real estate market, the organicists failed to explain how their ideas related to those of orthodox economics.

At the opposite intellectual pole, those influenced by conventional microeconomics would, if they were to pay any attention to organicist ideas, likely dismiss or reject them. Given economic assumptions, conventionally trained economists would have to take the view that market-led real estate transactions in themselves generate good urban form, and that the planner's role is simply that of developing the rules of the game that fix market imperfections (Moore, 1978). According to this reasoning, a property owner's decision to build a building can have effects on neighbors and passers-by, effects to which these external parties did not agree in any market transaction. According to this *market-failure* concept, the urban features that onlookers enjoy or dislike are *spillovers* (effects spilling across the bounds of private property) or, what is more or less the same, *externalities* (effects external to market transactions). This market-failure theory lets us recognize garbage-strewn lots and dilapidated buildings as nuisances (negative externalities) displeasing to neighbors, and well tended gardens and fine architecture as benefits (positive externalities) for which passers-by did not pay. This conventional economic thinking does offer a limited rationale for public interventions in the real estate market, typically through tax incentives, side payments between individuals, government incentives, voting procedures, and abstract regulations. In making room for such interventions, orthodox economic thought may come in handy in physical planning meant only to resolve simple spillovers; however, since it still conceives of such economic failure as the aggregated result of self-interested individual actions, it does not, and inherently cannot, provide intellectual tools for guiding design. Making assumptions diametrically opposed to those of the organicists, orthodox market-failure theory, though widely thought of as a foundation of policy analysis and even planning, fails as a coherent intellectual foundation for urban design. It fails because it ignores the integrity (noncommodifiability) of the built environment (Sternberg, 1996).

Though an urban designer may, to some extent, indeed be concerned about a building's distinctly identifiable spillover effects on neighboring parcels, as by overshadowing or blocking a view, his or her greater concern is the building's broader interrelationships: with street walls, roads and avenues, neighborhood, land gradient, views, and other landscape features. The designer is concerned, furthermore, not just with neighbors observing from fixed points, but with onlookers moving by and perceiving the building from near and far, from varying angles and with respect to its various perceptible interrelationships with other structures. The building exerts its effects on beholders for whom it is one of a series of urban experiences—it is part of the experience of an urban whole. Orthodox theories of market failure do not appreciate this "organic" relationship between a building and its urban surroundings. They cannot serve as the theoretical foundation for a planning field that seeks to reintegrate built form. In contrast to schools of policy analysis built on market-failure theory, urban design requires concepts through which it can recognize and work with the cohesive interrelationships that constitute the built environment. Urban designers need to base their work on intellectual principles through which they can recognize, sustain, and reconstitute environmental integrity.

While recognizing the market forces that generate the built environment, Karl Polanyi's work establishes a theory that can inquire into environmental integrity without succumbing to the weaknesses of organicism. This is true even with regard to urban design, a subject Polanyi did not write about. It turns out that the great writers about urban design, such as Camillo Sitte, Edmund Bacon, Kevin Lynch, and Jane Jacobs, depended on an ill-formed organicism. The rest of this article argues that we can reinterpret

organicist ideas in urban design and thereby restore this important stream of thought to its rightful place at the heart of planning thought. We can do so by reformulating the problem as follows: Urban design has as its special concern the non-commodifiability of the human experience of the city.

Though the great writers about urban design are not especially known for their interest in economic questions (with the exception of Jane Jacobs), they implicitly recognize that it is the integrity of the urban experience across property boundaries that the urban designer should seek to reassert. Gordon Cullen (1961) writes, for example, that urban design is an "art of relationship" (p. 10) that seeks to weave together environmental elements like buildings, trees, landscape, and traffic. Using such elements, "we can manipulate the nuances of scale and style, of texture and colour and of character and individuality, juxtaposing them in order to create collective benefits" (p. 14). Or as Edmund Bacon (1974) puts it, "Movement through space creates continuity of experience" (p. 34). The very challenge Bacon sets down for the field of urban design is to create such "experiential continuity" (p. 294). Indeed, principal authors have long recognized that the designer should strive to integrate urban form across private property lines (on the general importance of property to planning, see Krueckeberg, 1995). These authors have often relied on concepts of the "organic" to make their point. As we shall see, however, each has emphasized a different facet—a different integrative principle—of the urban whole, whether good form, legibility, vitality, or meaning.

Good form

In Camillo Sitte's classic work *City Planning According to Artistic Principles* (1965, first published in Vienna in 1889) and much later in Edmund Bacon's *The Design of Cities* (1974), good urban design was to be based on artistic principles of *good form*.

Responding to the 19th-century's new city building, which tried to maximize the salability of properties through abstractly rationalized land subdivision, Camillo Sitte (1965) provided one of the first book-length treatments of urban physical planning in market society. Anticipating the ideas of the next generation of planning theorists, he advocated planning because the making of public spaces had become an impersonal, mechanistic project, one that was overtaking the formerly "organic" city.

"Should one be satisfied then," Sitte asks rhetorically, "to place this mechanically produced project, conceived to fit any situation, into the middle of an empty place without organic relation to its surroundings or to the dimensions of any particular building?" (p. 75). Indeed, he was certain that one should not.

Formalist ideas like Sitte's can be seen in the works of the recent generation of urban designers, such as Allan Jacobs' (1993) fine writing on street definition. Edmund Bacon (1974) adds a number of additional guides to good form, demanding that good design should interlock and interrelate buildings across space.

Bacon stresses that the human experience of this articulated space happens along an axis of movement. To define this axis, the designer may strategically place small and large buildings to create scale linkages receding in space; or insert in the landscape an arch, gate, or pair of pylons that set the frame of reference for structures appearing on a recessed plane. The designer may also repeat similar forms in diminishing perspective, as an arch may be placed deep behind another arch, to create unifying form in space and foster the human experience of penetrating into depth. And the designer may use stairs, ramps, and other changes in gradient to engage the participant in the satisfaction of experiencing ascent and descent.

Though such spatial relationships may be elementary to an architect working on a single property, they are problematic to the urban designer, who lacks the architect's comprehensive control over her medium. The urban designer's realm contains multiple properties owned by separate owners, with differing interests, who commission buildings from disparately motivated architects. Indeed it is this condition that sets up the urban designer's formal compositional challenge: to use proportion, enclosure, interlocking points, recession planes, penetration in depth, and ascent and descent, among other formal relationships, to sustain a satisfying experiential continuity across properties. As these interrelationships escape the confines of the individual property, the urban designer faces the further challenge that she must work in a politicized environment, so that despite the designer's partial dependence on an architectural heritage, her work belongs squarely in the planning discipline.

Of these formal interrelationships across buildings, proportion may be the longest recognized, since it can be traced back to classical architecture, yet the least well understood. Writing in 1909, English town planner Raymond Unwin (1994), whose work drew heavily on Sitte, declared that we "need to establish relation and proportion between parts of our design" (p. 176). But what proportions should we favor? We can infer from Sitte that principles of proportion—of relative dimension—need not arise from mystical Pythagorean formulas, but from insight into the beholder's experience of space. The operations of the land market do not reliably generate proportionate relationships across parcel boundaries. Whether any economic actor wants it or not, formal spatial relationships transcend—literally rise above and cross over—formal property lines and use rights. Urban form is a non-commodifiable resource. Relation and proportion at the urban scale cannot arise through the impersonal mechanism of the market; they must be willfully brought into existence through planning—through a design intelligence exercised on the collective behalf.

Legibility

For Kevin Lynch, too, the city's designer had to deal with the experiential quality of the city, what he often called the "sensuous qualities" or simply "sense" of place (Banerjee & Southworth, 1991, p. 6). Through a career spanning several decades, he was remarkably persistent in searching for the concepts that could inform and guide the design of cities. Of all the ideas he experimented with, the most distinctive and enduring was legibility.

As explained in *The Image of the City* (Lynch, 1960), a legible city is one whose constituent parts "are easily identifiable and are easily grouped into an over-all pattern" (p. 3). A distinctive and ordered environment helps the resident orient himself, place parts of the city into coherent categories, and acquire a sense of security that he can relate to the surrounding urban world. Hence, the city should be made "imageable," both in the sense that it projects distinctions and relationships that the observer can comprehend and in the sense that it complies with the observer's "mental picture" of the city (p. 6).

Compared to Sitte, who favors spatial effects (such as obliquely related streets entering a plaza) whose explanation escapes the naive viewer, Lynch suggests clearly comprehensible interrelationships, even recommending perpendicular or other rectilinear relationships that users can remember and identify with.

As compared to Lynch's later works, which are theoretically more ambitious but less distinct in content, his early book firmly establishes legibility as one integrative principle underlying the urban inhabitant's experience of the city.

Moreover, in this early work Lynch (1960) makes clear that nodes, edges, etc. are of little concern in themselves. Rather, they are design elements in achieving something that the haphazard work of developers, owners, and architects individually could not achieve. These elements are crucial in the "interrelation of parts into a whole" (p. 108). The planner who uses the concepts properly "would deal with the interrelations of elements, with their perception in motion, and with the conception of the city as a total visible form" (p. 116). As formal interrelationships are a city's collective asset to Sitte and Bacon, so legibility is in Lynch's early work. It crosses property boundaries, escaping market commodification, to constitute an integral whole, a whole that can be shaped through the exercise of design intelligence.

Vitality

Whereas Sitte, Bacon, and Lynch conceive of urban design from the perspective of the solitary beholder, Jane Jacobs is preeminent among those who have a more gregarious concept of the urbanite who partakes of city life because of its vitality. In *The Death and Life of Great American Cities* (1961), one of the most lucid books in our field, Jacobs forcefully knocks down the vapid mid-century planning that artificially separates uses, creates dead vacant zones, and (as in American "urban renewal" programs) tries to renew cities through urban clearances, thereby destroying the diversity on which urban health rests.

At the heart of Jacob's argument is the idea that a bustling street life is essential to a good city, and vital streets need "a most intricate and close grained density of uses that give each other mutual support" (p. 14). She holds, moreover, that certain conditions nourish these interrelationships among uses.

Especially since her ideas are popular, it needs to be said that concepts for texturing streets to make them more vital do not by any means exhaust urban design ideas. A good city should offer not only bustling mixed use areas, but also residential areas purposefully designed for quiet streets and undisturbed home life. Density can be taken to excess, since it can produce congestion that actually hampers a street's vitality. And a streetscape can, after all, be engaging when one is alone to experience it; a formalist like Bacon (1974) appreciates the perspectival features of, say, Brasilia, especially when there is no one else there to distract him. Just as Sitte and Bacon focus on form and Lynch's writings of 1960 stress legibility, so Jacobs, too, should be understood to have focused on one integrative principle: vitality. We can best appreciate her ideas about vitality when we do not elevate them into an all-purpose, single-minded design goal.

As do other prominent writers on urban design, Jacobs elaborates primarily on one facet of the neighborhood or street as an experiential whole—in her case the urban texturing that generates vibrant activity. In keeping with all planning thought, she stresses that the conditions that generate a good place can be shaped through public or other nonmarket guidance. And like much contemporary planning, she retains the ambivalent relationship to private markets: She recognizes that free real estate markets are essential for urban diversity, but sees that these markets operating on their own cannot effectively create the textural conditions on which vital places depend. Unhampered markets can undermine or even destroy urban vitality, replacing diverse places with exclusive uses, so that, as she puts it, planners should actively plan for diversity (Jacobs, 1961). Indeed, though a property owner may make decisions that add to density, fine grain, and permeability, that owner is one of many owners interacting through an anonymous market mechanism, a mechanism that cannot in itself generate consistent density, grain, and permeability, and may just as well undermine them with box stores, parking lot entrances, empty lots, and blank walls. Working alongside the real estate market, the planner's task is to foster textured interrelationships among many disparate properties.

Meaning

In reaction to modernism that focused on building forms that are pure and impersonal, streets that are little more than conduits for traffic, and urban patterns replicated around the world without regard to locality and context, a new generation of thinkers has stressed still another integral facet of the city: its capacity to exhibit history, tradition, nature, nationality, or other themes that heighten meaning and solidify identity. In professional design practice, *purposeful thematization* is now widespread, extending from shopping malls to festival market places to urban waterfronts (Gottdiener, 1997; Sternberg, 1999). But most writers on this topic disdain mere thematization and assert that design for meaning should be rooted in indigenous character, something the planner should come to comprehend through the study of local landforms, local history, and local culture.

Of the writers who stress design for indigenous meaningfulness, possibly the most influential is Norbert-Schulz (1979). He writes that "nature forms a comprehensive totality, a 'place,' which according to local circumstances has a particular identity" (p. 10), an identity that he sometimes refers to as a "spirit." As dwellers in a place contend with living forces of nature, the place gives rise to mythologies through which it becomes meaningful. By studying the locality and making dwellings that, as it were, emerge from this natural folk-spirit, architects affirm and sustain local identity. Though Norbert-Schulz overtly addresses architects, it is clear through out his work that he actually has in mind a special kind of designer, one who does not conceive of the built structure in isolation. Rather, this designer understands that buildings should express the indigenous spirit and that this spirit emanates from the whole place—from its land, materials, myths, and traditions.

Urban landscapes necessarily accrue multiple meanings, as they accumulate objects referencing varied cultural sources. Here there is a franchise restaurant, there a monumental stadium, and nearby there are an over-grown lot, a broken street lamp, half-covered cobble-stone, a busy highway ramp, and an abandoned art deco post office, all overshadowed by a newly rising office tower. Urban landscapes are jumbled, inchoate, repetitive, and stereotyped. Urban designers must constantly work with these cultural bits and pieces, rough assemblages, and haphazard juxtapositions, since individual property owners, when they site and design their buildings, cannot—through the atomized market process alone—shape the meanings of the urban whole. However, in trying to reconstitute cohesive meaning, the urban designer need not impute to the place an organically indigenous spirit. The multifarious origins of environmental meaning point up one of the limits of organicism: The phenomenology of dwelling and the organicist tradition might lead us in search of a *volk*-spirit, a putative cultural and historical unity.

We need not do so. As urban designers, we can seek integrity of meaning across properties, without imposing indigenous correctness. In one place, the local identity we wish to articulate may well derive from strands of local history, but in another that identity might best evolve from today's living culture. Things made new or imported from afar may better express the aspirations of the place than trivial legends dressed up as history (see Sternberg, 1999). And the result should not be a homogenization of meaning. Working with boundaries, transitions, reflections, gradations, contrasts, complements, and interruptions, planners can set out to create coherent interrelationships among urban objects, without requiring that they conform to supposed indigenous origins. In shaping the urban cultural experience, planners should indeed respond to the market's tendency toward the fragmentation of meaning, but need not do so just through appeals for cultural unity; they can instead design to make diversity cohere.

Toward integrative foundations

The foregoing passages do not by any means exhaust the urban designer's integrative task in the city. A fuller discussion of an integrative theory of urban design would also consider *comfort*, the total of sun angles, microclimate, wind exposure, walking distances, rest stops, traffic barriers, and other outdoor elements that deliver intimacy and security, or otherwise exposure and discomfort, in the public realm. Comfort is another integrative dimension of the urban experience.

As we have seen, each of the pioneering writers on urban design has focused on one of these integrative facets of the built city. Walking or driving through the city, Sitte's and Bacon's observer experiences relative proportion, openness or enclosure, penetration into height, and ascent or descent. Lynch's urban traveler finds her way with respect to paths, edges, nodes, landmarks, and districts. Jacobs' urbanite lingers in the street through the combined effects of mixed use, fine grain, density, and permeability. And Norbert-Schulz's urban dweller finds meaning in buildings' and landscapes' references to history, myth, and nature.

Each of us combines in one human being these abstract urban observers. As I walk, I react to the scale of a building in relation to the scales of others and to that of my own body, in all their proportionate interrelationships, heightening my awareness of self in space. To make my way toward my destination, I draw geographical inferences and impose cognitive maps that orient myself in, and make sense of, the structures through which I move. Drawn and reassured by vitality on the street, I come out to join that urban commerce, and thereby contribute my own presence to the city's life. The landscape features I pass become meaningful to me through their capacity to express cultural referents, whether local or foreign. And my determination to continue walking depends on how well the landscape responds to my flagging strength, my desire for shelter, my need for rest, and my wavering curiosity.

Because all these capacities to experience are combined in one beholder, the designer's task is that of integrating them, though perhaps still stressing one facet of the urban experience or another. So the integrative principle that each of our pioneering authors stresses should not be confused with principles of composition. Foremost among these principles of composition is *continuity*. As Bacon (1974) writes, "The purpose of design is to affect the people who use it, and in an architectural composition this effect is a continuous, unbroken flow of impressions that assault their senses as they move through it" (p. 18). Cullen (1961) stresses "serial vision as the urban designer's fundamental concern" (p. 11). Bacon (1974) goes so far as to make continuity of experience part of his definition of architecture. He declares in bold type that the architect's purpose in urban design is to define the urban participant's sequence of experiences. As we have seen here, that participant's experience of the city coheres according to several integrative principles, which can be understood separately or in combination. Nodes and enclosure, fine grain and ascent into space, mixed use and myth, permeability and relative proportion—guided by explicit integrative principles, the urban designer must compose across experiential domains to produce a continuity of experience.

The urban designer's task is distinct from that of the architect (one working on a single property) because form, legibility, vitality, meaning, and comfort each act on observers across property lines and across the public-private divide. In our market-driven world, our experience coheres—or fails to cohere—across space that is otherwise segmented by ownership, use rights, and admission criteria. Operating according to an impersonal and autonomous logic, real estate markets slice up and subdivide the urban environment into self-contained compartments, generating cities that are incoherent and fragmented. Urban designers' primary role is to respond to this economic fact by reasserting the cohesiveness of the urban experience.

In designing any particular place, we should be able to declare the integrative principles—whether form, legibility, vitality, meaning, comfort, or other principles (this article has not exhausted them)—through which we want to make the place cohere. While these principles do have an economic rationale, a planning theory drawn from conventional economics is starkly incapable of deriving such principles. And the organic tradition is too gross and undiscerning to serve as a good guide. We need a theory of planning through which designers can recognize experiential integrity and begin to rebuild the coherence of urban form.

Urban design as a field of planning

Working with ideas drawn from Karl Polanyi and the organicists, this article has presented an integrative theory of urban design, though in incipient and preliminary form. With proper elaboration, could it meet the five challenges listed at the beginning of this article? First, as we have seen, the theory does reveal that the seemingly divergent schools of urban design have in common a set of principles for reintegrating environments that would otherwise be fragmented by market commodification.

Second, the theory is substantive, not procedural. The questions of process that procedural planning theory addresses are nonetheless essential to planning practice. Skilled in integrative principles of form, vitality, etc., the urban designer must still make her way within the organizational contexts of professional practice, negotiate and resolve disagreements, muddle along within the constraints of human knowledge, grapple with complex ambiguities, survive in a world of power imbalances, and present ideas with rhetorical force (see Forester, 1989; Innes, 1998). Like other planners, urban designers must interact with communities and constituencies in formulating plans (see Schneekloth & Shibley, 1995). So planners, including urban designers, must still look to procedural theory, though it is an incomplete tradition in planning thought. Substantive theory is its essential complement; this article has presented one attempt at a substantive theory.

Despite its focus on urban design, the integrative theory presented here eschews the idea that the urban design subdiscipline is adequately circumscribed by concepts of space or physicality. After all, some kinds of space and most kinds of physical objects are very well allocated through market mechanisms. And several professional fields, including land use planning and some of environmental planning, seek to shape the built environment. What makes urban design distinctive is that it has origins in a rich intellectual heritage that inquires into the human experience of the urban realm. Drawing on this heritage, integrative theory responds to the third challenge by specifying some of the constituents (legibility, meaning, and so forth) of our experience of built form.

What characterizes urban design, moreover, is that it seeks to sustain environmental integrity, or if that integrity has been undermined, to repair it, thereby shaping those environmental features that resist commodification. Having this as its calling, urban design benefits both from architectural inquiry and, unexpectedly, from economic debates about the roles of planning in capitalism. Therefore, integrative theory answers the fourth challenge: It seeks to unify what would otherwise seem to be disparate and irreconcilable economic and architectural traditions. It must be clear, however, that microeconomic theories of market failure, so often seen as potential theoretical sources for urban planning, cannot possibly serve as intellectual foundations for urban design. No microeconomic analysis could possibly generate the principles of interrelatedness across properties. It is rather through an integrative theory of urban design that planners can help make, repair, or preserve those environmental realms that pure markets would otherwise undermine through fragmentation and commodification.

Fifth, the concepts that this theory generates are eminently practical. In response to varied urban contexts, planners can work with proportions and contrasts, edges and landmarks, permeability and fine grain, and imported vs. indigenous meanings—each as contextually appropriate to shape better a place. It would be absurd to impose, say, Sitte's turbine plazas as a blanket requirement. Sitte's concepts, like those of others reviewed here, must be seen as sources of personal insight—as inspirations for the making of better plans, not as mandates. It would be a fundamental misunderstanding to take them as all-purpose policy recommendations or blanket prescriptions. It would be a further mistake to think of them as another kind of top-down planning. By elucidating the integrative principles, we do not at all have to revert to the idea that plans emerge as an act of will, thereupon to be hierarchically imposed on the city.

Like other planners, urban designers have to work in varied and complex institutions, in the midst of the push and pull of electoral democracy, subjected to varying political and budgetary stresses. They must pay attention to others' views, engage in give and take, and act as politically astute advocates of their ideas, using their rhetorical capacities to argue for good design. The design ideas they advocate should, nonetheless, be well founded on substantive principles. Having learned to explicate the integrative principles underlying our experience of the city, as for example the formal relationships of balance and proportion exerting effects across property lines, the urban designer would be better prepared to articulate and prepare for public scrutiny the arguments implicit in good design.

References

Alexander, E. (1992). *Approaches to planning.* Philadelphia: Gordon and Breach.

Bacon, E. (1974). *The design of cities.* New York: Penguin.

Banerjee, T., & Southworth, M. (Eds.). (1991). *City sense and city design: Writings and projects of Kevin Lynch.* Cambridge, MA: MIT Press.

Barnett, J. (1974). *Urban design as public policy.* New York: Architectural Record Books.

Calthorpe, P. (1993). *The next American metropolis.* New York: Princeton Architectural Press.

Cullen, G. (1961). *Townscape.* London: Architectural Press.

Dalton, G. (Ed.). (1968). *Primitive, archaic and modern economies: Essays of Karl Polanyi.* Garden City, NY: Anchor.

Duany, A., & Plater-Zyberk, E. (1990). *Towns and town-making principles.* New York: Rizzoli.

Forester, J. (1989). *Planning in the face of power.* Berkeley: University of California Press.

Geddes, P. (1968 [1915]). *Cities in evolution.* London: Ernest Benn.

Gottdiener, M. (1997). *The theming of America: Dreams, visions, and commercial spaces.* Boulder, CO: Westview.

Hall, P. G. (1988). *Cities of tomorrow.* Cambridge, England: Blackwell.

Hill, D. R. (1985). Lewis Mumford's ideas on the city. *Journal of the American Planning Association, 51*, 407–421.

Innes, J. E. (1998). Information in communicative planning. *Journal of the American Planning Association, 64*, 52–63.

Jacobs, A. B. (1993). *Great streets.* Cambridge, MA: MIT Press.

Jacobs, J. (1961). *Death and life of great American cities.* New York: Random House.

Krueckeberg, D. A. (1995). The difficult character of property: To whom do things belong? *Journal of the American Planning Association, 61*, 301–309.

Lynch, K. (1960). *The image of the city.* Cambridge, MA: Technology Press and Harvard University Press.

Lynch, K. (1981). *Good city form.* Cambridge, MA: MIT Press.

Madanipour, A. (1997). Ambiguities in urban design. *Town Planning Review, 68*(3), 363–383.

Marx, L. (1990). Lewis Mumford, prophet of organicism. In T. P. Hughes & A. C. Hughes (Eds.), *Lewis Mumford: Public intellectual* (pp. 164–180). New York: Oxford University Press.

Moore, T. (1978). Why allow planners to do what they do? A justification from economic theory. *Journal of the American Institute of Planners, 44*, 387–398.

Mumford, L. (1964). *The highway and the city.* New York: Mentor Books.

Mumford, L. (1968). *The urban prospect.* New York: Harcourt, Brace and World.

Norbert-Schulz, C. (1979). *Genius loci: A phenomenology of architecture.* New York: Rizzoli.

Radin, M. J. (1996). *Contested commodities: The trouble with trade in sex, children, body parts, and other things.* Cambridge, MA: Harvard University Press.

Rowley, A. (1996). Mixed-use development: Ambiguous concept, simplistic analysis and wishful thinking? *Planning Practice and Research, 11*(1), 85–97.

Schneekloth, L. H., & Shibley, R. G. (1995). *Placemaking: The art and practice of building communities.* New York: Wiley.

Sitte, C. (1965 [1889]). *City planning according to artistic principles* (George R. Collins and Christiane Crasemann Collins, Trans.). New York: Random House.

Sorkin, M. (1992). *Variations on a theme park.* New York: Hill and Wang.

Sternberg, E. (1993). Justifying public intervention without market externalities: Karl Polanyi's theory of planning in capitalism. *Public Administration Review, 53*(2), 100–109.

Sternberg, E. (1996). Recuperating from market failure: Planning for biodiversity and technological competitiveness. *Public Administration Review, 56*(1), 21–29.

Sternberg, E. (1999). *The economy of icons: How business manufactures meaning.* Westport, CN: Praeger.

Sussman, C. (Ed.). (1976). *Planning the fourth migration.* Cambridge, MA: MIT Press.

Tyrwhitt, J. (Ed.). (1947). *Patrick Geddes in India.* London: Lund Humphries.

Unwin, R. (1994 [1909]). *Town planning in practice.* New York: Princeton Architectural Press.

Source and copyright

This chapter was published in its original form as:

Sternberg, E. (2000), "An Integrative Theory of Urban Design", *Journal of the American Planning Association*, **66** (3), 265–278.

Reprinted with permission from the *Journal of the American Planning Association*, copyright summer 2000 by the American Planning Association.

5

Postmodern urban form

A. Loukaitou-Sideris and T. Banerjee
[1998]

Various changes have remolded the form, character, and social functions of the North American downtown. Some of these changes had to do with the transformed nature of the economy, others with the way that people live, and still others with the way that the built environment was produced (Sudjic 1992).

The classic city form had a semantic unity; it was organized around a center within which the social practices of politics, religion, business, and culture were exercised (Gottdiener 1986). As the urban center progressively lost its role in daily life (Jackson 1980), and as its primacy ceased to be the important prerequisite for many activities, the downtown lost its significance as the unifying heart of the metropolis. Later, in response to a restructuring in the early 1970s (Soja 1989), the downtown tried to resurrect its original importance. The center became the command post of a global economy (Abbott 1993) dedicated to power, money, and modern technology (Jackson 1980).

The rise of a service economy—in which finance, marketing, and the rendering of personal services have become the cornerstones of economic activities—brought about a downtown rich in signature buildings, upscale marketplaces, convention centers, and entertainment facilities. Advances in communication and information technologies in the late twentieth century allowed global mobility and flexibility in the accumulation of capital and reduced the importance of geographic location. Thus, in addition to the global cities of the United States (New York, Los Angeles, Chicago), second-tier cities also got involved in an unprecedented competition to attract corporate investment in their downtowns (Boyer 1992). The active state involvement of the previous era declined in favor of the increased role and significance of the private sector. Policy makers turned overwhelmingly to market-based solutions. Privatization, commercialization, and deregulation became key words for a policy that led to an increasing polarization between the haves and have-nots (Hitters 1992). As some researchers have documented (Fainstein 1994; Sudjic 1992; Grönlund 1993; Deben, Musterd, and van Weesep 1992), similar socioeconomic processes occurred simultaneously in other parts of the Western world and led to similar spatial outcomes in downtowns.

As Henri Lefebvre (1971, 31) has argued, space is political and ideological, a product "literally filled with ideologies." If space is the product, urban design is the tool that shapes it. Urban design interprets, expresses, and legitimizes the socioeconomic processes that affect the building of cities and their spaces. In that respect, the contemporary American downtown is a product of purposeful design actions that have effectively sought to mold space according to the needs of a corporatist economy and to subordinate urban form to the logic of profit. A new urban design language has invented a new downtown urban form. Some (Jameson 1991) have argued that this language represents a complete break from modernism. Others (Harvey 1989; Berman 1986) described it as an evolutionary and transitional phase of modernism, as reflecting a late modern rather than a postmodern discourse. But even if the new language represents an evolution and not a replacement, its vocabulary, syntax, and semantics are quite different from those of modernism. In the following section we will discuss the characteristics that distinguish postmodern design from its modernist predecessor.

Postmodern design

During the post–World War II period the modernist ideals of rationality and functionalism, modulated by concern for social welfare, overwhelmingly dictated the shape and form of downtown buildings and spaces. By the 1960s, however, it was clear that the modern movement's original imperatives had been replaced by the imperatives of an advanced capitalist economy. The legacy of the movement was not social housing for workers but flagship buildings for corporations. The building skyline of all major American downtowns was outlined by the flat rooftops of monumental glass boxes.

In the late 1960s a new design ideology appeared as a commentary and a reaction to the primacy of the modern movement. Interestingly, the postmodernist polemic against modernism concentrated more on issues of style rather than substance. Postmodernism advocated a selective revitalization of older styles (Jencks 1977), often leading to a pastiche of vernacular architectonic elements. The overall effect has sometimes been characterized as aesthetic populism (Dear 1986). Postmodernist writings were critical of the anonymity, standardization, and placelessness of the International Style. Reacting against the aesthetic austerity and purity of form that modernism had espoused, they called for an architecture of "complexity and contradiction" (Venturi 1966) that would draw from commercial and vernacular landscapes, as well as from the world of television and advertising.

While postmodernism seemed to concentrate on aesthetics, the construction of witty "decorated sheds" (Venturi, Scott Brown, and Izenour 1977, 87), some looked beyond the playfulness, depthlessness, and superficiality of this new design ideology. Fredric Jameson (1991) was one of the first to argue that rather than being a temporary stylistic fad, postmodernism represented the "cultural logic of late capitalism"—it was the product of and response to a historical reality, the third expansion of capitalism around the globe. A postindustrial economy, characterized by an internationalization of fictive commodities and based on financial and business services, required an architecture for the consumer, identified as the white-collar office employee (Lash 1990).

The idioms that compose the language of postmodernism intend to serve the same need: to make space all the more appealing for consumers. Many consumer experts argue that a product is more easily liked if it is familiar. Hence, while modernism often intended to shock its audience by using new materials and vocabulary and by breaking with the past, postmodern design uses familiar elements borrowed from older styles. Arches, columns, pilasters, and pediments are historical quotations, but they also provide visual references to beloved and popular settings of the world (Italian piazzas, country towns, European hill towns, and so on). Umberto Eco (1985, 166) has called this practice the "new aesthetics of seriality," where the repetition of known and expected patterns and themes aims to relax, entertain, and even amuse the viewer. Eco explains that postmodern aesthetics avoid interruption, novelty, or shock and instead value the repeatable, familiar, and expected.

Often a product has to be attractive or entertaining in order to sell. The minimalism and austerity of modernism are replaced by a pastiche of colors and by stylish and highly ornamental materials that intend to attract, impress, and at the same time promote the feeling of affluence in a materialistic, capitalist society. The aesthetic result blends well with the purposes of commercial enterprise. The appearance of the signifier is enhanced through decoration, packaging, and advertising, while the meaning and substance of the signified become fuzzy.

Sometimes a product needs to achieve some distinction in order to sell. The universality and standardization of modernism are replaced by designs custommade for developers and their clients. Ironically, however, these designs do not show any particular sensitivity to the context, culture, or local history of places, but simply provide the decor for the act of consumption (Boyer 1992). Scott Lash has argued that this postmodernist idiom reveals a "de-semanticized historicity," since historical signifiers are utilized not for their relationship to the history of the setting but simply for their ability to produce an effect on the consumer (Lash 1990, 72).

A product should not scare its prospective consumers. In contrast to the political agenda of the early modern movement, postmodernism appears neutral and apolitical; it is interested in aesthetics rather than ethics, in the medium but not the message (Harvey 1989; Ellin 1996). Postmodern design eliminates feared and unwanted political, social, and cultural intrusions. Space is cut off, separated, enclosed, so that it can be easily controlled and "protected." This treatment succeeds in screening the unpleasant realities of everyday life: the poor, the homeless, the mentally ill, and the landscapes of fear, neglect, and deterioration. In the place of the real city, a hyperreal environment is created, composed by the safe and appealing elements of the real thing, reproduced in miniature or exaggerated versions.

The use of a postmodern urban design language has been the trademark of development in contemporary American downtowns. In what follows we will present the major themes that capture the tragedy of postmodern urbanism, and we will analyze their impact on the urban form of American downtowns.

From synoptic vision to a collage downtown

"Make no little plans," urged Daniel Burnham, setting the pace for modernist town planning and downtown design. The modernist ideal of the "machine city" envisioned an urban environment broken down into functional segments that constituted the parts of a coherent whole. Downtown was one constituent part, and planners tried to homogenize it, unify it, plan for its totality. Grand plans and designs and large-scale urban models were the dominant tools of modernist planning and architecture.

Postmodernism advocated a very different approach to downtown design. The coherent canvas of modernism was now broken down into incoherent fragments. A collage of unrelated settings and spaces started appearing in downtown environments as a result of an urban design praxis that was commissioned by private entities. Because of its private nature, urban design became disjointed, episodic, incrementalist, and fragmented. When megablocks in downtown got developed, they composed self-sufficient environments instead of being pieces in a unifying master plan, as modernism had dictated. The postmodernist settings were not linked to the city; they excluded it instead. Horton Plaza in San Diego, Rincon Center in San Francisco, California Plaza in Los Angeles, and all the other cases that we have discussed in this book aspire to form miniature cities within their city. As will be recalled, the developers of the Metropolis project in Los Angeles promoted their project as a city within a city. The episodic nature of their development, combined with the public sector's lack of overall vision for downtown, prevents these increments of change from becoming integrated into the city's urban tissue. They remain incoherent fragments, and together they compose a collage of downtown spaces. This market-driven urbanism places more emphasis on aesthetic appearance and promotes the idea of space as a set piece designed to complement only the building, but not necessarily the rest

of the city. This urban design is oblivious of its immediate context and the overall urbanism. Attention is given to the architectural style and form, the colors and texture (remember the forty-nine shades used in Horton Plaza), the seating and landscaping of specific buildings, but not to urbanistic objectives such as coherence, continuity, transitions, and pedestrian connections.

The difference between modernist and postmodernist urban design ideologies is well illustrated when we compare urban design documents of different eras. *Design for Development* (Community Redevelopment Agency 1968), produced by the Los Angeles CRA in the mid 1960s, provided the overall framework for the redevelopment of Bunker Hill in Los Angeles. The *Los Angeles Downtown Strategic Plan* (Community Redevelopment Agency 1993) is the recent product of an advisory committee appointed by the CRA and composed of downtown businesspeople; developers; housing and social service providers; residents; cultural institutions; and consultants for urban design, historic preservation, economic planning, and transportation. The document discusses the future of downtown Los Angeles and recommends programs and projects.

The first document aspires to be a grand unifying plan. It strives to plan and determine the form and uses of all twenty-nine blocks of the Bunker Hill landscape. Its authors note that

> It is important to realize as essential to the overall concept, that the land uses, circulation system, and urban forms proposed throughout are immeasurably interdependent. The Design for Development is predicated on the total cumulative effect of complementary uses, integrated circulation patterns, and the structuring and interplay of urban forms. (Community Redevelopment Agency 1968, I)

The rhetoric of the text attests to the urban designers' wish for unification, integration, and comprehensiveness. The major concepts of urban form, as described in the document, are:

> A carefully conceived interaction of building volumes and open spaces.

> A strategic arrangement of building forms.

> A project-wide organization which differentiates one zone of activity from another while expressing their necessary interdependence within the whole of the project and related Downtown area.

An integrated organization of all open spaces.

A pleasant landscape environment unifying public and private areas.

A comprehensive design of public improvements. (Community Redevelopment Agency 1968, 4)

An illustrative plan included in the document clearly reveals the designers' intentions. The twenty-nine blocks are consolidated in twenty-four superblocks. The high-rise towers are connected with skyways, street-level connections, and mid-block linkages. Planting and paving is provided to unify the whole. This is a master plan that, true to the doctrines of modernism, presumes that the whole Bunker Hill area can be uniformly designed like a building and that its environment can be shaped and controlled in an overarching manner.

There is no illustrative master plan in the downtown strategic plan (DSP) of the 1990s. An aerial map of the downtown projected for Los Angeles in the year 2020 shows only the proposed building sites: "actual locations and sequences of development projects will depend on thousands of decisions made by public and private interests" (Community Redevelopment Agency 1993, 2). The document describes downtown Los Angeles as a collection of districts (the financial core, the markets, the civic center, the convention center, and so on). It discusses general "district strategies" but not downtown-wide physical plans. In the place of a unifying urban vision, designers talk about small-scale architectural intervention and a series of "catalytic projects" inserted into the existing districts. But few of these projects address the specific social context, the history of the site, or the local cultures.

In an effort to selectively draw from an invented imagery of downtown's Spanish past, the DSP proposes four *avenidas* with planting and broad sidewalks—seen as "corridors of power and commerce" in the new downtown (Community Redevelopment Agency 1993, 126); and four civic plazas: Pershing Square, Market Square, South Park Plaza, and Saint Julian Commons. Pershing Square, redesigned by architect Ricardo Legoretta as a stage set, aspires to be the living room for the office district. The proposal for Market Square, envisioned as a covered urban mall in the tradition of Les Halles in Paris (Betsky 1993), seeks to "revitalize" the presently very successful and predominantly Latino Grand Central Market by providing an upscale and trendy shopping environment. In doing so, it colonizes a thriving Latino commercial district (Morton 1994). South Park Plaza is envisioned as an open space for a proposed housing district consisting of condominiums and upscale executive suites; while Saint Julian Commons is reserved for the denizens of the city's skid row district.

The plan legitimizes a collage downtown composed of unrelated districts and privately initiated and financed projects. The districts are not given the same emphasis. The plan includes an extensive discussion of how the CBD (where all new private investment has concentrated) can become more "livable," but there is very little about the connections to and development of the "other" downtown.

The visible hand of privatization in downtown development

Privatization, the extreme reliance on private initiative and investment, is to a great extent responsible for the uneven development of many downtowns. Even the design initiative has shifted from the public to the private sector. With declining fiscal resources, local governments have become increasingly dependent on private investments for improvements and amenities and are forced to rely heavily on regulations and entitlement processes to negotiate the outcome of design (Loukaitou-Sideris and Banerjee 1993). Design concepts have largely been dictated by the designers hired by the private sector. Governmental efforts to shape public environments through urban design and public policy have been largely abandoned in favor of private initiatives (Francis 1988). Private developers have become the city builders, and frequently it is private interest that determines what gets built where in downtown. It is only rarely that any strategic planning is done by the public sector regarding the form and character of downtown's public realm: on how much public space is needed, where it should be allocated, which models of public space can best serve the needs of different segments of the public. In the absence of a broader public vision or purpose, the private production of downtown settings remains a non sequitur in a shrinking public domain. This is the inevitable result of a weakened and passive public design and a total absence of public initiatives.

Privatization has also resulted in the weakening of downtown's public domain. Although corporate open spaces are presumed to be part of the public domain, there is considerable ambiguity about whether they actually are. Legally, the corporate open spaces remain private property. In San Francisco, the presumption of public domain is legislated: an official plaque that declares the publicness of plazas is required. In Los Angeles and many other downtowns, this presumption at best remains in the planners' visions, and is not an official requirement. But even in San Francisco, the formal requirement has not always succeeded in integrating plazas and other private open spaces into the public realm. These spaces are inward oriented, cut off from the street, detached, and isolated. They are created for the benefit of the office tenants and not for the general public.

We have seen that private interests have always played a role in downtown development, but the complete subjugation of urban design to market forces is a phenomenon of the last two decades. Downtown urban design, because it is determined by private interests, has become reactive and opportunistic rather than proactive. The public sector reacts to the initiatives of the private sector for downtown building. The developers' actions are opportunistic, predicated upon their expectations of market response. Their objectives are profit and good business—which are not always congruent with good city form and urban design. This philosophy is quite different from earlier urban design philosophies that relied on the strategic location and investment of public projects and improvements to stimulate civic pride, sense of community, and private investment in a desired pattern.

Finally, the lack of strategic planning and the dominance of the private over the public sector in the creation of downtown's public realm have resulted in some lost urban design opportunities for downtowns. For example, the inward orientation and fragmentation of most urban plazas and downtown open spaces are in conflict with urbanistic objectives for coherence, effective linking of districts, and pedestrian connections. Plazas effectively turn their backs on one another, closing the city outside. This tactic produces a noncohesive arrangement of open spaces and a fragmentation of the public realm.

The polarization of new and old in downtown

In their effort to create exclusive settings and spaces accessible to some but not all, contemporary patterns of urban design serve only a limited public. This result has contributed to a polarization between the public, but old and derelict, downtown for the indigent, and the new, private, and glamorous downtown of the corporate America. Increasingly, the new downtown has come to be at odds with the traces of the old downtown, the Main Street of yesteryear. The public life of the Main Street downtown is vestigial at best and has been totally transformed by the culture of the poor, the homeless, and the new immigrants. What is left of the earlier downtown is ignored or forgotten as indeed are many of its denizens. This polarization is all too apparent in the segregated urbanism of contemporary downtown, and is a challenge yet to be addressed by most urban designs and downtown plans.

Reviewing the downtown plans of six cities (Cleveland, Denver, Philadelphia, Portland, San Francisco, and Seattle) in the 1980s, Dennis Keating and Norman Krumholz (1991) express skepticism that any of these plans can change the pattern of uneven development that insulates revitalized downtowns from all the socioeconomic problems that plague their ailing downtown frames. It can be argued that postmodern urban design contributes to the widening of the gap between the private downtown of corporate America and the public downtown of the poor. This gap is reflected in the distribution of downtown open space. Maps of the downtown areas of San Francisco and Los Angeles clearly show that the corporate plazas are not located in the high-intensity pedestrian and transit corridors. There are very few open spaces in and around the old downtown. Los Angeles is both an embarrassment of riches and an embarrassment of deprivation. Since the downtown rebuilding has systematically segregated the contemporary downtown from the historic core, corporate plazas normally do not have to worry about integrating different classes of users. But the contrast between the old and the new should haunt public policy. Should public priorities keep fostering investment into the new downtown while neglecting the poor and more ethnically diverse parts of the city?

Polarization of space in downtown happens also at the microlevel. In contrast to the modernist design scheme that placed buildings within a limitless and abstract public space, the postmodernist approach is to enclose public space, to drastically separate the fragment of new development from its context. In the examples that we studied we found that an array of architectonic elements is often utilized to produce the desired effect of seclusion. Developments are surrounded by blank walls and impenetrable street frontages. Frequently, plazas are sunken below the street level and, thus, separated from the life and activity of the city fabric. The exterior gives few clues to the space within the private premises. Major entrance points to plazas and open spaces are often through parking structures. Doorways and openings that provide a direct link to the street are de-emphasized. The intention of design is to create a break, a sharp contrast, between the gray exterior space and the bright interior courts and atria.

Interactive and creative uses of retail have not been exploited in the postmodern design of discrete projects and places. In the old days, street-level retail enlivened the downtown area and contributed to the vibrancy of the streets, but now postmodern urban design creates commercial projects that are islands. These developments, which usually occupy several consolidated blocks, deny the surrounding streets by placing retail around interior ways, plazas, and atria. Street vendors are perceived as a nuisance for corporate tenants and are chased away to their "proper place"—the dirty streets and alleys of the old downtown.

Downtown as a collection of spectacles

The fragments that compose the contemporary downtown can be presented as a series of spectacles or as variations on a theme park. A great deal of attention is given to developing a certain mood for each space, to promoting a theme park–type setting, to packaging and advertising the product, and finally to managing and maintaining the theme park environment. Postmodern urban design seeks to create catalytic projects in downtown and present them as a collection of spectacles. Sometimes the themes are imported from other parts of the world, as is the case with the Bunker Hills Steps in Los Angeles or Horton Plaza in San Diego. Other times the themes derive from glimpses into the city's past. South Street Seaport in New York and Inner Harbor in Baltimore revive and gentrify parts of older harbors; Ghirardelli Square in San Francisco renovates the shell of an old factory; Faneuil Hall in Boston adapts the structure of an old market to contemporary retail needs. A theme can also be devised by packaging together different settings and architectural pieces.

The theme park–like settings that have mushroomed in the American downtowns create an idealized image of the public realm, which in reality

was never so clean, safe, or stratified. Postmodern urban design strives to screen out the problematic social and physical elements of downtown. As the developers of City Walk, an outdoor mall in Universal City, California, argued, "A new and improved Los Angeles is needed" because "reality has become too much of a hassle" (Wallace 1992). The produced spaces are designed for passive viewers, tourists, conventioneers, and busy office workers who want to browse, safe and undistracted, through a collection of spectacles that tries to substitute for the real city center. This simulation of urbanity that combines the ideal with the real provides the stage set for consumption and is packaged so as to intensify the attraction of commodities (Boyer 1992).

Packaging downtown settings

The majority of projects built in the new downtowns are associated with commercial activities. Their space is orchestrated so as to encourage and stimulate the act of consumption. Commerce has always been one of the primary uses of American downtowns. Markets and streets in downtown were characterized by their public nature. They often served as places for social encounters and as forums for public life and political activity.

Public debate and political controversy have no place in the settings of the new downtown. Owners and developers want their spaces to be apolitical. They separate users from unnecessary social or political distractions, and put users into a mood consistent with their purposes. The facilitation of consumption becomes the primary objective in the orchestration of space. At the same time the poetics of design is utilized to dress up downtown settings so that they stimulate the imagination and fantasies of tenants and clients. Built form becomes a marketable product, a commodity. Design becomes thoroughly integrated into the packaging, advertising, and marketing of downtown real estate. As David Harvey argues (1989, 87–88) the application of postmodern design creates a "veil" in downtown that entertains, but at the same time masks and diverts attention from pressing social problems that lie behind the veil.

Many have argued that there has been a shift to concerns that are politically benign and are cosmetic rather than substantive (Ellin 1996; Crilley 1993). The emphasis that postmodern urban design places on the aesthetics of settings, on the ornamentation, styling, and packaging of the signifiers, diffuses such political questions as: Who benefits and who loses from such design? Whose priorities and needs are followed? Whose history is represented? and What is the sociophysical context that should be respected?

The contextless downtown

Ironically, postmodernism has followed modernism in producing an acontextual downtown. Like postmodern architecture, postmodern urban design also tends to be context independent. Postmodernism criticizes the universality and standardization espoused by modernism and advocates instead the introduction of an eclectic combination of architectonic elements— sometimes whole settings from the past—as historic signifiers. The Spanish Steps of Rome find their way to the heart of downtown Los Angeles, and London's Burlington Arcade is recreated in a major commercial street of Pasadena, California. But these efforts are not attentive to the current realities and particularities or to the local history and culture of their context. As a result, they do not carry any particular meaning. Quite often, there is a recreation of an idealized past or present, a nostalgic selection of the safe and likable attributes, and an attempt to erase all the troubling elements. Spaces are created simply to impress their users. This attempt of postmodern urban design to reestablish historical meanings often results in deriding and trivializing those meanings (Lash 1990). The principal concern about this postmodern urban design is not one of style, which dominates architectural criticisms, but rather one of its missing connections, linkages, and continuity in space and time.

It is possible to explain postmodern urban form essentially as a true landscape of a market economy, where each project attempts to outperform its immediate competition in scale, scope, and novelty of themes, driven by imperatives of profit maximization and market success. Product differentiation is critical in a competitive environment. Autonomy from the context is the driving force behind such an urban design. Yet the architecture and imagery of contemporary downtown projects, urban malls, plazas, galleries, and the like is characteristically similar in most American downtowns. This paradox can be explained by the fact that the goals of commercial or corporate developers are similar everywhere, and these are the goals that are expressed and served through design. Moreover, the superstar architects employed to create signature buildings in downtowns around the globe produce the same standardized form independent of the local context. This results in a franchise culture: an urban form created by multinational corporations, which incorporates popular and well-known elements and is reproduced at downtown centers in New York, Chicago, Los Angeles, London, Paris, or Tokyo (Zukin 1991).

Production of form and practice of design

Finally, we must consider the practice of design, which has been one of our major themes. We have examined on several aspects of downtown design—from public art to the production and packaging of individual projects. We have seen how in the absence of overall vision and direction, the public component of downtown urban design has become ad hoc and opportunistic. Because of their weakened fiscal position, cities have little leverage in influencing the location, timing, or direction of development. They don't have the resources to initiate the priming action that was common in earlier days. The public component of urban design has been essentially reduced to managerial and brokerage functions and, where feasible, to exaction of public benefits. Cities have essentially taken a reactive rather than a proactive stance. And because of this reactive position, the public sector has become more defensive and protective than it was in the past. Much greater emphasis is now placed on procedures, design and environmental impact reviews, and other such entitlement processes. It is as if urban design in the public sector has amounted to a "minimax" strategy— that is, one that minimizes "maximum" losses—for protecting the public good and interest. As we have seen from our cases in San Francisco, developers and property owners have considered such managerial oversight as authoritarian and meddlesome and, sometimes, counterproductive in terms of overall design outcome.

Even where the public sector has demanded public benefits from downtown developers and corporate clients, such as plazas and public art, these benefits have been presented mainly as ameliorative measures or reduced to bureaucratic formulas. Take public art for example. Public art has become an integral element of public urban design. Many downtowns have accumulated an impressive collection of art pieces—albeit located mainly within the privately owned plazas and courts—but their public purpose and their effect on the appearance of the city remain undefined and undetermined. At best they serve as window dressing that compensates for bad design or an ugly streetscape.

Similarly when such money is spent on performing arts—outdoor concerts and shows—the benefit is only to momentarily enliven a plaza that otherwise has very little life of its own. Clearly these gestures have not served as the glue that connects and integrates the disparate pieces. But most importantly, as in the location of and access to corporate plazas, there is little equity in the distribution of this benefit. Like plazas, public art is also concentrated in the white-collar district. The art serves little educational purpose. We suppose this outcome has a Nietzschean logic—that is, you judge the welfare of society by looking not at the lot of the worst off but at how the elite class benefits from a policy. If downtown urban design is judged by this logic alone, there is no doubt the present outcome will score high.

If the public component of urban design is reduced to legislative, procedural, managerial, and opportunistic tasks, how much of the environmental quality concerns that have guided past urban design plans—structure and legibility, form, comfort and convenience, accessibility, health and safety, historic conservation, vitality, diversity, sociability, and so on (see Southworth 1989)—figure in the designer's thinking on individual projects for corporate clients? We tried to find an answer to this question in our discussion with the designers about their personal rationale and vision for various projects. We discussed how each design scheme is guided by a poetics of form and place. Whether a design is officially adopted by the developer client or not, the rhetoric of design plays an important role in the way the designer identifies the problem, defines the constraints, and develops the scheme. But very little of this poetics concerns the larger public realm or a larger public good or includes any of the values implicit in earlier design plans (Southworth and Southworth 1973; Southworth 1989). The poetics of design almost always finds some internal rationale—be it from the site, the building type, or the imperatives of the market. Even where the poetics is derived from some external referent, like Jerde's metaphor of an Italian hill town or an urban theater, the connection is abstract. The immediate context rarely figures in this poetics of form or in the legitimation of the immediate design proposal. We also sensed in several instances that the designer's instinct to serve a larger public purpose was squelched by the client's concern for cost, competition, or risk. In these instances the poetics of form seemingly has mitigated the cognitive dissonance between the designer's ideal and the imperatives of market.

While we have established that contemporary urban design has become an ad hoc collection of discrete projects with their own internal rationale, we are not quite ready to concede that these characteristics define postmodern urban design. If there is a postmodern ideology that includes an image of good society, it has yet to define the nature of urban design. What we have in fact is an urban design under a postmodern condition, or more appropriately an urban design of a market-driven landscape.

Still, there have been some deep and fundamental changes in how individual projects are conceived, designed, and promoted. We have found that contemporary project development is an open-ended process; the competition and approval processes are not finite. The projects carry a great deal of uncertainty and risk. It may take anywhere from five to ten years from the time a project is conceived to the time it is actually built. In the meantime, market demand may change, the state of the economy will inexorably fluctuate, and global economic trends or the federal deficit may influence availability of capital and the cost of borrowing money. The rules of the game—in terms of the entitlement process—may change as well. So the design process requires considerable flexibility.

Indeed the process of project development and design is, as we have pointed out, not unlike the production of a movie or a show. It is a collaborative process that involves many actors and experts. Even the end products—especially the open spaces, gallerias, and so on—are seen as stage sets where what matters is the design of the overall experience rather than the space itself. The script for the uses of an open space is equally as important as the design of the setting itself. We have seen also how the promotion and inauguration of a modern office complex resembles a Hollywood production and premiere. Ultimately the changing scope of design—the transformation from designing spaces to designing experiences—may define the scope of postmodern urban design. The real question is how the future urban design—call it postmodern or not—will address the social issues and mediate the conflicts and contradictions of a polarized city.

References

Abbott, Carl. 1993. Five Downtown Strategies: Policy Discourse and Downtown Planning since 1945. In *Urban Public Policy: Historical Modes and Methods,* edited by Martin V. Melosi. University Park: Pennsylvania State University Press.

Banerjee, Tridib. 1993a. Market Planning, Market Planners, and Planned Markets. *Journal of the American Planning Association* 59(3): 353–60.

Banerjee, Tridib, Genevieve Giuliano, Greg Hise, and David Sloane. 1996. Invented and Reinvented Streets: Designing the New Shopping Experience. *Lusk Review* 2(1): 18–30.

Berman, Marshall. 1986. Take It to the Streets: Conflict and Community in Public Space. *Dissent* 33(4): 476–85.

Betsky, Aaron. 1993. All Roads Lead Downtown. *L.A. Weekly*, November 12–18, 16–19.

Boyer, M. Christine. 1992. Cities for Sale: Merchandising History of South Street Seaport. In *Variations on a Theme Park: Scenes from the New American City and the End of Public Space*, edited by Michael Sorkin. New York: Hill and Wang.

Burnham, Daniel, and Edward Bennett. 1970. Reprint. *Plan of Chicago*. Edited by Charles Moore. New York: Da Capo Press. Original edition, Chicago: Commercial Club of Chicago, 1909.

Colquhoun, Alan. 1985. On Modern and Postmodern Space. In *Architecture, Criticism, Ideology*, edited by Joan Ockman. Princeton, NJ: Princeton Architectural Press.

Community Redevelopment Agency of Los Angeles. 1968. *Design for Development: Bunker Hill, Los Angeles, California*. Los Angeles: Community Redevelopment Agency of Los Angeles.

Community Redevelopment Agency of Los Angeles. 1993. *Los Angeles Downtown Strategic Plan, Final Draft*. Los Angeles: Community Redevelopment Agency of Los Angeles, June 10.

Crilley, Darrell. 1993. Megastructures and Urban Change: Aesthetics, Ideology, and Design. In *The Restless Urban Landscape*, edited by Paul Knox. Englewood Cliffs, NJ: Prentice Hall.

Dear, Michael J. 1986. Postmodernism and Planning. *Environment and Planning D: Society and Space* 4(3): 367–84.

Deben, Léon, Sako Musterd, and Joan van Weesep. 1992. Urban Revitalization and the Revival of Urban Culture. *Built Environment* 18(2): 85–89.

Eco, Umberto. 1985. Innovation and Repetition: Between Modern and Postmodern Aesthetics. *Daedalus* 114(4): 161–84.

Ellin, Nan. 1996. *Postmodern Urbanism*. Cambridge, MA: Blackwell.

Fainstein, Susan S. 1994. *The City Builders: Property, Politics, and Planning in London and New York*. Cambridge, MA: Blackwell.

Francis, Mark. 1988. Changing Values for Public Spaces: Addressing User Needs Is Crucial to Success. *Landscape Architecture* 78(1): 54–59.

Gottdiener, Mark. 1986. Recapturing the Center: A Semiotic Analysis of the Shopping Mall. In *The City and the Sign: An Introduction to Urban Semiotics*, edited by Mark Gottdiener and Alexandros Ph. Lagopoulos. New York: Columbia University Press.

Grönlund, Bo. 1993. Särtryck: Life and Complexity in Urban Space. *Nordisk Arkitekturforskning* 4: 49–70.

Harvey, David. 1989. *The Condition of Postmodernity: An Enquiry into the Origins of Cultural Change*. Cambridge: Blackwell.

Hitters, Erik. 1992. Culture and Capital in the 1900s. *Built Environment* 18(2): 111–22.

Jackson, John B. 1980. *The Necessity for Ruins, and Other Topics*. Amherst: University of Massachusetts Press.

Jameson, Fredric. 1991. *Postmodernism, or, The Cultural Logic of Late Capitalism*. Durham: Duke University Press.

Jencks, Charles A. 1977. *The Language of Post-Modern Architecture*. New York: Rizzoli.

Keating, W. Dennis, and Norman Krumholz. 1991. Downtown Plans of the 1980s: The Case for More Equity in the 1990s. *Journal of the American Planning Association* 57(2): 136–52.

Lash, Scott. 1990. Postmodernism as Humanism? Urban Space and Social Theory. In *Theories of Modernity and Postmodernity*, edited by Bryan S. Turner. Newbury Park, CA: Sage Publications.

Lefebvre, Henri. 1971. *Everyday Life in the Modern World*. Translated by Sacha Rabinovitch. New York: Harper & Row.

Loukaitou-Sideris, Anastasia, and Tridib Banerjee. 1993. The Negotiated Plaza: Design and Development of Corporate Open Space in Downtown Los Angeles and San Francisco. *Journal of Planning Education and Research* 13(1): 1–12.

Morton, Pat. 1994. Getting the "Master" out of the Master Plan. *The Los Angeles Forum for Architecture and Urban Design Newsletter*, no. 2.

Rybczynski, Witold. 1993. The New Downtowns. *The Atlantic Monthly* 271(5): 98–106.

Soja, Edward W. 1989. *Postmodern Geographies: The Reassertion of Space in Critical Social Theory*. New York: Verso.

Southworth, Michael. 1989. Theory and Practice of Contemporary Urban Design: A Review of Urban Design Plans in the United States. *Town Planning Review* 60(4): 369–402.

Southworth, Michael, and Susan Southworth. 1973. Environmental Quality in Cities and Regions. *Town Planning Review* 44(3): 231–53.

Sudjic, Deyan. 1992. *The 100 Mile City*. London: A. Deutsch.

Venturi, Robert. 1966. *Complexity and Contradiction in Architecture*. New York: Museum of Modern Art.

Venturi, Robert, Denise Scott Brown, and Steve Izenour. 1977. *Learning from Las Vegas*. Cambridge: MIT Press.

Wallace, Amy. 1992. Like It's So L.A.! Not Really. *Los Angeles Times*, February 29.

Zukin, Sharon. 1991. *Landscapes of Power: From Detroit to Disney World*. Berkeley: University of California Press.

Source and copyright

This chapter was published in its original form as:

Loukaitou-Sideris, A. and Banerjee, T. (1998), 'Postmodern Urban Form', in Loukaitou-Sideris, A. and Banerjee, T. (1998), *Urban Design Downtown: Poetics and Politics of Form*, University of California Press, Berkeley, 277–296.

Reprinted with permission of The University of California Press.

6

A procedural explanation for contemporary urban design

R. Varkki George
[1997]

A crisis of identity?

The task of designing urban places—where the designer is primarily concerned with the sensual, but particularly visual, qualities of these places—has traditionally been termed *urban design*. Long associated with architecture and urban planning, urban design in the US began to acquire a distinct but weaker identity in academia as each of these two disciplines lost interest in the issues that engage urban designers (Dagenhart & Sawicki, 1992). Despite this weak academic identity, urban design continues to remain alive in several ways. First, urban places continue to be designed in cities across the US. This is true even if, as Kreditor (1990b, p. 67) points out, there is not an 'urban design practice carried out by professional urban designers.' Second, issues of concern to urban designers continue to be discussed at meetings and conferences of planners and architects, when they meet together and separately.

Despite the apparent impossibility of a commonly agreed definition of urban design, it could be argued that a meaningful explanation for contemporary urban design is vital, and that it is worth trying to arrive at one. This paper will attempt to make the case for this point of view and for the belief that a meaningful explanation of urban design is crucial to training a new generation of effective urban designers and for inspiring research that can inform the future practice of urban design. There is support for this belief (Symes, 1982; Colman, 1988), and it is not hard to see why: can a teacher tell her or his students, 'I will not tell you exactly what urban design is (or, I will only give you a vague description), but I will teach you urban design?' What will guide researchers in identifying research questions—other than the obvious questions about the sensual qualities of urban places—the answers to which will help urban designers do their job better?

In the author's experience of teaching urban design over several years to different groups of sceptical students, it has been necessary to articulate and refine a procedural explanation for urban design that is both sufficiently general and specific at the same time. It is procedural in that it focuses more on the means that contemporary urban designers use to create urban places. It is general in the sense that it is applicable across different situations, and that it is not overly restrictive in what it subsumes. It is specific in the sense that it provides a reason for engaging in specific analytic and synthetic tasks.

This paper presents the author's procedural explanation: essentially, it is argued that contemporary urban design is a *second-order design endeavour*; that is, the urban designer is only indirectly responsible for producing built forms and the spaces in between them. Unlike other design professionals, today's urban designers rarely design built artefacts; rather, they are mostly engaged in designing the decision environment within which others (sometimes these are other design professionals) make decisions to alter or add to the built environment. While the term *second-order design* is new, many of the arguments and ideas used to support the use of this term can be found scattered in the discourse generated when urban design practitioners and scholars have gathered to discuss urban design (Goldberg *et al.*, 1962; Pittas & Ferebee, 1982, *Ekistics*, 1988; Kahn & Speck, 1990). In particular, this explanation builds on and recasts—in a more useful way—the ideas of Jonathan Barnett, Robert Shibley, and Richard Lai.

The first section of this paper reviews what has been established in the literature and in practice as the tactics used by contemporary urban designers in the design of urban places. The second section presents the case for why the term *second-order design* is a good explanation for these tactics. The choice of this term rather than any other is explained together with the reasons for such an approach to design given contemporary circumstances.

The descriptive theorizing in this paper is directed more towards making sense of contemporary urban design practice than towards postulating the characteristics of good urban design practice. Hence, this paper attempts to explain rather than define. Second, the term *contemporary* is used to delimit the historic scope of my explanation because words such as *modern* and *postmodern* come with too many distracting associations from architecture and philosophy.

Describing contemporary urban design

With the 1971 San Francisco urban design plan (City of San Francisco, 1971) came a significant change in the way urban designers seek to shape the built environment in cities. Previously, the future urban fabric, as envisioned by the urban designer, was completely described and specified using drawings the way an architect would describe and specify a building. Based on these drawings, builders would execute the construction of the structures thus specified. The work of Le Corbusier in Chandigarh is illustrative of this kind of an architectonic approach.

Rather than use an architectonic approach, the urban designers of San Francisco—and in other cities such as New York (Barnett, 1982b)—sought to realize their vision of the future by influencing decisions made by the various individuals and organizations intending to alter or add to the built environment. These tactics, collected and expressed in a document using words and pictures, were intended to ensure that decisions made by different decision makers at different points in time would collectively and eventually produce the intended built environment.

In the 25 years since the San Francisco urban design scheme was formulated, such tactics have been used more widely (Ray, 1984, Shirvani, 1990), but they have also evolved somewhat in response to lessons learned from previous applications.

The description of contemporary urban design developed in this section clarifies the aptness of the definitions proffered by Jonathan Barnett, Robert Shibley, and Richard Lai. Urban design is designing cities without designing buildings because the intention is to realize a desired state of the built environment, but without actually designing the components of the environment. Urban designers are not authors of the built environment, rather they create a decision environment that enables others to author the built environment. The invisible web that urban designers spin is the decision environment within which designers make design decisions: urban design involves manipulating and structuring this environment. Each definition is by itself not quite complete, but perhaps together they sufficiently describe contemporary urban design.

How is urban design different?

Clearly, urban design as described above is an unusual type of design endeavour; it is different from design endeavours such as architecture, landscape architecture, interior design, and product design. One could distinguish between urban design and the other types of design endeavours in terms of the scale of the designed product (Scott Brown, 1982).

A more useful, sufficient, and complete distinction, however, lies in the relationship between the designer and the designed object. All designers, except contemporary urban designers, have a direct relationship with the object that they design, as schematically depicted in Figure 6.1. These designers make the decisions that dictate and directly shape the object. In an intellectual sense, they have ownership over the object. As described in the previous section and depicted in Figure 6.2 however, contemporary urban designers have only an indirect relationship with the designed object. They shape the designed object by influencing decisions made by other designers who then directly shape the object; they design the decision environment within which other designers create the designed object. (In this case, the word *designer* is used to include both professional designers as well as non-designers whose decisions shape the built environment; this is because professional designers are responsible for only a fraction of additions and alterations to the built environment.)

What term can we use to describe the relationship between the contemporary urban designer and the designed object? Contemporary urban design appears to be a higher-order design activity in the sense that it is indirectly related to the designed object. The term *metadesign* offers itself as a candidate. Meta-activities are those that involve the recursive application of an activity: for example, meta-analysis is the analysis of other analyses, it is 'analysis of analyses;' hence, metadesign can be understood to mean 'design of designs.' In that sense, unfortunately, the term *metadesign* is clearly too grandiose, and using it to describe urban design may be overstating the scope and nature of contemporary urban design.

Another candidate, the term *second-order design*, appears to be more appropriate. Second-order relationships are indirect relationships in the sense that the related objects are one step removed from each other. Some examples from human relationships might help delineate the difference between meta and second-order relationships: grandparents can be described as metaparents (they are 'parents of parents'): the children of siblings, on the other hand, are second-order siblings (they are not 'siblings of siblings,' rather they are siblings once removed from each other). Contemporary urban design is design that is one step removed from the designed object; hence, it is second-order design. While architectural programming is another second-order design activity, most other professional design endeavours involve first-order design.

FIGURE 6.1
The relationship between the typical designer and the designed object.

Why a second-order approach to urban design?

Why is a second-order approach to urban design necessary? Does such an approach reduce urban design to what Shirvani (1990, p. x) contemptuously refers to as 'a mere bureaucratic process'? Can urban design still be a creative task? Does urban design have to be an enterprise distinct from architecture

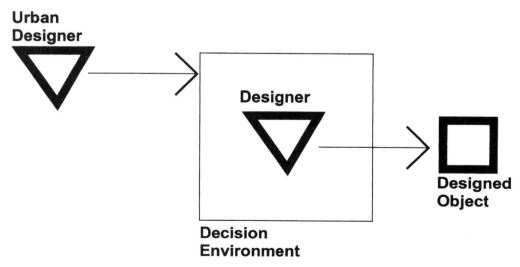

FIGURE 6.2
The relationship between the urban designer and the designed object.

and landscape architecture? It will be argued in this section that the circumstances under which urban design is practised today require a second-order approach. In the days of Pope Sixtus V and Baron Haussmann, and perhaps in the early part of this century, urban design could be a first-order design activity: very little about the project changed during the time it took to become reality; feudal systems allowed decision-making powers to be concentrated in the hands of a few individuals or even a single individual. In the more recent past, however, urban areas have been changing very rapidly, and this change is becoming even more rapid and widespread each passing year: it is hard to predict economic, technological, and social circumstances even a few years down the road. Compounding this rapid change, the increasing prevalence of democratic ideals necessitates increasingly distributed and perhaps decentralized decision-making powers.[1] Additionally, this distributed decision making presents the urban designer with multiple clients rather than the unitary client with which other designers interact. Further discussion of these issues is warranted.

Turbulent decision environment

As schematically illustrated in Figure 6.3, there is a difference between the decision environments encountered in first-order design and urban design.

Though complex endeavours in themselves, first-order design projects involve factors that are relatively stable over the time it takes to realize the design project. Factors such as function, climate, topography, and aesthetics are often extremely challenging to address, but nonetheless the nature of these factors can be expected in most cases to remain relatively stable while an object is being designed and constructed. Urban design projects involve these kinds of factors, but they also involve factors of an economic, political, social, and legal nature. These latter types of factors are liable to change significantly, particularly over the rather long time frame that most urban design projects take to be realized, thereby contributing to a turbulent decision environment. Second-order design is more appropriate to a turbulent decision environment because it is based on a strategic approach to decision making ('What do we *really* need to specify? What can we ignore?') rather than the comprehensive decision making that characterizes first-order design (where every aspect of the designed object must be specified).

Distributed decision making

In first-order design, the designer usually has control over, is involved in, or is directly responsible for all design decisions. In urban design, on the other hand, control over decisions that produce or alter

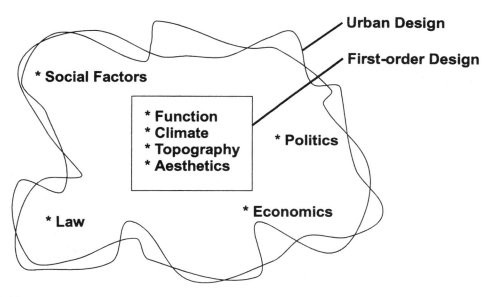

FIGURE 6.3
Different decision environments.

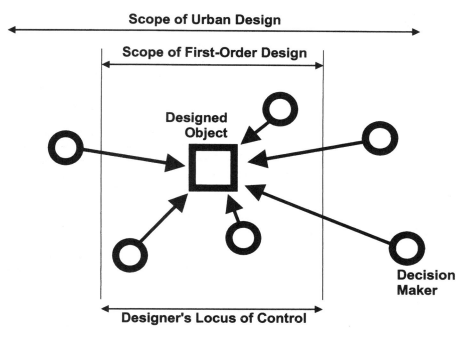

FIGURE 6.4
Different control over decision making.

the built environment is distributed across a wide range of private and public entities (Brown, 1982): decision making is 'complex and fractionated' (Scott Brown, 1982, p. 169). As a result, many of the decisions are outside the designer's locus of control. (This situation is graphically represented in Figure 6.4.) For instance, the built environment is affected when the owner of a parcel of land decides to renovate the structure on that parcel. It is also affected when a city official makes the decision to replace ageing light-posts in a residential neighbourhood or to redo the sidewalks in a commercial area. The urban designer can rarely participate directly in this myriad of decisions. Second-order design is appropriate to a situation characterized by distributed decision-making because the design solution is specified at a more abstract level and is, therefore, applicable across a wider range of situations than would be possible if the solution were specified in very concrete terms. To illustrate: where a neighbourhood is identified as historic through various public policy initiatives, property owners and city officials tend to make diverse first-order design decisions that preserve the historic aspects of the neighbourhood (whether this is good or bad in a particular instance is a different question altogether).

Multiple clients

No matter how large the scale of a project, first-order designers usually deal with a single client while urban designers deal with multiple clients (Barnett, 1982a). These multiple clients include the individual decision makers—individual property owners, developers, business interests, politicians—as well as relatively homogenous groups of these decision makers. A second-order approach to design is appropriate for dealing with multiple clients because a range of acceptable solutions is usually specified rather than a single solution: the likelihood of satisfying multiple interests and points of view is increased.

Conclusion

How satisfactory an explanation does the notion of second-order design provide? Does it, as Kreditor (1990a, p. 157) warns, 'disappoint and discourage further discussion'? In the author's opinion, this is far from the case. First, the explanation is sufficient to describe contemporary urban design. It is inclusive in terms of our ability to use this idea to explain the assorted activities and projects for which we use the term *urban design*. It provides a coherent rationale for this assortment that we find so hard to delimit and describe in a succinct manner. Second, rather than terminating further development of an urban design discourse, it prompts fresh questions about why we do certain things and how we can do them differently and better.

Notes

1. This is not to suggest that all urban design endeavours of the past 50 years have been democratic. As the anonymous referee points out, Nelson Rockefeller in Albany (and others would add Robert Moses in New York) oversaw urban design endeavours that were far from democratic. Still, in the past 30 or 40 years, there is a much greater pressure on urban designers to be less autocratic.

References

Alexander, C. *et al.* (1987) *A New Theory of Urban Design* (New York, Oxford University Press).

Alterman, R. & Corren, N. (1996) Designing design control: dimensions and dilemmas, Paper presented at the *Joint International Congress of the Association of Collegiate Schools of Planning and the Association of European Schools of Planning*, Toronto, Canada (July).

Appleyard, D. (1982) 'Three kinds of urban design practice', in: M. Pittas & A. Ferebee (Eds), *Education for Urban Design* (Boston, MA, Hutchinson Ross).

Attoe, W.C. & Logan, D. (1989) *American Urban Architecture. Catalysts in the Design of Cities* (Berkeley, CA, University of California Press).

Bacon, E.N. (1988) Bringing us back to our senses: The new paradigm for teaching design, *Ekistics, 55* (328–330), pp. 110–120.

Barnett, J. (1982a) For case studies and internships, in: M. Pittas & A. Ferebee (Eds), *Education for Urban Design* (Boston, MA, Hutchinson Ross).

Barnett, J. (1982b) *Introduction to Urban Design* (New York, Harper & Row).

Barnett, J. (1986) Architectural education: Teaching urban design now that clients really want it, *Architectural Record*, 174, p. 49.

Becker, J. (1992) The validation of computer simulations for design guidelines dispute resolution, Proc. of the International Symposium on Design Review, Cincinnati, OH (October).

Boyer, M.C. (1990) Erected against the city: The contemporary discourses of architecture and planning, *Center*, 6, pp. 36–43.

Brown, L. (1982) An urban designer speaks, in: M. Pittas & A. Ferebee (Eds), *Education for Urban Design* (Boston, MA, Hutchinson Ross).

Choate, C.L. (1994) The Ransom Place Information System: A hypermedia information system for preservation planning, unpublished Masters Thesis, Department of Urban and Regional Planning, University of Illinois at Urbana-Champaign (Champaign, IL).

City of San Francisco, Department of City Planning (1971) The Urban Design Plan for San Francisco (May).

Colman, J. (1988) Urban design: A field in need of broad educational innovation, *Ekistics*, 55 (328–330), pp. 106–109.

Dagenhart, R. & Sawicki, D. (1992) Architecture and Planning: The divergence of two fields, *Journal of Planning Education and Research*, 12(1), pp. 1–16.

Ekistics (1988) Professional education and training: Urban-rural planning and management; urban design; architecture, 55 (328–330), pp. 4–156 (Athens, Greece, Doxiadis Associates/Athens Center of Ekistics).

George, R.V. (Forthcoming) *HyperSpace*: Communicating ideas about the quality of urban spaces, *Journal of Planning Education and Research*.

George, R.V. & Campbell, M.C. (1994) Architectural design controls: Is the whole greater than the sum of its parts? Paper presented at the *36th Conference of the Association of Collegiate School of Planning*, Philadelphia, PA (July).

Goldberg, J., Montgomery, R. & Weismantel, W. (Eds) (1962) *Education for Urban Design*. Proc. of a conference held at Washington University School of Architecture (St. Louis, MO).

Gutman, R. (1988) *Architectural Practice: A Critical View* (Princeton, NJ, Princeton Architectural Press).

Hack, G. & Canto, M. (1990) Collaboration and context in urban design, *Center*, 6, pp. 74–85.

Hall, A. (1996) *Design Control: Towards a New Approach* (Oxford, Butterworth-Heinemann).

Hamnett, S. (1988) The current interest in urban design: Implications for planning education in Australia, *Ekistics*, 55 (328–330), pp. 101–105.

Hinshaw, M.L. (1992) Transforming suburbia through urban design; case study: Bellevue, Washington, Proc. of the International Symposium on Design Review, Cincinnati, OH (October).

Hough, M. (1992) Place-making and design review, Proc. of the International Symposium on Design Review, Cincinnati, OH (October).

Jacobs, A.B. (1982) Education for successful practice, in: M. Pittas & A. Ferebee (Eds), *Education for Urban Design* (Boston, MA, Hutchinson Ross).

Jacobs, A. & Appleyard, D. (1987) Toward an urban design manifesto, *Journal of the American Planning Association*, Winter, pp. 112–120.

Kahn, T.D. & Speck, L.D. (Eds) (1990) *Architecture vs Planning. Collision and Collaboration in the Design of American Cities* (published as Volume 6 of *Center*; New York, Rizzoli).

Knack, R.E. (1984) Staking a claim on urban design, *Planning*, 50 (10), pp. 4–11.

Kreditor, A. (1990a) The neglect of urban design in the American academic succession, *Journal of Planning Education and Research*, 9(3), pp. 155–164.

Kreditor, A. (1990b) Urban design: A victim of American academic tastes, *Center*, 6, pp. 64–71.

Lassar, T.J. (1989) *Carrots and Sticks: New Zoning Downtown* (Washington, DC, Urban Land Institute).

Lai, R. (1988) *Law in Urban Design and Planning* (New York, Van Nostrand Reinhold).

Lightner, B.C. (1992) A survey of design review practice in local government, Unpublished manuscript, School of Planning, University of Cincinnati (Cincinnati, OH).

Lynch, K. (1982) City design: What it is and how it might be taught, in: M. Pittas & A. Ferebee (Eds), *Education for Urban Design* (Boston, MA, Hutchinson Ross).

Moudon, A.V. (1992) A catholic approach to organizing what urban designers should know, *Journal of Planning Literature*, 6(4), pp. 331–349.

Nasar, J.L. (1988) The effect of sign complexity and coherence on the perceived quality of retail scenes, in: J.L. Nasar (Ed.) *Environmental Aesthetics: Theory, Research, and Applications* (New York, Cambridge University Press).

Pittas, M. & Ferebee, A. (Eds) (1982) *Education for Urban Design* (Boston, MA, Hutchinson Ross).

Rand, A. (1971) *The Fountainhead* (New York, New American Library).

Ray, G.H. (1984) *City Sampler: Catalogue of Urban Environmental Design Tools and Techniques in Local Government* (Washington, DC, Community Design Exchange).

Robertson, J.T. (1982) The current crisis of disorder, in: M. Pittas & A. Ferebee (Eds), *Education for Urban Design* (Boston, MA, Hutchinson Ross).

Scott Brown, D. (1982) Between three stools: A personal view of urban design practice and pedagogy, in: M. Pittas & A. Ferebee (Eds), *Education for Urban Design* (Boston, MA, Hutchinson Ross).

Selby, R.I. (1992) Design of a splendid city: A case study of urban synergy. Paper presented at the *34th Annual Meeting of the Association of Collegiate Schools of Planning*, Columbus, OH (October).

Shibley, R. (1982) Urban design as performing art, in: M. Pittas & A. Ferebee (Eds), *Education for Urban Design* (Boston, MA, Hutchinson Ross).

Shirvani, H. (1985) *The Urban Design Process* (New York, Van Nostrand Reinhold).

Shirvani, H. (1990) *Beyond Public Architecture: Strategies for Design Evaluations* (New York, Van Nostrand Reinhold).

Stamps, A.E. (1991) All buildings great and small: Design review from high rise to houses, *Environment and Behavior*, 23(5), pp. 402–420.

Stamps, A.E. (1994) Comparing preferences of neighbors and a neighborhood design review board, *Environment and Behavior*, 26(3), pp. 616–629.

Symes, M. (1982) Urban design education in Britain and America, in: M. Pittas & A. Ferebee (Eds), *Education for Urban Design* (Boston, MA, Hutchinson Ross).

Toon, J. (1988) Urban planning and urban design, *Ekistics*, 55 (328–330), pp. 95–100.

Trache, H. (1996) The design dimension of local land use plans: A review of current French practice. Paper presented at the *Joint International Congress of the Association of Collegiate Schools of Planning and the Association of European Schools of Planning*, Toronto, Canada (July).

Source and copyright

This chapter was published in its original form as:

Varkki George R (1997), 'A Procedural Explanation for Contemporary Urban Design', *Journal of Urban Design*, **2** (2), 143–161.

Reprinted with permission of Taylor & Francis Ltd (http://www.tandf.co.uk/journals)

Section Two

The morphological dimension

Appreciation of urban morphology – that is, the layout and configuration of urban form and the processes giving rise to them – helps urban designers be aware of local patterns of development and processes of change. Morphologists have shown that settlements could be seen in terms of several key elements and, in addition, emphasised the difference in their temporal stability (e.g. Conzen, 1960). Buildings, and particularly the land uses they accommodate, are usually the least resilient elements. Although more enduring, the plot pattern also changes over time as plots are subdivided or amalgamated. The street or cadastral pattern tends to be the most enduring element. Many urban design writers have attempted to analyse and understand these changing patterns and the reasons for them.

A key tool for analysing urban form has been the figure-ground diagram – an early advocate of which was Colin Rowe. In *Collage City*, Rowe and Koetter (1979) described the 'spatial predicament' of the Modernist city as one of 'objects' and 'texture'. Objects are sculptural buildings standing freely in space, while texture is the background matrix of built form defining space. Rather than privileging the positive space or the positive building, they recognised situations where one or the other would be appropriate and that the situation to be hoped for would be '… *one in which both buildings and spaces exist in an equality of sustained debate. A debate in which victory consists in each component emerging undefeated*' (Rowe and Koetter, 1979: 83).

In practice, however, common observations have drawn attention both to the lack of well-defined positive space and to the important role played by more mundane and relatively anonymous buildings that define space – Kelbaugh (2002: 99), for example, defines these as 'background' or 'collateral' buildings, which '… *gain their strength from the public space they define*'. In the absence of explicit concern for the spaces between the buildings, many environments are simply random collections of individual buildings rather than synergistic combinations of buildings and spaces. In practice, the spaces between object-buildings need to be – but often are not – expressly designed; the spaces between buildings-defining-spaces have less need to be expressly designed.

This Section presents a set of three chapters. The first chapter, Chapter 7, is **Roger Trancik's** 'What is lost space?', which forms a chapter in his 1986 book, *Finding Lost Space: Theories of Urban Design* (Van Nostrand Reinhold, New York) – a highly accessible, but curiously neglected book in the urban design canon. The chapter develops from the recognition

that there are essentially two types of urban space system, which can be referred to as 'traditional' and 'Modernist'. Traditional urban space consists of buildings as constituent parts of urban blocks, where the blocks define and enclose positive, external space – that is, 'figural space'. Modernist urban space conventionally consists of freestanding 'pavilion' (or 'object') buildings in landscape settings – that is, 'figural buildings'. Trancik's chapter explains how Modernist ideas of urban space design, combined with development practices during the twentieth century, created a phenomena he aptly describes as 'lost' space: '… *individual buildings isolated in parking lots and highways*' (Trancik, 1986: 21). Trancik's chapter both presents his concept of 'lost space' – a useful way of conceiving the transformation of urban space in the late part of the twentieth century – and then gives some explanation about why it came about, emphasising as causes the automobile and the highway; the Modern Movement in architecture; urban renewal and zoning; the privatisation of public space; and changing patterns of land use in urban areas.

Chapter 8 is **Leslie Martin's** 'The grid as generator', the opening essay in his book, *Urban Space and Structures* (Cambridge University Press, Cambridge), co-edited with Lionel March, his fellow researcher at the then Centre for Land Use and Built Form Studies (now the Martin Centre) at the University of Cambridge. Attempting to provide a strong theoretical basis for urban space design, the book represented an extraordinary breakthrough in urban research, by demonstrating how cadastral patterns and block sizes affect the distribution of urban space and the sustainability of urban form over time. The chapter explores relationships that Raymond Unwin had begun to grasp (but had not developed) in his pioneering pamphlet *Nothing Gained By Overcrowding* (1912). From a somewhat different perspective, Le Corbusier also examined similar relationships in his Plan Voisin for Paris in the 1920s. Martin examined different configurations of built form and open space, in order to explore the desirability of the outcomes. Rather than prescribing preferred options and layouts, he stressed the importance of being aware of what options were possible. For example, small block sizes are often advocated for reasons such as urban vitality, permeability, visual interest and legibility (Jacobs, 1961: 191–99; Krier 1990: 198), while larger block structures may be more efficient in terms of the distribution of built form and open space. By examining the densities and land use intensities of different development patterns, Martin was able to provide mathematical arguments supporting the principles of larger block sizes and perimeter rather than pavilion development.

Chapter 9 is **Douglas Kelbaugh's** 'Typology: An architecture of limits', published as a chapter in his 2002 book, *Repairing the American Metropolis* (University of Washington Press, Seattle). Focusing on a discussion of limits and constraints in design and how, for example, site and programmatic constraints may actually make the design process easier, this chapter presents a valuable argument about functionalism and typology and the more general shift from Modernism to contemporary ideas of urban space design. Typology formalises the processes of learning from experience and precedent and revives a traditional way of looking at function. While, for functionalists, the design process starts with analysis of the problem at hand, typologists look at how design problems have been solved in the past, especially in similar physical and cultural milieus, and assert that typology is a better point-of-departure when designing a building or part of a city.

It is important to note, however, that the use of types and typology have generally been more readily accepted among the urban design community than among the architectural community. This relates both to urban design being a 'second-order' design activity (see Section One) and to the value placed on originality and novelty within the architectural community. Kelbaugh makes a very valuable commentary on the relationship between scale and originality in design. He asserts that typology has 'shifted the scale at which the freedom to invent occurs' and argues that: '*Getting the types right for a given street, neighbourhood, or community is usually more important than the architectural brilliance of individual buildings.*' Indeed, at the start of his chapter, he quotes Andres Duany's comment on the 'appalling' win/loss ratio of Modernist architecture:

> '*I would have no problem with modernist architecture were it not for its appalling win-to-loss ratio. I am not prepared to tolerate the thirty million modernist buildings that have destroyed the cities of the world in exchange for the three thousand (or is it three hundred?) undeniable masterpieces of modernism*' (cited in Kelbaugh, 2002: 94).

Kelbaugh's argument is that not only did architectural Modernism pursue novelty and originality for their own sake, but that it also pursued them at the wrong scales.

Matthew Carmona and Steve Tiesdell

7

What is lost space?

Roger Trancik
[1986]

The problem of urban design today

In today's cities, designers are faced with the challenge of creating outdoor environments as collective, unifying frameworks for new development. Too often the designer's contribution becomes an after-the-fact cosmetic treatment of spaces that are ill-shaped and ill-planned for public use in the first place. The usual process of urban development treats buildings as isolated objects sited in the landscape, not as part of the larger fabric of streets, squares, and viable open space. Decisions about growth patterns are made from two-dimensional land-use plans, without considering the three-dimensional relationships between buildings and spaces and without a real understanding of human behavior. In this all too common process, urban space is seldom even thought of as an exterior volume with properties of shape and scale and with connections to other spaces. Therefore what emerges in most environmental settings today is unshaped antispace.

The approach proposed in this text falls between the design of site-specific buildings and that of the urban land-use plan. It is centered on the concept of *urbanism* as an essential attitude in urban design, favoring the spatially connected public environment over the mere *master planning* of objects on the landscape. This approach calls for making figurative space out of the lost landscape. As professionals who permanently influence the urban environment, architects, urban planners, and landscape architects have a major responsibility to meet the challenge of redesigning lost spaces that have emerged over the last five decades or so in most major American and European cities. Understanding the concept of antispace as a predominant spatial typology is essential in contemporary urban design practice.

Every modern city has an amazing amount of vacant, unused land in its downtown core—hundreds of acres in most major American cities. For instance in Pittsburgh, Pennsylvania, there are 4,930 acres of industrial land, 260 acres of underutilized railroad land, and 17.5 miles of riverfront available for redevelopment today within the city boundaries.[1] As the movement to suburbia during the fifties and sixties drew industry and people to the periphery, previously viable downtown land became desert. Over the past few years, radically changing economic, industrial, and employment patterns have further exacerbated the problem of lost space in the urban core. This is especially true along highways, railroad lines, and waterfronts, where major gaps disrupt the overall continuity of the city form. Pedestrian links between important destinations are often broken, and walking is frequently a disjointed, disorienting experience. It is important first to identify these gaps in spatial continuity, then to fill them with a framework of buildings and interconnected open-space opportunities that will generate new investment. Identification of the gaps and overall patterns of development opportunities should be done before any site-specific architecture or landscape architecture is designed and as a key element in urban land-use planning.

Designers of the physical environment have the unique training to address these critical problems of our day, and we can contribute significantly toward restructuring the outdoor spaces of the urban core. Lost spaces, underused and deteriorating, provide exceptional opportunities to reshape an urban center, so that it attracts people back downtown and counteracts sprawl and suburbanization.

Lost space defined

What exactly is lost space and how does it differ from positive urban space, or 'found' space? Lost space is the leftover unstructured landscape at the base of high-rise towers or the unused sunken plaza away from the flow of pedestrian activity in the city. Lost spaces are the surface parking lots that ring the urban core of almost all American cities and sever the connection between the commercial center and residential areas. They are the no-man's-lands along the edges of freeways that nobody cares about maintaining, much less using. Lost spaces are also the abandoned waterfronts, train yards, vacated military sites, and industrial complexes that have moved out to the suburbs for easier access and perhaps lower taxes. They are the vacant blight-clearance sites— remnants of the urban-renewal days—that were, for a multitude of reasons, never redeveloped. They are the residual areas between districts and loosely composed commercial strips that emerge without anyone realizing it. Lost spaces are deteriorated parks and marginal public-housing projects that have to be rebuilt because they do not serve their intended purpose. Generally speaking, lost spaces are the undesirable urban areas that are in need of redesign— antispaces, making no positive contribution to the surroundings or users. They are ill-defined, without measurable boundaries, and fail to connect elements in a coherent way. On the other hand, they offer tremendous opportunities to the designer for urban redevelopment and creative infill and for rediscovering the many hidden resources in our cities.

The causes

There are five major factors that have contributed to lost space in our cities: (1) an increased dependence on the automobile; (2) the attitude of architects of the Modern Movement toward open space; (3) zoning and land-use policies of the urban-renewal period that divided the city; (4) an unwillingness on the part of contemporary institutions—public and private—to assume responsibility for the public urban environment; and (5) an abandonment of industrial, military, or transportation sites in the inner core of the city.

The automobile

Of all these factors, dependence on the automobile is the most difficult to deal with, since it is so deeply ingrained in the American way of life. It has resulted in an urban environment in which highways, thoroughfares, and parking lots are the predominant types of open space.

Mobility and communication have increasingly dominated public space, which has consequently lost much of its cultural meaning and human purpose. A staggering percentage of urban land in major

FIGURE 7.1
Washington, D.C. Aerial Photograph. Valuable urban lands are often given over to the excessive movement and storage of automobiles. (Courtesy: Marvin I. Adleman)

modern cities is devoted to the storage and movement of automobiles—in Los Angeles and Detroit as much as 75 to 80 percent. Partly because of this, buildings are separated, encompassed by vast open areas without social purpose. Streets, no longer essential urban spaces for pedestrian use, function as the fastest automobile link, regardless of social cost. At the outskirts of the city the street has become the 'strip,' the square a parking lot framed by unrelated buildings.

Modern Movement in design

Also contributing to lost outdoor space was the Modern Movement in architectural design. At its zenith from 1930 to about 1960, this movement was founded on abstract ideals for the design of free-standing buildings; in the process it ignored or denied the importance of street space, urban squares and gardens, and other important outdoor rooms.

In the Piazza Navona District of Rome, streets and square are carved out of the building mass, giving direction and continuity to urban life and creating physical connections, meaningful places. In Houston, Texas, on the other hand, the urban form consists of separate buildings floating among parking lots and roadways. An identifiable ring of lost space encircles the urban core and spatially segregates surrounding residential areas—a typical pattern of most American cities (fig. 7.3).

How did this happen? Designers and builders influenced by the Modern Movement abandoned principles of urbanism and the human dimension of outdoor space established in the urban design of cities of the past. The profile of the Medieval or Renaissance city, our most important historic urban design models, is generally low and horizontal, and there is usually a close connection between life inside the buildings and activity on the street. With the advent of the mechanical elevator and new technologies of construction, the modern city has become an environment of high-rise towers removed from street life. Activities on the streets of Manhattan have little to do with the functions of the high-rises above.

The social and commercial role of the traditional street has been further undermined by such Modern Movement design features as enclosed malls, mid-block arcades, and sunken or raised plazas. These have siphoned shopping and entertainment off the street, which no longer functions as a gathering place. The modern city dweller is forced to create a social life on personal, controllable territory instead of engaging in a communal existence centered around the street. As a consequence, individual attitudes toward the use of urban space have been radically altered.

With the loss of a collective sense of the meaning of public space, we have also lost the sense that there are rules for connecting parts through the design of outdoor space. In the traditional city, the

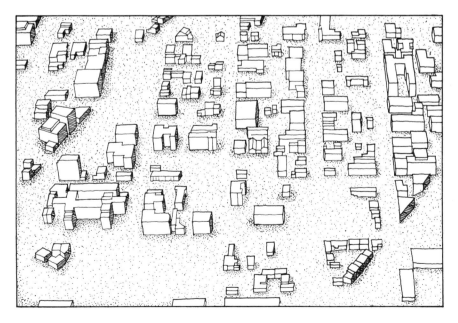

FIGURE 7.2
Washington, D.C. Diagram of the same site as fig 7.1, showing how roadways and parking lots have destroyed the consistency of the urban fabric. Without the paved surfaces buildings have little if any relationship to one another.

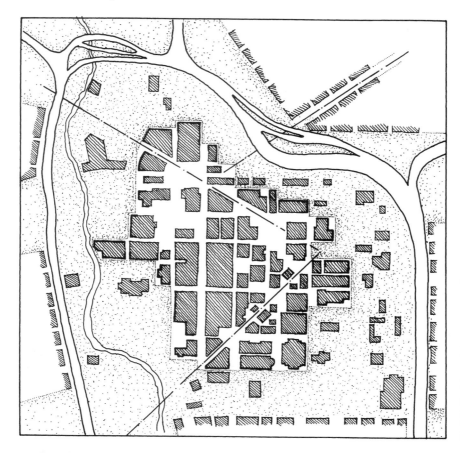

FIGURE 7.3
Diagram of the Form of the Typical American City. The high-rise core (hatched area) is surrounded by a belt of parking lots and highways created during urban renewal (stippled areas)—a ring of lost space that segregates downtown from residential neighborhoods. This diagram is based on the form of downtown Syracuse, New York.

rules were clear. Buildings were subordinate to the more powerful collective realm—to an implicit vocabulary of design and a deference to the larger order of things. The 'manners and rules of a place' gave instructions on how to connect.[2] One of the challenges to urban design in our times is to redevelop a sense for the rules and, in doing so, to bring back some richness and variety to public life—important ingredients in cities of the past.

In criticizing the form of the modern city, the intention is not to imply that the architecture and urban design of the last half-century has been an utter failure or that the works of many great designers should be rejected out of hand. Functionalism, which laid the groundwork for our loss of traditional space, became obsessed with efficiency, but, like any great historical movement, it was most concerned with meanings and the problem of giving man an existential foothold. The ethics of modernism have proved inadequate, and its synthetic vision and preemptive dogma no longer constitute the dominant

frame of reference in city design. Renewed interest in historicism and the traditional city, which were neglected by the Modernists, has reintroduced the grammar of ornament, metaphor, and style, which can reunite the many aspects of building as an art responsive to the larger issues of contemporary society.[3]

Zoning and urban renewal

The loss of traditional qualities of urban space has also been the result of zoning policies and urban-renewal projects implemented during the 1950s and 1960s. These closely allied approaches to planning were well-intentioned, if ultimately misguided, responses to urban decay. The impulse was to clear the ground, sanitize, and promote human welfare through the segregation of land uses into discrete zones and the substitution of high-rise towers for ground-level density. Urban-renewal projects rarely corresponded in spatial structure to the evolved community pattern they replaced, nor did they respond to the social relationships that gave meaning to community existence. Zoning legislation had the effect of separating functions that had often been integrated. Discrete districts segregated living space from working space. Isolated 'superblocks' formed by urban-renewal plans closed off historic streets, drastically affecting the scale of the city. Abstract notions of compatible uses created urban areas that could no longer accommodate physical or social diversity, and that therefore were no longer truly urban. Both zoning and urban renewal substituted functional for spatial order and failed to recognize the importance of spatial order to social function.

Privatization of public space

The sanctity of private enterprise has also contributed significantly to lost space in our urban centers. While the economic health of a city strengthens its downtown, it also creates a heavy demand for floor space in the center, thereby pushing toward the vertical city. A byproduct has been the appropriation of public space for private expression. Each site is seen as a place for 'image' buildings as a potential corporate flagship. The very idea of modestly fitting into the collective city is antithetical to corporate aspirations and the chest-beating individualism of the American way.

We have transformed the city of collective spaces into a city of private icons. Regulations intended to define the broader urban vocabulary and to govern individual projects are regularly waived if they do not suit the whims of the particular developer. The continuities of streets are broken by ill-placed buildings, height ordinances are frequently violated, and varied materials and facade styles compete stridently for attention. The city becomes a showplace for the private ego at the expense of the public realm.

In cities of the past, the designs for streets, squares, parks, and other spaces in the public realm were integrated with the design of individual buildings. 'Standards for the integration of architecture and urban spaces were set by the patrons and builders of the Renaissance—that model society architects should take as their most important precedent.'[4] But in the modern city, each element is the responsibility of a different public or private organization, and the unity of the total environment is lost. Various development and urban-renewal projects are, by and large, put together separately, without an overriding plan for public space. The result is a patchwork quilt of private buildings and privately appropriated spaces, usually severed from an historical context.

As government has become more departmentalized and private interests more segregated from public, the feeling that there is a framework of common concern has been lost. Competition between a fragmented system of government decision making, bureaucratic regulations, community participation, and the sacred cow of private money, together with a mayoral scramble for limited federal tax dollars, has made a shambles of the orderly interrelationship of a city's buildings, open spaces, and circulation. Further, the institutional neglect of the public realm is a monumental problem both because of minimal investment in maintaining public space and a general lack of interest in controlling the physical form and appearance of the city. In any redesign of urban space the conflict between public good and private gain must be resolved.

Changing land use

The final major cause of lost space has been the pervasive change in land use in most American cities over the past two decades. The relocation of industry, obsolete transportation facilities, abandoned military properties and vacated commercial or residential buildings have created vast areas of wasted or underused space within the downtown core of many cities. These sites offer enormous potential for reclamation as mixed-use areas, especially since the exodus from the inner city seems to be reversing. The obsolete shipping or rail yard frequently occupies a desirable waterfront site. The abandoned warehouse, factory, or wholesale outlet may have attractions as centrally located, architecturally interesting, and relatively inexpensive housing. Vacant land can be temporarily used for productive urban gardens, commercial horticulture, or neighborhood playgrounds. For the developer, advantages in reusing such sites are obvious; however, the contribution that well-conceived spatial changes might make to the urban fabric of the entire city offers social advantages that go far beyond those of economic gain.

Redesigning lost space

The five factors we have discussed—the highway, the Modern Movement in architecture, urban renewal and zoning, competition for image on the part of private enterprise, and changing patterns of land use in the inner city—have, then, together created the dilemma of modern urban space. Most striking has been the unwillingness or inability of public institutions to control the appearance and physical structure of the city. This has resulted in the erosion of a collective framework and visual illiteracy among the public. The government must institute strong policies for spatial design, the public must take part in shaping its surroundings, and designers must understand the principles underlying successful urban space.

In order to address the lost-space question, designers should create site plans that become generators of context and buildings that define exterior space rather than displace it. In a successful city, well-defined outdoor spaces are as necessary as good buildings, and the landscape architect, in concert with architects and planners, should contribute to their creation.

The history of city design shows that exterior urban space, if conceived of as figural volume rather than structureless void, can reverse the unworkable 'figure-ground' relationships between buildings and open spaces of the modern city. A lesson we can learn from traditional, preindustrial, cities is that exterior space should be the force that gives definition to the architecture at its borders, establishing the walls of the outdoor room. People's image of and reaction to a space is largely determined by the way it is enclosed. People like rooms. They relate to them daily in their homes and at work. This probably explains why tourists and residents enjoy the structured urban rooms of Europe in cities such as Rome, Venice, and Paris or the garden rooms of Villa Lante, Vaux-le-Vicomte, and Versailles.

In urban design the emphasis should be on the groups and sequences of outdoor rooms of the district as a whole, rather than on the individual space as an isolated entity. Special attention should be given to the residual spaces between districts and the wasteland at their edges. We need to reclaim these lost spaces by transforming them into opportunities for development; infill and recycling can incorporate such residual areas into the historic fabric of the city. Existing public plazas, streets, and parking lots that are presently dysfunctional and incompatible with their contexts can be transformed into viable open spaces. These design and development strategies can also provide the impetus to attract people back to the center. By identifying lost spaces in the city as opportunities for creative infill, local governments can allocate funding to stimulate private investment through 'enterprise zones' and other community-development programs.

One of the major requirements therefore is to design environments in which individual buildings are integrated with exterior public space so that the physical form of the city does not fall victim to separation caused either by zoning or by a dictatorial circulation system. How can we do this—how can we give structure to our urban spaces so that they provide a unifying framework for groups of buildings of disparate architectural form and style? In order to find the answer, we should look closely at the traditional city, particularly at the principle of enclosure that gives open space its definition and connection, creating workable links between spaces (fig. 7.4). We need to return to the theories and models of urban space that worked in the past and to develop a design vocabulary based on these successful precedents for today's cities. Maybe we 'finally have to understand that history and environment

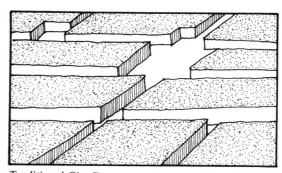

Traditional City Form

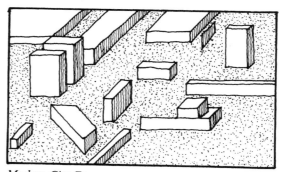

Modern City Form

FIGURE 7.4
Traditional and modern urban form. These drawings illustrate the spatial structure of traditional cities *(above)* and the fragmentary form of the modern city *(below)*. In the traditional city, urban blocks direct movement and establish orientation; in the modern city, the fragmentary and confused structure creates disorientation. (Drawing based on diagrams by Rob Krier)

are the two faces of architecture, that no building stands alone';[5] 'and that architectural solutions however brilliant cannot overcome the limitations of the urban fabric in which they are placed.'[6]

We have introduced the importance of the outdoor environment as a social and physical space and some of the causes of its decline in the modern city. The most basic act in urban landscape design should be to establish the spatial framework of public design 'rules' for streets, squares, and open spaces prior to the design of individual buildings. This code of rules should accommodate a diversity of building styles and forms. It should also express the rules of scale and character for making coherent, visible connections between new and old uses, buildings, and activities. It takes more than good architects and landscape architects to create good cities; it takes good rules—rules that may not guarantee quality in every instance, but that help prevent disasters.[7] In the end, the streets and squares of our cities should once again become spaces for social discourse, taking precedence over the movement and storage of automobiles.

The points stressed most strongly here are that an expertise in urban design can only be developed by: (1) studying historic precedents and the way in which modern space has evolved; (2) developing an understanding of the underlying theories of urban spatial design; and (3) developing skills in synthesizing and applying these in the design process.

Notes

1. Urban Design International Conference Syllabus. Pittsburgh, Pennsylvania, Oct., 1984.
2. Jaquelin Robertson, Harvard University GSD Lectures, Dec. 4, 1981.
3. Harry Cobb, Harvard University GSD Lectures, Dec. 4, 1981.
4. James Steward Polshek, Preface in Deborah Dietsch and Susanna Steeneken, eds. *Precis: Architecture in the Public Realm.* Columbia University Graduate School of Architecture and Planning, New York: Rizzoli International Publications, Inc. Vol. 3. 1981, p. 3.
5. Ada Louise Huxtable, 'The Troubled State of Modern Architecture,' *AD.* 1/2, London, 1981, p. 16.
6. Charles Jencks, *Modern Movements in Architecture.* New York: Doubleday, 1973, p. 299.
7. Robert Campbell, 'The Choice: Learn from the Past or Fail in the Future.' *The Boston Globe Magazine,* Nov. 11, 1984, p. 35.

Source and copyright

This chapter was published in its original form as:

Trancik, R. (1986), 'What is Lost Space?', in Trancik, R. (1986), *Finding Lost Space: Theories of Urban Design,* Van Nostrand Reinhold, New York, 1–20.

Copyright 2007. Reprinted with permission of John Wiley & Sons, Inc.

8

The grid as generator[†]

Leslie Martin
[1972]

1

The activity called city planning, or urban design, or just planning, is being sharply questioned. It is not simply that these questions come from those who are opposed to any kind of planning. Nor is it because so many of the physical effects of planning seem to be piecemeal. For example roads can be proposed without any real consideration of their effect on environment; the answer to such proposals could be that they are just not planning at all. But it is *not* just this type of criticism that is raised. The attack is more fundamental: what is being questioned is the adequacy of the assumptions on which planning doctrine is based.

What are those assumptions? To put this in the most general terms, they resolve themselves into two powerful lines of thought. The first, which stems from the work of the Viennese writer Camillo Sitte, whose book *City Planning according to Artistic Principles* was published in 1889, can be called the doctrine of the visually ordered city. To Sitte the total city plan is the inspired and the all encompassing work of art. But Sitte went further: civic art must be an expression of the life of the community, and finally 'works of art cannot be created by committee but only by a single individual' (Collins 1965).[‡] The planner then is the inspired artist expressing in the total city plan the ambitions of a society. There are indeed many who, though not prepared to accept this total – it would not be inaccurate to say this totalitarian – role of the

planner, have nevertheless been profoundly influenced by Sitte's doctrine of the visually ordered city. The doctrine has left its mark on the images that are used to illustrate high density development of cities. It is to be seen equally in the layout and arrangement of Garden City development. The predominance of the visual image is evident in some proposals that work for the preservation of the past: it is again evident in the work of those that would carry us on, by an imagery of mechanisms, into the future. It remains central in the proposals of others who feel that, although the city as a total work of art is unlikely to be achieved, the changing aspect of its streets and squares may be ordered visually into a succession of pictures. The second line of doctrine is severely practical. It can be called the doctrine of the statistically ordered city. We know it well. It is the basis of those planning surveys in which uses are quantified, sorted out and zoned into particular areas; population densities are assessed and growth and change predicted. It is the raw material of the outline analyses and the town maps of the 1947 Act.

Now it is precisely these two aspects of planning (the first concerned with visual images and the second with procedure, and sometimes of course used in combination by planners), that were so sharply attacked by Mrs Jane Jacobs in her book *The Death and Life of Great American Cities* (1961). For Mrs Jacobs, both 'the art of city planning and its companion, the pseudo-science of city planning, have not yet embarked on the effort to probe the real world of

[†] Some parts of 'The grid as generator' were used in the Gropius Lecture at Harvard University in June 1966. The argument was developed later into the theme delivered at the University of Hull under the title, 'The Framework of Planning', as the inaugural lecture by Leslie Martin as Visiting Ferens Professor of Fine Art. It is presented here in essentially that form.
[‡] See also a review of both Sitte 1889 and Collins 1965 in L. March (1966).

living'. For her a city can never be the total work of art, nor can there ever be the statistically organised city. Indeed, to Mrs Jacobs, the planning of any kind of order seems to be inconsistent with the organic development of cities which she sees as a direct outcome of the activities of living. Planning is a restrictive imposition: the areas of cities 'in which people have lived are a natural growth … as natural as the beds of oysters'. Planning, she says, is essentially artificial.

It is of course just this opposition between 'organic' growth and the artificial nature of plans, between living and the preconceived system within which it might operate, that has been stressed so much in recent criticism. Christopher Alexander in a distinguished essay 'A city is not a tree' puts the point directly when he says:

> I want to call those cities that have arisen spontaneously over many many years 'natural cities'. And I shall call those cities or parts of cities that have been deliberately created by planners 'artificial cities'. Siena, Liverpool, Kyoto, Manhattan, are examples of natural cities. Levittown, Chandigarh and the British New Towns are examples of artificial cities. It is more and more widely recognised today that there is some essential ingredient missing in the artificial cities (Alexander 1966).

Let us consider this. First of all would it be true to say that all old towns are a kind of spontaneous growth and that there have never been 'artificial' or consciously planned towns in history? Leaving on one side ancient history, what about the four hundred extremely well documented cases of new towns (deliberately planted towns) that Professor Beresford has collected for the Middle Ages in England, Wales and Gascony alone (Beresford 1967)? What about the mediaeval towns such as those built in Gascony between 1250 and 1318 on a systematic gridiron plan? All these towns were highly artificial in Alexander's sense. The planted town, as Professor Beresford observes, 'is not a prisoner of an architectural past: it has no past'. In it the best use of land meant an orderly use, hence the grid plan. In siting it and building it estimates had to be made about its future, about its trade, its population, and the size and number of its building plots. This contributes a highly artificial procedure.

But it is of course by no means uncommon. Indeed it is the method by which towns have been created in any rapidly developing or colonial situation. A recent book by John Reps, *The Making of Urban America* (1965) is a massive compendium of the planting of new towns throughout America, practically all of them based on highly artificial gridiron plans. He points out that there is a sense in which not merely cities but the whole of Western America is developed within an artificial frame: 'the giant gridiron imposed upon the natural landscape by … the land ordinance of 1785'.

The coloniser knows that the natural wilderness has to be transformed: areas must be reserved for agriculture as well as plots for building. The man-made landscape is a single entity: cities and their dependant agricultural areas are not separate elements. All these things are matters of measure and quantity. They are interrelated between themselves and numbers of people. The process demands a quality of abstract thought: a geometry and a relationship of numbers worked out in advance and irrespective of site. The 20-mile square plan for the proposed colony of Azilia, the plans of Savannah and Georgetown, are typical examples of this kind of thought. William Penn's plan for Philadelphia, the plans of such towns as Louisville, Cincinnati, Cleveland, New York City itself, Chicago and San Francisco, are all built on the basis of a preconceived frame.

In the case of the mediaeval towns described by Beresford, whilst some failed, a high proportion succeeded in their time. In a large number of American cities, the artificial grid originally laid down remains the working frame within which vigorous modern cities have developed. It is quite clear then that an artificial frame of some kind does not exclude the possibility of an organic development. The artificial grid of streets that was laid down throughout Manhattan in 1811 has not prevented the growth of those overlapping patterns of human activity which caused Alexander to describe New York as an organic city. Life and living have filled it out but the grid is there.

And this brings us closer to the centre of Alexander's main argument What he is criticising in the extended content of his essay, is the notion that the activities of living can be parcelled out into separate entities and can be fixed for ever by a plan. The assumption is common in much post-war planning. Consider an example. Housing is thought of in terms of density: 75, 100, 150 people per acre. That will occupy an area of land. Housing requires schools and they need open space: that will occupy another specific area. These areas in turn may be thought to justify another need: an area for recreation. That is one kind of thought about planning. But alternatively an effort may be made to see the needs of a community as a whole. It may be discovered that the way housing is arranged on the ground may provide so much free space that the needs of schools or recreation will overlap and may even be contained within it (Martin 1968).

In the first instance the uses are regarded as self-contained entities: Alexander equates this kind of thinking with an organisation like that demonstrated by a mathematical tree. In the second instance the patterns of use overlap: the organisation in this case is much closer to a far more complex mathematical structure: the semi-lattice. The illustration of the separate consideration of housing, schools and open space is elementary. But it is Alexander's argument that whole towns may be planned on this basis. And it is this attempt to deal with highly complex and overlapping patterns of use, of contacts and of communications in a way which prevents this overlap from happening that Alexander deplores. Hence the title of his paper: 'A city is not a tree'. In this sense of course he is correct. But the argument can be put in a different way. It can be argued that the notion (implied by Mrs Jacobs) that elaborate patterns of living can never develop within a preconceived and artificial framework is entirely false. This can be developed by saying that an 'organic' growth, without the structuring element of some kind of framework, is chaos. And finally that it is only through the understanding of that structuring framework that we can open up the range of choices and opportunities for future development.

The argument is this. Many towns of course grew up organically by accretion. Others, and they are numerous and just as flourishing, were established with a preconceived framework as a basis. Both are built up ultimately from a range of fairly simple formal situations: the grid of streets, the plots which this pattern creates and the building arrangements that are placed on these. The whole pattern of social behaviour has been elaborated within a limited number of arrangements of this kind and this is true of the organic as well as the constructed town. Willmott and Young, studying kinship in the East End of London (1957), were able to show that everywhere elaborate patterns of living had been built up. All these elaborations, and a great variety of needs, were met within a general building pattern of terraces and streets. Change that pattern and you may prevent these relationships from developing or you may open up new choices that were not available in the original building form.

The grid of streets and plots from which a city is composed, is like a net placed or thrown upon the ground. This might be called the framework of urbanisation. That framework remains the controlling factor of the way we build whether it is artificial, regular and preconceived, or organic and distorted by historical accident or accretion. And the way we build may either limit or open up new possibilities in the way in which we choose to live.

The understanding of the way the scale and pattern of this framework, net or grid affects the possible building arrangements on the land within it, is fundamental to any reconsideration of the structure of existing towns. It is equally important in relation to any consideration of the developing metropolitan regions outside existing towns. The pattern of the grid of roads in a town or region is a kind of playboard that sets out the rules of the game. The rules outline the kind of game; but the players should have the opportunity to use to the full their individual skills whilst playing it.

2

How does the framework of a city work? In what way does the grid act as a generator and controlling influence on city form? How can it tolerate growth and change?

The answer to these questions is best given by historical examples, and in order to give the argument some point we can deliberately choose the most artificial framework for a city that exists: the grid as it has been used in the United States, and so well illustrated by Reps (1965).

We can start with the notion that to the coloniser the uncultivated wilderness must be tamed into a single urban–rural relationship. In the plan for the proposed Margravate of Azilia (the forerunner of the colony of Georgia) the ground to be controlled is 20 miles square, or 256,000 acres. Implicit in the subdivisions of this general square is a mile square grid; and out of the basic grid the areas for farmland, the great parks for the propagation of cattle and the individual estates are built up. At the centre is the city proper.

The Margravate was never built, but the concept of the single urban–rural unit and the principle of a grid controlled land subdivision within this remains. In the County map of Savannah, Georgia, made in 1735, a grid of (slightly less than) one mile square sub-divides a rectangle nearly 10 miles long and 6 miles deep. Thirty-nine of these squares remain wooded areas: within this primary subdivision, further subdivisions create farms of 44 acres and 5-acre garden plots. These are the related grid systems of the city region. On the river front within this main system is the city itself.

Now it is this city grid of Savannah that can be used as a first example of a city grid. A view of Savannah in 1734 illustrated in John Reps' book describes the principle: the plots and streets of the embryo city are being laid out: some buildings are complete. The unit of the Savannah grid is square: it is called a ward and is separated from its neighbours by wide streets. Within each square (or ward) building plots for houses are arranged along two sides, the centre itself is open, and on each side of this open square are sites for shops and public buildings. Savannah grew by the addition of these ward units. In 1733 there were four units: in 1856 no less than twenty-four. The city became a chequer board of square ward units, marked out by the street pattern. But within this again, the plaid is further elaborated. The central open spaces of each ward are connected in one direction by intermediate roads, in the other direction the central areas become a continuous band of open spaces and public buildings. Here is a unit grid with direction and orientation.

The second example of a grid is absolutely neutral. It lays down an extensive and uniform pattern of streets and plots. The whole process can be illustrated in one single large scale example. In 1811 the largest city grid ever to be created was imposed upon a landscape. The unlikely site for this enterprise was an area of land between two geophysical provinces in which a succession of tilts, uplifts and erosions had brought through the younger strata two layers of crystalline rock. These appeared as rocky outcrops under a thin layer of soil and vegetation. Into their depressions sands and gravels had been deposited by glacial action to create swampy areas through which wandered brooks and creeks. Some of these still wander into the basements of the older areas of what is now Manhattan.

In 1613 the original Dutch settlement was limited to the tip of the island. In 1760 there was little expansion beyond this and contemporary illustrations depict to the north a rolling landscape. Taylor's plan of 1796 shows the first modest growth of a city laid out on a gridiron pattern. Surveys in 1785 and 1796 extending up the centre of Manhattan set out the basis for a grid, and in 1811 the special State Commissioners confirmed this in an 8 ft long plan which plotted the numbered street system of Manhattan as far north as 155th Street. The plan showed 12 north–south avenues each 100 ft wide and 155 cross streets each 66 ft wide. The size of

the rectangular building plots set out by this grid are generally 600 ft by 200 ft. There were some public open spaces. (Central Park was of course carved out later.) And it is this framework that has served the successive developments of the built form from 1811 to the present day.

The third example of a city grid is of interest because of its dimensional links with the land ordinance, suggested by Thomas Jefferson and passed by Congress in 1785. Under that ordinance a huge network of survey lines was thrown across all the land north and west of the Ohio river (Robinson 1916). The base lines and principal meridians of the survey divided the landscape into squares 36 miles each side. These in turn were subdivided into 6-mile squares or townships and further divided into 36 sections each one mile square. The mile squares are then subdivided by acreage: the quarter section 160 acres with further possible subdivisions of 80, 40, 20, 10 or 5 acres. The 5-acre sites lend themselves to further division into rectangular city blocks (not unlike those of Manhattan) and subdivision again into lots or building plots.

In 1832, according to Reps (1965), Chicago was not much more than a few log cabins on a swamp. The railway came in the mid-century and by the seventies and eighties a mile square grid had been extended over a considerable area of the prairie and the city framework had developed within this through a plaiting and weaving of the subdivisions that have been described.

Here then are three types of grid, that of Savannah, the gridiron of Manhattan and that of Chicago. Each one is rectangular. Each one has admitted change in the form and style of its building. Each one has admitted growth, by intensification of land use or by extension. Savannah, as it grew, tended to produce a green and dispersed city of open squares (Fig. 8.1). In Manhattan, the small scale subdivision of the grid and the exceptional pressure to increase floor space within this, forced buildings upwards. Chicago spread, continually opening out the pattern of its grid. In each case the influence of the original grid remains: each one offers different possibilities and choices of building and of living.

In order to trace the influence of the grid, we can examine the building arrangement that developed within it in New York. We can identify at once what might be called the streets and the system that is established by the grid. If we now use the language of the urban geographers, we know that this defines the general plot pattern. The building arrangement develops within this (Conzen 1962).

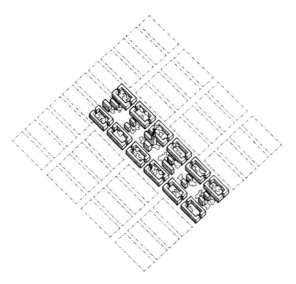

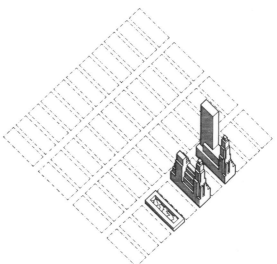

FIGURE 8.1
The basic plot layout of Manhattan is shown in the dotted lines. On this, four wards of the Savannah type of development have been superimposed. The example shows the effective way in which this layout opens up broad bands of green space and public buildings running across the developed areas.

FIGURE 8.2
The basic plot layout of Manhattan is shown again in the dotted lines. The building forms show three stages of development including the original 4–6-storey perimeter form with a garden at the centre which was characteristic of the city in the 1850s, and two examples of the more intensive development during the present century.

The stages of this latter process can be traced in the early plans of Manhattan produced in 1850. The grid of roads is already built. Within this general plot pattern the separate building plots are being established. To the north, on the building frontier, there is a line of huts and shacks. Further south more permanent but separate buildings are being built. And in the most developed area further towards the tip of Manhattan the full building arrangement has solidified into connected terraces of four to six-storey houses arranged around the perimeter of the site and enclosing private gardens. Views of Manhattan in the 1850s show a city developed in this way: and this pattern of building arrangement can still be seen in many areas. At this point the building land is replete. A balance is maintained between the plot, the amount of building that it can reasonably support and the street system that serves this.

But as the pressure for floor space increases, the building form changes intensively at certain nodal points (Fig. 8.2). Deeper and higher perimeter buildings first of all submerge the internal garden space. A process of colonisation of the individual building plots begins, so that larger areas of the general plot are covered by higher buildings. In 1916 the first single building to occupy an entire city block rose a

sheer 600 ft; its roof space almost exactly equalled the area of its ground plan. It was this building that most clearly illustrated the need for the comprehensive zoning ordinances adopted that year, after arduous study and political compromise, to safeguard daylight in streets and adjoining buildings. But the grid now exerts a powerful influence: the limited size of the grid suggests the notion that increased floor space in an area can only be gained by tall buildings on each separate plot. The notion suggests the form; the regulations shape it into ziggurats and towers. Under the regulations that prevailed until recent years, if all the general building plots in central Manhattan had been fully developed, there would have been one single and universal tall building shape. And, to use an old argument by Raymond Unwin (1912), if the population of those buildings had been let out at a given moment, there would have been no room for them in the streets. The balance between area of plot, area of floor space and area of street has disappeared.

Now these descriptions of the grid, which have been used as a basis for the argument, have exposed the points at which it can be, and has been, extensively attacked for more than a century. A grid of any kind appears to be a rigid imposition on the natural landscape. It is this reaction against the grid that is voiced by Olmstead and Vaux writing in support of their design for Central Park in 1863: 'The time will come when New York will be built up, when all the grading and the filling will be done and the picturesquely varied rocky formation of the island will have been converted into formations for rows of monotonous straight streets and piles of erect buildings' (Reps 1965).

In their opposition to the grid, the relief from its monotony became a specific aim. Central Park itself is an attempt to imitate nature and to recreate wild scenery within the grid.[†] The garden suburb with its curving streets is one form of attack on the grid system, and an attempt to replace it. And at the end of the century, the Chicago Fair (1893), Cass Gilbert's schemes in Washington (1900), and the plans for San Francisco (1905) and Chicago (1909) by Burnham are another attempt to transform the urban desert by means of vistas and focal points, into the 'city beautiful'. However, we recognise at once a contrast. The various types of grid that have been described opened up some possible patterns for the structure of a city but left the building form free to develop and change within this. The plans of the garden city designers or those concerned with making the 'city beautiful' are an attempt to impose a form: and that form cannot change.

It is not possible to deny the force behind the criticisms of the grid. It can result in monotony: so can a curvilinear suburbia. It can fail to work: so can the organic city. What has been described is a process. It is now possible to extract some principles. Artificial grids of various kinds have been laid down. The choice of the grid allows different patterns of living to develop and different choices to be elaborated. The grid, unlike the fixed visual image, can accept and respond to growth and change. It can be developed unimaginatively and monotonously or with great freedom. There can be a point at which the original grid fails to respond to new demands (Fig. 8.3). As in Manhattan, it congeals. And it is at this point that we must try to discover from the old framework a new ordering principle that will open up new opportunities for elaboration by use.

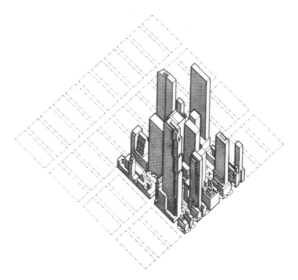

FIGURE 8.3
The illustration shows building plot development in its most intensive form.

It is precisely this that Le Corbusier underlined when he paid his first visit to New York in 1935 and made the comment: 'What about the road?' (Le Corbusier 1939, 1947.) The diagrams by which he illustrates this remark show the regenerative process that is necessary (Fig. 8.4). By increasing the size of the street net in Manhattan, Le Corbusier shows that the grid ceases to restrict. New building arrangements become possible and the balance between plot, building and street can be restored.

3

In the case of these American cities the grid or framework can be regarded as an ordering principle. It sets out the rules of the environmental game. It allows the player the freedom to play with individual skill. The argument can now be extended by saying that the grid, which is so apparent in the American examples, is no less controlling and no less important in cities nearer home that would normally be

---

[†] This movement which began with gardens, was less appropriately applied to city layout. In Olmstead's words, 'lines of roads were not to press forwards'. Their curving forms suggest leisure and tranquility. Compare this with the almost contemporary (1859) statements by Cerda in his plan for Barcelona in which there is 'a reciprocal arrangement between that which is contained' (building plot and arrangement) and 'that which contains' (grid and street system). 'Urbanisation is an appendix to universal movement: streets are for movement but they serve areas permanently reserved and isolated from that movement which agitates life' (the environmental area).

called organic: London, Liverpool or Manchester. They too have a network of streets and however much the grid is distorted, it is there. At a certain scale and under certain pressures the grid combined with floor space limits and daylight controls is just as likely to force tall building solutions. And it is just as likely to congeal. It lends itself just as readily to regenerative action. The theoretical understanding of the interaction between the grid and the built form is therefore fundamental in considering either existing towns or the developing metropolitan regions.

The process of understanding this theoretical basis rests in measurement and relationships and it goes back certainly to Ebenezer Howard. Lionel March has recently pointed out a number of interesting things about Howard's book *Tomorrow: a peaceful path to real reform* first published in 1898. It is a book about how people might live in towns and how these might be distributed. But the important thing is that there is no image of what a town might look like. We know the type of housing, the size of plot, the sizes of avenues. We know that shopping, schools and places of work are all within walking distance of the residential areas. On the basis of these measurements we know the size of a town and the size of Howard's cluster of towns which he calls a city Federation. We know the choice that is offered

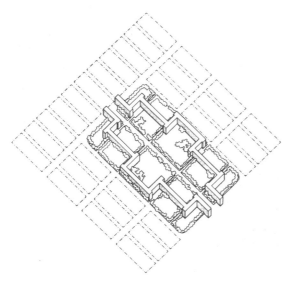

FIGURE 8.4
Change in the scale of the grid. Le Corbusier's proposals for dwellings with setbacks (from his proposals for a city for 3 million people) are superimposed on the Manhattan grid and open up new possibilities in the building form.

and we know the measurements that relate to these. If we disagree with the choice we can change the measurements. Lionel March (1967) took Howard's open centred city pattern linked by railways and showed that it could be reversed into a linear pattern linked by roads and that such patterns could be tested against the land occupied by our present stock of building and our future needs.

Now that is theory. It contains a body of ideas which are set down in measurable terms. It is open to rational argument. And as we challenge it successfully we develop its power. The results are frequently surprising and sometimes astonishingly simple. Ebenezer Howard's direct successor in this field was Raymond Unwin. The strength of his argument always rests in a simple demonstration of a mathematical fact. In an essay 'Nothing gained by overcrowding' (Unwin 1912), he presents two diagrams of development on ten acres of land. One is typical development of parallel rows of dwellings: the other places dwellings round the perimeter. The second places fewer houses on the land but when all the variables are taken into account (including the savings on road costs) total development costs can be cut. From the point of view of theory, the important aspect of this study is the recognition of related factors: the land available, the built form placed on this, and the roads necessary to serve these. He demonstrated this in a simple diagram.

Unwin began a lecture on tall building by a reference to a controversy that had profoundly moved the theological world of its day, namely, how many angels could stand on a needle point. His method of confounding the urban theologians by whom he was surrounded was to measure out the space required in the streets and sidewalks by the people and cars generated by 5-, 10- and 20-storey buildings on an identical site. The interrelationship of measurable factors is again clearly demonstrated. But one of Unwin's most forceful contributions to theory is his recognition of the fact that 'the area of a circle is increased not in the direct proportion to the distance to be travelled from the centre to the circumference, but in proportion to the square of that distance'. Unwin used this geometrical principle to make a neat point about commuting time: as the population increases round the perimeter of a town, the commuting time is not increased in direct proportion to this.

The importance of this geometrical principle is profound. Unwin did not pursue its implications. He was too concerned to make his limited point about low density. But suppose this proposition is subjected to close examination. The principle is demonstrated again in Fresnel's diagram (Fig. 8.5) in which each successive annular ring diminishes in width but has exactly the same area as its predecessor. The outer band in the square form of this diagram has exactly the same area as the central square. And this lies at the root of our understanding of an important principle in relation to the way in which buildings are placed on the land.

Suppose now that the central square and the outer annulus of the Fresnel diagram are considered as two possible ways of placing the same amount of floor space on the same site area: at once it is clear that the two buildings so arranged would pose totally different questions of access, of how the free space is distributed around them and what natural lighting and view the rooms within them might have. By this process a number of parameters have been defined which need to be considered in any

theoretical attempt to understand land use by buildings.

This central square (which can be called the pavilion) and the outer annulus (which can be called the court) are two ways of placing building on the land. Let us now extend this. On any large site a development covering 50% of the site could be plotted as forty-nine pavilions, as shown in Fig. 8.6, and exactly the same site cover can be plotted in court form. A contrast in the ground space available and the use that can be made of it is at once apparent. But this contrast can be extended further: the forty-nine pavilions can be plotted in a form which is closer to that which they would assume as buildings (that is low slab with a tower form over this). This can now be compared with its antiform: the same floor space planned as courts (Fig. 8.7). The comparison must be exact; the same site area, the same volume of building, the same internal depth of room. And when this is done we find that the antiform places the same amount of floor space into buildings which are exactly one third the total height of those in pavilion form (Martin and March 1966).

This brings the argument directly back to the question of the grid and its influence on the building form. Let us think of New York. The grid is developing a certain form: the tall building. The land may appear to be thoroughly used. Consider an area of the city. Seen on plan there is an absolutely even pattern of rectangular sites. Now assume that every one of those sites is completely occupied by a building: and that all these buildings have the same tower form and are twenty-one storeys in height. That would undoubtedly look like a pretty full occupation of the land. But if the size of the road net were to be enlarged by omitting some of the cross streets, a new building form is possible. Exactly the

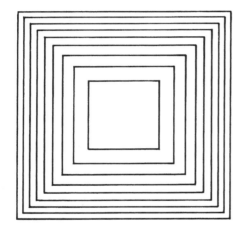

FIGURE 8.5

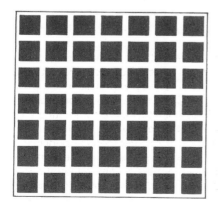

FIGURE 8.6

same amount of floor space that was contained in the towers can be arranged in another form. If this floor space is placed in buildings around the edges of our enlarged grid then the same quantity of floor space that was contained in the 21-storey towers now needs only 7-storey buildings. And large open spaces are left at the centre.

Let us be more specific. If the area bounded by Park Avenue and Eighth Avenue, and between 42nd and 57th Street is used as a base and the whole area were developed in the form of Seagram buildings 36 storeys high, this would certainly open up some ground space along the streets. If, however, the Seagram buildings were replaced by court forms (Fig. 8.8) then this type of development while using the same built volume would produce buildings only 8 storeys high. But the courts thus provided would be roughly equivalent in area to Washington

Square: and there could be 28 Washington Squares in this total area. Within squares of this size there could be large trees, perhaps some housing, and other buildings such as schools.

Of course no one may want this alternative. But it is important to know that the possibility exists, and that, when high buildings and their skyline are being described, the talk is precisely about this and not about the best way of putting built space on to ground space. The alternative form of courts, taken in this test, is not a universal panacea. It suggests an alternative which would at once raise far-reaching questions. For instance, the open space provided in the present block-by-block (or pavilion) form is simply a series of traffic corridors. In the court form, it could become traffic-free courts. In this situation the question which needs answering is: at what point do we cease to define a built area by streets and corridors? At

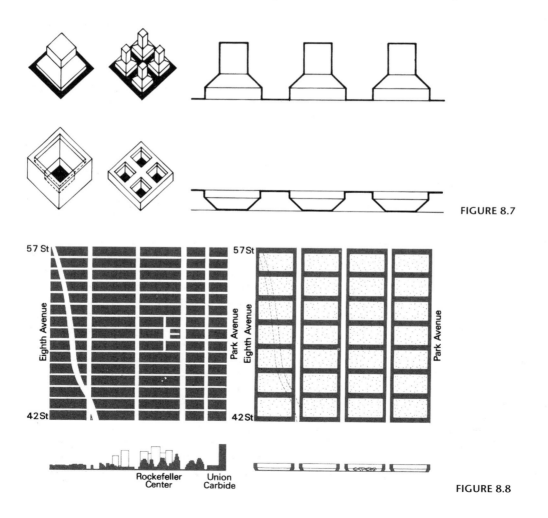

FIGURE 8.7

FIGURE 8.8

what point could we regard a larger area as a traffic-free room surrounded by external traffic routes?

In all this the attempt has been simply to give a demonstration of procedure. The full repercussions of the questions are not obvious. They are highly complicated. But the factual aspect of the study establishes a better position from which to understand the nature of the complication and the limits of historical assumptions. What is left is something that can be built upon and needed decisions are brought back to the problem of the built form of an urban area not merely of a building. Here, the choice of the built form is critical in a number of ways, not least as a means of securing a new unity of conception.

Take for instance the question of the size of the road net. Professor Buchanan has looked at this from another angle (Ministry of Transport, 1963). Looking at cities in relation to traffic, he saw that most of them are built up from a collection of localities. He called these 'environmental areas'. These areas are recognisable working units. They are areas in which a pattern of related uses holds together: local housing, shopping, schools, etc., would be one obvious example. These areas are recognisable in Manhattan just as clearly as they are in London. They form, in Professor Buchanan's terms, 'the rooms of a town'. They need to be served by roads but they are destroyed when roads penetrate and subdivide them. His solution was to try to recognise and define these working areas and to place the net of roads in the cracks between them. By estimating the amount of traffic that might be generated by the buildings in such areas, Professor Buchanan was able to suggest some possible sizes for the networks. He had in fact by this procedure redefined the grid of a town in terms of modern traffic.

Here then is a proposition for a framework within which we can test out some possible arrangements of the built form. Professor Buchanan selected St Marylebone as one of his test areas. This happens to adjoin the main London University site (already defined as a precinct in the London Plan) and this in turn is contiguous with the area around the Foundling Estate which has been used in some Cambridge studies of the built form (Fig. 8.9). All three areas are approximately equal in size. The Foundling area (bounded on the north and south by Euston Road and Theobalds Road, and on the west and east by Woburn Place and Grays Inn Road), is about 3700 ft from north to south and 2000 ft wide. It developed a cohesion of its own. How did this happen?

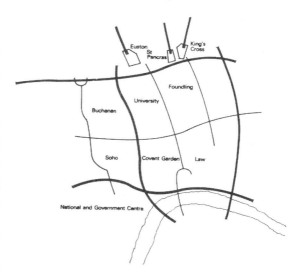

FIGURE 8.9
Environmental areas and road networks as suggested by Buchanan.

This in turn can be related back to the main line of argument. In 1787 the whole of this area consisted of open fields: there were no controlling features. A plan of 1790 divides the land into building plots by its network of streets and squares. The subsequent history, so well traced by Olsen (1964), shows the development and elaboration within this pattern. By 1900 the area could have been described by the language that Mrs Jacobs applies to Greenwich Village. The intellectuals were there: so were the working Londoners: so were the Italians around their hospital in Queen Square. There were handsome houses; tenements and mews; hotels and boarding houses. The area had its own Underground station and its own shopping area along Marchmont Street. It served a complex community.

By 1960 the balance within the original pattern had radically altered. Fast moving traffic using the small scale grid of streets had subdivided the area. Site by site residential development at a zoned density of 136 people to the acre produces only one answer: tall blocks of flats. Redevelopment of sites for offices created taller and thicker buildings. The hospitals, which needed to expand, were hemmed in by surrounding development. The pattern congealed.

In this situation only a new framework can open up a free development. And if Professor Buchanan's surrounding road net is accepted as a basis for the development of the environmental area, the problem

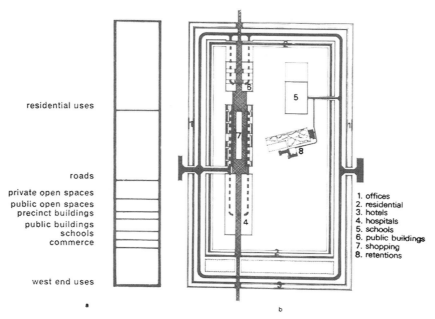

residential uses

roads

private open spaces
public open spaces
precinct buildings
public buildings
schools
commerce

west end uses

1. offices
2. residential
3. hotels
4. hospitals
5. schools
6. public buildings
7. shopping
8. retentions

a

b

FIGURE 8.10a
Quantities of built and open space in the Foundling Area.
FIGURE 8.10b
Possible geometric layout of the same quantities of built space in perimeter form.

can be seen within a new unifying context. What sort of advantages could a rearrangement of the built form now create? Professor Buchanan in his study area outlined three possible solutions with progressive standards of improvement. The merit of this is that it sets out a comparative basis of assessment. But even his partial solution leads to an extensive road and parking system at ground level. From the point of view of the pedestrian the position is made tolerable by the use of a deck system to create a second level. Above this again, some comparatively tall buildings are required to rehouse the built space that is at present on the ground. This kind of image of the architecture of cities has a considerable history in modern architecture and has been much used as an illustration of central area reconstruction. But, as Professor Buchanan himself asks, what building complications does it produce and what sort of an environment does it create? Is it in fact worth building?

Professor Buchanan's range of choices could in fact be extended by applying some of the theoretical work which has been described. And when this is done the results are significantly different. The boundaries of the total area that are being considered have been defined by this new scale of the road network: the grid. Within this, the existing floor space can be assessed (Fig. 8.10): 34% of the site is occupied by housing: 25% by roads: 15% by office and commercial use: 12% is open space. In addition there is an important shopping street, a major hospital and several schools and educational buildings. With this information available it can be considered at a theoretical level how this might be disposed in a new building arrangement.

First, the shopping street, Marchmont Street, could be established as a north/south pedestrian route associated with the Underground and some housing. If all the office space which is at present scattered throughout the area could be placed in a single line of buildings around the perimeter of the area (where some of it already is), it need be no higher than eight storeys. All the housing at present in the area could be placed within another band of buildings sited inside this and no higher than five storeys. Of course it could be arranged on the ground to include other forms and types of housing. But in theory, the bulk of the building at present covering the area could be placed in two single bands of building running around its edge, leaving the centre open, which would be a park-like area

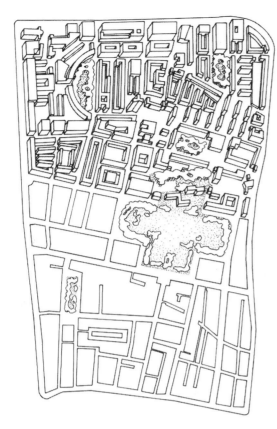

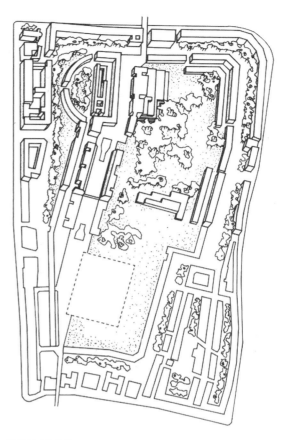

FIGURE 8.11a
The existing plot layout and building development in
an area of London that might be regarded as an
environmental room. But it is subdivided by roads
and the limited size of the building plot increasingly
forces development upward.

FIGURE 8.11b
The same area as that in 8.11a. The road network
is now enlarged and runs around the boundary of
the area. Theoretically an entirely new disposition
of buildings is possible and the illustration shows
exactly the same amount of floor space in a new
form. Tall buildings are no longer necessary: the
buildings themselves have a new freedom for
development and a considerable area of open space
is discovered.

about the same size as St James's Park (Fig. 8.11).
Precisely the same amount of floor space would
have been accommodated. There need be no tall
buildings, unless they are specifically wanted. All
the housing could look onto a park. Buildings such
as schools could stand freely within this. There
would be a free site and a park-like setting for new
hospital buildings.

All that may sound theoretical and abstract. But
to know what is theoretically possible is to allow
wider scope for decisions and objectives. We can
choose. We can accept the grid of streets as it is. In
that case we can never avoid the constant pressure
on the land. Housing will be increasingly in tall flats.
Hospitals will have no adequate space for expansion. Historic areas will be eaten into by new building.

A total area once unified by use will be increasingly
subdivided by traffic. We can leave things as they
are and call development organic growth, or we
can accept a new theoretical framework as an outline of the general rules of the game and work
towards this. We shall know that the land we need
is there if we use it effectively. We can modify the
theoretical frame to respect historic areas and elaborate it as we build. And we shall also know that the
overlapping needs of living in an area have been
seen as a whole and that there will be new possibilities and choices for the future.

References

Alexander, C. (Feb. 1966). A City is Not a Tree, *Design*.

Beresford, M. (1967). *New Towns of the Middle Ages*, Lutterworth Press (London).

Collins, G. R. and C. C. (1965). *Camillo Sitte and the Birth of City Planning*, Random House.

Conzen, M. R. G. (1962). The Plan Analysis of an English City Centre, in *Proceedings of the I.G.U. Symposium in Urban Geography*, Royal University of Lund (Lund, Sweden).

Howard, Ebenezer (1898). *Tomorrow: A Peaceful Path to Real Reform*, republished 1945, as *Garden Cities of Tomorrow*, Faber.

Jacobs, J. (1961). *The Death and Life of Great American Cities*, Random House.

Le Corbusier (1939). *Oeuvres Complètes 1934–1938*, Girsberger (Zurich).

Le Corbusier (1947). *When the Cathedrals Were White*, Routledge (London).

March, L. (April 1966). Heavens on Earth, *Cambridge Review*.

March, L. (Aug. 1967). Homes Beyond the Fringe, *R.I.B.A. Journal*.

Martin, L. (Aug. 1968). Education Without Walls, *R.I.B.A. Journal*.

Martin, L. and March, L. (April 1966). Land Use and Built Forms, *Cambridge Research*.

Ministry of Transport (1963). *Traffic in Towns* (The Buchanan Report), Her Majesty's Stationery Office.

Olsen, D. J. (1964). *Town Planning in London*, Yale University Press.

Reps, J. W. (1965). *The Making of Urban America*, Princeton University Press.

Robinson, C. M. (1916). *City Planning*, Putnam.

Sitte, Camillo (1889). *City Planning According to Artistic Principles*, translated by Collins, G. R. and C. C. (1965). Phaidon Press.

Unwin, R. (1912). Nothing to be Gained by Overcrowding, in Creese, W. L., ed., 1967, *The Legacy of Raymond Unwin: A Human Pattern for Planning*, MIT Press (Cambridge, Massachusetts).

Willmot, P. and Young, M. (1957). *Family and Kinship in East London*, Routledge.

Source and copyright

This chapter was published in its original form as:

Martin, L. (1972), 'The Grid as Generator', in Martin, L. & March, L. (1972) (editors), *Urban Space and Structures*, Cambridge University Press, Cambridge, 6–27.

Cambridge University Press, reproduced with permission from the author and publisher.

9

Typology: an architecture of limits

Douglas Kelbaugh
[2002]

Limits are essential to freedom. Physical limits can liberate and constrain us at the same time: traveling on skis or bicycle frees us to move with much greater speed than on foot, but it severely limits the ability to turn sharply, not to mention the ability to operate, say, a lawn mower. Other examples are not so obvious: being trapped in a snow-bound airport may at first seem imprisoning. If there is the slightest hope of flying, the situation can be one of high anxiety. But if there is absolutely no chance of flying, there can be a reassuring calm as social barriers fall and a free camaraderie settles in—a rare moment of freedom, community, and equality. This irony also applies to mental activities, especially cognitive ones such as sorting sensory data and classifying information. Epistemological limits, i.e., ones that limit our ways of knowing the world, are essential. Likewise, site and programmatic constraints actually make the design process easier. Unconstrained freedom is anathema to designers, who need limits as much as civilization itself needs rules, traditions, and conventions. A blank piece of paper may be welcome to an artist, but it can be intimidating to a designer.

The deeper question is whether these limits are primarily intellectual fences that we erect as boundaries to make cognition of, and in, a complex world manageable. Do limits simply act as navigational devices as we negotiate and construct reality? Or do limits in themselves embody essential truths about the world? Although the point may be unprovable, this chapter contends that limits are more than a pragmatic necessity and do embody basic truths about life, as well as offer lasting insights into the world. They are fundamental to the human condition in general and to design in particular. The categories vary from time to time and culture to culture, but limits per se seem to be more than transitory and superficial constructs. Like the sensory screens and mental templates through which our world rushes in every day, they help make the complex data and stimuli of life understandable.

Limits are part of a classical, zero-sum conception of reality. This is a world view in which we can't have it all, in which there is tragedy as well as happiness, in which there are finite resources and a limited number of times to get it right. It acknowledges that we all have within us the capacity to be cruel, perverse, and stupid, as well as kind, generous, and wise. This limited view of the human condition, with its full recognition of the dark as well as the bright side of human nature, is fundamentally different from the progressive and open-ended optimism of Modernism (which to a large extent grew out of logical positivism). The classical point of view emphasizes harmony and balance, rather than originality and freedom. Convention takes on as much or more importance as invention. Tradition is valued as much or more than innovation.

Classicism, which has seen balance and harmony as an ideal since early Antiquity, recognizes that it is possible to take an idea too far. It would argue that many Modernist buildings are too single-minded, that they sometimes pursue a single concept to exhaustion in the name of internal consistency and purity. High-tech architects, for example, are driven to make structures ever more lightweight and articulated. They can lose their sense of balance in their drive to defy physical forces and achieve elegance. It is a matter of time before one of their tensile roofs, trussed walls, or delicate handrails dramatically fails, just as Beauvais Cathedral collapsed when its late medieval builders pushed its nave too high. The failure will not come as a result of misunderstanding gravity, wind, or seismic forces. It will come as a result of the relentless competitive push to perfect one idea or aesthetic sensibility at the expense of all others. If catastrophic, such a failure could represent the same kind of culmination and gamble as Beauvais and would serve as a reminder to us about the dangers of single-minded architectural excess and the importance of balance.

Every life (or design) experience is not a growth experience, as some contemporary pundits would have it. Nor is life foolproof, fail-safe, or no-fault. Without wisdom and discipline, we make mistakes, some of which are irrevocable, even fatal. This is not to say there is no room in the classical view for optimism and growth. Classicism is not so much pessimistic about human nature and perfectibility as it is realistic. It acknowledges and tries to reconcile the conflicted, dualistic nature of the human condition, something with which contemporary American culture has trouble dealing. As the late humanist Allan Bloom pointed out: "The images cast helter-skelter on the wall of our cave … present high and low, serious and frivolous, without distinction or concern for harmonizing contrary charms."[1]

Limited space, limited form

There was a noticeable shift in the 1970s and 1980s from treating both architectural space and natural resources as unlimited and open-ended to treating them as finite and bounded. A sense of finitude was perhaps the one and only convergence of environmentalist, regionalist, and Postmodernist design—a happy and significant conjunction given the divergence and pluralism of contemporary architectural thought. The Modernist conception of architectural space—Cartesian, universal, and continuous—gave way during those two decades to a static and finite conception, which was sometimes also specific to site and region. This non-Modernist or Postmodernist (even anti-Modernist) conception was a more hierarchical and classical representation of the world. Despite its tectonic and social shortcomings, it was more than a knee-jerk reaction to Modernism and was based on a more realistic and balanced understanding of human and ecological forces. Balance and harmony may be values that are too bland for today's media, but they have been of vital importance to

Postmodernists, as well as environmentalists, Neo-Traditionalists, and New Urbanists.

During this same period, there was also a shift from treating architectural form and space as abstract and asymmetrical toward treating them as figural and symmetrical. Figural forms are finite by definition, and natural forms are often symmetrical. The residual space often left over around Modernist "object" buildings has been rejected in favor of background buildings that enclose positive outdoor space. This figure/ground reversal represents a profound paradigm shift in urban design—perhaps the most important overt formal difference between Modernism and what preceded and has followed it. The outdoor "rooms" of urban streets and squares have become more valued than freestanding buildings surrounded by either the empty windswept plazas around downtown office towers or the grass perimeters and parking lots of suburban office parks.

Background or collateral buildings gain their strength from the public space they define. They also get strength from figural composition and detailing of the facades rather than from the bold footprints, gymnastic sections, and minimalist elevations that often characterize Modernist buildings. The quintessential Modernist building was like a prismatic Modernist sculpture—a freestanding, abstract, minimalist object in unbounded universal space. The stand-alone building has given way to the infill building, where more design attention is lavished by the architect on the composition of facade than on the logic of the plan or the bravado of the section.

By opposing the two axes on which there have been these diametric shifts, a map is created on which the work of influential twentieth-century architects can be plotted. The contemporary celebrities have staked out extremist positions, which get media attention. The "Modern Masters" who have stood the test of time occupied a more balanced, centrist position. Le Corbusier, Mies, Aalto, and Louis Kahn seemed to be driven more by philosophical, social, technological, and formal ideas and values that were bigger than themselves. Or so it seems after the passage of time, which has exalted their position in history but also covered up or at least dimmed some of their architectural sins.

No one working today in any architectural mode—whether it be Postmodernist, Regionalist, New Urbanist, Deconstructivist, or Neo-Modernist—seems to have yet achieved a comparable maturity, mastery, and wholeness, with the possible exception of some high-tech firms. Today's stars seem mainly interested in aesthetic ideas and formal expression, as well as promotion of themselves, rather than ideas and ideals bigger than themselves. Even their interest in theory seems strategic and self-serving, consorting with academic theorists and critics who propound and/or interpret theory that gives their work license and legitimacy. The academy has validated and encouraged extremist, self-referential architecture with theory that has been too quick to drop long-standing institutional and cultural values. The media merry-go-round pushes star architects to the edge, while slowly and surely eroding the general credibility and relevance of the profession, especially its more responsible practitioners who have resisted this centrifugal force.

Was there also a change in design methods that corresponded to the shift on these two axes? Or was this shift simply a measure of changing style and sensibilities? Although methodological changes are less heralded than stylistic ones, this chapter argues that there has been an equally dramatic and important change in design methods. One of the most notable methodological changes has been the decline of functionalism and the rise of interest in precedent, context, and typology.

Functionalism

Functionalism, in this context, means a design mode that not only strives rationally to accommodate the programmatic needs and aspirations of a building's users, but also to express and embody those needs and aspirations architecturally. It has been one of the hallmarks of modernity and the most recent step in the philosophical march that started in the late seventeenth century with the Enlightenment and continued into this century as Logical Positivism, which sought to eliminate subjectivity in its quest for the precision and predictability of science. This philosophical tradition has given little credence to anything that cannot be measured. Metaphysics has little if any place in functionalism. "No doubt the Logical Positivists had sought to show that the classical metaphysical problem had either to be dismissed entirely, since no solution to it could be verifiable, or else transposed it into problems in the logic of science."[2] After this close embrace of metrics, the spiritual and cultural sterility of functionalist buildings is not surprising.

For the functionalist, the design process starts with analysis of the problem at hand. Before attempting any synthesis, the designer must first dissect and analyze the user, the user's program, the building systems and technics, the climate, and the site. Functionalist architects start with an empty piece of paper—literally, a carte blanche—and license to do just about anything formally. They commence with diagrams of uses and their adjacencies. If they are true to the tenets of the Modern Movement, they only look forward, never back to historical examples—free of any preconceptions about how a building might be configured or what it might look like. No books on architectural history would be found on the drafting table, unless it was a monograph of a hallowed architect, perhaps Le Corbusier's *Oeuvre Complet.* The functionalist ideal would have the program and technology design the building by themselves, driven by their own transparent logic. Each building program is addressed as unique, requiring fresh learning and a new start. "Following their functionalist theory, they believe[d] every new design problem to consist of unprecedented requirements of various kinds, including a unique site, a unique set of functional demands, and a unique architectural form which would precisely solve this set of requirements and no others."[3]

Since functional requirements change quickly in modern society, buildings are often designed to be adaptable over the years and flexible during the daily or weekly cycle. Therefore, functionalists argue that architectural composition should visually express as well as physically accommodate these temporal changes. Thus, buildings should be designed not only to anticipate change, but to read as incomplete or adaptable when first built. Building additions have always occurred incrementally, but the additions, like the host buildings, were usually treated before the Modern Movement as discrete compositions; additions were used to further unify or reinforce an already complete composition or start a new one. Think of the myriad wings of the Louvre or the many additions to the United States Capitol. Buildings tried to be compositionally complete at all times—before and after the intervention. Modernists, however, would sometimes intentionally leave a building's composition open-ended, almost as if construction had been interrupted and was waiting expectantly for the next phase to relieve the tension. The Pompidou Center in Paris is an example of a building that is intended to feel unfinished. Because these open-ended and adaptable buildings or complexes are not fully able to anticipate the future, they often end up being developed in unpredictable ways. The typical hospital complex suffers from such disjoined development. As Stewart Brand says in *How Buildings Learn,* "All buildings are predictions. All predictions are wrong."[4]

After more than a half-century of Modernism, its buildings are standing all over the globe and can be and have been broadly and fairly judged. As individual buildings the best ones are, to be sure, magnificent and powerful, some of the most creative and stunning designs of all time. One has only to visit the better works of Wright, Le Corbusier, Aalto, Mies, Kahn, and Eero Saarinen and many of their disciples to realize the strengths of Modernism. Almost every American skyline is a robust testimony to both the masculine strength and pervasiveness of Modernism. But Andres Duany effectively if cavalierly nails Modernist architecture when he points out its appalling win-loss ratio, i.e., thirty million Modernist buildings that have destroyed the cities of the world versus the three thousand, at best, that are masterpieces.

Although Modernism produced some of the greatest individual buildings of all time, it failed outright to produce good streets or good cities. Its buildings, because of their obligatory originality and direct expression of the interior, weren't likely to speak the language of neighboring buildings, especially traditional ones. If not by demolition, they related to their context by contrast and counterpoint—often a simplistic formal strategy used by Modernists that became a blanket defense for ignoring abutting buildings. Along with the upheaval of neighborhoods and cities by urban renewal, the automobile, and zoning, the Modern Movement produced buildings that ignored each other and their older neighbors.

Functionalism sought to be internally consistent and coherent. Concerned with the unity and integrity of the individual building, which it saw as the inalienable building block of the city, Modernism's primary canon was to express clearly and honestly the internal logic of the building's program, as well as its materials and structural systems. Style, per se, was forbidden—whether invented or copied. (Ultimately, it proved inescapable even to the most die-hard Modernists.) Functionalism reserved new forms to express new technical or programmatic developments and did not permit willful and arbitrary formalism. But even its best examples had trouble relating to the surrounding fabric of the city, not only in its historic districts but also in new districts. In the latter cases, the problem was uniformity and scalelessness rather than discord with the context, because there was no traditional urban fabric with which to contrast. This inability to achieve consistency or even sympathy with neighbors was perhaps Modernism's biggest shortcoming.

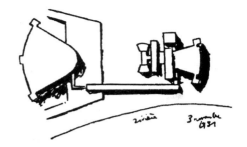

Modernism celebrated buildings as freestanding objects. These sculptures were often wonderfully composed, with the abutting urban fabric acting as a backdrop off which they were set as new and clean interventions. However, when the same principles of composition were applied to large areas of old cities, they proved problematic. And when applied to whole new towns, where there was no traditional urban fabric to act as a foil, these principles of composition were even more unsuccessful. In short, Modernist architecture and urbanism worked better as the exception than the rule. Its open plan, so successful at the architectural scale, failed to work at the urban scale.

As functionalism strove to be a "styleless" aesthetic, it did not typically produce buildings of a scale and richness around which popular affection and memories could easily develop. Instead it often produced cold and faceless buildings. As a consequence, our cities lost much of their ability to nurture and transmit values of place, nature, history, and craft. In the hands of genius, it could reach the sublime, but in the hands of everyday practitioners Modernism fell short of what everyday architects have done in other periods. "For modernism had not produced a style which could simply be drawn upon by lesser practitioners, as had classical or Gothic architecture. Instead it had produced too much freedom—almost anything could be attempted. ... Such freedom could constitute a breath-taking release in the hands of the masters—in the hands of followers it could easily become a new imprisonment."[5]

The average building was more urbanistically responsive and responsible in the nineteenth century, when architecture was more normative. Modernism's best solo buildings may be more virtuoso performances, but the typical fabric and its overall orchestration were better in previous eras. This past harmony was to a large extent the result of designers and builders being guided by a tacit understanding of convention and precedent. Among the most important conventions was architectural typology.

AIA Gold Medalist Cesar Pelli has this to say about the breakdown of contemporary rules and expectations, many of them born of functionalism:

In trying to understand our art we may keep in mind that not only buildings that flaunt their aesthetic intentions are artistically valuable; so are many modest structures that have been designed with love and care.... The contemporary rules for designing and judging architecture put such a premium on original talent that only a handful of architects have been able to master them. Examples from the past demonstrate that when rules and expectations are reasonable, most architects can design good buildings. Any society should expect that architects' rules will produce good buildings most of the time. This is what a healthy architecture does. The evidence of the majority of our buildings suggests that there is something wrong with today's rules. They do not suit our cities and need to be reconsidered. The final result of our work is making cities. It is our greatest responsibility. If we do not make beautiful, enjoyable, and workable cities, we are not going to be worth much in that history that we all prize, no matter how brilliant our individual efforts may be.[6]

Typology?

Typology is an idea that the Modern Movement intentionally abandoned.

Typology—the study and theory of architectural types—revived a traditional way of looking at function in the 1970s and 1980s. Theorists asserted that it was a better point of departure than Modernist functionalism when designing a building. Typologists like Leon Krier argued that almost any spatial problem at hand has been solved in the past. They defended enduring and commonplace architectural types that have evolved over time rather than following the mandate of the Modern Movement to discover new forms latent in program, site, or technology. In architectural education, typology brought academics to see their discipline more and more as a traditional language and not as an artistic and technical field in which invention is valued more than convention. Although the center of gravity of architectural theory later moved on to Deconstructivism and to social and environmental concerns, the idea of type remains alive as a result of Postmodernism.

Designers who utilize a typological approach may admit that a design problem can present unprecedented social issues and new technical opportunities, but they also know that human nature, human needs, and the human body haven't changed; nor has climate (yet) or geography (much). They also believe that cultural continuity is more desirable than constant change. Because archetypes represent origins, a return to typology is an attempt to recover purity and continuance, privileging tradition over endless progress.

Typologists look at how the design problem at hand has been solved in the past, especially in similar physical and cultural milieus. They visit built examples in the field. They visit the library, unashamed of learning from the history books that were not allowed any influence in the functionalist's office. They ask if there is a normative or standard architectural type that has evolved over time to solve the problem. If, for instance, the problem is a house, there are many types to draw on. Some types are ancient: the country villa and the atrium house. Some are high architecture: the palazzo and the Palladian villa. Some are low: the sharecroppers' cabin and the garage apartment. Some are prehistoric and universal: yurt, thatched hut, house on stilts, and tree house. Some are national: center-hall colonial, Cape Cod cottage, ranch house, split-level, and bi-level. Some are regional and colloquial: New England "salt box," Charleston "single," New Orleans "shotgun," Philadelphia "trinity," Seattle "box," Florida "cracker," Baltimore "stoop," and so on. Some are from other countries: Dublin "Georgian," Sydney "terrace," Bengalese "bungalow," New Zealand "villa," and Russian "dacha," to name a few.

Type

An architectural type is not an easy thing to explain. It is like a three-dimensional template that is copied over and over in endless variations. It is a norm, an abstraction, not an actual building. It is not usually the kind of abstraction that is ordained from on high or that springs whole from a single designer or builder. Rather a type is rooted in the commonplace, the unselfconscious, even the unconscious. It is idealized in its archetype, which is its purest or most exemplary expression. A type devolves as a characteristic and typical representation of the archetype. It can be vernacular or high-style architecture. Even in the latter case, its origin cannot usually be traced to a single architect.

An architectural type is morphological, although it can also be characterized by specific materials (e.g., a Georgian townhouse is brick). It must be distinguished from building type, which refers to function rather than form. The distinction between architectural types and building types is as important as it is confusing. The word "type" is sometimes employed loosely to refer to a functional building type with no standard morphology or configuration, such as an office building or apartment house. Other times it is used to refer to an architectural type with a standard morphology, such as the Italian palazzo, an example that may help explain this commonly misunderstood difference.

In its ideal or archetypal configuration, the palazzo is a four-sided, three-story urban domicile with other buildings abutting on either side and with a squarish courtyard, which is reached through a front portal and which provides light and air to a rusticated ground floor, a piano nobile (second floor), top floor, and possible attic. There are many inflections, distortions, and variations: the footprint might be rectangular or trapezoidal, the courtyard circular, skewed, or multiple, the site might be a corner or midblock, and the piano nobile may be repeated on the third floor. More to the point, the function can change and has changed over time. This basic configuration has been adapted or built anew to house offices, institutions, or apartments, among other things. Functional flexibility—the fact that different uses can be poured into its immutable form—is what makes the palazzo an architectural type rather than a building type.

An example of a modern architectural type is the American gas station, with its cantilevered canopy, pump islands, cashier room, and service bays. Although it has increasingly been adapted to fruit stand, video store, or adult bookstore, it is not a type likely to be built anew to house these or other new functions. This is because its archetype is a very specific configuration designed for the all-weather vending of fuel and the indoor servicing of automobiles. Form and function are not so loosely matched as in the palazzo, temple, or townhouse, which have proven such versatile and lasting types. At the rate at which gas stations are changing to convenience stores—vending sugar as well as gasoline and without maintenance or repair services—the classic version may soon be on the historic register. The motel, the airport terminal, the multi-level stadium with cantilevered tiers of seating (especially ones with an operable roof), and the parking garage are other modern architectural types. Also highly specific in

configuration, they will not be easily adapted to or reincarnated for new uses.

When a type is realized as individual built form, it is often referred to as a model. A model has inflections and idiosyncrasies that accommodate and express its particular site and crafting. It is not a clone, which has no individuality and is the mechanical product of a prototype. Prototypes are part of an industrial paradigm, wherein standardized design and mass production crank out clones that are exactly identical or in which the differences are too random, too superficial, or too small to constitute true models. In speculative housing, changing the color of the cladding or brick, flipping the garage from one side to the other, or adding shutters to the front facade are usually too artificial to make a type into a model. The model is a thoughtful accommodation of a building type to a specific site and a personal expression of its designer, builder, or owner—not just a marketing ploy.

If architectural types keep working well, they remain alive and are reproduced in new models and are filled and refilled with new and different uses. But if no longer functional or meaningful, they lose their vitality and degenerate into hollow or sentimental stereotypes. This has been the fate, for example, of the contemporary ranch house or split-level, which is now built with superficial variations all over the country in countless suburban subdivisions. Although the bungalow was also built around the country, there were more genuine differences from region to region. At least it seems that way today. Perhaps their differences now seem more genuine (and appealing, like many historic buildings) simply because of their better craftsmanship and materials, as well as heavier, more substantial construction. Their variations were also greater because homebuilders back then built two or three houses at a time, rather than two or three hundred, as they often do now. They didn't all suffer, for instance, standard contemporary aluminum windows with snap-in plastic muntins or sliding glass doors, so oblivious to climate and craft.

Perhaps the most easily understood example of type and model is the human body. The human being is a single biological species with a single physical template (two legs, two arms, one head, etc.), but it keeps reproducing in miraculous morphological variety. There are two sexes, a relatively limited range of skin and hair color, and three basic body types, but no two of today's six billion models of the type are the same. This is not to mention the other billions of humans who have already come and gone. Differences of millimeters in facial structure or half-inches in body height are immediately recognizable; friends can be spotted at once in a crowd. (Identical twins are harder but still possible to differentiate, although they are genetically more like clones of a prototype than models of a type.)

Not only are subtle differences appreciable, humans do not tire of looking at each other. Indeed, we look at thousands of faces every year and are never bored by the next one that comes into our cone of vision. We are intrigued not just by visual differences and superficial details. We are interested in and drawn to the person behind the face, just as we appreciate authentic differences in a building's facade that promise differences inside. The ability of variations on a single theme to hold our interest is remarkable. Those architects who argue that typology makes architecture inherently less free and creative fail to recognize this immense human capacity to appreciate subtle physical differences and minute details. Indeed, it can be argued that type increases the ability to generate and appreciate difference and therefore actually liberates morphological creativity at the small scale. Later in this chapter, it will be argued that typology is also liberative at the scale of the neighborhood, town, city, and metropolitan region.

The limits of originality

Although Modernists eschewed the concept and tradition of typology, they would acknowledge the importance of prototype and stereotype and might also admit to three morphological types: centroidal, linear, and field or scattered. These basic categories are objective and abstract diagrams, as inevitable as they are devoid of function or history.

Modernists would also admit to functional types, such as office building or apartment house, but not in a way that prefigures a building's form. They tended to invent new architecture types with every new program. Indeed, Modernist architectural education taught an architecture of ideas, self-discovery, and self-expression, rather than one of learning from and building on exemplary precedent. (I can remember starting with "bubble diagrams" or paper cutouts of functional areas as a method of rationally arranging adjacent parts of a floor plan.) In the 1960s, studying a magazine article or book about a relevant architect or architectural type would have been looked at askance—a prohibition so well understood and inculcated that there would not have been the

need for the instructor to announce it. It was also understood that the inventive use of both functionalist architectural language and technology was far more valued than adapting or transforming an existing architectural type.

As a result of this forced functional and formal creativity, a generation of architects lost the decorum and discipline to do straightforward, nonheroic buildings when the program was ordinary and modest. (As an architecture student and young practitioner, I was looking to design architecture that was good but also attention-getting as opposed to simply good. Only later, with the insights of Critical Regionalism and New Urbanism, did I realize that the personal need, even duty, to be *always and forever* inventive and unique made me part of the problem, not the solution, of contemporary American architecture and urbanism.) To refrain from conspicuously creative and original statements when they were not necessary became and continues to be an act of architectural courage in both architecture schools and in our media-saturated society (which is why I admire Andres Duany and Elizabeth Plater-Zyberk's early, unequivocal assertion while they were still architecture students that the emperor of Modernist architecture was not wearing any clothes. They also asserted that traditional American architecture and urbanism were being foolishly overlooked. These were radical and embarrassing things to say at the time). The overthrowing of tradition, long the third rail in architectural discourse, became the curse rather than the blessing of Modernism.

The time and the place for idiosyncrasy and originality are when the program or site or both are unusual. Designers need not feel compelled to be constantly innovative with every commission, at least not at the scale of the whole building, on which Modernist invention usually focused. Typology means creativity is more often exercised at a smaller or larger scale than the individual building, such as at the scale of the window or of the neighborhood. It means that all building types are not equally conducive to originality. Housing, because it is a place of rest and retreat, tends to be more conservative and less inventive technologically, structurally, and morphologically than other building types. But its detailing can be personally expressive and idiosyncratic. It also has had a relatively unchanging program. It numerically compromises the bulk of the urban fabric, and consequently best plays a more subdued role in the city.

The types with which to be most architecturally inventive and expressive are places of recreation, entertainment, and work, where people extend themselves. Architects who radically innovate or experiment with private houses, especially when they are second homes, are acting within a long and fertile design tradition, going back in the western world at least to Palladio's villas if not Hadrian's. But those that take similar liberties with multifamily housing for anonymous users or with wild insertions of single-family houses in residential neighborhoods forget that home and community are about haven and familiarity, not stimulation and striving. When a talented architect such as Rem Koolhaas conducts exciting and creative experiments like the Congrexpo at Euralille, it's a reasonable and exciting proposition. But when he experiments in Fukuoka, Japan, with new architectural types for housing that ends up looking like a nightclub from the street, it's not all right. (It is no wonder that this project went begging in the market.) Residential communities are more socially fragile than business centers—or, for that matter, airports, convention centers, entertainment centers, and sports arenas. Architects must know the right type and time and place to thumb their noses at convention. Not all parts of the city are equally appropriate for experimentation. Most neighborhoods are brittle and need stability more than innovation.

A major contributor to excessive experimentation has been and continues to be schools of architecture. It is important that schools be a progressive and critical force in the discipline and practice of architecture. It is also important that every architecture student be pushed to experiment and speculate. However, it shouldn't be mandatory on, and need not be fundamental to, *every* design exercise and project. Thinking and designing out of the box normally makes more sense in the advanced studios during the later years of the curriculum. To experiment and invent is heady, fun, and positive, but needs to be encouraged at the right time and place. To do it habitually is like eating nothing but dessert—tasty but not very nutritional. Somehow architectural education has come to just that, a hypoglycemic diet of making interesting form. Moreover, the manipulation of form is usually within a predictable "house style" that prevails within the school. Style per se is okay, even beneficial, and ultimately unavoidable. It helps students (or practicing architects) deal with and bring order to the daunting number of variables that they will undoubtedly face. But an architectural style needs to be buildable, adaptable, humane, liberative, and ultimately meaningful. Recent styles, especially those based on fractal and deconstructed geometry, may be dramatic and seductive, but they

often are arbitrary and unworkable when they encounter building practice, the human user, and physical context.

Typology can also be an act of efficiency and economy for the designer. It is considerably easier to start with a time-tested architectural type and modify it into a suitable model than to try to invent a new type (or at least an unrecognizable version of an existing type) with every architectural commission. A typological point of departure is quicker in that it draws on types that are finite in number. It does not start out with the near-infinite architectural possibilities that a functional analysis or "bubble diagram" of the building's program permits. The Modernist insistence on starting from scratch is very expensive. It often overtakes the architectural fee and exhausts the design team and client before the design has climbed very high toward perfection on the curve of diminishing returns, where additional design time and effort result in less improvement. Typological designers can climb higher on that quality curve because they waste less time and fee in discovery at the outset. Economy of means and of time encourages architects to embrace typological design.

"Form follows function" was the rallying cry of Modernism. Although it may have achieved this correspondence at the building scale, it often ignored the connection between form and function at the urban scale. Because many Modernist buildings are creative translations of one-of-a-kind programs into unforeseen and never-before-seen forms, materials, and structural systems, they are often unrecognizable as urban elements. Most people would not recognize Frank Lloyd Wright's Guggenheim as a museum, for example. Nor would most people recognize Le Corbusier's Ronchamp Chapel as a church.

On the other extreme, commercial Modernism has recently put complex or mixed programs under one roof, sometimes in a single large volume. These inexpensive sheds, warehouses, pre-engineered metal buildings, tilt-up boxes, and "big boxes" tend to be so large, unarticulated, and generic as to be mute megaboxes in the cityscape. They lack the tectonic quality of traditional market halls and sheds. These warehouses offer the same potential for adaptability for which palazzos and townhouses have been praised, but they are built of much lower quality construction in dumbed-down configurations. Space is not made for particular uses but is simply made available. The huge metal and concrete boxes could house a discount mart, tennis courts, or dairy cows. This reduction in the number of architectural types is more acute in suburbia, where building is even more expedient and repetitive.

Typological design is also less likely to produce visual chaos in the built environment than Modernism. Buildings of the same type naturally tend to rhyme more with each other over time and space. Cities can once again be more legible and therefore more understandable to their inhabitants and guests. They are vital not because they are a breathless collection of novel and exciting buildings, but because they are an understandable hierarchy of buildings that are big and small, important and unimportant, vernacular and monumental, background and foreground. When understandable to their citizens, cities can again help record, legitimize, transmit, and extend the values of culture and community.

Does typology dull architectural creativity? No, but it does put limits on it. Like many ordering systems, it can actually liberate and unleash more coherent creativity. The type offers a known framework in which creative change can take place, either during the initial design process, during construction, or after occupancy. It frees the designer to concentrate on changes that truly make a difference rather than on the superficial or arbitrary invention of form. It limits originality for its own sake—the kind of novelty into which commodification, marketing, and avant-gardism can degenerate. The Modernist imperative to innovate ultimately became just as tyrannical as the former imperative to follow tradition. Typologists can be original and go beyond the ordinary, but only at the appropriate scale and when extraordinary circumstances warrant it. They do not feel that they must be original with every design problem. On the other hand, they must guard against being too slavish or derivative in their replication of a given type.

Typology has a different attitude toward change over time than Modernism. High-style Modernist buildings tend to be unique responses to specific programs for particular users. With the exception of some high-tech and most loft buildings, they usually start out specialized, with interiors and exteriors that are hard to adapt to the subsequent uses that will be invariably asked of the building. Types are not overspecialized and are usually more adaptive. The palazzo, the basilica, the Georgian townhouse, the Cape Cod cottage, and the loft warehouse are examples of versatile architectural types. Not all types are this adaptable, but most buildings based on types are general enough to be customized over time. In a sense, they start out conservative, conventional, and traditional and become radicalized

over their life. High-style Modernist buildings, on the other hand, often start out as radical and are made to become more normal over time as they are changed by their users.

A question of scale (toward a theory of scale)

Typology has also shifted the scale at which the freedom to invent occurs. Instead of sculpting a figural statement (a "duck" in Robert Venturi and Denise Scott Brown's terms) at the building scale, a hallmark of the Modern Movement, a typological design is often concerned with the room. Rooms with a capital "R" take on the importance that Modernism tended to lavish on the circulation system. (Such elements as stair towers, corridors, and elevator shafts are often externally expressed as bold and conspicuous elements in Modernist buildings.) Related to this re-emerging interest in discrete rooms is a renewed emphasis on architectural elements such as the door, column, and window, which need not be thought of as standardized components.

At the middle scale—that of public space—typology also brings discipline and hierarchy to creativity. Typical alley, street, avenue, and boulevard sections, as well as time-tested block configurations, are deployed in site-specific ways. Spatial variety is possible at the urban scale, because public spaces are treated as particularized outdoor rooms that can also be site-specific. They are not treated as generic streets and plazas. Nor are neighborhoods, districts, cities, and regions seen in standard or universal terms. In a sense, typology trades freedom, uniqueness, and creativity at the scale of the building, neighborhood, street, and block for freedom, uniqueness, and creativity at the scale of the architectural details and of the whole city. It's a trade that makes for more predictable buildings but less predictable cities.

Although Modernist buildings are free, original, and creative at the building scale, their details tend to be standard and generic; their hollow-metal door jambs and steel and aluminum knobs, window jambs and trim, railings, and light fixtures are typically uniform from project to project. Indeed, Modernism actually championed standardized industrial production. Perhaps the pioneers of the Modern Movement instinctively and subconsciously realized that, with the advent of standardized mass production, they had better be creative at a larger scale.

Modernist functional or Euclidean zoning segregated the city into zones of single uses, greatly

	DETAILING	BUILDING	STREET/BLOCK	N'HOOD/CITY/REGION
Modernist	Standard	Unique	Unique	Standard
Typological	Unique	Standard	Standard	Unique

reducing the number of both building and architectural types with which to shape the city. Urban blocks became superblocks; while curvilinear and cul-de-sac streets made irregular blocks in suburbia. Bulk zoning requirements, especially set-back regulations, resulted in oversized and windswept streets (which encouraged cars to drive too fast) and gigantic plazas (which encouraged pedestrians to walk too fast). These public zones are residual rather than positive space. And they are usually empty of pedestrians. As stated earlier, traditional typology reverses this figure/ground relationship, trading figural object buildings for figural public spaces. And, when regionalist architectural, street, and block types are respected, neighborhoods, cities, and regions are particular and unique. The reversals are consistent across the board, at four scales shown in the table above.

Although tradition and precedent were ideologically and stylistically eschewed at all scales, the Modern Movement was especially free and creative at the two middle scales, i.e., the building and the street/block. It put its most fertile eggs primarily in one basket, the individual building. Architectural details and components were standard and generic, while building plans and sections were very creative and particular. Modernism also tended to experiment with urban design, often with oversized superblocks, streets, and plazas, which were sometimes raised above or sunken below street level. At the largest scale, suburban and urban neighborhoods and districts are more standardized; indeed, contemporary cities have grown to look and feel more and more alike as they become zoned and themed for tourists and commodified for residents by national and international corporations, retail chains, and banks. Mass tourism, by trying to standardize the experience of travelers, dilutes authentic local urban character.

Conversely, typology breeds more predictable and anonymous design at the middle scales of the individual building and of the street and block, but blossoms at the small and large scales. This predictability at the building and block scale is one of the key architectural phenomena that makes urban design possible. Without it, there is no way for urban designers to make meaningful and effective plans. It also encourages rich, idiosyncratic architectural detailing. The reason that a typologically driven architect is more creative with the smaller, more private compositions of architecture—the windows, the doors, and the trim—is that they are less prescribed than the overall building configuration is by the architectural type. Precedent, repetition, and predictability are viewed as positive traits and good points of departure at the scale of the building. At the scale of the city, however, the uniformity of zoning yields to mixed-use neighborhoods and districts that can be unpredictable in the composition of the mix. As with architectural details and elements, the city becomes a rich hierarchical array of architectural types, streets, and public spaces, while the individual building becomes better behaved, that is, less autonomous and egotistical. And when the architectural and urban typologies are rooted in the region, the neighborhood, the city, and the metropolitan region are all better able to resist standardization and universalization.

A question of hierarchy

If Modernism bleached variety out of architectural detailing and neighborhood, Postmodernism artificially restored it. It started dressing a single architectural type in different garbs, often trying to pump up the importance of a building or trying to be contextual where there was no distinctive context. This dress code often inflated the visual importance of a building beyond its programmatic importance in the city or townscape, adding further confusion to the built environment. Like signing an unimportant document with a grand flourish, it overembellished everyday buildings. Indeed, architects were hired to put their signatures on mundane, commercial buildings. Postmodernism overreacted to functionalism. To quote Leon Krier:

Whatever the pretensions of its forms, a supermarket is no less or more significant, whether wrapped in architectural, nautical or commercial dressing. Its very typological and social status will forever prevent it from becoming culturally significant. The reverse is also true: however beautiful and dignified an historical city center may be, it cannot survive for long its transformation into a shopping, business or leisure zone. In the same way even the largest housing scheme cannot become a city or public monument.... its functional monotony and uniformity simply do not provide the typological materials for significant monumental and urban gestures.[7]

Background and foreground buildings

Making the distinction between background and foreground buildings is another way of linking architecture and function. Here function is defined as urban coherence and legibility rather than the accommodation of a building's program. Putting private and commercial functions in foreground, monumental buildings is inappropriate. Putting important public functions in background, vernacular buildings is equally wrong. The local post office often looks like it could be a warehouse, and conversely the drug store looks like it might be the post office.

Monumental buildings need not be large in size. They need only be civic in presence. Sometimes stature is enhanced by miniaturization, color, or refinement rather than grand size. A figural, low-rise city hall can tame surrounding high-rise buildings into backdrop roles. (High-rise buildings tend to be perceived as background buildings at street level and as foreground buildings when seen against the sky from a distance.) The inner temples at Japan's Ise Shrine are but one famous example of the power of smallness and refinement. Teahouses are another example from that country which so values propriety. In Philadelphia, Independence Hall makes dwarfs of much larger surrounding buildings, as do gemlike colonial buildings such as the Old State House in downtown Boston and Neo-Gothic churches in the canyons of New York's Wall Street district. Neighborhood libraries and firehouses are small, but they also can command a strong public presence.

Expression by type

The appropriate expression of each and every building's importance is a critical part of restoring meaning and clarity to both architecture and the city. The hierarchy of civic importance and the distinction of

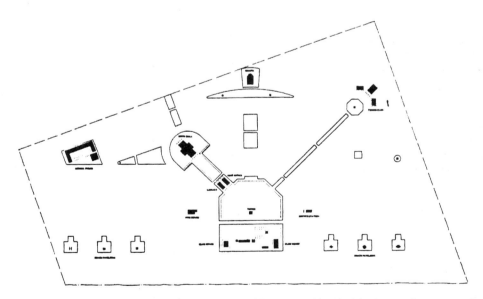

With a clear distinction between residential and public buildings, Seaside, Florida, is zoned more typologically than functionally. This Neo-Traditional resort community trades uniformity of function within a zone for a variety of architectural types within a neighborhood. A common architectural language is also prescribed in its codes, which reinforce a hierarchy of building and street types. For instance, only public buildings can be white; all houses must be colored, have picket fences, etc. Public buildings are far less constrained by the code. They are treated as figural monuments, with foreground buildings set off against the background residential buildings. (Duany and Plater-Zyberk)

the public from the private realm have become confused. The revival of mixed-use buildings and mixed-use zones has begun to exacerbate the problem and begs a different kind of urban order. As it jumbles land uses again, the city becomes more typologically chaotic, with residential, institutional, commercial, recreational, and industrial architectural types cheek-to-jowl. Bolder architectural figuration, size, and color are needed to stand out from the more variegated cityscape, much like a church or city hall stands out in the mixed-use fabric of an Italian hill town. A raised megastructure or megaform is one strategy to stand out in the sprawling urban/suburban smear, which Kenneth Frampton likens to the natural wilderness that architecture once was expected to tame and civilize.

It is also important to be clear about what functions are foreground and background in individual buildings that mix uses, especially if any of the uses are important public ones. If, for instance, a public conference center or civic hall is embedded in a commercial or residential building, its entrance elevation should be expressed as more important and dignified.

Location by type

Getting the right architectural type in the right place becomes more critical than getting the right use in the right place. Uses move around, transform, and become obsolete at a faster rate and in more unpredictable ways than architectural types change. It is clearly good urban practice to mix and remix uses, in both mixed-use buildings and mixed-use zones, but not to mix up architectural types or to confuse their hierarchy of importance. A grand hall or iconic tower should be reserved for important locations in the city as much as for important functions. Big boxes, even if they house institutional uses such as a church, should not be built on honorific sites. The architectural type trumps the building type in the mixed-use, Postmodernist city, unlike in the functionally zoned or Euclidean-zoned Modernist city, where the building type was the increment of planning and development. For instance, the "loft building" becomes more important than the more generic "apartment building" or "office building."

Variety by type

There has been a decrease in the absolute number of architectural types, especially in suburbia. As a

growing range of functions is housed in generic big boxes, tilt-up warehouses, and pre-engineered metal sheds, there are fewer and fewer architectural types with which to shape and articulate the built environment. It could be argued that this dumbing down of the palette while scaling up in size is a straightforward way to deal with increasing programmatic complexity and mixing under one roof. However, a smaller menu for architects, engineers, and urban designers makes for a less informed, less articulate place. Ultimately, it makes for an urban monoculture, however rich or lean the architectural mix inside the big boxes or however much their syncopated facades falsely mimic main street. Genuinely new architectural types that accommodate and express new conditions, sensibilities, and purposes need to emerge, much as the gas station, the motel, the airport terminal, the live-work loft, the storage rental building, and the retractable-roof stadium emerged during the last century.

Construction by type

When this simplified palette of buildings are not built to last because of short-term investment strategies, the city soon is as shoddily built as it is architecturally mute or fake. Important and honorific architectural types, because they tend to occupy the most important sites and to outlast specific uses, are usually designed and built with more care and expense. The more dispensable background architectural types, such as big boxes, which typically occupy less privileged locations, can be designed and built more cheaply. Taken together, the strategy of type and of foreground/background buildings offers some hope for reversing the decline in the quality of the built environment.

Typology and tradition

A purely functionalist architecture also makes for historical sterility. The break with tradition that Modernism sponsored, including but not limited to eschewing typology, was simply too abrupt. Modernists scoff at the notion of tradition, telling us that traditions are invented, thereby implying they can be as easily replaced as they are discarded. But as Roger Scruton contends, a "real tradition is not an invention; it is the unintended byproduct of invention, which also makes invention possible. Our musical tradition is one outstanding example of this. No single person created it. Each contributor built on previous achievements, discovering problems and solving them through the steady expansion of the common syntax."[8] Architectural types, from the Greek temple to the Charleston "Single" to the Las Vegas casino, offer a parallel tradition in another medium.

By embracing traditional architectural types and inflecting them with new programmatic needs and new materials, designers honor past generations, with whom we partner to make cities. "The dead and the unborn are as much members of society as the living. To dishonor the dead is to reject the relation on which society is built—the relation of obligation between generations. Those who have lost respect for their dead have ceased to be trustees of their inheritance. Inevitably, therefore, they lose the sense of obligation to future generations. The web of obligations sinks to the present tense."[9] The architecture of the "now generation," with its difficulty in deferring gratification and its reluctance to make long-term commitments, has weakened if not broken this chain of caring. By working with inherited architectural types—however freely and imaginatively—the chain is repaired and strengthened. The sudden quantum jumps that chaos theory describes as necessary to evolution may be liberative and necessary from time to time, but most change is incremental and evolutionary, not cataclysmic.

Embracing the benefits of typology does not mean the end of functionalism per se. Obviously, buildings must continue to function operationally and economically. But not at all costs and not at the loss of urban decorum. In recent decades, function as a design methodology and as the sole or primary organizing device for building plans and sections has fortunately given up much of its preeminence to contextualism and typology (and, alas, to formalism). Typology *functions* better in urbanistic terms by better addressing the architectural needs of the mixed-use city and sustaining a degree of continuity and tradition in architecture. It is the link between architecture and urbanism, between the past and the present, that was missing in Modernism.

Architectural types are to urban designers what walls, doors, windows, and columns are to architects. Typology is the vocabulary for the language of urban form. Without a typological language, designing cities in coherent, predictable, and collaborative ways over time becomes impossible. If urban design is too big to be mastered by a single professional and therefore requires teamwork, there needs to be a design language for intra- and inter-professional communication. And if urban design is correctly defined by urbanists Alan Simpson and David Lewis as "three dimensional policy," a common language of form is needed for communication between design professionals on the urban design team and elected officials, community leaders, citizens, etc. As urbanist Jonathan Barnett points out, without the ability to approximate the footprint, height, and bulk of buildings before they are designed and built by others, the urban designer is rendered helpless and toothless in proposing urban design plans and guidelines. When architects base their work, however loosely, on known architectural types, the urban designer can roughly anticipate how development will take shape, without unduly restricting the design freedom of the architect in shaping individual buildings. Architects, in turn, can more effectively and intelligently interpret urban design plans and guidelines if they speak the same typological language. There is room for invention of new or radically altered types, but when invention of both building and architectural types is rife or the norm, as it has become with some architects, urban design becomes difficult if not futile.

Getting the types right for a given street, neighborhood, or community is usually more important than the architectural brilliance of individual buildings. A collection of beautifully designed buildings does not a city make. Witness a World's Fair with many pavilions designed by their country's star architects. They don't necessarily add up to a sense of place or community. Columbus, Indiana, has individual masterpieces by many of the nation's most distinguished and talented architects. But a trophy collection does not necessarily confer coherence on a town or city (which is why it is good that this enlightened town has more recently commissioned leading architects to do both smaller and more background architectural types and building types). At the moment, most American cities suffer more from typological confusion than architectural mediocrity. However, the right architectural typology alone cannot provide for a good built environment. It takes both good design and the right types to imbue the built environment with the splendid magic and power of which architecture and urbanism are capable.

Is our individualistic architecture beginning to abate in favor of a less atomistic architecture and urbanism? For no other reason than the arithmetic pressure of population growth, has the fulcrum slowly but inexorably begun to shift from rugged individualism to urbanity? The promising return of residents to our downtowns begins to suggest such a shift. In any case, we must reassess the scales at which we should be bold and innovative. We have begun to understand and appreciate that architecture need not re-invent itself every generation and certainly not for every new problem or program it addresses. We have started to downsize our expectations and to realize—as players in a classical play realize—that the physical world is finite and must be fashioned out of limited resources, energy, space, forms, and architectural types in a limited amount of time. There is neither the luxury of endless time nor the bottomless resources to pursue casually, cavalierly or experimentally our architectural and urban agenda.

Typology versus critical regionalism

If Critical Regionalism celebrates and reinforces what is unique and enduring, typology provides us with a connection to something bigger and more universal. It connects our buildings to our city and region as well as to architecture and urbanism around the world. It also provides us with the building blocks—the DNA, if you will—to shape a city that is more than a collection of its pieces. In a secular culture, the city may be the biggest and most long-lived thing to which many people can hope to connect. The city was made for us by people who preceded us, and we make it for people who follow us. It is both unique and great. Both needs—to be unique and to be part of some great idea or large group—seem to be a major part of the modern Western psyche. It could be argued that typology, because it allows regional variation on universal types, answers both of these needs. But it no longer speaks loudly enough about the regional differences, which are quickly becoming extinct around the globe. Regional architectural types are not strong enough alone to withstand mass culture and to resist the commodification of architecture that ignores or erases regional and local differences. For this, we need a rooted and judicious regionalism.

The tension and friction between these two proclivities can be fertile. Because Critical Regionalism is critical, even disdainful, of popular culture, it is not always conducive to city making. More concerned about place than community, it is very compelling at the architectural scale, but its critical stance can be counterproductive when trying to make a street or neighborhood. In making its critiques of popular culture, Critical Regionalism perpetuates an avant-garde attitude toward culture, with its endless over-turning of tradition by an artistic elite. In striving to be authentic, pure, and timeless, Critical Regionalism sets itself apart from the norm. This stance may produce good, even profound, architecture, but not necessarily good neighborhoods, towns, or cities. A townsperson knows the importance of a collective framework or covenant that brings people together in less critical and more tolerant ways. This means the city needs many background buildings that behave in predictable, normal ways and that honor their context for every foreground architectural/artistic statement. In short, we must beware of architectural snobbery when designing whole communities and be aware that architectural typology and precedent can help us make our communities more coherent.

Complex, self-defining systems like society, cities, and culture need competing ideas and contradictory forces to invigorate and regulate themselves. Although there must always have been social tension and disharmony, other periods and cultures have inspired and liberated the human spirit to higher civic achievements and fostered a greater sense of a community. (Although this unity may have come at the expense of stigmatizing and warring with an enemy.) Americans seem particularly saddled for better or worse with an equally strong need both to individuate and to be part of a group. Rebelliousness and egotism are joined against connectedness and community, liberty against equality. If we are to design for both the individual and the group, if we are to express what is local and what is universal in our built environment, then regionalism and typology must engage in continuous dialogue.

Notes

1. Allan Bloom, *Love and Friendship,* p. 211 (New York: Simon and Schuster, 1993).
2. John Passmore, "The End of Philosophy," *Australasian Journal of Philosophy* 74 (March 1996):1–19.
3. Mark Gelernter, "Teaching Design Innovation through Design Tradition," *Proceedings,* ACSA Annual Meeting, Miami, 1988.
4. Stewart Brand, *How Buildings Learn: What happens after they're built,* p. 178 (London: Phoenix Illustrated, 1997).
5. Bryan Appleyard, *Richard Rogers: A Biography,* p. 65 (London: Faber and Faber, 1986).
6. Cesar Pelli, *Observations for Young Architects,* pp. 10–12 (New York: Monacelli Press, 1999).

7. Krier, *Architectural Design,* p. 61.
8. Roger Scruton, "Rousseau and the Origins of Liberalism," *The New Criterion* (October 1998):8
9. Ibid., p. 12

Source and copyright

This chapter was published in its original form as:

Kelbaugh, D. (2002), 'Typology: An Architecture of Limits', in Kelbaugh, D. (2002), *Repairing the American Metropolis*, University of Washington Press, Seattle, 94–132.

Reprinted with permission of The University of Washington Press.

Section Three

The perceptual dimension

Since the early 1960s an interdisciplinary field of environmental perception has developed and there now exists a significant body of research on people's perception of their urban environment. The initial work on environmental images was extended and reinforced by a body of work focusing on the experiential 'sense-of-place' and 'lived-in' experiences associated with the urban environment, which explored how people perceive environments and experience places. With sense-of-place came the parallel phenomena of 'placelessness' and concepts of 'invented' and 're-invented' places, entraining ideas of 'authenticity' and the construction/manufacture of place and place values. More recently, the field has been supplemented by work on symbolism and meaning in the built environment.

This section presents a set of five chapters. The first chapter, Chapter 10, is from **Edward Relph's** 1976 book, *Place and Placelessness*. If we see contemporary urban design as being about place-making, then Relph's book was one of the first to focus on the psychological and experiential sense-of-place. His book was also one of the first in the urban design field to draw on phenomenology – the philosophical investigation and description of conscious experience. Relph (1976: 8) argued that, while 'amorphous' and 'intangible', whenever we feel or know space, there is typically an associated sense or concept of 'place'. Thus, for Relph, places were essentially centres of meaning constructed out of lived experience. By imbuing them with meaning, as individuals or as groups, people change 'spaces' into 'places'. Relph also considered it unrealistic to investigate place without also considering 'placelessness', which he defined as the 'casual eradication of distinctive places' and the 'making of standardised landscapes'. Appreciation of the concept of 'placelessness' helps the activity of urban design by providing a frame of reference. Whereas sense-of-place tends to be associated with something of intrinsic value, placelessness is generally viewed negatively, evoking what some commentators refer to as a 'narrative-of-loss'. The extract reproduced here is the first part of a longer discussion on the identity of places. Parallels are also apparent with, for example, Trancik's discussion of lost space (see Chapter 7) and with critiques of market-led urban design (see Chapter 5).

Chapter 11 is **Kevin Lynch's** *Reconsidering the Image of the City*, originally written in 1984 and republished in Tribid Banerjee and Michael Southworth's 1991 edited collection of Lynch's work, *City Sense and City Design: Writings and Projects of Kevin Lynch* (MIT Press, Cambridge, Mass). This chapter is Lynch's own reflection on his earlier book, *The Image of the City* (1960), which had been a key work in both the field of urban imagery and the emerging field of urban design. Without diminishing its status as a classic text, Lynch's essay is important in putting it into its historical context and in showing how he reflected upon and developed his earlier work. Lynch had initially been interested in legibility (i.e. how people orientated themselves and navigated within cities), but soon adjusted his focus to the theme of the city's mental image. Observing that cities had districts or landmarks or pathways that were easily identifiable and easily grouped into an overall pattern, led him to the concept of 'imageability' and the identification of his famous five key physical elements – paths, edges, districts, nodes and landmarks. Although his original study had been based on a very small sample of people, it was later replicated in various contexts and Lynch argues that the basic ideas held. However, some of the work following on from Lynch had been highly critical of his findings and his methods. To some extent this is unfair because Lynch had explicitly offered it as a 'first initial sketch'. He nevertheless addresses these criticisms in this chapter.

Chapter 12 is **Paul Knox's** 'The social production of the built environment: Architects, architecture and the post-Modern city', originally published in *Progress in Human Geography* in 1987. Knox has played an important role in making the concept of meaning more readily accessible to an urban design audience. In this chapter, he presents an important discussion of the role of socially constructed meaning in the production of the built environment and, by extension, in urban design practice. In this respect, this chapter builds on Kevin Lynch's three attributes of environmental images – *identity* (i.e. recognition of an object as a separable entity – a door); *structure* (e.g. the door's position in the wall); and *meaning* (e.g. recognition of a 'door' as a hole for getting in and out of). Lynch established that meaning was unlikely to be consistent across disparate groups of people. Similarly, Knox establishes that socially constructed meaning is a complex phenomenon, but a vital component of designers' understanding of place and the significance of their actions.

One of the responses to 'placelessness' and the standardisation and homogenisation of place (i.e. in the face of trends such as globalisation, mass culture, etc.) is a deliberate 'manufacturing' of difference or, in terms more specific to urban design, the 'invention' – and sometimes 'reinvention' – of places. While invented places are those that are wholly invented (such as Disneyland), 're-invented places' are those that start from a basis in reality, but generally involve a significant degree of change, distortion and loss of authenticity. Accordingly, Chapter 13 is **Jan Sircus's** short paper, 'Invented places', which was published in *Prospect* in 2001. Sircus (2001: 31) likens sense-of-place to a brand that connotes certain expectations of quality, consistency and reliability. The influence of theme parks and invented places is widespread and pervasive and, as Sircus suggests, Disneyland is the quintessential invented place. The (supposedly) artificial creation or manufacture of 'places' and place values in ways that draw upon the techniques of theme parks – usually to further the purposes of consumption – occurs in a variety of settings, including shopping malls, historic districts, urban entertainment districts, central city redevelopments and tourist destinations (see Relph, 1976; Zukin, 1991; Hannigan, 1998). Providing a good discussion of the phenomena, Sircus's paper is additionally valuable because its author worked as an architect and as a senior Disney 'Imagineer'. By presenting a difference perspective, the paper highlights the apparent disjuncture between the 'elitist' concerns of critics and the more popularist desires, made manifest by the popularity of such places. As Sircus argues, place is neither good nor bad simply because it is 'real' rather than surrogate or 'authentic' rather than pastiche – people enjoy both; they are not inevitability fooled by the invention and 'fakery' and, furthermore, it may not matter to their experience.

This leads on to Chapter 14, **Sharon Zukin's** 'Learning from Disney World' – a chapter from her 1995 book, *The Cultures of Cities* (Blackwell, Oxford). A valuably critical article about what urban design might have to learn from Disney World and from theme parks generally, the paper has two themes. The first relates to the making places vis-à-vis theme parks (i.e. inventing/reinventing places). The second relates to control and management strategies, which, in turn, moves the discussion onto the social dimension of urban design. The lesson here – and from the previous selection – is that all design involves a process of imagining changed outcomes, either by changing existing places or by creating places anew. The theme park might be at one end of a continuum of authenticity, while incremental alterations to existing urban environments might be at the other, but this immediately raises debates about precisely what is meant by authenticity: is authenticity resident, for example, in the environment or is it constructed in the mind of the beholder? An answer – but certainly not the end of the debate – is that authenticity is in the experience rather than in the object (Ashworth, 1997). Moreover, the original design of places is only one contribution to the perception of them, because the way places are managed and controlled over time also impacts on sense-of-place. Again, Disney World may be one extreme, but much of the so-called 'privatised' public realm (see Section Four) exhibits similar characteristics.

Matthew Carmona and Steve Tiesdell

10

On the identity of places

Edward Relph
[1976]

There are two major reasons for attempting to understand the phenomenon of place. First, it is interesting in its own right as a fundamental expression of man's involvement in the world; and second, improved knowledge of the nature of place can contribute to the maintenance and manipulation of existing places and the creation of new places. The real difficulty lies, however, not in the justification of the study of place, but in the development of adequate concepts and approaches for this. These must be based on the recognition that, as Wagner (1972, p.49) expresses it: "Place, person, time and act form an indivisible unity. To be oneself one has to be somewhere definite, do certain things at appropriate times." Given this fusion of meaning, act, and context, it has sometimes been suggested that generalisations about places cannot be formulated. "Both region and writer, person and place, are unique", declares Hugh Prince (1961, p.22), "and it is in their distinctive qualities that we find their essential character." From this it follows that to capture, comprehend and communicate 'essential character' depends largely on artistic insight and literary ability. Such an approach is well illustrated in the work of many novelists and other artists, for example Ronald Blythe's *Akenfield* (1969), a study of an English village through the verbatim accounts of its inhabitants, or Lawrence Durrell's essays (1969) about the Greek Islands collected under the title *The Spirit of Place*. An alternative method is that of systematic and objective description and analysis in which places are considered only in terms of their general properties, for instance as gap towns, commuting centres, central places or points in isotropic space. In fact neither approach offers much towards an understanding of places as phenomena of experience: the former is too specific and the latter is too general. What is required is an approach and attendant set of concepts that respond to the unity of 'place, person, and act' and stress the links rather than the division between specific and general features of places.

It is the purpose in this chapter to examine one such set of concepts and methods relating to the notion of 'identity' of place. This examination is based on the recognition that while places and landscapes may be unique in terms of their content they are nevertheless products of common cultural and symbolic elements and processes (Wagner, 1972, p.5). Identity of place is as much a function of intersubjective intentions and experiences as of the appearances of buildings and scenery, and it refers not only to the distinctiveness of individual places but also to the sameness between different places.

The identity of places

The notion of identity is a fundamental one in everyday life. Heidegger (1969, p.26) has written: "Everywhere, wherever and however we are related to beings of every kind, identity makes its claim upon us." Thus we recognise the identities of people, plants, places, and even nations. Possibly because it is so fundamental, identity is a phenomenon that evades simple definition, although some of its main characteristics are apparent. In particular the difference yet relationship between 'identity of' and 'identity with' should be noted. The identity of something refers to a persistent sameness and unity which allows that thing to be differentiated from others.

Such inherent identity is inseparable from identity with other things; Erik Erikson (1959, p.102), in a discussion of ego identity, writes: "The term identity ... connotes both a persistent sameness within oneself ... and a persistent sharing of some kind of characteristic with others." Thus identity is founded both in the individual person or object and in the culture to which they belong. It is not static and unchangeable, but varies as circumstances and attitudes change; and it is not uniform and undifferentiated, but has several components and forms.

Kevin Lynch (1960, p.6) defines the identity of a place simply as that which provides its individuality or distinction from other places and serves as the basis for its recognition as a separable entity. This tells us only that each place has a unique address, that it is identifiable. Ian Nairn (1965, p.78) offers some expansion of this: he recognises that "there are as many identities of place as there are people", for identity is in the experience, eye, mind, and intention of the beholder as much as in the physical appearance of the city or landscape. But while every individual may assign selfconsciously or unselfconsciously an identity to particular places, these identities are nevertheless combined intersubjectively to form a common identity. Perhaps this occurs because we experience more or less the same objects and activities and because we have been taught to look for certain qualities of place emphasised by our cultural groups. Certainly it is the manner in which these qualities and objects are manifest in our experience of places that governs our impressions of the uniqueness, strength, and genuineness of the identity of those places.

It is clear that rather than being a simple address in a gazetteer or a point on a map, identity is a basic feature of our experience of places which both influences and is influenced by those experiences. What is involved is not merely the recognition of differences and of samenesses between places—but also the much more fundamental act of identifying sameness in difference. And it is not just the identity *of* a place that is important, but also the identity that a person or group has *with* that place, in particular whether they are experiencing it as an insider or as an outsider.

In the following discussion identity is considered in terms of, first the constituent components of the identity of places; second, the links between individual, group, and mass images of places and the identities of those places; and finally, the ways in which identities develop, are maintained, and change.

The components of the identity of places

If we consider places only in terms of their specific content, they present a remarkable diversity—one in which common elements are not readily apparent. Furthermore, our experiences of places are direct, complete, and often unselfconscious; if there are component parts, they are experienced in the fullness of their combinations. However, from a rather less immediate perspective one can distinguish elements, bound together but identifiable nevertheless, that form the basic material out of which the identity of places is fashioned and in terms of which our experiences of places are structured. These are like the fundamental components of a painting—the canvas, the paint, the symbols, each irreducible to the other but inseparable. Albert Camus' essays on North Africa are used here to demonstrate the components of the identity of place, but almost any description or direct observation of a particular place would serve just as well.

In his essays on the life and landscape of Algeria Albert Camus (1955, 1959) uses a clearly structured approach in his accounts of places. Both when he is describing his own experiences and when he is describing as an observer he reveals not only what appear to be the basic components of the identity of all places, but also the interweaving of these. Consider for example his account of Oran (1955, pp.130–131):

"Oran has its deserts of sand: its beaches. Those encountered near the gates are deserted only in winter and spring. Then they are plateaus covered with asphodels, peopled with bare little cottages among the flowers ... . Each year on these shores there is a new harvest of girls in flower. Apparently they have but one season ... . At eleven a.m., coming down from the plateau, all that young flesh, lightly clothed in motley materials, breaks on the sand like a multi-coloured wave ... . These are lands of innocence. But innocence needs sand and stones. And man has forgotten how to live among them. At least it seems so, for he has taken refuge in this extraordinary city where boredom sleeps. Nevertheless, that very confrontation constitutes the value of Oran. The capital of boredom besieged by innocence and beauty ..."

Here Camus makes quite clear the major features of the landscape around Oran. First there is the bountiful physical setting of sand, sea, and climate and buildings. This provides the backdrop to the ostensible, observable activities of the people, yet is complemented by and influences those activities. But embracing and infusing both of these is a set of meanings for Camus—particularly the opposition of innocence and boredom.

These three components of place that are so apparent in Camus' writings—the static physical setting, the activities, and the meanings—constitute the three basic elements of the identity of places. A moment's reflection suggests that this division, although obvious, is a fundamental one. For example it is possible to visualise a town as consisting only of buildings and physical objects, as it is represented in air photographs. A strictly objective observer of the activities of people within this physical context would observe their movements much as an entomologist observes ants, some moving in regular patterns, some carrying objects, some producing objects, some consuming objects, and so on. But a person experiencing these buildings and activities sees them as far more than this—they are beautiful or ugly, useful or hindrances, home, factory, enjoyable, alienating; in short they are meaningful. The first two of these elements can probably be easily appreciated, but the component of significance and meaning is much more difficult to grasp.

The meanings of places may be rooted in the physical setting and objects and activities, but they are not a property of them—rather they are a property of human intentions and experiences. Meanings can change and be transferred from one set of objects to another, and they possess their own qualities of complexity, obscurity, clarity, or whatever. All this is well illustrated in an example quoted by Stephan Strasser (1967, pp.508–509). In 1084 St. Bruno went to the French Alps to establish himself as a hermit there. Before his arrival the environment was quite neutral to him; it was what it was without meaning. But by seeking in those mountains a place to meditate St. Bruno and his followers made them meaningful in terms of this intention—they became 'dangerous' or 'safe', 'useful', or 'inhospitable'. And subsequently as their intentions changed, as they found a suitable site and began to look for land for cultivation, or as his followers now try to get rid of troublesome tourists, so their situation was modified. In other words the meaning of the situation, of the place, was defined by the intentions of St. Bruno and his followers. This is, of course, a very straightforward example; meaning is much more complex than this for intentionality is itself very complicated, involving both individual and cultural variations

which reflect particular interests, experiences and viewpoints. But the example of St. Bruno does serve to demonstrate that places can only be known in their meanings.

The three fundamental components of place are irreducible one to the other, yet are inseparably interwoven in our experiences of places. In explicating this experience, however, they can be identified as distinctive poles or focuses, and they can be further subdivided within themselves. Thus the physical component can be understood as comprising earth and sea and sky, and a built or created environment, each of which offers its own characteristic possibilities for experience (Dardel, 1952). Similarly activities and functions can be distinguished as being creative or destructive or passive, as communal or individual. The relative weighting of each of these subcomponents may be of considerable importance in establishing the identity of particular places— thus we recognise coal-mining towns or mountain villages. Artists, photographers, and novelists may even compress identity into one small feature which somehow captures the essence of a place; Wallace Stegner (1962) found that for him the spirit of his former home town of Whitemud on the Prairies was expressed above all in the smell of wolf-willow.

Such selection or concentration of the identity of a place into one feature depends, of course, on local circumstances and on the purposes and experiences of the author, and is not especially relevant to the present, more general discussion. What is significant here is the way in which physical setting, activities, and meanings are always interrelated. Like the physical, vital, and mental components of behaviour that Merleau-Ponty (1967) identifies, it is probable that they constitute a series of dialectics that form one common structure. Physical context and activities combine to give the human equivalent of locations within the 'functional circle' of animals (see Cassirer, 1970, p.26); setting and meanings combine in the direct and empathetic experience of landscapes or townscapes; activities and meaning combine in many social acts and shared histories that have little reference to physical setting. All of these dialectics are interrelated in a place, and it is their fusion that constitutes the identity of that place. Physical appearance, activities, and meanings are the raw materials of the identity of places, and the dialectical links between them are the elementary structural relations of that identity.

This analysis of the components of identity of place is not, however, complete. There is another important aspect or dimension of identity that is less tangible than these components and dialectics, yet serves to link and embrace them. This is the attribute of identity that has been variously termed 'spirit of place', 'sense of place' or 'genius of place' (*genius loci*)—all terms which refer to character or personality. Obviously the spirit of a place involves topography and appearance, economic functions and social activities, and particular significance deriving from past events and present situations—but it differs from the simple summation of these. Spirit of place can persist in spite of profound changes in the basic components of identity. Rene Dubos (1972, p.7) writes: "Distinctiveness persists despite change. Italy and Switzerland, Paris and London have retained their respective identities through many social, cultural and technological revolutions." The spirit of place that is retained through changes is subtle and nebulous, and not easily analysed in formal and conceptual terms. Yet at the same time it is naively obvious in our experience of places for it constitutes the very individuality and uniqueness of places. D. H. Lawrence (1964, p.6) wrote:

> "Different places on the face of the earth have different vital effluence, different vibration, different chemical exhalation, different polarity with different stars; call it what you like. But the spirit of place is a great reality."

Types of identities of places

The identity of a place is comprised of three interrelated components, each irreducible to the other— physical features or appearance, observable activities and functions, and meanings or symbols. There is an infinite range of content within each of these and numberless ways in which they can combine. Hence there is no discernible limit to the diversity of identities of places, and every identifiable place has unique content and patterns of relationship that are expressed and endure in the spirit of that place.

But it is not feasible to argue that uniqueness and the individuality of identity are the only important facts in our experiences of places. While each place is unique and has a persistent sameness within itself, at the same time it shares various characteristics with other places. In terms of our experiences this sharing does display certain consistences that make it possible to distinguish a number of types of identities of places.

1. From the individual perspective or sociality in communion of existential insideness places are

lived and dynamic, full with meanings for us that are known and experienced without reflection.
2. For empathetic insiders, knowing places through sociality in community, places are records and expressions of the cultural values and experiences of those who create and live in them.
3. From the standpoint of behavioural insideness place is ambient environment, possessing qualities of landscape or townscape that constitute a primary basis for public or consensus knowledge of that place.
4. In terms of incidental outsideness it is usually selected functions of a place that are important and the identity of that place is little more than that of a background for those functions.
5. The attitude of the objective outsider effectively reduces places either to the single dimension of location or to a space of located objects and activities.
6. The mass identity of place is a consensus identity that is remote from direct experience for it is provided more or less ready-made by the mass media. It is a superficial identity, for it can be changed and manipulated like some trivial disguise so long as it maintains some minimum level of credibility. It is also pervasive, for it enters into and undermines individual experiences and the symbolic properties of the identities of places.
7. For existential outsiders the identity of places represents a lost and now unattainable involvement. Places are all and always incidental, for existence itself is incidental.

With the exception of existential outsideness which replaces all the others, these various types of identity are not discrete, nor mutually exclusive, nor unchanging. Thus we may know our home town as dynamic and full of meaning, yet be quite capable of also viewing it as professional planners or geographers from the perspective of objective outsideness, and also participate in its mass identity. For each setting and for each person there are a multiplicity of place identities reflecting different experiences and attitudes; these are moulded out of the common elements of appearance and activities and the borrowed images of the media through the changing interactions of direct observation with preconceptions.

The identity of place is not a simple tag that can be summarised and presented in a brief factual description. Nor can it be argued that there is a real or true identity of a place that relates to existential insideness. Indeed an outsider can in some senses see more of a place than an insider—just as an observer of argument gains a perspective not available to those arguing, even though he misses the intensity of being involved in that argument. Identity is, in short, neither an easily reducible, nor a separable quality of places—it is neither constant and absolute, nor is it constantly changing and variable. The identity of place takes many forms, but it is always the very basis of our experience of *this* place as opposed to any other.

References

Blythe R, 1969 *Akenfield* (Harmondsworth: Penguin Books)

Camus A, 1955 *The Myth of Sisyphus* (New York: Vintage Books)

Camus A, 1959 *Noces suivi de l'Eté* (Paris: Editions Gallimard)

Cassirer E, 1970 *An Essay on Man* (Toronto: Bantam Books)

Dardel E, 1952 *L'Homme et La Terre: Nature de Realité Géographique* (Paris: Presses Universitaires de France)

Dubos R, 1972 *A God Within* (New York: Charles Scribner's Sons)

Durrell L, 1969 *The Spirit of Place* (New York: Dutton)

Erikson E, 1959 "Identity and the life-cycle" *Psychological Issues* **1** (1)

Heidegger M, 1969 *Identity and Difference* (New York: Harper and Row)

Lawrence D H, 1964 *Studies in Classic American Literature* (London: Heinemann)

Lynch K, 1960 *The Image of the City* (Cambridge, Mass: MIT Press)

Merleau-Ponty M, 1967 *The Structure of Behaviour* (Boston: Beacon Press)

Nairn I, 1965 *The American Landscape* (New York: Random House)

Prince H, 1961 "The geographical imagination" *Landscape* **11** 22–25

Stegner W. 1962 *Wolf-Willow* (New York: The Viking Press)

Strasser S, 1967 "Phenomenology and the human sciences" in *Phenomenology: The Philosophy of Edmund Husserl* Ed J J Kockelmans (Garden City, N Y: Doubleday)

Wagner P L, 1972 *Environments and Peoples* (Englewood Cliffs N J: Prentice-Hall)

Source and copyright

This chapter was published in its original form as:

Relph, E. (1976), 'On the Identity of Places', in Relph, E. (1976), *Place and Placelessness*, Pion, London, 44–62.

Reprinted with permission of Pion Limited, London.

11

Reconsidering the image of the city

Kevin Lynch
[1984]

The Image of the City was published over 20 years ago, and it is still listed in bibliographies. It is time to wonder what it led to. The research was done by a small group with no training in the methods they used, and no literature to guide them. Several motives led them to the study:

1. An interest in the possible connection between psychology and the urban environment, at a time when most psychologists—at least, those in the field of perception—preferred controlled experiments in the laboratory to the wandering variables of the complicated, real environment. We hoped to tempt some of them out into the light of day.
2. Fascination with the aesthetics of the city land-scape, at a time when most U.S. planners shied away from the subject, because it was "a matter of taste" and had a low priority.
3. Persistent wonder about how to evaluate a city, as architects do so automatically when pre-sented with a building design. Shown a city plan, planners would look for technical flaws, estimate quantities, or analyze trends, as if they were contractors about to bid on the job. We hoped to think about what a city should be, and we were looking for possibilities of designing directly at that scale.
4. Hope of influencing planners to pay more atten-tion to those who live in a place—to the actual human experience of a city, and how it should affect city policy.

These motives found an early outlet in an erratic seminar on the aesthetics of the city in 1952, which considered, among several other similar themes, the question of how people actually found their way about the streets of big cities. Various other unconnected ideas sprouted during a subsequent fellowship year spent walking the streets of Florence, which were recorded in some brief and unpublished "Notes on City Satisfactions." These ideas matured during 1954, when I had the opportunity of work-ing with Gyorgy Kepes on a Rockefeller grant devoted to the "perceptual form of the city." As we walked the Boston streets and wrote notes to each other, and as I listened to his torrent of ideas on per-ception and daily experience, the minor theme of city orientation grew into the major theme of the mental image of the environment.

Undoubtedly, there were many other less explicit influences: from John Dewey, with his emphasis on experience, to ideas of the "transactional" psychol-ogists, with their view of perception as an active transaction between person and place. I had done fairly extensive reading in psychology, without find-ing much that was helpful. I had always learned much more from stories, memoirs, and the accounts of anthropologists. We were not then aware of K. E. Boulding's key study, *The Image*,[1] which was published at the same time as our own work and became an important theoretical underpinning of it. The role of the environmental image was an idea in the air, however.

The first study was too simple to be quite respectable. We interviewed 30 people about their mental picture of the inner city of Boston, and then we repeated the exercise in Jersey City (which we guessed might be characterless) and Los Angeles (booked as the motorized city). We took Boston because it was there, and we knew it and liked it. We asked people what came to their mind about the city, and to make a sketch map of it, and to take imaginary trips through it. We asked them to describe its distinctive elements, to recognize and place various photographs, and (with a small sample) to go on actual walks with us. Later, we stopped people in the streets and asked for directions to places. Meanwhile, other members of the team, uncontaminated by all this interview work, surveyed the town, in order to make some guesses about what a typical image would be, given the physical form.

This small group of informants produced an astonishing flood of perceptions. At times, as we listened to their tapes and studied their drawings, we seemed to be moving down the same imaginary street with them, watching the pavements rise and turn, the buildings and open spaces appear, feeling the same pleasant shock of recognition, or being puzzled by some mental gray hole, where there should have been some piece of the city. Our conclusion—or perhaps the hardening of our preconceived notion—was that people had a relatively coherent and detailed mental image of their city, which had been created in an interaction between self and place, and that this image was both essential to their actual function, and also important to their emotional well-being. These individual images had many common features—similarities that arose from common human strategies of cognition, common culture and experience, and the particular physical form of the place that they live in. Thus, an observer, familiar with the local culture and with the general nature of city images, could, after a careful study of the town, make predictions about likely common features and patterns of organization in the mental images of that place. We developed methods for eliciting these mental images from people, as well as a way of classifying and presenting them. We asserted that the quality of that city image was important to well-being and should be considered in designing or modifying any locality. Thus, orientation had been expanded into a general method of analyzing place, and a vivid and coherent mental image had been elevated to a general principle of city design. Later, this idea was expanded further, to include a vivid image of time as well as place.[2]

All of this from talking to 30 people! It was not surprising that there were sharp criticisms. The obvious remark was that the sample of people was far too small, and too biased, to permit of such sweeping assertions. Our handful of interviewees were all young, middle-class people, and most of them were professionals. The attack was well mounted; and yet it failed. The original work has by now been replicated in many communities, large and small, in North and South America, Europe, and Asia, because the method is cheap and rather fun to do. In every case, the basic ideas have held, with the important proviso that images are much modified by culture and familiarity, as was predicted in our original speculations. But the existence and role of the place image, its basic elements, and the techniques of eliciting and analyzing it seem astonishingly similar in some very diverse cultures and places. We were lucky.

A second criticism was that the techniques of office and field interview, of photo recognition, and of map drawing were inadequate to get at the true mental image, so deeply lodged in the mind. Map drawing, in particular, is too difficult for most people, and thus it is a very misleading index of what they know. Even just talking may be an exercise in pleasing the interviewer more than a revelation of inner patterns, many of which may be inaccessible to the person.

In principle, the comment is just. What is in the mind is an elusive thing. Environmental psychologists are busy debating the relative merits of various tricks for entering that fascinating realm. But one can reply that, although each method may elicit only a piece of the internal picture, and that may be distorted as well as partial, yet, if a sufficient array of probes is employed, a composite picture develops that is not very far from the truth. Of course, it may only be the tip of the iceberg, whose base is hidden far below, but the tip is the tip of a real iceberg, nonetheless. Luckily for us, the environmental image is usually not a painful subject for most people, something to be defended by unconscious barriers. People like to talk about it.

The possibility remains that the image brought forth for discussion in an interview is not the same one that is used in actually operating in a city. This possibility can be checked only by working with people as they actually move about, as we did in our street interviews. But even if the two images were disjunctive (which does not seem to be the case), the interview image can still have an important social and emotional role.

A method war erupted over map drawing, which was one of the techniques we used that seemed at first to take everyone's fancy. Drawing is indeed an unfamiliar act, as compared with talking, not only for most interviewees, but also (which may be the real problem) for most interviewers as well. Yet I cling to the value of drawing as a means of expression, especially of spatial ideas, despite our cultural down-grading of visual communication (a downgrading that may now be reversed, at least in a passive sense, for the current TV generation). Much can be read from amateur maps, in supplement to verbal comments, if one allows for common drafting difficulties. Drawings convey emotional tone as well as substance, just as actual speech does.

Whereas researchers worried over our methods, designers were fearful that these same methods might usurp their central creative skill—that a "science of design" might suddenly seize their territory. Image analysis would then lead automatically to form decisions, untouched by the free imagination. But their fears were quite unfounded. Analysis can describe a present situation and its consequences, and even—much more uncertainly—predict the consequences of some altered arrangement, but it is powerless to generate new possibilities. This is the irreplaceable power of the creative mind. Image studies, although they may threaten designer pretenses about how other people feel about places, are no more threatening to the central act of design than is an analysis of structure or of climate. On the contrary, perception studies could support and enrich design.

The most critical attack of all was that the study was overblown, if it meant to identify a basic principle of place quality. It focused on way finding, which was surely a secondary problem for most people. If lost in a city, one can always ask the way or consult a map. The study may have analyzed the nature of the way-finding image accurately enough. But it only assumed its importance and never demonstrated it. What do people care if they have a vivid image of their locality? And aren't they delighted by surprise and mystery?

This was a more direct hit. The study never proved its basic assumption, except indirectly, via the emotional tone of the interviews: the repeated remarks about the pleasure of recognition and knowledge, the satisfaction of identification with a distinctive home place, and the displeasure of being lost or of being consigned to a drab environment. Succeeding studies have continued to collect this indirect evidence. The idea can be linked to the role of self-identity in psychological development, in the belief that self-identity is reinforced by a strong identity of place and time. A powerful place image can be presumed to buttress group identity. The pleasures of perceiving a complex, vivid landscape are frequently experienced and recorded. Mature, self-confident people can cope with drab or confused surroundings,

but such places are crucial difficulties for those internally disoriented, or for those at some critical stage of their development.[3] It is reasonable to think that a featureless environment deprives us of some very important emotional satisfactions. These convictions have been reinforced by many expressions of popular culture, as well as findings in psychology, art, and the sociology of small groups. (As to the role of surprise and disorder, I return to that below.) Nevertheless, it is true that this central assumption remains an assumption, however it may be shored up by anecdote, personal experience, or its connection to the structure of other ideas.

If these four criticisms—of sample size, method, design usurpation, and basic relevance—were the important ones made at the time, there were also other unremarked cracks in our structure, which only opened up later. The first, and most immediately dangerous, was the neglect of observer variation, which we passed over in order to show the effect of physical variation. This neglect was deliberate and explicit, as the role of visual form had been widely ignored, and it was also important to show that a given physical reality produces some common images of place, at least within one culture. Image variation among observers—due to class, age, gender, familiarity, role, and other such factors—was expected to be a finding of subsequent studies. Indeed, it was. Broader samples, such as those interviewed by Appleyard in Ciudad Guayana,[4] made clear how social class and habitual use cause people to see a city with very different eyes.

What was not foreseen, however, was that this study, whose principal aim was to urge on designers the necessity of consulting those who live in a place, had at first a diametrically opposite result. It seemed to many planners that here was a new technique—complete with the magical classifications of node, landmark, district, edge, and path—that allowed a designer to predict the public image of any existing city or new proposal. For a time, plans were fashionably decked out with nodes and all the rest. There was no attempt to reach out to actual inhabitants, because that effort would waste time and might be upsetting. As before, professionals were imposing their own views and values on those they served. The new jargon was appropriated to that old end, and its moral was stood on its head. Instead of opening a channel by which citizens might influence design, the new words became another means of distancing them from it. Indeed, the words were dangerous precisely because they were useful. They afforded a new way of talking about the qualities of large-scale form, for which designers had previously had only inarticulate feelings. Thus, the words seemed true in themselves.

Fortunately, designers have gone on to other fashions, and accumulating studies have made it evident how differently a low-income teenager thinks of a city from a middle-class professional (just as both see a compact, labyrinthine city very differently from one that sprawls over an extensive grid). The perception of a city is a transaction between person and place, which varies with variations in each factor, but which has stable rules and strategies. Armed with a sense of those strategies, and a set of analytical methods, a designer can help citizens to understand what they see and value and can thus help them to judge proposed changes. In their work in Cambridgeport, Carr and Herr[5] showed how these same image techniques could be used as a means of participation. In a few cases, image studies are now used in that way, but the first effect on city design was often pernicious.

Our second omission, less easy to repair, was that we elicited a static image, a momentary pattern. There was no sense of *development* in it—of how that pattern came to be, nor of how it might change in the future, as the person matured, her or his function changed, her or his experience enlarged, or the city itself was modified. The dynamic nature of perception was denied. Once again, the study unwittingly fed a designer illusion: that a building or a city is something that is created in one act, then to endure forever.

It is far more exhausting to analyze how an image develops, because this requires a longitudinal analysis. Yet that will be a necessity, if we mean to get a true understanding of this dynamic process and to link these studies to fundamental research in developmental and cognitive psychology. Some starts have been made: Denis Wood on the growth of the image of London among teenage visitors,[6] Banerjee's comparison of the images of newcomers and old inhabitants,[7] and Smith's replication of the original Boston studies,[8] which showed how 10 years of physical change had affected the public image of that place. The track of image development in the maturing person and also the path of change as one becomes familiar with a place are both progressions (or regressions) that stand in need of close analysis.

The static view is mistaken not only as a matter of understanding, but also as a matter of value. We are pattern makers, not pattern worshipers. Unless we are mentally at risk, our great pleasure is to *create* order, in an ascending scale of complexity as we

mature. This is the pleasure that designers so enjoy—and so often deny to others. The valuable city is not an ordered one, but one that can be ordered—a complexity whose pattern unfolds the more one experiences it. Some overarching, patent order is necessary for the bewildered newcomer. Beyond that, the order of a city should be an unfolding order, a pattern that one progressively grasps, making deeper and richer connections. Hence our delight (if we are internally secure) in ambiguity, mystery, and surprise, as long as they are contained within a basic order, and as long as we can be confident of weaving the puzzle into some new, more intricate pattern. Unfortunately, we do not have any models for an unfolding order.

Third, the original study set the meaning of places aside and dealt only with their identity and their structuring into larger wholes. It did not succeed, of course. Meaning always crept in, in every sketch and comment. People could not help connecting their surroundings with the rest of their lives. But wherever possible, those meanings were brushed off the replies, because we thought that a study of meaning would be far more complicated than a study of mere identity. This original renunciation is now itself being renounced, particularly in the studies of environmental semiotics, in which the technical analysis of meaning in language is applied to the meaning of place. Interesting as this work is, it labors under the difficulty that places are not languages: their primary function is not the communication of meaning, nor can their elements be so neatly parsed into discrete signifiers. Nevertheless, if it can free itself of that analogy—if places can be considered in their own nature, and not as silent speech—the study of environmental meaning will undoubtedly bring rich results for city designers. Some promising advances have been made, by Appleyard just before his death,[9] Rapoport,[10] and others. If only it were not so difficult!

Last, perhaps, I would criticize our original studies because they have proved so difficult to apply to actual public policy. This difficulty is strange, because the principal motive of the whole affair was to change the way in which cities were shaped: to make them more responsive to their inhabitants. To my chagrin, the work seems to have had very little real effect of that kind, except for the first flurry of misuse, now so happily faded away.

To my surprise, on the contrary, the work led to a long line of research in other fields: in anthropology and sociology to some extent, and to a larger degree in geography and environmental psychology.

Golledge and Moore's *Environmental Knowing,*[11] and Evans' review article, "Environmental Cognition,"[12] summarize this extensive work and lay out the current debates and preoccupations. The original findings have been extended, corrected, built upon, and superseded. In that sense, the work has fulfilled its function. That function was largely unforeseen, except for our hope of attracting perceptual psychologists to an interest in the urban environment. The work has become a small part of a much larger, and intellectually more fascinating, study of the nature of human cognition. Environmental psychology and cognitive geography are now well-established areas of concern in their general fields. Cognitive anthropology is maturing. The function of the human brain is the central mystery, and the study of humankind's perception of its environment has a valid place in it.

On the other hand—ironically—the early work has had only a minor impact on actual city design. Although researchers were quick to take up the idea, and many amateur city-lovers as well, fewer professionals have done so, saving only that early spurt, cited above. Those that have tried it in real situations report that the results are interesting, but hard to put to use. A soil survey or an analysis of a housing market leads quite easily into city design. Why should an analysis of the image of place, first motivated by design preoccupations, fail to do so?

One reason is that there are many mental images of the city. If one is concerned with an area used by many diverse people, it may be difficult to set out the common problems, and these problems may not be central to the concerns of any one group. Therefore, these techniques are more telling in smaller, more homogeneous communities, or in dealing with tourists, who are more dependent on overt visible clues. Yet, even in complex metropolitan areas, certain images are apparently very widely held.

I think that a deeper reason for this lack of application lies in the special place of aesthetics in our culture. Aesthetics is thought to be something separate from the rest of life (which it is not), and the perceptual form of something is believed to be solely an aesthetic issue (which it is not, either). Aesthetics can be considered a sacred issue—the highest goal of human activity once basic wants are satisfied. Or it may seem to be a secondary affair, subordinate to more fundamental needs. In either case, it is thought special, idiosyncratic, and not subject to rational debate. Thus, it is not an appropriate concern for public policy, or at least, it must be dealt with separately, gingerly, and at late stage of decision. Urban design, which tries to deal with public aesthetic issues in conjunction with other "functional" issues (as if seeing were not functional!), holds only an uneasy position in this country. By custom and by institution, public policy at larger scales deals with economic and social ends, whereas perceptual questions are addressed at the level of small territories, or of single buildings. Decision makers often base their choices on a strong personal image of the environment, but this image is implicit and is not tested against others. Politicians do not base their campaigns on explicit sensuous issues, although such questions are often hidden motives in political battle, and even though there is the pervasive, inarticulate public response to the way localities look. What is usually called *urban design* today is more often large-scale architecture, which aims to make an object in one sustained operation, according to the will of a gifted professional. It may even be no more than a visible gloss, applied to a development "package" to help it glide along the rails of decision. True city design—dealing directly with the ongoing sensed environment of the city, in collaboration with the people who sense it—hardly exists today.

This quirk in our view of the world limits what we do. A public agency is unlikely to support a costly piece of analysis that deals with "mere aesthetics," and it is also unlikely to see how the results might fit into its decisions. The agency will be cautious about deciding anything on what seem to be such arbitrary grounds. The professional, in his or her turn, may prefer to cloak aesthetic judgments in the more dignified mantle of other criteria, and so keep his or her aesthetic underbody as safe as possible from defiling amateur hands.

Some attempts have been made to apply image surveys to city policy in this country, notably in San Francisco,[13] Dallas,[14] and Minneapolis.[15] These attempts are dissected in Yata's "City Wide Urban Design Policies."[16] They are not convincing examples of the effectiveness of this particular technique. More work has been done in other countries, notably in Japan, in Israel, and in Scandinavia. In this country, again, there is some application of the method in tourist areas, where images may equate with dollars, or at the local neighborhood level, where a settled and vocal group have an explicit stake in the quality of their surroundings.

But decision makers—and many professionals— still find the technique peculiar. Despite the continuing notoriety of the early study, it has been an enthusiasm of researchers in other fields, or of amateurs and contemplatives, or of beginners in the profession. I tried, in *Managing the Sense of a Region*,[17] to show how such studies and issues could actually be applied to public management decisions in complicated urban regions. For the most part, however, these were speculations, rather than actual experiences.

It may be that there is some characteristic of the analysis that adapts it for research, but not for policy. This characteristic is not yet apparent to me. It is ironic that a study launched with the primary aim of affecting policy seems to have missed its target and hit another one. I remain in hope that the flight is not yet over.

Notes

1. Ann Arbor: University of Michigan Press, 1956.
2. Kevin Lynch, *What Time Is This Place?* Cambridge: MIT Press, 1972.
3. H. F. Searles, *The Non-Human Environment.* New York: International University Press, 1960.
4. Donald Appleyard, *Planning a Pluralist City: Conflicting Realites in Ciudad Guyana.* Cambridge: MIT Press, 1976.
5. Phillip B. Herr et al., *Ecologue/Cambridgeport Project.* MIT Department of Urban Studies and Planning, 1972.
6. D. Wood and R. Beck, "Talking with Environmental A, an Experimental Mapping Language." In *Environmental Knowing: Theories, Research, and Methods,* ed. G. T. Moore and R. G. Golledge (Stroudsburg: Dowden, Hutchinson and Ross, 1976).
7. Tridib Banerjee, "Urban Experience and the Development of the City Image." Ph.D. dissertation, Department of Urban Studies and Planning, MIT, 1971.
8. B. A. Smith, "The Image of the City 10 Years Later." Master's thesis, Department of Urban Studies and Planning, MIT, 1971.
9. In his incomplete and unpublished manuscript "Identity, Power, and Place."
10. Amos Rapoport, *The Meaning of the Built Environment: A Nonverbal Communication Approach.* Beverly Hills: Sage, 1982.
11. G. T. Moore and R. G. Golledge (eds.), *Environmental Knowing: Theories, Research, and Methods.* Stroudsburg: Dowden, Hutchinson and Ross, 1976.
12. G. Evans, "Environmental Cognition." *Psychological Bulletin* 88, no. 2(1980): 259–287.
13. San Francisco Department of City Planning, *San Francisco Urban Design Study* (8 vols.) and *Urban Design Plan* (1969–1971).
14. Dallas Department of Urban Planning, *The Visual Form of Dallas* (1974).
15. Minneapolis Planning Commission, *Toward a New City* (1965).
16. Tsutomo Yata, "City-Wide Urban Design Policies." Ph.D. dissertation, Department of Urban Studies and Planning, MIT, 1979.
17. MIT Press, 1976.

Source and copyright

This chapter was published in its original form as:

Lynch, K. (1984), *Reconsidering the Image of the City*, in Banerjee, T. and Southworth, M. (1991) (editors), *City Sense and City Design: Writings and Projects of Kevin Lynch*, MIT Press, Cambridge, Mass., 247–256.

Reproduced with kind permission from Springer Science and Business Media.

12

The social production of the built environment: architects, architecture and the post-Modern city

Paul L. Knox

[1987]

It has been clear for some time that processes of urban development in the world's core economies have been responding to a new and distinctive set of economic, social, demographic and political forces. Some of the major influences on this new phase of urbanization are the result of changes which have been developing throughout the postwar period as capitalism has entered a 'late' or 'advanced' stage (Mandel, 1975). These changes include a shift away from manufacturing employment to service employment, an increasing dominance of big conglomerate corporations, and an internationalization of corporate activity. These developments have precipitated important social transformations: the creation of a 'new' petite bourgeoisie (Carchedi, 1975; Giddens, 1973), for example. These social transformations, in turn, are being reproduced in space through property markets that are both reflected and conditioned by the built environment (Lefebvre, 1974; Gottdiener, 1985).

As these fundamental socioeconomic transformations have been gathering momentum, other shifts – in technology, in demographic composition, and in cultural and political life – have been taking place: the entry of the baby-boom generation into housing and labour markets, the changing structure and composition of private households, the development of advanced telecommunications and new high-technology industries, the articulation of the

liberal/ecological values of the middle-class youth counterculture, the retrenchment of public expenditure with the rise of the 'New Right', and the system-shock precipitated by the OPEC oil embargo of 1973, for example. Gappert (1979), noting both the uncertainty within major economic and political institutions and the altered mood and disposition of America's middle classes, has labelled the overall condition as 'postaffluent'. Lyotard (1984), writing in the wake of French 'post-Marxism', takes a still broader view of all these shifts and transformations. The world's core economies, he argues, now exhibit a 'post-Modern' condition, in which the economic rationality and cultural Modernism of industrial capitalism are widely rejected but have not been clearly displaced by a new aesthetics, a new economics, or new politics.

Theoretical orientations and labels notwithstanding, it is clear that urban change must be seen in relation to these major transformations and shifts. This paper – reviews the recent literature on architects and architecture – agents and outcomes of change in the built environment that have received surprisingly little attention from geographers – in the context of these broader changes. Compared with other related fields, research on this topic has for a long time been impoverished, with an overwhelming emphasis on microscale interactions between architecture and human behaviour and an equally overwhelming emphasis on the deterministic interpretation of people-environment relationships. With a few important exceptions (see, for example, King, 1980; Millon and Nochlin, 1978; Norberg-Schultz, 1975; Saint, 1983; Tafuri, 1976), the built environment has automatically been assigned the role of an independent variable, 'explaining' everything from people's perceptual acuity to their social networks and their propensity to indulge in deviant behaviour (see, for example, Ankerl, 1981; Coleman, 1985; Curran, 1983; Zeisel, 1975). At its worst, the literature falls away into the bourgeois high-art category of coffee-table products. What has most often been overlooked or discounted in studies of architects and architecture is the relationship of both the built environment and people's behaviour to the broader context of economic and social organization and, in particular, to the imperatives of property capital. By focusing on individual behaviour, and taking the built environment as a product of 'design', many studies have under-rated the broader context of social and economic forces (as modulated and amplified by institutions) and overplayed the roles of architects. This clearly goes down well with the profession itself, but the net result is that theories about architecture remain weakly developed: a situation that has led several writers to urge the pursuit of a new approach in which the built environment is regarded as a reflection of economic, social and political relationships within society and as a means through which these relationships are reproduced, sustained, or modified (Appleton, 1979; Dickens, 1980; 1981; King, 1984; Korllos, 1980). As Darke and Darke (1981) have pointed out, such an approach need not throw the baby out with the bathwater: the built environment does inhibit, facilitate, precipitate and modify both individual and group behaviour. What is needed is an approach which encompasses the reciprocal relationships between individuals, the built environment, and society at large (Knox, 1984). This paper represents an attempt to review some of the ideas and empirical evidence relevant to such an approach, looking successively at interpretations of architecture as culture and as politics, the role of architects and architecture in relation to capital accumulation and circulation, legitimation and social reproduction, and the role of architects as 'urban managers'.

The following sections of this paper review recent analyses of architecture and architectural practice which are relevant to the interpretation of architecture in the context of the social production of urban space.

Architecture as culture

As King (1984) notes, one of the most common approaches to the built environment in the social sciences has been through comparative studies in which 'culture' is treated as an independent variable to 'explain' various aspects of the built environment (see, for example, Rapoport, 1982; Zelinsky, 1973). Such an approach can throw up interesting issues and provide informative vignettes, but too often it falls into the trap, as Duncan (1981) points out, of reifying culture, mistakenly transforming a conceptual abstraction into an active force which relegates people into passive agents of culture and which obscures economic, social, psychological, ideological and political factors. Moreover, in focusing on particular settings and case studies, the 'culturological' approach tends to neglect the *flows* – of capital, labour, ideas, etc. – which relate to the dynamics of economic, social and, indeed, cultural change.

But by no means all analyses of architecture as culture exhibit such shortcomings. Rowntree and Conkey (1982), for example, provide a case study of historic preservation (in Saltzburg, Austria) which demonstrates how the promotion of certain elements of the built environment can alleviate cultural stress 'through the creation of shared symbolic structures that validate, if not actually define, social claims to space and time' (p. 459). Rowntree and Conkey do not extend their analysis into the post-Modern period, but their approach would lend itself well to an analysis of the ways in which those under stress as a result of the structural transition to an advanced, postaffluent capitalism are beginning to affect the cultural landscape. In a very different vein, Jakle (1983) has also brought a dynamic perspective to architecture as culture, analysing the changing popularity of revival themes in American domestic architecture, as reflected by illustrations of model houses in the *American Builder*. Jackle's analysis links the first rise of Early and Colonial American styles, for example, with the desire among sections of middle-class America, buffeted by the Depression and conditioned by isolationism, for 'an elemental return to American basics' (p. 35).

Jackle's analysis underlines the fact that revival styles were important long before the arrival of the post-Modern period. This, in turn, raises the question of whether the reassertion of neovernacular styles and regional specificities in post-Modern architecture amounts to anything more than a manifestation of what the Frankfurt school called the 'culture industry' (Frampton, 1982; Habermas, 1975). Could it, on the other hand, be part of a broader reevaluation of the past, a dialectical recovery of certain values that represent a genuine move towards a post-Modern culture (Knesl, 1984)? According to Knesl, architecture represents an important catalyst for cultural change because of its ability to connect the 'life-praxis' of the world of everyday action to the realm of ideas, ideology and aesthetics. The embryo post-Modern condition, argues Knesl, is distracted, not yet fixed to a specific cultural framework and therefore open to the integration of life-praxis and ideas in a variety of ways. Among these, Knesl suggests, the emerging elements of post-Modern architecture represent, collectively, an answer to the distraction, ennui, hostility and powerlessness of contemporary urban society. Thus, for example, the revival of classicist spatial order offers 'comforting formal stability', contextualist architecture offers 'a spatial cloak of identity and predictability', and the use of metaphor and ironic reference offers a flexible, 'multisuggestive' imagery (Knesl, 1984, 16).

Architecture as politics

Just as architecture can be seen as a product of culture, so it can be seen, in parallel, as the product of politics. What gets built is strongly conditioned by the structure and dynamics of political power in society; how and where it gets built is subject to a host of laws, codes, standards and regulations that reflect the interests of political powers and pressure groups (see, for example, Perin, 1977). Architecture can also be seen as a product of politics in a more dramatic sense. Paris provides a good example, the politics of the built environment being acted out among the legacies of some celebrated examples of the manipulation of public architecture for political purposes during the nineteenth century (Evenson, 1979; Harvey, 1979; 1985). In Gaullist Paris, forced modernization took the form of forced Modernism, reaching a climax with the *urbanisme* of the *grands ensembles* of Sarcelles, Pompidou's Musée Beaubourg, and the proposal to develop Les Halles as the hub of a new regional Metro, dominated by a world trade centre. In the new political and socioeconomic climate of the mid-1970s, Giscard d'Estaing was able to dramatize his commitment to the new politics of environmental concern by cancelling the Les Halles project and replacing it with a green space to be designed by the contextualist Ricardo Bofill. Before this could materialize, however, Jacques Chirac had seized upon l'*affaire des Halles* to score

points in the mayoral elections; he, in turn, cancelled the half-built green space and replaced it with a pastiche of commercial and residential developments in the style of an amusement park. Meanwhile, the burden of defining and monumentalizing Mitterand's socialism in the capital has fallen to the new 'popular opera', to be built, symbolically, at the Place de la Bastille (Trilling, 1985).

At a more general level, Knesl (1984) argues that architecture has an important *potential* role to play in the politics of advanced capitalism. The emergence of factionalized, grass-roots social movements, he suggests, calls for an architectural syntax to foster 'innovative forms of life-praxis' that would, in turn, foster self-determination and 'help to keep larger-scale political organs responsive to local situations' (p.11). This seems a dangerously close parallel to the idealistic and determinist philosophy of the Modernists; perhaps it is no coincidence that Knesl's only example draws on the work of Van Eyck, whose work is more functionalist than anything else (Prak, 1984). Nevertheless, as Gutman (1985) points out, the transition to an advanced capitalist society will inevitably affect architecture as politics at the level of public policy 'because there are so many issues of cultural, social and economic policy in advanced industrial societies that impinge on architectural ideas and practice' (p. 86). Gutman cites issues such as whether there should be increased funding for landmark preservation programmes; what government policy should be with respect to allocating funds between 'high culture' and 'popular culture' projects; and the design requirements of the increasing numbers of marginal and atypical households.

Architecture as zeitgeist

The general idea of the built environment as a product of the *zeitgeist*, or spirit of the age, has a long history in urban studies. Lewis Mumford's fundamental argument was that:

> in the state of building at any period one may discover, in legible script, the complicated processes and changes that are taking place within civilization itself (1938, 403).

Ruth Glass (1968, 48) described the city in terms of 'a mirror . . . of history, class structure and culture'; while Ray Pahl's Weberian approach was set in the context of a built environment that emerges as

the result of conflicts . . . between those with dif-
ferent degrees of power. . . . As the balance of
power changes and ideologies rise and fall, so
the built environment is affected (1975, 151).

One specific example of architecture as *zeitgeist*
which has been explored in the recent literature is
the expression of the 'metropolitan spirit' of the
interwar period in the architecture of Otto Wagner,
Daniel Burnham, the Deutscher Werkbund and
Antonio Sant'Elia (Larsson, 1984). Another is the
expression of America's changing political mood
through the medium of federal architecture – from
Jeffersonian classicism, through Beaux Arts grandeur
to contemporary Modernism (Craig, 1978). In terms
of the emerging *zeitgeist* of the post-Modern era, a
good example is provided by the 'signature' structures and decor of chains of fast food restaurants in
the United States (Langdon, 1985). The bold, mod-
ernistic forms and brash interiors characteristic of
America's first restaurant chains, Langdon observes,
did not sit well with the environmentalism and
increased consumer sophistication of the late 1960s
and early 1970s. Consequently, the big chains began
to embark on major refits, with new buildings, surrounded by landscaped lawns and shrubbery, fea-
turing wood, brick, earth-tone carpeting, and
up-market artwork with local themes, all capped by
a mansard roof (in natural-looking tiles) to hide the
heating, ventilating and air-conditioning equipment while providing 'human scale'. McDonald's,
who pioneered the mansard roof format for fast
food restaurants, have sought to exploit the post-
Modern taste for neovernacular styles by developing a range of 16 stock facade alternatives – from
Country French to Village Depot – that can be
applied to the exterior of its standard building configurations.

It takes only a short step from this kind of view of
architecture as *zeitgeist* to deploy a crude form of
Marxist theory in which the built environment is
seen as part of the superstructure that is produced
by – and that helps to sustain – the dominant relations of production. The history of architecture can
thus be linked to a critical history of urban-industrial
society, revealing a dialectic of intellectual and artistic responses to the *zeitgeist* of successive moments
of capitalist development. Thus, for example, the
Art Nouveau and Jugendstil architecture of the late
nineteenth century can be seen as the architectural
expression of the romantic reaction to what
Mumford (1961, 470) called the 'palaeotechnic' era
of the Industrial Revolution; a reaction which was

first expressed in the Arts and Crafts movement. By
1900, the Art Nouveau style was firmly established
as the snobbish style, consciously elitist, for all 'high'
architecture. The Modern movement can be interpreted as a dialectic response to this elitism (Bloch,
1977), with post-Modernism being the latest,
incipient dialectical response to the transformation
of Modernism into the glib Esperanto of the
International style (Frampton, 1980; Tafuri, 1980).

Despite the appealing symmetry of such interpretations, it must be recognized that, in detail,
shifts in architectural styles do not always fit a neat
chain of cause and effect (Banham, 1975). The spatial and temporal fluidity of the social meaning of
built form, combined with the idiosyncracies and
impulses of architects, their clients, and the users of
the built environment, means that the production
of the built environment inevitably enjoys a degree
of relative autonomy from the dominant social
order (Dickens, 1980). In short, architecture, like
other components of the social superstructure, is
contingent rather than determined: a product of
complex interactions between structure and human
agency (Gottdiener, 1985). Whitehand's work
(1983; 1984) on the architecture of commercial
redevelopment in postwar Britain illustrates this
contingent quality very well. Comparing two
provincial centres – Northampton and Watford –
Whitehand found that, whereas Modern styles rapidly supplanted neo-Georgian and Art Deco styles in
Northampton after the second world war, neo-
Georgian styles continued to dominate in Watford
until the property boom of the 1960s, when styles
in both cities became predominantly Modern. More
recently, post-Modern styles have been featured in
Northampton, whereas redevelopment in Watford
has continued to use Modern styles. Whitehand
traces these differences to variations between the
two cities in the involvement of local versus non-
local finance, in the activity of national speculative
property development companies, in the involvement of owner-occupiers versus property speculators, in the proportion of office as opposed to chain
store redevelopment, and in the use of local rather
than outside architectural firms. This contingent
nature of architecture means of course that it cannot be assumed to be straightforwardly functional
for capitalism at any given moment of development. Nevertheless, the idea that architecture, as
part of the social superstructure, serves, at least in
general terms, to sustain, legitimize and reproduce
the relations of production seems to offer several
themes relevant to the analysis of urban geography.

Architecture and the accumulation and circulation of capital

Although very interesting relationships have been proposed between architecture, the building industry and processes of capital *circulation and accumulation* (Harvey, 1975; 1981; Lefebvre, 1970), their actual operation remains to be documented, and the proposed relations have, for the most part, still to be operationalized and empirically validated. The links between the building and construction industry and overall postwar growth in *consumption* are widely acknowledged, as are the distinctive characteristics of the building and construction industry. For a variety of reasons, the organization and division of labour in the industry seem not to have followed general trends. As Marco puts it:

> In contrast to goods like cars, electrical appliances or even furniture (products for houses, for which there is a very close link between the extension of the market and the growth of productivity), the development of construction has been subject to a logic 'exogenous' to the dominant economic process. The extension of the market has been much more the result of general economic conditions than of gains in productivity implemented inside the sector. That is why it is possible to say that the action of the worker in construction has been rationalized and not industrialized (Marco, 1984, 31).

At the same time, the significance of land and land ownership means that fixed capital which is invested in construction tends to remain subordinate to circulating capital; and the overall productivity of the construction industry has been declining as a result of compositional changes in the types of structures that are being built (Bowlby and Schriver, 1986). In this context, any means of adding exchange value, stimulating consumption and fostering the process of capital accumulation is critical.

The architect, by virtue of the prestige and mystique socially accorded to creativity, adds exchange value to buildings through his or her decisions about design,

> so that the label 'architect designed' confers a presumption of quality even though, like the emperor's clothes, this quality may not be apparent to the observer (Darke and Darke, 1981, 12).

The professional ideology and career structure which rewards innovation and the ability to feel the pulse of fashion (see below) also serves to promote the circulation of capital. The upper middle classes, in short, can be encouraged to move from their comfortable homes into new ones through the cachet of fashionable or distinctive design, and part of the architect's role is to 'manufacture' new designs: style for style's sake, the *zeit* for sore eyes. In some US cities, new housing for upper income groups is now promoted through annual exhibitions aimed at selling 'this year's' designs, much like the automobile industry's carefully planned obsolescence in design. As one of the key arbiters of style in contemporary capitalist society, the architect is in a powerful position to stimulate consumption by merchandising the up-market end of the built environment. As Rubin observes:

> in the ideology of American aesthetics, it is understood that those who make taste make money, and those who make money make taste (1979, 360).

Mattson's study (1982) of main street storefront remodelling in America provides a good example of a very direct link between architectural style and the circulation of capital in one particular context. His research shows how main street storefronts have been repeatedly remodelled in order to stimulate business. In the 1930s, an amendment to the National Housing Act insured lenders up to 20 per cent of $50 000 for loans to up-date any kind of income-producing property. 'In line with the tenets of Modern architecture', writes, Mattson (1982, 42), 'the new store fronts displayed smooth, clean functional surfaces. . . . By the end of the decade, streamlined forms with sweeping, curvilinear lines had become the fashion'. The style became known as 'Depression Modern'. After the second world war, main street merchants were once again impelled to remodel store fronts in order to entice busy, automobile-riding customers back from the new commercial strips and shopping centres. New storefront designs now focused on merchandise visibility, with exuberant features such as vertical fins, glass-encased display islands and cantilevered window displays to attract passers-by; facings became more like giant billboards advertising the names of businesses in huge, easy-to-read lettering. Later, in response to the same social forces as the fast food chains described by Langdon (1985), main street storefronts were remodelled again, with pastiche, neovernacular motifs, mansard roof 'equipment screens', rusticated brick and stone veneers, and ersatz carriage lamps, imitation cedar shingles and shakes, window frames and wagon wheels designed to appeal to the values of the new locus of spending power: Venturi's middle-middle classes.

Finally, it is worth noting that architectural design is playing an important role in the current decollectivization/recapitalization of housing in Britain and the United States. Symes (1985) cites the example of architects who were given the task, under an urban development grant, of eradicating the public-housing image of a vandalized local authority estate, so that the apartments would be more marketable when put up for sale. The result was the addition of a combination of 'private' elements (garages, entrance lobbies and driveways) and post-Modern elements (pitched, pantiled roofs, timber handrails and balconies, and landscaping) to the structurally sound concrete-and-steel 'boxes' of failed Modernism.

Architecture, legitimation and social reproduction

Because of the rich and powerful symbolism inherent in urban design, architecture is readily interpreted in terms of sociopolitical legitimation. Tafuri's critical history of the architecture of industrial capitalism (1976; 1980), for example, takes as its central theme the idea that architecture has repeatedly veiled and obscured the realities of capitalist social relations. Porphyrios, developing this theme, puts the argument as follows:

> Architecture as a discursive practice owes its coherency and respectability to a system of social mythification. In other words, a given architectural discourse is but a form of representation that naturalizes certain meanings and eternalizes the present state of the world in the interests of a hegemonical power (Porphyrios, 1985, 16).

Architecture, in this view, is transparent to ideology (Dickens, 1980; 1981). As ideology, the social function of architecture is to insert the agents of an aesthetic culture into activities that support or subvert (in varying degrees) the dominant relations of production. Architecture, in this sense, comprises not only elements of building knowledge and tenets of design, but also a whole process of symbolization. 'Reality', as Porphyrios puts it, 'gives to architecture a set of rules and productive techniques while, in its turn, architecture gives back to reality an imaginary coherence that makes reality appear natural and eternal' (1985, 16).

At a less abstract level, it is clear that all social acts must take place in settings; when these acts are subject to ambivalence, contradiction and conflict – as many are – settings can help to establish clarity, to suggest stability among flux and to create order amid uncertainty. In this sense, the built environment serves to legitimize existing socioeconomic distinctions in several ways. The settings created for government offices, for example, contain clear messages to the clients who come regularly to transact business in them:

> The businessmen, lawyers and interest group representatives who negotiate contracts, arrange for government subsidies or bargain about administrative rules and the disposition of administrative proceedings do so for the most part in well-appointed, comfortable, sometimes lavish offices and conferences rooms. . . . The settings are major contributors to the definition of such proceedings as the responsible implementation of the law by experts and professionals, *though critics may see some of these transactions as a problematic use of public funds to subsidize those who already have most of what there is to get in money, status and influence. . . .*
>
> Another class of clients, exemplified by welfare recipients, emotionally disturbed people, and public-school students, is explicitly defined as being in need of 'help' and by comparison gets very little of it. The settings in which they deal with bureaucrats define the worth of the clients as eloquently as do the bureaucratic offices discussed above, but in the opposite way. *Waiting rooms are typically crowded and often drab and uncomfortable.* The dependency of the client on the power and goodwill of the authority is reflected in the physical arrangements (Edelman, 1978, 2–3, emphases added).

Like these examples, much of the symbolism of the built environment has to do with power (or the lack of it), with some of the most obvious and direct examples being associated with big business and big government (Appleyard, 1979; Appleton, 1979; Hughes, 1980; Millon and Nochlin, 1978; Woodward, 1982). Nevertheless, as Eco (1980, 12) points out, 'every usage is converted into a sign of itself', so that most structures, even though their symbolism may not be intended, have a 'secondary function', individually or collectively, which is connotative of something. It follows that the symbolism of the built environment is complex and often contradictory. The 'signature of power', according to Lasswell (1979), is manifest in two ways: through a 'strategy of awe', intimidating the audience with majestic displays of power; and through a 'strategy of admiration', aimed at diverting the audience with spectacular and histrionic design effects. It will be recognized, however, that it may not always be desirable to display power. Symbolism may, therefore, involve 'modest' or 'low profile' architectural motifs; or carry deliberately misleading messages for the purposes of maintaining social harmony (Hill, 1980). Neither is power the only kind of message to convey. Various elements of counter-ideology can create or take over their own symbolic structures and settings, as illustrated, for example, by the public housing projects of the Spaarndammerbuurt district of Amsterdam, the vacant lot in Berkeley, CA, that became People's Park, and the many buildings that have been listed, preserved and conserved as a result of the efforts of pressure groups of various kinds (Rowntree and Conkey, 1980). It must also be recognized that there are important differences, sometimes, between the intended meaning and the perceived meaning of architecture, that perceived meanings can vary with the audience or users, that concepts of audience held by architects and their clients will help to determine the kinds of messages that are sent, and that the social meaning of architecture is not static (Agrest, 1977; Baudrillard, 1971; Cable, 1982; Knox, 1984).

Gutman (1972) observes that the literature on architectural symbolism conventionally distinguishes three levels of symbolic meaning:

> syntactical *meaning, or the meaning that an element of form or style acquires by virtue of its location in a chain of form or style elements;* semantic *meaning, or the meaning it acquires because of the norm, idea or attitude that it represents or designates; and* pragmatic *meaning, or the meaning that is understood in relation to the architect, the client or the social group that invents or interprets the building's form or style (Gutman, 1972, 299, emphases added).*

The first of these has involved the pursuit of Barthes's (1967; 1973) concept of the city as a language written through the built environment and read by inhabitants through use and cognitive imagery. This has channelled a great deal of effort towards developing a theory of signs—semiotics or semiology—(Blonsky, 1985; Broadbent *et al.*, 1980; and Jencks, 1980; Cable, 1981; Gottdiener, 1983; Gwin and Gwin, 1985; Hillier *et al.*, 1976; Hillier and Hanson, 1984; Krampen, 1979; Minai, 1984; Preziosi, 1979a; 1979b); but most of this work is highly codified

and mechanistic, deliberately and systematically abstracting symbols from their historical and social context. This, as Dickens (1980) observes, fosters the 'fetishism' of design, focusing attention on buildings and architects rather than on the sets of social relations that surround the production and meaning of buildings. What is needed is a theory of signs and symbols which directly confronts the fundamental questions of communication by whom, to what audience, to what purpose and to what effect? There is a good deal of evidence of one kind or another to support Edelman's conclusion that the built environment affirms

> established social roles by encouraging those who act and those who look on to respond to socially sanctioned cues and to ignore incompatible empirical ones. Spaces reaffirm a dialectic of hierarchical distinctions (Edelman, 1984, 4).

But a great deal of work needs to be done before we are close to being able to specify the role and significance of architecture in legitimation (Francis, 1983).

The same conclusion applies to architecture and social reproduction, although again there are sufficient examples and pieces of evidence to point fairly convincingly to the overall role of workplace and residential settings in reproducing and 'structurating' class relations (Giddens, 1984; Parkin, 1981; Cullen and Knox, 1981). Perhaps the most compelling example to be documented in any detail is that of the way in which socially-created gender roles have been defined and sustained through housing design and urban planning (Duncan, 1981; Hayden, 1984; Wright, 1981).

Architects as urban managers

Architects, like other exchange professionals and design professionals involved in the production of the built environment, can be regarded as urban managers, 'middle dogs' who exercise, in a neo-Weberian sense, a certain degree of autonomy and control over patterns of urban development in ways that reflect their distinctive professional ideologies and career structure (Leonard, 1982). What, then, is known about the relative importance and autonomy of architects in the production of the built environment, about the values and world views of architects, about the influence of their professional organization and career structure on urban outcomes; and about the implications of the postaffluent, post-Modern period for all of these?

Architecture, like other professions, has been engaged in a century-long struggle for professional turf, social status, financial rewards and control over the labour process through legal monopoly powers (Kostof, 1977). Although the professionalization of architecture was achieved largely among the new technical developments, new ideas about business organization and new opportunities brought by the Industrial Revolution, it was the architect's pretensions to art and aesthetics that clinched the profession's individuality, status and legitimacy (Larson, 1983). Architects' emphasis on the artistic aspects of their work was partly a defensive strategy in the struggle for turf with engineers and other building specialists, but it was also because of the status associated with creativity, the lure of immortality attached to the authorship of important works of art, and the appeal of establishing an inspirational role directed, ostensibly, at social good rather than personal enrichment. Consequently, the lumpen-intelligentsia of architecture has always rated its members on their artistic achievements, the authoritative trade magazines – *Architectural Design, Progressive Architecture, Architectural Review, Domus, Werk* – have always stressed the aesthetic over the practical, and schools of architecture have consistently instilled an ethic of aesthetic avant-gardism (Gutman, 1985a; Prak, 1984).

It did not take long, in the cloisters of Modernist idealism, for this orientation to narrow into a vain arrogance. Clients, other professionals and users were systematically excluded, and often patronized. Corbusier, for example, suggested that people would have to be 'reeducated' to appreciate his urban vision, while Walter Gropius felt that it would be useless to consult the beneficiaries of his utopian designs for workers' housing because they were 'intellectually undeveloped'. Mies van der Rohe, asked if he ever submitted alternative schemes to a client, replied:

> *Only one. Always. And the best one that we can give. That is where you can fight for what you believe in. He doesn't have to choose. How can he choose? He hasn't the capacity to choose . . . (quoted in Prak, 1984, 95),*

Armed with these attitudes, architects were able to maintain a resolute hold on the wrong end of the determinist stick, with consequences that became written into the social as well as the physical fabric of the city (Jacobs, 1961).

But advances in technology and engineering posed dilemmas for an artistically-oriented profession.

American architects, for example, have repeatedly ceded the technical side of the building process to specialists – from engineers to interior designers (Ventre, 1982); yet, in order to maintain their self-appointed role as leaders of the building team, they have had to acquire a wide range of technical skills: in order to coordinate artistic design with code requirements and structural engineering constraints, for example. These skills have come to be reflected in the division of labour within larger architectural practices; but architectural educators and the professional press have persisted with the aesthetics of design to the virtual exclusion of the pragmatic and policy-related issues of building – a trend which Gutman (1985) suggests is linked to the rise of post-Modernism.

Meanwhile, the rise of big business and big government brought further dilemmas. The size of private practices and government departments that came to serve the big corporate and public clients fostered the division of architectural labour (and so effectively restricted opportunities for artistic expression) while drawing more and more architects into managerial and bureaucratic roles (Cullen, 1983). These trends were accentuated both by the property boom of the 1960s and by the political conservatism that accompanied the economic slump of the late 1970s (Saint, 1983). One outcome of the trend towards architect/managers and architect/entrepreneurs, according to Saint, has been a reaction against the influence of the 'prima donna art-architect'. The erosion of this influence, in turn, has made it easier for the eclecticism of post-Modernism to flourish.

Nevertheless, it was the spell of art that successfully legitimized the profession, and aesthetics remain a major element of architects' education and professional socialization. It is not surprising, therefore, to find that architects have a distinctive set of values that are dominated by a blend of artistic design and environmental determinism (Blau, 1984; Lipman, 1969; Prak, 1984; Salaman, 1974; Valadez, 1984). Blau's survey of New York architects (1984) reveals some interesting detail to this generalization, however. One particularly striking aspect of her findings relates to the differences which exist between the values and orientations of principals and those of rank-and-file architects. Principals, it seems, are much more business-minded, with aesthetic values that weaken rapidly in the face of economic austerity. Rank-and-file architects, on the other hand, are strongly committed to liberal, humanist and socially responsible values, as well as being favourably disposed (somewhat ambiguously) towards both artistic approaches and technical solutions.

This cleavage is reflected in the relative autonomy of architects. Many rank-and-file architects, according to Blau (1984), feel that they have little or no 'voice' because of their specialization in routine tasks outside the realm of decisions about design. The voice of principals and senior architects, meanwhile, is often closely circumscribed by the conservatism of other urban managers (Halper, 1967; Prak, 1984). Goodman (1972) wrote that

> our economic system has reduced the architect to the role of providing culturally acceptable rationalizations for projects whose form and use have already been determined by real-estate speculation.

Yet the relative autonomy of design itself, noted above, leaves architects with a significant influence on urban outcomes. Moreover, architects effectively act as arbiters, in many circumstances, between developers and builders (Dickens, 1979); and those – like Richard Siefert, John Portman and the notorious John Poulson – who have been able to make the transition to architect/entrepreneurs have been able to act as master coordinators of urban change and redevelopment, with profound implications in terms of 'who gets what, when and where'.

With the crisis of Modernist architecture, the role of architects as urban managers is in flux:

> As the forces of late capitalism make themselves increasingly felt, profit for the professions becomes a motive more compelling than status or class, and the interest of architects falls into line with that of the construction industry (Saint, 1983, 160).

At the same time, of course, competition from engineers, building programmers, construction managers, facilities managers, interior designers, home-builders and package dealers has become more intense, fostering the transition of the architect from a principled professional into a hustler (Banham, 1982). The internationalization of the economy under advanced capitalism, meanwhile, appears to have become as much a threat as an opportunity for architects: between 1980 and 1983, design services imports to the US grew by 300 per cent (Ventre, 1986). Some architects, in response to these pressures, have sought to capitalize on the 'contextual' emphasis of post-Modernism to stake a claim on urban design, only to find themselves in a new turf conflict with planners and landscape architects (Knack, 1984).

The outcome of such trends is important not only for the profession itself but also for the form and dynamics of the post-Modern city. As Gottdiener (1985) emphasizes, the design of the built environment is an important element of the productive forces of society, not just a reflection of them. 'The question of control over spatial relations and design', he asserts, 'represents the same revolutionary importance to society as the struggle over the control of the other means of production, because both ownership relations and relations of material externalization – that is, the production of space – are united in the property relations which form the core of the capitalist mode of production' (1985, 124–25). The economic and social operation, as well as the aesthetics, of the post-Modern city will thus depend in part on the interactions between the profession and the opportunities and constraints, stimuli and deterrents, of the postaffluent phase of advanced capitalism.

References

Agrest, D. 1977: Architectural anagrams: the symbolic performance of skyscrapers. *Oppositions* 11, 26–51.

Allen, J.A. 1983: *The romance of commerce and culture.* Chicago: University of Chicago Press.

Allsopp, B. *A modern theory of architecture.* London: Routledge and Kegan Paul.

Ankerl, G. 1981: *Experimental sociology of architecture.* New Babylon: De Gruyter.

Appleton, I. 1979: The urban political context of architecture. *Edinburgh Architecture Research* 6, 98–98.

Appleyard, D. 1979: The environment as social symbol. *Ekistics* 46, 272–81.

Banham, R. 1975: *The age of the masters.* London: Architectural Press.

1982: The architect as gentleman and the architect as hustler. *RIBA Transactions* 1, 33–38.

Barthes, R. 1967: *Elements of semiology.* London: Cape.

1973: Seminology and urbanism. *Via* 2, 155–57.

Baudrillard, J. 1981: *For a political economy of the sign.* St Louis, Missouri: Telos Press.

Blau, J. 1984: *Architects and firms.* Cambridge, Massachusetts: MIT Press.

1987: Where architects work: a change analysis, 1970–1980. In Knox, P.L., editor, *The design professions and the built environment*, Beckenham: Croom Helm.

Bloch, E. 1977: *Der geist der utopie.* Frankfurt a/M: Suhrkamp.

Blonsky, H. 1985: *On signs.* Baltimore: Johns Hopkins University Press.

Bontinck, I. 1978: Cultural dimensions of architecture and town planning in Europe: town planning, architecture and the quality of life. *International Social Science Journal* 30, 560–90.

Bowlby, R.L. and Schriver, W.R. 1986: Observations on productivity and composition of building construction output in the United States, 1972–1982. *Construction Management and Economics* 4, 1–18.

Broadbent, G. 1975: The road to Xanadu and beyond. *Progressive Architecture* September, 68–83.

1980: Architects and their symbols. *Built Environment* 6, 10–28.

Broadbent, G., Bunt, R. and Jencks, C. 1980: *Signs, symbols and architecture.* Chichester: John Wiley.

Brolin, B.C. *The failure of modern architecture.* London: Studio Vista.

Cable, C. 1981: *Semiotics and architecture.* Monticello, Illinois: Vance Bibliographies #P565.

1982: *Symbolism in architecture.* Monticello, Illinois: Vance Bibliographies #A596.

Carchedi, G. 1975: On the economic identification of the new middle class. *Economy and Society* 4, 1–86.

Carter, E. Politics and architecture: an observer looks back at the 1930s. *Architectural Review*, November, 325–28.

Coleman, A. 1985: *Utopia on trial: vision and reality in planned housing.* London: Hilary Shipman.

Corbusier, Le 1927: *Toward a new architecture.* Translated by F. Etchells. London: Architectural Press.

Craig, L.A. 1978: *The federal presence: architecture, politics and symbols in US government building.* Cambridge, Massachusetts: MIT Press.

Cullen, J. 1983: Structural aspects of the architectural profession. In Pipkin, J., La Gory, M. and Blau, J., editors, *Professional and urban form.* Albany: SUNY Press, 280–98.

Cullen, J.D. and Knox, P.L. 1981: 'The triumph of the eunuch': Planners, urban managers and the suppression of political opposition. *Urban Affairs Quarterly* 17, 149–72.

Curran, R.J. 1983: *Architecture and the urban experience.* New York: Van Nostrand Reinhold.

Darke, R. and Darke, J. 1981: Towards a sociology of the built environment. *Architectural Psychology Newsletter* 11, 1–2.

Dear, M. 1986: Post-Modernism and planning. *Environment and Planning D: Space and Society* 4, 367–84.

Dickens, P. 1979: Marxism and architectural theory: critique of recent work. *Environment and Planning B* 6, 105–17.

1980: Social science and design theory. *Environment and Planning B* 7, 353–60.

1981: The hut and the machine: towards a social theory of architecture. *Architectural Design* 51, 111–23.

Duncan, J. 1981: From container of women to status symbol: the impact of social structure on the meaning of the house. In Duncan, J., editor, *Housing and identity,* Beckenham: Croom Helm.

Eco, U. 1980: Function and sign: the semiotics of architecture. In Broadbent, G., Bunt, R. and Jencks, C., editors, *Signs, symbols and architecture,* Chichester: John Wiley, 11–69.

Edelman, M. 1978: Space and the social order. *Journal of Architectural Education* 32, 2–7.

Evenson, N. 1979: *Paris: A century of change.* New Haven: Yale University Press.

Forty, A. and Moss, H. 1980: A housing style for troubled consumers: the success of neovernacular. *Architectural Review* 996, 73–78.

Frampton, K. 1980: *Modern architecture: a critical history.* London: Thames and Hudson.

1982: Place, production and architecture. *Architectural Design* 52, 28–45.

Francis, R. 1983: Symbols, images and social organization in urban sociology. In Pons, V. and Francis, R., editors, *Urban social research: problems and prospects.* London: Routledge and Kegan Paul, 115–45.

Fusch, R. and Ford, L.R. 1983: Architecture and the geography of the American city. *Geographical Review* 73, 324–40.

Gans, H.J. 1983: Toward a human architecture: a sociologist's view of the profession. In Pipkin, J., La Gory, M. and Blau, J., editors, *Professionals and urban form,* Albany: SUNY Press, 303–19.

Gappert, G. 1979: *Post-affluent America.* New York: New Viewpoints.

Giddens, A. 1973: *The class structure of advanced societies.* New York: Harper.

1984: *The construction of society: outline of the theory of structuration.* Cambridge: Polity Press.

Glass, R. 1968: Urban sociology in Great Britain. In Pahl, R. E., editor, *Readings in urban sociology,* Oxford: Pergamon, 21–46.

Gold, J.R. 1984: The death of the urban vision? *Futures* 16, 372–81.

Goodman, R. 1972: *After the planners.* Harmondsworth: Penguin.

Gottdiener, M. 1983: Urban semiotics. In Pipkin, J., La Gory, M. and Blau, J., editors, *Remaking the city.* Albany: SUNY Press, 101–14.

1985: *The social production of urban space.* Austin: University of Texas Press.

Groat, L. and Canter, D. 1979: Does post-Modernism communicate? *Progressive Architecture*, December, 84–87.

Gutman, R. 1972: *People and buildings.* New York: Basic Books.

1983: Architects in the home-building industry. In Pipkin, J., La Gory, M., and Blau, J., editors, *Professionals and urban form.* Albany: SUNY Press, 208–33.

1985a: Educating architects: pedagogy and the pendulum. *The public interest* 80, 67–91.

1985b: *The design of American housing.* Washington DC: Publishing Center for Cultural Resources.

Gwin, W. and Gwin, M. 1985: *Semiology, symbolism and architecture.* Monticello, Illinois: Vance Bibliography #A1346.

Habermas, J. 1975: *Legitimation crisis.* Boston: Beacon Press.

Halper, J.B. 1967: The influence of mortgage lenders on building design. *Law and Contemporary Problems* 32, 269.

Harvey, D. 1975: Class-monopoly rent, finance capital and the urban revolution. In Gale, S. and Moore, E., editors, *The manipulated city,* Chicago: Maaroufa Press.

1979: Monument and myth. *Annals, Association of American Geographers* 69, 362–81.

1981: The urban process under capitalism: a framework for analysis. In Dear, M. and Scott, A.J., editors, *Urbanization and urban planning in a capitalist society,* New York: Methuen, 91–122.

1985: *Consciousness and the urban experience.* Oxford: Basil Blackwell.

Hayden, D. 1984: *Redesigning the American dream.* New York: W.W. Norton.

Hill, R. 1980: Architecture: the past fights back. *Marxism Today* 24, 21–25.

Hillier, B. and Hanson, J. 1984: *The social logic of space.* Cambridge: Cambridge University Press.

Hillier, B. *et al.* 1976: Space syntax. *Environment and Planning B*, 3, 147–85.

Horowitz, M. 1985a: Artist employment in 1984. Research Division Note 11. Washington DC: National Endowment for the Arts.

1985b: Artists' real earnings decline 37 per cent in the 1970s. Research Division Note 13. Washington DC: National Endownment for the Arts.

Hughes, J. 1980: *The shock of the new.* New York: Knopf.

Jacobs, J. 1961: *The death and life of American cities.* New York: Vintage.

Jackson, B. 1970: *The politics of architecture: A history of modern architecture in Britain.* London: Architectural Press.

Jakle, J.A. 1983: Twentieth-century revival architecture and the gentry. *Journal of Cultural Geography* 4, 28–43.

Jameson, F. 1985: Architecture and the critique of ideology. In Ockman, J., editor, *Architecture, criticism, ideology,* Princeton: Princeton Architectural Press, 51–87.

Jencks, C. 1977: *The language of post-Modern architecture.* London: Academy Editions.

1983: Post-Modern architecture: the true inheritor of Modernism. *RIBA Transactions* 2, 26–41.

King, A.D. editor, 1980: *Buildings and society: essays on the social development of the built environment.* London: Routledge and Kegan Paul.

1983a: Culture and the political economy of building form. *Habitat International* 6, 237–48.

1983b: The world economy is everywhere: urban history in the world system. *Urban History Yearbook 1983* 7–18.

1984: The social production of building form: theory and research. *Environment and Planning D* 2, 429–46.

Knack, R.E. 1984: Staking a claim on urban design. *Planning* 50, 4–11.

Knesl, J.A. 1984: The powers of architecture. *Environment and Planning D* 2, 3–22.

Knox, P.L. 1984: Symbolism, styles and settings: the built environment and the imperatives of urbanized capitalism. *Architecture et Comportement* 2, 107–22.

Korllos, T.S. 1980: Sociology of architecture: an emerging perspective. *Ekistics* 47, 470–75.

Kostof, S. editor, 1977: *The architect: chapters in the history of the profession.* New York: Oxford University Press.

1985: *A history of architecture: settings and rituals.* New York: Oxford University Press.

Krampen, M. 1979: *Meaning in the urban environment.* London: Pion.

Krier, L. and Culot, M. 1978: The only path for architecture. *Oppositions* 14, 39–43.

Krier, L. and Vidler, A. 1978: *Rational architecture: the reconstruction of the European city.* Brussels: Archives d'architecture moderne.

Langdon, P. 1985: Burgers! Shakes! *Atlantic Monthly,* December, 75–89.

Larson, M.S. 1983: Emblem and exception: the historical definition of the architect's professional role. In Pipkin, J., La Gory, M. and Blau, J., editors, *Professionals and urban form,* Albany: SUNY Press, 49–86.

Larson, M.S., Leon, G. and Bollick, J. 1983: The professional supply of design: a descriptive study of architectural firms. In Pipkin, J., La Gory, M. and Blau, J., editors, *Professionals and urban form.* Albany: SUNY Press, 251–79.

Larsson, L.O. 1984: Metropolis architecture. In Sutcliffe, A., editor, *Metropolis 1890–1940,* Chicago: University of Chicago Press.

Lasswell, H. 1979: *The signature of power.* New York: Transaction Books.

Lefebvre, H. 1970: *La revolution urbaine.* Paris: Gallimard. 1974: *La production de l'espace.* Paris: Anthropos.

Leonard, S. 1982: Urban managerialism: a period of transition? *Progress in Human Geography* 6, 190–15.

Lipman, A. 1969: The architectural belief system and social behaviour. *British Journal of Sociology,* 20, 190–204.

Lyotard, J.F. 1984: *The post-Modern condition.* Minneapolis: University of Minnesota Press.

MacEwan, M. 1974: *Crisis in architecture.* London: RIBA Publications.

McKean, C. 1984: Society and architecture: the controlling of both. *The Planner* 70, 18–21.

McLeod, M. 1985: Introduction. In Ockman, J. editor, *Architecture, criticism, ideology,* Princeton: Princeton Architectural Press, 7–11.

McQuade, W. 1979: Why all those buildings are collapsing. *Fortune,* November 19, 58–66.

Mandel, E. 1975: *Late capitalism.* New York: Velos.

Marco, D. 1984: The role of intellectuals as agents in the transformation of processes of work and production. In *The production of the built environment.* Proceedings of the 5th Bartlett International Summer School, Geneva. London: Bartlett School of Architecture.

Mattson, R. 1983: Storefront remodelling on Main Street. *Journal of Cultural Geography* 3, 41–55.

Millon, H.A. and Nochlin, L. editors, 1978: *Art and architecture in the service of politics.* Cambridge, Massachusetts: MIT Press.

Minai, A.T. 1984: *Architecture as environmental communication.* New York: Walter de Gruyter.

Montgomery, R. 1985: The rapid recent expansion of American architecture employment. Architecture Employment Working Paper 85–1. Berkeley: Department of City and Regional Planning.

1961: *The city in history.* Harmondsworth: Penguin.

Mumford, L. 1983: *The culture of cities.* New York: Harcourt, Brace and World.

Norberg-Schulz, C. 1975: *Meaning in western architecture.* New York: Praeger.

Pahl, R. 1975: *Whose city?* Harmondsworth: Penguin.

Parkin, F. 1971: *Class, inequality and political order.* London: New Left Books.

Pawley, M. 1983: The defence of Modern architecture. *RIBA Transactions* 2, 50–5.

Perin, C. 1977: *Everything in its place.* Princeton: Princeton University Press.

Porphyrios, D. 1985: On critical history. In Ockman, J., editor, *Architecture, criticism, ideology,* Princeton, Princeton Architectural Press, 16–21.

Portoghesi, P. 1982: *After Modern architecture.* New York: Rizzoli.

Prak, N.L. 1984: *Architects: the noted and the ignored.* Chichester: John Wiley.

Preziosi, D. 1979a: *Architecture, language and meaning: the origins of the built world and its semiotic organization.* The Hague: Mouton.

—— 1979b: *The semiotics of the built environment: an introduction to architectonic analysis.* Bloomington: Indiana University Press.

Rapoport, A. 1982: *The meaning of the built environment.* Beverly Hills: Sage.

Ravetz, A. 1980: *Remaking cities.* Beckenham: Croom Helm.

Rowntree, L.B. and Conkey, M.W. 1980: Symbolism and the cultural landscape. *Annals, Association of American Geographers,* 70, 459–74.

Rubin, B. 1979: Aesthetic ideology and urban design. *Annals, Association of American Geographers* 69, 339–61.

Saint, A. 1983: *The image of the architect.* New Haven: Yale University Press.

Salaman, G. 1974: *Community and occupation.* Cambridge: Cambridge University Press.

Sternlieb, G. and Hughes, J.W. 1986: Demographics and housing in America. *Population Bulletin* 41, 1, 1–35.

Symes, M. 1985: Urban development and the education of designers. *Journal of Architectural and Planning Research* 2, 23–38.

Tafuri, M. 1976: *Architecture and utopia: design and capitalist development.* Cambridge, Massachusetts: MIT Press.

—— 1980: *Theories and history of architecture.* New York: Harper and Row.

Trilling, J. 1985: Architecture as politics. *Atlantic Monthly,* February, 26–35.

Valadez, J. 1984: Diverging meanings of development among architects and three other professional groups. *Journal of Environmental Psychology* 4, 223–28.

Ventre, F. 1982: Building in eclipse, architecture in secession. *Progressive Architecture,* December, 58–61.

—— 1986: Competition conditions affecting export of design and construction services. Paper presented to 10th Triennial Congress of the International Council for Building Research Studies and Documentation, Washington, DC.

Venturi, R., Brown, D.S. and Izenour, S. 1972: *Learning from Las Vegas: the forgotten symbolism of architectural form.* Cambridge, Massachusetts: MIT Press.

Venturi, R. and Rauch, J. 1976: Signs of life: symbols in the American city. *Aperture* 77, 49–78.

Whitehand, J. 1983: Architecture of commercial redevelopment in postwar Britain. *Journal of Cultural Geography* 4, 41–55.

—— 1984: *Rebuilding town centres: developers, architects and styles.* Occasional Paper #19. Birmingham: Department of Geography, University of Birmingham.

Wolfe, T. 1981: *From Bauhaus to our house.* New York: Farar, Straus, Giroux.

Woodward, R. 1982: Urban symbolism. *Ekistics* 295, 285–91.

Wright, G. 1981: *Building the American dream: a social history of housing in America.* New York: Pantheon.

Zelinsky, W. 1973: *Cultural geography of the United States.* Englewood Cliffs: Prentice-Hall.

Ziesel, J. 1975: *Sociology and architectural design.* Russell Sage Social Science Frontiers Occasional Series #6. New York: Russell Sage.

Source and copyright

This chapter was published in its original form as:

Knox, P. (1987), 'The social production of the built environment: architects, architecture and the post-Modern city', *Progress in Human Geography*, **11**, 354–78.

Reprinted with permission of Edward Arnold (Publishers) Ltd (www.hodderarnoldjournals.com).

13

Invented places

Jan Sircus
[2001]

"Minas Tirith was such that it was built on seven levels, and delved into the hill, and about each was set a wall, and in each wall was a gate. But the gates were not set in a line... so that the paved way that climbed towards the Citadel turned first this way and then that across the face of the hill."

"... the floor was paved with stones of many hues; branching runes and strange devices intertwined beneath their feet. They saw now that the pillars were richly carved, gleaming dully with gold and half-seen colours. Many woven cloths were hung upon the walls, and over their wide spaces marched figures of ancient legend...." (*'The Lord of the Rings'* – J.R.R. Tolkien)

In our minds we climb the curving path, up towards the Citadel of Minas Tirith. In our minds we enter the Great Hall of runes and carved pillars. In our minds these places unfold, step by step, image by image, in a richly portrayed sequence of experiences. Places spawned by the imagination of J.R.R. Tolkien. Invented places.

Invented places spring from the creative minds of author, artist or architect. Often pure fantasy, they are the 'other worlds' of Oz, Star Wars, Dynotopia, and Myst. Yet their inspiration is the world we inhabit. Authors and artists freely borrow from the crafts, technology and architecture of ancient civilisations, recent history, and contemporary society. They blend cultures and imagery creating new, credible visions of place, as in the stories of Jules Verne and George Lucas, the movies *Bladerunner*, or *Dune*, and the architecture of Arcosanti and Las Vegas.

Common to the most successful invented places are 'theme' and 'story'. The theme is the overriding 'big idea' (such as 'The Movies' in Universal Studios' theme park) gluing together the story or stories being told. The theme establishes the context. The story provides the content.

An invented place may be themed as an authentic or symbolic recreation of a past time and place; its

sights and sounds, its colour and texture. For example, the Ancient Rome of the movie *Gladiator*, or Prince Charles's 'Thomas Hardy style' rural town of Poundbury, or a totally magical fantasy like Barry's Never Never Land in *Peter Pan*. While we stay in each story, while we 'suspend disbelief', it all works. When the reader or viewer is jarred by contradiction or distraction, the world falls apart; the place loses credibility, or at best becomes confusing and even chaotic. Successful places stay in one story at a time.

In the real world, Disneyland is the quintessential invented place. It creates reality out of fantasy in ways that are often symbolic and subliminal; digging deep down into the user's psyche, connecting with cross-cultural archetypal images and multigenerational, hard-wired memories. It is successful because it adheres to certain principles of sequential experience and storytelling, creating an appropriate and meaningful sense of place in which both activities and memories are individual and shared. Disneyland provides 'safe' adventures in a 'safe' environment, reaffirming our ability to survive and grow in a world of risks and conflict.

Many interpretations of place might not work for the cultural élite, who demand authenticity, but most places, real or invented, have a pop-culture audience.

And, like novels, real world places must know their audience before the story is written. It's common sense taken to the level of brand marketing. Every place is potentially a brand. In every way as much as Disneyland and Las Vegas, cities like Paris, Edinburgh, and New York are their own brands, because a consistent, clear image has emerged of what each place looks like, feels like, and the story, or history it conveys.

Place has meaning and memories. Place is not passive. Place is not good or bad simply because it's real vs. surrogate, authentic vs. pastiche. People enjoy both, whether it's place created over centuries, or created instantly. A successful place, like a novel or movie, engages us actively in an emotional experience orchestrated and organised to communicate purpose and story.

Story is a strong metaphor for place. It becomes the organising principle and the shared memory. Sometimes the place creates the story, as in Edinburgh, where characters and events have shaped the outcome. Sometimes story is the basis upon which place is created, as in the movies, or at Disneyland. It was no accident that the original creators of Disneyland were art directors and production designers from the Disney Studio, the Imagineers, adept at translating story into place in theatrical and emotionally engaging ways.

Over the years the Imagineers have followed certain principles fundamental to creating a successful place. These principles are concerned with structure and theme (organisation of ideas and people flow), sequence experience (telling of story or purpose), visual communication (details, symbols, and magnets), and participation (through the senses, action, and memory).

The first of these principles is structure and theme. Structure in this context is about planning organisation. It's about flow and Gestalt (memorable pattern). People like simple, logical flowplans. It's easier to follow a sequence of events, easier to orient, and makes people feel more comfortable, more in control. They aren't threatened; they lower their defences and enjoy themselves more. Circuitous sidetracks or dead ends are fine if they're short and consistent with the story. Decision points should be limited. Too much choice creates stress and confusion.

The structure should reflect the 'theme'. A Movie Studio theme will have a grid layout. An Adventure theme will be looping and circuitous. A Discovery theme may be molecular in structure and branching.

In many cultures the 'shape' of a place has additional meaning. For some, the Mandala, or circle, is a key organising shape, reflecting fundamental spiritual ideologies and primordial truths. It is universally symbolic, representing both the Hero's Journey of leaving and returning home, and the circular nature of life. The circle is a safe, comfortable shape, reinforcing harmony and unity. Disneyland is circular, with a central hub and radiating spokes or paths taking guests on circular, looping journeys into different lands and stories, one at a time.

Circular plans are common in European cities, for practical reasons of defence, surrounding a strong point, or castle, and straddling some natural feature such as a hill or river. Their story reflects a need for protection and reassurance, like a memory of the womb and connection to the umbilical cord. Early Edinburgh had a simple, anthropomorphic Gestalt. The High Street was the spinal cord of the Old Town, connecting the strong head, the Castle, with the rest of the body, branching out to either side with the heart at the Lawnmarket. And, just as Disneyland is organised as distinct, separate stories and lands (Adventureland, Frontierland, etc.), central Edinburgh has a similar structure. On the one side, Holyrood Park and the Old Town, on the other James Craig's Georgian New Town and the port of Leith. Each area of the city is distinctively different in its form, function, and feel. Each has its own, clearly legible story. It's part of what makes Edinburgh a successful place.

The second principle is sequential experience. Experiencing a place is much like following a river … "which flows, now fast, now slow, now placidly between broad banks … now halted by a dam, now debauching into an ocean" (Eric Bentley, *The Life of the Drama*). The experience unfolds emotionally, in a physical sequence.

In moviemaking, storyboarding of sequential images is used linearly to describe a single point of view of action and settings. In a place-making story, sequences are experienced in multiple ways, from different directions and different points of view. There may not be a classic beginning, middle, and end, or plot points. It is interactive story. All the more reason to keep it simple, clear, and consistent.

In a spatial sequence, like a movie, gradual transitions (dissolves), sudden changes (jump cuts), or new perspectives (different point of view), control the narrative. Each creates a different emotional response. In a spatial narrative, elements of the place can be story points. A small tunnel becomes a 'crossing over' or start of something new, like Alice's rabbit hole. A labyrinth or steep stair can represent an ordeal, a rickety bridge or dead end a test, and multiple doors or passageways represent dilemmas or choices. There are many such devices, all with associative meanings. Imagine arriving centuries ago at the foot of the Edinburgh High Street, entering under the portcullis arch of the Netherbow gate. The road ahead climbs steeply up through a canyon of tenements, past innumerable archways of wynds and closes, past John Knox's house, beyond the soaring crown of St Giles, beyond the stalls and pens of the Lawnmarket, and on to the powerful embattlements of the Castle, and another gateway. The harsh, unpredictable outer world has been replaced by the fabric of an historic inner world, whose sequential layout reinforces the interdependent relationship and hierarchy of commerce, faith, and politics; a narrative about power and control. Main Street and the Castle at Disneyland have a similar spatial construct, but the narrative is one of harmony and reassurance. The difference is symbolised through the visual communication.

Visual communication is the third key principle. The full meaning or story of a place is only apparent if it can be read; if it's visually legible. Without that legibility the place may be interpreted inappropriately and sometimes not at all. The challenge for invented places is to make the place legible for the audience, by communicating through both subtle and enhanced sights and sounds. It involves the careful use of scale, colour, texture and detail in ways that make the story self-evident and credible. It may be the reproduction of an authentic national pavilion, like Japan, at EPCOT, or an African village in Disney's Animal Kingdom, or interpreting an animated tale like *Snow White* or *Toy Story*. Even when the solution involves 'tricks' of scale-change (to make people feel more comfortable) or forced perspective (inducing exaggerated feelings of awe) or there is a highly theatrical, abstract presentation of facades or landscaping, the creative process and story considerations are the same. Legibility is key.

In older places, the meanings of symbols often change or are forgotten and stories are constantly evolving, or being reinterpreted. The original legibility may be lost on today's audience. Cities move with the times, creating their story in part from the fabric of today. In some cases, new architecture preserves the original narrative, interpreting the past in contemporary ways, or by being a bold statement that adds a new twist to an old story. Too often the outcome is a pointless departure that is out of context or cheaply executed. The shambles of facades and bad signage along Edinburgh's Princes Street is an example of chaos and banality that has almost destroyed the original narrative, a romanticised cornucopia of

Victorian and Edwardian commercial 'palaces'. The nineteenth-century Victoria Street in the Old Town is also a romanticised 'invention', recreating the baronial splendour of Scottish stories in Walter Scott's *Waverley* novels, but it works. Similarly the 'invented' New Town is a complete and consistent story, but is now suffering from forests of parking meters and some poorly scaled window replacements (a different story). Yet in its time it was no more or less a pastiche than Poundbury. It gives the impression of ancient classicism, but without the need to slavishly use ancient technology. The imposing neo-classical street facades are strictly two-dimensional, like a stage set. The back sides are a cheaper, more functional vernacular. It's about impressions, not substance. It's been that way in every revival period. A need to engage the present with memories and meanings anchored in readable images of the past.

Another key place-making and visual communication necessity is the visually compelling focal element, or 'emotional magnet'. It's what Walt Disney irreverently called a 'wienie'. It may be an isolated tower, or a castle, or some interesting event. It keeps people moving; enticing them through spaces to a specific destination point. A wienie is more than simply a landmark, because it embodies meaning and elicits an emotional response and an action. In Disneyland, each Land, each story, has at least one major wienie and often several subordinate ones. They are often visible from within another Land, beckoning, and reminding that another story and place await.

European cities like Edinburgh are full of 'wienies'. The spires and domes of churches and banks, and the towers and battlements of castles, all act to move people through a city. They provide orientation markers and goals, over and beyond their original significance as symbols of power. Invented places need similar markers and emotional magnets.

Successful places can be either rich on detail and authentic, or boldly abstracted and theatric, providing they have clear visual communication that is easily understood and is congruent with the story. The uninteresting, banal places do not communicate and in that respect are simply pastiches.

There is, however, a balance that needs to be struck between providing a rich, meaningful experience that can be re-visited and new discoveries made, and one that creates informational overload. The presentation and access to the experience needs its own hierarchy, allowing people to make their own choices about how deep and how broad they want to go. It helps make the experience less risky, more controllable, and more enjoyable.

Participation in a story usually takes place via characters and action. They are the connecting link that allows us to identify with our own world and experiences. On one level, the buildings themselves can be considered characters, whose very juxtaposition can create harmony or conflict. But a more literal interpretation depends on the living characters that inhabit these places, without whom the place is but a shell. Historic places are rife with characters of infamy and legend, remembered by prose, song, and art. What would Edinburgh be without its 'Old Town' stories of Burke and Hare, Deacon Brodie, or Greyfriars Bobby, or the 'New Town' memories of Lister, Simpson and Conan Doyle? These 'sons of Reekie', and the many others immortalised by story and statue throughout the city, provide a kind of 'streetmosphere' in much the same way as the walk-around storybook characters of a theme park. They awake memories, often related to childhood, and early fantasies. They make the stories accessible.

In story places, people also participate through sound and smell as well as sight. These other senses are extremely potent stimuli of memory. If any sensory input is inconsistent the place suffers. Imagine Disneyland smelling of fish and the music being techno-rap. It just doesn't work. This kind of participation can be the difference between success and failure. At Disneyland and in Las Vegas the music is as carefully choreographed as the flow of spaces. Music is there to provide the right ambience and emotional emphasis at just the right moment and place, in the same way as a movie score. The occasional fiddler and bagpiper on the Royal Mile though often annoying to locals, achieves the appropriate result for Edinburgh's tourists.

In summary, all places are to some degree invented, but the successful ones are characterised by planning, building design and programme that is clearly integrated with story. Story makes places more meaningful and more accessible. Story is both an individual and a shared experience. It's what connects us as human beings and defines our cultures. Like places, story may come about over time, or may arise instantaneously. It doesn't matter which, providing the particular story and place are consistent and immersive.

It doesn't mean the whole world should be a theme park. But there are lessons to be learnt from these experientially successful, cross-cultural, operationally intense places. Derived from a lineage including fairs, expos, museums and heritage-sites and the places of fictional story, theme park design is part art, part science. Theme parks have influenced a host of places in the urban environment, like Las Vegas, and innumerable retail entertainment centres around the world. The theme park epitomises the 'invented place', but it does so with a nod to some of the great places of history; places like Edinburgh, the 'Athens of the North', 'Auld Reekie'.

Source and copyright

This chapter was published in its original form as:

Sircus, J. (2001), 'Invented Places', *Prospect*, **81**, Sept/Oct, 30–35.

Reprinted with kind permission of the author Jan Sircus.

14

Learning from Disney World

Sharon Zukin
[1995]

Disneyland and Disney World are two of the most significant public spaces of the late 20th century. They transcend ethnic, class, and regional identities to offer a national public culture based on aestheticizing differences and controlling fear. The Disney Company is an innovator of global dimensions in the symbolic economy of technology and entertainment; it also exerts enormous influence on the symbolic economy of place in Anaheim and Orlando. The world of Disney is inescapable. It is the alter ego and the collective fantasy of American society, the source of many of our myths and our self-esteem.

Learning from Disney World is a humbling experience, for it upsets many of the assumptions and values on which a critical understanding of modern society is based. Not least is the assumption that production, rather than culture, is the motor driving the economy. Yet the entertainment provided at Disney World relies on an extensive work force and an expansive network of material resources. These in turn feed the urban development of the surrounding towns and counties, establishing an image of regional growth that attracts more jobs, more migrants, and more houses. Disney World itself has become a base for attempting synergy with other areas of a service economy. Given the planning capacity of Disney managers and employees, would a Disney Medical Center be out of line? There is, already, a Walt Disney Cancer Institute at Florida Hospital in Orlando, but building a hospital on the grounds of Disney World itself would not be inconceivable.

People have also learned they can derive social benefits from visual coherence. The landscape of Disney World creates a public culture of civility and security that recalls a world long left behind. There are no guns here, no homeless people, no illegal drink or drugs. Without installing a visibly repressive

political authority, Disney World imposes order on unruly, heterogeneous populations – tourist hordes and the work force that caters to them – and makes them grateful to be there, waiting for a ride. Learning from Disney World promises to make social diversity less threatening and public space more secure.

For many years, critics have dissected the public culture that Disneyland and Disney World embody. In the early 1960s, before civility became an issue, the architect Charles Moore (1965, 65) wrote that Disneyland offers "the kind of participation without embarassment" that Americans want in a public space. People want to watch and be watched, to stroll through a highly choreographed sequence of collective experiences, to respond emotionally with no risk that something will go wrong. Although Moore praised Disneyland for creating a coherent public space in "the featureless private floating world of southern California," he anticipated the harsher criticisms of European intellectuals, who have tended to write about Disney World since it opened, in 1971, as a simulation of history for people who prefer fakes because they *appear* more sincere (Eco 1986 [1975]; Baudrillard 1986). Disney World works because it abstracts both the technical and architectural elements of a place and the emotions that places evoke. "The more openly fake the buildings are, the more comfortable we are with them" (Goldberger 1992b).

By contrast, North American intellectuals criticize Disney World because it is not "hyperreal," but too real. Between 1982, when EPCOT (the Experimental Prototype Community of Tomorrow) opened, and 1985, when the new corporate management of the Disney Company revitalized the theme park by commissioning new rides and planning new hotels, Disney World began to be understood as a powerful visual and spatial reorganization of public culture. Its exhibits make social memory visible, and its means of establishing collective identity are based strictly on the market. Moreover, its size and functional interdependence make Disney World a viable representation of a real city, built for people from the middle classes that have escaped from cities to the suburbs and exurbs. It is an aestheticization of an urban landscape built without the city's fear or sex – and with its own, Disney money. Moreover, the insular theme park complex suggests very strongly that a separate, smaller city can be walled off within a larger city. While Disney World is an autonomous place with its own price of admission, a walled-off real city – like a gated residential community – promises to control the menace of strangers.

Nevertheless, the vision has its critics. Mike Wallace (1985) accuses the narrative behind the attractions of bleaching the conflicts out of American history. Steven Fjellman (1992) describes the paid amusements as a bazaar of commodity fetishism. While Alex Wilson (1992) calls the architecture and physical layout a supersuburb that eliminates the city, Michael Sorkin (1992, 208) thinks Disney World is an elaborate modernist utopia that reshapes the city into "an entirely new, antigeographical space." Like television, which provided the original Disneyland with a national audience of wannabe Mouseketeers, visual communication at Disney World "erode[s] traditional strategies of coherence."

The fascinating point is that Disney World idealizes urban public space. For city managers seeking economic development strategies and public philosophers despairing of the decline of civility, Disney World provides a consensual, competitive strategy. Take a common thread of belief, a passion that people share – without coming to violence over it – and develop it into a visual image. Market this image as the city's symbol. Pick an area of the city that reflects the image: a shimmering waterfront commercial complex to symbolize the new, a stately, Beaux Arts train station to symbolize renewal, a street of small-scale, red-brick shops to symbolize historical memory. Then put the area under private management, whose desire to clean up public space has helped to make private security guards one of the fastest-growing occupations.

Visual culture, spatial control, and private management make Disney World an ideal type of new public space. From the 1950s to the 1970s, this space was usually found in suburban shopping malls. From the 1970s, however, as conservative national governments reduced urban renewal funds and competition for private-sector investment discouraged local governments from urban planning, this new public space has increasingly occupied the centers of cities. It has been shaped by both the expansionary strategies of real estate developers and the withdrawal from planning on the part of local governments. In this sense it is an emblem of the reshaping of the Welfare State.

But cities have never been able to control space so effectively as does corporate culture. Disney World admits the public on a paying basis. After getting local governments to pay for the infrastructure, the administration of the theme park secures the right to govern its territory autonomously. Disney World has its own rules, its own vocabulary, and even its own scrip or currency. Not only do these norms emphasize a surrender of consumers' identity to the corporate giant, they also establish a public culture of consumership. This is the model of urban space driving the public-private business improvement districts. Since Disney World provides its own security force and sanitation workers, the area they control is safer and cleaner than real city streets. Disney World has a mass transportation system, outdoor lighting, and street furniture; again, not surprisingly, all this works better than public facilities. Has Disney World been, all along, a not-so-subtle argument for privatizing public space?

"The Disney Company is America's urban laboratory," a journalist writes in the *Village Voice* (Ball 1991). So parts of Disney World have been used in many different places. There are visual and spatial elements of Disney World in urban festival marketplaces and shopping malls, museum displays, ski resorts, and planned residential communities. Moreover, Disney World's control over its labor force and their interaction with consumers have been taken as models for other service firms. The synergies between Disney's various corporate investments are a model for the symbolic economy based on media, real estate, and artistic display. And Disney World is a way of making the whole symbolic economy real, no matter what levels of unreality are explored. When you see Disney World, you have to believe in the viability of the symbolic economy. So learning from Disney World relates to a number of separate agendas: in theme parks, urban planning, service industries, and the symbolic economy as a whole.

A shared public culture

The production of space at Disneyland and Disney World creates a fictive narrative of social identity.

The asymmetries of power so evident in real landscapes are hidden behind a facade that reproduces a unidimensional nature and history. This is corporate, not alternative, global culture, created in California and replicated in turnkey "plants" in Florida, Japan, and France. We participate in this narrative as consumers. The products we consume are imported from other places. Because they are sold in a coherent visual scheme, they appear to perpetuate or reconstruct a place with its own identity. Main Street and EPCOT make obvious fictions for yesterday and tomorrow. But the experience of going to Disney World, and waiting to consume the various attractions, locates us in an endless present, when we are concerned only with getting somewhere and waiting to get back.

The big question is how we have come to use these public spaces to satisfy private needs. The need to be together, to be entertained, has created a mass market for high-quality consumer goods in high-status consumption spaces. The need to "connect," to form social communities, creates a market for many kinds of associations and convention centers for them to meet. Private corporations' desire to project a benevolent public spirit – helped along by zoning laws – creates large plazas, atria, or lobbies devoted to "public use," either through art exhibits or facilities for eating and shopping. People "experience" these spaces by seeing each other experiencing them. Disney World has become such a monumental phenomenon because it visualizes a public that comes together only in transitory, market situations.

At the same time, Disney products have become the logos of a public culture. Naturally, there have been some changes over the years. Mickey Mouse started out in 1928 as a cartoon character. The Great Depression was Mickey's formative childhood experience. In a Christmas tale published in 1934 (*Mickey Mouse Movie Stories* repr. 1988), Mickey and his dog Pluto walk hungrily through the snow on Christmas Eve. They pass a rich household, where the spoiled child amuses himself by teasing the butler, a dog dressed in a morning coat. The butler asks Mickey if he will sell his dog, which Mickey refuses to do. Mickey and Pluto then pass another house, where a poor family of kittens is asleep. Mickey rushes back to the first house, sells Pluto to the butler, and buys gifts for the kittens, which he leaves in their home. Warmed by his good deed, Mickey sits in the snow – where Pluto finds him, for he has run away from the rich child, dragging the rich family's Christmas turkey with him. How does this lean and hungry Disney symbol

relate to the sleek, self-satisfied mouse who is the mascot of a major transnational corporation?

During the 1980s, Mickey Mouse's ears were unashamedly stolen from popular culture by high-status arts, beginning with architecture. The architect Arata Isozaki designed part of the Team Disney Building at Lake Buena Vista, Florida (1987–90) in the shape of a giant pair of mouse ears – pop art fed back to a corporate sponsor. This design has been defended aesthetically as a pure geometric abstraction, in contrast to the anthropomorphic dolphins, swans, and mice used by the architect Michael Graves on other Disney corporate buildings (Asada 1991, p. 91). Once they are abstracted from the mass culture of Disney cartoons, however, mouse ears become symbols of a shared public culture. They even appear in a political cartoon on the Op-Ed page of the *New York Times* (June 5, 1992), worn by both a Republican elephant and Democratic donkey.

As Disney symbols are introduced into high culture, artists shake off the ironic detachment with which they might once have regarded them. When a modern dance company, Feld Ballets/New York, set two recent ballets to Mozart symphonies, they dressed the soloist in mouse ears and had the dancers sing "M-I-C-K-E-Y M-O-U-S-E" along with the 31st symphony (*New York Times*, February 29, 1992). While they do not offend in cultural performances, Disney symbols may be too suggestive for political affairs. A British painter, John Keane, caused an uproar in London in 1992 by exhibiting *Mickey Mouse at the Front*, a painting critical of the United States for mounting the Persian Gulf War (Porter 1992). The artist Bill Shiffer showed an assemblage, *New World Order*, in New York in 1993 that featured Mickey Mouse on top of a hammer and sickle, stars and stripes, cross, and Jewish star. Professional culture critics may even see Disney forms where none are intended. When the Sugar Cubes, a far-out rock group from Iceland performed recently in New York, the *New York Times* (April 20, 1992) described the lead singer's hair as pinned up in Mickey Mouse ears on each side of her head – or maybe they were just Viking braids.

Mickey Mouse infiltrated standard American English a long time ago. Yet the meaning is ambiguous because it joins irony and simulation. The adjective *Mickey Mouse* means both outlandish and false, "a caricature of normal practice . . . [and, as in the military, a] mindless obedience to regulations" (Rosenthal 1992). Despite this ambiguity, and his changing form, Mickey Mouse has become a criterion of authenticity in cultural production. He is both icon and exemplar, a talismanic Ralph Lauren that enables mass market reproductions to be discussed as high culture. Which is more authentic, the cultural critic of the *New York Times* has asked: an idealized version of the past or the real past with all its warts? "The Disney version, like Mr. Lauren's environments, corrects all the mistakes, and paradoxically gives you a much better sense of what the experience of being in a lavish Victorian seaside hotel ought to have been" (Goldberger 1992a, 34).

The spatial reality of virtual reality

The virtual reality of Disney World most resembles the metropolitan region of Orlando. Orlando's rapid growth since Disney World opened relates at least as much to the theme park and the tourist economy it spawned as to the proximity of high-tech industry at Cape Canaveral, low-wage labor, and open land. The theme park brought Orlando subjective legitimacy as a place where businesses and people wanted to be. "Spend less Orlandough," says a United Airlines poster in a travel agency window on Madison Avenue in New York. People are attracted to the city because it has the image of public space that Disney World projects. "People come here because they know it's going to be safe," says the head of Universal Studios, Florida. People need never worry about bad weather or crime. The author of a best-selling book of investment advice who lives in Orlando says, "The best place to live is where everybody wants to vacation" (quotes in "Fantasy's Reality," cover story, *Time* May 27, 1991, 52–59, on 54).

Besides helping to shape the growth of Orlando, Disney World influences the shape of other places. The commercial and critical success of planned residential communities with strict building and design rules, like Seaside, Florida, planned by the architects Andres Duany and Elizabeth Plater-Zyberk, show that people like benevolent authoritarianism, as long as it rules by imposing visual criteria. In smaller development projects, re-creating the 19th-century town green has been highly marketable. But the old town and town green represent more than aesthetic images; they embody broader strategies of social control. The organization of space is accompanied by a carefully planned distribution of population by age and income level. This goes hand in hand with acceptance of an internalized political authority. Ironically, the town government legislates a certain amount of diversity. No white picket fence

in Seaside may look like any other white picket fence. Other regulations control the density, size, and style of construction, as well as the use of space. Controlling diversity determines the aesthetic power of the place. In social class terms, this is a middle-class space, the equivalent of Disney World's Main Street. It reproduces the white middle-class exclusivity – the safe, socially homogeneous space – of the 1950s, within acceptable limits of aesthetic diversity.

Since four-fifths of the visitors to Disney World are grownups, the look of the place must appeal to what adults want. Disney World exemplifies visual strategies of *coherence*, partly based on uniforms and behavioral norms of conformity, and partly based on the production of set *tableaux*, in which everything is clearly a sign of what it represents in a shared narrative, fictive or real (see Boyer 1992). Disney World also uses a visual strategy that makes unpleasant things – like garbage removal, building maintenance, and pushing and shoving – *invisible*. Disney World uses *compression* and *condensation*, flattening out experience to an easily digestible narrative and limiting visualization to a selective sample of symbols. Despite all the rides and thrills, Disney World relies on *facades*. You cannot go into The Magic Kingdom, but it is a central place at Disney World.

These visual strategies have influenced the building of shopping complexes with historical themes like South Street Seaport in New York and shopping malls with amusements like the West Edmonton Mall in Canada. They also shape consumption space as a total experience, as at the Mall of America in Minnesota. But defining a consumption space by its look is especially suited to transnational companies in the symbolic economy, which try to synergize the sale of consumer products, services, and land. Disney World is, of course, the prime example. It is followed by the Ashley resort, or "recreational village," built by the Laura Ashley Company in Japan, where the home furnishings, fabrics, and fashion company designs and sells hotel rooms, restaurants, gardens, stables, helipads, apartments, and houses (Gandee 1991). The look is the experience of the place. Controlling the vision brings market power.

Disney World's strategies for organizing space also influence New York City's business improvement districts (BIDs). Their first goal is to *clean up* an area, to keep it free of litter that the city's sanitation services cannot control. They also secure space by erecting barriers or otherwise limiting public access and making rules about appropriate behavior. Private security guards help enforce that strategy. They control the public's mobility by keeping people moving through public space and organizing where and how they sit – and also determining who may sit. Another strategy of establishing social control is to influence norms of body presentation. The dress and grooming codes for employees at Euro Disney got a lot of attention in the press because they seemed to violate French culture. How could French men not be permitted to wear a beard? Or French women not to wear black stockings? Yet in every culture, dress rules are a means of managing socially engendered diversity. As an American visitor to Euro Disney, a long-time resident of Paris, observes, conforming to Disney's work rules made French workers seem to be "professionals"; it gave them an air of civility. "Perhaps one can conclude that class boundaries are erased at Euro Disney, if only for a few hours" (Zuber 1992, 15).

These social strategies have the political effect of creating an impression of trust among strangers. This differs from the fatalistic trust found among passengers aloft in an airplane – or below ground in a New York City subway car. It is comparable to the sociable but reserved behavior you find in small country "inns," where everyone trusts that the other guests are the same social type. Politically, it is important that these are all spaces to which you buy entry. The ticket price alone – at Disney World, a hefty, though not extraordinary, $35 a day – ensures some gate-keeping, some exclusivity, some sense of confidence that equal access is not threatening.

Establishing confidence by means of spatial controls creates a precedent for public-private partnerships and private developers in cities. Unable to wall off their sections of the city, they have to make them accessible to the public but do not want to encourage the disorder of loiterers, muggers, the homeless, and the unruly. Like Disney World, these agencies set up private jurisdictions over which they have nearly absolute control. They have fiscal and financial power to create "public" services. These differ from previous arrangements because the services do not supplement public goods: they *replace* public goods.

BIDs create a privatization of public goods that many city dwellers find attractive. The BIDs' political autonomy derives from their financial autonomy: in addition to paying legally required city and state taxes, the property owners assess themselves an additional local tax based on square footage, and these taxes are collected for them by the city government. The BIDs then use the money to fund public improvements that local governments cannot or will

not pay for. Activist BIDs develop because of the city government's inability to generalize improvement strategies – which is, of course, the problem with the BIDs themselves (see Wolfson 1992).

These BIDs create their own sense of place not only by re-creating the attentive municipal services of another era (such as sanitation and security), but also by following Disney's lead in identifying theme and style with social order. The extreme example is the BIDs' use of uniform design to reinforce their public identity. In 1992, the Times Square BID commissioned an award-winning theatrical costume designer to create uniforms for its private sanitation force (*The New Yorker*, July 6, 1992, 12). Jumpsuits and caps are bright red to match the trash cans; T-shirts and logos are purple to match the plastic liner bags. "Until now," says a member of the sanitation crew, "we wore the same dull-blue work pants and shirts that ten thousand other people wear in New York. But now when people spy you on the street, they'll know you're part of the Times Square team. These are sharp – I mean, this is Broadway, right?"

Property values lie at the heart of the BIDs' drive for public improvements. But property values do not merely reflect use, as David Harvey (1973) has written. Instead, they reflect Disney World values of cleanliness, security, and visual coherence. The 34th Street BID, on a heavily used shopping street between the Empire State Building and Macy's, hired retail consultants to write guidelines on proper storefront design because the stores' presentation of a public face was too messy (Griffith 1992). For years, 34th Street has been a "populist" shopping street, a magnet for working-class families of every ethnic group. But, since Macy's filed for a bankruptcy reorganization in 1991 and the Empire State Building was bought by a private investor in 1992, the bazaar look has not projected a desirable image. Signs were oversize, up to six stories high, and merchandise spilled out onto the street from stalls at newsstands and through open windows. Images of brand names, store names, logos, and murals were overwhelming. So the BID decided to push the enforcement of municipal regulations. BID employees reported such violations as awnings that were too big, illegal sidewalk stalls, and newsstands that "have turned into bazaars," as an assistant commissioner of the city's Department of Consumer Affairs says. If found guilty by an administrative law or Criminal Court judge, violators face fines, jail terms, and suspension of licenses. Ironically, the murals and signs and "carnival atmosphere" on 34th Street deplored by a retail consultant are the lively aesthetic element so desired – after years of public criticism – in the redevelopment of Times Square.

The BIDs' strategies for managing public space suggest what an important role vision plays in defining spatial identities. To some extent the importance of visualization reflects the cumulative influence of photography, film, and television from the end of the nineteenth century, but it also reflects the influence of Disney World on public culture. In New York, advocates of both historic preservation and new construction accuse each other of "Disneyitis" (see Gill 1991), as they try to regulate, or free from regulation, aesthetically or narratively incoherent segments of the city. Occasionally these efforts are too strenuous. In a village on the eastern end of Long Island, where many affluent New Yorkers have vacation homes, some old-time residents criticized the village improvement association for "trying to turn Water Mill into Disneyland," by cutting down two trees on the village green to preserve a windmill that is a national historic landmark (*New York Times*, December 30, 1991).

The general question behind "Disneyitis" is which visual strategy – historic preservation, imitation, or imaginative recreation – is morally legitimate. While strategies based on theme may be transparent, techniques of simulation decontextualize the production of space and so may be difficult to decode in a critical way. Moreover, simulation is economically productive, for it provides opportunities to develop new products and a market edge, as well as to export work to new markets, especially in Japan and Southeast Asia. By the same token, simulation gives art and architecture critics something to discuss, rhetorical grist for the critics' mill. The architecture critic of the *Boston Globe* defends a new, pseudo-neo-Georgian office tower in Boston by the architect Robert A. M. Stern because it "is architecture for an age of simulation" (Campbell 1992). He also praises the way the social diversity and unruliness of the work force contradict the apparent aesthetic harmony and political coherence that real neo-Georgian architects aimed for in the early 20th century. Between post-modern architecture and the new informality, public space enshrines spontaneity and chaos – but to what purpose and at what cost? "A long-haired messenger boy in bicycle tights . . . transforms the building at once, by his mere presence, into a stage set. . . . An attorney in running shoes and earmuffs simply by being here alchemizes [the building] into a museum representation of a dead culture, becoming, herself, a tourist in that museum."

Disney's symbolic economy

The sponsorship of marine culture at Disney World represents an integration of primary products and visual symbols. Like Disney World itself, this symbolic economy accepts incongruities that violate historic material forms, both economic and ecological. Buy "fresh salmon steak, farm raised and grain fed," as a supermarket poster in New York proclaims. In the symbolic economy, employers hire a work force with cultural capital or higher education to do productive labor and provide a labor-intensive service called fun. Because of language requirements, business establishments use "European" employees in front regions in direct contact with customers and "minority" employees in the back. The Disney World model suggests that a local or regional economy can be created on a primary base of services, which spin off real estate development, attract other "clean" businesses, and generate creative business services like advertising and entertainment (Zukin 1990).

This model of the symbolic economy creates its own internal stratification, with low-wage workers, temporary workers, and unionized workers performing low-status tasks of maintenance, security, and food preparation. One of the crucial social issues is how this model handles status disparities. Much of the burden is borne by corporate culture and job security, but the cost may be employee burnout, achievement limited to the benefits provided by the firm, and vulnerability to corporate mind control. Will producing fun create a different kind of personal identity than producing widgets?

The corporate managers that took over the Disney family business in 1985 have bet on the development and diversification of new mass culture products: Hollywood films, syndicated television programs, and videocassette releases of old Disney movies. They have also taken on the role of hotel developer at Disney World and expanded the theme park by building new rides, linking them with such high-price talent as Michael Jackson, Steven Spielberg, and George Lucas, and multiplying "participation agreements" with large corporate sponsors. Corporate synergies are not new to Disneyland. Back in the 1950s, Walt Disney received a $500,000 investment and a loan guarantee of $4.5 million from the television network ABC to build Disneyland.

In return, the network owned one-third of the park and got to show Disney's first weekly television program. Walt Disney also sold Coca-Cola an exclusive soda concession for Disneyland; Kodak bought exclusive rights to sell film at the park. Under a

Disney license, Hollywood-Maxwell sold underwear from a corset shop on Main Street, and a building company sold real estate from another store. At EPCOT, the large corporations that sponsor pavilions invested $75 million apiece in construction funds and guaranteed operating expenses for ten years.

Under CEO Michael Eisner and CFO Frank Wells, the new Disney management negotiated a new contract with Kodak so that Kodak paid for part of the construction costs of the Michael Jackson ride as well as for theater renovations at Disneyland and Disney World. General Motors, which had its own pavilion, The World of Motion, and also supplied Disney World's "official car," paid a share of the costs of joint advertising campaigns. A new corporate sponsor, Metropolitan Life Insurance Company, agreed to spend almost $90 million for a health-theme pavilion at EPCOT.

> By late 1988, the Disney Channel was also achieving Eisner's goal of cross-promotion for other company ventures. Kids watching Winnie the Pooh or Mickey Mouse cartoons became a target market for Disney toys. Showing episodes of The Mickey Mouse Club, which had been filmed at the Disney-MGM Studios Theme Park, enticed 14-year-olds into pressuring their parents to take them to Orlando (Grover 1991, 150).

In any event, the Disney World theme park is almost infinitely expandable even within the southern tier of the United States. While Disney World has helped to create a new transatlantic and Latino tourist zone in south Florida, a completely new Disneyland in Anaheim, Westcot Center, will focus on "our humanity, our history, our planet, our universe." The new Disneyland resort will include Westcot, the original Disneyland, a resort hotel district, a centralized Disneyland Plaza linking the old and new theme parks, and Disney Center, a commercial area for shopping and strolling around a lake.

The virtual reality of Disney World is expandable not only in economic and geographical terms. Visually, too, Disney World is a model of how to think about the past and how to reproduce it. While technology aids this process, Disney World's real attraction is that it is a new social space, an alternative to cities. The conceptual challenge Disney World raises to public culture reflects the fact that a completely artificial space, a space that has never been a real place to live, can so resonate with social desires.

Disneyland and its marketing world developed together with broadcast television. Like Niagara Falls and Yellowstone National Park (Sears 1989), Disney World emerged at a crucial point – after the Vietnam War, before the fall of the Berlin Wall, during the Decade of Greed – when American identity was contentious, divided, unfocused on a patriotic vision. Because there is no longer a public identity that cities embody, the artificial world of Disney has become our safe place, our cities' virtual reality.

Cities impose visual coherence in many ways: by using zoning to impose design criteria for office buildings, by making memory visible in historic districts, by interpreting the assimilation of ethnic groups in street festivals, by building walls to contain fear. Disney World is not only important because it confirms and consolidates the significance of cultural power – the power to impose a vision – for social control. It is important because it offers a model of privatization and globalization; it manages social diversity; it imposes a frame of meaning on the city, a frame that earlier in history came from other forms of public culture. That frame is now based on touring, a voyeurism that thrives on the video camera and the local television news.

It is unreasonable to propose that people sit at home and cultivate their gardens, but Disney World raises serious questions about the social and political consequences of marketing culture, from cultural tourism to cultural strategies of urban development.

References

Asada, Akira. 1991. "Discussion." *Anyone*, ed. Cynthia C. Davidson. New York: Rizzoli.

Ball, Edward. 1991. "Theme Player." *Village Voice* (August 6): 81.

Baudrillard, Jean. 1986. *Amérique*. Paris: Grasset.

Boyer, M. Christine. 1992. "Cities for Sale: Merchandising History at South Street Seaport." *Variations on a Theme Park: The New American City and the End of Public Space*, ed. Michael Sorkin, pp. 181–204. New York: Hill and Wang.

Campbell, Robert. 1992. "Architecture View: A Logo of the Past on the Screen of the Present." *New York Times* (August 6).

Eco, Umberto. 1986 [1975]. "*Travels in Hyperreality.*" *Travels in Hyperreality*, trans. William Weaver, pp. 1–58. New York: Harcourt Brace Jovanovich.

Fjellman, Steven. 1992. *Vinyl Leaves*. Boulder, CO: Westview.

Gandee, Charles. 1991. "Gandee at Large: Nick Ashley: Life After Laura." *HG* (April): 212.

Gill, Brendan. 1991. "The Sky Line: Disneyitis." *The New Yorker* (April 29): 96–99.

Goldberger, Paul. 1992a. "25 Years of Unabashed Elitism." *New York Times* (February 2).

Goldberger, Paul. 1992b. "A Curious Mix of Versailles and Mickey Mouse." *New York Times* (June 14).

Griffith, Joseph P. 1992. "Commercial Property: 34th Street Partnership. A Carrot and a Stick to Tone Down the Garishness." *New York Times* (June 28).

Grover, Ron. 1991. *The Disney Touch: How a Daring Management Team Revived an Entertainment Empire.* Homewood, IL: Business One Irwin.

Harvey, David. 1973. *Social Justice and the City.* Baltimore: Johns Hopkins University Press.

Moore, Charles. 1965. "You Have to Pay for the Public Life." *Perspecta,* nos. 9–10: 57–106.

Porter, Henry. 1992. "London Diary." *New York Observer* (February 2).

Rosenthal, Jack. 1992. "Mickey Mousing." *New York Times Magazine* (August 2).

Sears, John F. 1989. *Sacred Places: American Tourist Attractions in the Nineteenth Century.* New York: Oxford University Press.

Siegel, Fred. 1992. "Reclaiming Our Public Spaces." *City Journal* (Spring): 35–45.

Sorkin, Michael. 1992. "See You in Disneyland." *Variations on a Theme Park,* ed. Michael Sorkin, pp. 205–32. New York: Hill and Wang.

Wallace, Mike. 1985. "Mickey Mouse History: Portraying the Past at Disney World." *Radical History Review* (32): 33–57.

Wilson, Alexander. 1992. *The Culture of Nature: North American Landscape from Disney to the Exxon Valdez.* Oxford: Blackwell.

Wolfson, Howard. 1992. "New York Bets on BIDs." *Metropolis* (April): 15, 21.

Zuber, Martha. 1992. "Mickey-sur-Marne: une culture conquérante?" *French Politics and Society* 10: 1–18.

Zukin, S. 1990 "Socio-spatial prototypes of a New Organization of Consumption: The Role of Real Cultural Capital," Sociology 24: 37–56.

Source and copyright

This chapter was published in its original form as:

Zukin, S. (1995), 'Learning from Disney World', in Zukin, S. (1995), *The Cultures of Cities*, Blackwell, Oxford, 49–77.

Reprinted with permission of Blackwell Publishing.

Section Four

The social dimension

It is difficult to conceive of 'space' as being without social content and, equally, to conceive of society without a spatial milieu. The relationship is, therefore, best conceived as a continuous two-way process in which people create and modify spaces while at the same time being influenced in various ways by those spaces. By shaping the built environment, urban designers influence – inhibit, facilitate, precipitate and modify, but do not determine – patterns of human activity and, therefore, of social life.

This section presents a set of five chapters exploring the social dimension of urban design – that is, the relationship between space and social/urban experience. The first is from **Jan Gehl's** 1971 book *Life Between Buildings: Using Public Space* (Arkitektens Forlag, Skive). Gehl's work is based on extensive observational analysis over many years, much of it in Copenhagen (Denmark). Through his work, Gehl has been able to directly influence the design and management of public space in the city. As a result, and despite its climate, Copenhagen is an extremely 'livable' place, with high quality public spaces. Gehl has now applied his ideas to a large number of European cities, including London. Presented in a very accessible form, Gehl illustrates how the environmental quality of public spaces affects the intensity of their use. Arguing that outdoor activities in public spaces can be divided into three categories – 'necessary' activities; 'optional' activities and 'social' activities – he contends that, through design and within certain limits – regional, climatic, societal – it is possible to influence *how many* people use public spaces, *how long* individual activities last, and *which* activity types can develop. The crux of Gehl's argument is that when public spaces are of poor quality, only strictly necessary activities occur. When public spaces are of higher quality, necessary activities take place with approximately the same frequency – although people choose to spend longer doing them – but, more importantly, a wide range of optional (social) activities also tends to occur.

Chapter 16 is **Jane Jacobs'** 'The uses of sidewalks: safety', originally published in her 1961 book *The Death and Life of Great American Cities* (Penguin, Harmondsworth). Jacobs was an early critic of functional zoning arguing that the vitality of city neighbourhoods depended on the overlapping and interweaving of activities and that understanding cities required dealing with combinations or mixtures of uses as the 'essential phenomena'. Like Gehl, much of Jane Jacobs' analysis was based on observational research: in Jacobs' case through personal observation of the neighbourhoods in which she

lived – Greenwich Village, New York and Rittenhouse Square, Philadelphia. The influence of this inevitably subjective and impressionistic approach to investigating urban design has nevertheless been profound, providing an early and devastating critique of Modernist urban space design. Part of the classic urban design canon, the essence of Jacob's book, and arguably her major contribution to urban design, is her emphasis on vitality. Focusing on the cardinal importance of a mix of land uses and activities to create lively, vital public places and outlining four conditions she considered indispensable to the generation of 'exuberant diversity' in a city's streets and districts, this selection encapsulates that contribution.

Chapter 17 is **Tridib Banerjee's** 'The future of public space: beyond invented streets and reinvented places', originally published in the *Journal of the American Planning Association* in 2001. This short article offers a straightforward argument in the form of a series of useful points and succinct observations. Banerjee argues that the boundary between public space and quasi-public space is often difficult to define precisely as a result of privatisation, globalisation and the communications revolution. As well as issues of space, issues of access and accessibility must be considered together with whether or not the setting constitutes 'neutral' ground (and in what sense). Given the somewhat slippery nature of definitions of 'public' space, Banerjee recommends urban designers focus on the broader concept of 'public life' (i.e. the socio-cultural public realm of people and activities), rather than the narrower one of 'public spaces' (i.e. the physical public realm of buildings and spaces). Banerjee's concern, therefore, is with 'social space' (i.e. spaces that support social interaction and public life) regardless of whether it is genuinely 'public' space or private space that is publicly accessible. He argues that while planners have traditionally associated public life with public spaces, public life increasingly flourishes in private places, such as coffee shops and bookstores – that is, in Oldenburg's 'third places' (see below).

Chapter 18 is **Ray Oldenburg's** 'The character of third places', drawn from his 1989 book *The Great Good Place: Cafés, coffee shops, bookstores, bars, hair salons and the other great hangouts at the heart of a community* (Marlowe & Company, New York – second edition published 1999). As highlighted in the previous selection, Oldenburg's concept of the third place provides a useful way of enhancing the understanding of informal public life and its relation to the public realm. Oldenburg argues that, while seemingly 'amorphous and scattered', informal public life is actually highly focused and emerges in 'core settings'. His term third place, therefore, signifies the '... *great variety of public places that host the regular, voluntary, informal, and happily anticipated gatherings of individuals beyond the realms of home and work*'. Oldenburg's central thesis is that to be 'relaxed and fulfilling', daily life must find its balance in three realms of experience – 'domestic', 'work' and 'social'. Drawing on contemporary US society, he argues that because people's expectations of work and family have 'escalated beyond the capacity of those institutions to meet them', people need the release and stimulation that more sociable realms can provide. Hence, the need for – and emergence of – third places. Oldenburg's paper is particularly valuable for its identification of the desirable qualities of third places (which can also be regarded as core qualities of the public realm).

As Oldenburg establishes some of the desirable qualities and social trends resulting from transformations of public space, then the New York journalist **Paul Goldberger** has reminded us of a darker side. Accordingly, the final chapter in this section is his essay 'The Rise of the Private City', which originally appeared in J. Vitullo-Martin's 1996 edited book *Breaking Away: The Future of Cities: Essays in Memory of Robert F. Wagner Jnr* (The Twentieth Century Fund Press, New York). The essay provides an important

and focused discussion of trends in contemporary urban development in terms of its product or outcome and warns against the suburbanisation of the urban and the blurring of traditional differences between the city and the suburb. It is particularly valuable in its contribution of the concept of 'urbanoid' environments – the pseudo-street, the pseudo-square, the pseudo-plaza. As with humanoids that have some human qualities without being human, urbanoid environments have some urban qualities without actually being urban. In Goldberger's words, they '... *purport to offer some degree of urban experience in an entertaining, sealed-off, private environment*'. For Goldberger, authentic urban environments require the mixing of different classes of people in public space and can be contrasted with the disengagement and private space of suburban environments. Goldberger's paper, therefore, ultimately reiterates Don Mitchell's question about the 'end of public space':

> *Have we created a society that expects and desires only private interactions, private communications, and private politics, that reserves public spaces, solely for commodified recreation and spectacle? (Mitchell, 1995: 110).*

> *Matthew Carmona and Steve Tiesdell*

15

Three types of outdoor activities; Outdoor activities and quality of outdoor space

Jan Gehl
[1971]

Three types of outdoor activity

An ordinary day on an ordinary street. Pedestrians pass on the sidewalks, children play near front doors, people sit on benches and steps, the postman makes his rounds with the mail, two passersby greet on the sidewalk, two mechanics repair a car, groups engage in conversation. This mix of outdoor activities is influenced by a number of conditions. Physical environment is one of the factors: a factor that influences the activities to a varying degree and in many different ways. Outdoor activities, and a number of the physical conditions that influence them, are the subject of this book.

Greatly simplified, outdoor activities in public spaces can be divided into three categories, each of which places very different demands on the physical environment: *necessary activities, optional activities, and social activities.*

Necessary activities include those that are more or less compulsory – going to school or to work, shopping, waiting for a bus or a person, running errands, distributing mail – in other words, all activities in which those involved are to a greater or lesser degree required to participate.

In general, everyday tasks and pastimes belong to this group. Among other activities, this group includes the great majority of those related to walking.

Because the activities in this group are necessary, their incidence is influenced only slightly by the physical framework. These activities will take place throughout the year, under nearly all conditions, and are more or less independent of the exterior environment. The participants have no choice.

Optional activities – that is, those pursuits that are participated in if there is a wish to do so and if time and place make it possible – are quite another matter.

This category includes such activities as taking a walk to get a breath of fresh air, standing around enjoying life, or sitting and sunbathing.

These activities take place only when exterior conditions are optimal, when weather and place invite them. This relationship is particularly important in connection with physical planning because most of the recreational activities that are especially pleasant to pursue outdoors are found precisely in this category of activities. These activities are especially dependent on exterior physical conditions.

When outdoor areas are of poor quality, only strictly necessary activities occur.

When outdoor areas are of high quality, necessary activities take place with approximately the same frequency – though they clearly tend to take a longer time, because the physical conditions are better. In addition, however, a wide range of optional activities will also occur because place and situation now invite people to stop, sit, eat, play, and so on.

In streets and city spaces of poor quality, only the bare minimum of activity takes place. People hurry home.

In a good environment, a completely different, broad spectrum of human activities is possible.

	Quality of the physical environment	
	Poor	**Good**
Necessary activities	●	●
Optional activities	·	⬤
'Resultant' activities (Social activities)	·	●

Graphic representation of the relationship between the quality of outdoor spaces and the rate of occurrence of outdoor activities.

When the quality of outdoor areas is good, optional activities occur with increasing frequency. Furthermore, as levels of optional activity rise, the number of social activities usually increases substantially.

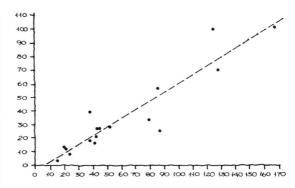

The more time people spend outdoors, the more frequently they meet and the more they talk.

Chart plotting the relationship between the number of outdoor activities and frequency of interactions. (Street life studies in Melbourne [1].)

Social activities are all activities that depend on the presence of others in public spaces. Social activities include children at play, greetings and conversations, communal activities of various kinds, and finally – as the most widespread social activity – passive contacts, that is, simply seeing and hearing other people.

Different kinds of social activities occur in many places: in dwellings; in private outdoor spaces, gardens, and balconies; in public buildings; at places of work; and so on; but in this context only those activities that occur in publicly accessible spaces are examined.

These activities could also be termed "resultant" activities, because in nearly all instances they evolve from activities linked to the other two activity categories. They develop in connection with the other activities because people are in the same space, meet, pass by one another, or are merely within view.

Social activities occur spontaneously, as a direct consequence of people moving about and being in the same spaces. This implies that social activities are indirectly supported whenever necessary and optional activities are given better conditions in public spaces.

The character of social activities varies, depending on the context in which they occur. In the residential streets, near schools, near places of work, where there are a limited number of people with common interests or backgrounds, social activities in public spaces can be quite comprehensive: greetings, conversations, discussions, and play arising from common interests and because people "know" each other, if for no other reason than that they often see one another.

In city streets and city centers, social activities will generally be more superficial, with the majority being passive contacts – seeing and hearing a great number of unknown people. But even this limited activity can be very appealing.

Very freely interpreted, a social activity takes place every time two people are together in the same space. To see and hear each other, to meet, is in itself a form of contact, a social activity. The actual meeting, merely being present, is furthermore the seed for other, more comprehensive forms of social activity.

This connection is important in relation to physical planning. Although the physical framework does not have a direct influence on the quality, content, and intensity of social contacts, architects and planners can affect the possibilities for meeting, seeing, and hearing people – possibilities that both take on a quality of their own and become important as background and starting point for other forms of contact.

This is the background for the investigation in this book of meeting possibilities and opportunities to see and hear other people. Another reason for a comprehensive review of these activities is that precisely the presence of other people, activities, events, inspiration, and stimulation comprise one of the most important qualities of public spaces altogether.

If we look back at the street scene that was the starting point for defining the three categories of outdoor activities, we can see how necessary, optional, and social activities occur in a finely interwoven pattern. People walk, sit, and talk. Functional, recreational, and social activities intertwine in all conceivable combinations. Therefore, this examination of the subject of outdoor activities does not begin with a single, limited category of activities. Life between buildings is not merely pedestrian traffic or recreational or social activities. Life between buildings comprises the entire spectrum of activities, which combine to make communal spaces in cities and residential areas meaningful and attractive.

Both necessary, functional activities and optional, recreational activities have been examined quite throughly over the years in different contexts. Social activities and their interweaving to form a communal fabric have received considerably less attention.

Outdoor activities and quality of outdoor space

Life between buildings is discussed here because the extent and character of outdoor activities are greatly influenced by physical planning. Just as it is possible through choice of materials and colors to create a certain palette in a city, it is equally possible through planning decisions to influence patterns of activities, to create better or worse conditions for outdoor events, and to create lively or lifeless cities.

The spectrum of possibilities can be described by two extremes. One extreme is the city with multistory buildings, underground parking facilities, extensive automobile traffic, and long distances between buildings and functions. This type of city can be found in a number of North American and "modernized" European cities and in many suburban areas.

In such cities one sees buildings and cars, but few people, if any, because pedestrian traffic is more or less impossible, and because conditions for outdoor stays in the public areas near buildings are very poor. Outdoor spaces are large and impersonal. With great distances in the urban plan, there is nothing much to experience outdoors, and the few activities that do take place are spread out in time and space. Under these conditions most residents prefer to remain indoors in front of the television or on their balcony or in other comparably private outdoor spaces.

Another extreme is the city with reasonably low, closely spaced buildings, accommodation for foot traffic, and good areas for outdoor stays along the streets and in direct relation to residences, public buildings, places of work, and so forth. Here it is possible to see buildings, people coming and going, and people stopping in outdoor areas near the buildings because the outdoor spaces are easy and inviting to use. This city is a living city, one in which spaces inside buildings are supplemented with usable outdoor areas, and where public spaces are allowed to function.

It has already been mentioned that the outdoor activities that are particularly dependent on the quality of the outdoor spaces are the optional, recreational activities, and by implication, a considerable part of the social activities.

It is these specially attractive activities that disappear when conditions are poor and that thrive where conditions are favorable.

The significance of quality improvement to daily and social activities in cities can be observed where pedestrian streets or traffic-free zones have been established in existing urban areas. In a number of examples, improved physical conditions have resulted in a doubling of the number of pedestrians, a lengthening of the average time spent outdoors, and a considerably broader spectrum of outdoor activities [2].

In a survey recording all activities occurring in the center of Copenhagen during the spring and summer of 1986, it was found that the number of pedestrian streets and squares in the city center had tripled between 1968 and 1986. Parallel to this improvement of the physical conditions, a tripling in the number of people standing and sitting was recorded.

In cases where neighboring cities offer varying conditions for city activities, great differences can also be found.

In Italian cities with pedestrian streets and automobile-free squares, the outdoor city life is often much more pronounced than in the car-oriented neighboring cities, even though the climate is the same.

A 1978 survey of street activities in both trafficked and pedestrian streets in Sydney, Melbourne, and Adelaide, Australia, carried out by architectural students from the University of Melbourne and the Royal Melbourne Institute of Technology found a direct connection between street quality and street activity. In addition, an experimental improvement of increasing the number of seats by 100 percent on the pedestrian street in Melbourne resulted in an 88 percent increase in seated activities.

William H. Whyte, in his book *The Social Life of Small Urban Spaces* [3], describes the close connection between qualities of city space and city activities and documents how often quite simple physical alterations can improve the use of the city space noticeably.

Comparable results have been achieved in a number of improvement projects executed in New York and other U.S. cities by the Project for Public Spaces [4].

In residential areas as well, both in Europe and the United States, traffic reduction schemes, courtyard clearing, laying out of parks, and comparable outdoor improvements have had a marked effect.

In summarizing the studies, a close relationship between outdoor quality and outdoor activities can be noted.

In at least three areas, it appears possible, in part through the design of the physical environment, to influence the activity patterns in public spaces in cities and residential areas. Within certain limits – regional, climatic, societal – it is possible to influence *how many* people and events use the public spaces, *how long* the individual activities last, and *which* activity types can develop.

The fact that a marked increase of outdoor activities is often seen in connection with quality improvements emphasizes that the situation found in a specific area at a certain time frequently gives an incomplete indication of the need for public spaces and outdoor activities, which can indeed exist in the area. The establishment of a suitable physical framework for social and recreational activities has time after time revealed a suppressed human need that was ignored at the outset.

When the main street in Copenhagen was converted to a pedestrian street in 1962 as the first such scheme in Scandinavia, many critics predicted that the street would be deserted because "city activity just doesn't belong to the northern European tradition." Today this major pedestrian street, plus a number of other pedestrian streets later added to the system, are filled to capacity with people walking, sitting, playing music, drawing, and talking together.

It is evident that the initial fears were unfounded and that city life in Copenhagen had been so limited because there was previously no physical possibility for its existence.

In a number of new Danish residential areas as well, where physical possibilities for outdoor activity have been established in the form of high-quality public spaces, activity patterns that no one had believed possible in Danish residential areas have evolved.

Just as it has been noted that automobile traffic tends to develop concurrently with the building of new roads, all experience to date with regard to human activities in cities and in proximity to residences seems to indicate that where a better physical framework is created, outdoor activities tend to grow in number, duration, and scope.

Notes

1. Gehl, Jan. 'The Residential Street Environment.' *Built Environment* 6, no. 1 (1980): 51–61.
2. Gehl, Jan. 'Mennesker og trafik i Helsingør' (Pedestrians and Vehicular Traffic in Elsinore). *Byplan* 21, no. 122 (1969): 132–33.
3. Whyte, William H. *The Social Life of Small Urban Spaces*. Washington D.C.: Conservation Foundation, 1980.
4. *Planning Public Spaces Handbook*. New York: Project for Public Spaces, Inc., 1976.

Source and copyright

This chapter was published in its original form as:

Gehl, J. (2001 is fifth edition, first published 1971), 'Three Types of Outdoor Activities' and 'Outdoor activities and quality of outdoor space', in Gehl, J. (1996), *Life Between Buildings: Using Public Space*, Arkitektens Forlag, Skive, 11–16; 17–31; 32–40.

Reprinted with kind permission of the author Jan Gehl.

16

The uses of sidewalks: safety

Jane Jacobs
[1961]

Streets in cities serve many purposes besides carrying vehicles, and city sidewalks – the pedestrian parts of the streets – serve many purposes besides carrying pedestrians. These uses are bound up with circulation but are not identical with it and in their own right they are at least as basic as circulation to the proper workings of cities.

A city sidewalk by itself is nothing. It is an abstraction. It means something only in conjunction with the buildings and other uses that border it, or border other sidewalks very near it. The same might be said of streets, in the sense that they serve other purposes besides carrying wheeled traffic in their middles. Streets and their sidewalks, the main public places of a city, are its most vital organs. Think of a city and what comes to mind? Its streets. If a city's streets look interesting, the city looks interesting; if they look dull, the city looks dull.

More than that – and here we get down to the first problem – if a city's streets are safe from barbarism and fear, the city is thereby tolerably safe from barbarism and fear. When people say that a city, or a part of it, is dangerous or is a jungle, what they mean primarily is that they do not feel safe on the sidewalks.

But sidewalks and those who use them are not passive beneficiaries of safety or helpless victims of danger. Sidewalks, their bordering uses, and their users, are active participants in the drama of civilization versus barbarism in cities. To keep the city safe is a fundamental task of a city's streets and its sidewalks.

This task is totally unlike any service that sidewalks and streets in little towns or true suburbs are called upon to do. Great cities are not like towns only larger; they are not like suburbs only denser. They differ from towns and suburbs in basic ways, and one of these is that cities are, by definition, full of strangers.

To any one person, strangers are far more common in big cities than acquaintances. More common not just in places of public assembly, but more common at a man's own doorstep. Even residents who live near each other are strangers, and must be, because of the sheer number of people in small geographical compass.

The bedrock attribute of a successful city district is that a person must feel personally safe and secure on the street among all these strangers. He must not feel automatically menaced by them. A city district that fails in this respect also does badly in other ways and lays up for itself, and for its city at large, mountain on mountain of trouble.

Today barbarism has taken over many city streets, or people fear it has, which comes to much the same thing in the end. 'I live in a lovely, quiet residential area,' says a friend of mine who is hunting another place to live. 'The only disturbing sound at night is the occasional scream of someone being mugged.' It does not take many incidents of violence on a city street, or in a city district, to make people fear the streets. And as they fear them, they use them less, which makes the streets still more unsafe.

To be sure, there are people with hobgoblins in their heads, and such people will never feel safe no matter what the objective circumstances are. But this is a different matter from the fear that besets normally prudent, tolerant, and cheerful people who show nothing more than common sense in refusing to venture after dark – or in a few places, by day – into streets where they may well be assaulted, unseen or unrescued until too late.

The barbarism and the real, not imagined, insecurity that gives rise to such fears cannot be tagged a problem of the slums. The problem is most serious, in fact, in genteel-looking 'quiet residential areas' like that my friend was leaving.

It cannot be tagged as a problem of older parts of cities. The problem reaches its most baffling dimensions in some examples of rebuilt parts of cities, including supposedly the best examples of rebuilding, such as middle-income projects. The police precinct captain of a nationally admired project of this kind (admired by planners and lenders) has recently admonished residents not only about hanging around outdoors after dark but has urged them never to answer their doors without knowing the caller. Life here has much in common with life for the three little pigs or the seven little kids of the nursery thrillers. The problem of sidewalk and doorstep insecurity is as serious in cities which have made conscientious efforts at rebuilding as it is in those cities that have lagged. Nor is it illuminating to tag minority groups, or the poor, or the outcast with responsibility for city danger. There are immense variations in the degree of civilization and safety found among such groups and among the city areas where they live. Some of the safest sidewalks in New York City, for example, at any time of day or night, are those along which poor people or minority groups live. And some of the most dangerous are in streets occupied by the same kinds of people. All this can also be said of other cities.

Deep and complicated social ills must lie behind delinquency and crime, in suburbs and towns as well as in great cities. This book will not go into speculation on the deeper reasons. It is sufficient, at this point, to say that if we are to maintain a city society that can diagnose and keep abreast of deeper social problems, the starting point must be, in any case, to strengthen whatever workable forces for maintaining safety and civilization do exist – in the cities we do have. To build city districts that are custom made for easy crime is idiotic. Yet that is what we do.

The first thing to understand is that the public peace – the sidewalk and street peace – of cities is not kept primarily by the police, necessary as police are. It is kept primarily by an intricate, almost unconscious, network of voluntary controls and standards among the people themselves, and enforced by the people themselves. In some city areas – older public housing projects and streets with very high population turnover are often conspicuous examples – the keeping of public sidewalk law and order is left almost entirely to the police and special guards. Such places are jungles. No number of police can enforce civilization where the normal, casual enforcement of it has broken down.

The second thing to understand is that the problem of insecurity cannot be solved by spreading people out more thinly, trading the characteristics of cities for the characteristics of suburbs. If this could solve danger on the city streets, then Los Angeles should be a safe city, because superficially Los Angeles is almost all suburban. It has virtually no districts compact enough to qualify as dense city areas. Yet Los Angeles cannot, any more than any other great city, evade the truth that, being a city, it *is* composed of strangers not all of whom are nice. Los Angeles's crime figures are flabbergasting. Among the seventeen standard metropolitan areas with populations over a million, Los Angeles stands so pre-eminent in crime that it is in a category by itself. And this is markedly true of crimes associated with personal attack, the crimes that make people fear the streets.

Here we come up against an all-important question about any city street: how much easy opportunity does it offer to crime? It may be that there is some absolute amount of crime in a given city, which will find an outlet somehow (I do not believe this). Whether this is so or not, different kinds of city streets garner radically different shares of barbarism and fear of barbarism.

Some city streets afford no opportunity to street barbarism. The streets of the North End of Boston are outstanding examples. They are probably as safe as any place on earth in this respect. Although most of the North End's residents are Italian or of Italian descent, the district's streets are also heavily and constantly used by people of every race and background. Some of the strangers from outside work in or close to the district; some come to shop and stroll; many, including members of minority groups who have inherited dangerous districts previously abandoned by others, make a point of cashing their pay-cheques in North End stores and immediately making their big weekly purchases in streets where they know they will not be parted from their money between the getting and the spending.

Meantime, in the Elm Hill Avenue section of Roxbury, a part of inner Boston that is suburban in superficial character, street assaults and the ever-present possibility of more street assaults with no kibitzers to protect the victims, induce prudent people to stay off the sidewalks at night. Not surprisingly, for this and other reasons that are related (dispiritedness and dullness), most of Roxbury has run down. It has become a place to leave.

I do not wish to single out Roxbury or its once fine Elm Hill Avenue section especially as a vulnerable area; its disabilities, and especially its great blight of dullness, are all too common in other cities too. But differences like these in public safety within the same city are worth nothing. The Elm Hill Avenue section's basic troubles are not owing to a criminal or a discriminated against or a poverty-stricken population. Its troubles stem from the fact that it is physically quite unable to function safely and with related vitality as a city district.

This is something everyone already knows: a well-used city street is apt to be a safe street. A deserted city street is apt to be unsafe. But how does this work, really? And what makes a city street well used or shunned? Why is the sidewalk mall in Washington Houses, which is supposed to be an attraction, shunned? Why are the sidewalks of the old city just to its west not shunned? What about streets that are busy part of the time and then empty abruptly?

A city street equipped to handle strangers, and to make a safety asset, in itself, out of the presence of strangers, as the streets of successful city neighbourhoods always do, must have three main qualities:

First, there must be a clear demarcation between what is public space and what is private space. Public and private spaces cannot ooze into each other as they do typically in suburban settings or in projects.

Second, there must be eyes upon the street, eyes belonging to those we might call the natural proprietors of the street. The buildings on a street equipped to handle strangers and to ensure the safety of both residents and strangers must be oriented to the street. They cannot turn their backs or blank sides on it and leave it blind.

And third, the sidewalk must have users on it fairly continuously, both to add to the number of effective eyes on the street and to induce the people in buildings along the street to watch the sidewalks in sufficient numbers. Nobody enjoys sitting on a stoop or looking out a window at an empty street. Almost nobody does such a thing. Large numbers of people entertain themselves, off and on, by watching street activity.

In settlements that are smaller and simpler than big cities, controls on acceptable public behaviour, if not on crime, seem to operate with greater or lesser success through a web of reputation, gossip, approval, disapproval, and sanctions, all of which are powerful if people know each other and word travels. But a city's streets, which must control not only the behaviour of the people of the city but also of visitors from suburbs and towns who want to have a big time away from the gossip and sanctions at home, have to operate by more direct, straightforward methods. It is a wonder cities have solved

such an inherently difficult problem at all. And yet in many streets they do it magnificently.

It is futile to try to evade the issue of unsafe city streets by attempting to make some other features of a locality, say interior courtyards or sheltered play spaces, safe instead. By definition again, the streets of a city must do most of the job of handling strangers, for this is where strangers come and go. The streets must not only defend the city against predatory strangers, they must protect the many, many peaceable and well-meaning strangers who use them, ensuring their safety too as they pass through. Moreover, no normal person can spend his life in some artificial haven, and this includes children. Everyone must use the streets.

On the surface, we seem to have here some simple aims: to try to secure streets where the public space is unequivocally public, physically unmixed with private or with nothing-at-all space, so that the area needing surveillance has clear and practicable limits; and to see that these public street spaces have eyes on them as continuously as possible.

But it is not so simple to achieve these objects, especially the latter. You can't make people use streets they have no reason to use. You can't make people watch streets they do not want to watch. Safety on the streets by surveillance and mutual policing of one another sounds grim, but in real life it is not grim. The safety of the street works best, most casually, and with least frequent taint of hostility or suspicion precisely where people are using and most enjoying the city streets voluntarily and are least conscious, normally, that they are policing.

The basic requisite for such surveillance is a substantial quantity of stores and other public places sprinkled along the sidewalks of a district; enterprises and public places that are used by evening and night must be among them especially. Stores, bars, and restaurants, as the chief examples, work in several different and complex ways to abet sidewalk safety.

First, they give people – both residents and strangers – concrete reasons for using the sidewalks on which these enterprises face.

Second, they draw people along the sidewalks past places which have no attractions to public use in themselves but which become travelled and peopled as routes to somewhere else; this influence does not carry very far geographically, so enterprises must be frequent in a city district if they are to populate with walkers those other stretches of street that lack public places along the sidewalk. Moreover, there should be many different kinds of enterprise, to give people reasons for criss-crossing paths.

Third, storekeepers and other small businessmen are typically strong proponents of peace and order themselves; they hate broken windows and holdups; they hate having customers made nervous about safety. They are great street watchers and sidewalk guardians if present in sufficient numbers.

Fourth, the activity generated by people on errands, or people aiming for food or drink, is itself an attraction to still other people.

This last point, that the sight of people attracts still other people, is something that city planners and city architectural designers seem to find incomprehensible. They operate on the premiss that city people seek the sight of emptiness, obvious order, and quiet. Nothing could be less true. People's love of watching activity and other people is constantly evident in cities everywhere. This trait reaches an almost ludicrous extreme on upper Broadway in New York, where the street is divided by a narrow central mall, right in the middle of traffic. At the cross-street intersections of this long north–south mall, benches have been placed behind big concrete buffers and on any day when the weather is even barely tolerable these benches are filled with people at block after block after block, watching the pedestrians who cross the mall in front of them, watching the traffic, watching the people on the busy sidewalks, watching each other. Eventually Broadway reaches Columbia University and Barnard College, one to the right, the other to the left. Here all is obvious order and quiet. No more stores, no more activity generated by the stores, almost no more pedestrians crossing – and no more watchers. The benches are there but they go empty in even the finest weather. I have tried them and can see why. No place could be more boring. Even the students of these institutions shun the solitude. They are doing their outdoor loitering, outdoor homework, and general street watching on the steps overlooking the busiest campus crossing.

Once a street is well equipped to handle strangers, once it has both a good, effective demarcation between private and public spaces and has a basic supply of activity and eyes, the more strangers the merrier.

Strangers become an enormous asset on the street on which I live and the spurs off it, particularly at night when safety assets are most needed. We are fortunate enough, on the street, to be gifted not only with a locally supported bar and another around the corner, but also with a famous bar that draws continuous troops of strangers from adjoining neighbourhoods and even from out of town. It is famous because the poet Dylan Thomas used to go there, and mentioned it in his writing. This bar, indeed, works two distinct shifts. In the morning and early afternoon it is a social gathering place for the old community of Irish longshoremen and other craftsmen in the area, as it always was. But beginning in the mid afternoon it takes on a different life, more like a college bull session with beer, combined with a literary cocktail party, and this continues until the early hours of the morning. On a cold winter's night, as you pass the White Horse, and the doors open, a solid wave of conversation and animation surges out and hits you; very warming. The comings and goings from this bar do much to keep our street reasonably populated until three in the morning, and it is a street always safe to come home to. The only instance I know of a beating in our street occurred in the dead hours between the closing of the bar and dawn. The beating was halted by one of our neighbours who saw it from his window and, unconsciously certain that even at night he was part of a web of strong street law and order, intervened.

A friend of mine lives on a street uptown where a church youth and community center, with many night dances and other activities, performs the same service for his street that the White Horse bar does for ours. Orthodox planning is much imbued with puritanical and Utopian conceptions of how people should spend their free time, and, in planning, these moralisms on people's private lives are deeply confused with concepts about the workings of cities. In maintaining city-street civilization, the White Horse bar and the church-sponsored youth centre, different as they undoubtedly are, perform much the same public street-civilizing service. There is not only room in cities for such differences and many more in taste, purpose, and interest of occupation; cities also have a need for people with all these differences in taste and proclivity. The preferences of Utopians, and of other compulsive managers of other people's leisure, for one kind of legal enterprise over others is worse than irrelevant for cities: it is harmful. The greater and more plentiful the range of all legitimate interests (in the strictly legal sense) that city streets and their enterprises can satisfy, the better for the streets and for the safety and civilization of the city.

Bars, and indeed all commerce, have a bad name in many city districts precisely because they do draw strangers, and the strangers do not work out as an asset at all.

This sad circumstance is especially true in the dispirited grey belts of great cities and in once fashionable or at least once solid inner residential areas gone into decline. Because these neighbourhoods are so dangerous, and the streets typically so dark, it is commonly believed that their trouble may be insufficient street lighting. Good lighting is important, but darkness alone does not account for the grey areas' deep, functional sickness, the great blight of dullness.

The value of bright street lights for dispirited grey areas rises from the reassurance they offer to some people who need to go out on the sidewalk, or would like to, but lacking the good light would not do so. Thus the lights induce these people to contribute their own eyes to the upkeep of the street. Moreover, as is obvious, good lighting augments every pair of eyes, makes the eyes count for more because their range is greater. Each additional pair of eyes, and every increase in their range, is that much to the good for dull grey areas. But unless eyes are there, and unless in the brains behind those eyes is the almost unconscious reassurance of general street support in upholding civilization, lights can do no good. Horrifying public crimes can, and do, occur in well-lighted subway stations when no effective eyes are present. They virtually never occur in darkened theatres where many people and eyes are present. Street lights can be like that famous stone that falls in the desert where there are no ears to hear. Does it make a noise? Without effective eyes to see, does a light cast light? Not for practical purposes.

Suppose we continue with building, and with deliberate rebuilding, of unsafe cities. How do we live with this insecurity? From the evidence thus far, there seem to be three modes of living with it; maybe in time others will be invented but I suspect these three will simply be further developed, if that is the word for it.

The first mode is to let danger hold sway, and let those unfortunate enough to be stuck with it take the consequences. This is the policy now followed with respect to low-income housing projects, and to many middle-income housing projects.

The second mode is to take refuge in vehicles. This is a technique practised in the big wild-animal reservations of Africa, where tourists are warned to leave their cars under no circumstances until they reach a lodge. It is also the technique practised in Los Angeles. Surprised visitors to that city are forever recounting how the police of Beverly Hills stopped them, made them prove their reasons for being afoot, and warned them of the danger. This technique of public safety does not seem to work too effectively yet in Los Angeles, as the crime rate

shows, but in time it may. And think what the crime figures might be if more people without metal shells were helpless upon the vast, blind-eyed reservation of Los Angeles.

People in dangerous parts of other cities often use automobiles as protection too, of course, or try to. A letter to the editor in the *New York Post* reads,

> *I live on a dark street off Utica Avenue in Brooklyn and therefore decided to take a cab home even though it was not late. The cab driver asked that I get off at the corner of Utica, saying he did not want to go down the dark street. If I had wanted to walk down the dark street, who needed him?*

The third mode, was developed by hoodlum gangs and has been adopted widely by developers of the rebuilt city. This mode is to cultivate the institution of Turf.

Under the Turf system in its historical form, a gang appropriates as its territory certain streets or housing projects or parks – often a combination of the three. Members of other gangs cannot enter this Turf without permission from the Turf-owning gang, or if they do so it is at peril of being beaten or run off.

The technique of dividing the city into Turfs is not simply a New York solution. It is a Rebuilt American City solution. At the Harvard Design Conference of 1959, one of the topics pondered by city architectural designers turned out to be the puzzle of Turf, although they did not use that designation. The examples discussed happened to be the Lake Meadows middle-income project of Chicago and the Lafayette Park high-income project of Detroit. Do you keep the rest of the city out of these blind-eyed purlieus? How difficult and how unpalatable. Do you invite the rest of the city in? How difficult and how impossible.

Like the Youth Board workers, the developers and residents of Radiant City and Radiant Garden City and Radiant Garden City Beautiful have a genuine difficulty and they have to do the best they can with it by the empirical means at their disposal. They have little choice. Wherever the rebuilt city rises the barbaric concept of Turf must follow, because the rebuilt city has junked a basic function of the city street and with it, necessarily, the freedom of the city.

Under the seeming disorder of the old city, wherever the old city is working successfully, is a marvellous order for maintaining the safety of the streets and the freedom of the city. It is a complex order. Its essence is intricacy of sidewalk use, bringing with it a constant succession of eyes. This order is all composed of movement and change, and although it is life, not art, we may fancifully call it the art form of the city and liken it to the dance – not to a simple-minded precision dance with everyone kicking up at the same time, twirling in unison and bowing off *en masse*, but to an intricate ballet in which the individual dancers and ensembles all have distinctive parts which miraculously reinforce each other and compose an orderly whole. The ballet of the city sidewalk never repeats itself from place to place, and in any one place is always replete with new improvisations.

The strangers on Hudson Street, the allies whose eyes help us natives keep the peace of the street, are so many that they always seem to be different people from one day to the next. That does not matter. Whether they are so many always-different people as they seem to be, I do not know. Likely they are. When Jimmy Rogan fell through a plate-glass window (he was separating some scuffling friends) and almost lost his arm, a stranger in an old T-shirt emerged from the Ideal bar, swiftly applied an expert tourniquet and, according to the hospital's emergency staff, saved Jimmy's life. Nobody remembered seeing the man before and no one has seen him since. The hospital was called in this way: a woman sitting on the steps next to the accident ran over to the bus stop, wordlessly snatched the dime from the hand of a stranger who was waiting with his fifteen-cent fare ready, and raced into the Ideal's phone booth. The stranger raced after her to offer the nickel too. Nobody remembered seeing him before, and no one has seen him since. When you see the same stranger three or four times on Hudson Street, you begin to nod. This is almost getting to be an acquaintance, a public acquaintance, of course.

I have made the daily ballet of Hudson Street sound more frenetic than it is, because writing it telescopes it. In real life, it is not that way. In real life, to be sure, something is always going on, the ballet is never at a halt, but the general effect is peaceful and the general tenor even leisurely. People who know well such animated city streets will know how it is. I am afraid people who do not will always have it a little wrong in their heads – like the old prints of rhinoceroses made from travellers' descriptions of rhinoceroses.

On Hudson Street, the same as in the North End of Boston or in any other animated neighbourhoods of great cities, we are not innately more competent at keeping the sidewalks safe than are the people who try to live off the hostile truce of Turf in a blind-eyed city. We are the lucky possessors of a city order that makes it relatively simple to keep the peace because there are plenty of eyes on the street. But there is nothing simple about that order itself, or the bewildering number of components that go into it. Most of those components are specialized in one way or another. They unite in their joint effect upon the sidewalk, which is not specialized in the least. That is its strength.

Source and copyright

This chapter was published in its original form as:

Jacobs, J. (1961), 'The Uses of Sidewalks: Safety', in Jacobs, J. (1961), *The Death and Life of Great American Cities*, Penguin, Harmondsworth, 39–65.

Copyright 1961 by Jane Jacobs. Used by permission of Random House, Inc.

17

The future of public space: beyond invented streets and reinvented places

Tridib Banerjee
[2001]

What is the future of our public space? Not an unreasonable question to ask as we stand at the threshold of a new century. A hundred years ago this question probably would not have crossed our minds. There was then no reason to be concerned about the future of public space, for it was a time when the urban park systems of many major U.S. cities were experiencing remarkable growth (Rybczynski, 1999). In contrast, we have seen very little expansion of parks and open space systems in American cities in recent decades. Amenities that contribute to the livability of cities are now in short supply. The stock of open spaces has not kept up with population growth, especially in older core cities. While some suburbs at the edges of metropolises have added new open space, the overall metropolitan outcome has been uneven and unequal. While the wealthy suburbs flaunt their bridle paths, golf courses, jogging trails, tennis courts, and nature reserves,[1] more-moderate-income, older, and inner-city communities struggle to keep up with the growing demand for baseball diamonds, basketball courts, and soccer fields.

The shortage and inequity in the distribution of urban open space are symptomatic of larger transformations of public space and, indeed, of the public realm. Under way for some time, these changes reflect political, economic, and technological changes and make us wary. Because we do not fully grasp their implications, three key and interrelated trends continue to provoke our collective anxiety.

- First, there is a general agreement that we are experiencing a steady withering of the public realm, a trend recently exacerbated by a worldwide campaign for market liberalism and downsizing governments. As a result, we are witnessing a corresponding and palpable decline in the levels of goods and services historically provided by the government. As the traditional role and the fiscal capacity of government have shrunk, the role of the private, and to a limited extent, that of the nonprofit sectors has increased. While the growing involvement of the nonprofit sector has mitigated some of the slack created by the withdrawal of government, privatization—the "commodification" of public goods and emergence of local governments as entrepreneurs—seems to be the order of the day.
- Second, emerging conflicts and tensions at the local level over the economy, environment, and equity are becoming a by-product of a larger restructuring of the global economy characterized by growth of transnational corporate power, international labor mobility, polarized local and global economies, and subservience of local public interest to interests of global capital.
- Finally, the dizzying pace of the information and communication technology revolution is contributing to profound changes in the traditional concepts of place and community, local versus global interests, individual and group identities, and the nature of daily commerce and social relations.

Collectively, these trends represent fundamental shifts in the way public life and space are conceptualized and in the values associated with them. I argue in this article that the future designs and plans for public space must be based on an understanding of the causes and consequences of these trends and the changing nature of public life.

Social values of urban open spaces

Any discussion of the future of public spaces must necessarily begin with a retrospective view of the evolution of values and symbolism associated with urban open spaces in the past century. In the second half of the 19th century, most major cities of America—initially Boston, Chicago, New York, and San Francisco and later Buffalo, Detroit, Kansas City, Louisville, and Rochester—acquired large chunks of land within the city and transformed them into major urban parks or park systems.[2] A legacy of these turn-of-the-century cities, today they continue to serve as a major civic resource. Indeed, as Rybczynski (1999) points out, the urban park systems are probably the only exception to the otherwise privatized world of city building, where private monuments, department stores, railroad stations, skyscrapers, sports stadiums, and the like have dominated the American cityscape. The park system represented an attempt to humanize the utilitarian form of American cities. This was reflected in Frederick Law Olmsted's designs for parks and his writings about creating order and structure in the expanding industrial cities of the late 19th and early 20th centuries.[3] According to Rosenfield (1989), a scholar of American rhetoric, "the public park served for the nineteenth-century urban democracy much the same function that civic oratory or eloquence served in traditional republican societies: to celebrate institutions and ideological principles thought to be the genius of those cultures" (p. 222). He argues further that in the American context public parks served to inspire republican virtue in several forms: civic pride; social contact, especially between people from diverse backgrounds; a sense of freedom; and finally, common sense (as in aesthetic standards and public taste). Thus the civilizing virtues of public parks extolled in Olmsted's designs and writings can be more broadly interpreted to include democratic ideals, good citizenship, civic responsibilities, and, ultimately, the essential social compact that constitutes the core of civil society.

Such rhetorical interpretations of the urban park, while elegant and uplifting, begged the very question of class, ethnicity, and income inequality. Social contact, especially with people of different backgrounds, was acknowledged as one of the values of open space, but almost in denial of the everyday reality of the class and ethnic ecology of American cities and the conflicts and contradictions it represented. For example, the urban parks created in the latter half of the 19th century served mainly as pleasure grounds of the upper-class elite (Cranz, 1989). Because many were located on the periphery of the city, they remained domains of the rich and the elite, beyond the reach of the poor and the working class.[4]

In the progressive era of the early 20th century, health, hygiene, and recreational opportunities for the public, especially the working class living in the congested inner cities, became the principal reasons for open space. Easy access to open space was often integral not only to metropolitan or regional planning concepts (see Sussman, 1976), but also to community- and neighborhood-scale design, epitomized by Clarence Stein's famous Radburn Plan (see Parsons, 1999) and Clarence Perry's Neighborhood Unit concept (see Banerjee & Baer, 1984).[5] These secular objectives, inspired by Ebenezer Howard and the English Garden Cities, were proposed as an antidote to the crowded and polluted environment of the industrial city. In their 1933 Athens Charter, the International Congress of Modern Architecture (CIAM [its acronym in French]) strongly endorsed the provision of urban open spaces as an essential principle of modern town planning, referring to open spaces as the lungs of the city.

Thus the Olmstedian view of civic pride and republican virtue that inspired the earlier parks systems of American cities was transformed into a more secular and communitarian view of a public realm advanced by the progressive ideas of the CIAM and Regional Plan Association of America. Since then, parks and open space in American cities have been identified with recreation, physical and mental health, communion with nature, and the like, making them a public good and service.

As a public good, standards for purveying open space would become codified through parks and recreation standards officially adopted nationwide. In the late 1940s the Committee on Hygiene and Healthful Housing of the American Public Health Association (1948) published *Planning the Neighborhood,* a book of standards that codified the open space requirements in urban areas and promoted local and neighborhood parks in proximate relationship with the local schools. Eventually these standards became the principle for open space and the community facilities elements of general plans, required by state enabling legislation or the 701 Program of the U.S. Department of Housing and Urban Development (HUD). In promoting the public service aspect, parks departments were now more directly involved in programming and organizing recreational events, and their focus was more on social utility of parks than on their earlier aesthetic merits and civilizing aims. Thus, Forest Park in St. Louis, originally designed in 1880 in the Olmstedian tradition, was redone at the turn of the century as a collection of golf courses, tennis courts, museums, zoos, and other such utilitarian facilities (Heckscher, 1977).[6]

Thus, what began as part of a grand civic design movement gradually became more populist, more institutionalized, and more bureaucratized as part of planning the rational city (see Boyer, 1983). In the absence of sufficient capital budgets, however, open space requirements as postulated in city general plans remained advisory and mainly unrealized. Furthermore, budget cuts of the mid-1970s had a disastrous effect on cities' ability to even keep up the current stock. New York City, with some 26,000 acres of public parks, is a case in point: Its maintenance staff was cut almost in half during this period (Siegel, 1992). With declining maintenance, parks became vulnerable to abuses and were shunned by the public. Studies conducted in the 1970s questioned the validity of contemporary open space standards given the lack of use of parks in the inner city (Gold, 1972).

Furthermore, in recent years, market protagonists have begun to challenge the very assumption that parks and open spaces, along with such other public facilities and services, necessarily have to be a public good (see Richardson & Gordon, 1993, for example). Indeed, financially strapped cities are already forced to rely on private resources to create open spaces like the corporate plazas commonplace in downtown America today (see Loukaitou-Sideris & Banerjee, 1998). Meanwhile, privately owned shopping malls continue to capture much of the public life in America while its Main Street languishes. Privatization of public life and spaces is the focus of the following section.

Decline of the public realm: a narrative of loss

In common parlance, public space is associated with parks, playgrounds, or systems of open space

that are obviously in the public realm. But not all open spaces are in the public realm, and for that matter not all public spaces may be open, in the sense of being either alfresco or accessible and free. Many years ago Kevin Lynch (1972) asked these questions quite succinctly: How open are our open spaces? Are they accessible physically as well as psychologically? Are they widely available and amenable to user control? Are they distributed equally or equitably in an urban region? If they are not, then are they all truly public or democratic?[7]

In recent years the concern for public space has extended beyond the questions of adequacy and distributive equity of parks and open spaces. They are now subsumed under a broader narrative of loss[8] that emphasizes an overall decline of the public realm and public space. Several themes characterize this narrative of loss, some focusing on the public space and public life, other on aspects of social capital and civil society. Discussions that focus on the atrophy of American public life have sought to find historical causes and culprits. These include, in chronological order, the early resistance of American Puritanism to pleasure and decadence associated with public life; the advent of industrialization that preordained the dominance of the automobile; the flight of the American middle class from the inner city; the Modern movement in architecture, which glamorized the urban grid; and the economics of cheap and expedient land development (Hitt et al., 1990). To these one could add zoning, suburban shopping malls and office parks, strip malls, and urban sprawl, all of which have been the subject of critical writings in recent years (Garreau, 1991; Kowinski, 1985; Kunstler, 1993). Others concede that the kind of social cohesion necessary for enduring public life typical of many homogeneous cultures is difficult to obtain in the U.S., where the public remains heterogeneous and pluralistic (Hitt et al., 1990; Sennett, 1988).

It has been suggested also that the decline of the public realm is paralleled by a corresponding decline in the public spirit, which resides in the very core of our collective intuitions of civil society. Using Jane Jacobs' term "social capital" to describe the civic virtue that constitutes the spirit of trust and citizenry, Putnam (1993) has argued that such civic formations as "singing groups" and "soccer clubs" actually may improve local governance in modern societies. Yet, echoing the narrative of loss, Putnam (1995, 1996) has also suggested that since World War II there has been a precipitous decline in the civic spirit in the U.S. He attributes this decline to the growing exposure to television (and today, one supposes, the Internet) and the privatization of leisure activities.[9]

Still another aspect of this narrative of loss involves public incivilities and loss of territorial control as explanations for the retreat of the general public from spaces in the public realm. According to this view, the steady decline in the quality and supply of public spaces is a product of a general decline of civility and decorum in public spaces. The "broken window" syndrome—weakened social control and lack of enforcement—is widespread in the inner city, and panhandlers, drug-dealers, and the homeless have expropriated public spaces. The presence of graffiti, trash, and vandalism intimidate the general public. According to one protagonist, such public spaces should be recaptured through strict regulation of land use and behavior in public (Ellickson, 1996).[10]

Privatization of public life and spaces

For many observers, the sense that the public realm is declining is further corroborated by a growing trend of what is commonly described as "privatized" public spaces. (Or should we say "publicized" private spaces, as some might wonder?) Seemingly an oxymoron, the term is used commonly to describe the corporate plazas and open spaces, shopping malls, and other such settings that are increasingly popular destinations for the public. Of course, none of these privately owned and managed spaces is truly public, even though they might have been created through incentive zoning programs of an earlier era, in exchange for additional Floor Area Ratio (FAR) for the developer and the property owner (see Frieden & Sagalyn, 1989; Loukaitou-Sideris & Banerjee, 1998). There is a presumption of "publicness" in these pseudo-public spaces. But in reality they are in the private realm. In many parts of downtown business districts, a thin brass line or a groove cut in the sidewalk, often accompanied by an embedded sign, makes it clear that the seemingly unbounded public space is not boundaryless after all. The owner has all the legal prerogatives to exclude someone from the space circumscribed by sometimes subtle and often invisible property boundaries. The public is welcome as long as they are patrons of shops and restaurants, office workers, or clients of businesses located on the premises. But access to and use of the space is only a privilege, not a right. In San Francisco, the planning department requires owners to post a sign declaring that the space is

"provided and maintained for the Enjoyment of the Public [sic]"[11] but any expectation that such spaces are open to all is fanciful at best. Many of these spaces are closely monitored by security guards and closed circuit television cameras, which has prompted critics such as Mike Davis (1990) to refer to them as "fortress" environments. Because of their designs, locations, and management policies,[12] for the most part corporate open spaces remain insular and mostly empty, save for perhaps a lunchtime crowd and occasional clusters of smokers. Heroic efforts like San Francisco's to the contrary, limitations of public access and use of such spaces have been taken for granted in most cities.

Shopping malls, however, are a different story. Over the last 50 years, shopping malls have become the "new downtown" (Rybczynski, 1993) and replaced the Main Street culture of America to become perhaps the most ubiquitous and frequently visited places today (Kowinski, 1985). When the kind of public activities typical of downtown public spaces—distribution of leaflets, political discussions and speeches, solicitation for funds or signatures, sale of home-baked cookies, voter registration, and the like—started to occur in the shopping malls, their managers responded by excluding such activities and people. Legal challenges ensued. The issue of public access in shopping malls has been tested in the U.S. Supreme Court and the highest courts of seven different states (for details, see International Council of Shopping Centers, 1987). The critical question in all of these court cases was whether the shopping centers, by dint of becoming a de facto downtown, could also be considered the kind of public forum that the downtowns once represented. As of 1987, only Massachusetts and Washington courts had ruled in favor of requiring public access, while Connecticut, New York, North Carolina, Michigan, and Pennsylvania allowed denial in their decisions (International Council of Shopping Centers, 1987). In sum, more often than not shopping centers are not to be construed as public forums.[13] The same principle applies to corporate plazas.

Collectively, the shopping malls, corporate plazas, arcades, galleries, and many such contrived or themed settings create an illusion of public space, from which the risks and uncertainties of everyday life are carefully edited out. The distinction thus created between the private and public are not unlike Mircea Eliade's (1987) notion of sacred and profane spaces, or Mary Douglas' (1980) treatise on purity and danger as the basis for separating the unwanted from our public experience. Thus the sanctity of the private spaces is preserved by excluding what Lofland (1989) refers to as the "unholy" and "unwashed"—the panhandlers, the winos, the homeless, and simply the urban poor. In many cities, in the name of pedestrian safety or extreme weather, public agencies have planned and built networks of underground tunnels, sky bridges, and pedways to connect these insular corporate spaces. This has created what Trevor Boddy (1992) calls the "analogous city," or a city of contrived urban spaces that keeps out the poor and undesirables.

It seems that proliferation of such insular and protected spaces has extended beyond the business and shopping districts of the city. In recent years we have seen a phenomenal growth of gated communities throughout the U.S. (Blakely & Snyder, 1997). When asked why they chose to live in gated communities, most respondents spoke of the need for safety and a search for community, presumably one that is based on homogeneity and cohesion. The result is the spread of a "club phenomenon," an apt metaphor used some years ago by Charles Tiebout (1956) and his colleagues to explain the political economy of metropolitan fragmentation involving multiple autonomous municipalities (Ostrom et al., 1961).[14] The study by Blakely and Snyder suggests that this tendency to live in club-like communities with common spaces and facilities arises from a fear of strangers, especially of those who come from a different class, culture, ethnicity, or national origin, and not just a concern for personal and property safety.

Interestingly, the search for utopia in such controlled communities has become both an object and a subject of the expanding domain of the entertainment industry. The life portrayed in the movie *The Truman Show*, filmed in the original New Urbanist icon of Seaside, Florida, is a caricature of programmed but insular private and public life in a controlled setting. While the utopian life may be an object of entertainment in *The Truman Show*, The Disney Corporation takes the search for utopia seriously in the planning and development of Celebration, a planned new community not too far from Disney World in another corner of Florida. Only 3 years old, this company town is an edited New Urbanist utopia that emulates the quintessence of the 18th, 19th, and early 20th century American towns, and a clear departure from Walt Disney's initial dream of a high-tech utopia. Although, as Kurt Andersen (1999) points out, "Celebration is the real EPCOT—the quasi-democratic, postmodern fulfillment of Walt's totalitarian, late-modern vision" (p. 74). Entertainment-based corporate vision even provides the script for uses of the "public" realm and

space, such as Disney music or Christmas carols piped in through loudspeakers installed in the streets or fake snow falling in the downtown at night (Andersen, 1999).[15]

If Celebration successfully combines the communitarian ideals—the "trap," as David Harvey (1997) would argue—and a hyper-reality, as suggested by Umberto Eco (1990), that only Disney can so effectively and professionally construct and orchestrate, what does it presage about the future of the public realm? Andersen (1999) speculates that Celebration may in fact set the stage for reinventing the suburb and may influence public taste to demand similar buildings and places in the future. The real question is whether such products will come packaged only in the form of insular and gated communities. If that happens to be the trend, the democratic ideals of public space and the public realm will no doubt atrophy further. Yet the brand of public life offered by Disneyland and its cohorts continues to intrigue such noted observers as Charles Moore (1965) and Umberto Eco (1990), who concede that while contrived, these settings offer clean, efficient, and predictable encounters and experiences. The entry fee guarantees that and, in the words of Charles Moore, "You have to pay for public life" (p. 57). The public seems to agree and be willing. Disney's command of the future of public life and space may in fact be a *fait accompli*, according to some observers (see Ghirardo, 1996).

Invented streets: a public life of *flânerie* and "third places"

The sense of loss associated with the perceived decline of public space assumes that effective public life is linked to a viable public realm. This is because the concept of public life is inseparable from the idea of a "public sphere" (Habermas, 1989) and the notion of civil society, where the affairs of the public are discussed and debated in public places. The domain of the public sphere is seen to exist between the privacy of the individual and domestic life and the state (or the government).

But there is another concept of public life that is derived from our desire for relaxation, social contact, entertainment, leisure, and simply having a good time. Individual orbits of this public life are shaped by a consumer culture and the opportunities offered by the new "experience economy" (Pine & Gilmore, 1999). The settings for such public life are not necessarily public spaces. According to Ray Oldenburg

(1989), such settings can be called "third places," as opposed to the first place of home or the second place of work or school. These are places such as bars or taverns, beauty salons, pool halls, sidewalk cafés, and the like. There are culture-specific third places—the pubs of England, sidewalk cafés of Paris, and beer gardens of Germany, for example—that have been historically associated with the culture and urbanism of different cities. Today, Starbuck's coffee shops, Barnes and Noble or Borders bookstores, health clubs, video rental stores, and various combinations thereof have become major icons of the third place in many American cities.

Theme parks are the epitome of the invented place and capture some aspects of our collective public life, but they are not third places. Created often as facsimiles of some distant place or time—past or future—theme parks are corporate productions within the tourism and entertainment industry. The art of contrivance, the special effects, and the stage sets are all by-products of the film industry, and it should not be any surprise that many of the theme parks are created and managed by subsidiaries of Disney, Universal Studios, MGM, and the like (see Fjellman, 1992). Much has been written recently about the role of corporate theme parks in leading the way for the packaging and selling of urban places, including the recently built fantasy environments of Las Vegas (Boyer, 1992; Gottdeiner, 1998; Hannigan, 1998; Huxtable, 1997; Sorkin, 1992). Relatively less has been said about the reasons why these contrived settings are so successful in drawing the public, other than that they provide entertainment, an essential ingredient of the experience economy (Moustafa, 1999; Pine & Gilmore, 1999).

Looking, gazing, and watching are all part of our normal stimulus-seeking behavior, as any textbook in cognitive theory would confirm. The cultural and social context of this behavior, however, has received much attention in the critical literature on the urbanism of modernity. Many of the writings focus on the relationship between the observer and the environment, and how the built form was created and shaped to facilitate the display of merchandise for mass consumption. The setting for these analyses is usually Paris in the late 19th century, immediately after its Haussmanian transformation. The subject of this literature is the *flâneur*, the person who engages in *flânerie*, "the activity of strolling and looking" (Tester, 1994, p. 1). The arcades of Paris are considered the epitome of settings for such activities, and their forms and functions have become a subject of writings on comparative urbanism (see Geist, 1983).

These arcades were the earliest forms of privatized public places and the precursor of modern department stores, shopping malls, and the invented streets—streets created as stage sets—of the Western world.

Today, it is the appropriate mix of *flânerie* and third places that dictates the script for a successful public life. The new shopping malls are now designed to encourage *flânerie* and "hanging out." Horton Plaza in San Diego, City Walk in Universal City, and Two Rodeo in Beverly Hills are all examples of these invented streets that attempt to combine *flânerie* with a third place.

The same formula is also applied to reinvented streets and places like Third Street Promenade in Santa Monica, Quincy Market in Boston, South Street Seaport in New York, Fremont Street in Las Vegas, Harborplace in Baltimore, and of course the most celebrated reinvention of the century, Times Square in New York City. Without doubt they are themed environments: Horton Plaza uses metaphors such as "Italian Hill Town"; CityWalk claims to be an interpretation of Los Angeles itself; Two Rodeo tries to look like a European shopping street; and Times Square has become a multimedia tribute to America's communication and entertainment industries. These reinvented places usually derive their design metaphors and marketing rhetoric from the history of the place, as is the case for South Street Seaport, Quincy Market, and Harborplace. In all of these cases, the attempt is to create a public life of *flânerie* and consumerism; whether it actually takes place in a private or public space does not seem to matter. The line between public and private spaces blurs very easily, as was the case in the Parisian arcades.

In the tradition of earlier civic design, American architects and planners often romanticized European urban spaces, and tried to recreate them in American cities, but without success (see Dyckman, 1962). The expectation was that if we design the space, activities will happen. This type of physical determinism proved wrong time and again, but the practice still continues in the urban design of civic centers and similar public spaces. Yet, the success of these invented streets and reinvented places demonstrates—as the developers have discovered, if unwittingly—a shift of emphasis from form to function—that being *flânerie*. Not that form does not matter, but it need not be tied to formal layouts of Apollonian spaces of exclusive civic and institutional uses. The message is that the form is only a stage set that can be easily changed and embellished to accommodate celebrations, happenings, and other such ephemera (see Schuster, 2001). There is no need to copy European urban form. The American city can be the model now: New Orleans Square in Disneyland, CityWalk in Universal City, Hollywood Boulevard or New York Street in Disney World, New York New York in Las Vegas.

"Convivial cities" and "insurgent citizenship" in a globalizing era

Lisa Peattie (1998) has argued that while planners usually seem to be obsessed with creating or restoring a sense of community, they have given very little attention to conviviality as a planning goal. Conviviality, Peattie argues, is more than just feasting and fun, drinking and good company. Using Illich's (1973) original definition of conviviality as "autonomous and creative intercourse among persons, and the intercourse of persons with their environment" (p. 11), Peattie (1998) speaks of sociable pleasures as purposeful activities. And these may include not just singing in pubs, street dancing, or tailgate parties, but also "small-group rituals and social bonding in serious collective action, from barn raisings and neighborhood cleanups to civil disobedience that blocks the streets or invades the missile site" (p. 246). Clearly, many of these communal public actions typically happen in existing public spaces—streets, squares, parks, and other open spaces or in such public buildings as school auditoriums or community centers—thus reasserting the role and sustenance of the public realm. However, one wonders whether Peattie's ideal of democratic conviviality that bonds people in communal public actions is becoming increasing vestigial and episodic in the face of a market propensity to service conviviality needs in the form of a growing number of third places in invented streets and spaces. Is the typical consumer public completely co-opted by the public life of third places and invented streets?

But there is hope still for Peattie's ideal. In a perverse way this hope stems from a globalizing economy that produces several tensions and contradictions. It is reflected in the recent demonstrations against the World Trade Organization meeting in Seattle, the International Monetary Fund/World Bank meeting in Washington, and the Asian Development Bank meeting in Bangkok. The tensions symbolize powerlessness of the local public over global corporate interests; inexorable trends of cultural homogenization; growing income polarization; environmental degradation on a local and global scale; a crisis of cultural, local, and social identities in

multiethnic urban communities; and the like. These demonstrations are expressions of frustration over a lack of local control, which increasingly leads to mobilization at the local and neighborhood level. An example of such local activism is the recent charter reform of the City of Los Angeles, which mandates the formation of neighborhood councils. As such initiatives occur, it can be expected that much of the interest will focus on improving the livability of local streets and neighborhoods and the shared public realm. In some cities, community activism helped convert abandoned or vacant lots into vest-pocket parks or neighborhood playgrounds. In many inner-city neighborhoods, immigrant communities have brought street life back into the community. There is a general growth in the neighborhood-based non-profit groups that are taking charge of community improvements—from affordable housing to small business development—and thus infusing conviviality and creating third places even in poorer neighborhoods that the conventional market sees as too risky for investment. Thus, the claim to local public space can arise from a variety of insurgent citizenship and community initiatives (see Holston, 1995; Sassen, 1995). Could this be the beginning of a movement to reclaim the public realm at the community level?

The communication and information technology revolution

The recent revolution in communication and information technology has made it possible for us to isolate ourselves from the public life and spaces even further. We are now all citizens of cyberspace and cybercommunities ("cyborgs," according to Mitchell, 1995) where conventional concepts of public space and place are increasingly becoming outmoded. The *terra cognita* of the "City of Bits" has very little bearing to the territorial city of senses, or for that matter our conventional concepts of public and private spaces. What concerns many is whether this cybercity and its cyberplaces may totally obviate the social life of real places and communities. For it is now possible to conduct many of our daily activities—work, shopping, business transactions, socializing—through the Internet, minimizing the need for face-to-face communication or travel. Thus, the transaction costs of living in cities can be minimized by belonging to a network society, which further reduces the need for public encounters in public spaces.

Indeed, we now wonder how communication technology might revolutionize our ways of living, and what effect it might have on conventional urban form. We can now shop with the click of a mouse. But will that obviate construction of new shopping malls? Will e-commerce lead to the closing of older, languishing shopping centers and malls? What will be the alternative uses of such spaces? If more and more workers stay home and telecommute, will that lead to a stronger sense of localities and local public spaces? Will it lead to the revival of the community main streets and third places?

The communication technology revolution may also presage other developments that could further negate public life and the public realm. The cyborgian life might lead to greater isolation, withdrawal, and anomie. It may lead to what former Labor Secretary Robert Reich (1991) had referred to as the secession of the successful, now to an analogous city in cyberspace. Seemingly, the duality of a public city of the poor and dependent population and a private city of the successful will continue on the two sides of the digital divide.

Epilogue

I would not want to end this essay with the impression that public initiatives are totally dead as far as public space is concerned. This is not quite the case. It seems that throughout the United States, scattered efforts are underway to create new open space under local, state, and federal initiatives of various sorts. Certainly the economic growth and prosperity of the 1990s has helped to finance such initiatives. The 1991 Intermodal Surface Transportation Efficiency Act and more recently the Transportation Equity Act for the 21st Century, authorized by Congress in 1998 to fix America's aging infrastructure, have created new opportunities to transform inner-city transportation rights of way for productive public space. Boston's "Big Dig" is a case in point. Putting the city's central artery underground will create 27 acres of new ground space in a premier downtown location, of which three quarters or about 20 acres will remain open. Earlier, San Francisco created major waterfront promenades and access by demolishing the Embarcadero Freeway. The Freeway Park that Seattle built in the 1970s to link the Capitol Hill neighborhood to the downtown is another example of a creative public project to produce new open space over transportation infrastructure.

Similarly, public efforts to create parks and open spaces in conjunction with safe neighborhoods or land and water conservation programs continue, and seemingly are gaining strength. A detailed review of such programs currently existing at the federal and local levels is not possible within the scope of this article. But the recent passage of Proposition 12 in California that allows the State to raise $2.1 billion through general obligation bonds to spend on the acquisition, development, and protection of new and existing cultural, natural, and recreational areas is a case in point. In the metropolitan areas of California, the State's $854-million budget for the first year has provided a major boost for parks and recreation projects. Whether such initiatives will spread throughout the country to signal a new revival of civic and public values remains to be seen. Let's hope they do.

Notes

1. According to Southworth and Parthasarathy (1996) large quantities of open space are in public ownership in suburbia, but not all of it is accessible to the public. It belongs to public utilities, water districts, or is simply not suitable for development. They note also that public space is often used for ornamental or aesthetic purposes.

2. In most instances these were designed by Frederick Law Olmsted and Calvert Vaux.

3. S. B. Sutton (1971), editor of Olmsted's writings, comments, "Olmsted believed, with his contemporaries, in the spiritual progress of man. As a landscape architect he tried, above all, to civilize the city; his parks simulated nature in response to the needs of an urban population" (p. 1). For a discussion on Olmsted's views implicit in his open space plan for Los Angeles, see Hise and Deverall (2000).

4. In fact, sports and games typically enjoyed by the urban working class and various ethnic groups were overtly discouraged from these urban spaces (Cranz, 1989). Scholars of modernity would also point out today that while women were considered an essential element of the family functions of the pleasure garden, they were probably not expected to be there on their own, as in any other public spaces (Fraser, 1993; Friedberg, 1994).

5. The Radburn Plan itself represented an attempt to organize housing around a public realm of a unified system of parks and open spaces. In 1928 Stein (quoted in Parsons, 1999) wrote:

   The backbone of all our cities and towns has been the highways, the means of getting from place to place. In this New Town the backbone of the community will be the parks. All houses will face on gardens. Every child will be able to walk to school without crossing a single road. Every house will be within a minute's walk of a park as wide as a New York City block. Here the little tots may amuse themselves in the sand. Here the younger children may play in safety. Here the grown children and adults may enjoy themselves with tennis, quoits, or other sports, and here those who want quiet and escape from the mad movement of the automobile may walk for a mile or more in parks out of sight of highways. (p. 150)

6. In 1911 the St. Louis Parks Department ceased to exist and became the Division of Parks and Recreation of the Department of Public Welfare.
7. Although Lynch did not quite use the term "public," the sense was quite implicit in his discussions.
8. A term used by Margaret Crawford, currently at Harvard University Graduate School of Design, in a video interview conducted at USC in 1996.
9. Not all agree with Putnam's conclusion. Lemann (1996), for example, argues that while Americans might be bowling alone, they are increasingly "kicking in groups," referring to the growing popularity of youth soccer and parents' involvement in such group activities.
10. In recent years, City authorities in New York and San Francisco, have adopted aggressive programs to remove homeless people from major public spaces. Although denounced by homeless groups, these rules make it difficult for the homeless to assemble in some parks, subway stations, and bus and train terminals. In Los Angeles, Pershing Square was reclaimed through an expensive face lift.
11. From a plaque posted at the entrance to Grabhorn Park in San Francisco (see Loukaitou-Sideris & Banerjee, 1998, p. 204).
12. For detailed discussions of these issues, see Loukaitou-Sideris and Banerjee (1998).
13. The International Council of Shopping Centers (1987) has conducted extensive surveys of policies on what is allowed and what is not, including types of groups and various constraints.
14. For a more recent discussion of the Tieboutian club phenomenon, see Heikkila (1996).
15. For the original stories in the two books on Celebration reviewed by Andersen, see Ross (1999) and Frantz and Collins (1999).

References

American Public Health Association, Committee on Hygiene of Housing. (1948). *Planning the neighborhood.* Chicago: Public Administration Service.

Andersen, K. (1999, September 6). Pleasantville: Can Disney reinvent the burbs? *The New Yorker*, pp. 74–79.

Appleyard, D. (1981). *Livable streets.* Berkeley: University of California Press.

Banerjee, T., & Baer, W. C. (1984). *Beyond the neighborhood unit: Residential environments and public policy.* New York: Plenum Press.

Blakely, E., & Snyder, M. G. (1997). *Fortress America: Gated communities in the United States.* Washington, DC: Brookings Institution Press.

Boddy, T. (1992). Underground and overhead: Building the analogous city. In M. Sorkin (Ed.), *Variations on a theme park* (pp. 123–153). New York: Noonday Press.

Boyer, M. C. (1983). *The rational city: The myth of American city planning.* Cambridge, MA: MIT Press.

Boyer, M. C. (1992). Cities for sale: Merchandising history at South Street Seaport. In M. Sorkin (Ed.), *Variations on a theme park* (pp. 181–204). New York: Noonday Press.

Cranz, G. (1989). *The politics of park design: A history of urban parks in America.* Cambridge, MA: MIT Press.

Davis, M. (1990). *City of quartz: Excavating the future in Los Angeles.* New York: Verso.

Douglas, M. (1980). *Purity and danger: An analysis of concepts of pollution and taboo.* London: Routledge.

Dyckman, J. W. (1962). The European motherland of American urban romanticism. *Journal of the American Institute of Planners, 28,* 277–281.

Eco, U. (1990). *Travels in hyperreality.* Orlando, FL: Harcourt, Brace & Company.

Eliade, M. (1987). *The sacred and the profane: The nature of religion.* San Diego: Harcourt, Brace, Jovanovich.

Ellickson, R. C. (1996). Controlling chronic misconduct in city spaces: Of panhandlers, skid rows, and public space zoning. *Yale Law Review, 105*(5), 1165–1248.

Fjellman, S. M. (1992). *Vinyl leaves: Walt Disney World and America.* Boulder, CO: Westview Press.

Frantz, D., & Collins, C. (1999). *Celebration, U.S.A.* New York: Holt

Fraser, N. (1993). Rethinking the public sphere: A contribution to the critique of actually existing democracy. In B. Robbins (Ed.), *The phantom public sphere* (pp. 1–32). Minneapolis: University of Minnesota Press.

Friedberg, A. (1994). *Window shopping: Cinema and the postmodern.* Berkeley: University of California Press.

Frieden, B., & Sagalyn, L. H. (1989). *Downtown Inc.* Cambridge, MA: MIT Press.

Garreau, J. (1991). *Edge city: Life on the new frontier.* New York: Doubleday.

Geist, J. F. (1983). *Arcades: The history of a building type.* Cambridge, MA: MIT Press.

Ghirardo, D. (1996). *Architecture after modernism.* London: Thames and Hudson.

Gold, S. M. (1972). Nonuse of neighborhood parks. *Journal of the American Institute of Planners, 38,* 369–378.

Gottdeiner, M. (1998). *The theming of America.* Boulder, CO: Westview Press.

Habermas, J. (1989 [1962]) *The structural transformation of the public sphere: An enquiry into a category of bourgeois society.* Translated from German by Thomas Burger. Cambridge, MA: MIT Press.

Hannigan, J. (1998). *Fantasy city.* New York: Routledge.

Harvey, D. (1997, Winter/Spring). The new urbanism and the communitarian trap. *Harvard Design Magazine,* <http://www.gsd.harvard.edu/hdm/harvey.htm>.

Heckscher, A. (1977). *Open spaces: The life of American Cities.* New York: Harper & Row.

Heikkila, E. (1996). Are municipalities Tieboutian clubs? *Regional Science and Urban Economics, 26,* 203–226.

Hise, G., & Deverall, W. (2000). *Eden by design: The 1930 Olmsted-Bartholomew plan for the Los Angeles region.* Berkeley: University of California Press.

Hitt, J., Fleming, R. L., Plater-Zyberk, E., Sennett, R., Wines, J., & Zimmerman, E. (1990, July). Whatever became of the public square? *Harper's Magazine,* pp. 49–53, 56–60.

Holston, J. (1995). Spaces of insurgent citizenship. *Planning Theory, 13,* 35–51.

Huxtable, A. L. (1997). *The unreal America: Architecture and illusion*. New York: New Press, distributed by W.W. Norton.

Illich, I. (1973). *Tools for conviviality*. New York: Harper & Row.

International Council of Shopping Centers. (1987). *Public access: The rights of shopping centers to restrict the use of malls for political and other noncommercial activities*. New York: Author.

Jacobs, A. B. (1993). *Great streets*. Cambridge, MA: MIT Press.

Koenig, H. (1995, December). The French mirror. *Atlantic Monthly*, pp. 95–106.

Kowinski, W. S. (1985). *The malling of America: An inside look at the great consumer paradise*. New York: Morrow.

Kunstler, J. H. (1993). *The geography of nowhere: The rise and decline of America's man-made landscape*. New York: Simon & Schuster.

Lemann, N. (1996, April). Kicking in groups. *Atlantic Monthly*, pp. 22–26.

Lofland, L. (1989). The morality of urban public life: The emergence and continuation of a debate. *Places, 6*(1), 18–23.

Loukaitou-Sideris, A. (1995). Urban form and social context: Cultural differentiation in the meaning and uses of neighborhood parks. *Journal of Planning Education and Research, 14*(2), 101–114.

Loukaitou-Sideris, A., & Banerjee, T. (1998). *Urban design downtown: Poetics and politics of form*. Berkeley: University of California Press.

Lynch, K. (1972) (1990). Openness of open spaces. In T. Banerjee & M. Southworth (Eds.), *City sense and city design: Writings and projects of Kevin Lynch* (pp. 396–412). Cambridge, MA: MIT Press.

Mitchell, W. (1995). *The city of bits*. Cambridge, MA: MIT Press.

Moore, C. (1965). You have to pay for the public life. *PERSPECTA, 9/10. The Yale Architecture Magazine*, pp. 58–97

Moudon, A. V. (Ed.) (1987). *Public streets for public use*. New York: Van Nostrand Reinhold.

Moustafa, A. A. (1999). Transformations in the urban experience: Public life in private places. Unpublished Ph.D. dissertation, University of Southern California.

Oldenburg, R. (1989). *The great good place: Cafés, coffee shops, community centers, beauty parlors, general stores, bars, hangouts, and how they get through the day*. New York: Paragon House.

Ostrom, E., Tiebout, C., & Warren, R. (1961). The organization of government in metropolitan areas: A theoretical inquiry. *American Political Science Review, 55*, 831–842.

Parsons, K. C. (Ed.) (1999). *The writings of Clarence Stein: Architect of the planned community*. Baltimore: Johns Hopkins University Press.

Peattie, L. (1998). Convivial cities. In J. Friedmann & M. Douglass (Eds.), *Cities for citizens: Planning and the rise of civil society in a global age*. Chichester, NY: John Wiley & Sons.

Pine, J. B., & Gilmore, J.H. (1999). *The experience economy: Work is theatre and every business a stage*. Boston: Harvard Business School.

Putnam, R. D. with Leonardi, R., & Nanetti, R.Y. (1993). *Making democracy work: Civic traditions in modern Italy*. Princeton, NJ: Princeton University Press.

Putnam, R. D. (1995, January). Bowling alone: America's declining social capital. *Journal of Democracy, 6*(1), 65–78.

Putnam, R. D. (1996, Winter). The strange disappearance of civic America. *The American Prospect, 24*[On-line]. Available: <http://www.prospect.org/archives/24/24putn.html>.

Ramati, R. (1981). *How to save your street*. Garden City, NJ: Dolphin Books.

Reich, R. B. (1991, January 20). Secession of the successful. *New York Times Magazine*, pp. 16–17.

Richardson, H. W., & Gordon, P. (1993). Market planning: Oxymoron or common sense. *Journal of the American Planning Association, 59*, 347–352.

Rosenfield, L. W. (1989). Central park and the celebration of civic virtue. In T. Benson (Ed.), *American rhetoric: Context and criticism* (pp. 221–266). Carbondale: Southern Illinois Press.

Ross, A. (1999). *The Celebration chronicles*. New York: Ballantine.

Rybczynski, W. (1993). The new downtowns. *Atlantic Monthly, 271*(5), 98–106.

Rybczynski, W. (1999, Summer). Why we need Olmsted again. *Wilson Quarterly, 23*(3), 15–21.

Sassen, S. (1995). Whose city is it? Globalization and the formation of new claims. *Public Culture, 8*, 205–223.

Schuster, M. (2001). Ephemera, temporary urbanism and imaging. In L. J. Vale & S.B. Warner, Jr. (Eds.), *Imaging the city: Continuing struggles and new directions*. New Brunswick, NJ: Rutgers University Center for Urban Policy Research Press.

Sennett, R. (1988). The *civitas* of seeing. *Places, 5*(4), 82–84.

Siegel, F. (1992). Reclaiming our public spaces. In Philip Kasinitz (Ed.), *Metropolis: Center and symbol of our times*. New York: New York University Press.

Sorkin, M. (Ed.) (1992). *Variations on a theme park*. New York: Noonday Press.

Southworth, M., & Parthasarathy, B. (1996). The suburban public realm: Its emergence, growth and transformation in the American metropolis. *Journal of Urban Design, 1*(3), 245–263.

Sussman, C. (1976). *Planning the fourth migration: The neglected vision of the Regional Planning Association of America*. Cambridge, MA: MIT Press.

Sutton, S. B. (Ed.) (1971). *Frederick Law Olmsted. Civilizing American landscapes: Writings on city landscape*. Cambridge, MA: MIT Press.

Tester, K. (Ed.) (1994). *The flâneur*. New York: Routledge.

Tiebout, C. M. (1956). A pure theory of local expenditures. *Journal of Political Economy, 64*, 416–424.

Source and copyright

This chapter was published in its original form as:

Banerjee, T. (2001), "The Future of Public Space: Beyond Invented Streets and Reinvented Places", *Journal of the American Planning Association*, **67**, 9–24.

Reprinted with permission of the *Journal of the American Planning Association*, copyright Winter 2001 by the American Planning Association.

18

The character of third places

Ray Oldenburg
[1989]

Third places the world over share common and essential features. As one's investigations cross the boundaries of time and culture, the kinship of the Arabian coffeehouse, the German *bierstube*, the Italian *taberna*, the old country store of the American frontier, and the ghetto bar reveals itself. As one approaches each example, determined to describe it in its own right, an increasingly familiar pattern emerges. The eternal sameness of the third place overshadows the variations in its outward appearance and seems unaffected by the wide differences in cultural attitudes toward the typical gathering places of informal public life. The beer joint in which the middle-class American takes no pride can be as much a third place as the proud Viennese coffeehouse. It is a fortunate aspect of the third place that its capacity to serve the human need for communion does not much depend upon the capacity of a nation to comprehend its virtues.

The wonder is that so little attention has been paid to the benefits attaching to the third place. It is curious that its features and inner workings have remained virtually undescribed in this present age when they are so sorely needed and when any number of lesser substitutes are described in tiresome detail. Volumes are written on sensitivity and encounter groups, on meditation and exotic rituals for attaining states of relaxation and transcendence, on jogging and massaging. But the third place, the people's own remedy for stress, loneliness, and alienation, seems easy to ignore.

But there is far more than escape and relief from stress involved in regular visits to a third place. There is more than shelter against the raindrops of life's tedium and more than a breather on the sidelines of the rat race to be had amid the company of a third place. Its real merits do not depend upon being harried by life, afflicted by stress, or needing time out from gainful activities. The escape theme is not erroneous in substance but in emphasis; it focuses too much upon conditions external to the third place and too little upon experiences and relationships afforded there and nowhere else.

Though characterizations of the third place as a mere haven of escape from home and work are inadequate, they do possess a virtue—they invite *comparison*. The escape theme suggests a world of difference between the corner tavern and the family apartment a block away, between morning coffee in the bungalow and that with the gang at the local bakery. The contrast is sharp and will be revealed. The *raison d'être* of the third place rests upon its differences from the other settings of daily life and can best be understood by comparison with them. In examining these differences, it will not serve to misrepresent the home, shop, or office in order to put a better light on public gathering places. But, if at times I might lapse in my objectivity, I take solace in the fact that public opinion in America and the weight of our myths and prejudices have never done justice to third places and the kind of association so essential to our freedom and contentment.

On neutral ground

The individual may have many friends, a rich variety among them, and opportunity to engage many of them daily *only* if people do not get uncomfortably tangled in one another's lives. Friends can be numerous and often met only if they may easily join and depart one another's company. This otherwise obvious fact of social life is often obscured by the seeming contradiction that surrounds it—we need a good deal of immunity from those whose company we like best. Or, as the sociologist Richard Sennett put it, "people can be sociable only when they have some protection from each other."[1]

In a book showing how to bring life back to American cities, Jane Jacobs stresses the contradiction surrounding most friendships and the consequent need to provide places for them. Cities, she observed, are full of people with whom contact is significant, useful, and enjoyable, but "you don't want them in your hair and they do not want you in theirs either."[2] If friendships and other informal acquaintances are limited to those suitable for private life, she says, the city becomes stultified. So, one might add, does the social life of the individual.

In order for the city and its neighborhoods to offer the rich and varied association that is their promise and their potential, there must be *neutral ground* upon which people may gather. There must be places where individuals may come and go as they please, in which none are required to play host, and in which all feel at home and comfortable. If there is no neutral ground in the neighborhoods where people live, association outside the home will be impoverished. Many, perhaps most, neighbors will never meet, to say nothing of associate, for there is no place for them to do so. Where neutral ground is available it makes possible far more informal, even intimate, relations among people than could be entertained in the home.

Social reformers as a rule, and planners all too commonly, ignore the importance of neutral ground and the kinds of relationships, interactions, and activities to which it plays host. Reformers have never liked seeing people hanging around on street corners, store porches, front stoops, bars, candy stores, or other public areas. They find loitering deplorable and assume that if people had better private areas they would not waste time in public ones. It would make as much sense, as Jane Jacobs points out, to argue that people wouldn't show up at testimonial banquets if they had wives who could cook for them at home.[3] The banquet table and coffee counter bring people together in an intimate and private social fashion—people who would not otherwise meet in that way. Both settings (street corner and banquet hall) are public and neutral, and both are important to the unity of neighborhoods, cities, and societies.

If we valued fraternity as much as independence, and democracy as much as free enterprise, our zoning codes would not enforce the social isolation that plagues our modern neighborhoods, but would require some form of public gathering place every block or two. We may one day rediscover the wisdom of James Oglethorpe who laid out Savannah such that her citizens lived close to public gathering areas. Indeed, he did so with such compelling effect that Sherman, in his destructive march to the sea, spared Savannah alone.

The third place is a leveler

Levelers was the name given to an extreme left-wing political party that emerged under Charles I and expired shortly afterward under Cromwell. The goal of the party was the abolition of all differences of position or rank that existed among men. By the middle of the seventeenth century, the term came to be applied much more broadly in England, referring to anything "which reduces men to an equality."[4] For example, the newly established coffeehouses of that period, one of unprecedented democracy among the English, were commonly referred to as levelers, as were the people who frequented them and who relished the new intimacy made possible by the decay of the old feudal order.

Precursors of the renowned English clubs, those early coffeehouses were enthusiastically democratic in the conduct and composition of their habitués. As one of the more articulate among them recorded, "As you have a hodge-podge of Drinks, such too is your company, for each man seems a Leveller, and ranks and files himself as he lists, without regard to degrees or order; so that oft you may see a silly Fop, and a wonder Justice, a griping-Rock, and a grave Citizen, a worthy Lawyer, and an errant Pickpocket, a Reverend Noncomformist, and a canting Mountebank; all blended together, to compose an Oglio of Impertinence."[5] Quite suddenly, each man had become an agent of England's newfound unity. His territory was the coffeehouse, which provided the neutral ground upon which men discovered one another apart from the classes and ranks that had earlier divided them.

A place that is a leveler is, by its nature, an inclusive place. It is accessible to the general public and does not set formal criteria of membership and exclusion. There is a tendency for individuals to select their associates, friends, and intimates from among those closest to them in social rank. Third places, however, serve to *expand* possibilities, whereas formal associations tend to narrow and restrict them. Third places counter the tendency to be restrictive in the enjoyment of others by being open to all and by laying emphasis on qualities not confined to status distinctions current in the society. Within third places, the charm and flavor of one's personality, irrespective of his or her station in life, is what counts. In the third place, people may make blissful substitutions in the rosters of their associations, adding those they genuinely enjoy and admire to those less-preferred individuals that fate has put at their side in the workplace or even, perhaps, in their family.

Further, a place that is a leveler also permits the individual to know workmates in a different and fuller aspect than is possible in the workplace. The great bulk of human association finds individuals related to one another for some objective purpose. It casts them, as sociologists say, in roles, and though the roles we play provide us with our more sustaining matrices of human association, these tend to submerge personality and the inherent joys of being together with others to some external purpose. In contrast, what Georg Simmel referred to as "pure sociability" is precisely the occasion in which people get together for no other purpose, higher or lower, than for the "joy, vivacity, and relief" of engaging their personalities beyond the contexts of purpose, duty, or role.[6] As Simmel insisted, this unique occasion provides the most democratic experience people can have and allows them to be more fully themselves, for it is salutary in such situations that all shed their social uniforms and insignia and reveal more of what lies beneath or beyond them.

Necessarily, a transformation must occur as one passes through the portals of a third place. Worldly status claims must be checked at the door in order that all within may be equals. The surrender of outward status, or leveling, that transforms those who own delivery trucks and those who drive them into equals, is rewarded by acceptance on more humane and less transitory grounds. Leveling is a joy and relief to those of higher and lower status in the mundane world. Those who, on the outside, command deference and attention by the sheer weight of their position find themselves in the third place enjoined, embraced, accepted, and enjoyed where conventional status counts for little. They are accepted just for themselves and on terms not subject to the vicissitudes of political or economic life.

Conversation is the main activity

Neutral ground provides the place, and leveling sets the stage for the cardinal and sustaining activity of third places everywhere. That activity is conversation. Nothing more clearly indicates a third place

than that the talk there is good; that it is lively, scintillating, colorful, and engaging. The joys of association in third places may initially be marked by smiles and twinkling eyes, by hand-shaking and back-slapping, but they proceed and are maintained in pleasurable and entertaining conversation.

A comparison of cultures readily reveals that the popularity of conversation in a society is closely related to the popularity of third places. In the 1970s, the economist Tibor Scitovsky introduced statistical data confirming what others had observed casually.[7] The rate of pub visitation in England or café visitation in France is high and corresponds to an obvious fondness for sociable conversation. American tourists, Scitovsky notes, "are usually struck and often morally shocked by the much more leisurely and frivolous attitude toward life of just about all foreigners, manifest by the tremendous amount of idle talk they engage in, on promenades and park benches, in cafés, sandwich shops, lobbies, doorways, and wherever people congregate." And, in the pubs and cafés, Scitovsky goes on to report, "socializing rather than drinking is clearly most people's main occupation."

American men of letters often reveal an envy of those societies in which conversation is more highly regarded than here, and usually recognize the link between activity and setting. Emerson, in his essay on "Table Talk," discussed the importance of great cities in representing the power and genius of a nation.[8] He focused on Paris, which dominated for so long and to such an extent as to influence the whole of Europe. After listing the many areas in which that city had become the "social center of the world," he concluded that its "supreme merit is that it is the city of conversation and cafés."

In a popular essay on "The American Condition," Richard Goodwin invited readers to contrast the rush hour in our major cities with the close of the working day in Renaissance Italy: "Now at Florence, when the air is red with the summer sunset and the campaniles begin to sound vespers and the day's work is done, everyone collects in the piazzas. The steps of Santa Maria del Fiore swarm with men of every rank and every class; artisans, merchants, teachers, artists, doctors, technicians, poets, scholars. A thousand minds, a thousand arguments; a lively intermingling of questions, problems, news of the latest happening, jokes; an inexhaustible play of language and thought, a vibrant curiosity; the changeable temper of a thousand spirits by whom every object of discussion is broken into an infinity of sense and significations—all these spring into being, and then are spent. And this is the pleasure of the Florentine public."[9]

The judgment regarding conversation in our society is usually twofold: we don't value it and we're not good at it. "If it has not value," complained Wordsworth, "good, lively talk is often contemptuously dismissed as talking for talking's sake."[10] As to our skills, Tibor Scitovsky noted that our gambit for a chat is "halfhearted and . . . we have failed to develop the locale and the facilities for idle talk. We lack the stuff of which conversations are made."[11] In our low estimation of idle talk, we Americans have correctly assessed the worth of much of what we hear. It is witless, trite, self-centered, and unreflective.

If conversation is not just the main attraction but the sine qua non of the third place, it must be better there and, indeed, it is. Within its circles, the art of conversation is preserved against its decline in the larger spheres, and evidence of this claim is abundant.

Initially, one may note a remarkable compliance with the rules of conversation as compared to their abuse almost everywhere else. Many champions of the art of conversation have stated its simple rules. Henry Sedgwick does so in a straightforward manner.[12] In essence, his rules are: (1) Remain silent your share of the time (more rather than less). (2) Be attentive while others are talking. (3) Say what you think but be careful not to hurt others' feelings. (4) Avoid topics not of general interest. (5) Say little or nothing about yourself personally, but talk about others there assembled. (6) Avoid trying to instruct. (7) Speak in as low a voice as will allow others to hear.

The rules, it will be seen, fit the democratic order, or the leveling, that prevails in third places. Everyone seems to talk just the right amount, and all are expected to contribute. Pure sociability is as much subject to good and proper form as any other kind of association, and this conversational style embodies that form. Quite unlike those corporate realms wherein status dictates who may speak, and when and how much, and who may use levity and against which targets, the third place draws in like manner from everyone there assembled. Even the sharper wits must refrain from dominating conversation, for all are there to hold forth as well as to listen.

Whatever interrupts conversation's lively flow is ruinous to a third place, be it the bore, a horde of barbaric college students, or mechanical or electronic gadgetry. Most common among these is the noise that passes for music, though it must be understood that when conversation is to be savored, even Mozart is noise if played too loudly. In America, particularly, many public establishments reverberate with music played so loudly that enjoyable conversation is impossible. Why the management chooses to override normal conversation by twenty decibels is not always obvious. It may be to lend the illusion of life among a listless and fragmented assembly, to attract a particular kind of clientele, because management has learned that people tend to drink more and faster when subjected to loud noise, or simply because the one in charge likes it that way. In any case, the potential for a third place can be eliminated with the flip of a switch, for whatever inhibits conversation will drive those who delight in it to search for another setting.

As there are agencies and activities that interfere with conversation, so there are those that aid and encourage it. Third places often incorporate these activities and may even emerge around them. To be more precise, conversation is a *game* that mixes well with many other games according to the manner in which they are played. In the clubs where I watch others play gin rummy, for example, it is a rare card that is played without comment and rarer still is the hand dealt without some terrible judgment being leveled at the dealer. The game and conversation move along in lively fashion, the talk enhancing the card game, the card game giving eternal stimulation to the talk. Jackson's observations in the clubs of the working-class English confirm this. "Much time," he recorded, "is given over to playing games. Cribbage and dominoes mean endless conversation and by-the-way evaluation of personalities. Spectators are never quiet, and every stage of the game stimulates comment—mostly on the characteristics of the players rather than the play; their slyness, slowness, quickness, meanness, allusions to long-remembered incidents in club history."[13]

Not all games stimulate conversation and kibitzing; hence, not all games complement third place association. A room full of individuals intent upon video games is not a third place, nor is a subdued lounge in which couples are quietly staring at backgammon boards. Amateur pool blends well into third place activity generally, providing that personality is not entirely sacrificed to technical skill or the game reduced to the singular matter of who wins. Above all, it is the latitude that personality enjoys at each and every turn that makes the difference.

Accessibility and accommodation

Third places that render the best and fullest service are those to which one may go alone at almost any time of the day or evening with assurance that acquaintances will be there. To have such a place available whenever the demons of loneliness or boredom strike or when the pressures and frustrations of the day call for relaxation amid good company is a powerful resource. Where they exist, such places attest to the bonds between people. "A community life exists," says the sociologist Philip Slater, "when one can go daily to a given location and see many of the people he knows."[14]

That seemingly simple requirement of community has become elusive. Beyond the workplace (which, presumably, Slater did not mean to include), only a modest proportion of middle-class Americans can lay claim to such a place. Our evolving habitat has become increasingly hostile to them. Their dwindling number at home, seen against their profusion in many other countries, points up the importance of the accessibility of third places. Access to them must be *easy* if they are to survive and serve, and the ease with which one may visit a third place is a matter of both time and location.

Traditionally, third places have kept long hours. England's early coffeehouses were open sixteen hours a day, and most of our coffee-and-doughnut places are open around the clock. Taverns typically serve from about nine in the morning until the wee hours of the following morning, unless the law decrees otherwise. In many retail stores, the coffee counters are open well before the rest of the store. Most establishments that serve as third places are accessible during both the on and off hours of the day.

It must be thus, for the third place accommodates people only when they are released from their responsibilities elsewhere. The basic institutions—home, work, school—make prior claims that cannot be ignored. Third places must stand ready to serve people's needs for sociability and relaxation in the intervals before, between, and after their mandatory appearances elsewhere.

Those who have third places exhibit regularity in their visits to them, but it is not that punctual and unfailing kind shown in deference to the job or family. The timing is loose, days are missed, some visits are brief, etc. Viewed from the vantage point of the establishment, there is a fluidity in arrivals and departures and an inconsistency of membership at any given hour or day. Correspondingly, the activity that goes on in third places is largely unplanned, unscheduled, unorganized, and unstructured. Here, however, is the charm. It is just these deviations from the middle-class penchant for organization that give the third place much of its character and allure and that allow it to offer a radical departure from the routines of home and work.

As important as timing, and closely related to it, is the location of third places. Where informal gathering places are far removed from one's residence, their appeal fades, for two reasons. Getting there is inconvenient, and one is not likely to know the patrons.

The importance of proximate locations is illustrated by the typical English pub. Though in the one instance its accessibility has been sharply curtailed by laws that cut its normal hours of operation in half, it has nonetheless thrived because of its physical accessibility. The clue is in the name; pubs are called locals and every one of them is somebody's local. Because so many pubs are situated among the homes of those who use them, people are there frequently, both because they are accessible and because their patrons are guaranteed the company of friendly and familiar faces. Across the English Channel sociable use of the public domain is also high, as is the availability of gathering places. Each neighborhood, if not each block, has its café and, as in England, these have served to bring the residents into frequent and friendly contact with one another.

Where third places are prolific across the urban topography, people may indulge their social instincts as they prefer. Some will never frequent these places. Others will do so rarely. Some will go only in the company of others. Many will come and go as individuals.

The regulars

The lure of a third place depends only secondarily upon seating capacity, variety of beverages served, availability of parking, prices, or other features. What attracts the regular visitor to a third place is supplied not by management but by the fellow customers. The third place is just so much space unless the right people are there to make it come alive, and they are the regulars. It is the regulars who give the place its character and who assure that on any given visit some of the gang will be there.

Third places are dominated by their regulars but not necessarily in a numerical sense. It is the regulars, whatever their number on any given occasion, who feel at home in a place and set the tone of conviviality. It is the regulars whose mood and manner provide the infectious and contagious style of interaction and whose acceptance of new faces is crucial. The host's welcome, though important, is not the one that really matters; the welcome and acceptance extended on the other side of the bar-counter invites the newcomer to the world of third place association.

A low profile

As a physical structure, the third place is typically plain. In some cases, it falls a bit short of plain. One of the reasons it is difficult to convince some people of the importance of the third place is that so many of them have an appearance that suggests otherwise. Third places are unimpressive looking for the most part. They are not, with few exceptions, advertised; they are not elegant. In cultures where mass advertising prevails and appearance is valued over substance, the third place is all the more likely *not* to impress the uninitiated.

Several factors contribute to the characteristic homeliness of third places. First, and recalling Emerson's observation, there are no temples built to friendship. Third places, that is, are not constructed as such. Rather, establishments built for other purposes are commandeered by those seeking a place where they can linger in good company. Usually, it is the older place that invites this kind of takeover. Newer places are more wedded to the purposes for which they were built. Maximum profits are expected and not from a group of hangers-on. Newer places also tend to emerge in prime locations with the expectation of capitalizing on a high volume of transient customers. Newer places are also more likely to be chain establishments with policies and personnel that discourage hanging out. Even the new tavern is not nearly as likely to become a third place as an older one, suggesting that there is more involved than the purpose for which such places are built.

Plainness, or homeliness, is also the "protective coloration" of many third places. Not having that shiny bright appearance of the franchise establishment, third places do not attract a high volume of strangers or transient customers. They fall short of the middle-class preference for cleanliness and modernity. A place that looks a bit seedy will usually repel the transient middle-class customer away from home and protect those inside from numerous intrusions by one-time visitors. And, if it's a male third place in which women are not welcome, a definite seediness still goes a long way toward repelling the female customer. Many otherwise worn and aging structures, I should point out, are kept meticulously clean by owners devoted to the comfort and pleasure of their customers. It is the first impression of the place that is at issue here.

Plainness, especially on the inside of third places, also serves to discourage pretention among those who gather there. A nonpretentious decor corresponds with and encourages leveling and the abandonment of social pretense. It is part of a broader fabric of nonpretention, which also includes the manner of dress. Regulars of third places do not go home and dress up. Rather, they come as they are. If one of them should arrive overdressed, a good bit of ribbing, not admiration or envy, will be his desert. In the third place, the "visuals" that surround individuals do not upstage them.

The plainness and modesty surrounding the third place is entirely fitting and probably could not be otherwise. Where there is the slightest bit of fanfare, people become self-conscious. Some will be inhibited by shyness; others will succumb to pretention. When people consider the establishment the "in" place to be seen, commercialism will reign. When that happens, an establishment may survive; it may even thrive, but it will cease to be a third place.

Finally, the low visual profile typical of third places parallels the low profile they have in the minds of those who frequent them. To the regular, though he or she may draw full benefit from them, third places are an ordinary part of a daily routine. The best attitude toward the third place is that it merely be an expected part of life. The contributions that third places make in the lives of people depend upon their incorporation into the everyday stream of existence.

The mood is playful

The persistent mood of the third place is a playful one. Those who would keep conversation serious for more than a minute are almost certainly doomed to failure. Every topic and speaker is a potential trapeze for the exercise and display of wit. Sometimes the playful spirit is obvious, as when the group is laughing and boisterous; other times it will be subtle. Whether pronounced or low key, however, the playful spirit is of utmost importance. Here joy and acceptance reign over anxiety and alienation. This is the magical element that warms the insider and reminds the outsider that he or she is not part of the magic circle, even though seated but a few feet away. When the regulars are at play, the outsider may certainly know neither the characters nor the rules by which they take one another lightly. The unmistakable mark of acceptance into the company of third place regulars is not that of being taken seriously, but that of being included in the play forms of their association.

A home away from home

If such establishments as the neighborhood tavern were nearly as bad as generations of wives have claimed them to be, few of the ladies should have found much reason to be concerned. The evil houses would have fallen of their own foul and unredeeming character. In fact, however, third places compete with the home on many of its own terms and often emerge the winner. One suspects that it is the similarity that a third place bears to a comfortable home and not its differences that poses the greater threat. Aye, there's the rub—the third place is often more homelike than home.

Using the first and second definitions of *home* (according to my Webster's), the third place does not qualify, being neither (1) the "family's place of residence" or (2) that "social unit formed by a family living together." But the third definition of home as offering "a congenial environment" is more apt to apply to the average third place than the average family residence. The domestic circle can endure without congeniality, but a third place cannot. Indeed, many family nests are brutish places where intimacy exists without even a smattering of civility.

Obviously, there is a great deal of difference between the private residence and the third place. Homes are private settings; third places are public. Homes are mostly characterized by heterosocial relations; third places most often host people of the same sex. Homes provide for a great variety of activities, third places far fewer. Largely, the third place is what the home is not, yet, there clearly exists enough similarity to invite comparison.

Summary

Third places exist on neutral ground and serve to level their guests to a condition of social equality. Within these places, conversation is the primary activity and the major vehicle for the display and appreciation of human personality and individuality. Third places are taken for granted and most have a low profile. Since the formal institutions of society make stronger claims on the individual, third places are normally open in the off hours, as well as at other times.

The character of a third place is determined most of all by its regular clientele and is marked by a playful mood, which contrasts with people's more serious involvement in other spheres. Though a radically different kind of setting from the home, the third place is remarkably similar to a good home in the psychological comfort and support that it extends.

Notes

1. Richard Sennett, *The Fall of Public Man* (New York: Alfred A. Knopf, 1977), 311.
2. Jane Jacobs, *The Death and Life of Great American Cities* (New York: Random House, 1961), *55*.
3. *Ibid.*
4. O.E.D. Noun definition no. 2.
5. Robert J. Allen, *The Clubs of Augustan London* (Hamden, Conn.: Archon Books, 1967), 14.
6. Georg Simmel, in *On Individual and Social Forms*, ed. Donald N. Levine (Chicago: The University of Chicago Press, 1971), Chapter 9.
7. Tibor Scitovsky, *The Joyless Economy* (New York: Oxford University Press, 1976), Chapter 11.
8. Ralph Waldo Emerson, *Essays and Journals* (New York: Doubleday, 1968), *158*.
9. Richard Goodwin, "The American Condition," *The New Yorker* (28 January 1974), *36*.
10. William Wordsworth, "The Art of Conversation," in *Wordsworthian and Other Studies*, ed. Ernest de Selincourt. (New York: Russell & Russell, 1964), 181–206.
11. *Ibid.*
12. Henry Sedgwick, *The Art of Happiness* (New York: Bobbs-Merrill, 1930), Chapter 17.
13. Brian Jackson, *Working Class Community* (London: Routledge & Kegan Paul, 1968) Chapter 4.
14. Slater, Philip E. 'Must marriage cheat today's young women' *Redbook Magazine* (February 1971).

Source and copyright

This chapter was published in its original form as:

Oldenburg, R. (1999), "The Character of Third Places', in Oldenburg, R. (1999), *The Great Good Place: Cafés, coffee shops, bookstores, bars, hair salons and the other great hangouts at the heart of a community*, second edition, Marlowe & Company, New York, 2–42. (First edition published 1989.)

Copyright 1989, 1997, 1999 by Ray Oldenburg.

Appears by permission of the publisher, Marlowe & Company, A Division of Avalon Publishing Group.

19

The rise of the private city

Paul Goldberger
[1996]

"The street is a room by agreement," the architect Louis Kahn wrote, and this line, with Kahn's characteristically gentle, poetic tone to it, tells all. The street is the building block of urban design and, by extension, of urban life; the city with vibrant street life is the city that works as a viable urban environment. It is the street, not the individual building, that is the key to making a city work as a piece of design, for the street is, as Kahn put it, the true room of the city—more even than its ceremonial plazas and squares. Indeed, if plazas, to paraphrase Napoleon's famous remark about St. Mark's Square, are the drawing rooms of cities, then streets are the kitchens, the places where the real life goes on.

Or so conventional urban theory would have it. Urbanists are trained to believe that a collection of buildings, however distinguished, does not a city make—witness Houston, say, or Minneapolis—but add a few great streets and you have something far more potent: New Orleans, perhaps, or San Francisco.

Even if there is no reason to believe this theory wrong—and who could question the intuitive sense that there is more urban energy to a city like San Francisco than to one like Phoenix?—it is increasingly inadequate as a way of discussing American cities at the end of the twentieth century. The traditional, dense city for which streets are the measure of success is less and less a design paradigm. It is increasingly being replaced by a model that values automobile access more than pedestrian accommodation, a model that seems designed to offer the ease and convenience of the suburbs. Yet this new model seems determined to demonstrate that it can offer many of the benefits of traditional cities: a variety of shops, restaurants, and public gathering places; facilities for the performing and visual arts,

and the general level of excitement and stimulation associated with older, street-oriented cities.

It is worth noting that both Dallas and Seattle, as well as Charlotte, Minneapolis, and numerous other successful examples of the new urbanism, provide middle-class residents with close-in neighborhoods of detached houses with ample, and private, yards, allowing them to live what is essentially a suburban life within city limits.

The desire is clearly to have certain benefits of an urban place—energy, variety, visual stimulation, cultural opportunities, the fruits of a consumerist culture—without exposure to the problems that have always come along with urban life: specifically, crime and poverty. It seems inherently clear that achieving a quasiurban environment that is free of these problems results in places that are not only primarily middle class but also primarily white. Indeed, while segregation may not be the goal, it is surely the result of the new urbanism—though, given the ample presence of middle-class blacks and Hispanics in many of the areas that can be called examples of the new urbanism, it must be said that this segregation is generally more class-driven than race-driven. But it is no exaggeration to say that the new urban paradigm can be defined, in part, by the desire to provide some measure of urban experience without encouraging the mixing of different classes of people: making the city safe for the middle class.

This represents a sea change in attitude from the premise on which traditional cities have always been based. It is not that they do not value safety (though they have not always been successful in providing it), but rather that they emerge from the premise that both security and more uplifting values such as visual and intellectual stimulation emerge naturally out of the juxtaposition of different people and different cultures in close physical proximity. Traditional cities view engagement as a virtue. The new urban paradigm is the precise opposite; it sanctions disengagement, denying the premise of the traditional city even as it professes to celebrate the virtues of urbanity.

In its social attitude, the new urban paradigm is less truly urban than it is a kind of blurring of traditional differences between the city and suburb. This blurring exists all the more in what may be the purest examples of all of the new urban model, those clusters of shopping malls, hotels, and high-rise office buildings built on the outskirts of older cities, often at the intersection of major freeways. These so-called edge cities (an awkward term; I have always preferred the less high-sounding "out-town") would seem to have every quality of cities except streets. Such places as City Post Oak in Houston, Tyson's Corners outside Washington, Buckhead north of Atlanta, and Las Colinas outside Dallas are gleaming and relatively new, and represent an attempt to take on the more benign characteristics once associated with larger cities without acquiring any other qualities of urban downtowns. The message is obvious: urbanity is attractive, so long as it can be rendered friendly and harmless by excluding poverty and all that is associated with it—crime, drugs, and violence.

Paradoxically, what might be called suburban values have by now come to play a significant role in defining the urban experience. This is true not only in areas outside of cities, but in entire urban regions, often even including portions of older central cities themselves. By suburban values I mean much more than matters of geography, and much more than accommodation to the automobile, though this is surely a part of it: no longer need a suburbanite's night at the symphony naturally be combined with a stroll on a city street or a visit to an urban cafe or restaurant. The orchestra hall in many places is just as likely to be driven to, and driven home from, as it is to be walked to along city streets.

Underlying this are two much more subtle, but ultimately far more profound, aspects of suburban values: the presumption of disengagement and, going hand-in-hand with this, an acceptance, even an elevation, of the notion of private space. Indeed, the truly defining characteristic of our time may be this privatization of the public realm, and it has come to affect our culture's very notions of urbanism.

Suburbs have traditionally valued private space—the single-family, detached house, the yard, even the automobile itself—over public space, which they have possessed in limited enough quantities under the best of circumstances. And most suburbs now have even less truly public space than they once did. Not only are malls taking the place of streets in the commercial life of many small towns, the privatization of the public realm has advanced even more dramatically with the huge increase in the number of gated, guarded suburban communities, places in which residential streets are now technically private places rather than public ones. In literally thousands of such communities, entire neighborhoods become, in effect, one vast piece of private property.

The rise of suburban values means much more than the growth of suburban sprawl, then. It has meant a change in the way public and private spaces work in both suburbs and cities. And it has meant that many cities, even ones that pride themselves on their energy, prosperity, and urbanity have come to take on certain characteristics once associated mainly with the suburbs. Now in both city and suburb, expressions of urbanity, which we might define as the making of public places where people can come together for both commercial and civic purposes, increasingly occur in private, enclosed places: shopping malls, both urban and suburban; "festival marketplaces" that seem to straddle the urban/suburban models; atrium hotel lobbies, which in some cities have become virtual town squares; lobbies of multiplex cinemas, which often contain a dozen or more theaters and thus exist at significant civic scale, and office building galleries, arcades, and lobbies.

Private places all, yet they serve the function that was once reserved for public places such as the street, the town square, and the park. The magnificent and civilized balance Louis Kahn evoked in his musing on the street—a balance established over time, across the generations, not only between commercial and civic concerns but also between different architects who knew the street belonged to none of them individually but was in and of itself a part of the commonweal—is essentially a thing of the past. It is gone because it emerges from the implicit assumption that the street is a public place. The great streets of the great cities of the world are all arenas in which private enterprise has made what might almost be called a kind of sacrificial gesture, in which architects have worked together to create a sense of place that is larger and more consistent, not to mention considerably more complex, than anything any individual building can possibly attain.

This is not to say that such a balance between public and private concerns is not respected today. But it is rarely imitated. Indeed, genuine street life exists today mainly where it has managed to survive. There are significant numbers of great old streets in American cities, many of which are healthy both as economic entities and as expressions of a lively urban culture (the two often go hand in hand). But there are few, if any, great new ones. There is no late twentieth-century equivalent of Madison Avenue, or Newbury Street, or North Michigan Avenue. Indeed, North Michigan Avenue in Chicago, for all its continued power as a majestic urban boulevard, seems as much an example of the new form of urbanism as the old: it is intersected by several large vertical shopping malls, punctuation marks of the new urbanism amid the old.

Our culture now creates what might be called urbanoid environments with a vengeance. From the South Street Seaport in New York, where a mall and food court sit on the edge of the most vibrant traditional cities in the world; to Grand Avenue in Milwaukee, where an interior mall has brought some modest, but limited, commercial activity to a troubled downtown, to Horton Plaza in San Diego, a kind of pseudo theme park-urban mall, we are awash from coast to coast in places that purport to offer some degree of urban experience in an entertaining, sealed-off, private environment. That they exist and prosper stands as proof that our culture has not discarded the most important urban value of all, the desire for physical proximity to others in a shared place. But even as these urbanoid environments show that we crave the satisfactions being in public places can give us, they make it equally clear that we are inclined to satisfy those cravings in places very different from traditional streets.

The urbanoid environment—the pseudo-street, the pseudo-square, the pseudo-piazza—is at bottom a kind of theme park, and in this sense, a descendant of that Southern California project from the 1950s that surely had more long-term influence on the American urban landscape than Le Corbusier: Disneyland. The architect Charles Moore was perhaps the first to see Disneyland's significance in terms of American attitudes toward public space; in 1965, in an essay entitled "You Have to Pay for the Public Life," he wrote: "Disneyland, it appears, is enormously important and successful just because it recreates all the chances to respond to a public environment, which Los Angeles in particular does not any longer have. It allows play-acting, both to be watched and to be participated in, in a public sphere. In as unlikely a place as could be conceived, just off the Santa Ana Freeway, a little over an hour from the Los Angeles City Hall, in an unchartable sea of suburbia, Disney has created a place, indeed a whole public world, full of sequential occurrences, of big and little drama, of hierarchies of importance and excitement, with opportunities to respond at the speed of rocketing bobsleds or of horse-drawn streetcars. . . . No raw edges spoil the picture at Disneyland; everything is as immaculate as in the musical comedy villages Hollywood has provided for our viewing pleasure for the last three generations. . . . Everything works, in a way it doesn't seem to any more in the world outside."

As we seek to find places in which "everything works," Disneyland, and the private, pseudo-urban environment that it represents, has become the model. We see it in the biggest of the sprawling suburban malls, where the parade of shops, itself a series of changing stage sets in the manner of Disneyland, gives way every few hundred yards to some form of entertainment—often children's rides right out of an amusement park. CityWalk in Universal City, California, a pseudo-city street of shops and entertainment produced by Disney's competition, raises the curious question: Is it a city street masquerading as a theme park, or a theme park masquerading as a city street? We are not quite sure.

There is nearly as remarkable an ambiguity in the upmarket version of CityWalk, 2 Rodeo Drive in Beverly Hills. That is Disneyland's Main Street for grownups; instead of cute little shops selling mouse ears and stuffed animals, there are mock Art Deco and Spanish Colonial buildings, selling Tiffany jewelry and Hermes scarfs, all lined up on a make-believe street over underground parking. If nothing else, it is proof that the theme park has come a long way. Once a protected pretend-city, it has now broken out of its gates to become a kind of mutated urban form. Charles Moore showed us how the theme park "wanted" to be a city—we see now how the world outside its gates wants to be a theme park. Is it the real city playing at being entertaining, or entertainment playing at being a city?

The same question might be asked of a new Disney venture, the planned rehabilitation of the historic New Amsterdam Theater on West 42nd Street in New York, one of the first efforts in the city's long-planned Times Square renewal effort to show signs of life. That the Walt Disney Company, a private corporation whose innovative designs have all but created the new, private urban paradigm, would step in to restore a landmark theater off Times Square when public efforts to push an urban renewal project for Times Square ahead have so far borne so little fruit, might seem to be a metaphor for the moment. In this case a city is not looking to Disney for inspiration, but quite literally turning over a piece of the urban fabric to it.

Such places as CityWalk, 2 Rodeo Drive and virtually every urban mall in any city are sources of entertainment as much as commercial interaction. Indeed, it is no exaggeration to say that a key characteristic of the urban impulse right now is that it has become more closely wedded to the entertainment impulse than ever before. In an age in which electronic media have come to render many kinds of face-to-face contacts unnecessary, people are as likely to go to a public place in search of relief from boredom as anything else. But this is hardly unprecedented in the history of cities, which, after all, have always been in part sources of entertainment. Nineteenth-century Paris, that high point of Western urbanity, was an entertaining public culture; strolling on a boulevard or sitting in a cafe to watch the world go by were both forms of entertainment. There have always been close ties between the urban impulse and the entertainment impulse. The city grew up as a marketplace, but it flourished also as a stimulating, entertaining environment.

What, in the face of competition from out-towns, suburbs, and suburbanized cities in which disengagement is valued above engagement, is the traditional, dense, truly urban city to do? If there is anything that older, street-oriented cities can offer, it is a sense of authenticity, a sense that their pleasures, if not as instantly easy or comfortable as those of the new urban paradigm, are at least real. They are authentic. They are places not made out of whole cloth; they exist in time, they grow and change, like living beings. "In a city, time becomes visible," Lewis Mumford has said, and that is the one thing that the new urban paradigm has not managed to figure out how to replicate. In the mall and the theme park, things are ever new, ever perfect: there is no sense of the ravages of time, but also no sense of its depths.

There is open space in the suburbs, but not of the richness and complexity of Central Park; there is culture in Costa Mesa, but not with the powerful interaction between performance and city that exists at Lincoln Center or Carnegie Hall; there is big public space in suburban malls, but it is not capable of being as continually enriched and revived and redefined as the gestalt of Madison Avenue. Streets are not only rooms, as Kahn said; they are also arteries, carrying people and things and, most important of all, a sense of time. It is in the very nature of a street that it is different from one year to the next, while the most important quality of a mall is that it tries to remain the same.

Cities can offer reality, then: the reality of time as well as the reality of engagement. Whether that will be enough to satisfy a generation brought up to value other things—to value convenience and ease and entertainment over what older cities can offer—remains to be seen. Longevity—the mere act of survival—is clearly not enough for a city to possess, or Buffalo, Detroit and St. Louis would occupy the same role in American urban culture that Seattle, Dallas and San Diego do. Cities must appear vital and possessed of an urgent present, even as they also possess deep and resonant pasts; they must truly make the whole arc of time visible, from embracing and enlivening the past to holding out the promise of a future.

This is a noble ambition, and perhaps this notion in and of itself marks the difference between traditional urbanity and the new urban paradigm. Cities have great reach: They inspire and ennoble, and they surely challenge. The new urban paradigm seems to shrink from challenge, preferring to embrace ease and comfort. It is the familiar and the tame that are acceptable, not the new and different.

But it is clear that, whatever short-term economic benefits may come from the new urban paradigm's fondness for imitating suburbs, the ability of this model to have a real impact on the condition of older cities is limited indeed. Baltimore is a good case in point: its Inner Harbor project has managed to bring middle-class suburbanites into the city limits, and it has encouraged a considerable amount of benign thinking about the notion of the city. But the Inner Harbor is really an island unto itself, with little connection, either physical or conceptual, with the rest of the city. The prosperous Inner Harbor throws off tax dollars which affect the rest of the city, but it does not change the basic nature of Baltimore. We should be grateful that it has not remade the rest of the city in its suburban image, but its lack of connection also means that it has had little effect on the city's deeper problems. It is numb to the city's traditional urban virtue of engagement.

Cities must play to their strengths, and their greatest strength is authenticity. It is no small irony that Disney, the company that has done so much to devalue authenticity in the new urban paradigm, would be taking on the restoration of the New Amsterdam Theater in New York, a building whose very selling point is its authenticity. The New Amsterdam is real, with a long and distinguished history, and it is in a very real and very troubled place, 42nd Street. Conceptually at least, it is best to think of Disney mainly as a source of financing here, since what is planned for the New Amsterdam is really quite un-Disneyesque. As the New Amsterdam is restored, this will not be the invention of a make-believe past; it will be the reinvigoration of a very real one. This is the kind of remake of an urban icon that more cities need.

Does the spread of the new urban paradigm mean that the glass of urbanism is half empty or half full? The urban impulse is obviously alive in this country, even if it is being fulfilled in a manner that is more contained, more controlled, and ultimately less free than traditional streets and public open spaces have been. There must be a reason that urbanity is now highly prized in this culture, even if it is so often expressed in a manner that would seem to contradict the values of the traditional city. But what are the consequences of the new urbanism? Does it ultimately matter that so many public places today are not, technically, very public?

With their resources strained, it is all most cities can do to maintain the public places that they have (and many are not even able to do that adequately). In a climate that makes it impolitic to devote significant public funds to the creation of new public places, most cities have welcomed the willingness of the private sector to create what is, in effect, a new public realm. Indeed, more than a few of the products of the new urbanism, such as atrium lobbies and public arcades in office buildings, are mandated by zoning codes designed to encourage the creation of public space within private buildings. To cash-starved urban officials, allowing public places to become a function of private enterprise is a fair price to pay; they see the alternative as having no new public places at all.

Yet as the new urbanism turns over financial responsibility for public places to the private sector, it implicitly cedes control of the public realm as well. No matter how strict a municipality's regulations may be in requiring open access for all, both the design and the user population can fairly be described as likely to be more homogeneous than in "real" public places, especially in the new out-towns. Good news for the urbanophobe, perhaps, who moves cautiously into urban life from a safe suburban refuge, but far less encouraging for those who value the harsher edge of traditional urban environments. Public places that are not truly public almost invariably possess a measured quality that makes them different from older streets, parks, esplanades and squares. They may be cleaner and safer, but they have a tendency to be flatter and duller; the voltage is almost always reduced. Everything is so right that it becomes, by consequence, wrong, for no matter how physically handsome these places may be, they are almost always missing a certain kind of serendipity, the randomness that provides the element of surprise that is so critical to a real urban experience.

This failing is most obvious in such examples of the new urbanism as open outdoor plazas, interior atriums, and office-building lobbies that double as public arcades. Architecture is almost always at the forefront here, but for all the determination of private developers and the city officials regulating their work to maintain a high standard of design, few of these places manage to transcend the limitations of this now-common genre and project any real sense of traditional urbanity. Their role as private places ultimately overshadows their public mission, whatever the architectural achievement they represent. They are, for the most part, upright and dull, bespeaking good taste above all. And if rampant propriety and dullness are less likely to be the case in many of the more purely commercial examples of the new urbanism, such as theme parks, which at least offer a high level of visual stimulation and occasionally even wit, even the most entertaining of such places possesses none of the complexities and inconsistencies of real urban form. They are not made over time, like real streets; they are manufactured by designers, seeking to reproduce and package and make in an instant something that elsewhere developed over generations.

It is the role of all places to consume culture, but it is the privilege of a special few to create culture. Those places that manage to create culture in a more than incidental way tend, almost always, to be great cities: New York and Los Angeles rank above all others in this country in this regard, and it is no accident that they are both complicated, rough, difficult cities, profoundly original in their physical makeup and highly diverse in their population. Los Angeles may have spawned Disneyland, but it is not itself Disneyland, any more than New York is the "festival marketplace" of the South Street Seaport. New York and Los Angeles may be as different in their physical form as they are in their climate, but they share an intensity and a power, not to mention a certain sense of disorder—even, if this is not too extreme a word, anarchy.

Is it their extraordinary complexity that makes both of these cities so attractive to younger artists, musicians, writers, painters, dancers and architects? Or the way in which each borders on chaos? This is not the place in which to answer the question of why particular kinds of environments seem to encourage creativity. But it seems impossible to argue that it is large, difficult, "real" cities that are most hospitable to the creation of culture, as opposed to the consumption of it.

The new urban paradigm seems to celebrate consumption of culture, not creation. The Costa Mesa Performing Arts Center in Orange County may rival Los Angeles in the artistic events it presents, but it has spawned no community of artists and performers around it to challenge that of Los Angeles, any more than the new suburban cultural facilities around New York have made a dent on the role of New York City as a cultural incubator. The "festival marketplace" of the South Street Seaport may be an economic boon to the lower Manhattan neighborhood, but its shops and cafes are filled with consumers of culture, not with the makers and shapers of it.

Cities that have the capability of making culture—New York, Los Angeles, to a certain extent Seattle, San Francisco, perhaps Boston and Miami—have little to fear from the new urbanism. They are incubators, creators of culture, and as such possess what might be called the ultimate form of urban authenticity. They can make what the new urbanism can only imitate. Their economies will ebb and flow, but it is difficult to believe that the new urbanism can replace the essential role these cities, and others like them, play.

But many older cities, those not lucky enough to possess the power of shaping culture, are highly vulnerable to the lure of the new urban paradigm. They can offer little that the middle class truly wants, and thus they seek refuge in trying to save themselves by becoming ever more suburbanized. Atlanta, Charlotte, Dallas, Denver, Phoenix—these cities are already heavily suburban in feeling, and it is hard to believe that they will develop in a different way over the next generation. And whatever happens to the cores of these older cities, it is all the more likely that more and more commercial business will be done in out-towns, those clusters of high-rise buildings that stand as the new urban paradigm's alternative to the old commercial centers.

Intimately tied to consumerism, to entertainment, and to popular culture, the urbanism of today seeks to provide a measured, controlled, organized kind of city experience, which is the precise opposite of the rough-edged, somewhat disorganized reality of older streets and older cities. The new American urbanism is packaged for easy use; it disdains the randomness, the difficulty, and the inconsistency of real cities. It is without hard edges, without a past, and without a respect for the pain and complexity of authentic urban experience. It is suburban in its values, and middle class to its core. That it exists at all, for all its flaws, is probably a good thing, given how determined this country seemed at the peak of the frenzy of urban renewal in the 1960s to eschew any kind of urban life altogether. Yes, we seek an urbanism still. What we do not have—yet—is a true public realm.

Source and copyright

This chapter was published in its original form as:

Goldberger, P. (1996), "The Rise of the Private City', in Vitullo-Martin, J. (1996) (Editors), *Breaking Away: The Future of Cities: Essays in Memory of Robert F. Wagner, Jnr*, The Twentieth Century Fund Press, New York, 135–147

Reprinted with permission of The Century Foundation.

Section Five

The visual dimension

Architecture and urban design are among the very few truly inescapable – and, therefore, public – art forms. With movements such as 'City Beautiful' in the US and 'Townscape' in the UK establishing a predominantly visual perspective on development, the visual dimension of urban design was perhaps its dominant dimension until at least the 1960s. Even the Modern Movement can be criticised for its preoccupation with the visual expression of many of its key concepts rather than with the essence of the concepts themselves. The expression of function, for example, was often more important than buildings or places actually being functional. While the visual composition of both architecture and urban space is a vitally important component of the urban design remit, and profoundly affects the human qualities of places, it needs to be understood alongside the other dimensions discussed in this book.

This section presents a set of four chapters exploring the spatial and visual character of urban environments/design. Chapter 20 is **Gordon Cullen's** introduction to the first edition (1961) of his book *Townscape* (Architectural Press, London – second edition published 1971). While a number of writers have made significant contributions to contemporary townscape theory (e.g. Sitte, 1889; Sharp, 1946; 1948; Gibberd, 1953; Worskett, 1969; Tugnutt and Robertson, 1987), the modern 'townscape' approach has always been closely associated with Gordon Cullen. Cullen's beautifully illustrated essays on the subject initially formed a series of articles in the *Architectural Review* during the mid and late 1950s and subsequently appeared in book form as *Townscape* (1961), later republished as *The Concise Townscape* (1971).

One of the classic urban design texts, Cullen's introduction succinctly encapsulates his main ideas and his contribution to urban design. His argument was a contextualist one in which the whole was greater than the sum of the individual parts. Moreover, he argued that the urban environment is not typically experienced as a static composition. It is experienced in some form of dynamic, emerging, unfolding and temporal sequence. To describe this, Cullen conceived the concept of 'serial vision', further arguing that the urban environment should be considered and designed from the point of view of the moving person (see also the discussion of time in Section Seven).

Chapter 21 is drawn from **Edward T. White's** 1999 book, *Path–Portal–Place: Appreciating Public Space in Urban Environments* (Architectural Media Ltd, Tallahassee). Like Cullen's work, White presents a well-illustrated discussion of the key visual and spatial qualities of the urban environment. This little known contribution to the urban design literature is useful in the way it succinctly summarises these key concepts. The article's value is its three-part structure, focusing on 'path', 'portal' and 'place'. Path equates to 'street' and may be regarded as a more movement-oriented space. Place equates to 'square' and, in turn, may be regarded as a more static space. Portal refers to thresholds and transitions between spaces and between the public and private realms.

The urban environment's visual-aesthetic character derives from the combination of its spatial and visual qualities. The visual qualities derive from the surfaces that define the space – that is, the design of surrounding buildings (i.e. the walls to the urban space); the design of the floor; and the design of the array of street furniture within the space. Chapters 22 and 23 both concentrate on façade design and the design of 'urban' architecture generally. 'Urban' architecture can be considered to be architecture that responds to and contributes positively both to its context and to the definition of the public realm. This generally excludes the design of buildings as freestanding objects in space except as an occasional element. The value of both chapters lies not only in reminding urban designers of the importance of architectural design in contributing to the character of urban spaces, but in also reminding architects and their clients of the 'urban obligations' of their designs and developments – that is, in Tibbalds' words, the place matters most (see Section One).

Chapter 22 is **Sherban Cantacuzino's** 'Buildings in depth', which originally formed part of the Royal Fine Art Commission's inquiry, *What Makes a Good Building?* (1994) (RFAC, London).[1] The RFAC report brought together a number of the 'great-and-the-good' to discuss what makes a good building and to identify some guiding principles. The process identified six criteria – 'order and unity', 'expression', 'integrity', 'plan and section', 'detail', and 'integration'. However, recognising the need to avoid turning generally desirable principles into dogmatic imperatives, the report stressed that a building could embody every criterion and still not be a 'good' building, and, conversely, could be a 'good' building

---

[1] The functions of the Royal Fine Art Commission were taken over by the Commission for Architecture and the Built Environment, formed in 2000.

without complying with any of the criteria. Six further dimensions of the sixth criterion – integration – or, as it is sometimes disparagingly (and incorrectly) called, 'fitting in', were also identified – 'siting', 'massing', 'scale', 'proportion', 'rhythm', and 'materials'. The criteria provide a framework to discuss, and perhaps also to evaluate, the visual success of urban architecture and urban development generally.

Chapter 23 is **Peter Buchanan's**, 'A report from the front', originally published in the *Architects Journal* in 1988. The preface to Buchanan's article stated that:

> *'Late twentieth century capitalism in the UK, at least for the moment, has the confidence and cash to care about its face in the public domain. . . . Not all patrons want to hide the complex yet banal realities of contemporary life. They simply want something better than what reductive Modernists have offered to date.'*

Recognising the problem of 'repetitive, boring elevations, prefabricated for speedy erection' and, *inter alia*, going beyond the visual-aesthetic role of façades, Buchanan outlines the qualities that façades should have. The article is valuable in reminding us that most façades are designed by architects for private interests, and that these private interests may be very different to the public interest of good place-making. While, at one level, a paper evidently of its time (the property boom of the late 1980s), it also presents a set of universal lessons for urban architectural design – that façades should help to create a sense-of-place; mediate between inside and out, private and public space, and provide gradations between the two; have windows that suggest the potential presence of people and that reveal and 'frame' internal life; have character and coherence that both acknowledge conventions and enter into a dialogue with adjacent buildings; have compositions that create rhythm and repose and hold the eye; have a sense of mass and materials, which should be combined with an expression of the form of construction; have substantial, tactile and decorative materials, which are natural and which weather gracefully; and have decoration that distracts, delights and intrigues.

Matthew Carmona and Steve Tiesdell

20

Townscape: introduction

Gordon Cullen
[1961]

There are advantages to be gained from the gathering together of people to form a town. A single family living in the country can scarcely hope to drop into a theatre, have a meal out or browse in a library, whereas the same family living in a town can enjoy these amenities. The little money that one family can afford is multiplied by thousands and so a collective amenity is made possible. A city is more than the sum of its inhabitants. It has the power to generate a surplus of amenity, which is one reason why people like to live in communities rather than in isolation.

Now turn to the visual impact which a city has on those who live in it or visit it. I wish to show that an argument parallel to the one put forward above holds good for buildings: bring people together and they create a collective surplus of enjoyment; bring buildings together and collectively they can give visual pleasure which none can give separately.

One building standing alone in the countryside is experienced as a work of architecture, but bring half a dozen buildings together and an art other than architecture is made possible. Several things begin to happen in the group which would be impossible for the isolated building. We may walk through and past the buildings, and as a corner is turned an unsuspected building is suddenly revealed. We may be surprised, even astonished (a reaction generated by the composition of the group and not by the individual building). Again, suppose that the buildings have been put together in a group so that one can get inside the group, then the space created between the buildings is seen to have a life of its own over and above the buildings which create it and one's reaction is to say 'I am inside IT' or 'I am entering IT'. Note also that in this group of half a dozen buildings there may be one which through reason of function does not conform. It may be a bank, a temple or a church amongst houses. Suppose that we are just looking at the temple by itself, it would stand in front of us and all its qualities, size, colour and intricacy, would be evident. But put the temple back amongst the small houses and immediately its size is made more real and more obvious by the comparison between the two scales. Instead of being a big temple it TOWERS. The difference in meaning between bigness and towering is the measure of the relationship.

In fact there is an *art of relationship* just as there is an art of architecture. Its purpose is to take all the elements that go to create the environment: buildings, trees, nature, water, traffic, advertisements and so on, and to weave them together in such a way that drama is released. For a city is a dramatic event in the environment. Look at the research that is put into making a city work: demographers, sociologists, engineers, traffic experts; all co-operating to form the myriad factors into a workable, viable and healthy organization. It is a tremendous human undertaking.

And yet . . . if at the end of it all the city appears dull, uninteresting and soulless, then it is not fulfilling itself. It has failed. The fire has been laid but nobody has put a match to it.

Firstly we have to rid ourselves of the thought that the excitement and drama that we seek can be born automatically out of the scientific research and solutions arrived at by the technical man (or the technical half of the brain). We naturally accept these solutions, but are not entirely bound by them. In fact we cannot be entirely bound by them because the scientific solution is based on the best that can be made of the average: of averages of human behaviour, averages of weather, factors of safety and so on.

And these averages do not give an inevitable result for any particular problem. They are, so to speak, wandering facts which may synchronize or, just as likely, may conflict with each other. The upshot is that a town could take one of several patterns and still operate with success, equal success. Here then we discover a pliability in the scientific solution and it is precisely in the *manipulation of this pliability* that the art of relationship is made possible. As will be seen, the aim is not to dictate the shape of the town or environment, but is a modest one: simply to *manipulate within the tolerances*.

This means that we can get no further help from the scientific attitude and that we must therefore turn to other values and other standards.

We turn to the *faculty of sight*, for it is almost entirely through vision that the environment is apprehended. If someone knocks at your door and you open it to let him in, it sometimes happens that a gust of wind comes in too, sweeping round the room, blowing the curtains and making a great fuss. Vision is somewhat the same; we often get more than we bargained for. Glance at the clock to see the time and you see the wallpaper, the clock's carved brown mahogany frame, the fly crawling over the glass and the delicate rapier-like pointers. Cézanne might have made a painting of it. In fact, of course, vision is not only useful but it evokes our memories and experiences, those responsive emotions inside us which have the power to disturb the mind when aroused. It is this unlooked-for surplus that we are dealing with, for clearly if the environment is going to produce an emotional reaction, with or without our volition, it is up to us to try to understand the three ways in which this happens.

1. Concerning OPTICS. Let us suppose that we are walking through a town: here is a straight road off which is a courtyard, at the far side of which another street leads out and bends slightly before reaching a monument. Not very unusual. We take this path and our first view is that of the street. Upon turning into the courtyard the new view is revealed instantaneously at the point of turning, and this view remains with us whilst we walk across the courtyard. Leaving the courtyard we enter the further street. Again a new view is suddenly revealed although we are travelling at a uniform speed. Finally as the road bends the monument swings into view. The significance of all this is that although the pedestrain walks through the town at a uniform speed, the scenery of towns is often revealed in

a series of jerks or revelations. This we call SERIAL VISION.

Examine what this means. Our original aim is to manipulate the elements of the town so that an impact on the emotions is achieved. A long straight road has little impact because the initial view is soon digested and becomes monotonous. The human mind reacts to a contrast, to the difference between things, and when two pictures (the street and the courtyard) are in the mind at the same time, a vivid contrast is felt and the town becomes visible in a deeper sense. It comes alive through the drama of juxtaposition. Unless this happens the town will slip past us featureless and inert.

There is a further observation to be made concerning Serial Vision. Although from a scientific or commercial point of view the town may be a unity, from our optical viewpoint we have split it into two elements: the *existing view* and the *emerging view*. In the normal way this is an accidental chain of events and whatever significance may arise out of the linking of views will be fortuitous. Suppose, however, that we take over this linking as a branch of the art of relationship; then we are finding a tool with which human imagination can begin to mould the city into a coherent drama. The process of manipulation has begun to turn the blind facts into a taut emotional situation.

2. Concerning PLACE. This second point is concerned with our reactions to the position of our body in its environment. This is as simple as it appears to be. It means, for instance, that when you go into a room you utter to yourself the unspoken words 'I am outside IT, I am entering IT, I am in the middle of IT'. At this level of consciousness we are dealing with a range of experience stemming from the major impacts of exposure and enclosure (which if taken to their morbid extremes result in the symptoms of agoraphobia and claustrophobia). Place a man on the edge of a 500-ft. cliff and he will have a very lively sense of position, put him at the end of a deep cave and he will react to the fact of enclosure.

Since it is an instinctive and continuous habit of the body to relate itself to the environment, this sense of position cannot be ignored; it becomes a factor in the design of the environment (just as an additional source of light must be reckoned with by a photographer, however annoying it may be). I would go further and say that it should be exploited.

Here is an example. Suppose you are visiting one of the hill towns in the south of France. You climb laboriously up the winding road and eventually find yourself in a tiny village street at the summit. You feel thirsty and go to a nearby restaurant, your drink is served to you on a veranda and as you go out to it you find to your exhilaration or horror that the veranda is cantilevered out over a thousand-foot drop. By this device of the containment (street) and the revelation (cantilever) the fact of height is dramatized and made real.

In a town we do not normally have such a dramatic situation to manipulate but the principle still holds good. There is, for instance, a typical emotional reaction to being below the general ground level and there is another resulting from being above it. There is a reaction to being hemmed in as in a tunnel and another to the wideness of the square. If, therefore, we design our towns from the point of view of the moving person (pedestrian or car-borne) it is easy to see how the whole city becomes a plastic experience, a journey through pressures and vacuums, a sequence of exposures and enclosures, of constraint and relief.

Arising out of this sense of identity or sympathy with the environment, this feeling of a person in street or square that he is in IT or entering IT or leaving IT, we discover that no sooner do we postulate a HERE than automatically we must create a THERE, for you cannot have one without the other. Some of the greatest townscape effects are created by a skilful relationship between the two, and I will name an example in India, where this introduction is being written: the approach from the Central Vista to the Rashtrapathi Bhawan[1] in New Delhi. There is an open-ended courtyard composed of the two Secretariat buildings and, at the end, the Rashtrapathi Bhawan. All this is raised above normal ground level and the approach is by a ramp. At the top of the ramp and in front of the axis building is a tall screen of railings. This is the setting. Travelling through it from the Central Vista we see the two Secretariats in full, but the Rashtrapathi Bhawan is partially hidden by the ramp; only its upper part is visible. This effect of truncation serves to isolate and make remote. The building is withheld.

We are Here and it is There. As we climb the ramp the Rashtrapathi Bhawan is gradually revealed, the mystery culminates in fulfilment as it becomes immediate to us, standing on the same floor. But at this point the railing, the wrought iron screen, is inserted; which again creates a form of Here and There by means of the screened vista. A brilliant, if painfully conceived, sequence.[2]

3. Concerning CONTENT. In this last category we turn to an examination of the fabric of towns: colour, texture, scale, style, character, personality and uniqueness. Accepting the fact that most towns are of old foundation, their fabric will show evidence of differing periods in its architectural styles and also in the various accidents of layout. Many towns do so display this mixture of styles, materials and scales.

Yet there exists at the back of our minds a feeling that could we only start again we would get rid of this hotchpotch and make all new and fine and perfect. We would create an orderly scene with straight roads and with buildings that conformed in height and style. Given a free hand that is what we might do . . . create symmetry, balance, perfection and conformity. After all, that is the popular conception of the purpose of town planning.

But what is this conformity? Let us approach it by a simile. Let us suppose a party in a private house, where are gathered together half a dozen people who are strangers to each other. The early part of the evening is passed in polite conversation on general subjects such as the weather and the current news. Cigarettes are passed and lights offered punctiliously. In fact it is all an exhibition of manners, of how one ought to behave. It is also very boring. This is conformity. However, later on the ice begins to break and out of the straightjacket of orthodox manners and conformity real human beings begin to emerge. It is found that Miss X's sharp but good-natured wit is just the right foil to Major Y's somewhat simple exuberance. And so on. It begins to be fun. Conformity gives way to the agreement to differ within a recognized tolerance of behaviour.

Conformity, from the point of view of the planner, is difficult to avoid but to avoid it deliberately, by creating artificial diversions, is surely

---

[1] The President's Residence, lately Viceregal Lodge.
[2] It was the cause of bitterness between Lutyens and Baker.

worse than the original boredom. Here, for instance, is a programme to rehouse 5,000 people. They are all treated the same, they get the same kind of house. How *can* one differentiate? Yet if we start from a much wider point of view we will see that tropical housing differs from temperate zone housing, that buildings in a brick country differ from buildings in a stone country, that religion and social manners vary the buildings. And as the field of observation narrows, so our sensitivity to the local gods must grow sharper. There is too much insensitivity in the building of towns, too much reliance on the tank and the armoured car where the telescopic rifle is wanted.

Within a commonly accepted framework—one that produces lucidity and not anarchy—we can manipulate the nuances of scale and style, of texture and colour and of character and individuality, juxtaposing them in order to create collective benefits. In fact the environment thus resolves itself into not conformity but the interplay of This and That.

It is a matter of observation that in a successful contrast of colours not only do we experience the harmony released but, equally, the colours become more truly themselves. In a large landscape by Corot, I forget its name, a landscape of sombre greens, almost a monochrome, there is a small figure in red. It is probably the reddest thing I have ever seen.

Statistics are abstracts: when they are plucked out of the completeness of life and converted into plans and the plans into buildings they will be lifeless. The result will be a three-dimensional diagram in which people are asked to live. In trying to colonize such a wasteland, to translate it from an environment for walking stomachs into a home for human beings, the difficulty lay in finding the point of application, in finding the gateway into the castle. We discovered three gateways, that of motion, that of position and that of content. By the exercise of vision it became apparent that motion was not one simple, measurable progression useful in planning, it was in fact two things, the Existing and the Revealed view. We discovered that the human being is constantly aware of his position in the environment, that he feels the need for a sense of place and that this sense of identity is coupled with an awareness of elsewhere. Conformity killed, whereas the agreement to differ gave life. In this way the void of statistics, of the diagram city, has been split into two parts, whether they be those of Serial Vision, Here and There or This and That. All that remains is to join them together into a new pattern created by the warmth and power and vitality of human imagination so that we build the home of man.

That is the theory of the game, the background. In fact the most difficult part lies ahead, the Art of Playing. As in any other game there are recognized gambits and moves built up from experience and precedent.

New Delhi 1959

Source and copyright

This chapter was published in its original form as:

Cullen, G. (1971), 'Introduction', in Cullen, G. (1971), *The Concise Townscape*, second edition, Architectural Press, London, 7–17. (First edition published 1961.)

With permission from Elsevier.

21

Path–portal–place

E. White

[1999]

These are the three kinds of public space considered in this discussion. They are our primary objects of attention together with the ways we can know and appreciate a place. Paths, portals, and places make up the majority of meaningful exterior space in urban environments. The places are the plazas, courts, gardens, and parks. Portals are the gateways into the places. And paths are the boulevards, avenues, streets, walks, and alleys that connect the places and knit the city together.

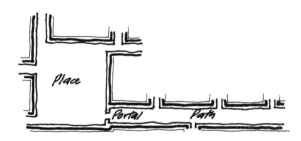

Good paths and portals are also kinds of places. Distinctions will be made here for the sake of discussion by defining paths as primarily dedicated to movement and having linear configurations. Portals are the points where paths meet places. And places are the urban rooms of the city where pedestrian life is invited, accommodated, and experienced. Places tend to be stable shapes such as squares, rectangles, circles, and ovals.

Path

Paths in urban settings are devoted to circulation. They are about moving from place to place. Pathways involve experiences of approach, anticipation, invitation, and arrival. Movement to and from urban places is a ritual of procession, a participation in the belonging of city life, and a threshold of transformation where paths open into places. To walk a good path to a successful urban place is to savor the expectation of reaching the destination, of our first glimpse of the place as we approach, of the quickening as the gravitational pull of the place becomes stronger, of crossing the portal where not-place becomes place, and of moving into the space where we are transformed into citizens. The invitational power of good plazas, squares, courts, and gardens flows out down the paths that lead to them. In most urban environments, pedestrian pathways correspond with vehicular ones. The extent to which a path is devoted to foot versus wheel traffic is read by the proportion of ground plane devoted to sidewalk and street and by restrictions on vehicular use. Some paths with stingy walks are clearly vehicular domains. Other paths are mainly walkway, all pedestrian with little or no vehicular activity. The character of a pedestrian-vehicular path is strongly affected by the volume, speed, and type of vehicular traffic. An urban artery may be a primary vehicular movement channel carrying any and all kinds of wheeled conveyances. An alley way may be an intimate path wide enough for only single file pedestrian traffic. Between these extremes we have wide boulevards

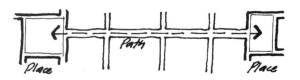

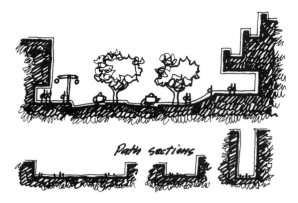

Path sections

entice and tease, inviting us to come see what's around the bend.

with bands of street-landscape-parking-walkways, typical streets with bordering walks, and paths where pedestrians share space with bicycles.

Paths can be described in terms of their physical attributes (container), use (activity), and feel (ambience). We may also understand them by their historical significance.

Container

Physically, cross sections through a path reveal the configuration of the pathspace, the profile of the ground plane, and the sectional character of the building facades that enfront the path. An urban pathway is typically a simple channel, a linear slot carved through solid city form. The channel can be wide and shallow, equally wide and deep, or deep and narrow. It can be simple and essentially rectilinear in section or more gymnastic and convoluted. The architectural personality of a path is determined by the building facades that form the boundaries of the space. Facade widths, heights, transparency, material, color, texture, window pattern, composition, and ornamentation are attributes that contribute to path character. In plan, paths can be straight, bent, curved, jogged, or meandering, each offering its own unique experience as we move along its route. Straight paths reveal their destinations or converge to distant vanishing points. Other path plan geometries

Path configurations

Activity

By definition, most of the activity in a path space is movement. Paths accommodate circulation between origins and destinations. Pedestrian flow ranges from slow, strolling, low-volume traffic to crowded, rapid, purposeful, half-jogging. Some paths are devoted only to circulation, with no activating storefronts or building uses or sidewalk functions to invite us to slow down and stay awhile. Others are enlivened by window displays, interesting shops, sidewalk cafes, courtyards, and street vendors. These paths are essentially linear plazas, destinations in themselves, places to come, be, and participate in urban life. Certain pathway spaces serve as sites for periodic civic events such as parades, flea markets, farmer's markets, craft fairs, speeches, art shows, concerts, and welcoming dignitaries. On these occasions, path is transformed to urban room, a place not just for circulation but for being and belonging. User demographics, foot traffic volume, direction and pace, vehicular use profile, and storefront activation tend to be cyclical, contributing to the rhythm and pulse of the town. Cycles can be seasonal (tourists), yearly (college students), monthly (store sales), weekly (farmer's market), weekday/weekend (off-work shoppers), day/night (party life), and morning/afternoon (rush hours). The rich overlay of these rhythms infuses path spaces with very real identities as living organisms.

The spatial distribution of activity types and intensities along a path is often varied and uneven. Many paths have zones of greater or lesser action intensity and areas where certain kinds of activities tend to occur or not occur. Action hot spots and cool spots may be due to the locations of building types along the street (museum), location of exterior functions (sidewalk cafe), connections to feeder paths (intersection node), and positions of public transportation

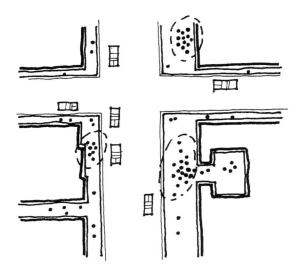

by a kind of rubbing friction that builds up an electrical charge. If handled improperly, heavy vehicular presence can degrade the pedestrian experience. In these unfortunate instance, speed feels dangerous and threatening, noise assaults the senses, and belching exhausts are anything but life-affirming.

The feel of a path involves its sense of purpose, its reason for being, and role in the tapestry of city places. A street might serve as the axial/ceremonial approach to an important building or monument, as a linear collection of the town's art galleries, or as the main vehicular arterial to the city center. A path could be where all the apartment garages face, where trucks make deliveries and collect trash, or where street vendors congregate. Ambience is the sum of our memories, expectations, emotions, sensations, preferences, choices, and actions. A synthesis of properties of place and human possibilities and processes. Our experience of atmosphere is as much about us as about qualities of the path. Experience in urban paths is shaped by both the physical place and our anticipation, readiness, alertness, mindfulness. The extent to which our perceptual apparatus is open or closed, sensitive or numb. We can be engaged with path qualities with all our senses and sense-making capability or preoccupied with place-eclipsing thoughts that situate us in our minds instead of the built environment. Path feel is affected by our environmental preferences, our positive and negative predispositions to scale, composition, material, crowds, traffic. Personal leanings regarding visual, audial, olfactory, tactile and taste environments map onto the particulars of this path, and the two interact to produce our sense of place, energy, and mood.

stops (buses, subways). Along the length of a street there might be one center of action or several. One side of the street may be busy while the other side is quiet. Activity is also distributed in bands across the section of a path. There is often a band of stationary activity such as window shoppers standing at store windows or people sitting at sidewalk cafes. On wider paths we sometimes find two streams of movement, one faster and one slower. Or the two bands may be pedestrians moving in opposing directions. Bands can also accommodate bicycles, strollers, and other small-wheeled vehicles. Finally, a sidewalk could have areas where groups of people huddle for conversation or where scooters and bicycles are parked. These linear streams of activity come and go, ebb and flow over time cycles and in response to contextual factors such as weather and special events.

Ambience

Path ambience is strongly affected by type, volume, and speed of vehicular traffic that shares the space with pedestrians. Atmosphere is likewise driven by these same attributes of foot traffic. A street can be noisy and smoggy with multiple lanes of speeding traffic composed of every conceivable kind of vehicle. Or there may be only slow-moving bicycles in a narrow alley. An urban pathspace might accommodate large bustling crowds of tourists walking briskly, bumpingly, ten abreast. Or only an occasional, solitary, doddling old man with his grey-muzzled dog. Vehicular and pedestrian activity creates energy, vitality. Movement, stimulation, and aliveness are created

Historical significance

The feel of a path and our emotions when we're there are affected by the historical significance of the place. A street may be especially important to the town's story. It could mark an ancient route that early settlers used, that revolutionaries stormed down to take the palace, or that victorious armies paraded along on their way back into the city. The impact of historical significance on path ambience and on the community regard for the path is dependent on our awareness of its history. When a road has a significant past that is understood and appreciated, history becomes a tangible context, a medium in which the present place, present functions, and present attributes are situated. The spirits of important events and people are very alive there, and they combine with our immediate experience to create a deeper and richer emotional content. A sad, run-down street is all the sadder when we know that it was once a grand and glittering avenue in a distant heyday. A narrow, nondescript alley becomes sacred if we are aware that a famous poet lived there. And a generous, landscaped boulevard is more interesting when we understand its story as an early rutted wagon trail.

The good path

Analytical efforts to understand urban pathways are frequently followed by evaluation. Our orientation shifts from careful attention and study to appreciation, judgments about goodness and success. What makes a path good? Successful pedestrian paths are a pleasure to move on and be in. They draw us into the life of the city. We feel the joy and satisfaction of citizenship when we're there. The good path entices us along with interesting destinations and invites us to linger in inviting places on the way. Successful pathspace enjoys a meaningful purpose in the city path network. It links important places, takes us to significant sites, and may itself be a magnet for urban activity. Paths are richer places when they have a story, a genealogy. Experience in a pathspace is enhanced when we know that important things happened there. Good paths nourish our senses. The visual environment is beautiful, interesting, and legible. The materials are a pleasure to touch, walk on, sit on. Agreeable aromas and sounds fill the air. Positive circulation spaces are about something. They have a theme. A path may be the collection point for the city's jewelry shops or the main ceremonial approach to city hall. Successful streets are appropriately defined and scaled by enclosing buildings that are well designed, carefully detailed, and faithfully maintained.

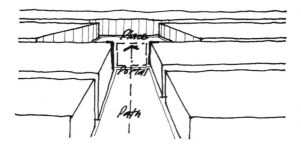

Portal

Portals in urban environments are about transition and transformation. Points in paths where we move into and out of plazas, gardens, and courts. Portals are gateways, thresholds, those wonderful places where outside becomes inside. We are changed when we pass through portals. Our very being is realigned like iron filings by a magnetic field. We are altered by virtue of entering public space, becoming urban citizens at a loftier level and feeling the heightened intensity of a higher belonging. Portals are where the path experience of moving toward, of becoming, shifts to the place experience of arriving, of being. This alchemical quality of portals endows them with mystery and magic. Urban gateways culminate rituals of procession toward significant city locales. They are the doorways that draw us along paths, as visible

invitations, apertures that frame our view to plazas. A portal channels our vision into an urban place as we approach and orchestrates the unfoldment of our view of the space as we enter. Like all doorways, portals are points of orientation, places where we collect ourselves and get our bearings. On entry, we scan the space for possibilities, options, invitations. And we decide our next move within the place. Portals sometimes occur at path midpoints or as freestanding elements in boulevards. In these instances, they may mark boundaries in city districts or serve as commemorative monuments. Portals are sometimes inadvertently formed by overhead events such as bridges or by path-flanking elements like matching buildings.

In this section, we will concentrate on pedestrian entryways to urban space. The same taxonomy will be employed as was used to discuss paths. Organizing categories include container-activity-ambience, historical significance, hybrids, scale of attention, and the good portal.

Container

As physical urban entities, portals can be deliberately planned as gateways, or they can just appear, as undesigned points where paths happen to connect to places. The deliberate marking of an entry to a public space may assume many forms. Archways, gates, and lintels spanning columns are walked through and under at plaza portals. A plaza entry might be accentuated with flanking columns, pillars, or pilasters with no overhead component. Sometimes a matched pair of buildings serves to create the sense of gateway. A portal could be established more subtly with a ground level change, material shift, altered paving pattern, or variation in landscaping. Moving from an unlandscaped path into a court filled with trees can create the transformational experience vital to a good portal. Of course, the essential transformation at any portal is a spatial one, moving from a narrow, linear, dynamic path experience into a more generous, stable, urban place experience.

When portal has been specially designed as doorway to urban room, its physical configuration and qualities are of interest. Plan, section, elevation, and perspective are useful tools in this regard.

A plan shows the portal width, length, shape, and position in relation to the path and place that it

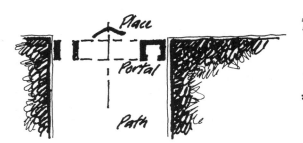

connects. Plan view also indicates solid-void relationships, whether the portal mass contains stairs, interior spaces, or secondary passages. In plan, a portal's relation to adjacent buildings is understood. Does the portal physically touch the buildings? Float as freestanding element in the path? Sit in the plaza and extend past the mouth of the path?

Sections through portals can be taken across the path opening or on axis with the path. Cross sections reveal the height, width, and shape of the portal aperture and the configuration of the architecture that forms the opening. Is the portal opening arched? Square? Rectangular? Is the boundary of the opening simple or complex? Are there niches, side doors, cornices? Portal sections along the path axis indicate the length or depth of the gateway as well as its height. Some gateways are only as deep as a wall thickness or column, essentially only planes through which we move into the plaza. Other are longer, more tunnel-like. There may even be a series of portals through which we pass into the urban space at

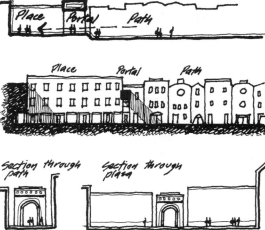

the path's end. Longitudinal sections show the elevational character of the inside surfaces of the portal and any profile configurations that happen on the portal ceiling. When extended, longitudinal sections reveal relations between the portal, the path it terminates, and the urban space it serves.

A portal's elevation may simply be the two building facades between which the opening into the plaza occurs. A portal situated between path-flanking building facades will have only two elevations. Portal elevations are frequently shown as aspects of sections through paths and plazas. An elevation can indicate the dimension, scale, and character of the portal facade, its relation to adjacent buildings, and the figure-ground character of the portal opening and its architectural frame. The architecture of the gateway might extend to the height of the flanking buildings, rise above them, or drop below them.

Perspective views offer the advantage of showing what we see when we look through the portal opening as well as the architecture of the portal itself. The perspective view might be down the axis of the path to the portal and into the plaza. Or perhaps toward the portal from the plaza and up the path beyond. A perspective series will illustrate the experience of approaching the portal, arriving at it, and moving through it to the plaza. The same applies to the plaza exiting experience. Perspectives provide the most holistic simulation of portal use because all urban surfaces are included in the point of view. Ground plane, path facades, overhead elements, freestanding elements in the pathspace, portal, and plazaspace beyond all happen together in perspective relationship.

Activity

The primary activity associated with gateways is moving through, a transition from path to place. Attention to activity at portals can be extended to include anticipation of first view of the portal; preview glimpses of it from distant paths; initial full look at the portal; the experience of moving toward it, arriving at it, passing through it, and feeling its presence behind on entering the plaza. If the portal is only as deep as a wall or column, moving through it takes only a moment. Extended portals like tunnels take longer to get through. Some urban doorways require some special activity such as opening a gate, climbing or descending steps, or shifting direction before entering the plaza. A portal opening can be as wide as its path space or some narrower dimension. Openings that are narrower than the path leading to them will funnel pedestrian movement down to a tighter aperture and may result in crowding, congestion, turbulence, and slower movement. These are not necessarily negative experiences and could contribute to the drama of entering the destination space. Portals are often sites for parades, pageants, speeches and civic ceremonies, especially when they have historical significance, or their architecture serves as a stage-like setting. Our interest in the portal might warrant study of particular aspects of movement through the opening. Examples are total traffic count, entry count versus exit count, movement speed, flow smoothness or turbulence, crowding, and congestion. Demographic considerations such as gender, age, dress, ethnicity, disabilities, and national origin could be relevant. Attention to spatial distribution of the movement streams across the portal opening involve us in questions like: What part of the aperture do most people use? Does crowding happen mainly at the center of the opening? Do entering users move through at the middle and exiting users at the edges? Activity types, intensities, demographics, and spatial distribution will have rhythms and patterns that vary cyclically over a year, season, month, week, and day. Rhythm responds to contextual factors like weather, tourist season, the economy, holidays, day-evening use, working hours, and special events. When a portal has depth (tunnel) or offers areas for stationary activity in it or around it, we may be concerned with non-circulation behaviors such as standing, sitting, queuing, selling, talking. More elaborate gateways might offer invitations to climb to raised vantage points at landings or rooftops.

Ambience

The energy of an urban portal is produced, in part, by the ambience moved through in the path to reach the gateway, in part by what's happening at the portal itself, and in part by what is seen in the plaza through the opening. As a component of path, portal participates in the mood of path. As a component of plaza, portal also participates in the ambience of that space. The energy of path and plaza may be similar or contrasting. For instance, both may be peaceful or noisy. Or one may be bustling, and the other quiet. Both path and destination might be slow paced and reverent in mood while the energy at the portal is crowded and pressured. This possibility of multivalent ambience creates an interesting complexity of moods around some portals. They can have a wonderful multiplicity of personalities, one from the plaza side, one from the path side, and a third at the portal itself. In this sense a gate can be far more than a transition between pathspace and placespace. It also can be a transition between vastly difficult urban energies.

We normally imagine portals in terms of entry as opposed to exit, and so the ambience of a gateway might begin with its gravitational pull, the power of its invitation to approach and move through into the public space beyond. We can feel this sense of anticipation even before the portal is actually seen. Knowing the entry to a great plaza is just around the bend creates an anticipatory tension that is released at our first glimpse of the portal. This tension-release experience is repeated as we move along the path to the portal and through to the plaza. Even though our ultimate destination is the space beyond the portal, the gateway can be a kind of destination, an object of attention in itself. Gateways may be understood in terms of experiential distance. There is a point of first encounter. Initial contact with the portal might be from several blocks away or at close range such as turning a corner and being in the gate's shadow. When there is an experience of procession to portal and when the portal is marked architecturally (arch, columns), we sense the gradual revelation of its form, detail, and surface as we draw closer. This gradation of disclosure is enriched by the view into the urban space that is framed by the gate opening. On approach, the portal aperture grows larger, revealing more and more of the plaza beyond. On passing through, the architecture of the gateway slides past and behind our peripheral vision, and perception is filled only with the plazaspace. The position of the portal in the plaza geometry affects the character of the framed view to plaza as we approach and the gradual revelation of the full plaza place when we enter. The dynamics of disclosure and the arrival experience are quite different when an urban space is entered on axis, off axis, at a corner, from behind the anchoring building, or parallel to its front facade. The plaza is framed differently and presents itself differently from each of these portal positions.

The emotional power of a gateway is intensified when all our senses are engaged in the experience. We feel the quickening of pace as we draw near, hear plaza sounds growing in clarity and level, take in the ever richer scents of the approaching destination, feel the path texture underfoot. Our whole body tastes the plaza.

Historical significance

Ambience is sometimes flavored and amplified by history. The portal may be the site of ancient traditions, rituals, celebrations. Perhaps it is the city entry where visiting dignitaries were once welcomed, the setting for the town's political speeches, or the ceremonial gate that sanctified the city's soldiers as they marched out to engage enemies. The significance and atmosphere of history is magically present here and now when we know the past of the place. We participate somehow in those historic events, rituals, transformations. Feelings of celebration, joy, sadness, fear, or weighty meaning associated with the past still linger at the place. And we sense them as we pass through the portal. Regard, respect, reverence are deepened if understanding of present urban role, function, and quality is underlaid with appreciation of history.

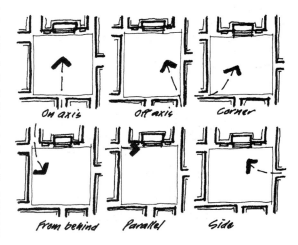

On axis   Off axis   Corner

from behind   Parallel   Side

The good portal

An urban entryway may be considered successful because of its beauty as an object or because of its role in the town form. A triumphal arch might not function as an actual portal but nonetheless be an elegant urban ornament. The goodness of a functioning portal is largely based on the success of the path and place it connects. It is difficult to describe a gateway as successful if it serves as an invitation to a dead and unattractive plaza. Portals need not be deliberately designed to be good. Unplanned building configurations can shape a beautiful garden entry experience and become a fitting terminus for a street. If there is evidence of design attention in the making of the gateway, we may consider the application of the success criteria discussed earlier. The headings of Definition, Identity, Character, Beauty, Habitability, Significance, Connectedness, and Sensuality guide us to telling questions about portal success. Is the portal well-formed? Does it have shape, a sense of entity, thereness? Does the gate possess presence? Is it memorable as an element and experience in its own right? What is the energy quality there, the feeling tone? Is it supportive of the pathspace and placespace that it joins? Does the portal offer an aesthetic experience? Are we moved emotionally by its attributes? Is urban life affirmed by the portal? Does the entryway have a history that deepens our experience there? How does the portal relate to other portals, paths, and places? Is it part of a larger pattern? Questions like these can lead us to personal value positions and attitudes about portal success.

Place

Places in cities are the plazas, courtyards, gardens, and parks. They are the destinations to which paths take us, the urban rooms into which we move through portals. In dense town form, places are the voids between the solidity of building, relief and release from the compression of streets. Whereas path is linear and portal is point between path and place, place has spatial volume, roomlike stability of shape and proportion.

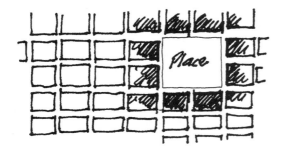

Path is about anticipation, expectation, approach. Portal is about transition, threshold, entry, arrival, disclosure, orientation. Place is about joining, being, belonging. While path invites us to move and portal to move through, place invites us to stay, to settle in and participate in the city life there. Some urban places are dedicated to vehicular traffic or parking, but we are interested here in spaces for pedestrian use. An urban space may have been deliberately planned or may have evolved unselfconsciously over many years with no comprehensive design attention ever devoted to it. A grand plaza today could have had humble beginnings as the site of the town market in the early days of the city's history. The enlargement and shaping of urban places often happens in conjunction with the construction of major civic buildings or as a power gesture by a new government regime. When spaces are planned, they frequently are dedicated to and named for important events or people in the town's history.

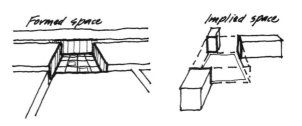

Container

Aspects of the physical presence of urban places that we tend to notice on first encounter are spatial volume, building facades, freestanding elements in the space, and ground plane.

Spatial volume is the open area contained by the buildings, its sectional, dimensional, scalar qualities. Spatial volume has shape, length, width, height, proportion. It has edge conditions that are sharply defined and planar or convoluted and rambling. A plaza space can be fully formed and defined by boundary buildings or barely inferred by a few structures that only imply the space.

The building facades that shape an urban space can occur as several types of enclosing fabrics. There may be no featured buildings and no comprehensive effort to plan the facades as a total composition. One or more of the plaza facades could be designed as a coherent unity. A single building might be featured, anchor the space, provide a focus, and establish the space's theme and character. There could be several featured structures that contribute to the identity of the place. An urban space can be formed by continuous abutting facades or an ensemble of freestanding structures.

Attributes of plaza elevations can be understood hierarchically. We may appreciate the facade along a space's edge in terms of its overall height and length, its general coloration and its roof profile. Attention might move to the material palette, massing articulations and surface treatment such as window pattern, pilasters, columns, cornices, and balconies. We scan the elevation for building doorways, window displays, and gaps between structures that offer exit and entry options. Our intensity of focus, level of attention paid to facade detail, and kinds of elevation information that interest us are influenced by our reasons for looking. Porches, awnings, arcades, and entrances are objects of intense scrutiny if it begins to rain.

Urban places often contain freestanding elements such as statues, sculpture, benches, pavilions, fountains, flags, or trees. They may represent important events, mark historic spots, define areas, answer visual axes, form part of a composition, anchor significant geometric positions, or organize space and activity. These elements can be strong contributors to the thematic power of the place or simply serve as decoration and functional scenery.

The ground plane in a plaza can be primarily paved or grassed. Combination hardscape-softscape spaces create patterns formed by their figural relationships. Paths may be differentiated as defined walks, or the space might be completely paved, offering strolling opportunities in all directions. Some plazas are sloped or multilevel. Ground materials are of interest too. What is the paving made of? What are its most noticeable qualities? Color, texture, unit shape, size and scale, finish, consistency versus variation, joinery, edge conditions, and patterns within the paving may catch our eye. Is there more than one material used? How are they arranged? Landscaping properties that can be appreciated are type, placement, condition and maturity of plant materials, subplaces in the space created by landscaping, geometric configurations, and water features. Ground-plane geometry is often responsive to the overall geometry

and configuration of the space and to the dimensions, composition, and entry positions of important facades.

Experientially, spatial volume, building facades, freestanding elements, and ground plane are perceived holistically, dynamically. Our understanding of place is composed of moving and stationary perspectives that register plaza elements and qualities in a rapid succession of immediate experiences, immediate memories, and immediate expectations. Our point of plaza entry, movement pattern in the space, and scanning configuration may be motivated and purposeful or guided only by the visual dynamics of the place. Are we there to take slides of the church? Searching for the entrance to the museum? The address of a friend? A particular shop? Or are we just strolling with no particular agenda?

Activity

Taxonomies can be useful in recognizing, understanding, and describing human activity in public spaces. These noticing/naming systems tend to occur at two levels. The first level of noticing activity involves immediately observable attributes of behavior. The second level moves to recognition of finer, more subtle activity distinctions and similarities.

First level noticing/naming categories for recognizing and describing action in urban space are active-inactive, vehicular-pedestrian, moving-stationary, native-tourist, and thematic-hybrid.

One of the first things we sense about a public space is its aliveness. Is something happening? Are people there? Or is the space vacant, dead? This deals with the extent to which people are present regardless of what they're doing. A plaza may be elegant as an architectural container but unactivated. People don't come because there is no reason to come. There are no animating purposes for the population to get there and stay there. Aliveness intensity can vary over time. Plazas are sometimes active during weekday working hours but dormant in the evenings and on weekends. Aliveness may mean the place is densely populated, activated with high-energy. Mardi Gras-like action. Aliveness can also take the form of small groups moving slowly in quiet reverence.

Vehicular-pedestrian is another category by which we make immediate sense of activity. Is the space primarily dedicated to vehicular traffic or to people on foot? If the space is shared by both, we quickly notice the domains claimed by each. A plaza can be alive with honking, grid-locked, agitated drivers or packs of loud, speeding, smoking scooters. The plaza is activated but not a very friendly environment for pedestrians. A space used exclusively as a parking lot is dead. Filled, not with people but with lifeless machines.

Moving-stationary refers to the extent to which the pedestrian activity in the place is primarily circulation and movement or staying put and doing things. A plaza can be full of motion with streams of people walking around and through the space. The place is kinetic, dynamic with the swirling energy of movement. Origins and destinations or just strolling for the joy of it. Or the place might be mainly activated by people engaged in stationary pursuits such as eating at outdoor cafes, sitting on benches, standing and talking, lying on the grass, or taking photos. Usually both stationary and moving activity are present, and we notice the extent of each and generally where each is happening. Aspects of movement elaborated on later in Ambience are speed, pace. Pedestrian circulation can be slow, smooth, even. At the pace of strolling and lingering. And it may be fast, darting, turbulent.

The native-tourist category helps us describe the plaza as a working space used by the local residents or a tourist destination, animated by out-of-towners. Many successful spaces accommodate both to some extent. The native-tourist distinction is particularly time-sensitive. Tourists may be noticeably present in the summer with the native population taking the place back in the fall, winter, spring. Or tourists might define plaza activity during the day, the locals in the evening.

Thematic-hybrid addresses the extent to which behaviors in the place are focused and organized around a central purpose or theme or are mixed and non-thematic. Thematic activity often results from a dominant function or building or can evolve as a town tradition. A plaza may be known for its shopping opportunities. Shopping can even be specialized as in high-fashion clothing, leather goods, jewelry, or antiques. Other themes frequently encountered include behaviors associated with restaurants, museums, churches, government, art galleries, and concert halls. Thematic action shaped by tradition is less determined by building types and functions and more by civic habit. A plaza might be where neighborhood children play, old men play board games, lovers stroll and cuddle on benches, residents come in the evening to share the day's gossip. Hybrid plaza activity is less pure in its constitution. There are several types of action happening together. These behavioral mixes can be mutually supportive as when they all contribute to the celebrative energy of the space. Or

they may be strange, even contradictory companions such as prostitutes roaming a church plaza.

Second-level categories for sensing, naming, and appreciating public place activity deal with behavioral attributes that are not as immediately noticeable as those attributes in the first-level categories. We have to look more closely or conduct survey research to harvest second-level information. First-level noticing/naming categories involve bipolar scales for describing activity characteristics. Second-level categories are open menus for seeing and understanding urban space behavior. They are behavioral type and description, spatial distribution, timing, sensitivity to contextual conditions, and demographics.

We will explore each of these categories as they apply to pedestrian activity.

Behavioral type and description involve us in the particulars of what's happening in the space. While a first-level observation might be that a plaza is populated with cart vendors attracting tourists, second-level study could address how many there are, what they are selling, merchandise price and quality, or vendor selling techniques and behavior. We might be interested in specific aspects of vendor activity such as vendor aggressiveness, willingness to negotiate price, most popular merchandise, profitability, and economic impact on the community.

Spatial distribution looks at where the vendors have positioned themselves in the space. Do they move around or stay in one location? Is there an understanding among the vendors about territory? Are their sites assigned, or do they select them? What are considered the prime spots and why? How do their locations relate to plaza circulation, entries to buildings, sun and shade, visibility and exposure, prestige, setting attractiveness, convenience? Are there patterns created by vendor positions? In what ways do vendors relate to and use plaza elements and qualities to enhance sales?

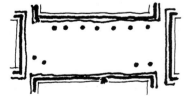

Temporal considerations involve changes in plaza activity over various time periods. Does the number of vendors remain the same over the year, or does the number change with the seasons? Is there a turnover in the kinds of vendors present? Are they absent altogether in the winter? Does the merchandise change in type or quality? How and why do vendor behaviors, spatial distribution, sensitivity to contextual conditions, and demographics change over the year, season, month, week, weekend, day-night, and holidays? Do prices rise and fall? When is business good? Slow? What are the meaningful time intervals for understanding vendor activity in the space?

Sensitivity to contextual conditions is closely related to time. Special events, weather, seasons, business cycles, pulse of plaza population density are contextual situations, climates within which the vendors operate. Vendor behavior may be more or less sensitive to these various contexts. More or less responsive to shifts in one, several, or all situational factors at the plaza. Do the vendors show up on rainy days? How much better is business when special events happen at the plaza? Are the vendors less aggressive when police are on patrol? Are prices more negotiable when the plaza is crowded?

The demographic aspect of activity addresses characteristics of the population using the space. Demographic interests might begin with readily observable factors. Examples are total head count: counts of the various population groupings; distribution of groups by space location, gender, ethnicity, general age categories, dress, body language and demeanor; use of environmental props (benches, railings); and gravitation to spatial features (fountains, building entries). Demographic understanding of urban space can also include information requiring closer observation, interviews, survey instruments. Information not apprehendable by casual observation alone. Where do the tourists come from? Where do the natives live? What is the demographic profile of space occupants in terms of income, occupation, marital status, children, religious/political preference? How do people feel about the space? Do they feel safe? Comfortable? Inspired? Proud? Alienated? Do they know where they are and how to find what they need? Do they like the place? Why?

Our interest in the aspects of activity mentioned above may apply to a moment in time or over an extended period. The moment could be as specific as a Saturday lunch hour in the heart of the tourist season. Attention to activity over longer periods tries to understand how behavior changes in relation to time. When does the tourist season begin and end? What days and times attract the largest and smallest crowds? Is there a shift in population demographics from daytime to evening? Do people feel safe at some times but not others?

Ambience

Place ambience is shaped by the character and condition of the architecture forming the space, by the activity and energy there, and by a wide variety of contextual circumstances. Mood and atmosphere can be flavored by factors like reputation, symbolism, and place name.

The words we use to describe for ourselves the architectural character of a plaza serve to create a component of the space's ambience. Buildings may be heavy, austere, light, ornate, opaque, transparent, inviting, foreboding. We could feel intimately embraced or oppressed by the enclosing structures. Is the space completely enclosed by buildings? Are there gaps between the facades? Key buildings in plazas establish place theme, and theme translates to ambience. A church, palace, museum, city hall, or theater can set the tone and energy in a space.

Building age affects mood. An ancient place feels different from a new place. Care, maintenance, and condition influence ambience too. A plaza formed by buildings covered with pigeon droppings is difficult to soak up with our senses. Ground plane can be a strong mood-shaping element. Is the plaza floor grass? All paved? Is movement controlled by a walk system, or are we free to move in any direction? What are the texture, pattern, and condition of the paving material? The architecture of a plaza includes its landscaping. Plazas lined with trees, canopied by tree groves, spatially articulated by tree groupings have a mood unlike spaces with no landscaping at all.

Vine-covered walks, window pots, trees peeking over cloister gates, glimpses into lush private patios can soften the severity of a plaza hardscape. How do we describe the space landscape to ourselves? Tropical? Spare? Thriving? Dormant? Mature? Nurtured with care? Is the place ornamented with flowers and filled with the aroma of blossoms?

Activity pace and energy help create space atmosphere and feel. We quickly notice if a place is devoted to pedestrians or vehicles, how crowded it is, who owns the space, what people are doing, demeanor, and movement intensity. All senses appreciate the energy of plaza action. We see what's happening. Feel the jostle of the crowd and pavement under foot. Hear the tour guides, church bells, musicians, conversations. Smell the roasting chestnuts, chimney smoke, food, buggy horses. And taste the cappuccino, pastries, cafe fare.

Emotions are influenced by action. Feeling safe, threatened, invigorated, proud, joyful, confused, hassled, frustrated, peaceful can be responses to crowdedness, chaotic action, disorientation, noisy traffic, or being alone in the space at 3:00 a.m. We resonate with the space's energy, especially if it is strong, consistent, and pervasive.

Contextual circumstances affecting ambience were discussed earlier under Path and Portal. They apply to Place too. Temperature, wind, sun, clouds, rain, snow form context for buildings and activities. Early morning, mid-morning, lunch time, late afternoon, early evening, late evening. Each has an energy and feel. Ambience is often noticeably different on holidays, Mondays, Fridays, weekends, and Sundays. Tourist season, vacation time for locals, agricultural rhythms in the country around the town. Christmas buying frenzy, and special city events all cause inflections in place atmosphere. Yearly, seasonal, monthly, weekly, daily cycles manifest mood clues like banners, flags, posters, closed restaurants, turned-off fountains, and darkened windows.

Lighting joins weather, calendar, clock, season, and events as strong influence on space feel. Natural light can be soft and diffuse or sharp and intense. The blue of early morning light sets a different scene from the gold light of sunset. Geography, weather, season, time of day shape natural light together with the configuration of the space. Sun angle, intensity, and color rendition constantly change, producing many moods over a single day. And how is the space lit at night? By store display windows? Flickering gas lamps? White globe clusters on ornate iron poles? Down lights nestled in shrubs? Dramatic up lighting on key facades? Fountain lighting? Each of these illumination methods and fixture placement strategies contributes to evening ambience and draws attention to particular space elements and attributes.

Historical significance

The historical significance of a public space is invisible, yet powerful as a contextual factor affecting ambience. A kind of knowing that infuses all our other appreciations of the place. The shape of plaza history might include a person or group, a series of events or single happening, an extended evolutionary process, or a powerful idea. What role did the place play in the genealogy of the town? How has the space been used since first human contact? Did an important person live there? Is it where citizens assembled in times of civic crisis? Celebrations? Executions? Pronouncements? Was this the site of a revolutionary speech? Riot? Assassination? Triumphal return of soldiers? Often, historical significance is not singular but plural and layered, perhaps beginning

before there was a human settlement and spanning to present time. History contributes to ambience by being a lens through which we take in the tangibles of the site. Or a curtain behind experience whose color reflects onto all we engage with our senses. History can be embedded in a building, a spot on the plaza floor, a tree, a balcony. Somehow, magically, the spirits, echoes, energies, and emotions of history are here, mixing with and flavoring present experience. What was is co-creator of atmosphere with what is. Then is homogenized with now, resulting in a then-now ambience.

A place's past can extend and reinforce present-day energy and mood, or it can contrast, even contradict present ambience. The site might be the location where political power was first consolidated and where the seat of government is situated today. A wonderful cathedral may celebrate the site of an ancient miracle. When history contrasts with contemporary atmosphere, the juxtaposition of yesterday and today can be humorous, poignant, inspiring, tragic. Gross injustice and suffering marked by a magnificent monument. A gambling casino on the site where the town was founded. A mega department store sited where the tiny ancient town market used to be. A marvelous museum for the work of an artist who died penniless. A single, simple flame at the grave of a complex hero.

Our own present mood, health, emotions, mind state, recent experience, expectations, and personal history form another kind of contextual filter through which we behold place. Memories of the space when we were last there tilt the feel of this visit in their direction. Aesthetic preferences, political affiliation, religious opinions, moral values are ingredients in our appreciation of atmosphere and place history. Are all our senses in good health, and are we using them all to engage the place? Is our attention on the space and activity, or are we preoccupied with personal problems? Are we inclined to compare the site with other favorite places? Is this locale the culminating experience in our stroll, or is the best yet to come? We are complex instruments for appreciating ambience because there are so many kinds of filters in us through which a place is experienced. No wonder we differ in our opinions and descriptions of urban spaces.

Place reputation, symbolism, and name join contextual considerations as factors affecting ambience. These are identity-shaping issues, the way a site is known.

Reputation is the accumulated history of opinions about a place, a strong influence on what we anticipate experiencing there. Reputation fosters a predisposition toward appreciating ambience in particular ways. A tendency to alertness for certain place elements and qualities. A plaza might have a reputation of being dangerous at night, a hive of pick pockets, an assembly of great restaurants, being sadly deteriorated, or lovingly maintained. We tend to see what we expect to see. Symbolism and meaning are ambience components. What does the place stand for? Refer to? Bring to mind? Symbolism can be multiple and layered or singular and focused. A plaza can be about a benevolent ruler who built the space. Or it might be the logo of an age, legacy to a designer, emblem of a political ideology, and exemplar of an historic style. Whatever the place represents becomes party to ambience, just as real in fashioning feeling tone as the physical fabric.

A plaza name can be telling, definitive, evocative with regard to atmosphere and mood. Place name predisposes us to see the place in a particular way, especially if we know the story behind the name. Names of people, buildings, events, functions, ideas are frequently employed to identify urban space. What a place is called can establish a boundary within which meaning and mood are experienced. Town hero, cathedral, military victory, banking center, celebration of freedom. Each of these themes pervasively flavors all that is in and at a place.

We conclude our discussion of place with attention to hybrid place, scale of attention, and the good place.

The good place

What is a good place? What makes it good or not so good? Earlier we applied success criteria to path and portal. Now we apply definition, identity, character, beauty, habitability, significance, connectedness, and sensuality to place.

A successful place is well defined, providing a sense of arrival, of culminating experience. Its space is clearly distinct from the path spaces leading to it. We know we've arrived at a there-space. The shape and dimensions paradoxically provide enclosure, embrace, containment and release, freedom and openness. Boundary conditions are clear, well-formed, legible, making a defined urban room.

Good place has distinguishing qualities that establish a unique identity. Something that makes the site special. One of a kind. The way we differentiate a place from other places can be by its architectural elements and landscape, by activities and dominant uses, by atmosphere and mood. What is it about the space that is noticeable, remarkable, memorable? A single compelling facade? An encircling arcade? Doorways and windows? The area might be filled with roving musicians, noisy tourists, or neighborhood children playing soccer. A space's signature can be its intense festivity, chaotic swirl, somber reverence.

Successful places have strength of character. Unmistakable personality profiles. A space may be proud or humble, flamboyant or reserved, pretentious or sincere. Place theme is clear, reinforced by architecture and surfaces, actions and events, atmosphere and mood. We inhabit the space on its terms, immersed in its energy and demeanor. The site's chemistry impresses us. It is alive, orderly, regal. Or gentle, delicate, elegant. The place has body language, complexion, facial expression, hand gesture, vocal inflection. It has attitude, posture, and clothes to match.

Great urban rooms are beautiful. They offer us the gift of their own unique elegance. A plaza can be pretty, handsome, a rich jumble of complexity, or a graceful, reassuring orderliness. An environment of agreeable tensions or serene refuge. Beautiful places are special, extraordinary. Their aesthetic quality startles us and floods over the edges of expectations. Beauty invites us to expand our being, who we are, in order to fully take it in. To stretch our senses to appreciate its intensity. An aesthetic experience satisfies, it fits and fills a void in our soul. It pleases, renews, enlivens, elevates, affirms.

A good public space is habitable. It generously accommodates life, supports its housed activities. It empowers, enables, encourages people to come and participate. Everything about the locale invites, welcomes, promotes a climate of safety, convenience, choice. Place location, scale and configuration, composition and surfaces, furniture and accessories, ornamentation and landscaping all symbiotically combine as supportive setting for human intention and action. Habitability success is measured by sustained human presence, by aliveness and vitality day and night, year round.

Great places have historical weight, gravity of significance. They played meaningful roles in the town's evolution. These sites are rich with myths, spirits, echoes of times past. When we're in these spaces, we're in their history. Their stories are as palpable as the air, and like a breeze on our face, we feel the ancient energies that are still there. Pride, reverence, gratitude, sadness, admiration are emotions that historical place can engender in us today. We resonate with old vibrations that are still very alive in the present.

Good public places enjoy connectedness, relatedness to immediate surroundings and to the broader community beyond. The space participates in a network, set, series, pattern that is larger than itself. It has a role, a function in the town's family of places. Successful urban space is well situated geometrically, experientially, aesthetically in the city's path system. There are interesting and meaningful routes of arrival and departure, views to and from the place, engaging continuities and discontinuities with the neighborhood. A good place asks to be seen in a larger context to fully understand and appreciate it.

A successful place is sensual. All our senses are awakened, invited to take the site in, to touch the space in many ways. To be there is a multidimensional experience. Views, sounds, scents, textures, tastes, movement, time all create individual impressions and combine into holistic memories. We appreciate the space experientially, with our bodies, not just with our minds. Cool doorknobs, freshly baked bread, misty breeze in our face, organ music from an open chapel door, coffee, and pastry mix with what we see to form a sensual occasion. Sensuality translates to emotions, feelings, higher levels of mindfulness. Sights, sounds, and scents foster immediate and direct impressions and remind us of past experiences that have their own emotional content. Great places call us to alertness, aliveness, full use of all dimensions of our humanity.

Source and copyright

This chapter was published in its original form as:

White, E. (1999), 'Path–Portal–Place', in White, E. (1999), *Path–Portal–Place, Appreciating Public Space in Urban Environments,* Architectural Media Ltd, Tallahassee, 57–96.

Reprinted with kind permission of the author.

22

What makes a good building?

S. Cantacuzino/The Royal Fine Art Commission [1994]

Buildings in depth

If the appreciation of architecture is largely a matter for the eye, the practice of architecture is grounded in reality – social, economic and physical. A building to be successful must not only be pleasing to the eye but withstand the forces of nature and fulfil its purpose. Architecture, therefore, is far from being a pure art which can be judged in terms of aesthetics only – of composition, balance, scale, proportion, rhythm silhouette texture, contrast, etc. That architecture was a far more complex and contradictory art than, say, sculpture, was recognised by Vitruvius when he said that all building must possess the qualities of *utilitas, firmitas,* and *venustas,*[1] later translated into "commodity, firmness and delight",[2] of which only the last is concerned with pure aesthetics.

It follows that we cannot make a fair judgement of a building without knowing a good deal more about the building than the appearance from outside. We must distinguish, for example, between building types. What makes a good power station does not necessarily make a good office building. Judging the merits of a design requires knowledge of the building's function, of the way the building responds to specific needs like energy efficiency, of the way the building is constructed and the materials with which it is built and of the way it fits into the overall plan of the area. Design, as the Royal Fine Art Commission pointed out long ago, covers the plan and form of the building as well as the elevational treatment of the façade.[3] A building therefore is a totality. It is much more than its external look. Its façade must not only address the street or

square in front of it but also bear some relation to the plan and section which lie behind it.

To speak of misrepresentation, deceit or falsification is not a moral judgement. Both functional and structural misrepresentation are common in architecture and may be justified by the result. At Trinity College library and Emmanuel College Chapel, both in Cambridge and by Sir Christopher Wren, the external appearance misrepresents the internal arrangement, but does this with the clear purpose of presenting an harmonious façade to the courtyard in which each building stands. Structural misrepresentation is even more common: of historical structural forms only the Gothic pointed arch is self-supporting. Unlike the round arch of Roman, Byzantine and Renaissance architecture, it does not have to be embedded, as Coventry Patmore noted, "in heavy masses of wall in order to make it constructively good and artistically beautiful".[4]

Palladio's churches in Venice are a good example of façades which express the plan and section of the building. Palladio took the traditional church plan of a central nave flanked by two aisles and expressed in section by lean-to roofs over the aisles butting into the nave walls which rise to carry a higher pitched roof over the nave. The principal space of the tall nave and the subsidiary lower spaces of the aisles are expressed on the west fronts of these churches by a major central temple-front flanked by two half temple-fronts. The interpenetration of the two temple-fronts produces an effect of great unity, reflecting the spatial unity and climax of the interior at the domed crossing and apsidal east end of the church. These west fronts, therefore, not only address the lagoon or the *campi* in an appropriate manner, but also perfectly express the form and purpose of the church.[5]

Expression

Churches and temples have always claimed high significance on a symbolic and emotional plane. The majority of the buildings designed today cannot do so. To monumentalise a power station or an office block is to debase the currency of architectural values by pretending that they are something other than what they are. It renders the buildings themselves ridiculous as was only too apparent in the scheme for Paternoster Square in which the office buildings were criticised by the Royal Fine Art Commission as "a series of large and separate 'palaces' fitted into an informal street pattern".[6] The street plan might have generated instead a proper street architecture as in Georgian streets and squares where the whole is greater than the sum of its parts. Although direct architectural expression of the function of an office block may produce a satisfactory solution in the right hands, it has too often done little more than emphasise the inhuman quality of the building type. "An office block", as the Royal Fine Art Commission has remarked, "requires a special delicacy in its architectural treatment to dissipate the oppressive effect of the 'human filing cabinet' both in respect of those who use the offices and of the passer-by".[7]

With power stations "a straight forward expression of the practical requirements is usually aesthetically the best".[8] In 1948 the Royal Fine Art Commission was pleased to note an increasing realisation of the fact that, handled with imagination, a simple housing for the large-scale electrical equipment involved can be much more impressive than a cathedral-like structure. In the case of Bankside Power Station the Commission considered the design eminently suitable for the site but believed that the site was inappropriate for an industrial building of this kind. "Its use for such a purpose struck at the root of good town planning and zoning principles, and necessitated a departure, in some respects, from the Commission's view that the architectural treatment of such buildings should be more functional and less monumental".[9]

Bankside and Battersea power stations, both cathedral-like structures, are much admired today, and the latter is even "listed". Many people would like both stations preserved and adapted to new uses. This is not so much an indication of a change of fashion as confirmation of the lasting tendency

for the public to judge buildings superficially by their external appearance only, and perhaps also of the lasting quality of Sir Giles Gilbert Scott's designs of the envelope. The fact is that the external appearance of early industrial buildings has usually expressed practical requirements and purpose in a direct and straightforward manner, and this way of designing today's industrial buildings must remain the most appropriate, even if it does not necessarily exclude other ways.

Planning and aesthetics

In assessing the merits of a building it can be helpful to distinguish between the building looked at in isolation and the wider aspects, usually regarded as planning matters, of environmental impact, setting, fitting into a given context, spaces between buildings and other aspects of civic design. Use, density, bulk, height, open space are all considered to be planning matters, yet all planning decisions have aesthetic implications. To accept, for example, a single large building with a single use on a whole city block, rather than break up the site with several buildings and uses, has implications of scale, rhythm and silhouette which are aesthetic issues.

It is generally accepted that high buildings, if ill-designed and wrongly sited, can have a disastrous effect by overshadowing fine streets or buildings, destroying famous skylines or causing damage to open spaces like parks, squares or river bank. Yet there is little systematic effort by planning authorities to study the effect at planning application stage and so prevent unpleasant surprises. The larger the open spaces and the lower the surrounding buildings are, the greater is the threat. The vast courtyards of Beijing's Forbidden City, one of UNESCO's World Heritage sites, will remain intensely vulnerable to high buildings in the surrounding areas of the city as long as the Chinese economy is booming and planning regulations based on the simple geometry of lines of vision are not applied.

The London parks are not on the World Heritage list but, as the Royal Fine Art Commission pointed out when faced with proposals for the Hilton and Royal Lancaster hotels, "such parks provide the only places of escape from walls and pavements to trees and grass, and it would be wrong to destroy the illusion of rural surroundings that most of them still retain. It would be an irreparable loss to London and indeed to the country as a whole, if these Parks were to become, like Central Park, New York, mere gaps in a solidly built-up area, with no real escape from the sight of bricks and mortar, or glass and concrete".[10] Thirty-five years later the threat of high buildings around the London parks has receded and it is the relentless pressure from the motor car, as well as a tendency to municipalise, which now endanger "the illusion of rural surroundings".

Context

Fitting new buildings into their context and conversely protecting the setting of existing buildings is nowadays a subject of great concern. This is a reaction to the post-war period when public awareness of these problems was inadequate. There is now a fear of contrast, dissonance and even counterpoint. Yet there are plenty of examples of modern-looking buildings which have become accepted, even admired in their setting. The Royal Fine Art Commission first commented on this subject in relation to the 1947 Town and Country Planning Act. "The question of the appropriateness of new buildings to their architectural surroundings and, indeed, the whole quality of their design, are now matters on which the Planning Authority may exercise its powers of control under the Act. The exercise of these powers can help to raise the general standard of architecture; they can also go far to stultify creative energy and imagination".[11] While the Commission repeatedly called for the new work to be sympathetic in scale and character to that already existing, it also made the point that the new work should be at least as good an example of contemporary design as the older work was of its own period.[12]

The Commission has also underlined the importance of the site and the need to study and understand it. In urban areas it has stressed the need for a critical appreciation of the merits of existing buildings and has urged that "new buildings should not generally be treated as the first instalment of an entirely new piece of civic design, with the implied suggestion that we must put up with the resulting muddle until the whole area has been rebuilt; this may never happen. Each generation will have its own ideas, and in England particularly it is this variety which gives interest and vitality to our towns and cities".[13] These words were written in 1956 but went unheeded during the next twenty years of comprehensive urban redevelopment. In a particular sense they remain unheeded today by planning authorities who compel the architect to design quaint brick buildings with mansards and bay windows, not realising that a place like the Market Square at Lavenham has every architectural style, material and method of construction and is marvellous because it was built by people who had good judgement and confidence in it.

The context and setting of a building are often considered nowadays to be of paramount importance. A greenfield site is just as much a context as a built-up urban area. Whether on a greenfield site or in a town there is the need for something appropriate to site, circumstances and function, but which must also encompass the original and innovative, great architecture on the cutting edge of the art and therefore initially unfamiliar like the Palace of Westminster, the Eiffel Tower and the Lloyds Building, which were all reviled when they were new. Context or the need for integration is only one of a number of factors, and to set too much store by it could deny the opportunity of innovation and excitement in architecture and continue to force many of Britain's most talented architects to build abroad.

There is the need for critical appreciation of the qualities of existing buildings and it is essential to get the basics right, like height, massing and silhouette, before considering elevational treatment. Appropriate designs are often quite ordinary, and therefore familiar and more readily accepted by planning officers. The genuinely original and innovative design, however, must also be recognised and a judgement made whether the resulting contrast is tolerable.

The Royal Fine Art Commission's view has been consistent over the years. In 1960 it looked primarily to such questions "as whether the new work preserves the scale of the setting and whether its colour and texture and general outline harmonise with its surroundings. A good solution is far more likely to be reached by an architect who has these points firmly in mind rather than by one who starts from the assumption that all will be well if either he builds in the original style of if he puts up a building designed in an unmistakably modern manner".[14] This is not support for anodyne contextualism but criticism of the architect who designs from outside inwards, deciding on the style of a building before considering function and purpose, structure and materials and the appropriate use of technology. The criticism is as relevant today as it was thirty years ago.

Judging designs

Criticism and judgement of architecture require knowledge, understanding and skill. They must illuminate the work criticised. The critic's medium is language; and words, Margaret Drabble has said, are as peripheral to architecture as pictures are to novels.[15] The difficulty of expressing a visual art in words makes the literary-minded English resort to witty metaphors. The Royal Fine Art Commission, English Heritage, planning authorities and amenity societies criticise designs rather than finished buildings. Only at this stage can influence on, and control of, design be exercised.

Traditionally the architect communicates by simulating a three-dimensional building in two dimensions with plan, section and elevation; or by greatly reducing the scale with three-dimensional models. The critic has to be able to interpret the architect's design, and this is best done from plan, section and elevation which the lay critic has difficulty in understanding. Models, which are more easily understood, are deceptive, and the more realistic the model, the more deceptive it is. The monochrome model, favoured by architects, is useful in assessing the form, massing and silhouette of a building, both in itself and in relation to its surroundings. The highly realistic model favoured by developers and planning authorities, emphasises the elevational treatment – the outer face and only part of a building most people ever see – at the expense of the organisation and form, bringing out the superficial, often Disneyland character of so much development today.

Understanding the plans, sections and elevations of a building is hard work but essential for a critic to be able to make a sound judgement. An easier and increasingly popular way of communicating with a lay public is by means of computer images, which makes it possible to simulate all the spaces of a building in sequence as if one was walking through them. By way of example, Stirling and Wilford's design for no.1 Poultry in the City of London has a beautiful plan and section, but the arguments about the relative merits of the existing and proposed buildings have been conducted almost entirely at the superficial level of external appearances. Perhaps the virtual reality of computer images would have helped even the most prejudiced to appreciate the consequences on the façades of the plan and section and to understand the building in three dimensions.

Appropriate and good buildings

Is an appropriate building necessarily a good building? English Heritage recently proposed as one of their criteria for the listing of post-war architecture, "intelligence, ingenuity or innovation in the planning and siting of a building".[16] The original Thorn

House in London by Andrew Renton of Sir Basil Spence & Partners consisted of a simple, strong statement: a vertical slab contrasted with a low, horizontal base, for which the prototype is Skidmore Owing & Merrill's Lever House in New York. The concept is never likely to result in an appropriate building in the sense of a good fit, because it breaks up the traditional street which consists of continuous narrow-fronted buildings producing a vertical rhythm. The vertical slab, which is much taller than the existing buildings in the neighbourhood and so out of scale, together with the low horizontal base, work against the traditional street scene and produce a sharp contrast.

At the time of building in the early nineteen-sixties there were not many people who thought respecting or fitting in with the traditional urban pattern of much importance. The Royal Fine Art Commission agreed with the county council that a tower block "would do no damage and might help to redeem what has become a somewhat depressed area ..."[17] The argument then prevailed that the whole street would in due course be rebuilt anyhow. Since then the attitude to our built surroundings has changed and people now see merit in preserving the street and other traditional urban spaces.

Conclusion

The criteria which have been proposed are not intended to be a check-list. The architect does not design in compartments or under separate headings, so that the critic's assessment of the design should also not be made under separate criteria. From what has been said it must be clear, in any case, that the criteria are inextricably bound up with one another. Choice and use of materials will affect rhythm, proportion, scale; massing is bound up with the plan and section; integrity underlies all the criteria. A building may embody every criterion and still not be a good building. Conversely it may be a good building without complying with any of the criteria if the architect is a good designer. The informed eye will quickly spot a good building irrespective of rules or guidelines.

The criteria, moreover, are objective values exhibiting facts which are not coloured by the feelings or opinions of the person making a judgement. To say that a building is good is not the same as saying "I like it". Judgements about design may be partly subjective, but the degree of subjectivity is reduced by scholarship and experience. The consensus which forms the basis of the Royal Fine Art

Commission's judgements is reached by a combination of experienced designers and informed laymen who have first-hand information on each case. Therefore the consensus, even if flawed from time to time, has a degree of authority.

In its assessment of a scheme the Royal Fine Art Commission looks for quality and not for a particular style, which is a matter of taste. It is possible to be objective about quality; taste, on the other hand, remains largely subjective – a matter of personal feelings or opinions. Quality is also enduring, while taste and fashion change. Though undefinable, quality is immediately recognisable.

Wholesale demolition and comprehensive redevelopment was a fashion of the 'sixties and' seventies just as contextualism and façadism are fashionable today. The practice of façadism has developed under commercial pressure from developers who want to build as much floor space as possible behind the façades of listed buildings. Unless there are overriding reasons for retaining the external fabric, it may be preferable to replace the listed building by a first-rate piece of new architecture. But the argument that a good design for a new building helps to justify the demolition of the existing building on the site requires making a judgement about the quality of a new design. It is an argument which is not admitted in official circles, yet making judgements about existing buildings which are going to be listed is accepted practice.

What makes a good building is, quite simply, a good brief, a good client and a good architect – in other words, enlightened architectural patronage. The public – the man in the street – sometimes frustrates enlightened patronage by denying approval and putting pressure on the local authority to refuse planning permission. The public awakening which has taken place over the last twenty-five years, and the public participation which has followed, demand a sense of responsibility which cannot be acquired without an adequate education in visual and environmental matters. While patronage will always remain the privilege of the few, it can no longer operate without support from the man in the street. A better educated public, therefore, becomes a prerequisite of enlightened patronage.

To achieve a good building by means of a good brief, a good client and a good architect is not a simple matter, and requires great effort and passionate commitment. The answer, in the end, must be in the quality of the architecture and in the patron who is prepared to search for quality and take risks.

Notes

1. Vitruvius, *De Architectura,* Bk I, chap iii
2. Sir Henry Wotton, *Elements of Architecture*
3. *Sixth Report of the Royal Fine Art Commission, 1937,* page 8
4. Coventry Patmore, 'Street Architecture', *National Review 5* (1987), page 61
5. For a full discussion of Palladio's church façades see Rudolf Wittkower, *Architectural principles in the Age of Humanism,* London 1949, pages 80 to 87
6. Minutes of the 731st meeting of the Royal Fine Art Commission, 5 June 1991
7. *Eleventh Report of the Royal Fine Art Commission, 1952,* page 4
8. Ibid., page 5
9. *Eighth Report of the Royal Fine Art Commission, 1946–47,* page 13
10. *Sixteenth Report of the Royal Fine Art Commission, 1958–59,* page 8
    Fifteenth Report of thee Royal Fine Art Commission, 1957, page 5
11. *Ninth Report of the Royal Fine Art Commission, 1948–49,* page 8
12. For example in the *Eleventh Report of the Royal Fine Art Commission, 1952,* page 4
13. *Fourteenth Report of the Royal Fine Art Commission, 1955–56,* page 11
14. *Seventeenth Report of the Royal Fine Art Commission, 1959–60,* page 12
15. To the architect John Winter while on a Royal Institute of British Architects Jury
16. Reported in *Building Design,* 2 April 1993, page 3
17. *Fourteenth Report of the Royal Fine Art Commission, 1955–56,* page 6

Source and copyright

This chapter was published in its original form as:

RFAC/Cantacuzino, S. (1994), *What Makes a Good Building? An inquiry by the Royal Fine Art Commission,* RFAC, London, 18–48.

Reprinted with kind permission of the Royal Fine Art Commission, RFAC, London.

23

A report from the front

Peter Buchanan
[1988]

All around us facades are becoming more figurative and flamboyant. They are sprouting gables and pediments, columns and arches, cornices and voussoirs, string courses and colour banding, even towers and turrets, all in a polychrome palette and in a promiscuous mix of varying textured materials from flashy modern to warm or noble (or reconstituted) traditional. This is justified as respect for context, history and human values, and as concern with communication (symbolism) and self-recognition (anthropomorphism). But despite all this, and despite the money and design time lavished on them—even if only by keen and callow year-out students—facades are not seen as a fit subject for serious and unembarrassed discussion.

Though not without good reason, most architects associate facade design with sham and cynicism, with hiding the complex yet banal realities of contemporary life, and with pandering to the lowest-common-denominator populism that pleases planners, councillors and now, possibly, Prince Charles. Compounding unease at such expediency, architects also feel that elaborate and self-conscious facade design betrays the moral spirit of Modernism. Though this constitutes a profound misunderstanding of Modernism (Le Corbusier and Aalto, to name but two, were brilliant facadists), the lack of recent deep thought about, and practice in, facade design means that most of those now being built are clumsy, confused and unconvincing.

But the reasons for facades becoming more richly composed and modelled are legitimate and compelling. We are witnessing a fundamental change in the urban architecture of commerce as facades once again become a major, if not the crucial, concern in design. That they are usually so badly designed may

be cause for embarrassment but not for ignoring them, or for treating them only with the contemptuous mirth or despair that so many provoke. With care and critical attention things can only improve. It is in this spirit that this article faces up to facades and treats them to serious but, we hope, entertaining discussion as something more than gaudy gift wrappings.

Back to the street

Renewed concern with decorative and figurative facades came initially from the rediscovery of the street, and with it, context and history. CIAM and the Charter of Athens had grossly oversimplified the city into little more than an agglomeration of separately zoned functions, freestanding and formally minimalist buildings, and isolated nuclear families, linked only by transport and communication systems. But inevitably the essence of the city was rediscovered in what was being lost—its complex continuities in space and time, in both physical presence and lingering associations. The seamless fabric of the traditional building-lined streets and squares sheltered citizens and their communities psychically as well as physically, and also proffered, in addition to visual delight, all sorts of images and messages with which to furnish meanings and memories.

Dismayed and disoriented by the destruction and discontinuities of reductive Modernism, the public, then the planners, and now the Prince all demand conservation and some reconnection of buildings to each other and to recognisable and memorable convention. The more thoughtful of these people want substantial, tactile and decorative materials which reveal their origins in nature and which weather gracefully. These materials have a past and a future; they are not flimsy, cold or slick man-made materials that only deteriorate visually with denting, dirt and discolouration. There is a desire for windows in walls that suggest that people may lean out of them, and not for smooth, tinted glass skins that sever the street from the life within where people are either oblivious of or desperately trying to ignore those outside. And they want decoration that distracts and delights, intrigues and informs, and not a blank reflectivity— even if it duplicates buildings around it and the clouds scudding by.

Concessions to such demands made so far by developers and their architects are, as often as not, grotesque and disconcertingly paper-thin rather than substantial. But the demands remain reasonable and are bound to intensify. Inevitably architects are going to have to learn to think about, understand, design and detail facades that are neither boring nor bombastic, that are neither mere mimicry and parasitic pastiche nor meaningless collages of random historical elements or those replicated or abstracted from neighbours. Instead, facades will have to have a character and coherence of their own and each will have to acknowledge, if not kowtow to, conventions in order to enter as an equal into a dialogue with its neighbours beside it and across the street.

In desperation some architects will play their trump card and say that such facades cost too much. But this argument is a con. Compared with traditional construction that out-performs and outlasts them, metal and glass skins are extravagantly expensive, as are the workmanship and shuttering costs of unadorned, no-detail, Modernist construction. As proof of both parts of this assertion, look behind many now shabby metal or concrete main elevations to the subordinate side ones: built in cheap block or brick, they are still immaculate.

Big Bang blocks

Certainly the cost and the thickness of the facade were often critical factors in tall, shallow office towers with their huge external wall area. Yet these towers have largely been rejected as an urban solution and rendered obsolete by technological change and the demand for larger floor areas. The post-Big Bang office blocks are reinstating street lines as they hug the perimeters of the block and fit into allowed areas within a reasonable cornice line. And because the external wall to floor area is so small and the interior

so highly serviced, huge increases in the cost of the facade constitute a proportionately small supplement to the total cost. Facades that are rich in material detail and even craftsmanship are now affordable. More than that, several factors are combining to insist that architects exploit this opportunity.

Inside, the office building has become simply a stack of structural trays placed at intervals sufficient for packing in an ever-burgeoning profusion of electrical and mechanical services. The 'people spaces' between the trays belong to the specific culture of each tenant, and are designed by others. The developers' architects can only display their flair on the exterior. With very fluid, high-interest finance, the considerations of early preletting and the quick enclosure of the frame within a high-profile exterior are of more concern to developers and funding institutions than the actual capital building costs. Hence the adoption of what has been called 'the fiscal facade' of factory-made panels fixed, already glazed, on a scaffoldless site. Traditional materials and construction, though much cheaper and not necessarily extending total construction time, are rejected because they do not offer such speed in the creation of an advertising face unmarked by scaffolding.

Creating an outdoor room

But facades, whether fiscal prefab or trad-built, carry responsibilities beyond furnishing buildings with an image and identity. They should also impart these to the outdoor spaces they face and help to create some sense of place there. And as so many contemporary buildings offer little sense of interior or place within, architects should feel compelled to seize the opportunity offered by the recontainment of the street, and by the ample budget for facade-making, to reestablish some sense of place in streets and squares without. Facades must once again face up to their dual role of not just enclosing and expressing the interior, but also of addressing and articulating external space, making outdoor rooms.

That facades should have these two roles is so obvious that it is extraordinary that reductive Modernism recognised only the one and ignored even the purely functional responsibilities to exterior space. Such reductionism was fuelled by the silly charge of formalism (extraordinary, too, that this is still heard today) that was levelled at anything of sufficiently arresting composition to play a commanding role in external place-making. At an extreme, much evident in avant-garde and academic circles, this inability to compose very large building facades, has led to the ultimate formalism of buildings becoming wildly expressive sculpture, gesticulating at the space which they stir and agitate rather than anchor and articulate. The MOMA Deconstructivist show and the 'Grand Buildings' competition were good examples of the genre. Exciting as this may be, is it architecture? Most architecture, after all—even the greatest—has consisted of mainly rectilinear spaces within simple rectilinear volumes crowned by prisms of roof—and the occasional hemisphere. The difference between good and bad architecture in large degree was publicly judged by the composition of the facade.

In its dual role, the facade imparts character to the rooms within as well as to the spaces without. Inside, it does this by admitting and modulating light and by editing and framing views out. Windows and doorways not only permit inhabitants to look and leave, but also to display themselves appropriately framed. The facade, then, is a mediating element, shaping the character of spaces inside and out and serving almost as an active joint between them. It often does this most effectively through itself being an ordered collection of smaller intermediary places. Within, these places may be window seats, deep-revealed windows or bay windows that are also expressed externally. Without, they include porticos, balconies, the aedicules that frame each window as a separate and special inhabitable place, and the columns or pilasters that frame space, if only millimetres thick, against the wall.

The articulation of these external elements, and their size and relationship to each other, largely determine the character of a facade and how effectively it commands the space it confronts. For a facade to anchor fluid space and contribute to a sense of rooted place, it must arrest the eye and also the space that would otherwise slip by. A facade of clearly articulated places obviously has immense advantages over any taut skin. Composition is critical too: visual rhythms that hold the attention played against proportions that create repose; a commanding central focus played against end pieces that stop the composition from dissipating away.

A sense of mass and materiality are important too: tangible mass roots a building and the spaces within and around; material with grain and texture offers a visual porosity that applies a certain friction to slow the eye and space. Also critical is the expression of statics and construction to allow an empathetic appreciation of how forces resolve themselves down into the ground and, in counterpoint, how

the various elements are supported and secured in position.

Search for a contemporary language

Together, all these factors in facade composition encourage the viewer not to just notice, but in various ways to engage (to subliminally interact in the imagination) with the facade. Of course, all these expressive complexities are difficult to realise in the increasingly prevalent fiscal facade. And they are especially difficult to realise when everybody knows that behind the facade are simply vast open areas of interminably altering lightweight partitions. A pastiche traditional facade (which some may think the argument so far was advocating) will be obviously phoney. The solution can only be sought in a contemporary language, which will, probably nevertheless (like that of Le Corbusier and Aalto) allude to and play with that of history and convention.

The search for richness

A historical facade may pull the ground up into a reticulated base and meet the sky with an entablature, above which are statuary and such symbolic elements as domes and pediments. Between base and cornice, floors and rooms are arranged in strict hierarchy. Expressed is a connection between heaven and earth and associated cosmic and social hierarchies. However much we may appreciate such historic facades, we—apart from Quinlan Terry and his cronies—no longer subscribe to the belief systems and so cannot convincingly make them. This is why modern architecture, no matter how tall, no longer connects ground and sky but severs the connections with pilotis below and plant rooms above. Instead, its identical and often roomless floors reach out to the horizon at which they stare in a perfect expression of a rational, non-hierarchic democracy. With each implying a relation only to the horizon (or sun, space and greenery, rather than the complexities of heaven and earth, street and neighbours), such buildings are fundamentally anti-urban and literally deracinated, and alienating. A more deeply satisfying and sustaining architecture needs to be predicated on a richer belief system (or at least conceptual system). These are available to us, both in the humanism manifest in the best Modern architecture and now in the 'myths' of leading edges of science, whether it be biology's Gaia hypothesis or the archetypal symbolism of Jungian psychology. Taken together they might furnish a contemporary conceptual system rich enough to guide the composition of facades in whose faces we may see our own complex aspirations and noble perfectibility.

Source and copyright

This chapter was published in its original form as:

Buchanan, P. (1988), 'A Report From The Front', *Architects Journal*, **188**, 21–27.

Reprinted with kind permission of the author.

Section Six

The functional dimension

Although the 'visual' and the 'social usage' traditions of urban design thought each had a 'functionalist' perspective, it was interpreted differently. In the visual-artistic tradition, the human dimension was often abstracted out and reduced to technical or aesthetic criteria, such that the functioning of the environment could be considered in terms of, for example, 'traffic flow', 'access' and 'circulation'. In the social-usage tradition, there was a concern for the functioning of the environment in terms of how people used it. Consideration of the functional dimension reinforces the notion of urban design as a design process. As design criteria have to be satisfied simultaneously, in any design process there is a danger of narrowly prioritising a particular dimension – aesthetic, functional, technical or economic – and of isolating it from its context and from its contribution to the greater whole. Appleyard (1991: 8), for example, argues that while the economist sees the resolution of differences in terms of 'compromise' and 'trade-offs', the urban designer offers creative ingenuity and adds value through the resolution of differences.

This section presents a set of five chapters. In essence, the chapters discuss how places 'work' – that is, how people use spaces and environments – and how urban designers can make 'better' places. Chapter 24 is **Jon Lang's** 'Functionalism', from his 1994 book *Urban Design: The American Experience* (Van Nostrand Reinhold, New York). This chapter is valuable in attempting to redefine functionalism in the face of Modernism's (mis-)use of the term. Lang takes the stance that there is little wrong with a functionalist agenda *per se*, providing one defines the range of functions that urban design should seek to address. For Lang, this amounts to far more than how a development looks (i.e. whether or not it looks functional) and, instead, encompasses how a design performs against a range of fundamental human needs. According to the argument, urban design should be about designing for these human needs, which, borrowing from Abraham Maslow (1962), Lang defines as physiological, safety and security, affiliation, esteem and self-actualisation needs.

As successful places support and facilitate the activities of people, the design of urban spaces should be informed by an awareness of how people use them. Accomplished urban designers generally develop a detailed knowledge of urban spaces, places and environments based upon both intuition and firsthand experience, and many of the best commentaries on the use of the public realm are based on direct observation of people in public spaces (e.g. Jacobs, 1961; Gehl, 1971; Whyte, 1980; Cooper Markus and Sarkissian, 1986; Project for Public Space, 2001). As the Project for Public Space (2001: 51) advise: '*When you observe a space you learn about how it is actually used, rather than how you think it is used.*' Accordingly, Chapter 25 is from **William 'Holly' Whyte's** *The Social Logic of Small Urban Spaces* (1980). Originally published as a booklet, Whyte's work was subsequently published as a more substantial book, *City: Rediscovering the Centre* (1988). One of the classic urban design canon, Whyte's analysis has been of particular interest in terms of how people use public spaces. A trained sociologist whose interests initially focused on the quality of rural open spaces (LaFarge, 2000), Whyte used photographic studies of a range of New York's urban spaces to observe how public space is actually used. In particular, he observed that the constituency for public space is mainly local and that the provision of public space creates its own demand, but also, conversely, that many of New York's urban spaces were little used and did not justify the extra floorspace given to developers as part of the city's incentive zoning regulations. The Project for Public Space – a non-profit, research and campaigning body established in 1975 – has continued and developed Whyte's work (see www.pps.org).

Chapter 26 is from **Stephen Carr, Mark Francis, Leanne Rivlin and Andrew Stone's** 1992 book *Public Space* (Cambridge University Press, Cambridge), which presents a discussion of 'Needs in public space' drawing on a wide range of research. Its principal value is in synthesising research on the use of public spaces into a five-part organisation of what people tend to do in and need from public spaces. Carr, *et al.*, argue that as well as being 'meaningful' (i.e. allowing people to make strong connections between the place, their personal lives, and the larger world), and 'democratic' (i.e. protecting the rights of user groups, being accessible to all groups and providing for freedom of action), public spaces should be 'responsive' – that is, designed and managed to serve the needs of their users. They identify five primary needs that people seek to satisfy in public space – 'comfort', 'relaxation', 'passive engagement with the environment', 'active engagement with the environment', and 'discovery' – which are used to structure their paper.

Chapter 27 is **Richard MacCormac's** 1994 essay 'Understanding transactions', originally published in the *Architectural Review*. In this paper, MacCormac explores cross-sections through urban areas – in his case, two cross-sections in central London – looking in particular at form and function and seeking to '... *explore the way that cities can be made up of successfully* *co-existent functions of different sorts that find their right place'*. His chief observation is that land uses are symmetric across streets and asymmetric across blocks. In another paper, MacCormac uses an analogy with the game of dominoes where each end of a domino has different numbers of spots, but where the game is played by joining the ends of dominoes with equal numbers of spots. From these observations he later develops a notion of the 'osmotic' properties of streets – the manner in which activities within buildings percolate through and infuse the street with life and activity, noting that some land uses have very little relation to people in the street, while others involve and engage people. Characterising the activity generated by different land uses as their 'transactional' quality, he draws a distinction between 'local' and 'foreign' transactions. Foreign transactions are carried out on a regional or national scale and are not part of the street they inhabit and have very little impact on street life because the activity is essentially internalised. Local transactions, on the other hand, are peculiar to place and sensitive to change, have a significant impact on street life, have active frontages and generate many comings and goings. This does not suggest that some uses are unnecessary or have no place within an urban area – merely that they should have less claim to frontage onto the street and onto public space. MacCormac's paper, thereby, offers a more theoretical background and context for the concept of 'active frontages' in urban design.

Chapter 28 is **Bill Hillier's** 1996 essay 'Cities as movement economies', originally part of his 1996 book *Space is the Machine* and subsequently published

as a paper in *Urban Design International*. Hillier's work has been one of the most important contributions to the development of theory in urban design over the past 25 years. With colleagues at University College London's Space Syntax Laboratory (www.spacesyntax.com), Hillier (Hillier and Hanson, 1984; Hillier, 1988, 1996a, 1996b; Hillier, *et al.*, 1993) has extensively explored and theorised the relationship between the pattern of movement and the configuration of urban space (i.e. the topology of its route network, which is analysed through the use of an axial map). Hillier argues that the configuration of space, particularly its effect on visual permeability, is important in generating movement. From an analysis of the structure of the urban grid (and irrespective of all other factors – including the distribution of land uses – that can be expected to affect movement), he claims to be able to account for, and effectively predict, the distribution of movement within a network. Space Syntax is now widely used as an analytic and design tool, while the theories behind its use continue to be developed by Hillier and others. The ideas, however, are not without their critics – for a fascinating exchange of views see Hillier and Penn (2004), Ratti (2004a; 2004b) and Steadman (2004). For the advancement of urban design as a field, such debate and critique is eminently healthy and Hillier's work challenges urban designers to think critically about the relationship between the configuration of space, movement and land uses.

Matthew Carmona and Steve Tiesdell

24

Functionalism

Jon Lang
[1994]

Despite the criticism that Modernism has received over the years, "Form follows function" remains a good slogan for architecture and urban design provided one redefines *function*. Ultimately, what a designer regards as the range of functions of an urban design is a political not an empirical question, but we have an increasingly well developed positive understanding of people and their environments on which to base such positions. Recent research has considerably enhanced our understanding of the functions that the built environment can possibly serve. A powerful way of considering these possibilities is through an understanding of human needs. This is the position that the Modernists took. Our advantage is that the range of human needs can now be established from empirical research and the clinical experience of psychologists, as well as from introspective analyses. Any statement of the human needs served by the built environment will remain fragmentary because our understanding is incomplete. It always will be, but we can now define functionalism more completely than the Modernists did. In order to understand this assertion, it is necessary to first understand the Modernist concept of functionalism. This understanding will put a revised concept into perspective.

The traditional concept of function in architecture

Twentieth-century urban design ideas have become closely related to the concept of functionalism of the Bauhaus, the de Stijl movement in Holland, and to the Rationalism of Le Corbusier (Trancik 1986).

During the third decade of the twentieth century, Walter Gropius and Le Corbusier argued for an architecture comparable to the functional purity of airplanes, ships, and grain elevators (Le Corbusier 1923; Wingler 1969). Functionalism in architecture came to mean technical efficiency in building construction, with ease and efficiency in the movement of people (i.e., the least movement or fewest actions) as the basis for the internal planning. Functional urban design was thus seen as hygienic, cost efficient, and efficient in the circulation of people and traffic flow while conveniently providing the basic necessities of life (see also Le Corbusier 1948). Sometimes the way climate, but more frequently the way air conditioning and energy consumption as a whole, are handled are items whose performance has to be efficient. The aesthetic quality of the environment, particularly its symbolic aspects, became a byproduct of attaining other ends.

This definition of functional buildings and urban designs is a very limited one, as people like Gropius began to recognize in the 1960s (Gropius 1962), but it is still the basis for much urban design, particularly that based on the speed of vehicular and pedestrian traffic flows. Designs based on purely Modernist functional requirements turn out dull places and, moreover, those that are inefficient in many respects, including their adaptability to change (J. Jacobs 1969). This result is not because traffic engineers and efficiency experts are involved, but because their ends become primary, partly because their studies are understandable, quantifiable, and efficient. As Aldo van Eyck noted:

Instead of the inconvenience of filth and confusion, we have now the boredom of hygiene.

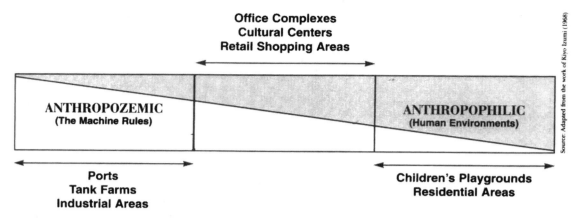

FIGURE 24.1
Anthropozemic and anthropophilic environments

The material slum has gone—but what has replaced it? Just mile upon mile of unorganized nowhere, and nobody feeling he is somewhere (Smithson 1969).

There were a number of early groups of critics of the Bauhaus concept of functionalism. One of them was the influential group, Team 10, whose members tried to base their designs on a greater range of human needs than their predecessors (Smithson 1968; Smithson and Smithson 1970). Another was Buckminster Fuller. To him the Bauhaus innovations were mere fashions without a knowledge of science behind them. In Fuller's opinion, the Bauhaus simply

peeled off yesterday's exterior embellishment and put on instead the formalized novelties of quasi-simplicity permitted by the same hidden structural elements of modern alloys which had permitted the discarded Beaux-Arts garments (quoted in McHale 1961).

Much the same argument is today leveled at the work of architects such as Norman Foster and Richard Rogers. The striving for structural and technological dexterity has become an end in itself without a major understanding of issues of solar heat gain, or of the wearing and weathering of the built environment. Places such as the Beaubourg Centre, Place Pompidou, in Paris, which visually appear to be technologically advanced, illustrate this point (Broadbent 1990). The concern is with the symbolism of functionality, not functionality itself. Despite their criticisms, no new concept of functionalism that can be used as a working base for urban design emerged

from the writings of Team 10, Buckminster Fuller, or the recent Neo-Rationalist designers.

Some critics have said the Modern designs are too functional. This point is conceded provided one has a very narrow definition of function. Other critics (e.g., Fitch 1980 and Newman 1980b) say that Modern designs have not been functional enough. This position is the one accepted here. It assumes that the definition of function of the Modernist was simply too narrow. It was based on too narrow a definition of the human being, too simple a model of people and life, and a strong antiurban bias (Wood, Brower, and Latimer 1966; Stringer 1980; Ellis and Cuff 1989).

If urban design is to serve people well, it must be concerned with the needs of people, and thus the mechanisms they use to meet those needs. The term "mechanism" needs to be interpreted broadly. Not only does it mean the patterns of the built environment, it extends to include other people and other animals, the flora of the world, and the machines people have developed to aid themselves in meeting their needs/desires. A functional environment is not simply one that meet people's needs for ease of movement and access to sunlight, but one that meets the broad ranges of needs of many diverse people and the needs of their supportive machinery. All designs involve a tradeoff between the needs of one person and another, between the needs of people per se and the needs of their equipment (Izumi 1968). In some instances the machines required to support human life comfortably, in comparison to humans themselves, have a very low tolerance for variability in the conditions around them. In such situations, paradoxically, to meet human needs, the machines need to be considered more thoroughly than the direct needs of people themselves. Serving the machines indirectly serves humans.

The concept of functionalism that emerges from this line of thought is much more complex than that of the Modernists. It is also clear that defining the functions that an urban design complex or set of urban design policies is to achieve is a *wicked* problem not a *simple* one. A wicked problem is one in which it is impossible to know, given the limits of human rationality and comprehensiveness of knowledge, whether one has defined the problem wholly or not (Rittel 1971, 1984; Bazjanac 1974; Rittel and Webber 1984). Almost certainly it has not been completely defined.

Given the limits of human knowledge and rationality, urban design problems can only be partially defined (see Cartwight 1973). The functions to be served can only be partially defined; the definition is fuller than in the past. *Function* has been thought of in simple terms—in terms of a limited and completely defined set of variables. Kidding ourselves by having a simple model of the human being or by using ourselves as the model of the human being for urban designing is not helpful in attaining rich and satisfying urban designs for the broad range of people likely to use the places we design.

Human needs as the basis for concepts of functionalism

Listing all the functions that are to occur in a proposed development by type of activity is one way of organizing one's thoughts for urban designing (see Chapin and Kaiser 1979). It is a very pragmatic way of considering urban design problems and is the basis for the planning and design guidebooks that cut through the process of dealing with recurring problems by presenting design standards. The information in these books (e.g., DeChiara and Koppelman 1975, 1978) enables one to ascertain the spatial needs of many activities, and the configuration of the built environment required to make them possible. These guides enable urban designers to make decisions on matters with which they are unfamiliar and on which they have neither time nor need to do the basic research. The research has already been done. These books deal effectively with such fundamental functional requirements as the turning radii of various automobiles but not effectively with the philosophical issues of what goals should be established. They are not set within an intellectual framework for asking

serious questions about life and human problems and desires. Christopher Alexander and his colleagues recognized these limitations in the design of their pattern language (1977), which outlines not only the patterns of solutions but the problems they solve as well as the empirical and/or other evidence for the connection between problem and solution. The language, however, prematurely assumes that nature of a good world.

If the built environment is to serve human purposes one must have a good model of human needs to use as the basis for asking questions about what should be done—what functions should be served—in a specific circumstance (see Krupat 1985). The Rationalists among Modernists certainly recognized that a model of human needs was necessary to guide their thinking. For instance, in order to focus his thinking about the functions of architecture, Hannes Meyer used such a model (Meyer 1928; Wingler 1969). Meyer, who headed the Bauhaus for a short period in the 1930s until his radical political stance led to his replacement by the more politically conservative Mies van der Rohe, was particularly concerned with improving the residential habitat of people. Meyer identified the following human needs as the basis for design:

- sex life
- sleeping habits
- gardening
- personal hygiene
- protection against the weather
- hygiene in the home
- car maintenance
- cooking
- heating
- insulation
- service

Housing design, in this model, is reduced to the provision of shelter and the provision for a number of activities.

Le Corbusier's Radiant City is based on the human need for light, sunlight, and access to clean open air as well as the provision of a number of services, such as shopping, child care, and recreation (Le Corbusier 1934). Important as these functions are, his is largely an *organismic* model of the human being. Issues of territoriality, privacy, security, social action, and symbolic aesthetics, for example, fall outside the scope of such a model. Le Corbusier's design for the Unité d'habitation in Marseilles (Le Corbusier 1953), which came much later in his intellectual development, is

TABLE 24.1
Model of Human Needs

MASLOW (1987) HUMAN MOTIVATIONS	LEIGHTON (1959) ESSENTIAL STRIVING SENTIMENTS	CANTRIL (1965) PATTERNS OF HUMAN CONCERNS	GROSS (LEWIS 1977)	STEELE (1973)
		BASIC NEEDS		
Survival	Physical Security Sexual Satisfaction	Survival		Shelter and security
Safety and Security	Orientation in society	Security, Order		Social contact
Belonging	Securing of love	Identity	Belonging, Participation	Symbolic identification
Esteem	Recognition		Affection Status Respect Power	Growth Pleasure
Self-Actualization		Capacity for choice and freedom	Self fulfillment	
		COGNITIVE NEEDS		
Cognitive	Expressions of love, hostility, spontaneity		Creativity	Growth
Aesthetic			Beauty	Pleasure

Adapted from P. Peterson (1969), Lewis (1977), and Mikellides (1980b)

based on a considerably more complex model of the human being than his earlier work (see also Curtis 1986). Perhaps this added richness accounts for its success in terms of the lives of its inhabitants (Avin 1973; Schafer 1974).

The model of human needs has to be richer than that used by the Modernists. It also needs to be a model that can be used for asking questions about how human needs are manifested in different cultures. The failure of Modern architecture (and Post-Modern and Deconstructionist architecture, for that matter) to deal with questions of culture and design is so well documented now (e.g., Rapoport 1969; Perin 1970; Brolin 1976) and has led to a number of treatises on cultural factors in design (e.g., Rapoport 1977; Low and Chambers 1989) that there is no need to review it here. In contrast, Le Corbusier (1923) observed:

All men have the same organisms, the same functions. All men have the same needs. The social contract which has evolved through the ages fixes standardized classes, functions and needs producing standardized products.... I propose one single building for all nations and all climates.

At a very general level "all men" do, indeed, "have the same needs." However, Le Corbusier was wrong in assuming that the way in which these needs are manifested and can be met is universal. He comprehended neither the full range of human needs nor the individual differences that exist among people within and across cultures or, alternatively, he largely disregarded them in design. Designers need to be sensitive to and argue for environments that fulfill not only "general human needs" but also the specific needs of specific people within specific cultures.

It is clear now that urban design solutions have to be culture-specific. What makes the problem *wicked* is that it is impossible to specify with certainty the important variables of a culture to be used as the basis for design because cultures are always evolving. A general model of human needs has to be one that can be used to ask sensible questions in any culture.

Models of human needs

There are many reasons why psychologists shy away from the investigation of human needs. Not the least of these is that given by Kurt Lewin. He noted that there are as many needs as there are specific and distinguishable cravings. There are, however, generalizations one can make about groups of needs—categorizations of needs—that can be used as the basis for defining a functional urban design.

A number of models of human needs have been examined by designers (e.g., Alexander 1969; P. Peterson 1969; Mikellides 1980b). There is considerable overlap among the models, but each emphasizes a different aspect of human life. Abraham Maslow's hierarchical model of needs, which is, perhaps, the dominant, all-inclusive model, is presented as a "theory of human motivations" (Maslow 1987). Alexander Leighton (1959) describes needs in terms of "essential striving sentiments." Erik Erikson (1950) analyzes individual identities at each stage in the human life cycle. Hadley Cantril (1965) also focuses on stages in the life cycle as a basic determinant of human needs. All of these psychologists bring important insights to the analysis of human behavior, but ultimately it is Maslow's model that holds up as the best comprehensive view. Indeed, in thinking about design issues, most city planners and architects who are concerned with a user needs approach to design have turned to some adaptation of Maslow's hierarchy of human needs.

In 1954 Abraham Maslow proposed a hypothetical model of human behavior in his book *Motivation and Personality,* which has been recently updated by his colleagues (Maslow 1987). His hierarchical "holistic-dynamic theory" draws on the earlier psychological work of John Dewey and Gestalt theory as well as on the psychoanalytical literature. Maslow identifies five sets of *basic needs* from the most fundamental to the most esoteric in a hierarchy of prepotency. "The most prepotent goal will monopolize consciousness . . . and when a need is fairly well satisfied, the next prepotent [higher] need emerges." His hierarchy of basic needs begins with physiological needs—the need for survival. These are followed by safety and security needs, affiliation needs, esteem needs, and self-actualization needs. Maslow also identified a second set of needs, *cognitive and aesthetic needs,* which guide and shape the processes of attaining the other needs but also have a character of their own.

An examination of individual lives indicates that not everybody, consciously or subconsciously, orders the hierarchy in this way. In some instances people's behavior can still be explained in terms of the model, but in others the values they hold turn the model upside down. Some people hold beliefs that place other ends above the need for survival in the hierarchy. Many people have died for their beliefs. There are also people who seem to lead lives without the need for external approval and indeed thrive on censure. However, while they still perceive themselves as part of a class of people, this kind of life can hardly be ideal.

The consequences of looking at urban designers' tasks as the fulfillment of human needs in this way can only be illustrated by understanding the interrelationships among them. The interrelationships form a complex web that shows the futility of any simplistic model of the concerns of urban design (see Fig. 24.2). The full consequences of a functional urban design based on Maslow's model need to be developed in detail, but in order to understand the functions of cities, they need to be previewed here.

The basic human needs

Human needs are neither independent of each other nor mutually exclusive. They are, indeed, highly interdependent. Some needs have a biological basis, others are a product of the sociogenic environment, and many have a biological base that is very much culturally molded. Although the nature-nurture controversy is no longer at the center of psychological research, there are many processes that are still poorly understood. The rise of sociobiological research shows that many of the factors that we assumed were purely cultural may well have biological components at their basis after all (Wilson 1978). Suffice to say here that the prerequisite for the attainment of the full set of needs is having freedom of action within a moral order.

Physiological needs

The basic human need is for survival. To survive one needs life-sustaining inputs of oxygen, food, and water. One also needs to be able to sleep and to move around a territory to obtain the basic necessities of life. If the need for food, say, is unsatisfied, then all the capacities of a person are put into the service of hunger-satisfaction. The architectural need is for shelter from the extremes of heat and cold. Almost no urban design decisions are made only at this most basic level—they deal with higher-order needs that subsume the need for survival.

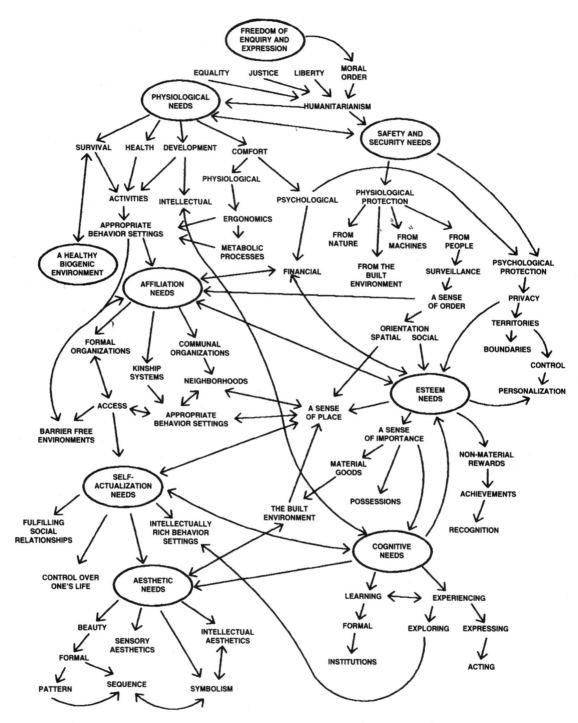

FIGURE 24.2
The hierarchy of human needs and design concerns

Extensions of the need for survival are not as fundamental for life but are very much sought after. People have a need to be healthy and to be comfortable. Comfort and health are psychological as well as physiological states. People are often prepared to trade off comfort and health for many other kinds of ends such as prestige, but having a comfortable environment and being healthy are also associated with self-esteem. Thus, in specifying how to design the built environment to meet physiological needs, much depends on individuals' expectations, which are, in turn, based on their habituation levels.

There are a number of other needs that might be regarded as semiphysiological—they have biological bases but are very much culturally attuned (P. Peterson 1969). One such need is sexual. Henry Murray (1938) regarded this as a basic physical need, but many people lead fulfilling asexual lives. The next level of needs in Maslow's hierarchy—safety and security needs—can also be seen as semiphysiological.

Safety/security needs

There is a need for harm-avoidance among all higher species of animals. This is really a self-protecting device. Sigmund Freud took the extreme position in dealing with harm-avoidance in his definition of the instinct for *self-preservation* (Freud 1949). He believed all human behavior is determined by the principle of avoiding pain and seeking pleasure. The urban design concern here is with the layout of environments that provide safe and secure settings in which people can pursue their lives.

Safety needs combine a diverse set of other needs. The broadest division is into physiological and physical safety needs and psychological needs. The former are concerned with attaining a security of knowing that one is safe from physical harm—from the natural elements, human elements, and from artificially created elements of the environments such as moving cars and structurally unsound buildings. Humans also have the need to be psychologically secure, to have control over the environment, to know where they are in space and in time, to not be socially or physically lost. In addition, there is a need for privacy from censure for carrying out various activities and for developing self-confidence. These needs clearly blur into the next higher set in Maslow's hierarchy, the need for affiliation.

The ways in which safety and security needs are fulfilled have much to do with the nature of the social organization of society, but the layout of the environment also affords or denies the possibility of many kinds of behavior that are necessary for them to be fulfilled. There are many examples that illustrate this observation. The layout of cities for defensive reasons is a major factor in design. Until the nineteenth century the major concern was with defense against outside invasion (A. Morris 1979). Now the concern is more for defense from one's fellow citizens (Newman 1972; Stollard 1991). The layout of the city and its precincts is also a major factor in finding one's way around, in orientating (Lynch 1960; Passini 1984). Fulfilling such needs gives one a feeling of security that results from being in control of situations.

Security is also obtained through being a member of a group—fulfilling the need for belonging. It is obtained through being part of a stable social order. When this stable social order starts to change—often in order to attain other social needs such as self-determination, or if the technological rate of change is so high that people get worried about their abilities to deal with the situation—there is a tendency to hold on to the symbols of the past. Thus there is, or at least appears to be, a correlation between major upheavals in the social order of a society and the degree of concern for the preservation of the existing environment—physical and institutional.

Affiliation needs

All individuals need to know who they are and to recognize themselves as distinct human beings—as having distinct identities. Identity-formation is a continuous process and has as much to do with the groups of which one is a member as much as one's own uniqueness. Our affiliation needs are met by knowing that we are members of a group and of a social and a moral order. These groups are diverse and based on such common characteristics as kinship, locality, and interests. People need to have a sense of belonging, community, and relatedness, as well as to receive affection and approval from other people. This category of needs includes the need to be with others—a desire to please and win affection. The costs of these needs being unmet may well be psychologically high, causing feelings of anxiety and often resulting in a withdrawal from society. Such isolation results in a lack of a feeling of psychological security.

Allied to the need for affiliation is the need for privacy. It serves the need for control of information flows about what one is doing and what others are doing. As such it is also a mechanism for fulfilling security needs, as already noted. Having privacy also helps to meet many other needs such as that of *counteraction* (Murray, 1938). Counteraction involves the active striving to obliterate a humiliation by regrouping and then striving again.

Affiliation needs are complex and interact with all other needs. Thus not only having available groups for us to join is important but also the displaying of symbols that show that we are indeed members. Some of these symbols are highly subtle and are largely unselfconscious; others are self-consciously designed. When we strive to be a member of a group we become very conscious of the symbols of membership, but once we are true members and accepted as such without perceived ambiguity, the symbols of membership are less important. The symbolic aesthetic of the places we inhabit is fundamental to our individual and group identities.

Urban designers tend to think of the consequence of people having a basic need for affiliation in terms of gathering places, of places to watch what is going on—the vicarious participation in the lives of others. It tends to be thought of in the romantic terms of English pubs, French cafes, and Italian plazas (Lennard and Lennard 1989). Similar places in the United States are still important for some people, but all kinds of identity-enhancing events bring people together either in person or through various media such as television. Innovations in communications technology have vastly changed the patterns of behavior related to affiliation needs (Brill 1989; Schmandt *et al.* 1990). The automobile as a means of bringing people together for a variety of purposes means that propinquity of like-minded people is less important than it once was. The telephone has had a similar impact. Urban designers need to understand these changes and potential changes and to design with them in mind rather than hanging on to a romantic view of life that has too frequently resulted in the creation of places that are unused and unloved (Jacobs 1961; Whyte 1980; Hitt 1990).

Esteem needs

All people need to have a stable, firmly based, usually high evaluation of themselves. People strive for competence, confidence, independence, and freedom of self-expression. There are two, often interrelated, types of esteem needs—to be in possession of self-esteem and to be held in esteem by others. One gets self-esteem through achievement and through the recognition by others of one's achievements. To get a sense of achievement one needs to be able to master tasks, to be able to manipulate, organize, or

own time, physical objects, or ideas, and, maybe, simply to look good—to be regarded as beautiful. John Atkinson and David McClelland (McClelland *et al.* 1953) identify three types of achievement: unique accomplishment, long-term involvement, and successful competition with a standard of excellence. Some people have a higher need for achievement than others. They strive harder in order to achieve esteem ends. Much depends on how one is socialized, so much is culturally dependent.

The fulfillment of esteem needs is manifested in many ways. It is shown, for instance, through having control of one's own life, and often over other people's lives, and having the symbols of control to display. The architectural mechanisms are diverse—many have to do with symbolic aesthetics, but they also have to do with territorial control, through real or symbolic barriers, over one's own space. Similarly, architectural and urban layout types and their artistic expression are often associated with specific groups of people. If we wish to be perceived as a member of that group we strive to use the appropriate architectural symbols. If we do not, we avoid those symbols.

Self-actualizing needs

Maslow (see 1987) has expressed dismay that the need for self-actualization has been interpreted as the need to be what one can be without regard for others. While there is the need to have freedom of action, to shake off restraints, and to be independent, there is also the need to provide succor to other people.

Once esteem needs have been met, people often sense a new discontent and restlessness in themselves unless they can be creative in what is best fitted for them. "A musician must make music, an artist must paint, a poet must write, if he is to be at peace with himself. What a man can be, is what he must be" (Maslow 1987). Carl Jung (1968) has termed this need "individuation," the process of striving toward individuality and self-realization. It may be accompanied by the striving for appropriate architectural symbols (Tyng 1969), but more likely for behavioral control and autonomy. Many people's lives get stuck at striving for esteem and never reach the self-actualizing stage (Maslow 1987). The full implications of these observations for urban design are unclear.

Cognitive and aesthetic needs

Striving to attain cognitive and aesthetic needs parallels the striving for the attainment of basic needs.

The need to be able to learn and the need for beauty are fundamental to human existence and to the attainment of basic needs.

Cognitive needs

Acquiring and categorizing knowledge is necessary for survival. One has to have some understanding of the world in order to survive in it in other than in a purely externally nurtured state. To behave successfully and to understand one has to learn. In any society there is a need for continuing to learn. Many formalized ways exist through the provision of educational institutions, but the opportunities to learn do not have to be organized in a formal way because the everyday world is full of wonder. The whole environment presents a universe to be explored and for testing one's knowledge and skills. It is a storehouse of information, available for use and for attaining understanding and wisdom. People strive to have access to it to the degree necessary for attaining their basic needs. Cognitive needs are thus basic to life. The higher the level of basic needs to be fulfilled, the more learning that is involved. At the highest level such processes are necessary for aesthetic reasons—to learn for the sake of learning. To be a fully self-actualized person there is also the need to understand, to organize, to analyze, to look for relationships and meanings, and to construct a system of values for their own sake and not for any external reward or expression of self.

Aesthetic needs

People have two sets of aesthetic needs: for beauty and for self-expression. It is clear that the aesthetic quality of the built and natural environments is an important mechanism in attaining a variety of ends— certainly a sense of belonging and a sense of self-esteem. Aesthetic needs are also, however, manifested more subtly than these needs. At every level of the fulfillment of basic needs there is also the need for beauty as it is defined within cultures. At the highest level, there is also a cognitive need to understand the aesthetic theories of artists for their own sake. Indeed, cognitive and aesthetic needs have, at that level, sometimes been regarded as the same need.

For some people there is a need to understand the creator's objectives in designing a building, in composing a piece of music, in appreciating the culturally defined standards of beauty for their own sake and not for any instrumental purpose they may serve. George Santayana (1896) called this activity

the intellectual level of aesthetic appreciation. It is neither basic nor acquired simply through experience, but it is sought after. It is "dealing with moral and aesthetic judgments as phenomena of the mind" (Santayana 1896).

Variability in needs fulfilment

While Maslow's model of a hierarchy of needs or motivations for behavior is widely accepted as a general statement about people, it must be recognized that there is considerable variability among individuals in the manifestation of these needs and in the mechanisms for fulfilling them. Some major differences depend on the nature of the individuals, their physiques and personalities, and some depend on their roles as members of a group who share a common characteristic such as their stage in life cycle or their socioeconomic status. There are also broader cultural differences that range from attitudes toward the world as a whole to attitudes toward the relationships between people and between people and objects. These cultural differences are partly a function of the terrestrial environment itself, but people are mobile and their cultures may be, temporarily at least, at odds with the biogenic environment (Vayda 1969). This categorization of individual differences is based on the "functional" sociology of Talcott Parsons (1966). It has been found to be a useful point of departure by a number of designers and by architectural theorists in thinking about how the built environment meets human needs and thus in understanding the utility of specific patterns of the built environment for diverse people (Cranz 1974; Michelson 1976; see also Lang 1987a).

The way we look at the world is motivated by our needs, which, in turn are affected by our competencies. Competence is easiest to understand in physiological terms (see Lawton 1977). What we are capable of perceiving, remembering, and doing depends on our physiological and mental abilities. Blind people simply are unable to perceive visual information. Colorblind people are unable to distinguish between certain colors. Mental competence is more difficult to define and understand. Drawing consequential conclusions about the design of public policies and/or the establishment of design goals and design guidelines is fraught with problems.

Personality type

Individuals differ uniquely in their physiological abilities and also in their personalities. Many personality traits/characteristics are stable and enduring, but people do change over time. One dimension of human personality that affects behavior and environmental choices is the degree to which a person is extroverted or introverted. This aspect of personality is complex and has at least two dimensions: the degree of a person's receptivity to outside information, and the degree to which a person is willing, or desires, to act on the environment—sociogenic and biogenic, natural and artificial. The degree to which one needs to express oneself outwardly through one's possessions and their nature depends on one's extroversion on the acting dimension (see Cooper Marcus 1974). Not everybody seeks self-esteem in this manner. While this type of expression is very much culture-bound, different individuals exhibit a greater or lesser need for self-expression within a culture.

We generally think of personality in terms of individuals rather than groups of people or nations, but there seems to be a relationship between the maturity (stage-in-life cycle) of a nation and the manifestation of its needs. After a colonial experience the need for self-esteem seems to be paramount and is architecturally expressed in the symbols of independence (Lang, in progress). In this sense personality and culture are closely related.

Stage-in-life cycle

The stage at which people are in their life cycles makes a major difference in establishing their needs and their competence to attain them. The infant's needs for succorance and security are more dominant than an adult's. The need for autonomy seems to be more dominant in adolescence than in adulthood (in the Western world, at least). Our ability to be mobile varies by our competencies and obligations at various stages in our life cycle (Hester 1975). As we age, many of our physiological competencies decrease and, for some elderly, so do mental competencies, but not to the degree that much folklore suggests (Lawton 1977). The decline in mental competence seems to be more related to diseases than to aging itself.

Some psychologists have taken a very strong developmental view of human needs (Erikson 1950; Cantril 1965). According to Erik Erikson (1950) each person goes through eight major life cycle stages, which are closely tied to specific needs. He presents these as a set of polar-opposite psychological states— healthy at one end and unhealthy at the other end. Unless the conflict at each stage is resolved in the healthy way, a person gets stuck at a stage in

intellectual development and there is a continuing need to resolve the conflicts. The eight stages are:

Basic Trust	— Mistrust	Infant
Autonomy	— Shame/Doubt	Infant
Initiative	— Guilt	Child
Industry	— Inferiority	Child
Identity	— Role Confusion	Adolescent
Intimacy	— Isolation	Young Adult
Generativity	— Stagnation	Adult
Ego Integrity	— Despair	Old Age

In *As You Like It*, Shakespeare presents seven stages (no pun intended) of man that are closer to being operational in terms of urban design than are those of Erikson: infant, schoolboy, lover, soldier, justice, elderly person, and finally, the senile one. At each stage in the life cycle, striving for the satisfaction of each basic need in Maslow's hierarchy differs because the focus of attention in one's life differs.

In developing urban design goals for total designs, all-of-a-piece designs, or design guidelines, many public interest questions arise. They are often so complex that it is essential to have a model more directly related to the services one needs today than either Erikson's or Shakespeare's model. William Michelson (1976) identifies the following stages in life cycle as important in raising questions about lifestyles and, more generally, about people's needs: infancy, childhood, adolescence, single adulthood (with roommates or family, but increasingly as a single person), child raising, empty nesters (adulthood after raising children), and old age. The behavioral opportunities, services, and aesthetic requirements to lead a fulfilled life once existed (more or less) at the local level at each stage, but as people's mobility has increased so the need for localization of activities has decreased. The degree to which this dispersion of behavior settings should occur has been a central urban design issue during this century. Neighborhood unit theory derives from it, as do many of Le Corbusier's urban design concerns (Marmot 1982).

Cultural setting and human needs

Expected and accepted behaviors and attitudes vary from culture to culture. A culture, by definition, has a system of beliefs about what behaviors are appropriate in different circumstances; it shares values and symbol systems. Cultures are unique because they have evolved and continue to evolve unselfconsciously in response to the peculiarities of their histories and of the terrestrial setting (Vayda 1969). Political action is one way of changing a culture self-consciously, but much change continues to result from unselfconsciously responding to changing world views, technological capabilities, and perceptions of how other cultures are evolving.

The attitudes toward both basic and cognitive needs and the degree to which they require fulfilling vary from culture to culture. Indeed, the beliefs about the way some needs should be fulfilled help define a culture. In some cultures, people seem to have a broad need for affiliation and use many symbols to denote their membership in various organizations. This may not be an attribute of all members of that society but may be a strong need for the majority. Similarly, a group of people may have a high need for achievement, and once attaining it they may have a high need for conspicuously consuming to display that achievement (see Reissman 1964). While this behavior is often a personality attribute of an individual, it can also be the personality attribute of a people—a culture.

Social roles within a culture

Each individual has a role to play within a culture. This role establishes a routine to a person's life. Needs are seen from the perspective of the role. Identifying them is not easy because roles overlap. The productive roles of individuals may well overlap the roles required at a stage in their life cycles—for instance, being a parent and a wage earner may occur simultaneously. Similarly, being a child in a family or being elderly are not only stages in life cycle but social roles. They are ways of establishing a place in society. In some societies the roles have traditionally been rigidly defined by gender and/or the role of one's parents, for instance. Although there is no place for it in the original Hindu Vedas, the caste system that evolved as a part of Hinduism and Buddhism rigidly assigns people of certain occupations to a specific place in the hierarchy of places in society. Although castism is illegal in both India and Japan, the roles of untouchables (Harijans in India, Eta in Japan) are still rigidly defined in both countries. Crossing social barriers is extremely difficult.

The daily routine of an individual may be a major factor in establishing how the basic necessities of life are met and also in what they wish to do with their spare time. A person isolated at home with children most of the day may have very different needs than a person who works on an assembly line or an executive who has a sedentary occupation. A general rule of thumb for a fulfilling life is that the activities occurring during breaks in the routine must satisfy needs complementary to those served by the routine.

Environmental setting

Cultures and all artificial physical environments exist within particular terrestrial settings. Each setting has a specific set of affordances. What one knows about the world and thus the perception of needs is shaped by these affordances. The geographic setting is thus part of the culture, shaping it and being shaped by it, and is the repository of the myths and memories of its inhabitants.

Human needs and the built environment

There are continuing attempts to take an empirical, human needs approach to urban design. This is apparent in the writings of Christopher Alexander, particularly his early work (e.g., 1969) and that of Alexander and his colleagues (1977, 1987), the writings of Kevin Lynch (1982, 1984), and the architectural work of architects such as Ralph Erskine (Egelius 1980a, 1980b), Herman Hertzberger (1980), and Charles Moore (Littlejohn 1984; Johnson 1986). It is now possible to give a much clearer portrayal of the relationship between the built environment and human needs fulfillment than the deterministic models of the Modern architects.

The concept of "affordance", borrowed from the work of psychologist James Gibson (1979), is increasingly used among designers because it adds conceptual clarity to the understanding of the link between the built environment, human behavior, and values and needs fulfillment. Any pattern of the built world affords certain activities or aesthetic interpretations. These patterns enlarge or constrain our options for behaviors—physical and mental—depending on the overall configurations and properties of the layout of the built environment.

To meet their needs, people must make behavioral choices. Such choices may be achieved in a number of ways. Individuals can adapt themselves either psychologically or physiologically to a situation; the former may often be difficult and stressful and the latter largely impossible. They can also manipulate the nature of a situation through social or institutional modifications. These changes may, in turn, necessitate making changes in their location in the physical environment or the structure of the built environment.

Urban designers' primary focus of concern is on the last choice, relocation, but such changes have to be seen in the context of the first two types of actions.

Relocation

For individuals, the first category of environmental change involves their relocation. The type of relocation varies by scale. At the small scale, it involves *micro-movements* to maintain an acceptable level of comfort in a situation through shifting of the body to another posture or to another place within the setting. At the larger scale, it involves the *macro-movements* of choosing another setting completely. The first type of relocation is below the scale of concern of an urban designer. The second is the type of change that is of primary importance in urban design. The question is: "What array of possible choices need to be provided in order for people to have an appropriate choice given their needs and potential needs?"

Environmental change

Changing the environment—that is, reconfiguring the environment—may involve: (1) changing the *micro-climate* by changing the temperature and other qualities of the air, the lighting and acoustical levels, and the nature of odors of a setting; (2) changing the *spatial configuration* of the setting(s) by changing the three-dimensional partitioning of space, and/or the nature of the partitions; (3) changing the *environmental hardware*—the furniture, plants, and other objects that define and control individual areas and the circulation within them; (4) changing those *environmental attributes* such as the materials, illumination, and colors of the elements that constitute the setting and give it its character and mood; and (5) changing the *symbolic attributes* of spatial configurations, materials, objects, and/or the position of these elements within the setting.

The basic concern in urban design is: (1) to identify/create and distinguish among possible future built environments, (2) to evaluate them given the resources that a society or an organization has available for building, (3) to consider/design ways of bringing them to fruition; and (4) to oversee their implementation.

Consequences for urban design

The concept of functionalism described here arises from an understanding of human needs. If one accepts it then a functional urban design responds to a much broader range of human needs than was traditionally considered under the rubric of functionalism. The most important departure from the past is the recognition that aesthetic display is a fundamental function of the built environment and should be considered as such. It competes with the other functions served by the built environment for the attention of the designer. It is not something added to the list of concerns when other functional requirements have been met. It must be recognized that aesthetic ends and other ends almost always have to be met to some degree for a design to be acceptable. A tradeoff among the requirements to meet each individual's needs in seeking environmental quality almost always exists, as there is never an infinitely elastic money supply with which to meet them. No design is able to totally meet all of everybody's needs simultaneously.

Considering human needs in an hierarchical manner as the basis for design requires great flexibility in the designer's thinking because it raises many questions. Designing by habit is easier. The design process requires creative thinking rather than the adaptation of a set of generic solutions or design principles that can be universally applied without much thought. The intellectual energy required of designers within the financial constraints placed on them is high.

Looking at human needs in the way proposed here as a basis for urban design inquiries and decisions raises questions about how tightly a pattern of the environment should cater to a specific set of behaviors. How well should the self-consciously designed environment *fit* an activity pattern or an aesthetic value of an individual or a group of people? It must, at least, *afford* the activity or the aesthetic demand. How specific or how tightly should the one fit the other? How *congruent* should the relationship between the pattern of the environment and the behavior be? How does one deal with potential future behavior changes? These are questions much debated when an architect moves away from designing for a specific person using his or her own values with a short-term future in mind to the more general, but fundamental, questions of urban design.

Urban designers like all other designers are always designing for the future. The future is always unknown, although there is much that we can predict with tolerable accuracy. The easiest way to deal with the unknown is to assume that tomorrow will be the same as today. For a short-run future this may be quite accurate. In the long run we know that there are likely to be substantial changes if the history of the past two hundred years is a guide. It is fortunate that history shows that people adapt the environment to their needs—and thus the city evolves. The role of the urban designers is to help shape these evolutionary processes so that problems are avoided and opportunities are not lost.

Major references

Note: The original chapter includes only a list of the major references cited in the text. These are reproduced below. The full list of references cited in the chapter can be found in the Bibliography to *Urban Design: The American Experience*.

Banham, Reyner (1960). *Theory and Design in the First Machine Age*. New York: Praeger.
Broadbent, Geoffrey (1978). "The Rational and the Functional." In Dennis Sharp, ed., *The Rationalists: Theory and Design in the Modern Movement*. London: Architectural Press, pp. 142–159.
Cranz, Galen (1974). "Using Parsonian Structural-Functionalism for Environmental Design." In William R. Spillers, ed., *Basic Questions in Design Theory*. New York: American Elsevier, pp. 475–484.
Lang, Jon (1987a). "Fundamental Processes of Human Behavior." In *Creating Architectural Theory*. New York: Van Nostrand Reinhold, pp. 84–100.
Maslow, Abraham H. (1943). "Theory of Human Nature." *Psychological Review* 50: 370–396.
—— (1987). *Motivation and Personality*. 3d ed. Rev. by Robert Frager, James Fadiman, Cynthia Reynolds, and Ruth Cox. New York: Harper & Row.

Source and copyright

This chapter was published in its original form as:

Lang, J. (1994), "Functionalism redefined", in Lang, J. (1994), *Urban Design: The American Experience*, Van Nostrand Reinhold, New York, 151–167.

Reprinted with permission of John Wiley & Sons, Inc.

25

The life of plazas

William H. Whyte
[1980]

We started by studying how people use plazas. We mounted time-lapse cameras overlooking the plazas and recorded daily patterns. We talked to people to find where they came from, where they worked, how frequently they used the place and what they thought of it. But, mostly, we watched people to see what they did.

Most of the people who use plazas, we found, are young office workers from nearby buildings. There may be relatively few patrons from the plaza's own building; as some secretaries confide, they'd just as soon put a little distance between themselves and the boss. But commuter distances are usually short; for most plazas, the effective market radius is about three blocks. Small parks, like Paley and Greenacre in New York, tend to have more assorted patrons throughout the day—upper-income older people, people coming from a distance. But office workers still predominate, the bulk from nearby.

This uncomplicated demography underscores an elemental point about good urban spaces: supply creates demand. A good new space builds a new constituency. It stimulates people into new habits—al fresco lunches—and provides new paths to and from work, new places to pause. It does all this very quickly. In Chicago's Loop, there were no such amenities not so long ago. Now, the plaza of the First National Bank has thoroughly changed the midday way of life for thousands of people. A success like this in no way surfeits demand for spaces; it indicates how great the unrealized potential is.

The best-used plazas are sociable places, with a higher proportion of couples than you find in less-used places, more people in groups, more people meeting people, or exchanging goodbyes. At five of the most-used plazas in New York, the proportion of people in groups runs about 45 percent; in five of the least used, 32 percent. A high proportion of people in groups is an index of selectivity. When people go to a place in twos or threes or rendezvous there, it is most often because they have decided to. Nor are these sociable places less congenial to the individual. In absolute numbers, they attract more individuals than do less-used spaces. If you are alone, a lively place can be the best place to be.

The most-used places also tend to have a higher than average proportion of women. The male-female ratio of a plaza basically reflects the composition of the work force, which varies from area to area—in midtown New York it runs about 60 percent male, 40 percent female. Women are more discriminating than men as to where they will sit, more sensitive to annoyances, and women spend more time casting the various possibilities. If a plaza has a markedly lower than average proportion of women, something is wrong. Where there is a higher than average proportion of women, the plaza is probably a good one and has been chosen as such.

The rhythms of plaza life are much alike from place to place. In the morning hours, patronage will be sporadic. A hot-dog vendor setting up his cart at the corner, elderly pedestrians pausing for a rest, a delivery messenger or two, a shoeshine man, some tourists, perhaps an odd type, like a scavenger woman with shopping bags. If there is any construction work in the vicinity, hard hats will appear shortly after 11:00 A.M. with beer cans and sandwiches. Things will start to liven up. Around noon, the main clientele begins to arrive. Soon, activity will be near peak and will stay there until a little before 2:00 P.M. Some 80 percent of the total hours of use will be concentrated in these two hours. In mid and late afternoon, use is again sporadic. If there's a special event, such as a jazz concert, the flow going home will be tapped, with people staying as late as 6:00 or 6:30 P.M. Ordinarily, however, plazas go dead by 6:00 and stay that way until the next morning.

During peak hours the number of people on a plaza will vary considerably according to seasons and weather. The way people distribute themselves over the space, however, will be fairly consistent, with some sectors getting heavy use day in and day out, others much less. In our sightings we find it easy to map every person, but the patterns are regular enough that you could count the number in only one sector, then multiply by a given factor and come within a percent or so of the total number of people at the plaza.

Off-peak use often gives the best clues to people's preferences. When a place is jammed, a person sits where he can. This may or may not be where he most wants to. After the main crowd has left, the choices can be significant. Some parts of the plaza become quite empty; others continue to be used. At Seagram's, a rear ledge under the trees is moderately, but steadily, occupied when other ledges are empty; it seems the most uncrowded of places, but on a cumulative basis it is the best-used part of Seagram's.

Men show a tendency to take the front-row seats, and, if there is a kind of gate, men will be the guardians of it. Women tend to favor places slightly secluded. If there are double-sided benches parallel to a street, the inner side will usually have a high proportion of women; the outer, of men.

Of the men up front, the most conspicuous are girl watchers. They work at it, and so demonstratively as to suggest that their chief interest may not really be the girls so much as the show of watching them. Generally, the watchers line up quite close together, in groups of three to five. If they are construction workers, they will be very demonstrative, much given to whistling, laughing, direct salutations. This is also true of most girl watchers in New York's financial area. In midtown, they are more inhibited, playing it coolly with a good bit of sniggering and smirking, as if the girls were not measuring up. It is all machismo, however, whether uptown or downtown. Not once have we ever seen a girl watcher pick up a girl, or attempt to.

Few others will either. Plazas are not ideal places for striking up acquaintances, and even on the most sociable of them, there is not much mingling. When strangers are in proximity, the nearest thing to an exchange is what Erving Goffman has called civil inattention. If there are, say, two smashing blondes on a ledge, the men nearby will usually put on an elaborate show of disregard. Watch closely, however, and you will see them give themselves away with covert glances, involuntary primping of the hair, tugs at the earlobe.

Lovers are to be found on plazas. But not where you would expect them. When we first started interviewing, people told us we'd find lovers in the rear places (pot smokers, too). But they weren't usually there. They would be out front. The most fervent embracing we've recorded on film has usually taken place in the most visible of locations, with the couple oblivious of the crowd.

Certain locations become rendezvous points for coteries of various kinds. For a while, the south wall of Chase plaza was a gathering point for camera bugs, the kind who like to buy new lenses and talk about them. Patterns of this sort may last no more than a season—or persist for years. Some time ago, one particular spot became a gathering place for raffish younger people; since then, there have been many changeovers in personnel, but it is still a gathering place for raffish younger people.

Self-congestion

What attracts people most, it would appear, is other people. If I belabor the point, it is because many urban spaces are being designed as though the opposite were true, and that what people liked best were the places they stay away from. People often do talk along such lines; this is why their responses to questionnaires can be so misleading. How many people would say they like to sit in the middle of a crowd? Instead, they speak of getting away from it all, and use terms like "escape," "oasis," "retreat." What people *do*, however, reveals a different priority.

This was first brought home to us in a study of street conversations. When people stop to have a conversation, we wondered, how far away do they move from the main pedestrian flow? We were especially interested in finding out how much of the normally unused buffer space next to buildings would be used. So we set up time-lapse cameras overlooking several key street corners and began plotting the location of all conversations lasting a minute or longer.

People didn't move out of the main pedestrian flow. They stayed in it or moved into it, and the great bulk of the conversations were smack in the center of the flow—the 100 percent location, to use the real-estate term. The same gravitation characterized "traveling conversations"—the kind in which two men move about, alternating the roles of straight man and principal talker. There is a lot of apparent motion. But if you plot the orbits, you will find they are usually centered around the 100 percent spot.

Just why people behave like this, we have never been able to determine. It is understandable that conversations should originate within the main flow. Conversations are incident to pedestrian journeys; where there are the most people, the likelihood of a meeting or a leave-taking is highest. What is less explainable is people's inclination to remain in the main flow, blocking traffic, being jostled by it. This does not seem to be a matter of inertia but of choice—instinctive, perhaps, but by no means illogical. In the center of the crowd you have the maximum choice—to break off, to continue—much as you have in the center of a cocktail party, itself a moving conversation growing ever denser and denser.

People also sit in the mainstream. At the Seagram plaza, the main pedestrian paths are on diagonals from the building entrance to the corners of the steps. These are natural junction and transfer points and there is usually a lot of activity at them. They are also a favored place for sitting and picnicking. Sometimes there will be so many people that pedestrians have to step carefully to negotiate the steps. The pedestrians rarely complain. While some will detour around the blockage, most will thread their way through it.

Standing patterns are similar. When people stop to talk on a plaza, they usually do so in the middle of the traffic stream. They also show an inclination to station themselves near objects, such as a flagpole or a statue. They like well-defined places, such as steps, or the border of a pool. What they rarely choose is the middle of a large space.

There are a number of explanations. The preference for pillars might be ascribed to some primeval instinct: you have a full view of all comers but your rear is covered. But this doesn't explain the inclination men have for lining up at the curb. Typically, they face inwards, toward the sidewalk, with their backs exposed to the dangers of the street.

Foot movements are consistent, too. They seem to be a sort of silent language. Often, in a shmoozing group no one will be saying anything. Men stand bound in amiable silence, surveying the passing scene. Then, slowly, rhythmically, one of the men rocks up and down: first on the ball of the foot, then back on the heel. He stops. Another man starts the same movement. Sometimes there are reciprocal gestures. One man makes a half turn to the right. Then, after a rhythmic interval, another responds with a half turn to the left. Some kind of communication seems to be taking place here, but I've never broken the code.

Whatever they may mean, people's movements are one of the great spectacles of a plaza. You do not see this in architectural photographs, which typically are empty of life and are taken from a perspective few people share. It is a quite misleading one. At eye level the scene comes alive with movement and color—people walking quickly, walking slowly, skipping up steps, weaving in and out on crossing patterns, accelerating and retarding to match the moves of the others. There is a beauty that is beguiling to watch, and one senses that the players are quite aware of it themselves. You see this, too, in the way they arrange themselves on steps and ledges. They often do so with a grace that they, too, must sense. With its brown-gray monochrome, Seagram's is the best of settings—especially in the rain, when an umbrella or two spots color in the right places, like Corot's red dots.

How peculiar are such patterns to New York? Our working assumption was that behavior in other cities would probably differ little, and subsequent comparisons have proved our assumption correct. The important variable is city size. As I will discuss in more detail, in smaller cities, densities tend to be lower, pedestrians move at a slower pace, and there is less of the social activity characteristic of high-traffic areas. In most other respects, pedestrian patterns are similar.

Observers in other countries have also noted the tendency to self-congestion. In his study of pedestrians in Copenhagen, architect Jan Gehl mapped bunching patterns almost identical to those observable here. Matthew Ciolek studied an Australian shopping center, with similar results. "Contrary to 'common sense' expectations," Ciolek notes, "the great majority of people were found to select their sites for social interaction right on or very close to the traffic lines intersecting the plaza. Relatively few people formed their gatherings away from the spaces used for navigation."

The strongest similarities are found among the world's largest cities. People in them tend to behave more like their counterparts in other world cities than like fellow nationals in smaller cities. Big-city people walk faster, for one thing, and they self-congest. After we had completed our New York study, we made a brief comparison study of Tokyo and found the proclivity to stop and talk in the middle of department-store doorways, busy corners, and the like, is just as strong in that city as in New York. For all the cultural differences, sitting patterns in parks and plazas are much the same, too. Similarly, shmoozing patterns in Milan's Galleria are remarkably like those in New York's garment center. Modest conclusion: given the basic elements of a center city—such as high pedestrian volumes, and concentration and mixture of activities—people in one place tend to act much like people in another.

Source and copyright

This chapter was published in its original form as:

Whyte, W.H. (1980), 'The Life of Plazas', in Whyte, W.H. (1980). *The Social Logic of Small Urban Spaces*, Conservation Foundation, Washington D.C., 16–23, Project for Public Spaces, New York, www.pps.org

Copyright W.H. Whyte estate. Reprinted by permission of the Albert LaFarge Literary Agency.

26

Needs in public space

S. Carr, M. Francis, L. G. Rivlin and A. M. Stone [1992]

In order to have effective design and management of public spaces it is essential to understand the role that those places play in people's lives, and why spaces are used or ignored. In our view, the human perspective has been neglected in both public space design and management. Places are proposed, built, and assessed with assumptions about what *should* be done in them. Much of this is based on the goals of space designers, their clients, and space managers and does not address people's needs or the ways that public places can function to serve these needs. All kinds of purposes have influenced the qualities of public spaces. For example, plazas often are designed for commercial reasons, to act as corporate emblems, to give builders and developers bonuses in the form of additional floors and space. Parks have taken their form from the past, acting as city emblems, often making statements about the city rather than its citizens. An understanding of the purposes of public places and their use by people is essential to any speculation about their qualities.

Using an open space may be the result of a deliberate plan, or it may be accidental and serendipitous, for example, stopping in a plaza that happens to be along a route, or pausing in one that is a shortcut to a destination. Chance discovery can uncover places worth a stop, and a brief pause may provide a new resource for future use. But the opposite effect also is possible. An uninviting or threatening setting may repel potential users, depositing an unfriendly memory of a place to be avoided in the future.

These incidental users probably make up a minority of the people we find in public places, although they cannot be ignored. Most people go to public open spaces for specific reasons. Some involve immediate needs – to get a drink of water, to eat lunch in a sunny area, or to rest. Others are long-range purposes and may be less obvious, for example, the need for a change or the opportunity to exercise.

The specific reasons drawing people to public areas reflect many aspects of life, especially urban life. A stop in a public place may enable a person to rest and escape from the confusion, noise, crowds and "overload" (Milgram, 1970) in the surroundings – a common need in complex, urban settings. In this instance the place becomes a haven, a "stimulus shelter" (Wachs, 1979), providing a contrast to the outside. It satisfies the periodic need people have to regroup their resources before moving on. In their study of Bryant Park, Nager and Wentworth (1976) classify a series of reasons users gave for coming to the park under the heading of "park as retreat." People used such words as "relaxing and comfortable," "tranquil, peaceful urban oasis, sanctuary" – words that we also have heard in our own interviews with users in Greenacre Park, another Manhattan green area. These same places also offer a contrast to the daily routine or a transition from the world of work to that of leisure, however brief the stop may be.

There are other reasons to stop, reflecting the need *to go to* rather than the need *to get away from*. Public areas also enable people to connect with others, to affiliate in some way with other people. This may occur in a very passive mode, as in cases where people position themselves to watch the passing scene, content to have their eyes follow the flow of strangers moving by. In other cases a more active participation is desired, where a place is used to meet friends.

Some users may seek specific activities hoping or certain that they will be available in a site. These may be bicyclers going to use paths in parks, people going to the beach to sun or swim, or the elderly in search of a bench. The intensity and nature of the activity may vary but there is an expectation that specific experiences will be possible in the place and that particular resources will be available.

Based on our review of past research and case study sites, five types of reasons seem to account for people's needs in public spaces: comfort, relaxation, passive engagement with the environment, active engagement with the environment, and discovery. Any one encounter with a place may satisfy more than one purpose. It is important to examine needs, not only because they explain the use of places but also because use is important to success. Places that do not meet people's needs or that serve no important functions for people will be underused and unsuccessful.

Comfort

Comfort is a basic need. The need for food, drink, shelter from the elements, or a place to rest when tired all require some degree of comfort to be satisfied. Without comfort it is difficult to perceive how other needs can be met, although people sometimes will endure major discomforts in attempts to enjoy themselves.

Relief from sun or access to sun is a major factor in the use of specific places, as indicated by our review of past research. Studies conducted in cool cities such as Seattle (Project for Public Spaces, 1978) and San Francisco (Bosselmann, 1983a, 1983b; Linday, 1978), with many overcast days, indicate that design of an outdoor space to allow maximum sunlight may be one of the most crucial factors in the success of the space. The San Francisco Downtown Plan (San Francisco Department of City Planning, 1985), heralded as a model for other cities, uses solar access to public spaces as a basis for controlling new development projects downtown. A film that included time-lapse footage made by Jamie Horwitz and Stephan Klein in 1977 traced the pattern of people sitting on the steps of the New York Public Library. The moving path of the January sun defined the places where people were sitting and the film caught this remarkable choreography.

Research in other parts of the country often stresses the need for some escape from the sun. A study of the Chicago First National Bank (Rutledge, 1976) indicates that lack of relief from the sun was a major source of user dissatisfaction; this situation is said to be "aggravated by the glare which

rebounded from the Plaza's unyielding reaches of granite" (p. 59). Research at Riis Park, a beach and landscaped shore in New York City (Madden & Bussard, 1977), suggests that even at a seaside recreation place, certain segments of the population may not value maximum exposure to sunlight. For these people, shade from trees, umbrellas, or some form of shelter is required. As people become more aware of the hazardous effects of the sun, the provision of shade will become essential. Shelter, whether from the sun, the rain, or inclement weather, is an important but frequently neglected element of open space design. Becker (1973, p. 453), in his evaluation of Sacramento's former downtown pedestrian mall, suggests that people who used the mall for extended periods of time were particularly bothered by the lack of "protection from the weather." An excellent but expensive form of multipurpose outdoor shelter is provided at New York's Greenacre Park, where a covered terrace on a section of the site provides shade and also contains an overhead heating element for cold days.

Comfortable and sufficient seating also is an important aspect of nearly any successful open space. Particularly important features of physically comfortable seating include the orientation of the seating, its proximity to areas of access, seating that is movable, seating for individuals and groups, seating that enables reading, eating, talking, resting and privacy, seats with backs, and, in the case of adults with children, seating in the sight line of play areas.

Comfort is also a function of the length of time people are to remain in a site. The steps of the New York Public Library or the Metropolitan Museum in New York could be adequate seating for the time it takes for a friend to arrive or for a view of the street performers below, but might not comfortably support an afternoon of sitting. A dramatic example of seating that does not accommodate users is provided by Clare Cooper Marcus (1978) in her observations of Minneapolis' Federal Reserve Plaza. During an observation session she found seven of the nine people in the plaza seated on the concrete floor instead of on the sculptural, rounded "sausage benches" that fill the plaza. It seems likely that other potential users chose not to go to the plaza at all.

In addition to physical comfort, seating should be designed so as to offer social and psychological comfort. For some years, William Whyte has been studying people in public places and he has been a careful documenter of the qualities of places that stimulate or frustrate people's needs. A major finding of his work, reported in *The Social Life of Small*

Urban Spaces (1980) and in *City* (1988), calls attention to the need for "sittable space" that is comfortable and properly oriented, spaces that have access
to sunlight, trees, water, and food, among other
amenities. In stressing this point, he states that it is
particularly related to choice: "sitting up front, in
back, to the side, in the sun, in the shade, in groups,
off alone" (1980, p. 28).

Some of these points will be further discussed later
in this chapter in a section dealing with the way
spaces are used. A useful finding from the research of
Project for Public Spaces (Madden & Bussard, 1977)
is that the people they studied preferred to be seated
facing pedestrian flow and avoided seating where
their backs were turned to all or part of this traffic.

Social and psychological comfort is a deep and
pervasive need that extends to people's experiences
in public places. It is a sense of security, a feeling that
one's person and possessions are not vulnerable.
Crime is a common concern and a reality in many
public places and cannot be ignored in an analysis of
their qualities. Across many cultures and times women
have been threatened in public spaces, making them
less comfortable to use. In a study of found or informal spaces, local neighborhood sites were especially
noted by women to be places where they felt safe,
surrounded by familiar faces in a neighborhood they
could trust (Rivlin & Windsor, 1986). But for many
women the streets in their home neighborhoods are
dangerous and local parks cannot be used. Their range
of movement is constrained by the challenges to their
safety, a condition little changed over the years.

Attention to features that reduce threats to safety
are likely to increase comfort in settings (Franck &
Paxson, 1989). In some cases this may involve space
management policies, the use of personnel to ensure
the security of users. In other cases design features
can enhance the openness, providing visual access
into the site. Concern for safety is one of the reasons
why people avoid parks or plazas that have barriers to
visibility. In their study of Bryant Park in New York,
Nager and Wentworth (1976) found that the very features that helped to make the park a pleasant sanctuary from the midtown noise and crowding, the
ornamental wall, fence, and shrubbery, obstructed
visual access, creating safety problems and discourag-
ing some people from going into the park.

Relaxation

Relaxation is distinguished from comfort by the
level of release it describes. It is a more developed

state with body and mind at ease. A sense of psychological comfort may be a prerequisite of relaxation –
a lifting of physical strains, moving the person to a
sense of repose. Relaxation frequently is cited by
designers as their intent in planning space, and the
description of a site as "relaxing" defines the experience possible in the place more than the physical
setting, although the two are clearly interrelated.

Urban open spaces, particularly parks, traditionally have been viewed in the United States as places
of relaxation and respite for the harried city dweller.
However, some authors have argued that this perspective has been overstressed. J. B. Jackson (1981)
claims that American designers and policy makers
have devoted too much attention to landscaped
parks, designed for relaxation and contemplation,
and have overlooked the public's need for active
recreation areas. Whyte (1980, 1988) has demonstrated convincingly that many users of small urban
parks and plazas seek liveliness and some form of
engagement with the life of a city, rather than
retreat from it. The growing interest in community
gardening also points to the need for the public
landscape to accommodate active recreation. Despite
the validity of these arguments, there is evidence
that people also look for spaces that accommodate
repose and relaxation and offer a brief pause from
the routines and demands of city life.

Research in a variety of public spaces indicates
that urbanites do frequently seek out settings for
relaxation. Becker (1973, p. 453) reports that a large
proportion of the users of Sacramento's downtown
pedestrian mall liked its "quiet relaxing atmosphere,"
although this was not what the retailers had desired.
In another dense and active context, Nager and
Wentworth (1976) found that interview respondents
in Bryant Park reported their most frequent activities as relaxing and resting. Users of Greenacre Park,
a Manhattan vest-pocket park (cited both by Burden,
1977, and in our own research), viewed the space
primarily as a place for relaxation.

In examining the factors that support relaxation,
the element of respite from or contrast to the adjacent
urban context appears to be prominent. Separation
from vehicular traffic, as in the case of pedestrian
malls, often makes it easier to be relaxed, although it
also may increase user concern about safety and security during low use times.

However, as we have noted, setting off a space
from adjacent streets and sidewalks can present safety
problems as well as benefits. Indeed, the Paseo del
Rio was generally considered unsafe in San Antonio
until, in the 1960s, commercial activities – especially

cafés and restaurants – began to appear along the river and it became a tourist attraction, greatly increasing the user population.

The importance of natural elements, especially water, in accentuating a contrast to the urban setting is a frequent theme in open space research. Studies of New York's Exxon Minipark and Greenacre Park have demonstrated the drawing power of simulated waterfalls for people seeking "a respite from the 'hustle-bustle' of the city" (Project for Public Spaces, 1978, p. 15). In her Greenacre Park study, Burden (1977) underscores the significance of the park's waterfall by describing what happens when it is turned off: "People halt conversations abruptly and make ready to leave. The sounds of the city suddenly fill the park, absorbing it and transforming an oasis into an adjunct of the street" (p. 33).

Natural features, such as trees and other greenery, were found to be the dominant factor in Bryant Park offering opportunities for retreat and relaxation (Nager & Wentworth, 1976). This is a view echoed in people's reactions to many open spaces. The opportunities to sit on grass, bask in the shade cast by a tree, or enjoy the greenery and flowers are greatly appreciated.

Although research bears out the importance of providing opportunities for relaxation in urban public spaces, not all spaces should be designed and managed with this in mind. Some sites should accommodate persons seeking liveliness and engagement with the city and its people.

Passive engagement

Passive engagement with the environment could lead to a sense of relaxation but it differs in that it involves the need for an encounter with the setting, albeit without becoming actively involved. This category includes the frequently observed interest and enjoyment people derive from watching the passing scene. This kind of encounter is indirect or passive, because it involves looking rather than talking or doing. There are many examples of places that serve this function and a popularity that testifies to this need.

People-watching is a frequently reported activity in small urban spaces. Whyte (1980, 1988) and his associates (Linday, 1978) indicate that it is the most popular activity in downtown plazas. According to Whyte (1980, p. 13), "What attracts people most, it would appear, is other people." In a study of San Francisco plazas, Linday (1978) found that the favorite sitting places were adjacent to the pedestrian flow,

in particular, near street corners. Similarly, R. L. Love (1973) found that the most frequently mentioned activity at two Portland fountains was "watching other people." She concludes, somewhat optimistically, that "The popularity of people watching, in conjunction with the heterogeneity of fountain visitors, points to the conclusion that through their visits to the fountains people do partake of the city's urbanity by being in contact with all the social types that contribute to it" (p. 193).

Other writers suggest that physical separations can facilitate visual contacts with people. Cooper Marcus (1978) states that observing others is the most popular activity at Minneapolis's Crystal Court, and that the provision of an upper balcony from which to look down at the crowd is particularly important. This elevated vantage point allows the observer to "watch people while avoiding eye contact" (p. 39). The terrace overlooking Rockefeller Center's skating rink is another heavily frequented viewing spot, especially in cool weather when skaters are below. Even when the recessed level is a restaurant, people look down into the space below. Cascades of steps leading to public buildings such as the Metropolitan Museum of Art in New York are popular if unplanned places for watching an array of city sights.

The open cafés of European cities, especially in France, are enjoyed as much for the opportunity to watch pedestrian traffic as for their refreshments. In the open cafés in mild weather and glass-enclosed ones in the cold seasons, patrons linger for hours over a drink or a coffee cup, which provides the excuse to observe the street scenes. This form of public activity has increased in popularity in the United States as restaurants have obtained permits to spill over onto the streets.

Another important attraction of public spaces is the opportunity to observe performers and formal activities. The scheduling of special events has become a popular management approach in many urban plazas and parks. In addition to the now commonplace scheduling of concerts and other formal events, several of the larger downtown complexes such as Boston's Faneuil Market, New York's South Street Seaport and San Francisco's Ghirardelli Square feature regular performances by street entertainers throughout the day. Although these events may strike some visitors as spontaneous, the artists generally are auditioned and issued permits by the management (Project for Public Spaces, 1984).

In parks outside downtown areas, observing games and sporting events offers a kind of passive engagement that often is sought. For example, baseball and basketball games in neighborhood parks may be surrounded by clusters of spectators. Designs for active recreation areas sometimes overlook this, failing to account for people who enjoy watching games in progress. Researchers at Riis Park in New York City (Madden & Bussard, 1977) found a lack of seating for spectators of handball and other games and noted that fences and bushes frequently blocked the view of such activities from adjacent areas.

People also are attracted to public spaces by various physical features. Fountains often function as a particular focus of interest. Rutledge (1976) observed that many people will walk down a flight of stairs to the sunken plaza, at Chicago's First National Bank, just to look at the large fountain there. Similarly, our research at Greenacre Park in New York indicates that viewing the dramatic waterfall was a major reason for coming to the park. This is also true for both Lovejoy and Forecourt Fountains in Portland, Oregon. In a study of the qualities people prefer in outdoor spaces, Buker and Montarzino (1983) found that water was the single most desired feature, mentioned by 98 percent of their interviewees.

Another type of passive engagement that concerns the physical and aesthetic qualities of a site involves viewing public art or a compelling landscape. It would be unfortunate to ignore this function, because it is an important aspect of the enjoyment of the public scene. The scenery and the panoramic views are features that draw people to national parks, but even users of vest-pocket parks speak of the pleasure of watching cascades of water.

Natural features, particularly vegetation, seem to attract people to urban places. In a linear park in downtown Yokohama, Japan, which offers three distinct types of settings, a "forest plaza" is "greatly enjoyed by the city dwellers" (Iwasaki & Tyrwhitt, 1978, p. 439). In our own study of Greenacre Park, the greenery and water were mentioned frequently by users as enjoyable qualities of the site. The opportunity to be close to plants, trees, flowers, and water is strongly desired by people and there is some evidence that these elements may have relaxing and "restorative" qualities (Hartig, Mang, & Evans, 1991; Kaplan, 1983, 1985; Kaplan & Kaplan, 1990).

Some urban spaces attract users because they offer splendid views. Francis and his associates (1984) report that many people came to Brooklyn's "drive-in" Grand Street Waterfront Park primarily to enjoy the panorama of the East River and Manhattan across the river.

Similarly, in their study of downtown Vancouver, Joardar and Neill (1978) found that waterfront places have a strong drawing power because of the vistas they offer. Unfortunately, until very recently, waterfronts in many cities have been largely ignored as public, open space resources. Mooney (1979) summarizes some of the problems in an article about the Mississippi River: "All too frequently locations for simple visual linkage with river activities have been usurped by marinas, parking lots, industrial blight and warehouses. With few exceptions, the urban edge of the Mississippi is uninviting to pedestrians" (p. 49).

With the development of waterfront parks such as the esplanade stretching along Battery Park City in Lower Manhattan, there is some hope that these policies are changing. New York City is planning the creation of an esplanade park from the Battery to Fifty-ninth Street, and other cities are building waterfront parks. However, one could complain that what is being done is too little and too late.

Active engagement

Active engagement represents a more direct experience with a place and the people within it. This function has a number of components. First, although some people find satisfaction in people-watching, others desire more direct contact with people – whether they are strangers in a site or members of their own group. Based on considerable research, primarily in New York City, William Whyte concluded that plazas in downtown areas "are not ideal places for striking up acquaintances, and even on the most sociable of them, there is not much mingling" (Whyte, 1980, p. 19). Yet Whyte notes that unusual features or occurrences in a plaza, such as an entertainer or a fine sculpture, will often result in what he calls "triangulation" whereby that special feature "provides a linkage between people and prompts strangers to talk to each other" (p. 94). In places other than the plazas of large, urban downtown areas, some degree of interaction between strangers may be more common. Christopher Alexander has pointed out the importance of the promenades, often centrally located shopping streets, common in older neighborhoods and small cities in Europe and Latin America where "people with a shared way of life gather together to rub shoulders and confirm their community" (Alexander et al., 1977, p. 169). Although Alexander suggests that promenades are used mainly by people who live within ten minutes' walking distance, some readers may be familiar with a variation of the promenade where teenagers and young adults with similar interests converge on a street and interact while driving cars slowly, sitting in cars, sitting on cars, and strolling.

Another type of space that is important in facilitating interaction between strangers is the small square or piazza, most commonly found in the old residential districts of Mediterranean cities. Alexander argues that with a few exceptions, such as Venice's Piazza San Marco and London's Trafalgar Square, such squares are most successful when they are under seventy feet in diameter (Alexander et al., 1977). In a plaza of this size people are able to "make out the faces and half hear the talk" (Alexander et al., 1977, p. 313) of those around them, which encourages a sense of social connection, increasing opportunities for interaction.

Public spaces also play a crucial role as a setting for socializing with relatives, neighbors, acquaintances, and friends. Although public space activities such as picnics and Sunday outings cut across class, less affluent people, particularly in cities, are clearly more dependent upon outdoor spaces close to home. The public spaces that play the most important social function in many older, working-class, and low-income neighborhoods are the streets and sidewalks (Fried & Gleicher, 1961; Jacobs, 1961). In fact, streets and sidewalks abound as public spaces supporting a range of child and adult activities. But some streets are more successful settings than others. In a study of informal or "found" public spaces we have observed places that are popular ones for street peddlers. The traffic of people is critical to drawing vendors to a site, but the width of the pavement and the attitudes of local shopkeepers are important factors as well.

The life of the street that Jane Jacobs (1961) has described so well as a complex mélange of tolerance, friendliness, mutual concern, and resources. However, young people are not necessarily welcome users of either commercial or residential streets. Whether it is casual "hanging out" by teenagers or the lively ball playing of younger children, complaints are commonplace. It may be easy to romanticize the streets as natural playgrounds for children as they are growing up but the reality often is less ideal. In the inner city the street is filled with dangers – vehicular and drug traffic, broken glass, and filth. In affluent areas the streets rarely are used for play. Children are transported to special play facilities – parks, gymnasiums, and the like – or they remain within their own homes. In both settings, the slum and the high-priced residential area, parents' fears for their children's safety make the street as a context for play and development an ideal rather than a reality.

But we can question whether this situation could be changed. The complex cultural and economic factors that underlie it cannot be ignored, but there are design and management alternatives that can alleviate some of the difficulties. The work of Appleyard (1981) has demonstrated that when residents were able to control the speed and volume of traffic on their streets, their use of the streets and attachments to them increased. Similarly, through the introduction of *woonerven*, zones where traffic is slowed down and play and planting areas introduced, many towns and cities in the Netherlands have made their streets safer and more pleasant. This approach has been adopted in other countries, as well, including in selected new developments in the United States.

During different stages in the life cycle, spaces assume a particular importance as a setting for interaction with friends and acquaintances. Parents caring for young children depend on nearby parks and playgrounds not only as facilities to occupy their children but also as places to enjoy contact with others, particularly other parents. Play areas that can accommodate a long social visit by parents supervising their children require comfortable seating arranged to enable face-to-face interaction, tables, running water, and ideally, restrooms.

Another group whose social life often centers around public spaces is the elderly. Brown, Sijpkes, and MacLean (1986) report that a number of elderly welfare recipients who frequent Complexe Desjardins, an indoor shopping center in downtown Montreal, "have refused to be moved further than a reasonable walking distance" (p. 170) away from the center. Groups of elderly people often are most concentrated in sitting areas around the perimeters of parks and other public areas. At this location there is a feeling of safety provided by passersby, and friends and acquaintances are most likely to be spotted.

In New York City's vest-pocket Greenacre Park, while the majority of users position their seats to view the waterfall at the back of the space, the elderly regulars are an exception. They seat themselves near the entrance, generally facing the street, so as to watch the pedestrian flow and greet acquaintances.

For adults, particularly young adults, considerable socializing occurs in the context of recreation. A study of a small park adjacent to a Delaware campus (Ulrich & Addoms, 1981) found that although students visited the park primarily to engage in sports activities, considerable socializing occurred there. The study did not reveal a strong connection between socializing and recreation at facilities such as the school gymnasium where, it can be assumed, athletic activities are pursued more for their own sakes.

In a comparative study of parks in Paris and Los Angeles, Lyle (1970) found large group activities such as picnics more common in Los Angeles. Linday's (1977) study of Central Park suggested that some Hispanics seek intense high-energy activities (such as dancing) while others seem to be seeking a "pastoral retreat."

Providing for active recreational needs is a predominant aspect of public place design. In recreation we also find regional, geographic, cultural, and age differences, both within and across spaces. People go to parks because ball playing, tennis, boating, and hiking are available and, although the public does vary in its preferences for these activities, they are generally popular. O'Donnell (1981) found that when youths were given the opportunity to select from among different amenities for a new park, as might be expected, they were strongly in favor of the development of recreational facilities in contrast with more passive options preferred by adults. Yet adults, too, are involved in active pursuits; jogging has become a popular exercise as enthusiasts find appropriate paths in likely and unlikely places. Bicycling also has increased and many parks provide paths for this active recreation.

Other cultural differences appeared in the contrast between parks in Los Angeles and Paris (Lyle, 1970). Active sports and games were spread over the parks in Los Angeles, whereas in Paris they were restricted to specific portions of the space. In addition, large group activities were more frequent in Los Angeles. Lyle also found considerably more variety of use in the local parks in Los Angeles when compared with those in Paris.

In some cases, activities enable participants to exercise both their bodies and their competitive desires. In other cases there seem to be other needs – for adventure, challenge, mastery, and perhaps even risk. Certainly the popularity of wilderness areas such as those frequented in Outward Bound courses attests to this quality. At the very least, they offer an extreme contrast to daily life, although risks are not necessarily unique to the wilderness.

Vigorous encounters with physical elements of a setting represent another dimension of active engagement. Here we are describing direct physical contact rather than just being within or moving across a place. One example can be found in the wading and frolicking found in some fountains – for example, Lovejoy and Forecourt in Portland (Love, 1973). This contact with water also formed part of the most

frequent activities on the original Sacramento Mall in California, now replaced by a more open transit mall (Becker, 1973). In his cross-city comparison, Lyle (1970) found people were actively involved with natural elements in Los Angeles, whereas Parisians were more apt to be viewers of the scene. From our own observations, the use of large, public fountains by children to float toy boats and feed fish, although common in Paris, is rare in the United States.

Although it is important to respect the needs of people with physical disabilities, public places could, and should, promote vigorous energetic use of the human body, something lacking in most present-day designs. The jogging paths, bicycle lanes, gardening plots, horseback riding paths, ice-skating rinks, and tennis courts are examples of some forms of active uses, and reflect the growing interest in exercise and health. But they are the exceptions rather than the rule in most public parks and are limited to a small portion of the public.

Another aspect of physical engagement involves manipulation of elements such as sculpture. There are examples of public art encouraging this activity, for example, the Calder sculpture in a Chicago plaza (Goldstein, 1975). In other cases, users may manipulate or alter fixed elements as a kind of protest against the lack of responsiveness of public places. This is especially apparent in the provision of seating, most of which is rigid and unyielding. Where movable chairs are available, they are used and appreciated.

Challenge and mastery are qualities that stimulate interest and use and are human needs that explain much of the use of public places. Yet most of the time this need is not acknowledged as sites are designed to minimize dangers and reduce the risks of liability of the space managers. People need to be able to test themselves, intellectually and physically, or they lose interest. These opportunities are especially critical to children because they are the foundation of the development of their cognitive abilities and their sense of competence (White, 1959). Florence Ladd has identified another developmental need. In an article entitled "City Kids in the Absence of ..." she argues that adventure should be provided for city teenagers (Ladd, 1975). These issues are major concerns in the design of children's play spaces, especially adventure playgrounds (Cooper, 1970; Nicholson, 1971). However, opportunities for healthy challenge and mastery are needed across the life cycle. Psychologists have shown that stimulation is essential throughout the years, including the later ones. Some of the deterioration of the elderly appears to come from the limited, uninteresting lives of many, due to physical problems, poverty, and restricted participation in the outside world. Yet most positive challenge has been removed from our public environment, although it may be one of the key reasons to have public space.

Their active qualities may be among the most important influences on the staying power of places, separating the ones that are boring and not worth a second visit from those of enduring interest. There are risks that are unnecessary and frightening and others that are stimulating and growth-producing, and it is the latter that should be identified and incorporated into public sites.

Ceremony, celebration, and festivity are other qualities that people often seek in urban public places. People require joyousness to refresh their lives. We speak here of a distinctive quality of life – the pleasure in engaging in a multifaceted activity that encompasses people-watching, socializing, being entertained, and consuming or buying food and other goods. The popularity of flea markets is one sign of this need where affordable merchandising and carnival spirit combine to draw crowds. Public places can become the stage of gatherings, special events and performances (Brower, 1977). For many decades this type of activity was characteristic of the market areas and entertainment strips of most American cities. With the growth of suburbs, the invention of television, and the increasing prominence of supermarkets and shopping centers, celebration became less a characteristic of American cities, while remaining prominent in many other parts of the world. The periodic events that attract large numbers, such as the yearly street fair in Brooklyn called "Atlantic Antic," the Italian saint day festivities, and the carnivals for which New Orleans is so noted, suggest that the capacity to enjoy is there, given the opportunity and the place. In these instances city streets become the fairgrounds for a wide range of pleasures.

Market areas providing the festivity of an earlier era still persist in many places. Philadelphians of all types gravitate to the Italian Market where vendors sell fresh produce, meat, poultry, and fish of all varieties, other foods, and bargain merchandise. In Seattle, for eighty years Pike Place Market has withstood many threats to its survival to retain its variety of shops and stalls in a seven-acre area overlooking Elliot Bay. New Yorkers still flock to the Lower East Side, especially on Sundays, to streets like Orchard, Delancey, and Essex, which specialize in discounted clothing and a wide variety of foods associated with this neighborhood. In many small towns residents visit weekend farmers' markets, which serve as a town center or gathering place (Sommer, 1981, 1989).

Farmers' markets have been returning to cities, as well. In New York City, eighteen locations host Greenmarkets that enable produce from regional farms to be sold by the people who grow it. Many visitors to these market areas are primarily in search of bargains or particular wares, but others are seeking engagement with the diversity of sights, sounds, and smells of these quintessential urban areas. In comparing the "behavioral ecology" of farmers' markets with that of supermarkets, Sommer (1981) finds the former friendlier, with more contacts with people.

Many merchants and planners are interested in this public design solution to revitalize areas of towns and cities. New retail spaces such as the Faneuil Hall Marketplace and Harborplace use prominent display of produce near entries to attract customers. However, these are not farmers' markets and the cost of food is much higher. These markets have much less social diversity and exchange than places like the Davis Farmers' Market.

While a handful of the old markets persist, a new phenomenon has recently arisen: a sort of in-town shopping mall, which nevertheless is quite different from the suburban prototype. Many of these places have adopted the name "market" – the Market at Citicorp in New York, Boston's Quincy Market, the Newmarket and Reading Station Market in Philadelphia – suggesting a parallel with the diverse, colorful, often chaotic marketplaces of an earlier era. Some of these "new markets" do bear similarities to their predecessors. For example, Quincy Market provides a wide variety of attractions, and on a busy day it is full of energy. Others, like the Market at Citicorp, are pleasant places to linger or pass through, but offer little that resembles the variety, excitement, and spontaneity of the old markets. In general, these contemporary, highly designed, largely artificial and costly to use "marketplaces" lack the liveliness, disorderliness, and unexpected possibilities of places like Philadelphia's Italian Market and New York's Lower East Side. It is odd to realize that pushcarts have largely disappeared from the Lower East Side but can be found in the South Street Seaport development in New York. One commentator (R. Campbell, 1980) accurately described these new markets as reflecting a yearning for the marketplaces and main streets of America's past but representing a very self-conscious re-creation of these prototypes. As Campbell states, these developments cater to people "who yearn for town life but who are not quite ready for the real city" (p. 48).

There is another kind of festivity common to public spaces that also seems to have considerable appeal, one that can be called ritual celebration. This is embodied in the convergence on Times Square to greet the New Year, the Fourth of July celebration in a town square, Chinese New Year in San Francisco, the Mardi Gras in New Orleans. The satisfaction here is in the predictable, shared experience that binds people together in the present and also allows them to feel part of history. Periodic communal celebration can be facilitated through environmental management. Some ritual celebrations, less geared toward a particular moment, can occur in settings that encourage more diffuse and varied forms of activity. Bacon (1981, p. 3) describes one such event, a day-long Fourth of July celebration that was designed as "a rambling, lazy family picnic day," spent in lower Manhattan.

Discovery

Discovery is the fifth reason for people's presence in public spaces and represents the desire for stimulation (Lynch, 1963) and the delight we all have in new, pleasurable experiences. Exploration is a human need. Forcing people to remain in confined, bare settings is a form of torture or punishment. For children, being deprived of stimulation can permanently stunt their intellectual and social development, as dramatically documented by Spitz (1945) and Goldfarb (1945).

In the context of urban public spaces, discovery has some specific meanings. It is the opportunity to observe the different things that people are doing when moving through a site, a quality that has been associated with San Francisco's Cannery (Burns, 1978). The visitor is able to move around and discover parts of the place – balconies that jut out, escalators, elevators, flags, strange or interesting people. In this example, the major aspects of discovery appear to be the diversity in the physical design and the changing vistas. Greenacre Park in New York often is cited as having a sense of discovery through its use of levels and the various sectors that visitors can find (Burden, 1977). It is very likely that these are unexpected vistas for the visitor only the first time in the park, although repeated use may uncover other things of interest. For discovery to continue to be part of someone's experience of familiar places, it would be essential to have changing physical qualities and changing human activity as well. Either people must bring the components of an interesting stay with them (in the form of equipment, books, or thoughts) or the place itself must provide the stimulation that enables users' interests to endure.

A sense of discovery can be enhanced by the design, as is clearly evident in the case of the Cannery in San Francisco where changes in perspective offer a succession of vistas to enjoy. Lynch (1963) suggests that contrast and juxtaposition of elements can provide a sense of pleasurable surprise that people enjoy, a quality that is epitomized by the Pompidou Centre. The management also can contribute by programming activities in a creative way. The streets in front of New York's Public Library on Fifth Avenue and along Bryant Park on Forty-second Street have been used for crafts fairs. Concerts have enlivened many moribund plazas. The experience of discovery can also contain a sense of mystery, as a photograph in Cullen's *Townscape* (1961) suggests. The caption reads: "From the matter-of-fact pavement of the busy world we glimpse the unknown mystery of a city where anything could happen or exist, the noble or the sordid, genius or lunacy" (p. 51).

The need for discovery often is met by travel, going to new places to discover their special qualities, to meet new people, to find new challenges from landscapes that contrast with familiar ones. Some places have been designed to create a sense of discovery as reflected in Tony Hiss's (1987, 1990) description of the entrance to Prospect Park, Olmsted's creative design for the borough of Brooklyn, New York. But discovery also can occur at home under conditions in which elements of known places change. A concert or flea market can transform a well-used plaza or park. Toys brought to a playground can introduce new opportunities for amusement. Some of these can be initiated by users, but most depend upon the support and instigation of space managers who can extend the opportunities for discovery beyond any individual user. Ultimately, the readiness for discovery lies within each of us, waiting to be evoked in public places by enlightened designs and management policies.

Summary

The various public space needs cover many aspects of human functioning. They include the physical comforts involved in relief from the elements, rest, and seating. Social needs address the stimulation surrounding people, escape from urban overload, and protection from the threats from others. People need to relax, to enjoy the respite offered by public places and have opportunities to enjoy natural elements with public places functioning as oases. While some persons seek out settings in which to relax, others gravitate toward physical and social challenges, active engagement with the public place and its occupants including interaction with others, shopping, participation in street life, and vigorous encounters such as sports, wading, and jogging. Other challenges can be found in places that support discovery, enabling opportunities for new experiences, new vistas that excite, educate, and delight.

This array of human needs, which no doubt could be supplemented by others, also should include opportunities for pure joy and fun, qualities missing from many places. The descriptions provide clues as to why some sites are filled whereas others are empty. Functionality, the usefulness of a site, provides a simple explanation of its success. But needs alone are not a sufficient reason for vitality. There are other qualities that constrain or facilitate open space experiences, and the different uses and rights of users of areas are essential ones.

References

Alexander, C., S. Ishikawa, M. Silverstein, M. Jacobsen, I. Fiksdahl-King, & S. Angel. 1977. A *Pattern Language*. New York: Oxford University Press.

Appleyard, D. 1981. *Livable Streets*. Berkeley: University of California Press.

Appleyard, D., & M. Lintell. 1977. The environmental quality of city streets: The residents' viewpoint. *American Institute of Planners Journal* 43: 84–101.

Bacon, K. 1981. Festivals: Hooking into the rhythm of city life. *Livability* 3: 3–4.

Becker, F. 1973. A class-conscious evaluation: Going back to Sacramento's pedestrian mall. *Landscape Architecture* 64: 295–345.

Bosselmann, P. 1983a. Shadowboxing: Keeping sunlight on Chinatown's kids. *Landscape Architecture* 73: 74–6.

Bosselmann, P. 1983b. Simulating the impacts of urban development. *Garten und Landschaft* 93: 636–40.

Brill, M. 1989a. Transformation, nostalgia and illusion in public life and public place. In I. Altman & E. Zube (Eds.), *Public Places and Spaces*, pp. 7–30. Vol. 10 of *Human Behavior and Environment*. New York: Plenum.

Brower, S. 1977. A year of celebration. Baltimore: Baltimore City Department of Planning.

Brown, D., P. Sijpkes, & M. MacLean. 1986. The community role of public indoor space. *Journal of Architectural and Planning Research* 3: 161–72.

Buker, C., & A. Montarzino. 1983. The meaning of water. Paper presented at the Fourth Annual Conference of the Wilderness Psychology Group. Missoula, Mont., August.

Burden, A. 1977. Greenacre Park. New York: Project for Public Spaces.

Burns, J. 1978. Evaluation: A classic recycling after II years. *AIA Journal* 67: 50–9.

Campbell, R. 1980. Lure of the marketplace: Real-life theater. *Historic Preservation* 63: 46–9.

Cooper, C. 1970. Adventure playgrounds. *Landscape Architecture* 60: 18–29, 88–91.

Cooper Marcus, C. 1978. Evaluation: A tale of two spaces. *AIA Journal* 67: 34–8.

Cullen, G. 1961. *Townscape*. New York: Van Nostrand Reinhold.

Francis, M. 1984. Mapping downtown activity. *Journal of Architectural and Planning Research* 1: 21–35.

Francis, M., L. Cashdan, & L. Paxson. 1984. *Community Open Spaces*. Washington, D.C.: Island Press.

Franck, K. A., & L. Paxson. 1989. Women and urban public space: Research, design, and policy issues. In E. Zube & G. Moore (Eds.), *Advances in Environment, Behavior and Design*, Vol. 2, pp. 122–46. New York: Plenum.

Fried, M., & P. Gleicher. 1961. Some sources of satisfaction in an urban slum. *Journal of the American Institute of Planners* 27: 4.

Goldfarb, W. 1945. Psychological privation in infancy and subsequent adjustment. *American Journal of Orthopsychiatry* 15: 247–55.

Goldstein, S. 1975. Seeing Chicago's plazas: Delight and despair. *Inland Architect* 19, 8: 19–23.

Hartig, T., M. Mang, & G. W. Evans. 1991. Restorative effects of natural environment experiences. *Environment and Behavior* 23: 3–26.

Hiss, T. 1987. Reflections: Experiencing places. *New Yorker*, June 22, pp. 46–68 and June 29, pp. 73–86.

Hiss, T. 1990. *The Experience of Place*. New York: Knopf.

Horwitz, J., & S. M. Klein. 1977. *Lunatics, Lovers and Bums: A Look at the Unintended Uses of the New York Public Library Entrance* [Ten minute Super 8 sound and color film]. New York: Graduate School, City University of New York.

Im, S. B. 1984. Visual preferences in enclosed urban spaces. *Environment and Behavior* 16: 235–62.

Iwasaki, S., & J. Tyrwhitt. 1978. Pedestrian areas in central Yokohama. *Ekistics* 273: 436–40.

Jackson, J. B. 1981. The public park needs appraisal. In L. Taylor (Ed.), *Urban Open Spaces*, pp. 34–5. New York: Rizzoli.

Jacobs, J. 1961. *The Death and Life of Great American Cities*. New York: Vintage.

Joardar, S. D., & J. W. Neill. 1978. The subtle differences in configuration of small public spaces. *Landscape Architecture* 68: 487–91.

Kaplan, R. 1983. The role of nature in the urban context. In I. Altman & J. Wohlwill (Eds.), *Behavior and the Natural Environment*, pp. 127–62. Vol. 6 of *Human Behavior and Environment*. New York: Plenum.

Kaplan, R. 1985. Nature at the doorstep: Residential satisfaction and the nearby environment. *Journal of Architectural and Planning Research* 2: 115–27.

Kaplan, R., & S. Kaplan. 1990. Restorative experience: The healing power of nearby nature. In M. Francis & R. Hester (Eds.), *The Meaning of Gardens*, pp. 238–43. Cambridge: MIT Press.

Ladd, F. 1975. City kids in the absence of . . . In *Children, Nature and the Urban Environment: Proceedings of a Symposium-Fair*, pp. 77–81. USDA Forest Service General Technical Report NE-30. Washington, D.C.: Government Printing Office.

Linday, N. 1977. Drawing socio-economic lines in Central Park. *Landscape Architecture* 67: 515–20.

Linday, N. 1978. It all comes down to a comfortable place to sit and watch. *Landscape Architecture* 68, 6: 492–7.

Love, R. L. 1973. The fountains of urban life. *Urban Life and Culture* 2: 161–209.

Lyle, J. T. 1970. People-watching in parks. *Landscape Architecture* 60: 51–2.

Lynch, K. 1963. *The Image of the City*. Cambridge: MIT Press.

Madden, K., & E. Bussard. 1977. Riis Park: A study of use and design. New York: Project for Public Spaces.

Milgram, S. 1970. The experience of living in cities. *Science* 167: 1461–8.

Mooney, R. T. 1979. Waterfronts: Building along the Mississippi. *AIA Journal* 68, 2: 47–53.

Nager, A. R., & W. R. Wentworth. 1976. Bryant Park: A comprehensive evaluation of its image and use with implications for urban open space design. New York: Center for Human Environments, City University of New York.

Nicholson, S. 1971. How not to cheat children: The theory of loose parts. *Landscape Architecture* 62, 1: 30–4.

O'Donnell, P. M. 1981. Houghton Park extension: User survey report. Paper presented at the meeting of the Environmental Design Research Association, Ames, Iowa, April.

Project for Public Spaces, Inc. 1978. Plazas for people: Seattle's First National Bank Plaza and Seattle Federal Building Plaza – a case study. 44 pp. New York.

Project for Public Spaces, Inc. 1984. *Managing Downtown Public Spaces*. Chicago: Planners Press, American Planning Association.

Rivlin, L. G., & A. Windsor. 1986. A study of found spaces. New York: Environmental Psychology Program, City University of New York. Unpublished report.

Rutledge, A. J. 1976. Looking beyond the applause: Chicago's First National Bank Plaza. *Landscape Architecture* 66: 22–6.

San Francisco Department of City Planning. 1985. *The San Francisco Downtown Plan*. San Francisco.

Sommer, R. 1981. The behavioral ecology of supermarkets and farmer's markets. *Journal of Environmental Psychology* 1: 13–19.

Sommer, R. 1989. Farmers' markets as community events. In I. Altman & E. Zube (Eds.), *Public Places and Spaces*, pp. 57–82. Vol. 10 of *Human Behavior and Environment*. New York: Plenum.

Spitz, R. A. 1945. Hospitalism: An inquiry into the genesis of psychiatric conditions in early childhood. *Psychoanalytic Study of the Child* 1: 53–74.

Ulrich, R. S., & D. L. Addoms. 1981. Psychological and recreational benefits of a residential park. *Journal of Leisure Research* 13: 43–65.

Wachs, J. 1979. Primal experiences and early cognitive intellectual development. *Merrill-Palmer Quarterly* 25: 3–42.

White, R. W. 1959. Motivation reconsidered: The concept of competence. *Psychological Review* 66: 313–24.

Whyte, W. H. 1980. *The Social Life of Small Urban Spaces*. Washington, D.C.: The Conservation Foundation.

Whyte, W. H. 1988. *City: Rediscovering the Center*. New York: Doubleday.

Source and copyright

This chapter was published in its original form as:

Carr, S., Francis, M., Rivlin, L.G. and Stone, A.M. (1992), 'Needs in Public Space', from Carr, S., *et al.* (1992), *Public Space*, Cambridge University Press, Cambridge, 87–136.

Cambridge University Press, translated with permission from the author and publisher.

27

Understanding transactions

Richard MacCormac
[1994]

This is a speculative study in its infancy. What has seemed important to me is to convert rather static observations about the nature of the European city into an understanding of it as a process, not simply as a product that exists in stasis. This would allow us to make better judgements about the nature of change and how we should guide change in old fabrics. I think that the unpopularity of what is called the 'modern environment' is partly to do with a deep sense of incongruity and a feeling that the nature of change is such that instead of affirming what exists and adding to it, the modern environment is perceived to have destroyed what was good and not to have improved on it. I want to investigate why.

The idea of looking at cross sections is to test a proposition about the traditional nature of the West End of London: it's hard to do in the City for reasons of rapidity of change. The validity of the proposition is yet to be established, though I have a sense that some of the things I am going to discuss were intentional in the development of the great land holdings, like the Bedford Estate.

The first example is north of where I work and live, in Spitalfields. In Cheshire Street market the Victorian houses are in multi-use. I managed to get them listed about three years ago to stop them being demolished – the borough planned to demolish everything here to build warehouses – partly to ensure the preservation of a social characteristic of this part of London. The key characteristic of this environment is that it supports what I call 'local transactions': people living behind their own front doors, restaurants and shops of all kinds and small local businesses and, of course, pubs. Local transactions are threatened if people who plan areas of this kind do not understand the threat which bland warehousing represents. Transactions

such as distributive warehousing on the Bethnal Green Road, and such functions as wholesale markets, banks and office buildings, are destructive of local character because they don't primarily serve local people and the transactions do not take place across the pavement. I call these 'foreign transactions' because they operate on a regional, national or international level. The warehouses do not belong to the road they are in because they abruptly interrupt its local character. They are incongruous.

I want to explore the way that cities can be made up of successfully co-existent functions of different sorts that find their right place. I want to try to understand architectural and urban structures as being rather like coral reefs that are re-inhabited over and over again. There seems to be a pattern in the relationships which recurs though the functions change. For example, in the eighteenth-century city, large houses on primary streets were inhabited by high income families and the mews behind serviced them. Today the houses might be offices of an international/national kind with a mews inhabited by people selling services to the primary users, like printing, employment agencies or sandwich bars.

Observations of this kind have prompted me to think about how to resolve the problem posed by the warehouse development on Bethnal Green Road. You organise the development so that the frontage to the road contains local transactions: chambers like buildings of a modest scale which have frequent access from the pavement and which contain small businesses, retailing, whatever. All these uses facing onto the road sustain the idea of the road as a place in which people can transact and the regional or national distribution function of the warehouses is relegated to its own hinterland. So there is a precinct

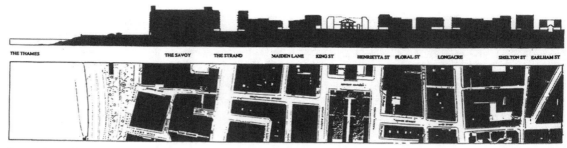

Savoy to Earlham Street plan and section

or service area behind the street. This belongs to the activities around it and confines them. The sections through the street and service yard are symmetrical while the section through the block between them is asymmetrical. So my proposition is that, traditionally, similar uses housed in a similar scale of building, faced each other across streets and the change of use and scale occurred within the block enabling a succession of adjacent streets to be different from one another. The symmetry in the street affirms its character as a place. It follows that the symmetry across the block characteristic of so much modern development produces either uniformity across the urban fabric as a whole or a series of places of ambiguous function and scale.

Disconcerted by the local borough planning policy for the Cheshire Street area, our office looked at how these ideas might be applied. We discovered that the existing section was intriguing, with the railway in a cutting going into Liverpool Street, bounded to the south by run-down warehousing looking into an existing plot of public open space called Allen's Gardens. We showed how the lively street character could be kept by preserving buildings and functions and how the hinterland could be developed for servicing warehousing without affecting the street scene.

We considered housing to be a more apt use to border the public open space which becomes the enclosed garden its name suggests. But we also perceived an economic side: that housing primes the site value, giving confidence to potential small scale investors in the little workshops and businesses between the housing and the railway. There is a sequence here, railway, small businesses giving acoustic protection to the housing, and the housing making an appropriate edge to the garden, to which it has a claim which small businesses don't. There's an idea here which is analogous to the game of dominoes where certain values attach to each other

and certain ones don't and it is this expression of congruity that is also part of my investigation of certain sections through the West End of London.

I would like to focus on two sections. The first is across London from the Thames to Centre Point. There is a general sense of congruity across the river with the Royal Festival Hall, the National Theatre, County Hall and so forth facing the Savoy Hotel, Shell Mex and Embankment Place on the north bank. All are equivalent kinds of set pieces. So there are symmetries of intention even across a river. All are responses to the symbolic status which the river carries into the city. For example the Savoy Hotel free-standing, with its palazzo section, is a type of Thames-side building that goes back to Roman times when villas were built here. If we look at what's happening sectionally on the north bank we find that on the slope from the Embankment itself up to the Strand we get an enormous change of scale, and a change of type through the section.

What happens is that the hotel changes from being a palazzo with all the other ones looking across the river to being a terraced structure which subsumes its rhetoric into that of the Strand and becomes equivalent to most of the other buildings lining the Strand – mostly stone or stucco-clad structures, five to seven storeys high. The Savoy Hotel itself is very interesting because there is a series of transformations within: it's actually rather like a Parisian Hôtel de Ville which invites you to get into the centre of the block where a lot of things are offered including the theatre. It gets its identity when entered from the Strand from its place of access. It has a special identity as a place rather than as an elevation to the street.

In this argument I am not concerned with architectural style, but with purpose and use, probably material to some extent, and with scale. I think many different architectural idioms are reconcilable with those conventions. Moving one street to the north, we find another character in Maiden Lane,

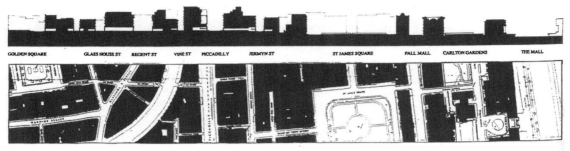

GOLDEN SQUARE   GLASS HOUSE ST   REGENT ST   VINE ST   PICCADILLY   JERMYN ST   ST JAMES SQUARE   PALL MALL   CARLTON GARDENS   THE MALL

St James's Park to Golden Square plan and section

which is a service street with solicitors, chambers, flats, occasional pubs, small businesses, a few shops, where the scale drops down from the Strand. The whole street is quite distinct and again there is a symmetry of use across the street and asymmetry across the block. And then another asymmetry occurs when you come up in scale to the much more public situation of the Covent Garden Piazza. Very little survived of the buildings of Inigo Jones's Piazza which was a symmetrical space of substantial scale into which the market was introduced. The church is on the axis of a wonderful central aisle through the Piazza. North is Long Acre, and here is a sectional change which goes from the large scale of the Piazza buildings down a bit to Floral Street which is a service street (I don't know quite what relationship it had to the Piazza originally but clearly a service function) and then up to Long Acre, a major street nearly equal to the Strand. We are beginning to see an alternation of scale and activity which while not universal is often a characteristic of these West End developments of seventeenth- to nineteenth-century origin.

Then we go through a series of warehouse blocks north of Long Acre which are another environment altogether and sometimes the exception to the rule, being asymmetrical across the street. This warehousing served the fruit and vegetable market originally and has now found a new use in housing small professional businesses, or impoverished professional activities (like architects).

And then you get a curious thing in Neal's Yard where the arrangements invert themselves. The service space which would have been for carts and dray-horses, at the back of buildings that looked out onto streets, has become an oasis of traffic-free activity. So the old coral reef, the old structure has suddenly been reinterpreted and inverted in a very positive way to create another kind of place.

Monmouth Street and Shaftesbury Avenue form the boundary to this area. This part of Shaftesbury Avenue is curiously without local transactions and dominated by large impersonal office buildings and to the north backs onto a desolate hinterland. Character changes again to small intensely used service streets off Charing Cross Road which are abruptly terminated by St Giles Circus. A terrible thing happened when Centre Point took out the end of the block of St Giles High Street, and joined onto the intersection of Oxford Street and Charing Cross Road. Consequently the fabric has been absolutely destroyed and amputated. The amputation is hidden by advertisements: commercial bandaging on the end of the block. It's that kind of disruption without any healing, which makes our modern interventions so crude, unresolved and ghastly. Which is not to say that you can't find places for this type of building. I actually rather like Centre Point, but the problem is contextual, a question of congruity – whether or not it should be there. Even if one were to argue that it should be there, there should be ways between the planning process and architectural process of establishing an environment for a total change of scale and of use.

The second section is of a very different sort and runs from St James's Park up to Golden Square in Soho again. The proposition gets a bit rough to the north of Regent Street, but what's interesting about thinking about London in this way is that you start to ask questions which produce very unexpected answers. Nash's intention was to have another 'Carlton House Terrace' on the other side of the Mall, a proposal which would have made the North boundary of St James's Park rather different. In other words the Mall was going to be a ceremonial axis to the Palace, like a great boulevard in St Petersburg. Carlton House Terrace has the rhetoric of facing the Park, but it is not entered from the Park side. A lot of modern buildings have a back and front, but country houses generally have two 'fronts', because they are entered from one side but they address themselves to the landscape park on the other. Nash's building does this very successfully. The garden at the back of the Pall Mall clubs is a slightly strange space, but it's very quiet and does have a special character, it is not entirely symmetrical – you don't enter clubs from this side, you enter them from Pall Mall.

Then there is a very strange thing, the block between St James's Square and Pall Mall is actually very thin – thinner than the depth of the block containing the clubs. This is because when St James's Square was developed in the 1660s, Pall Mall was already established as a primary street so the buildings on the south side of St James's Square originally presented their fronts to Pall Mall and their backs to St James's Square. Now some of them are back to back – in peculiar contrast to the social and architectural ambitions of the Square. St James's Square has its general symmetry, and then to the north you get the service condition. Apple Tree Yard, which is a mews between St James's Square and Jermyn Street, which again is symmetrical. So there is a symmetry of section through the block, from the primary activity of the square through the mews and up again to the scale of Jermyn Street.

Then we come to Norman Shaw's Piccadilly Hotel. In plan it is the meeting point between Piccadilly and Regent Street which forms a wedge-shaped block. So the hotel is constrained absolutely by an urban proposition which is to do with its palace-like relationship to Piccadilly and the crescent of Regent Street to the north. The hotel presents itself as such on its entrance side to Piccadilly but is entirely subsumed by the uses and rhetoric of Regent Street.

Then you cut through Regent Street to the back of Glasshouse Street, and you get the sense that even cities of the commercial power of London cannot sustain commercial activity in very long sections. There has to be quiet, and Glasshouse Street is very quiet, not a transactional street. It is a relatively low rental office street which collides with the old bit of Soho and then this part becomes dissonant.

Symmetries across places are perhaps generally a good thing, but my proposition does not depend upon symmetry occurring all the time. Off Regent Street, everything is dissonant and strange and interesting. Golden Square is full of amazing one-offs, talking very fast at each other, in a manner very uncharacteristic of the eighteenth-century urban ideal. Generally the surveyors, for example on the Bedford Estate in the eighteenth century, were sure that the long term value of the estates depended upon the style of the estate being maintained and upon leases that constrained people so that things like this couldn't happen, which is, in retrospect, interesting to our own situation.

One last point: for 10 years or so I've had reprints from Booth's London Poverty maps of 1889 on my wall. I suddenly realised that Booth's demographic record of wealth is always symmetrical across streets and shows change occurring across the block.

Source and copyright

This chapter was published in its original form as:

MacCormac, R. (1994), 'Understanding Transactions', *Architectural Review*, **194**, 1165, 70–73.

Reprinted with permission of Architectural Review, London.

This is an edited version of a talk given by Richard MacCormac to the Thursday Club in London.

28

Cities as movement economies

Bill Hillier
[1996]

The physical city and the functional city

It is a truism to say that how we design cities depends on how we understand them. In the late twentieth century, this truism has a disquieting force. Cities are the largest and most complex artefacts that humankind makes. We have learned long and hard lessons about how we can damage them by insensitive interventions. But the growth of knowledge limps painfully along through a process of trial and error in which the slow timescale of our efforts, and the even slower timescale of our understanding, make it almost impossible to maintain the continuity of experience and study which we might hope, in time, would give rise to a deeper, more theoretical understanding of cities.

Even so, a deeper theoretical understanding is what we need. We are at a juncture where fundamental questions about the future of our cities – should settlements be dense or sparse, nucleated or dispersed, monocentric or polycentric, or a mix of all types? – have been raised by the issue of sustainability.[1] It is widely acknowledged that to make cities sustainable we must base decisions about them on a more secure understanding of them than we have now. What is unclear is what we mean by a better understanding. Physically, cities are stocks of buildings linked by space and infrastructure. Functionally, they support economic, social, cultural and environmental processes. In effect, they are means–ends systems in which the means are physical and the ends functional. Our most critical area of ignorance is about the relation

of means to ends, that is of the physical city to the functional city. The fact that sustainability is about ends and the controls largely about means, has exposed our ignorance in this critical area.

One reason for this ignorance is the compartmentalization that has developed over the past quarter century among the disciplines concerned with the city. There is now a deep split between those who are preoccupied with analysis and control of the social and economic processes which animate the city, and who for the most part call themselves planners, and those concerned with physical and spatial synthesis in the city, who call themselves urban designers. This split is now, in effect, a split between understanding and design, between thought and action.

From the point of view of our ability to act on the city, there are two consequences. The first is a form–function gap: those who analyse urban function cannot conceptualize design, while those who can conceptualize design guess about function. The second is a scale gap. Planning begins with the region, deals reasonably with the 'functional city', that is the city and its 'dependences' (as the French say of outlying buildings) but barely gets to the urban area in which we live. Urban design begins with a group of buildings, gets to the urban area, but hesitates at the whole city for fear of repeating the errors of the past when whole city design meant over-orderly towns which never quite became places. Neither applies itself to our need to understand the city as a spatial and functional whole.

One effect of this disciplinary apartheid has been a complete failure to come to terms conceptually with what seems at first to be the simplest thing about the city: the fact that it is a large, apparently complex physical and spatial object, one which is at once a record of the functional processes which historically created it, and at the same time the strongest constraint on future development. Most attempts to use computers to model the ways in which cities work, for example, have dealt with the physical aspects of the city only at the grossest level, far above the level at which most interventions are made. Since the aim of an urban model is to try to bring the structural and dynamic complexities of cities as means–ends systems within the scope of reasoned decision-making about physical and spatial interventions, this has been a critical weakness.[2]

The fact that the physical city has proved most difficult to model effectively is probably due to two things. First, the physical and spatial structure of cities appears, for the most part, to be the rather disorderly outcome of a long history of small-scale, incremental changes which accumulate over time to produce patterns with neither geometrical nor functional simplicity. Until recently, the types of pattern that result from these quasi-organic processes have not seemed tractable to any obvious method of analysis. Consequently they were neglected. Second, the incremental ways in which economic and social processes create the city's physical and spatial patterns seem in themselves to be quite complex, involving feedback and multiplier effects, and interaction between different scales. Processes of urban growth and change seem to exhibit both 'emergence', by which unforeseen macro changes result from a series of micro changes, and the contrary effect, by which macro changes produce unforeseen effects at the micro scale. Again, until recently, there have not been obvious ways of modelling such processes.

The apparent intractability of the city as a physical and spatial object afflicts the synthesists as much as the analysts. If we look to urban designers for an analysis of the object of their design attention, we find much moral earnestness about such matters as the creation of 'places' as rich and complex as those found in traditional cities, but little analytical endeavour to understand how the physical and functional cities of the past gave rise to such 'places'. The current preoccupation with 'place' seems no more than the most recent version of the urban designer's preference for the local and apparently tractable at the expense of the global and intractable in cities. However, both practical experience and research suggest that the preoccupation with local place gets priorities in the wrong order. Places are not local things. They are

moments in large-scale things, the large-scale things we call cities. Places do not make cities. It is cities that make places. The distinction is vital. We cannot make places without understanding cities. Once again we find ourselves needing, above all, an understanding of the city as a functioning physical and spatial object.

Multifunctionality and the part–whole problem

Where should we then find a starting point for an enquiry into the form and functioning of cities, in the hope of founding a theory of cities as means–ends systems? In situations where new theories are needed, there is a useful rule. At every stage in the development of our understanding of phenomena, we already have in our minds some conceptual scheme through which we interpret and interrelate the phenomena that we see.[3] Usually there are irritating anomalies and problems at the edges of these conceptual schemes. The rule is that instead of keeping these problems at the edge of our field of vision, and accepting them as anomalies, we should bring them centre stage and make them our starting point. We should, in effect, start from what we cannot explain rather than what we think we can.

There are two such great anomalies in our current ways of seeing cities. The first is the problem of multifunctionality. Every aspect of the spatial and physical configuration of the city form seems to have to work in many different ways – climatically, economically, socially, aesthetically, and so on – with the additional difficulty that form changes only slowly while function changes rapidly. The second is the part–whole problem, or as some might prefer, the place–city problem, that is, the fact that in most cities made up of parts with a strong sense of local place it is almost impossible to make a clear morphological distinction between one part and another, at least not at the level at which it could inform design.

If the theory set out here is anywhere near right, then it will become clear that these two issues are rather more than closely related: they really are the same problem, because all functions relate to the form of the city through two generic functional factors – how we as individuals find the city intelligible, and how we move around in it. These generic factors are so powerful that all other aspects of function pass through them and influence the urban form through them. This is so because in cities, as in buildings, the relationship between form and function passes through space. How we organize space into configuration is the key both to the forms of the city, and how human beings function in cities.

The theory to be set out here is based on one central proposition: that the fundamental correlate of the spatial configuration is movement. This is the case both in terms of the determination of spatial form, in that movement largely dictates the configuring of space in the city, and in terms of the effects of spatial form, in that movement is largely determined by spatial configuration. The principal generator of the theory set out here is the discovery, through recent research, that the structure of the urban grid considered purely as a spatial configuration, is itself the most powerful single determinant of urban movement, both pedestrian and vehicular. Because this relation is fundamental and lawful, it has already been a powerful force in shaping our historically evolved cities, by its effect on land use patterns, building densities, the mixing of uses in urban areas and the part–whole structure of the city.[4]

The result now available suggests that socio-economic forces shape the city primarily through the relations between movement and the structure of the urban grid. Well functioning cities can therefore, it will be suggested, be thought of as 'movement economies'. That is, it is the reciprocal effects of space and movement on each other (and not, for example, aesthetic or symbolic intentions) and the multiplier effects on both that arise from patterns of land use and building densities, which are themselves influenced by the space–movement relation, that give cities their characteristic structures, and give rise to the sense that everything is working together to create the special kinds of wellbeing and excitement that we associate with cities at their best.

It will be suggested as a consequence of these arguments that our view of the city in the recent past has been afflicted by conceptions of space which are at once too static and too localized. We need to replace these by concepts which are dynamic and global. Both can be achieved through the configurational modelling of space, using the power it gives us both to capture the complexities of urban form, and bring these analyses to bear on design.

Form and function in space are not independent

We must begin by making a few basic observations about space and its relation to function. We tend to think of the form and function of space as two quite independent things. Space is a shape, and function

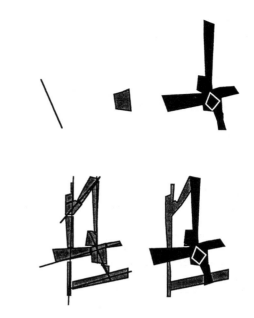

FIGURE 28.1

is what we do in it. Set up this way, it is hard to see why there should be any relation between the two, and even hard to see how any relation could be a necessary one.

But if we think a little more carefully about how human beings operate in space, we find everywhere a kind of natural geometry to what people do in space. Consider, for example, Fig. 28.1. At the most elementary level, people move in lines, and tend to approximate lines in more complex routes, as in the first figure. Then if an individual stops to talk to a group of people, the group will collectively define a space in which all the people the first person can see can see each other, and this is a mathematical definition of convexity in space, except that a mathematician would say points rather than people. The more complex shape of the third figure defines all the points in space, and therefore the potential people, that can be seen by any of the people in the convex space who can also see each other. We call this type of irregular, but well defined, shape a 'convex isovist'. Such shapes vary as we move about in cities, and therefore define a key aspect of our spatial experience of them.

There are relationships, then, between the formal describability of space and how people use it. These elementary relationships between the form of space and its use suggest that the proper way to formulate the relation is to say that space is given to us as

(a)

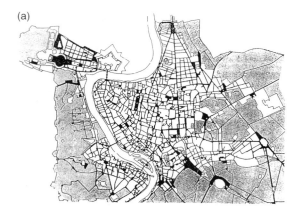

(b)

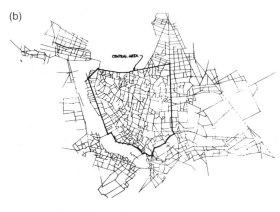

(c)

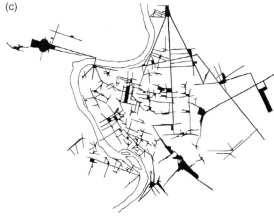

FIGURE 28.2
(a) Plan of Rome, Italy; (b) Axial map of Rome, Italy;
(c) Public open spaces in Rome.

a set of potentials, and that we exploit these potentials as individuals and collectivities in using space. It is this that makes the relation between space and function analysable, and to some extent predictable.

By dividing up urban space, which is necessarily continuous, in different formal ways we are likely to be dividing it up according to some aspect of how human beings function.

Consider, for example, Fig. 28.2a which is the plan of Rome, in which the customary representation with the buildings in black and the space white has been reversed to draw attention to the fact that it is the black structure of space that is our focus of concern.[5] Figure 28.2b is then one possible structure within Fig. 28.2, the fewest and longest lines that cover the open space of Rome, and therefore form its potential route matrix. Figure 28.2c is another such structure: all the convex elements we call public open spaces together with their isovists. By definition, this includes all the lines that pass through the spaces and relate them in the urban structure as a whole. Note how they link up to form global clusters. We immediately see how mistaken we would be to see Roman squares as local elements. The isovists show they also form a global pattern.

All these ways of looking at space can be seen as layers of spatial structuring, coexisting within the same plan, each with its own contribution to intelligibility and function. A spatial layout can thus be seen as offering different functional potentials. What is it like to move around in it? Does it have potential to generate interaction? Can strangers understand it? And so on. All these questions are about the relationship of space as formal potentials to different aspects of function. A layout can thus be represented as a different kind of spatial system according to what aspects of function we are interested in.

The shape of space in the City of London

Let us now look in more detail at a case that is much closer to home: the City of London, for no better reason than that it has been as often criticized as 'haphazard' as praised as 'organic' – but never explained properly. The plan of the 'square mile' (in fact it is neither square nor a mile) is shown in Fig. 28.3a using the black on white convention to emphasize that it is space we are looking at. Figure 28.3b homes in on one of the allegedly 'labyrinthian' back areas of the City between Cornhill and Lombard Street, taken from the Rocque map of 1746. We say allegedly because although it looks so in plan, it does not seem in the least labyrinthian to the person moving at ground level. On the contrary, it seems highly intelligible. How does this happen? The technique

(a)

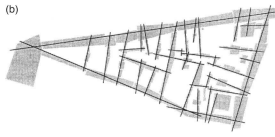

(b)

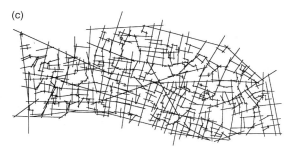

(c)

FIGURE 28.3
(a) Black and White illustration of the public open space of the City of London as it is today; (b) Close-up of the one and two dimensional space structure of the area between Cornhill and Lombard Street in 1677; (c) Axial map of the City of London as it is today.

is simple. The space structure is admittedly highly broken up into 'convex' spaces – but there are always lines which link the convex spaces together, usually several at a time. Sometimes the line 'just about' gets through the spaces formed by the buildings, sometimes more easily. But because people move in lines, and need to understand lines in order to know where they can go, this means that the space structure is easily intelligible from the point of view of movement.

In fact, the pattern is slightly subtler. There is for the most part a 'two-line logic' in that if you pass down a line that you can see from the main grid, the next line will take you either out of the back area again, or to some significant spatial event – say a larger piece of space or a significant building – within the

back area. This means that wherever you go, there is usually a point from which you can see where you have come from and where your next point of aim might be. This is the opposite of labyrinthian. As observation will confirm, the effect of this spatial technique is that the back areas become normally and naturally used for movement as part of the urban space pattern. There is no inhibition or sense of territorial intrusion in these areas.

This two-line logic is not the only constant property of these small-scale complexes. We also find that nearly every convex element, including the narrow ones that enter the back areas, as well as the fatter ones we find within the areas, has building entrances opening onto it. In the city, a fascinating cultural practice has augmented this: even in inclement weather, doors to buildings tend to be left open, often showing to the outside world one-way up stairs or down and another into the ground-level premises.

The effect of these apparent rules about how buildings relate to open space is to create two 'interfaces'. First, there is a close relation between those within the building, and those outside. Second, there is a natural mingling between those who are using the space outside the buildings, and those who are passing through. There is no sense of lack of privacy or intrusion. Nor is there any pressure to interact, though this is available if required. All we have is a relation of copresence between groups doing different things. Such copresence seems unforced, even relaxed. It is the product of a two-way relation from the convex spatial element: one into the building, the other to the larger scale through the line structure. The larger and smaller scales of space are held together by this spatial technique.

Now let us zoom out to the larger scale. Figure 28.3c is an 'axial map' of the city as a whole, that is, the least set of straight lines that pass through all the open space in Fig. 28.3a. The first thing we see when looking at the larger scale – that is at the longer lines – is that the tendency of lines 'just about' to pass through convex space is still there. It is just possible, in spite of the sinuous curves of the buildings, to see down Lombard Street from one end to the other, and it is just about possible to see from the Bank interchange through the whole of Cornhill into Leadenhall Street as far as Billiter Street. In both cases the line ends by striking the facade of a building at a very open angle, and from this it seems natural to infer continuation of potential movement in that general direction.

These improbably extended 'just about' lines create another effect which one must search a little to find, and perhaps go back to the old map to verify.

It is that if one enters any of the old City gates and proceeds following only a rule that requires you to take the longest line available at any time (without going back on yourself) then in each case from somewhere on the second line a line opens up from which the Bank interchange (the old centre of the City) can be seen. Again, we find a simple two-line logic underlying apparent complexity, and again we need have no doubt about its functional implication. It accesses the stranger to the heart of the city. An automaton could find the centre – so a stranger could.

However, when we compare the two levels at which we find this two-line logic, there is a geometric difference which we can summarize in a simple principle: the longer the line the more likely it is to strike a building facade at an open angle; the shorter the line, the more likely it is to strike a building at a right angle. This is exactly the opposite of the current rather pompous urban fashion to end major axes at right angles on major building facades. Historically this usually occurs where urban space is taken over for the symbolic expression of power, whereas the City's urban space structure is about the movement required to create a dense encounter field. The right angle relation of facade to line is used in the City, as it were, to illuminate the smaller-scale and spatially more complex areas, and to make them visible from the larger-scale grid. Thus we begin to see not only that there is an interior logic to the city's apparently disorderly grid, but that this inner logic is fundamentally about movement, and the potential that movement gives for creating copresence. We see that many of the properties of urban space that we value aesthetically are a product of this functional shaping of space.

These consistencies in spatial patterning show how the City is put together locally, and how it therefore works as a series of experiences. But the city also acquires a global form. To understand this, and why it is important, we must begin to formalize our understanding a little. It will turn out that the line pattern of the city is the most important to its global structure, and we must therefore begin by examining this if we wish to move the focus of our analysis from the local to the global. We may begin by a simple observation: that to go from any line to any other one must pass through a certain number of intervening lines (unless of course the origin line directly intersects the destination line). Each line thus has a certain minimum line 'depth' from another, which is not necessarily a function of distance. It follows that each line has a minimum average line 'depth' from all other lines in the system. Because lines will always be shallow from some lines and deep from others, one might expect that this would average itself out. The surprising thing is that it does not. There are substantial differences in the mean depth of lines from all others, and it is these differences that govern the influence of the grid on movement in the system: roughly, the less depth to all other lines, the more movement; and the more depth the less movement.

These configurational pictures of the City from the point of view of its constituent lines can be measured exactly through the measure of 'integration'. The 'integration value' of each line reflects its mean linear 'depth' from all other lines in the system. We can then map these integration values, and produce a global integration map of the whole of a city, as in Fig. 28.4a. We can also produce another highly informative map, one in which we calculate integration only up to three lines away from each line in every direction, and which we therefore call 'local integration', or radius-3 integration, in contrast to 'global' or radius-n integration (Fig. 28.4b).

Integration values in line maps are of great importance in understanding how urban systems function because it turns out that how much movement passes down each line is very strongly influenced by

(a)

(b)

FIGURE 28.4

(c)

(d)

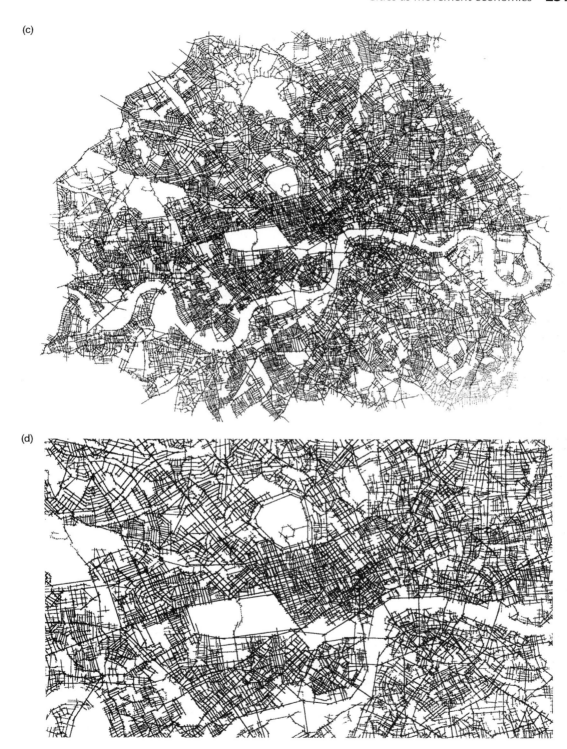

FIGURE 28.4
(*Continued*)

(e)

FIGURE 28.4

its 'integration value' calculated in this way, that is by how the line is positioned with respect to the system as a whole.[6] In fact, it is slightly more subtle and depends on the typical length of journeys. Pedestrian densities on lines in local areas can usually be best predicted by calculating integration for the system of lines up to three lines away from each line (radius-3 integration), while cars on larger-scale routes (though not in local areas, where radius-3 is the best predictor) depend on higher radius integration because car journeys are on the whole longer and motorists therefore read the matrix of possible routes according to a larger-scale logic than pedestrians.[7]

The principle of natural movement

This relationship between the structure of the urban grid and movement densities along lines can be called the principle of 'natural movement'. Natural

movement is the proportion of movement on each line that is determined by the structure of the urban grid itself rather than by the presence of specific attractors or magnets. This is not initially obvious, but on reflection does seem natural. In a large and well-developed urban grid people move in lines, but start and finish everywhere. We cannot easily conceive of an urban structure as complex as the city in terms of specific generators and attractors, or even origins and destinations but we do not need to because the city is a structure in which origins and destinations tend to be diffused everywhere, though with obvious biases toward higher density areas and major traffic interchanges. So movement tends to be broadly from everywhere to everywhere else. To the extent that this is the case in most cities, the structure of the grid itself accounts for much of the variation in movement densities.

We should then expect that the distribution of line intensity in axial maps will foreshadow densities

FIGURE 28.5
Axial map of Greater London within the North and South Circular Roads.

of moving people. Because the line intensities are really rough indices of precise numerical values, this proposition can of course be tested by selecting areas and correlating movement rates against integration values. However, because movement along a particular line is influenced in the main by its position in the larger-scale urban grid, we must take care to include enough of the whole urban grid in our analysis to ensure that each line in the area we are studying is embedded in all the urban structure that may influence its movement. We cannot then do better than to begin with the whole of an urban system, or at least a very large part of it in order to ensure that our study area is sufficiently well embedded.

In order to analyse an area in inner London, then, we begin with an axial representation of the very large part of London shown in Fig. 28.5, which covers the area approximately within the North and South

Circular Roads. Figure 28.4c–e is then a series of analyses of integration at different radii. Figure 28.4c is the radius-n analysis, and as such shows the most global structure of London, with a strong edge-to-centre pattern centred on Oxford Street, which is the most integrated line. Figure 28.4d is the radius-3 analysis, which highlights a much more localized structure, including most local shopping streets, but also picks out Oxford Street as the dominant integrator. This implies that Oxford Street is not only the strongest global integrator in London as a whole, but also the strongest local integrator of its surrounding area. Figure 28.4e is a radius-10 (or radius-radius) analysis, meaning that the integration analysis is set at the mean depth of the whole system from the main integrator, which in this case is 10. The effect of setting the radius of analysis at that of the main integrator is that each line is analysed at the same radius which is at the same time the maximum radius possible without differences in radius between lines. The effect of a radius-radius analysis is to maximize the globality of the analysis without inducing 'edge effect', that is the tendency for the edges of spatial systems to be different from the interior area because they are close to the edge. Taken together, the figures show a remarkably true-to-life functional picture of London as a whole, highlighting all the main in and out routes and shopping high streets.

The reason that a spatial analysis can give such a true-to-life functional picture is due to the powerful

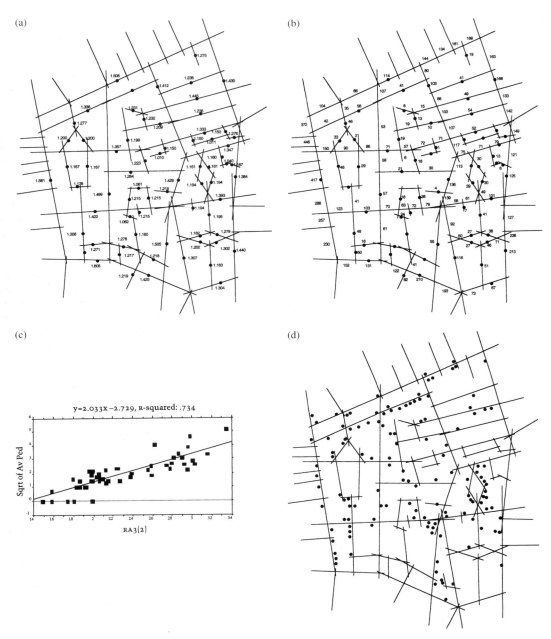

FIGURE 28.6

influence that natural movement – the tendency of the structure of the grid itself to be the main influence on the pattern of movement – has on the evolution of the urban pattern and its distribution of land uses. To test this properly we must translate back from graphics to numbers. Figure 28.6a selects a small area within the system, more or less coterminous with the named area of Barnsbury, and assigns precise 'integration values' to each line. Figure 28.6b then indexes observed movement rates of adult pedestrians on each line segment throughout the working day. Figure 28.6c is a scattergram plotting pedestrian movement rates against radius-3 integration. The R-squared value shows that about three-quarters of the differences between line segments in their movement rates are due to their configurational position in the larger-scale grid. Note, by the way, that we are still calculating integration with respect to a much larger system than that shown in Fig. 28.6a. Movement is not only largely determined by configuration, but also by configuration on a fairly large scale.

Readers can consult published texts for detailed results, but similar results have been achieved across a great range of studies, and even better (though slightly different) results have been found from studies relating vehicular movement to spatial configuration.[8] These studies show that the distribution of pedestrian movement in the urban grid is to a considerable extent determined by spatial configuration, with the actual levels also strongly influenced by area building densities (though the effects of building density are not in general found at the level of the individual line), while vehicular movement is strongly influenced by spatial integration in association with net road width, that is the width of the road less the permitted car parking. In the case of vehicular movement the second variable, net road width, does influence movement on a line-by-line basis and plays a more significant part in the larger scale road network.[9]

We may investigate another key component of successful urbanism, the informal use of open spaces for stopping and taking pleasure, by using a similar technique. Figure 28.7 is a 'convex isovist' representation of the City of London's few, informal open spaces, which vary remarkably in their degree of informal use. Attempts to account for the pattern of well and poorly used spaces in the City in terms of commonly canvassed explanations have been singularly unsuccessful. For example, some spaces hemmed in by traffic are several times better used than adjacent spaces without traffic, exposed spaces often perform better than spaces with good enclosure, some of

the most successful spaces are in the shadow of tall buildings, and so on. The only variable that correlates consistently with the degree of use of observed informal spaces is, in fact, a measure of the 'Roman property', noted in Fig. 28.2c, which we call the 'strategic value' of the isovist. This is calculated by summing the integration values of all the lines which pass through the body of the space (as opposed to skirting its edges). This makes intuitive sense. The primary activity of those who stop to sit in urban spaces seems to be to watch others pass by. For this, strategic spaces with areas close to, but not actually lying on, the main lines of movement are optimal. The main fault in most of the modern open spaces we have observed (with the most notable exception of Broadgate, which has the most successful spaces in the City of London) is that the designers have given too much attention to local enclosure of the space, and too little to strategic visual fields – yet another instance of an overly localized view of space. The general rule seems to be that a space must not be too enclosed for its size. The visibility field must be scaled up in proportion to the scale of the space.

Once we have the trick of correlating numbers indexing observed function with numbers indexing spatial patterns we can extend it to anything that can be represented as a number and located in space. When we do so, it turns out that everything seems to relate to space, and therefore to movement in some way: retail, building densities, indeed most types of land use seem to have some spatial logic which can be expressed as a statistical relation between spatial and function measures.

Now let us look at other aspects of how things are distributed in the urban grid. Take, for example,

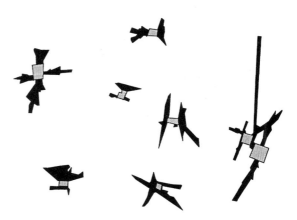

FIGURE 28.7
Convex isovists from eight City of London squares.

the well-known Booth map on London, in which socioeconomic classes are plotted from gold for the best off, through to red for merchant grade houses, then through pink to grey and black for the poorest. The most integrated streets are lined with red, and as you move into the less important, and less integrating streets, the grade of housing falls off, leaving the poorest in the most segregated areas. There is also a subtler organization concealed in the Booth map, one which provides an important clue to one of the hidden secrets of urban space: how different uses and economic classes are mixed in the same area by using a principle that can be summarized as 'marginal separation by linear integration'. If we look carefully we can see that different grades of housing – and in other situations we will find different land uses – may often be in close proximity but separated effectively by being on different alignments, often as part of the same urban block. The fundamental land use element is not the zone or even the urban block but the line: land use changes slowly as you progress along particular lines of movement, but can change quite sharply with ninety-degree turns onto different alignments. Since we know that the pattern of alignments is the fundamental determinant of movement, we can begin to see that the structure of the urban grid, the distribution of land uses, and built form densities are in the historically evolving city bound up with each other in a dynamic process centred on the relation of the grid structure to movement.

Which then is primary? Let us argue this through the spatial distribution of retail, the commonest non-residential land use. We may already have been suspected of having confused the effects of spatial configuration on movement with the effect of shops. Are not the shops the main attractors of movement? And do they not lie on the main integrators? This is of course true. But it does not undermine what is being said about the structure of the grid as the prime determinant of movement. On the contrary it makes the argument far more powerful. Both the shops and the people are found on main integrators, but the question is: why are the shops there? The presence of shops can attract people but they cannot change the integration value of a line, since this is purely a spatial measure of the position of the line in the grid. It can only be that the shops were selectively located on integrating lines, and this must be because they are the lines which naturally carry the most movement. So, far from explaining away the relation between grid structure and movement by pointing to the shops, we have explained the location of the shops by pointing to the relation between grid and movement.[10]

Now of course in a sense to say this is to say the obvious. Every retailer knows that you should put the shop where people are going to be anyway, and it is no surprise if we find that the structure of the urban grid influences at least some land uses as it evolves. It would be surprising if it were not the case. However, a little more than this is being claimed. It is being suggested that there is an underlying principle which, other things being equal, relates grid structure to movement pattern not only on the main lines in and out of a city, but also in the fine structure, and through this gives rise to a whole multiplicity of interrelationships between grid structure, land uses, densities, and even the sense of urban wellbeing and fear.

Multiplier effects and the movement economy

We can pursue this by thinking carefully about what it would take to produce this degree of agreement between grid structure, movement, land uses and densities. We find ourselves unavoidably led towards a theory of the general formation of the city through the functional shaping of its space by movement. Let us begin by considering that. An urban system, by definition, is one which has at least some origins and destinations more or less everywhere. Every trip in an urban system has three elements: an origin, a destination, and the series of spaces that are passed through on the way from one to the other. We can think of passage through these spaces as the by-product of going from *a* to *b*. We already know that this by-product, when taken at the aggregate level, is determined by the structure of the grid, even if the location of all the *a*'s and *b*'s is not.

Location in the grid therefore has a crucial effect. It either increases or diminishes the degree to which the movement by-product is available as potential contact. This applies not only to individual lines, but to the groups of lines that make up local areas. Thus there will be more integrating and less integrating areas, depending on how the internal structure of the area is married into the larger-scale structure of the grid, and this will mean also areas with more by-product and areas with less.

Now if cities are, as they were always said to be, 'mechanisms for generating contact', then this means that some locations have more potential than others because they have more by-product and this will depend on the structure of the grid and how they relate to it. Such locations will therefore tend to have higher densities of development to take advantage of this, and higher densities will in turn have a multiplier effect. This will in turn attract new buildings and uses, to take advantage of the multiplier effect. It is this positive feedback loop built on the relation between the grid structure and movement which gives rise to the urban buzz, which we prefer to be romantic or mystical about, but which arises from the coincidence in certain locations of large numbers of different activities involving people going about their business in different ways. Such situations invariably arise through multiplier effects generated from the basic relation between space structure and movement, and ultimately this depends on the structure of the urban grid itself. In other words, how the urban system is put together spatially is the source of everything else.

We may illustrate this negatively through a notorious case where the urban buzz does not occur, in spite of the coexistence in a small area of many major functions. The example is the area of the South Bank cultural centre in London, where within a few hundred metres can be found Europe's largest and most diverse cultural complex, a major international railway terminus, extensive office development, significant residential development and a famous riverside walk. Why do all these facilities not add up into an urban area with the qualities called for by these high-level facilities? It can only be the way it is put together. This is indeed the case. Our studies have shown that each of the various constituencies of space users – travellers, residents, office workers, tourists, concert goers and gallery visitors all use space in a different way and, as it were, move through the area largely on separate routes passing each other like ships in the night. It is the failure of the configuration of space to bring these different constituencies into patterns of movement and space use where all are prioritizing the same space, that deprive the area of the multiplier effects that occur when different constituencies of space use all spark off each other.

If these arguments are right, it means that all the primary elements of urban form – the structure of the urban grid, the distribution of land uses, and the assignment of development densities – are bound together in the historical city by the principle that relates the structure of the urban grid to the by-product of movement. It means that under certain conditions of density and integration of the grid structure things can happen that will not happen elsewhere. Movement is so central to this process that

we should forthwith cease to see cities as being made up of fixed elements and movement elements and instead see the physical and spatial structure as being bound up to create what we have called the 'movement economy', in which the usefulness of the by-product of movement is everywhere maximized by integration in order to maximize the multiplier effects which are the root source of the life of cities.

Urbanity, we suggest, is not so mysterious. Good space is used space. Most urban space use is movement. Most movement is through movement, that is, the by-product of how the grid offers routes from everywhere to everywhere else. Most informal space use is also movement related, as is the sense and fact of urban safety. Land uses and building density follow movement in the grid, both adapting to and multiplying its effects. The urban buzz, or the lack of it when it suits us, is the combination of these, and the fundamental determinant is the structure of the grid itself. The urban grid through its influence on the movement economy is the fundamental source of the multifunctionality that gives life to cities.

Disurbanism

The urban movement economy, arising from the multiplier effect of space, depends on certain conditions: a certain size, a certain density, a certain distribution of land uses, a specific type of grid that maintains the interface between local and global, and so on. Once this is spelled out, it is easy to see how thoroughly some of our recent efforts have disrupted it, so much so that we must think of many developments of recent years as an exercise in the spatial technique of disurbanism. 'Disurbanism' is intended to convey the reverse of the urban spatial techniques we have identified; the breaking of the relation between buildings and public space; the breaking of the relation between scales of movement; and the breaking of the interface between inhabitant and stranger.

Consider, for example, the integration map of an area around Barnsbury, which includes three housing estates around the Kings Cross railway lands site (the empty area), as in Fig. 28.8. The estates are easy to pick out: they are more complex and at a smaller spatial scale than the surrounding street-based areas, and each is marked by its density of light shaded, that is segregated, lines. If we try to plot these estates as dark point scatters of local against global integration,

FIGURE 28.8
Global integration map of King's Cross with three housing estates picked out in black and the scatters (in black dots) of the three housing estates within their within their larger context.

then we find that in each case the estate scatter forms a series of layers, each distributed in a more or less vertical pattern. Here we note three consequences of this type of spatial design. First, the estate is substantially more segregated than the rest of the urban surface and, what is more problematic, segregated as a lump. Good urban space has segregated lines, but they are close to integrated lines, so that there is a good mix of integrated and segregated lines locally. Second, there is a poor relation between local and global integration, that means a very unclear relation between the local and global structure. Third, the scatter does not cross the line to create a well-structured local intensification of the grid.

What this means in functional terms is that all interfaces are broken: between building and public space; between localized and less localized movement; and between inhabitant and stranger. Of course life is possible in such a place. But there is now evidence to suggest that we ought to be more pessimistic. Efforts to trace the effects that such designs can have over a long period on the type of life that goes on in them suggest that there is a pattern of long term development in which spatial designs create serious lacunas in natural movement, which then attract anti-social uses and behaviours. In extreme cases, where the lacunas of natural movement are the integration core of the estate itself, then the situation may become pathological.

These 'disurban' places arise from a poorly structured local configuration of space; as a consequence of which the main elements of the movement economy are lost. A similar pattern of loss can also arise through dispersion. If we move from an urban system that is dense and nucleated to one that is dispersed and fragmentary, it is obvious that the mean length of journeys will, other things being equal, increase. It is less obvious, but equally true, that the by-product effect will also be diminished. As dispersion increases, it becomes less and less likely that connected locations will benefit from the by-product of movement. In effect, as dispersion increases, the movement system becomes more like a pure origin–destination system. Instead of one journey accomplishing a number of purposes, more journeys, each one accomplishing fewer purposes, must be made to attain the same goals. These are the basic reasons why people travel farther in the country, and why most of this extra travel is in private cars.

A similar effect can arise even in a comparatively dense urban system through an urban design policy of replacing continuous urban structure with specialized enclaves. This will also tend to eliminate by-product. Enclaves are, almost by definition, destinations which are not available for natural movement. They form discontinuities in the urban grid. Because this is so they are in many ways comparable in their effects to physical dispersion, and similarly disruptive of the movement economy. Any tendency in an urban structure towards 'precinctization' must also be a tendency towards a lessening of the useful by-product, and therefore of the multiplier effect on which urban vibrancy depends.

These arguments suggest that the culturally sanctioned values that are embedded in attitudes towards urban design that until quite recently were taken for granted – lowering densities wherever possible, breaking up urban continuity into well-defined and specialized enclaves, reducing spatial scale, separating and restricting different forms of movement, even restricting the ability to stop travellers from moving and taking advantage of the by-product effect – are fundamentally inimical to the natural functioning of the city and its movement economy. It is not density that undermines the sense of well-being and safety in urban spaces, but sparseness; not large spatial scale, but its insensitive reduction; not lack of order but its superficial imposition; not the 'unplanned chaos' of the deformed grid, but its planned fragmentation. Without an understanding of the spatial and functional nature of the city as a whole, we are in danger of eliminating all the properties of density, good spatial scale, controlled juxtaposition of uses, continuity, and integration of the urban grid on which the well-ordering and well-functioning city depends.

Reflections on the origins of urbanism and the transformation of the city

These conclusions can only reinforce the thought with which we began: our interventions in the city can only be based on our understanding of the city. Where this understanding is deficient, the effects can be destructive, and this will be more the case according to the degree that this false understanding is held in place by a value system. The value system according to which we have been transforming our cities over much of the past century has always appeared as a kind of urban rationality, but it was never based on the study of the city. Where then did it come from?

Let us first reflect a little on the nature and origins of cities, why we have them and what made them possible. Towns, as physical objects, are clearly specialized forms of spatial engineering which permit large numbers of people to live in dense concentrations without getting on each other's nerves, and minimize the effort and energy needed for face-to-face contact with each other and with the providers for needs. Towns, we suggest, were in fact made functionally possible in the first instance by a transmutation in the way energy flowed through society It is most easily explained through the geographer Richard Wagner's distinction between two kinds of energy-related artifact: *implements* which transmit or accelerate kinetic energy, and *facilities* which store up potential energy and slow down its transfer.[11]

For example, a flint knife is an implement, whereas a dam is a facility. Whatever else made towns possible, there is no doubt that they were usually marked by a radical increase in facilities, most especially irrigation systems and food storage facilities.

What made towns possible socially was an invention we are so familiar with that we tend to take it for granted and forget it is there: the urban grid. The urban grid is the organization of groups of contiguous buildings in outward-facing, fairly regular clumps, amongst which is defined a continuous system of space in the form of intersecting rings, with a greater or lesser degree of overall regularity. Urban grids were never inevitable. In fact, the archaeological record reveals many proto-towns with quite different morphologies.

The urban grid was, however, the first powerful theorem of urban spatial engineering. Its crucial characteristic is that it is itself a facility – one that takes the potential movement of the system and makes it as efficient and useful as possible. The grid is the means by which the town becomes a 'mechanism for generating contact', and it does this by ensuring that origin–destination trips take one past outward-facing building blocks *en route*. That is, they allow the by-product effect to maximize contact over and above that for which trips are originally intended.

In the nineteenth century, however, under the impact of industrialization and rapid urban expansion, two things happened. First, to cope with sheer scale, the urban spatial grid was thought of as more of an implement than a facility. That is, it was seen as a means to accelerate movement in order to overcome size. Alongside this it was envisaged as a set of point-to-point origins and destinations, rather than as an 'all points to all points' grid, which is the product of an urban movement economy.

Second, the city began to be seen not as a grid-based civilization, but as the overheated epicentre of focal movement into and out of the city, and as such the most undesirable of locations. A social problem was seen in the disorderly accumulation, in and around city centres, of people brought in to serve the new forms of production. Big became synonymous with bad, and density became synonymous with moral depravity and political disorder. It was this that gave rise to much of the value system of nineteenth-century urban planning, as well as the more extreme proposals for the dispersion and ruralization of the city and its population.

Unfortunately, much of this nineteenth-century value system survived into the twentieth century, not so much in the form of consciously expressed beliefs

and policy objectives as in assumptions as to what constituted the good city. For much of the twentieth century, nineteenth-century anti-urbanism provided the paradigm for urban design and planning. It would be good to believe that this may have now changed, and that cities are again being taken seriously. But this is not the nature of human beliefs when they become embedded in institutional forms and structures. Many aspects of the nineteenth-century urban paradigm have not yet been dismantled, and are still to be found enshrined in everyday policies towards density, in novel ways of breaking up urban continuity into well-defined and specialized enclaves, in continuing to reduce spatial scale, and in separating and restricting different forms of movement. These relics of an outdated paradigm do not derive from an understanding of cities. On the contrary, they threaten the natural functioning and sustainability of the city.

Notes

1. The best recent review of these issues is Owens, S. (1992) Land-use planning for energy efficiency, *Applied Energy*, 43, 1–3, Special issue on the rational use of energy in urban regeneration, R. Hackett and J. Bindon (eds), Elsevier Applied Science. An important source on settlement forms on which she draws is P. Rickaby (1987) Six settlement patterns compared, *Environment & Planning B: Planning & Design*, **14**, 193–223. Significant recent contributions include Banister, D. (1992) Energy use, transport and settlement patterns, in M. Breheny (ed.) *Sustainable Development and Urban Form*, Pion; also Hall, P. (1994) Squaring the circle; can we resolve the Clarkian paradox? *Environment & Planning B: Planning & Design*, 21, s79–s94.
2. For a discussion see Batty, M. (1989) Urban modelling and planning: reflections, retrodictions and prescriptions, in B. Macmillan (ed.) *Remodelling Geography*, Basil Blackwell, Oxford, pp. 147–169. See also Batty, M. and Longley, P. (1994) *Fractal Cities*, Academic Press, London.
3. Hillier, B. *et al.* (1993) Natural movement: or configuration and attraction in urban pedestrian movement, *Environment & Planning B: Planning & Design*, **20**; and Penn, A. and Dalton, N. (1994) The architecture of society: stochastic simulation of urban movement, in N. Gilbert and J. Doran (eds) *Simulating Societies: The Computer Simulation of Social Phenomena*, UCL Press, London, pp. 85–125.
4. In this sense, it is an instance of what Ian Hacking calls 'the creation of phenomena', which then leads to the evolution of theory: Hacking, I. (1983) *Representing and Intervening*, Cambridge University Press, pp. 220–32.
5. The figures are taken from a case study carried out by Marios Pelekanos while a student on the MSc in Advanced Architectural Studies at the Bartlett School of Graduate Studies, UCL, in 1989.

6. Hillier, B. *et al*. 'Natural movement'. Op. cit.
7. Penn, A. *et al*. (1995) Configurational modelling of urban movement networks (submitted for publication, currently available from the Bartlett School of Graduate Studies).
8. See for example Penn, A. and Hillier, B. *Configurational modelling* (see note 7).
9. Penn, A. and Hillier, B. (see note 7).
10. This issue is discussed in greater detail in Hillier, B. *et al*. (1993) Natural movement (see note 3).
11. Wagner, P.L. (1960) *The Human Use of the Earth*, New York, Chapter 6. For a further discussion see Flannery, K. (1972). The origins of the village as a settlement type in Mesoamerica and the Near East: a comparative study, in P. Ucko *et al*. (eds) *Man. Settlement and Urbanism*, Duckworth, pp. 23–53.

Source and copyright

This chapter was published in its original form as:

Hillier, B. (1996), 'Cities as Movement Economies', *Urban Design International*, **1** (1), 41–60.

Reproduced with permission of Palgrave Macmillan.

Section Seven

The temporal dimension

Although sometimes considered to be a matter of working in three dimensions, urban design is four-dimensional – the fourth dimension being time. Time impacts on almost every aspect of urban design – on the way the environment is perceived (i.e. over time and on the move) (see Section Five); on the way places become imbued with meanings – over time (see Section Three); on how places last and adapt; how robust they are (i.e. on how places change over time); their morphological processes (see Section Two); and on the length of time that urban design processes take. Some of the most stimulating discussions of time are found in related fields such as cultural geography, philosophy, anthropology and phenomenology, but a number of theorists have also attempted to relate time factors directly to urban design.

This section presents a set of three chapters exploring the temporal or 'time' dimension of urban design. Chapter 29 is from **Peter Bosselmann's** 1998 book, *Representations of Places: Reality and Realism in City Design* (University of California Press, Berkeley). Building on Cullen's original work on serial vision, Bosselmann presents an excellent comparative discussion and presentation of the visual/aesthetic experience of moving through urban environments. Noting how Gordon Cullen and Ed Bacon's work showed how movement can be read and understood as a pictorial sequence (Cullen, 1961; Bacon, 1967), Bosselmann describes the rich and varied experience of a walk – measuring three-hundred-and-fifty metres and taking about four minutes – in central Venice. This walk is used to show how our perception of time passing and distance travelled differs from reality and is in part a function of the visual and experiential qualities of the environment we are moving through. Noting that the Venice walk seems both to be longer and to take more time than it actually does, he then assesses the aesthetic (and kinaesthetic) experience of the same length of walk in fourteen other cities. The perception of time varies in each as a direct consequence of visual-aesthetic qualities, particularly how monotonous or varied the experience is.

Chapter 30 is drawn from one of **Kevin Lynch's** less well-known books, *What Time is This Place?* (MIT Press, Cambridge Mass). Published in 1972 at a time when Modernist ideas were being questioned and replaced – or, at least, supplemented – by a greater focus on conservation, continuity and sense-of-place, the paper presents a valuable discussion of conservation – although Lynch tends to use the American term 'preservation' – and change. Urban environments and buildings are continuously and inexorably

changing, shaped and reshaped by technological, economic, social and cultural change. Furthermore, any intervention into the physical fabric of a place irreversibly changes its history for all time, becoming part of that history. Never static, the built environment stands as testament to processes of continuity, change and the passage of time within a particular place.

The emergence of conservation resulted in an increased concern and respect for the uniqueness of places and their history and, in large part, was instrumental in the evolution of the contemporary concept of urban design, which attempts to respond to the existing sense of place and stresses 'continuity-with' rather than a 'break-from' the past. In a world of rapid change, visual and tangible evidence of the past is valued for the sense-of-place and enduring qualities of its character and identity. Taken to extremes, however, extensive preservation and conservation can obstruct and even halt a city's evolution and development. Emphasising the necessity of adaptability, Lynch argues that environments that cannot be changed 'invite their own destruction' and that: *'We prefer a world that can be modified progressively against a background of valued remains, a world in which one can leave a personal mark alongside the marks of history'.*

To preserve the capacity for change, environments need to be capable of evolution. Thus, continuing in a similar vein as Lynch, working within established contexts requires an understanding of how environments adapt to change and, more importantly, why some environments adapt more successfully than others. Urban design often involves distinguishing between what is fundamental to the sense-of-place and should not change and what is less important and can change. The visual and physical continuity of valued places relates to issues of the 'obsolescence' of buildings and environments, the time frames of change, and the 'robustness' and 'resilience' of the built fabric and other physical attributes of that place. Accordingly, Chapter 31 is from **Stewart Brand's** 1994 book *How Buildings Age: What happens after they are built* (Penguin Books, Harmondsworth). Brand was not an urban design practitioner – he was trained as a biologist and army officer. His book was originally a six-part television series.

Already a classic, Brand's book presents an important discussion of how the different parts of a building age/change at different rates. He extends and develops Frank Duffy's series of layers of longevities (Duffy, 1990) to create a series of six systems – 'site', 'structure', 'skin', 'services', 'space plan', and 'stuff'.

The systems are differently paced – site and structure are the slowest, stuff and space plan are the quickest. As Brand suggests, the key to robust buildings – those able to accommodate change – is to allow the faster paced systems to change without the need for change in the slower paced systems (i.e. changing the services should not require change to the structure). Furthermore, a building's – and a place's – enduring character may be substantially embedded in its slower moving systems (see also the discussion of morphology in Section Two).

Matthew Carmona and Steve Tiesdell

29

Images in motion

Peter Bosselmann
[1998]

Painters in Western society have learned to represent the sense of movement by studying the human body. A painter's ultimate goal might be to paint landscapes or still lifes, but the drawing of the nude would be fundamental to any exploration of rhythmic relationships—the organization of shapes, linear movement, solidity, stability, mobility, equilibrium, and expressive character.[1]

Urban designers have no equivalent educational tradition, though the work of Gordon Cullen or Edmond Bacon has taught them that movement can be read and understood as a pictorial sequence. Critics of this approach argue that reliance on serial vision has led to overly picturesque designs. That claim is true if eye-level perspectives are the dominant form of imagining a place, but if these are combined with measured drawings such as maps, designers can learn important lessons about scale in city design. A designer who compares, for example, a plan view of a place with a pictorial sequence illustrating a walk through that place has a much better grasp of dimension.

The representation of pictorial sequences came late to Western culture. Chinese landscape painters perfected the representation of movement. The art historian George Rowley has written: "For the painters of landscape scrolls the principles of spatial design are conditioned through the isolation of motifs." For Rowley, motifs are picture elements a viewer can easily grasp in one single focus. The eyes, moving through the intervals between these elements, can overcome the isolation of each motif, tying adjacent motifs together. Thus the viewer is set free to "walk" through the landscape and observe the world in motion: "A scroll painting must be experienced in time like music or literature. Our attention is carried

along laterally from right to left, being restricted at any moment to a short passage which can be conveniently perused."[2]

The scroll tells a tale that can be interrupted and repeated. The walk through Venice on the pages that follow presents such a scroll, one that reads not from right to left, but from the bottom of the page to the top. At first, this direction seems counter-intuitive, especially when the accompanying written text is read top to bottom. But reading images is different from reading text. For the images to have the desired effect of pulling the reader into the space, the pictures themselves must be read from bottom to top. Western art traditionally represents conditions yet to be realized, the future and things associated with it—that is, hope, expectation, and so forth—in the upper portions of pictures. The present condition or position in space or time is shown in the middle of pictures; the past, what we have left behind, is shown at the bottom. An upward movement of the eyes implies progression; a downward movement, regression.[3]

In scanning the Venice images, the reader pieces them together and gains the illusion of movement through space. Reading the pictorial sequences quickly is similar to watching a motion picture film. Like a film, the pictorial sequences transport the viewer into the scene.

I walked along this route many times on the way to and from the Giudecca. Early in my stay, when one narrow alley looked like another, the bridges stood out as spatial elements, giving structure to my movements and expressing a rhythm. I remember the experience of rising at each bridge and gaining a better view for a few moments before "plunging" back to ground level. The squares along the walk defined

The walk starts on the Calle Lunga de Barnaba, in a typical Venetian alley: a dark, narrow passage about to open into a square. The pedestrian is drawn to the light beyond the passage, in the Campo Santa Barnaba. The pedestrian crosses the campo diagonally. Light reflects on the church facade and the stone pavement. Past a covered well, a bridge in the far corner of the campo gives new direction to the walk.

Beside the bridge is a shop selling mirrors. A large one on display in the window reflects the bridge and a young couple coming down the steps. The bridge arches high over the canal, reaching almost to the second story of nearby buildings. Signs announce the name of the bridge: Ponte Santa Barnaba at the Fondamente Rezzonico. At the highest point on the bridge, the pedestrian wants to take bearings.

But here the scroll technique shows its limits. The scroll continues on the obvious path down the steps into Calle de Bateche, but instead the pedestrian wants to look around. A glance to the left reveals the long straight Rio San Barnaba, with two more bridges in the distance. A Venetian might not remember the bridges' names but once oriented probably would know that they lead to another neighborhood near the large Campo San Marcherita, where an open-air market is held. The view to the right reveals the Grand Canal and perhaps the waterbus stopping at the Campo San Samuele on its way to the Rialto. The scroll, however, reveals none of this information.

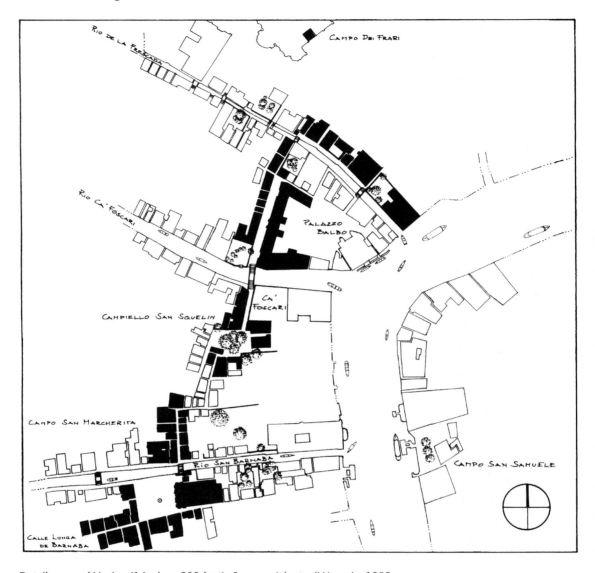

Detail, map of Venice (1 inch = 200 feet). Source: *Atlante di Venezia*, 1989.

the beginning and end of movement. Crossing a square gave me a sense both of balance and of anticipation of the next stretch of narrow alleys to be traversed before the next bridge and the next square.

The walk in Venice measures 1,060 feet, or approximately 350 meters. It takes four minutes to walk this distance—a very short time considering the many different physical spaces encountered. In Venice, buildings, squares, alleys, canals, and bridges are all crowded together in a very small area. To explore

the scale of Venice relative to the scale of other cities, I have overlaid the length of the walk in Venice on maps of other cities. The fourteen city maps that follow are all drawn to the same scale, one inch equals 200 feet, which is also the scale of the map accompanying the pictorial sequences. The fourteen city maps were selected to represent a wide range of urban scales. Some cities are finely scaled, like Kyoto or Barcelona. Others are large in scale, like Washington, D.C. Some cities have streets following regular grids; in other cities streets follow irregular patterns. The

The sequence of pictures leads down the steps and along Calle Boteche, a short, narrow street that turns right. (The walk skips a short section of the next alley.)

The sequence starts again at the corner of Calle Cappeler; the pedestrian turns right and—before seeing the square—senses the proximity of open space from the abundant light. A double row of trees marks a diagonal path across the Campiello del Squelin, where a bookstore sits on the square at the corner with the Calle Foscari.

Along the Calle Foscari a three-story-high wall on the right hides the garden of the Ca'Foscari; the palace itself faces the Grand Canal. The pedestrian's path parallels the Grand Canal behind the properties that face it.

The pedestrian sees the light falling on the facade of a building beside the Palazzo Balbo, on the other side of a large bridge with many steps, suggesting a wide span. Ponte Foscari "slides" into full view as the corner building on the left recedes. From the steps of the bridge, a landmark of the Polo district comes into view: the bell tower of the church of the Frari. From the bridge itself, the pedestrian looks down a street that is very wide and straight by Venetian standards.

Standing on top of the Ponte Foscari, the pedestrian takes a bearing once more. The view to the right again reveals the Grand Canal, looking closer than it looked from the Ponte Santa Barnaba and much wider as it bends eastward, but none of these sights is shown in the limited view of the images, which lead ahead down into the Calla Larga Foscari.

Four images suffice to convey the 80-meter length of the Calla Larga Foscari, a distance that has taken up to fourteen images in earlier sections of the walk when streets were narrower and more winding. Only when the pedestrian reaches what appears to be the dead end of this street does another pedestrian, stepping out of the narrow opening to an alley, show how the route continues, into the narrow Calle de la Dona Onesta.

The contrast between the wide Calle Foscari and the narrow Calle de la Dona Onesta is impressive. Half the length of the wide Foscari, Calle Onesta nonetheless appears longer. Light falls down into it from above a high garden wall; even more light falls onto a bridge, the cast-iron Ponte di Dona Onesta, that comes into view at the end of this narrow space. Steps to it rise suddenly from the alley.

From the bridge, the pedestrian sees a bookstore on the Fondamente del Fornu straight ahead and can read the covers of the books on display. But not for long, for the walk continues with a right turn on to the Fondamente del Fornu, where a row of beautiful buildings faces the Rio de la Frescada. The Grand Canal, visible once again, looks surprisingly distant; it has curved away from the pedestrian's straight path. On the canal one of the palazzi glimpsed from the bridge over the Rio Foscari again comes into view.

The distance covered in the walk in Venice equals that of a walk many Berkeley students take daily from the corner of Telegraph Avenue and Bancroft to Wheeler Hall (along the dotted line). This walk appears much shorter than the walk in Venice.

Detail, map of the Berkeley campus (1 inch = 200 feet). Source: University of California, 1987.

same four-minute walk applied to these fourteen city maps appears to take different amounts of time. In most cities, traveling the distance that is actually equivalent to the walk in Venice appears to take less time. In some of the cities, walking this distance comes close to the time it takes to walk in Venice.

For a designer, these comparisons are important. The dimensions and placement of urban elements influence the perception of time.

Thinking about time's embodiment in the physical world might bewilder most of us. The failure to grasp the elements that make one walk appear longer or

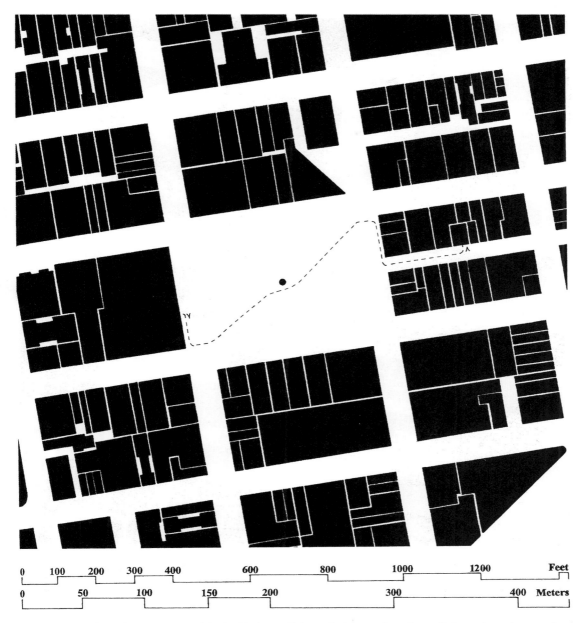

| 0 | 100 | 200 | 300 | 400 | 600 | 800 | 1000 | 1200 | **Feet** |

| 0 | 50 | 100 | 150 | 200 | 300 | 400 | **Meters** |

In San Francisco, the distance covered in the Venice walk is equivalent to that of a walk from the entrance of the St. Francis Hotel, through Union Square, past the Naval Monument, across Stockton Street, and into Maiden Lane to the Circle Gallery, designed by Frank Lloyd Wright——really a very short walk.

Detail, map of San Francisco's retail district (1 inch = 200 feet). Source: Department of City Planning, City of San Francisco, 1983.

shorter than another has astonished some of the most experienced city designers.

I do not have answers to explain all variables that alter the perception of time, but I found some interesting hints in the writings of the philosopher William James:[4] "Our heart-beats, our breathing, the pulses of our attention, fragments of words or sentences that pass through our imagination, are what

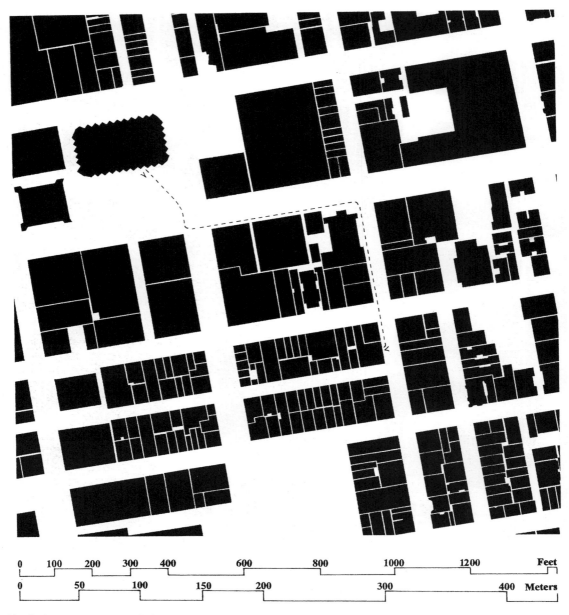

| 0 | 100 | 200 | 300 | 400 | | 600 | | 800 | | 1000 | | 1200 | **Feet** |

| 0 | | 50 | | 100 | | 150 | | 200 | | | 300 | | | 400 | **Meters** |

Also in San Francisco, a walk from the Bank of America Building along California Street, past Old St. Mary's Church, with a turn into Grant Avenue to a restaurant at the corner of Commercial Street appears to take a little longer than the previous walk in San Francisco but seems shorter than the walk in Venice.

Detail, map of San Francisco's Chinatown (1 inch = 200 feet). Source: Department of City Planning, City of San Francisco, 1983.

people this dim habitat" that he and others have called the twilight of our general consciousness. All of these elements have to do with rhythm. Even if we try to empty our minds, by sitting still, for example, with eyes closed, "some form of changing process remains for us to feel and cannot be expelled. Awareness of change is the condition on which our perception of time's flow depends." But there is no

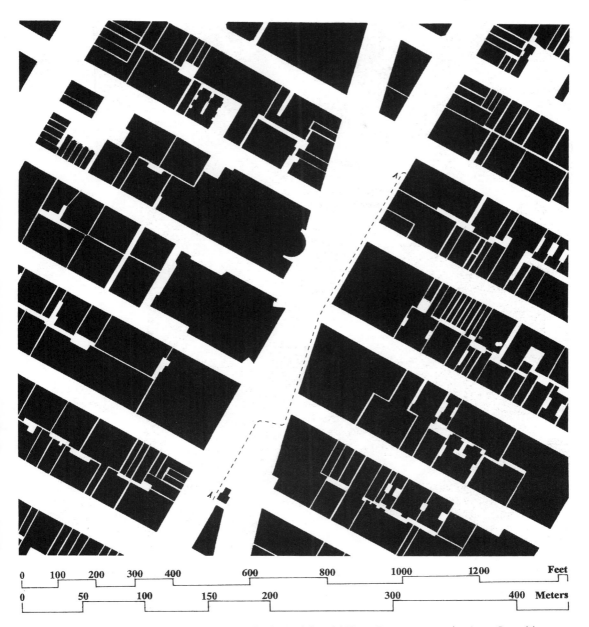

At Times Square in New York, a walk begins at the foot of the old Times Tower, passes the Army Recruiting Station, stops in the median strip between Broadway and Seventh Avenue for a good look at the square, chances it across Broadway, and proceeds along to the Palace, across from Duffy Square where tickets for same-day performances are sold. This is a quick walk.

Map of New York City's Times Square (1 inch = 200 feet). Source: Department of City Planning, City of New York, 1982.

reason to believe that sitting still and seeing nothing suffice to arouse the awareness of change. "The change must be of some concrete sort."

Pedestrians tell the length of their walks by the rhythmic spacing of recurring elements. The Venice walk has frequent and different types of rhythmic spacing. Other environments have produced fewer types of spacing, and the visible information engages walkers less frequently. Thirty-nine drawings of unequal spacing were needed to explain the

In Copenhagen, a pedestrian walks along Strøget from Nytorv, past York Passage, then catches sight of the grand old trees at the churchyard reaching into the streets at Helligaands Kirke, and walks to Amager Torv. The distance is the same as that of the walk in Venice, though it appears a little shorter.

Map of Copenhagen's main pedestrian street (1 inch = 200 feet). Source: Copenhagen General Planning Department; redrawn, 1989, by Allan Jacobs.

four-minute walk in Venice; far fewer drawings could explain most of the other walks. Successive acts of apperception and recognition influence one's sense of time. The walk through Venice necessitates many turns—through two squares, along several narrow alleys, across three bridges, and near a number of waterways. Pedestrians perceive change successively and adjust their knowledge—for example,

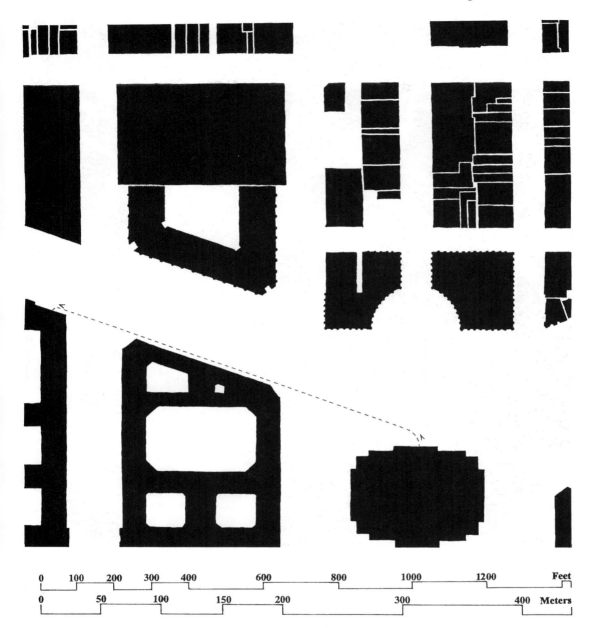

In Washington, D.C., a walk along Pennsylvania Avenue, from the National Archives to the Old Post Office, equals the distance of the walk in Venice but appears much shorter.
 Detail, map of Washington, D.C. (1 inch = 200 feet). Source: Allan Jacobs, 1989.

of bridges—to what they have already learned. But James warns that this observation is too crude. "To our successive feelings, a feeling of succession is added, that would be treated as an additional fact requiring its own special elucidation." A walk through Venice might be followed by a walk through Mestre, the nearest town on the mainland. Or, as here, a walk through Venice might be compared to

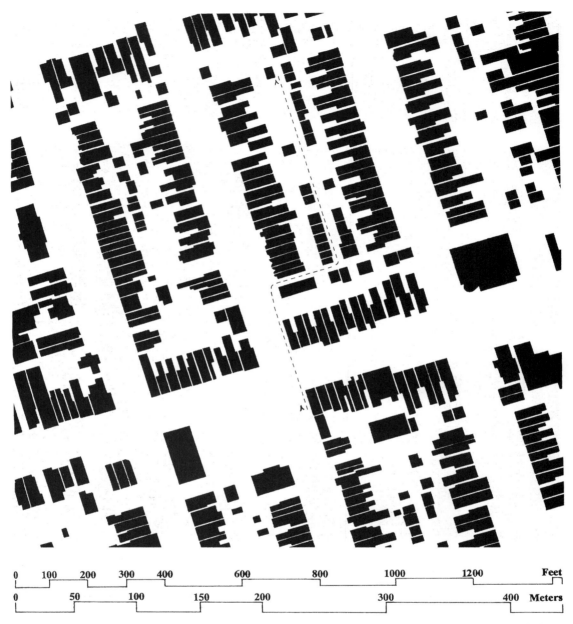

In an old neighborhood of Toronto, a walk equal in distance to the Venice walk takes a pedestrian along alleys from Ontario and Gerrard streets to the end of Milan Lane. Because there is much to see on this route along garages and yards in the rear of properties, this walk appears to take just as long as the Venice walk.
   Detail, map of Toronto (1 inch = 200 feet). Source: Department of Public Works, City of Toronto, 1990.

a walk in a place as far away as San Francisco, New York, or Kyoto—a comparison that requires large mental leaps in time and space. Even if these walks were known well, the sights they entail would have to be recalled; the images of Venice, in contrast, are still accessible to the reader in the pages of this book and can be looked at again. A consideration of rhythm in city design is valuable. The dimensions of

A walk through the old city of Kyoto, which was laid out 1,200 years ago, starts on Aya-no Koji Street, turns into one of the major old north-south streets called West Side of Tohin, passes the Aya Wishi Children's Playground, turns into Bukkō-ji Street, and almost reaches the entrance to the neighborhood shrine of the Suga Minister. This walk, a distance of two large cho's, appears a little longer than the walk in Venice.

Detail, map of Kyoto (1 inch = 200 feet). Source: Kyoto City Planning Department, 1985.

the physical objects and the setting of these objects in space influence the sense of time. Designers thus have remarkable power to affect the perception of time by arranging objects in space, by setting dimensions, designing textures, selecting color, and manipulating light.

0   100   200   300   400   600   800   1000   1200   **Feet**

0   50   100   150   200   300   400   **Meters**

To my great surprise, the walk in Venice equals a stroll through the Piazza Navona in Rome. Although I claim to know it well, I had underestimated its size, assuming that it took only half the time of the Venice walk; but, in fact, crossing the plaza takes four minutes.

Detail, map of the historic quarter, Rome (1 inch = 200 feet). Source: City of Rome, Map of the Centro Storico, 1985; redrawn by Allan Jacobs.

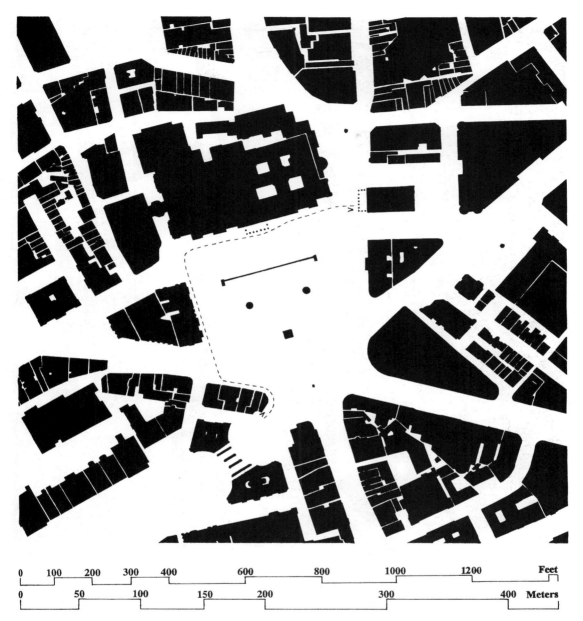

0	100	200	300	400	600	800	1000	1200	**Feet**
0	50	100	150	200		300		400	**Meters**

My surprise was even greater when the distance of the Venice walk was plotted out on a map of Trafalgar Square in London, from a point near the Arch of the Admiralty, past Canada House and the Venturi and Brown extension to the National Gallery, to St. Martin in the Fields. This stroll seems to cover a greater distance than the previous walks.

Detail, map of London (1 inch = 200 feet). Source: London Ordnance Survey.

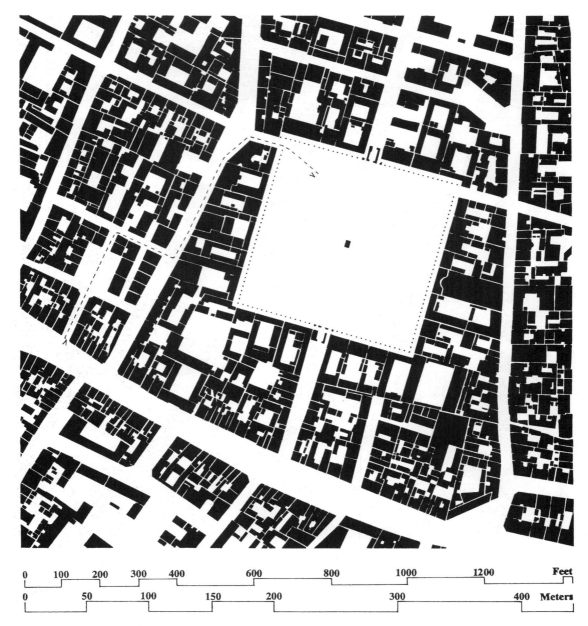

0   100   200   300   400   600   800   1000   1200   **Feet**

0   50   100   150   200   300   400   **Meters**

In Paris a walk starts at the beautiful symmetrically framed Place du Marché St. Catherine, off Rue Saint Antoine, turns right on Rue de Jarente, left on Rue Turenne, and right again to enter the Place des Vosges, where a statue of Louis XIII occupies the center of the square. The Paris walk appears to take longer than the walk in Venice.

Map of the Marais, Paris (1 inch = 200 feet). Source: Prefecture de Paris, Edition 1969.

0	100	200	300	400	600	800	1000	1200	**Feet**
0		50	100	150	200		300	400	**Meters**

A walk in Barcelona equal in distance to the Venice walk starts at the Plaza Reial and continues along the famous Ramblas, barely reaching the Sant Joseph Market, not quite halfway to the north end of the Ramblas, which is at the Plaza de Cataluña. The Ramblas is longer than I had remembered. I would have though that the equivalent of the Venice walk would have reached the Plaza de Cataluña.

Detail, map of Barcelona (1 inch = 200 feet). Source: Corporacio Metropolitana de Barcelona, 1983.

0   100   200   300   400   600   800   1000   1200   **Feet**

0   50   100   150   200   300   400   **Meters**

To match the distance of the walk in Venice, a home-owner in Orange County, California, might navigate a little more than halfway around the street that loops through the neighborhood, a walk much shorter than expected.

Map of a gated community in the City of Laguna Niguel, Orange County, California (1 inch = 200 feet). Source: Traced from a 1981 aerial photograph, Robert J. Lung and Associates.

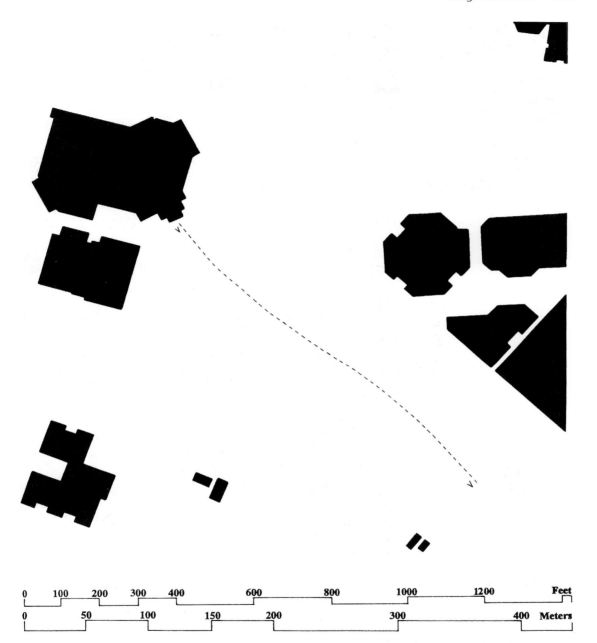

| 0 | 100 | 200 | 300 | 400 | | 600 | | 800 | | 1000 | | 1200 | | **Feet** |
| 0 | | 50 | | 100 | | 150 | | 200 | | | 300 | | | 400 | **Meters** |

A shopper at the Stanford Shopping Center in Palo Alto, California, might start at the Nordstrom department store and not get very far at all.

Map of the Stanford Shopping Center in Palo Alto, California (1 inch = 200 feet). Source: City of Palo Alto, Stanford Shopping Center, 1994.

Notes

1. George Rowley, *Principle of Chinese Painting* (Princeton, N.J.: Princeton University Press, 1947), 41.
2. Ibid., 61.
3. Christel Habbe, *Die Räumlichkeit der Topographie: Beiträge zum ländlichen Bau-und Siedlungswesen.* Bericht 33, Hannover University, 1991. See also Graf Karlfried von Dürckheim, "Untersuchungen zum gelebten Raum," in *Neue Psychologische Studien*, 6, ed. Felix Krüger (Munich: Beck'sche Verlagsbuchlandlung, 1930).
4. Quotations in this paragraph and the next are from William James, *Psychology: The Briefer Course*, ed. Gordon Allport (New York: Harper and Row, 1961), 147–153.

Source and copyright

This chapter was published in its original form as:

Bosselmann, P. (1998), 'Images in Motion' (Chapter Three), in Bosselmann, P. (1998), *Representations of Places: Reality and Realism in City Design*, University of California Press, Berkeley, 48–99

Reprinted with permission of The University of California Press.

30

The presence of the past

Kevin Lynch

[1972]

Throughout the world, but particularly in the economically advanced countries, fragments of an obsolete physical environment are lovingly preserved, or restored so that they may be preserved, as relics of time gone by. Such preservation is costly not only because it involves direct outlays of money and time but also because piecemeal retention causes endless difficulties for new development. In building a new library, for example, the Harvard Graduate School of Education recently paid $500,000 to move two rather small, old houses a few hundred feet.

Fierce political battles are fought over whether a building or set of buildings should be saved, since different groups place widely varying values on the remains. Because of the fixed and bulky nature of the objects and the strong personal attachments they arouse, their preservation is a far more strident affair than the preservation of movable objects, records, or customs. Nevertheless the resistance to the loss of historical environment is today becoming more determined as affluence increases and physical change itself is more rapid. And no wonder, since the past is known, familiar, a possession in which we may feel secure.

Preservation's past

Environmental preservation, at least as a widespread and coherent doctrine, is fairly new. Medieval masons razed an old building without a qualm, even though old, "historic" structures were then much rarer than now. In Tudor inventories, chattels called "old" were put at the foot of the list, implying they had little value. In Western Europe, at least, the idea of preservation first appeared about 1500, in the form of an

esoteric attraction to relict buildings, even to the point of the construction of sham ruins. By the eighteenth century an affection for the structures of the past was a widespread upper-class fashion, and by the nineteenth century it became part of the intellectual baggage of all middle-class travelers. In the same century, first in the United States and slightly later in Europe, organized movements sprang up to preserve historic landmarks for the public.

In the United States the first efforts were directed at saving particular buildings, especially the houses associated with patriotic figures.[1] Reinforcing national solidarity and pride was the chief reason for preservation. Specific motives ranged from attempts to prevent disunity before the Civil War and to reestablish it afterward, through the concern for "Americanizing" the immigrant, to the moves to magnify patriotic feelings during the twentieth-century wars. Relying on history to maintain coherence and common purpose in moments of stress and disunity is a familiar human tendency. The militant interest in black history is its most recent manifestation in America.

Later this patriotic emphasis merged with the enthusiasm for ruins of the romantic tradition, and architectural restoration became a basic principle of the movement. Connection with an established historic event and the quality of a building remain even today the chief criteria for preservation. The scientific motives of archaeology and the economic ones of tourist promotion appeared somewhat later. Perhaps most recently of all, in the United States at least, large segments of the population have come to feel that preservation is moral in itself and that environments rich in such features are more pleasant places in which to live. Patriotism and literary glamour have defined certain classic periods whose traces are most worth preserving: the late colonial and Revolutionary years in New England, the brief episode of pioneering in the forested interior, the antebellum days in the South, the period of exploration and cattle raising on the Great Plains (which passed so quickly), the mining era in the Western mountains, the years of the Spanish colonies in the Southwest, and, of course, the undefined background of the scattered and "timeless" Indian. Preservation has usually been the work of established middle- and upper-class citizens. The history enshrined in museums is chosen and interpreted by those who give the dollars.

Environments rich in historic remains often follow a particular pattern: once markedly prosperous, they then suffered a rapid economic decline and remained stagnant for long periods, though continuing to be occupied and at least partially maintained. Many now charming New England towns and farming areas were well-to-do in the early 1800s but in the later years of the century sank into the trough of the westward wave of national expansion. This stagnation must then be followed by a second period of wealth (whether belonging to the region itself or brought in by visitors) that can bear the costs of preservation.

The pattern can be seen not only in those small towns and rural regions that have decayed and then revived but also in the inner parts of large cities that have stagnated while the total urban region continued to prosper. Boston's Back Bay is one example of many. Natural decay is destructive of unoccupied old environment, but active development by subsequent generations is a far more rapid agent of disposal. And since if anything is preserved it tends to be the most expensive or most imposing or most symbolic of some classic period, the preserved environments tend to be very limited in extent. They represent the continuum of time in a spasmodic way and give a distorted view of the past since they are composed of the buildings of prosperous classes in prosperous times—times, furthermore, that quickly passed away. Such remains only reinforce that misguided view of history which sees it as consisting of sharp peaks of achievement separated by long, empty durations.

Preservation battle lines

There are several ways of dealing with a valued piece of an old environment.[2] What remains can simply be saved from destruction, perhaps by moving it away from danger. It can be restored by minor repairs and refurbishings. Or it can be rebuilt in as careful a copy of its "original" state as is currently known. This may

be done with original material, judiciously pieced out and refinished, or with covert new material, or even with obviously new material. Put another way, the patina of time may be retained, imitated, or removed. When there is a frank and complete reconstruction, using new material, on a new site, the aim may be an appearance of having just been built, an aim that may be carried out even to the details of equipment and perhaps the use of costumed actors. Such a reconstruction will often shock contemporary taste (Greek temples were gaudily painted in their day), and sometimes it will be made ridiculous by subsequent scholarship. But it can be a strong evocation of the past for a general audience.

The official priority rankings of historical societies usually range from the least to the most disturbance, that is, from preservation through restoration, reconstitution, and relocation to complete reconstruction. But this simple formula cloaks many subtleties and invites controversies. What, for example, happens to later historical additions to the original structure? Since historic structures are thought of as having been built all at one time and then potentially eternal, but have actually undergone a continuous process of physical change and human occupation, and since our view of history itself changes constantly, the controversies may be heated and scholastic. Robert Scott's Antarctic hut, unused since his fatal expedition sixty years ago, survives intact in the polar cold: papers, food, and equipment are just as they were. The effect is powerful—it corresponds to our wish to arrest the past—but we cannot easily reproduce the circumstances that created it.

Sometimes the historical object is reconstructed at regular intervals, preserving not the old materials but rather the ancient form. The 2000-year outline of the White Horse of Uffington is still visible on the downs because it is renewed by its annual "scouring." The temple at Ise, completely rebuilt with new material on a new site every twenty years, conserves the most primitive form of any building in Japan. Such periodic reconstructions, because they do not depend on a single effort, evade some of the issues posed here.

According to another doctrine, only the external historical shell need be preserved or reconstructed. It can then shelter current, active uses, and internal physical modifications suitable to those new uses are allowable. "Outsides" are public, historic, and regulated, while "insides" are private, fluid, and free. An aversion to an unused or "museum" environment is connected with this doctrine. Even then, there are difficult decisions to be made: the interior-exterior dichotomy is a convenient distinction to make, but what kinds of specific modifications are, in fact, allowable? In restoring the Nash terraces around Regent's Park in London for modern offices, the facades were rebuilt according to the original designs, but enough of the former internal arrangement was also imposed so that the view from the street would have the right sense of depth. How far can we go in subsidizing activities that are likely to survive in preserved surroundings? To what degree does contemporary utility, however discreetly provided, rupture the sense of historical integrity? The ceramic bathrooms of colonial Williamsburg come as a shock. And what is to be done where inside and outside are hard to separate, as in a large public building or in a landscape?

Strict preservation is the more pessimistic view. It considers any reconstruction as fraudulent and thinks of time as a process of regrettable but inevitable dissolution. We can protect only what still remains by a variety of means, principally passive but including removal to a protected place (then the loss of the museum itself can erase the concentrated harvest of generations!). The object to be preserved can be presented for better public view, but the process of decay is only slowed down—not stopped.

One may also take a purely intellectual view, aiming to learn as much and as accurately about the past as possible and only secondarily to preserve, use, or exhibit it. One is then justified in destroying remains by dissection or excavation or in reburying them then after inspection so that they are kept intact for later generations of scientists, even though they may not then be seen or used by the general public.

As vexing as the doctrine of preservation is the definition of its purpose. What pieces of the environment should we attempt to reconstruct or preserve, and what are the warrants for historical treatment? Are we looking for evidence of the climactic moments or for any manifestation of tradition we can find, or are we judging and evaluating the past, choosing the more significant over the less, retaining what we think of as best? Should things be saved because they were associated with important persons or events? Because they are unique or nearly so or, quite the contrary, because they were most typical of their time? Because of their importance as a group symbol? Because of their intrinsic qualities in the present? Because of their special usefulness as sources of intellectual information about the past? Or should we simply (as we most often do) let chance select for us and preserve for a second century everything that has happened to survive the first?

Such issues spring from confusions about how the past is perceived and what the nature of the endless process of environmental change is, as well as from disagreements about the purpose of preservation. Memory cannot retain everything; if it could, we would be overwhelmed with data. Memory is the result of a process of selection and of organizing what is selected so that it is within reach in expectable situations. There must also be some random accumulations to enable us to discover unexpected relationships. But serendipity is possible only when recollection is essentially a holding fast to what is meaningful and a release of what is not.

Every thing, every event, every person is "historic." To attempt to preserve all of the past would be life-denying. We dispose of physical evidences of the past for the same reason that we forget. To someone interested in action or understanding in the present, the past is irrelevant if a description of the present furnishes him with a better or more concise analysis on which he can base his action. Past events are indeed often relevant to present possibilities. They may explain causes or point to likely outcomes. Or they may give us a sense of proportion to help us bear our present difficulties. But these causes and probabilities must be created and disentangled from the heap of history. Indeed, there may be old wrongs and hatreds that are quite relevant to actions today, but from which the present must be severed.

"Man," Nietzsche said, "must have the strength to break up the past."[3] "History is a nightmare from which I am trying to awake," cried Stephen Dedalus in *Ulysses*.[4] New environments are often sought as escapes from servitude to the past, even if the freedom found thereby is sometimes less complete than it promised to be, and even if many valuable memories are lost in the severing. We prefer to select and create our past and to make it part of the living present.

The degree of restriction

Designers are aware that it is easier to plan when there are some commitments than it is when the situation is completely open. The building in the hills, the house in a dense city, and the interior in an old building are easier to create, and often more interesting and apt in their solution, than are their counterparts on flat plains, in open land, and in a new structure. The fixed characteristics restrict the range of possible solutions and therefore ease the agony of the design search. In addition, the accidental background permits solutions that are rich in form and full of contrast. Clearly, this is true only where the fixed elements are somehow valuable and do not completely inhibit desirable alteration. It is interesting to redesign the interior of an old warehouse for apartments, but not if the massive walls have no windows, or the ceiling heights are extremely low, or the rooms are perpetually damp. Nonphysical restraints may have similar effects. The unique institutions, values, or behavior of a group of users can be used as a principal source of strong character in a solution.

In an analogous way, older communities that have grown slowly have certain advantages for the inhabitant over new settlements. The older towns tend to be richer and more complex, with choices, services, and attachments better fitted to the plurality of needs and values of a diverse population. People will resist forcible removal from these older settlements, and signs of social stress often appear in the early days of the new towns to which they have moved. New housing can often be inserted more happily into existing communities than it can be erected on open ground since the former action can be taken without destroying the social fabric or losing access to the web of facilities.

Designers themselves are often found living in old houses in old districts, unless they have chosen to inflict their own personal designs on themselves. When they occupy old houses, however, they do not simply preserve them; they modify them by suppression and addition to enliven the surviving elements. Longevity and evanescence gain savor in each other's presence: "In a gourd that had been handed down for three centuries, a flower that would fade in a morning."[5] The old environment is seen as an opportunity for dramatic enhancement and becomes richer than it was. This is not preservation, or even simple addition, but a particular use of old and new.

It is the familiar connections, not all the old physical things themselves, that people want to retain, except where those things have a *personal* connection: their own furniture, the family mementos. One of the problems of the large new suburban communities is how to maintain some continuity of image and association despite the physical and social upheaval to which their inhabitants have been exposed. Since images and associations must be useful for both original and new inhabitants, the histories of the immigrants should be interwoven with the history of the new setting. When American families move to a new city, many go out of their way to find houses that in some manner remind them of their childhood homes, even as the Swedish immigrants to the United States looked for "Swedish" landscapes to settle in, and British colonists built British towns. (And thus a native of Calcutta, far from home but new to London, is struck by the nostalgic familiarity of the London scene. He sees the artifacts of home—the mailboxes, railings, details—that the British planners had in their time transplanted to ease their own nostalgia.)[6]

There seems to be some optimum degree of previous development in a changing environment, a degree most satisfactory owing to the low-cost and already depreciated resources that the environment provides, or to the rich variety of facilities and services catering to many preferences that it offers, or to the feeling of being at home that it fosters, or paradoxically, to the way in which it limits and simplifies choice. Yet while too little restraint confuses and impoverishes, too much is costly and frustrating. An environment that cannot be changed invites its own destruction. We prefer a world that can be modified progressively, against a background of valued remains, a world in which one can leave a personal mark alongside the marks of history.

Roots in time

Like law and custom, environment tells us how to act without requiring of us a conscious choice. In a church we are reverent and on a beach relaxed. Much of the time, we are reenacting patterns of behavior associated with particular recognizable settings. A setting may encourage a behavior by its form—a staircase has a shape that is made for going up or down—but also by the expectations associated with it—until recently it was not seemly for adults to sit on stairs. When place changes rapidly, as in a migratory move, people no longer "know how to behave." They must expend effort to test and choose a new form of behavior and to build group agreement. Thus, when change is wanted, a new setting supports the discontinuity. For social continuity it is useful to reenact behavior together in a setting of the past. Claude Lévi-Strauss tells how missionaries were able to disorient the culture of the Bororos by forcing them to abandon the traditional circular layout of their settlements.

Many symbolic and historic locations in a city are rarely visited by its inhabitants, however they may be sought out by tourists. But a threat to destroy these places will evoke a strong reaction, even from those who have never seen, and perhaps never will see, them. The survival of these unvisited, hearsay settings conveys a sense of security and continuity. A portion of the past has been saved as being good, and this promises that the future will so save the present. We have the sense that we and our works will also reach uninterrupted old age. After a catastrophe, the restoration of the symbolic center of community life is a matter of urgency: St. Paul's in burned London, or the "old city" in devastated Warsaw. Symbolic environment is used to create a sense of stability: threatened institutions celebrate their antiquity; kings proclaim their legitimate roots as well as their power. The English gypsies are avid collectors of china and family photographs.

There are striking differences in mood between groups with a valued past, in which they feel rooted, and groups that are living in an isolated present.

Might it also be possible to use environment to teach change instead of permanence—how the world constantly shifts in the context of the immediate past; which changes have been valuable, which not; how change can be externally effected; how change ought to occur in the future? Past flux might be communicated by marking out the successive locations of activities or populations or by representing the changing aspect of a single place. The lesson could be disturbing.

Saving the past can be a way of learning for the future, just as people change themselves by learning something now that they may employ later. If advanced education and upward mobility are to be important characteristics of the coming generations, then we might preserve for them a record of the changing educational environment and evidence of the social gaps that had been jumped before. If common ownership of property or an increased sense of public responsibility were desired for the future, then we might save the evidence of past commons. In other situations, we might preserve the corpus of herbal medicine or of technologies suited to more primitive resources or of ways of survival in a hostile environment. Just as we save plant varieties as the raw material of genetic innovation and to avert the disaster of a universal crop failure, so we may wish to save the skills and cultural solutions of the past in order to meet the demands of an uncertain future.

Ruins

There is a poignancy in evanescence, in something old about to disappear. Old toys, made for brief use, seemingly so fragile, associated with a passing and vulnerable phase of life, are much more emotive symbols than are permanent, serious memorials. In Japan there is an esthetic preference for that which decays and passes. Albert Speer, Hitler's architect, projected himself so far forward into the future as to design his grandiose structures with the hope that they would make noble ruins.

Ruined structures, in the process of going back to the earth, are enjoyed everywhere for the emotional sensations they convey.[7] This pleasurable melancholy may be coupled with the observer's satisfaction at having survived or be tinged with righteous triumph, esthetic delight, or intellectual enjoyment. One may loot the ruin or live in it or put one's name on it. Accumulated literary associations add depth to the experience; place names become pegs for layers of commentaries, as in the Chinese culture. But at base the emotional pleasure is a heightened sense of the flow of time.

Clever restoration obscures the essential quality of impermanent remains. A pleasantly ruinous environment demands some inefficiency, a relaxed acceptance of time, the esthetic ability to take dramatic advantage of destruction. A landscape acquires emotional depth as it accumulates these scars. Certain materials and forms age well. They develop an interesting patina, a rich texture, an attractive outline. Others are at their best only when clean and new; as they grow old, they turn spotted and imperfect.

Communicating the past

Historical knowledge must be communicated to the public for its enjoyment and education. Words and pictures convey much, but real things make the deepest impression. It is a sign of the verbal dominance of our civilization that we call any period without written documents "prehistoric." To be surrounded by the buildings and equipment of the past, or best of all to act as if we were in the past, is an excellent way to learn about it. The creation of skillful illusion requires one to move and concentrate structures and equipment or to counterfeit them. This ambience can then be peopled with live actors.

There are more than 125 museum villages and extensive city walking tours in the United States today, in forty-two of the fifty states. They re-create some particular period with the buildings and equipment of the time, often with simulated inhabitants who dress and act—even think—their parts. These reconstructions are tremendously popular. But they suffer some necessary limitations beyond cost, or information, or the availability of old artifacts, or accuracy in the light of changing scholarship. There can be problems of comfort (heavy wool clothes in the summer, for example, or the stink of indigo curing), or of social sanction (low-cut dresses, or the growing of hemp), or health and safety (dangerous tools and unsanitary conditions), or of isolation from what had been a total social and geographic system, or of the unwillingness or inability of present-day actors to take historic roles. There are modern myths to avoid, or temptations to sugarcoat the past, to forget the caste rigidity and social isolation of a military post, for example. How can children be induced to play the way they used to? Who wants to demonstrate a shameful or unwanted past, particularly if the show is for some presumably "superior" group of spectators? The villagers of delightfully retarded Stensjö, put on the national payroll when it became a Swedish historic area, soon wanted to enjoy modern facilities, and, when rebuffed, they simply moved away. Reconstructed environments exist today and not in the past time they mimic, and they are filled with modern tourists.

Passive demonstrations are the rule: the visitors gape and move on. Such enterprises would be even more effective if the observers were instructed to become the actors. The ordinary equipment of the time should be available for use. However clumsily, visitors might smooth with an adz, wear old clothes, cook and eat according to old recipes, dance the quadrille, plow with oxen, or warp a yardarm around. In that way they might begin to penetrate into some sense of the life of an earlier time. Were the visitors given the opportunity to live for a week as the people of that time lived and to suffer, at least temporarily, some of the real pleasures and penalties of adequate performance, the penetration would be deeper. A small group of high school students recently spent five days in a one-room cottage in the reconstructed Plimoth Plantation in Massachusetts.[8] They wore heavy Pilgrim clothes, ate the coarse Pilgrim food, cooked it over an open fire, hauled wood and water, scoured pots with sand, read and sewed by firelight. It was a difficult but instructive week. Even then, they knew they were not threatened by starvation, disease, or Indian attack.

The settings should illustrate not simply the "great" moments of the period but the full spectrum of its culture. Re-created pasts ought to be based on the knowledge and values of the present. We want them to change as present knowledge and values change, just as history is rewritten. One danger in the preservation of environment lies in its very power to encapsulate some image of the past, an image that may in time prove to be mythical or irrelevant. For preservation is not simply the saving of old things but the maintaining of a response to those things. This response can be transmitted, lost, or modified. It may survive beyond the real thing itself. We should expect to see conflicting views of the past, based on the conflicting values of the present. Diverse environmental museums might present divergent interpretations

of the Civil War, for example, or the Yankee and Irish views of what it was like in Boston in the 1850s. They would look at the conquest of the West through Indian eyes as well as those of the white pioneer. If so, it should be possible for a student to go from one presentation to the other, in the same way that he can compare different verbal interpretations. Environmental preservation has always had political as well as esthetic and educational motives. Groups in power save prominent symbols of their prestige, while others must be more discreet. But plural meanings could be made explicit in reconstruction.

The city itself can be a historical teaching device, an aim now served by the occasional guided tour or plaque. That "William Blake lived here" is trivial, unless the visible structure influenced what Blake did, or expressed his personality, or unless its location had some bearing on his personal history. The city can be enormously informative, since the pattern of remains is a vast if jumbled historical index. Signs, tours, guides, and other communications devices can bring out the latent history of a complex site, with little of the interference with present function that may be caused by massive physical reconstructions. The kingly bypass of a rebellious City of London by the water route from Westminster to the Tower can be demonstrated, or the successive flights of middle-class residents before the oncoming workingmen. Illustrated walks can be laid out, and crucial remains made visible—incorporated in other structures or underground or even underwater. The past can be shown in immediate relevance to the present: old-fashioned clothes in a clothing store, former work methods in a factory, previous illustrations of a site on the site itself. Indeed, the resources going into communication should be as large as, or larger than, those devoted to preservation.

The image of the physical environment has been used for centuries as a mental peg on which to hang material to be remembered, from the memory system of Simonides of Ceos in 500 B.C. to the imaginary walks of S. V. Shereshevskii in this century.[9] In the sixteenth century, Camillo actually built a memory theater in Venice, a wooden structure whose seats, gangways, and images had the sole purpose of symbolizing man's knowledge of the universe. Martin Pawley has recently suggested a "time house"—a family dwelling unit that automatically records and on request replays the sights and sounds of the life of the house. The thought that family life would be continuously watched and recorded is a little chilling, but it is quite reasonable to think that the real remains of a city, in conjunction with print, film, and recording, might consciously be used to retain and teach what we think to be instructive for the future. Could mute statues, for example, be associated with explanatory recordings or photographs that were available on request? Tommaso Campanella proposed that the walls of his utopia would illustrate the knowledge of history and the natural world. In a similar way the cathedrals vividly presented the Christian dogmas to the faithful.

Even now, environment interacts with other memory systems—with books and tales and film. Thus for an American in London for the first time but brought up on English children's stories, the names of streets and places are unsettlingly familiar. In the opposite case, a man-made environment may become completely detached from its previous meanings. For the medieval village that reoccupied it, the abandoned Diocletian palace at Spalato (the modern Split) must have simply been a natural landscape to be overcome. And furthermore quite false meanings may be attached to a place. So tourists enjoy the absurd but colorful tales that their guides fasten to the passing scene. The children of Manhattan, Kansas, now tell their own stories about the statue of Johnny Kaw, a "folk hero" hurriedly invented by the city fathers for a centennial celebration and as quickly forgotten by the elders. False history, which leads blacks to wear dashikis or former forest Indians to live in tipis—is also a means of mobilizing people to meet problems of today.

Present value

Thus there is something to say about archives, about the creation of special teaching areas, and about the uses of communication to teach environmental history. What can be said about preservation in extensive inhabited regions? Here the aim should be the conservation of present value as well as the maintenance of a sense of near continuity. Things are useful to us for their actual current qualities and not for some mystic essence of time gone by. We should save old houses if we cannot replace the equivalent space at a lower cost (recognizing that a possible increased consumption of natural resources in new building as compared with rehabilitation is a real, though often hidden, cost) or if we simply cannot reproduce valuable features of form or equipment. Often enough, old environment is worth conserving because it is completely amortized, or was built by cheap skilled labor or with materials now unobtainable, or was constructed to high standards for the affluent but was abandoned by them. Moreover, it may be a specially valuable artistic creation difficult to imitate

or may be part of a whole network of facilities and social connections that we cannot easily reconstruct. Taking rational account of existing values should not be clouded by dogma about the intrinsic goodness of old things. The most famous artists of the day protested vehemently against the erection of the Eiffel Tower. Cultures that produced fine environment were confident of their ability to create afresh, and we may notice in this connection the disdain for preservation, even of their own works, that is found among many creative artists.

If old environments are superior to new ones (sometimes they are, sometimes not), then we must study them to see what these superior qualities are, so that we can achieve them in a new way. Old buildings, even quite unremarkable ones, often have certain advantages over new structures, along with their typical disadvantages of poor utilities, an unsafe framework, a cramped floor plan, or expensive maintenance. They are likely to have a richer form, with the impress of many occupants, a well-adjusted fit between activity and form, a luxurious "wastefulness" of odd pieces of space, a more intimate scale, mellowed surfaces, and detail. Many of these qualities are reproducible in new construction, although at a cost of money and design attention. In regulating the replacement of older areas, the focus should be on identifying the present values in existing buildings and on insisting that new development equal or better those qualities before it is permitted to occur.

Present value will be particular to a certain group of people. Such a group is the necessary political base for restoration work. Areas that do not have a resident constituency—a partly abandoned nineteenth-century commercial district, for example—will be the most difficult to save. Then it is necessary to organize a nonresident base that is touristic or region-wide. Or the planner must be able to teach others to see the present values of an area, or, even harder, to persuade them that in another generation they will be valued.

When present value is not obvious, a careful analysis may be required to disentangle the valued qualities. For example, what and for whom are the present values of an existing slum environment, whose arrangements may support, but also enforce, a certain way of life? In Bath, as a contrasting example, a landscape analysis would reveal those qualities of space, scale, and facade texture that, if also achieved in new structures, would allow the replacement of many areas of the town which serve as a visual background for the more noteworthy structures and would do so without imitation and without loss. Historical areas are not so much irreplaceable as rarely replaced.

Fragmentary reminders

Where old structures cannot support present functions without impairing those functions, and unless they are of exceptional didactic or esthetic value, they can be cleared away, although their fragments may be used to enhance new buildings. We need not be so concerned about perfect conformity to past form but ought rather to seek to use remains to enhance the complexity and significance of the present scene. The contrast of old and new, the accumulated concentration of the most significant elements of the various periods gone by, even if they are only fragmentary reminders of them, will in time produce a landscape whose depth no one period can equal, although such time-deep areas may be achieved only in some parts of the city. The esthetic aim is to heighten contrast and complexity, to make visible the process of change. The achievement of the aim requires creative and skillful demolition, just as much as skillful new design.

We look for a setting that, rather than simply being a facsimile of the past, seems to open outward in time. To quote Vladimir Nabokov,[10] in his description of his years in Cambridge, England:

> Nothing one looked at was shut off in terms of time, everything was a natural opening into it, so that one's mind grew accustomed to work in a particularly pure and ample environment, and because, in terms of space, the narrow lane, the cloistered lawn, the dark archway hampered one physically, that yielding diaphanous texture of time was, by contrast, especially welcome to the mind, just as a sea view from a window exhilarates one hugely, even though one does not care for sailing.

Our new suburbs and new towns, on the other hand, seem all begun yesterday and completely finished then. There is no crevice through which one can venture back or forward.

We could enjoy these qualities even in the most ordinary areas, where there may be little of real distinction to be saved. Everywhere, even in regions to be swept clean for rebuilding, we can retain some environmental memories that go back at least to the first reminiscences of the living generation, say for sixty years. But since the generations overlap endlessly, and since current needs may require more or less demolition in any small region, it will be impossible to preserve a whole context. We then resort to saving symbols and fragments of a demolished environment, embedded in the new context for another generation.

Saved elements could be of many kinds, though they should not be random or trivial. Haphazard exhibits will create a sense of the past as chaos. Where possible, it is best to save something indicative of the old ambience: its scale, its spaces or pathways, its plantings. Where this is not possible, it is desirable to seek to keep things of high symbolic meaning or things that were directly connected with the actions of remembered people: crosses, seats, steps. But what is saved must be based on what users wish to remember or can connect with themselves. The implication is that the planner will seek to learn what inhabitants remember and wish to remember. Furthermore, since new urban development is almost always somehow constrained by previous patterns, we ought to make clear this influence of the past, marking the history of an environment on itself. Such patterns can be woven into a new design with little of the difficulty ordinarily associated with area-wide preservation. They could be part of our habitual concern for the character of a site.

Personal connection

If we examine the feelings that accompany daily life, we find that historic monuments occupy a small place. Our strongest emotions concern our own lives and the lives of our family or friends because we have known them personally. The crucial reminders of the past are therefore those connected with our own childhood, or with our parents' or perhaps our grandparents' lives. Remarkable things are directly associated with memorable events in those lives: births, deaths, marriages, partings, graduations. To live in the same surroundings that one recalls from earliest memories is a satisfaction denied to most Americans today. The continuity of kin lacks a corresponding continuity of place. We are interested in a street on which our father may have lived as a boy; it helps to explain him to us and strengthens our own sense of identity. But our grandfather or great-grandfather, whom we never knew, is already in the remote past; his house is "historical."

Most historical preservation, focused as it is on the classic past, moves people only momentarily, at a point remote from their vital concerns. It is impersonal as well as ancient. Near continuity is emotionally more important than remote time, although the distant past may seem nobler, more mysterious or intriguing to us. There is a spatial simile: feeling locally connected where we customarily range is more important than our position at a national scale, although occasional realization of the latter can impart a brief thrill. In this sense, we should seek to preserve the near and middle past, the past with which we have real ties. The family photograph or the heap of flowers in Dallas is a strong thing.

A humane environment commemorates recent events quickly and allows people to mark out their own growth. It is more human not only for the inhabitant but for the observer as well. He will sense its warmth and find in it a symbolic way of meeting its inhabitants. But there must also be some means of removing these marks as they recede in time or lose connections with present persons. This is forgetting again. There is a pleasure in seeing receding, half-veiled space or in detecting the various layers of successive occupation as they fade into the past—and then in finding a few fragments whose origins are remote and inscrutable, whose meanings lurk beneath their shapes, like dim fish in deep water. We do not wish to preserve our childhood intact, with all its personalities, circumstances, and emotions. We want to simplify and to pattern it, to make vivid its important moments, to skip over its empty stretches, sense its mysterious beginnings, soften its painful feelings— that is, to change it into a dramatic recital.

Personal connection is most effectively made by personal imprints on the environment. New customs might connect environment symbolically to personal experience. The stages of physical growth can be imprinted on our surroundings by height marks, foot or hand prints. Portraits and photographs may be mounted to give a place a visible genealogy. We are accustomed to marking death with a stone; can we also so signify birth? We could plant a tree in a community grove, a tree that gradually merges into the forest. Memorials may refer to a family or an individual or an age group: a gang or a school grade. Stones and trees may be carried with us when we move, to make a personal link to a new landscape, just as we bring familiar furniture with us to personalize our new interiors. Old inhabitants should be encouraged to record their memories of a place. The recording could then be made available nearby, in a branch library or a street information center. As in some primitive societies, burial might at first be in some nearby and conspicuous location, later removed to a marked place in a community site and, much later, when living kin are gone, to a common unmarked grave. Our distant and crowded cemeteries are devices for sealing away the dead from the living under the fiction of eternal remembrance.

There can be temporary memorials for recent events, to be replaced later by permanent markings,

if the event remains memorable. Our cities are mute about the persons for whom we care but littered with statues to generals and statesmen now in limbo.

Though the landscape should have the imprint of human events and seem connected with living persons, the imprints and connections must eventually fade away and be forgotten, just as human memories and generations fade.

Thus I propose a plural attitude toward environmental remains, depending on the particular motive. Where it is scientific study, there would be dissection, recording, and scholarly storage; where it is education, I propose unabashed playacting and communication; where it is the enhancement of present value and a sense of the flow of time, I should encourage temporal collage, creative demolition and addition; where it is personal connection, I suggest making and retaining imprints as selective and impermanent as memory itself. To preserve effectively, we must know for what the past is being retained and for whom. The management of change and the active use of remains for present and future purpose are preferable to an inflexible reverence for a sacrosanct past. The past must be chosen and changed, made in the present. Choosing a past helps us to construct a future.

Notes

1. Hosmer, Charles B., Jr. *The Presence of the Past: A History of the Preservation Movement in the United States before Williamsburg.* New York: Putnam, 1965.
2. Brandi, Cesare. *Teoria del Restauro.* Rome: Ediz. di storia e letteratura, 1963.
3. Nietzsche, Friedrich. *The Use and Abuse of History,* trans. Adrian Collins. New York: Liberal Arts Press, 1957 (orig. ed. 1873).
4. Joyce, James. *Ulysses.* New York: Vintage, 1961.
5. Kawabata, Yasunari. *A Thousand Cranes,* trans. Edward G. Seidensticker. New York: Knopf, 1959.
6. Banerjee, Tridib. Personal correspondence.
7. Macaulay, Rose. *The Pleasure of Ruins.* New York: Walker, 1953.
8. Rosenbloom, Joseph. "Student Pilgrims Work at Survival in Plimoth." *Boston Globe,* January 27, 1972.
9. Yates, Frances P. "Architecture and the Art of Memory." *Architectural Design 38* (December 1968), 573–578.
10. Nabokov, Vladimir. *Speak, Memory.* Baltimore: Penguin, 1969.

Source and copyright

This chapter was published in its original form as:

Lynch, K. (1972), "The Presence of the Past", *What Time is This Place?*, MIT Press, Cambridge Mass, 29–64.

Reprinted with kind permission of The MIT Press.

31

Shearing layers

Stewart Brand
[1994]

The leading theorist—practically the only theorist—of change rate in buildings is Frank Duffy, cofounder of a British design firm called DEGW (he's the "D"), and president of the Royal Institute of British Architects for 1993 to 1995. "Our basic argument is that there isn't such a thing as a building," says Duffy. "A building properly conceived is several layers of longevity of built components." He distinguishes four layers, which he calls Shell, Services, Scenery, and Set. Shell is the structure, which lasts the lifetime of the building (fifty years in Britain, closer to thirty-five in North America). Services are the cabling, plumbing, air conditioning, and elevators ("lifts"), which have to be replaced every fifteen years or so. Scenery is the layout

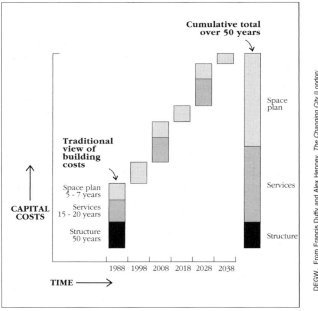

DEGW. From Francis Duffy and Alex Henney, *The Changing City* (London: Bullstrode, 1989), p. 61.

Over fifty years, the changes within a building cost three times more than the original building. Frank Duffy explains this diagram: "Add up what happens when capital is invested over a fifty-year period: the Structure expenditure is overwhelmed by the cumulative financial consequences of three generations of Services and ten generations of Space plan changes. That's the map of money in the life of a building. It proves that architecture is actually of very little significance—it's nugatory."[1] (I have translated Duffy's terms into my terms.)

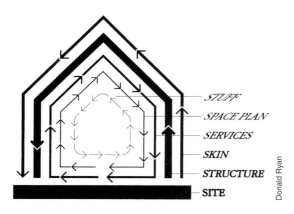

STUFF

SPACE PLAN

SERVICES

SKIN

STRUCTURE

SITE

Donald Ryan

Shearing layers of change. Because of the different rates of change of its components, a building is always tearing itself apart.

of partitions, dropped ceilings, etc., which changes every five to seven years. Set is the shifting of furniture by the occupants, often a matter of months or weeks.

Like the advertisers of *Architectural Digest*, Duffy and his architectural partners steered their firm toward the action and the money. DEGW helps rethink and reshape work environments for corporate offices, these days with a global clientele. "We try to have long-term relationships with clients," Duffy says. "The unit of analysis for us isn't the building, it's the use of the building through time. Time is the essence of the real design problem."

I've taken the liberty of expanding Duffy's "four S's"—which are oriented toward interior work in commercial buildings—into a slightly revised, general-purpose "six S's":

- SITE – This is the geographical setting, the urban location, and the legally defined lot, whose boundaries and context outlast generations of ephemeral buildings. "Site is eternal," Duffy agrees.
- STRUCTURE – The foundation and load-bearing elements are perilous and expensive to change, so people don't. These *are* the building. Structural life ranges from 30 to 300 years (but few buildings make it past 60, for other reasons).
- SKIN – Exterior surfaces now change every 20 years or so, to keep up with fashion or technology, or for wholesale repair. Recent focus on energy costs has led to reengineered Skins that are airtight and better-insulated.
- SERVICES – These are the working guts of a building: communications wiring, electrical wiring,

plumbing, sprinkler system, HVAC (heating, ventilating, and air conditioning), and moving parts like elevators and escalators. They wear out or obsolesce every 7 to 15 years. Many buildings are demolished early if their outdated systems are too deeply embedded to replace easily.

- SPACE PLAN – The interior layout—where walls, ceilings, floors, and doors go. Turbulent commercial space can change every 3 years or so; exceptionally quiet homes might wait 30 years.
- STUFF – Chairs, desks, phones, pictures; kitchen appliances, lamps, hair brushes; all the things that twitch around daily to monthly. Furniture is called *mobilia* in Italian for good reason.

Duffy's time-layered perspective is fundamental to understanding how buildings actually behave. The 6-S sequence is precisely followed in both design and construction. As the architect proceeds from drawing to drawing—layer after layer of tracing paper—"What stays fixed in the drawings will stay fixed in the building over time," says architect Peter Calthorpe. "The column grid will be in the bottom layer." Likewise the construction sequence is strictly in order: Site preparation, then foundation and framing the Structure, followed by Skin to keep out the weather, installation of Services, and finally Space plan. Then the tenants truck in their Stuff.

Frank Duffy: "Thinking about buildings in this time-laden way is very practical. As a designer you avoid such classic mistakes as solving a five-minute problem with a fifty-year solution, or vice versa. It legitimizes the existence of different design skills—architects, service engineers, space planners, interior designers—all with their different agendas defined by this time scale. It means you invent building forms which are very adaptive."

The layering also defines how a building relates to people. Organizational levels of responsibility match the pace levels. The building interacts with individuals at the level of Stuff; with the tenant organization (or family) at the Space plan level; with the landlord via the Services (and slower levels) which must be maintained; with the public via the Skin and entry; and with the whole community through city or county decisions about the footprint and volume of the Structure and restrictions on the Site. The community does not tell you where to put your desk or your bed; you do not tell the community where the building will go on the Site (unless you're way out in the country).

Buildings rule us via their time layering at least as much as we rule them, and in a surprising way. This idea comes from Robert V. O'Neill's *A Hierarchical Concept of Ecosystems.* O'Neill and his co-authors noted that ecosystems could be better understood by observing the rates of change of different components. Hummingbirds and flowers are quick, redwood trees slow, and whole redwood forests even slower. Most interaction is within the same pace level—hummingbirds and flowers pay attention to each other, oblivious to redwoods, who are oblivious to them. Meanwhile the forest is attentive to climate change but not to the hasty fate of individual trees. The insight is this: "*The dynamics of the system will be dominated by the slow components, with the rapid components simply following along.*"[2] Slow constrains quick; slow controls quick.

The same goes with buildings: the lethargic slow parts are in charge, not the dazzling rapid ones. Site dominates the Structure, which dominates the Skin, which dominates the Services, which dominate the Space plan, which dominates the Stuff. How a room is heated depends on how it relates to the heating and cooling Services, which depend on the energy efficiency of the Skin, which depends on the constraints of the Structure. You could add a seventh "S"—human Souls at the very end of the hierarchy, servants to our Stuff.

Still, influence does percolate the other direction. The slower processes of a building gradually integrate trends of rapid change within them. The speedy components propose, and the slow dispose. If an office keeps replacing its electronic Stuff often enough, finally management will insist that the Space plan acquire a raised floor to make the constant re-cabling easier, and that's when the air conditioning and electrical Services will be revamped to handle the higher load. Ecologist Buzz Holling points out that it is at the times of major changes in a system that the quick processes can most influence the slow.

The quick processes provide originality and challenge, the slow provide continuity and constraint. Buildings steady us, which we can probably use. But if we let our buildings come to a full stop, they stop us. It happened in command economies such as Eastern Europe's in the period 1945–1990. Since all buildings were state-owned, they were never maintained or altered by the tenants, who had no stake in them, and culture and the economy were paralyzed for decades.

Slow is healthy. Much of the wholesome evolution of cities can be explained by the steadfast persistence of Site. Property lines and thoroughfares in cities are inviolate even when hills are leveled and waterfronts filled in. After the Great Fire of London

in 1666, the city was rebuilt of brick, with widened streets but upon the old ground plan, and with meticulously preserved property lines. A wise move, says urban scholar Kevin Lynch: "Rebuilding was rapid and vigorous because each man could start again on his own familiar land."[3] Exactly the same thing happened two-and-a-half centuries later in San Francisco, after its earthquake and fire of 1906.

Different Site arrangements lead to different city evolutions. Downtown New York City, with its very narrow long blocks, is uniquely dense and uniquely flexible. Quick-built San Francisco is kept adaptable, congenial, and conservative over the decades by its modest lot sizes, according to urban designer Anne Vernez Moudon:

> Small lots will support resilience because they allow many people to attend directly to their needs by designing, building, and maintaining their own environment. By ensuring that property remains in many hands, small lots bring important results: many people make many different decisions, thereby ensuring variety in the resulting environment. And many property owners slow down the rate of change by making large-scale real estate transactions difficult.[4]

After Site comes Structure, at the base of which is the all-determining foundation. If it is out-of-square or out-of-level, it will plague the builders clear to the roof line and bother remodelers for the life of the building. If it is weak, it permanently limits the height of the building. If it lets in water or offers inadequate headroom for the basement, remedy is nearly impossible.

The mutability of Skin seems to be accelerating. Demographer Joel Garreau[5] says that in "edge cities" (new office and commercial developments on the periphery of older cities) developers are accustomed to fine-tune their buildings by changing rugs and facades—a typical "facadectomy" might go upscale from pretentious marble veneer to dignified granite veneer to attract a richer tenant. Developers expect their building Skins to "ugly out" every fifteen years or so, and plan accordingly.

The longevity of buildings is often determined by how well they can absorb new Services technology. Otis Elevator contractors don't bother to make money on their first installation. They know you'll be back soon enough for improved elevators; their profits are in the inevitable renovations. Energy Services such as electricity and gas are driven constantly toward greater efficiency by their sheer expense—30 percent of operating costs, equal over a building's life to the entire original cost of construction. Between the Energy Crisis of 1973 and 1990, the money spent on space heating in new American buildings dropped by a dramatic 50 percent.[6]

Even the home is no refuge from turnover in Services. Houses were revolutionized by the arrival of public water service around 1900, then by public electricity in the 1920s and 1930s, later by cable television in the 1970s. The two most renovated rooms in all houses are the kitchen and bathroom. Building historian Orlando Ridout says that in Maryland, you can find more whole houses from the 1700s than pre-1920 toilets. Whether it's the arrival of colored enamel in the 1920s, the advent of Jacuzzi baths in the 1970s, or guilt about water-wasting toilets in the 1980s, people keep making changes and expanding the significance of the bathroom in their homes. Likewise the kitchen, which has migrated from a back corner to the middle of home life, while stoves, refrigerators, and sinks are replaced as frequently as automobiles. Service-connected Stuff will not hold still.

The Space plan and Stuff are what building users have to look at and deal with all day, and they rapidly grow bored, frustrated, or embarrassed by what they see. Between constant tinkering and wholesale renovation, few interiors stay the same for even ten years.

A design imperative emerges: *An adaptive building has to allow slippage between the differently-paced systems of Site, Structure, Skin, Services, Space plan, and Stuff.* Otherwise the slow systems block the flow of the quick ones, and the quick ones tear up the slow ones with their constant change. Embedding the systems together may look efficient at first, but over time it is the opposite, and destructive as well.

Thus, pouring concrete on the ground for an instant foundation ("slab-on-grade") is maladaptive—pipes are foolishly buried, and there's no basement space for storage, expansion, and maintenance and Services access. Timber-frame buildings, on the other hand, conveniently separate Structure, Skin, and Services, while balloon-frame (standard stud construction) over-connects them.

All these shearing layers of change add up to a whole for the building, but how do they add up to a whole for the occupants? How can they change *toward* the humans in them rather than away, as so many seem to do? Here the leading theorist is Christopher Alexander. A long-time professor of architecture at the University of California, Berkeley, Chris Alexander is the author of an influential series of books from Oxford University Press which explore

in practical detail what it is that makes buildings and communities humane—or more precisely, what makes them become humane over time.[7]

A design professional of depth—his 1964 *Notes on the Synthesis of Form* is still in print—Alexander is inspired by how design occurs in the natural world. "Things that are good have a certain kind of structure," he told me. "You can't get that structure except dynamically. Period. In nature you've got continuous very-small-feedback-loop adaptation going on, which is why things get to be harmonious. That's why they have the qualities that we value. If it wasn't for the time dimension, it wouldn't happen. Yet here *we* are playing the major role in creating the world, and we haven't figured this out. That is a very serious matter."

Applying this approach to buildings, Alexander frames the design question so: "What does it take to build something so that it's really easy to make comfortable little modifications in a way that once you've made them, they feel integral with the nature and structure of what is already there? You want to be able to mess around with it and progressively change it to bring it into an adapted state with yourself, your family, the climate, whatever. This kind of adaptation is a continuous process of gradually taking care." You can recognize the result where that process is working, he writes. "Because the adaptation is detailed and profound, each place takes on a unique character. Slowly, the variety of places and buildings begins to reflect the variety of human situations in the town. This is what makes the town alive."[8]

While all buildings change with time, only some buildings improve. What makes the difference between a building that gets steadily better and one that gets steadily worse? Growth, apparently, is independent of adaptation, and spasmodic occupant-turnover can defeat adaptation.

Growth follows a simple goal of property owners: maximize what you control. The practice is ancient. In old cities of Europe and the Mideast, upper stories would jetty out farther and farther to increase the space on each floor, until neighbors could shake hands across the street from upper rooms. Now as then, more space in domestic buildings is equated with freedom. In commercial buildings, more space means profit. In institutional buildings, it means power. Everyone tries to get more than they're allowed. City councils often seem to discuss little else. But only sometimes are additions an improvement. Adding more rooms around the periphery of a building, for instance, often leaves the middle dark and desolate.

The opposite of adaptation in buildings is graceless turnover. The usual pattern is for a rapid succession of tenants, each scooping out all trace of the former tenants and leaving nothing that successors can use. Finally no tenant replaces the last one, vandals do their quick work, and broken windows beg for demolition. There are two forms of surcease. If there is a turnaround in local real estate, the succession of owners and tenants might head back upscale, each one adding value. Or the building may be blessed with durable construction and resilient design which can forgive insult and hard swerves of usage. A brick factory from the 1910s, with its intelligent daylighting and abundant space, can stand empty for a decade and still gain value.

Age *plus adaptivity* is what makes a building come to be loved. The building learns from its occupants, and they learn from it.

There is precedent for thinking this way. In classical Greece and Rome, *domus* meant "house" in an expanded sense:

> *People and their dwellings were indistinguishable: domus referred not only to the walls but also to the people within them. Evidence for this is found in inscriptions and texts, in which the word refers now to one, now to the other, but most often to both at once, to the house and its residents envisioned as an indivisible whole. The architectural setting was not an inert vessel; the genius of the domus, honored by a cult, was the protector of both the place and the people who lived in it.*[9]

That kind of bonding between building and inhabitants still occurs. We can consider seemingly opposite examples of it—two kinds of buildings that easily become loved. One, grand and deep, I call the High Road—durable, independent buildings that steadily accumulate experience and become in time wiser and more respected than their inhabitants. The other, quick and dirty, is the Low Road. Their specialty is swift responsiveness to their occupants. They are unrespectable, mercurial, street-smart.

Among buildings as within them, differences of pace are everything.

Notes

1. Francis Duffy, "Measuring Building Performance," *Facilities* (May 1990), p. 17.
2. R. V. O'Neill, D. L. DeAngelis, J. B Wade, T. F. H. Allen, *A Hierarchical Concept of Ecosystems* (Princeton: Princeton University Press, 1986), p. 98.
3. Kevin Lynch, *What Time Is This Place?* (Cambridge: MIT Press, 1972), p. 8.
4. Anne Vernez Moudon, *Built for Change* (Cambridge: MIT Press, 1986), p. 188.
5. Garreau is the author of *Edge City* (New York: Doubleday, 1991).
6. Rick Bevington and Arthur H. Rosenfeld, "Energy for Buildings and Homes," *Scientific American* (Sept. 1990), p. 77.
7. Alexander's "yellow books" from Oxford University Press, each with a variety of co-authors, are: *The Timeless Way of Building* (1979); *A Pattern Language* (1977); *The Oregon Experiment* (1975); *The Production of Houses* (1985); *The Linz Café* (1981); *A New Theory of Urban Design* (1987). A reviewer in *Architectural Design* called *A Pattern Language* "perhaps the most important book on architectural design published in this century."
8. Christopher Alexander, *The Timeless Way of Building* (New York: Oxford University Press, 1979), p. 231.
9. Yvon Thébert, "Private Life and Domestic Architecture in Roman Africa," *A History of Private Life*, 5 vols. (Cambridge: Harvard Univ. Press, 1985, 1987), vol. 1, p. 407.

Source and copyright

This chapter was published in its original form as:

Brand, S. (1994), "Shearing Layers", from Brand, S. (1994), *How Buildings Age: What happens after they are built*, Penguin Books, Harmondsworth, 12–23.

Reprinted with kind permission of the author.

Section Eight

Implementing urban design

The final section of this book explores the implementation of urban design. The first set of chapters in this section is concerned with the 'development' dimension of urban design. Awareness of the development process, particularly the balance between risk and reward that drives it, helps urban designers to gain a deeper understanding of both the context in which they operate and the forces acting upon the process by which their design policies, proposals and projects originate and are implemented. Furthermore, as they frequently need to argue the case for urban design, and more particularly the case for *better quality* urban design, their arguments are better – and more persuasive – when informed by this understanding.

The second set of chapters is concerned with the 'regulation' dimension. This is usually – but not necessarily – a public sector activity. The public sector is an important contributor to the quality of the built environment both in its own right and by influencing and requiring high quality development from the private sector. It is, therefore, necessary for urban designers to understand and use to their advantage the various public sector processes and available policy, regulatory and incentivising tools at their disposal. The public sector's role is much more than the rather narrow and limited concern with 'controlling' or 'guiding' design and development and increasingly focuses on facilitating and enabling good – or, at least, better – design.

The process of designing and producing the built environment involves a variety of 'actors' or decision-makers. In any given instance, the creation of the built environment – and the issue of design quality in respect of the development – is the result of a variety of agents, each with their own objectives, motivations, resources and constraints and all connected with one another in several different ways. To more fully understand the development process, it is necessary to identify the key actors, their motivations and objectives, and their relationships with each other. Accordingly, the first chapter is **Paul Knox and Peter Ozolins'** 'The built environment', from their 2000 edited book *Design Professionals and the Built Environment* (Wiley, London). Their paper presents a succinct and focused presentation of the main actors and decision-makers in the land and property development process.

Chapter 33 is **Sue McGlynn and Paul Murrain's** 'The politics of urban design', originally published in *Planning Practice & Research* in 1994. This paper takes the presentation of the different actors in the development process further by exploring power

relations between them – relations that are summarised in the form of a Powergram. Illustrating the powers of the various actors, McGlynn and Murrain's Powergram draws basic distinctions between actors who can exercise *power* to initiate or control development, those with a legal or contractual *responsibility* towards some aspect of development, and those with an interest or *influence* in the process. Although broad brush, the Powergram graphically illustrates how power is concentrated on the matrix's left-hand-side among the actors (i.e. developers and funders) able to initiate and control development in a very direct way. It also shows the wide-ranging interests of designers (but also their lack of any real power to either initiate or control development), and the lack of power wielded by the users of development (including the local community). Actors on the right-hand-side (i.e. designers and users) rely primarily on argumentation, alliances and participation to influence the process. Inevitably power relationships vary depending on a wide range of factors, including the development processes adopted, the political context, who the client is, and so forth. The Powergram is therefore a caricature, but its value lies in encouraging consideration of power relationships, and how different actors (particularly urban designers) can use the powers available to them to advantage.

McGlynn and Murrain's Powergram also highlights the apparent correspondence between the objectives of the designer and those of users and the general public. Urban designers may therefore be indirectly charged with representing users and the general public's views within the producer side of the development process. It is therefore necessary to look more closely at the urban designer's role. This is the focus of Chapter 34, which was originally a chapter in **Ian Bentley's** 1999 book, *Urban Transformations: Power, people and urban design* (Routledge, London). With McGlynn and Murrain (and Alan Alcock and Graham Smith), Bentley was one of the authors of *Responsive Environments: A manual for designers* (1985) – a major consolidation of and contribution to urban design thinking.

The importance of Bentley's chapter lies in its attempt to conceptualise the interaction of different development actors, particularly the interaction between the developer and the designer (architect). To describe the relationship, Bentley suggests a series of metaphors – 'heroic form-giver', 'master-and-servant', 'market signals' and 'battlefield'. For Bentley, the most convincing metaphor is the battlefield, which sees actors variously negotiating, plotting and scheming to achieve the development form they want. The opportunity space for negotiation, plotting and scheming is set by various considerations and constraints – or 'rules' – on the various development actors. In negotiating, the practical difficulty lies in knowing the limits of other actors' opportunity fields and a key question for the designer, for example, is to know how far developers can be pushed. Bentley argues that the more designers (or any other actors) understand other actors' opportunity fields – if, for example, designers understand financial feasibility calculations – the more effectively they can target their own resources.

Chapter 35 is **Allan Rowley's** essay 'Private-property decision makers and the quality of urban design' – an important early piece of research on different development actors' perspectives on the value of urban design. Originally published in the *Journal of Urban Design* in 1998, the paper looks in more detail at the motivations of different groups of development actors by examining the involvement of developers, investors and occupiers in urban design through a set of five case studies, six expert panels and a literature review. From the perspective of private-property decision-makers, it examines the role and importance of urban design considerations; the benefits of giving explicit attention to such considerations; factors constraining the promotion of good urban design; and incentives and other measures encouraging increased attention to urban design quality. It concludes that a better understanding of the relationship between urban design, the development process and the property industry is a prerequisite to achieving lasting improvements in the quality of the urban environment. While, in theory, 'good' (urban) design should add value to property development, Rowley argues that, in the UK at least, the notion that 'better-buildings-mean-better-business' is both new and debatable and that the dominant attitude in private property decision-making remains the 'appropriate' quality view (i.e. that higher-quality development, however defined, is unnecessary provided some sort of market exists for the development at a lower standard). The opposing attitude – the 'sustainable' quality view – is that high quality helps generate long-term commercial success.

Although written from a UK perspective, the lessons about how, in what circumstances, and to whom value is added by the design process are universal. Other work has since attempted to trace in a more systematic manner the potential value added by urban design (Carmona, *et al.*, 2000). To some degree, this body of work represents something of

a holy grail for designers, because if it can be shown that design adds value, and in what circumstances, then it is more likely that developers (and the public sector) will be willing to invest in it. Research therefore needs to examine the salience of design as a factor in developers' business strategies and especially in their appraisal of risk and reward (see Tiesdell and Adams, 2004).

Chapter 36 is **Brenda Case Scheer's** introduction to her 1994 edited book with Wolfgang Presier, *Design Review: Challenging Urban Aesthetic Control* (Chapman & Hall, New York). Usually based on restrictions of private property rights, systems of reviewing design and development invariably arouse great passions and sometimes controversy. Those who perceive themselves to be most directly affected – designers and developers – often make the most strident case against such forms of control, with some professionals demonstrably holding the inherently contradictory attitude that design controls should apply to everyone other than themselves. Design controls may be justified by the argument that they protect the composite values of all local property owners (i.e. that the maintenance of place quality benefits all property holders) and that they provide a more predictable – and, therefore, secure – investment environment. Case Scheer's paper articulates many of the perceived problems with public sector design control/review processes from an American perspective. Again, many of these critiques are universal in nature and should remind urban designers engaged in public sector regulation that their role has inherent dangers that need to be understood and guarded against. Discussions that present a more balanced view of the public sector role can be found in Punter and Carmona, 1997 and Carmona, 2001.

Chapter 37 is the penultimate chapter from **Andres Duany, Elizabeth Plater-Zyberk and Jeff Speck's** 2000 book, *Suburban Nation: The Rise of Sprawl and the Decline of the American Dream* (North Point Press, New York). This paper identifies lessons for inner-city/urban development through a comparison with – and critique of – suburban development patterns and designs. Acknowledging that suburban development is a 'well-honed science' and that new subdivisions 'outperform the city in category after category', the paper looks in detail at a selection of those categories – the 'amenity package', 'civic decorum', 'physical health', 'retail management', 'marketing techniques', 'investment security', and the 'permitting process'. Throughout this paper, the discussion is embedded in an appreciation of development process – the underlining ethos is that it is not necessary to agree with the values of the process nor with its products, but that it is necessary to better understand how and why they come about in order to be able to manipulate them and thereby achieve better outcomes.

Duany, et al., are closely associated with the New Urbanism movement – a movement that has received a mixed press and has gathered a lot of baggage that serves to obscure rather than to clarify central messages. In particular it is often reduced to debates about architectural style, as Duany, et al. (2000: 208) complain: *'For many architects, it is impossible to see past the pitched roofs and wooden shutters of Seaside and Kentlands to the progressive town planning concepts underneath.'* (see also Ellis, 2004; Calthorpe, 2005). Moreover, as they later state,

> *'. . . there is absolutely no incompatibility between traditional urbanism and modernist architecture – far from it: modernist architecture looks and works its best when lining the sidewalks of traditional cities. Some truly great places . . . consist largely of modernist architecture laid out in a traditional street network. These places do not suffer in any way from their modernist vocabulary, and neither do neighbourhoods that combine many different eras of architecture in a true urban fabric. Such is the power of the traditional street.'* (Duany, et al., 2000: 211–12).

But this mistaking of the part for the whole is not something that is exclusive to views on New Urbanism and pervades the urban design field more generally. Duany, et al.'s paper is simply about enabling good – or, at least, better – urban design. It therefore relates back to Francis Tibbalds' paper at the start of this Reader and to Tibbalds' golden rule that 'the place matters most'.

Matthew Carmona and Steve Tiesdell

32

The built environment

Paul Knox and Peter Ozolins
[2000]

The built environment in context

The built environment gives expression, meaning, and identity to the entire sweep of forces involved in people's relation to their surroundings. It provides cues for all kinds of human behavior, and it is symbolic of all kinds of political, social, and cultural elements. As a result, a building or other element of the built environment of a given period and type tends to be a carrier of the *zeitgeist*, or "spirit" of its time. Every city can therefore be "read" as a multilayered "text," a narrative of signs and symbols. If we think in this way of the city as a text, the built environment becomes a biography of urban change.

As Lewis Mumford put it: "in the state of building at any period one may discover, in legible script, the complicated process and changes that are taking place within civilization itself" (1938: 403). Thirty years later, sociologist Ruth Glass was to characterize the city as "a mirror . . . of history, class structure and culture" (1968: 21). Both comments point to the way that the built environment reflects the underlying relationships, tensions, and contradictions in society. Yet the built environment not only reflects the underlying structures of society—it also serves as one of the means through which they are sustained and legitimized. In this context, one of the most obvious roles for the built environment is in helping to stimulate economic consumption through product differentiation that is aimed at particular market segments. The designer, by virtue of the prestige and mystique socially accorded to creativity, adds exchange value to a building through his or her decisions about design. Thus, architects' professional values and career structure, which reward innovation and the ability to anticipate cultural change, also serve to promote the circulation of capital.

Another important role of the built environment is that of legitimation. A major theme in the literature on architectural history is the way that architecture has repeatedly veiled and obscured the realities of economic and social relations. The physical arrangement and appearance of the built environment can help to suggest stability amid change (or vice versa), to create order amid uncertainty, and to make the social order appear natural and permanent. Part of this effect is achieved through what political scientist Harold Lasswell (1979) calls the "signature of power." It is manifest in two ways: (1) through a "strategy of awe," intimidating the audience with majestic displays of power inherent in urban design and (2) through a "strategy of admiration," aimed at diverting the audience with spectacular and histrionic design effects. It must be recognized, however, that it may not always be desirable to display power. Legitimation may therefore involve modest or low-profile architectural motifs. On the other hand, it is by no means only "high" architecture that sustains the social order. The everyday settings of workplace and neighborhood also help to structure and reproduce class relations.

Meaning and symbolism

When we focus down from high-level generalizations, we find that people often endow buildings with meanings in ways that can be highly individualistic and often independent of their class or power. If, then, the built environment communicates different things to different people, or groups of people, we have to look more closely at questions of communication by *whom*, to *what audience*, to *what purpose*, and with *what results*. The first distinction to make here is the difference between the *intended* meaning of the built environment (on the part of designers and their clients) and its *perceived* meaning as interpreted by others. Often, of course, both intended and perceived meanings coincide. Lasswell's "signatures of power," for example, often serve to reassure the rich, strong, and self-confident while reinforcing feelings of deference among the poor and the weak. Nevertheless, some of the poor and the weak may be provoked and radicalized by such symbolism. The point is that much of the social meaning of the built environment depends on the audience. Meanwhile, of course, designers' and developers' preconceptions of the audience(s) help to determine the kinds of messages that are sent in the first place. It is therefore very important to look more closely at the roles and objectives of the various actors involved in the design and production of the built environment.

The design and production of the built environment

While architecture and urban design are important in contributing to the character of the built environment, much of the decision making about *what kind* of structure gets built, *when* and *where*, is in the hands not just of architects and urban designers but of others, such as developers and politicians. It is useful to think of the design and production of the built environment as a process that involves a variety of "actors" or decision-makers, each with rather different goals and motivations. As they interact with one another over specific development issues, they constitute an organizational framework for the evolution of the built environment.

One of the attributes of the built environment that makes it especially interesting is that it reflects, through its very creation, the decisions of form-givers such as landowners, financiers, developers, builders, politicians, and bureaucratic officials, as well as members of the design professions. The built environment must be seen as the culmination of land development processes that involve all of these key actors. Understanding the built environment requires us to identify the key actors, their motivations and objectives, their interpretations of market demand, and their relationships with one another.

In any given case, the creation of the built environment is the result of a variety of agents, all with their own objectives, motivations, resources, and constraints, and all connected with one another in several different ways. In a city of any size, there will be hundreds of major landowners, dozens of developers, and scores of builders. Some agents will act for themselves within the web of the development process; others will be representing groups of people, large corporations, or public agencies. Some agents may play more than one role at a time. Landowners may be actively involved in subdividing and building, for example; while city governments may act as both regulators and entrepreneurs. As long as we bear these caveats in mind, it is possible to sketch the agents that are typically involved in the creation of the built environment (see, for example, Baerwald, 1981).

Landowners

Landowners stand at the beginning of the chain of events involved in the design and production of the built environment. While different types of landowners behave in rather different ways, all of them influence the outcome of the city building process in two broad ways: (1) through the size and spatial pattern of parcels of land that are delivered to speculators and developers and (2) through conditions that they may impose on the subsequent nature of development. In terms of the size and spatial pattern of land parcels, much, of course, depends on the initial pattern of land holdings. The large *ranchos* and mission lands around Los Angeles, for example, have formed the basis of extensive tracts of uniform suburban development, while in cities along the Atlantic seaboard of the United States, where the early pattern of land holdings was fragmented, development has been more piecemeal.

Because many landowners often sell only part of their holdings at a time, they have a strong interest in what happens to the land they sell. In the past, it was very common for landowners to sell off parcels of land with contractual provisos—*restrictive covenants*—that limited the nature of subsequent development. Such covenants usually discriminated against low-status groups and socially undesirable land uses, sometimes in a very explicit way. With changed social attitudes and tougher laws against discrimination, restrictive covenants are now somewhat less common, but they have by no means disappeared. Rather, the practice has been to frame them obliquely, stipulating minimum plot sizes or residential densities, for example, and so ensure development for more affluent users.

Speculators

Speculators seek to buy relatively low-priced land just before it begins to appreciate rapidly in value and to sell it just as it reaches a peak. Sociologists John Logan and Harvey Molotch (1987) identified three very different kinds of speculators (or, as they called them, "place entrepreneurs"). The first is the "serendipitous entrepreneur"—someone who has inherited property or who has bought it with a particular use in mind and then finds that it would be more valuable sold or rented for some other use. The second is the "active entrepreneur"—the individual who hopes to anticipate changing patterns of land use and land values, buying and selling land accordingly. The prototypical active entrepreneur is a small- or medium-scale investor: individuals (not corporations) who attempt to monitor the investments and disinvestments of bigger players, using local social networks to find out who is going to do what, when, and where. The third is the "structural speculator"—the bigger player who relies not merely on an ability to anticipate changing patterns, but who also hopes to influence or engineer change for his or her own benefit. This individual may attempt, for example, to influence the route of a freeway or the location of a rapid transit stop, to change the zoning map or the master plan, or to encourage public expenditure on particular amenities or services.

Developers

The principal role of developers is in deciding upon the nature and form of new projects, platting large parcels of land into smaller lots, installing the infrastructure necessary for a particular use (e.g., streets, curbs, and gutters, sewer and water mains, gas and electric lines), and selling the lots to builders. These activities generally fall under the descriptive label of "subdivision." Many development companies, however, have extended their activities well beyond the business of subdivision to include land assembly and speculation, design, construction, and marketing. Because it is developers who must decide upon the *type* of project to be undertaken on a particular site, they can fairly claim to be the single most important group of form-givers.

Site selection and project conceptualization stand together at the very beginning of the developer's role. This first step is clearly very important to the outcome of the city-building process, since the developer is inscribing his or her judgment and interpretation onto the landscape. Other things being equal, developers will opt for what is easiest to produce and what is the safest bet in terms of effective demand—the middle of the market. Only a few will have both the nerve to gamble on innovative projects and the ability to persuade financiers and customers that the potential outweighs the risks. In terms of residential development, this conservative approach translates into housing for the "typical" household (or, at least, the developer's idea of the typical household).

Through the 1960s and 1970s this approach resulted in a preponderance of three-bedroom, single-family suburban housing, with little provision for atypical households—who were effectively excluded from new suburban tracts. Only in the 1980s, when marketing consultants caught up with the social shifts that had made the "typical" household a demographic minority, did developers begin to cater for affluent singles, divorcees, retirees, and "DINKs" (dual-income, no kids), adding luxury condominiums, townhouses, artists' lofts, and the like to their standard repertoire.

For most *commercial* and *industrial* development, on the other hand, the main criterion is the availability of sufficient land in an appropriate location; site costs are a secondary consideration. Indeed, as urban sprawl has accelerated and development companies have become larger, the whole question of the availability of land has increased in importance, even for residential developers. Some companies create *land banks*, partly as a speculative venture but mainly to ensure a supply of developable land (many of the parking lots on the edge of downtown areas, for example, are in fact held primarily for their speculative value rather than for their earning capacity as parking lots). Larger companies, with a compelling need to acquire land at a rapid rate (in order to keep their organizations fully employed), search out and bid for suitable land before it has been put on the market (and before any thought has been given to project conceptualization): a tactic known in the trade as "bird-dogging."

The final phase of predevelopment activities is that of determining *feasibility*. Typically, this phase requires coordination with local planners in order to check on compliance with zoning ordinances and legal codes, approaching community leaders in order to gauge reactions to the proposed project, undertaking detailed market analyses, drawing up alternative schematic designs ("schematics"), investigating any special technical issues arising from these schematics, and projecting costs and revenues for each of them.

Having completed the predevelopment activities, the developer moves into implementation: financing, marketing, design, and construction. *Financing* involves convincing others of the project's feasibility. Typically, the developer, just like the would-be homeowner, must put down part of the cost: the developer's *equity*. The remainder is sought from a bank or from some other backer or consortium of backers—pension funds, insurance companies, and the like—who may themselves require certain changes in the nature of the project. The development industry is highly "leveraged," meaning that the developer's equity often works out to be a much smaller proportion of the overall cost than the homeowner's equity.

The design and construction phase begins with the development of the project design based on the approved schematic design determining building materials and methods, then production of detailed contract drawings, followed by a bidding process in which general contractors are invited to bid for various aspects of the engineering, construction, and landscaping. Speed of operation is essential during this phase. Interest has to be paid on construction loans based upon a balance outstanding that increases as the project proceeds. Any delays in producing revenue from a project can result in significant losses due to increased interest payments, particularly when such delays occur toward the latter stages of construction. Once the construction is completed, the developer has to search for and manage tenants, collect rents, and generally maintain and administer the projects; or sell to new owners. This is the *facilities management* stage of the process.

Builders

As we have seen, developers sometimes extend their operations to include building; more often than not, however, general building contractors will be engaged by developers. At the same time, many small- and medium-sized building firms will undertake their own speculative land acquisition and development functions. Much depends, as with development companies, on the size and internal organization of the company. The typical large builder reduces costs through direct purchasing of materials in bulk, the maintenance of large inventories, the development of efficient subcontracting relationships, the retention of a specialized labor force, the use of federal financial aid and housing research, and the use of mass-production methods on large parcels of land.

As a result, large builders are inevitably concerned almost exclusively with construction for mass-market suburban development. Medium-sized companies cannot afford to pay the interest on large parcels of developed land, so their preferred strategy is to maximize profits by building at high densities (condominiums, apartment blocks) or by catering for the high-profit luxury end of the market (where the mass-production orientation of the big companies is a handicap). This strategy leaves small firms to use their more detailed local knowledge to scavenge for "custom" building contracts and smaller infill opportunities, whereupon they will assemble the necessary materials and labor and seek to build as quickly as possible, usually aiming at the market for larger, higher quality dwellings in neighborhoods with an established social reputation.

Consumers

Consumers—households, industrialists, retailers, and so on—represent the demand side of the development process. Consumer preferences and consumer behavior develop in a social context that is fundamentally competitive, though people's preferences are frequently created or manipulated by powerful investors and their associates working through advertising, public relations, and the mass media. It should also be stressed that people need not always react individually—as "consumers"—to the choices available to them: they may affect the development process collectively, through citizen-group protests over specific development projects, through involvement in pro-growth, no-growth, or slow-growth politics, or through involvement in residents' associations.

Real estate agents, financiers, and other professionals

Real estate agents, financiers, and other professionals are essential to the development process as facilitators, intermediaries, and specialized experts. A wide range of professionals is involved, including surveyors, market analysts, advertising companies, lawyers, title insurance companies, appraisers, property managers, engineers, ecologists, and geologists. The most important of them, however, are mortgage financiers and real estate agents, who stand at the center of the magic circle of "exchange professionals." Their activities go well beyond the actual *creation* of the built environment to encompass continuing processes of neighborhood change.

Government and regulatory agencies

The built environment forms a staple of local politics and the focus of a good deal of local policy. Local governments enact building codes and zoning regulations. They also invest heavily in the built environment. Indeed, the dynamism of many communities has depended since the early 1980s on an unprecedented form of "growth-machine" politics and unprecedented partnerships between development companies and public agencies. City governments in many Western countries have increasingly shifted to a new civic culture of entrepreneurialism that draws heavily on public—private partnerships, in which public resources and legal powers are joined with private interests in order to undertake development projects. This shift has fostered a speculative and piecemeal approach to the management of cities. Projects such as downtown shopping malls, festival marketplaces, new stadiums, theme parks, and conference centers have been subsidized by local governments (which in turn have leveraged additional funding from state and federal agencies) because they have been seen as having the capacity to enhance property values and generate retail turnover and employment growth.

Market trends

Like most other industries, the development industry has undergone some radical changes in the past 20 years. One of the most striking trends is the pursuit of product differentiation and niche marketing in the built environment. In the commercial sector, product differentiation has resulted in a variety of new formats for hotels: luxury/full service, executive conference resorts, extended-stay (with kitchen and laundry facilities en suite), economy-only, and all-suite. Developers of office buildings in the United States responded to the booming business climate of the 1990s by producing self-consciously luxurious buildings. Developments for retailing have similarly seen different formats for different market segments: upscale downtown gallerias and malls, for example, and "power centers" (community shopping centers located near regional shopping malls and dominated by specialized discount outlets). Another significant new "product line" for developers is the specialized mall: a medical mall, for example, that is crafted to provide busy, affluent consumers with one-stop shopping that offers physicians, counselors, therapists, medical laboratories, pharmacies, outpatient facilities, fitness centers, health food stores, and cafés.

Developers of business and industrial parks, meanwhile, have begun to offer "flexspace"—single-story structures with "designer" frontages, loading docks at the rear, and interior space that can be used for offices, R&D labs, storage, or manufacture, in any ratio. Old product lines can also be "treated" in order to enhance flexibility within the market. Business and industrial parks have been repackaged as "planned corporate environments" with built-in daycare facilities, fitness centers, jogging trails, restaurants and convenience stores, lavish interior decor, and lush exterior landscaping.

In the residential sector, some developers have repositioned themselves away from single-family "starter" homes to build more multifamily projects (that, like business parks, are packaged with services—in this case, security systems, concierge services, exercise facilities, bike trails, and so on) or more expensive homes for the "move-up" market. At the very top end of the residential market are speculative homes differentiated by the most lavish "designer" features. New "monster" homes in upscale neighborhoods in US cities typically stand on large lots, with circular drives and imposing gateways that create the unnerving effect of a landscape full of expensive funeral homes. The houses themselves average 600 to 1000 square meters and have elaborate master bedrooms, bathrooms with whirlpool tubs, saunas or steam cabinets, exercise rooms, "gourmet" kitchens, libraries with computer centers, two-story foyers, and 3 meter high ceilings.

Large, privately planned communities have also become popular with developers in many cities. They are a result of an extreme form of product differentiation and carefully targeted niche marketing. By exploiting new and more flexible zoning regulations, developers can put together projects that are attractive to a very profitable sector of the residential market while retaining scope for flexibility in the composition and timing of the development. Residents of such communities are offered sequestered settings with an extensive package of amenities that typically include tennis courts, a golf course, swimming pools, play areas, jogging courses, an auditorium, exercise rooms, a shopping center, a daycare center, and a security system symbolized by imposing gateways and operated by electronic card-key systems. The entire ensemble is typically framed in a carefully landscaped setting that might contain a lake stocked with waterfowl or a neo-conservationist assemblage of remnant woodland, an artificial wetlands environment, and plantings of wild flowers. We can "read" these "designer" neighborhoods as the product of our times, the carriers of our society's concern with materialism and social distinction.

Clearly, the importance of *design* in the built environment is increasing. As one developer put it, "My buildings are a product. They are products like Scotch Tape is a product, or Saran Wrap. The packaging of that product is the first thing that people see. I am selling space and renting space and it has to be in a package that is attractive enough to be financially successful" (quoted in Zukin, 1988: 437–8). Yet, of course, design can be—should be—so much more than packaging. It involves languages and ideologies that go well beyond the orbits of developers' worlds.

References

Baerwald, T. 1981. "The site selection process of suburban residential builders," *Urban Geography*, 2, 339–57.

Clay, G. 1974. *Close Up: How to Read the American City*. New York: Praeger.

Fainstein, S. 1993. *The City Builders*. Cambridge, MA.: Blackwell.

Glass, R. 1968. "Urban Sociology in Great Britain," in *Readings in Urban Sociology*, R. E. Pahl (ed.). Oxford: Pergamon, 21–46.

Lasswell, H. 1979. *The Signature of Power*. New York: Transaction Books.

Logan, J. and Molotch, H. 1987. *Urban Fortunes: The Political Economy of Place*. Berkeley: University of California Press.

Mumford, L. 1938. *The Culture of Cities*. New York: Harcourt, Brace and World.

Relph, E. 1987. *The Modern Urban Landscape*. London: Croom Helm.

Scully, V. 1988. *American Architecture and Urbanism*. 2nd edn. New York: Henry Holt.

Weiss, M. 1987. *The Community Builders*. New York: Columbia University Press.

Zukin, S. 1988. "The postmodern debate over urban form," *Theory, Culture, and Society*, 5, 435–52.

Source and copyright

This chapter was published in its original form as:

Knox, P. and Ozolins, P. (2000), 'The Built Environment', in Knox, P. and Ozolins, P. (2000) (Editors), *Design Professionals and the Built Environment: An Introduction*, Wiley, London, 3–10.

Reproduced by permission of John Wiley & Sons Limited.

The politics of urban design

Sue McGlynn and Paul Murrain
[1994]

Introduction

This paper seeks to emphasise and demonstrate that urban design is essentially a political matter—it involves us directly in making political choices through the representation and mediation of values and interests in the activity of design. The recognition of this role brings us immediately to a crucial problem in the practice of urban design, or rather a multi-layered series of problems. First, it is not part of the culture of the environmental professions to be explicit about values. Rather, the reverse is true—that values become an implicit part of the ideological baggage acquired in the course of professional training. This obfuscation of values is of particular concern where the very act of drawing 'town' and the built environment that results creates a political system in its own right. It allows certain things to happen for some people and constrains others. We would argue, therefore, that a clear statement of values and objectives would seem to be a precondition of advancing the legitimacy of environmental professions in general, and urban design in particular. The first section of this paper argues that all design exercises should start with the articulation of values by all participants, and offers an updated set of 'responsive' (Bentley *et al.*, 1985) qualities as a basis for urban designers' part of this exercise.

Second, and a direct consequence of the first problem identified, it is not part of the culture of the design professions to see themselves as being part of a wider political process. We will argue in the second section of this paper that it is essential to realize where the urban designer is located in the power structure of actors or stakeholders who have an interest in the realization of design and urban development, and whose interests the design is serving. Third, and perhaps even more fundamental, is the problem that, even if we can achieve greater clarity in the expression of our social and political values, there seems to be very little real understanding or knowledge of the relationship between values, design objectives and the design intentions derived from them, and the translation of these intentions into actual physical product. In the absence of a stronger theoretical development of urban design, there must be a radical change in the means by which design proposals are evaluated.

Some values for 'good' urban design

'Good' design can only exist relative to a set of values held by an individual, group or society in general. That is self-evident when one considers the arguments about what is 'good' in the products of the built environment professions. But how often are these differences expressed in terms of their overt connection to a set of values held by the various groups involved in the production of the built environment? What further complicates the issue, or perhaps gives the clearest demonstration of the problem, is the acknowledgement that the built environment is a political system *in its own right*. Try walking through a wall and you will notice that it is the physical fabric as well as the way that it is managed that sets constraints on what you can or cannot do (Bentley *et al.*, 1985). In urban design we talk often and glibly about 'democratic' town form. Again it seems self-evident that a good deal of democratic town form (to be defined shortly) has been produced by undemocratic political regimes throughout history. More recently and sadly, very undemocratic isola- tionist town form has been designed, built and managed by people who would genuinely claim to be interactive and essentially democratic in their own political persuasions.

As we cannot safely assume that an acceptable physical form will automatically result from good intentions, how does our claim to be democratic translate to the sort of town we should build? A most concise definition of democracy comes from the contemporary philosopher John Rawls that 'democ- racy arbitrates between conflicting freedoms'. For an urban designer this could be interpreted as 'design- ing achievable environments to support the interests of the widest publics who use them'; a definition put forward at the JCUD for a good few years now. A word allied to this has entered the urban design lan- guage more recently from the sustainability litera- ture (Elkin & McClaren, 1991) and rightly taken on great importance, namely *empowerment*—to author- ise and enable. But yet again when searching the burgeoning amount of 'sustainable' literature it is very hard to find clearly stated objectives translated into clear images and examples of *town form*, exist- ing or proposed.

If we are to counteract the inequalities inherent in the segregated and mono-functional forms of much post-war development we need to design envi- ronments which are lively, safe, sensorily rich, choice laden, economically and spatially efficient and eco- logically diverse. We believe that this can only be achieved through the promotion of mixed-use town forms. 'Good' mixed-use can therefore be defined as a finely grained mix of primary land uses, namely a variety of housing and workplaces with housing pre- dominant, closely integrated with other support services, within convenient walking distance of the majority of homes.

As co-authors of *Responsive Environments: a man- ual for designers* (1985), together with Ian Bentley, Alan Alcock and Graham Smith, we set out to be explicit about the values which underpinned our approach to urban design, and to provide a detailed explanation of the *form* implications of these social and political values. The idea of responsiveness is based on maximizing choice for the individual, but not at the expense of the collective. We argued that the design of a place affects the choices people can make at many levels:

- it affects *where people can go*, and where they can- not: the quality we shall call *permeability*;

- it affects the *range of uses* available to people: the quality we shall call *variety*;
- it affects how easily people can *understand* what opportunities it offers: the quality we shall call *legibility*;
- it affects the degree to which people can use a given place for *different* purposes: the quality we shall call *robustness*;
- it affects whether the detailed *appearance* of the place makes people aware of the choices available: the quality we shall call *visual appropriateness*;
- it affects people's *choice of sensory experiences*: the quality we shall call *richness*;
- it affects the extent to which people can put their *own stamp* on a place: we shall call this *personalization*.

It is now 9 years since publication of the book and at least 10 since it was written. Although we still hold to these qualities, it is not surprising that our ideas have evolved and been developed during this time through considerable debate by staff and students within the Joint Centre for Urban Design and else- where. Both of us make a critique of some aspects of *Responsive Environments* in our respective chapters of *Making Better Places: Urban design now* (Hayward & McGlynn, 1993). Through our experience in prac- tice and teaching we have reduced the original list to four fundamental qualities: permeability, variety (vitality, proximity and concentration), legibility and robustness (resilience). These four qualities deal with the spatial structure and use patterns of urban areas and have the most fundamental impact on opportu- nities for personal choice and equity of access, and are therefore the critical qualities in the achievement of democratic town form.

Ian Bentley (1990), in work he has been devel- oping with Ian Lyne at the JCUD, has initiated the inclusion of a new set of qualities which relate to the ecological impacts of urban forms and patterns of activity. Their work puts forward a further three basic qualities—resource efficiency, cleanliness and biotic support. The development of these qualities offers new ways in which patterns of land uses and spatial integration can aid the diversity and empowerment being sought in the value system described in this section. Many urban designers have been arguing for a return to a more democratic urban form for some time. However, the sustainability debate has given a welcome boost to these and related matters of social justice and ecological balance. What is more, they lead directly into the political arena as issues of resource efficiency, cleanliness and personal safety already feature strongly in many political programmes nationally and globally in a way that permeability, variety, legibility and robustness do not! The following section considers how urban designers are located within this wider political frame of reference and explores how this affects their ability to achieve the values and qualities discussed.

Where the power lies

The notions of social gain, community benefit and the public interest have featured largely in the rhetoric of the environmental professions. In the absence of explicitly stated values and objectives, professionals have been content to restrict evaluation primarily to their peer group, one which unsurprisingly is likely to share the same implicit value system. The history of the planning and architecture of post-war social housing is a good example of well-intentioned and socially conscious professionals making expansive claims of social and community benefit which the everyday experience of users has emphatically challenged.

In order to be able to develop an alternative evaluative process, we must be willing to make clear

and explicit statements of the values which underpin our design proposals. We must be willing and able to open up the design and decision making process to as wide a group of interests as possible and to develop methods which will facilitate a genuinely exploratory and interactive debate about this process. Lastly, we must be willing to identify who gains and who loses in this process.

The 'powergram' (McGlynn, 1993) shown in Figure 33.1 was designed to highlight both the very real conflict of values in the development process, and the huge potential to disadvantage the user groups because of the uneven distribution of power inherent in our political economy. On the vertical axis of the matrix are listed the physical components of the built environment which form the substance of negotiation and bargaining between actors in the design and development process. On the horizontal axis are the major actors in this process, categorized into the 'suppliers' of the basic commodities of development such as land and capital; the 'producers' from developers through to local government, the professional groups and urban designers; and lastly the 'consumers'—that is everyone who uses the environment. The diagram makes distinctions between actors who can exercise *power* to initiate or control development, actors who have a legal or contractual

Actors	Suppliers			Producers				Consumers
Elements of the built environment	Land owner	Funder	Developer	Local authority		Architects	Urban designers	Everyday users
				Planners	Highway engineers			
Street pattern	–	–	○	○	●	–	○	○
Blocks	–	–	–	–	–	–	○	–
Plots – subdivision & amalgamation	●	●	●	○ (in U.K.)	–	–	○	–
Land/building use	●	●	●	●	⊕	○	○	○
Building form – height/mass	–	●	●	●	–	⊕	○	○
– orientation to public space	–	–	○	⊕	–	–	○	○
– elevations	–	○	○	●	–	⊕	○	○
– elements of construction (details/materials)	–	○	●	⊕	–	⊕	○	○

Key: ● Power—either to initiate or control.   ○ Interest/influence—by argument or participation only
⊕ Responsibility—legislative or contractual   – No obvious interest

FIGURE 33.1
A 'powergram' for urban design (*Source:* McGlynn, 1993).

responsibility towards some aspect of development, and actors who have *interest or influence* in the process. Although somewhat simplistic in its categorization the powergram graphically illustrates that the power is concentrated in the left hand side of the matrix. These actors can initiate and control development in a very direct way, whilst those on the right hand side have to rely on argumentation, alliance and participation to have any influence in the process.

Although the matrix does expose a huge potential to disadvantage the user group in the process of development, it also reveals the close congruence of interest between urban designers and everyday users which each must exploit to increase their influence in the decision making and design process. Urban designers need to stress the political significance of this congruence of interest with user groups in the local development process, and must take a proactive role in gaining financial and political support for participatory exercises from local and central government and developers themselves. The ability to make convincing evaluations of how particular objectives will confer benefits for identified groups via the design process is essential if urban designers are to be effective in their alliance with everyday users.

However, there is a lamentable lack of good practice upon which to develop methods and techniques for enabling a genuinely exploratory and interactive debate between actors. One of the methods which, in a very concentrated way, tries to even out the imbalance illustrated in the 'powergram' is the design *charrette*, which, in a highly orchestrated forum, is designed for the open evaluation of design proposals.

Conclusion

In the context of this paper a key point to emerge is the role of the urban designer as an enabler of user involvement. The urban designer needs to be aware of the political, social and economic forces impacting on the situation, and be able to engage in the debate whilst having sufficient knowledge of the form implications of those forces such that he or she can lead a design team and produce, under great pressure, as many design outcomes as are deemed necessary to achieve consensus. This imposes an enormous responsibility on the role of the urban designer particularly in the current climate where interest groups which do not have great political

power are slowly but measurably demanding far greater input into the design process, wishing to scrutinize what is proposed by those with the power, and desiring to have someone to help them communicate their own responses via design alternatives. Enquiry by design is vital, and the design *charrette* provides a practical demonstration of the combination of knowledge and skills which urban designers must possess in order to be effective in the contribution which they can make to both the process and product of urban development.

References

Batchelor, P. & Lewis, D. (1985) *Urban Design in Action* (Chapel Hill, North Carolina State University).

Bentley, I. (1990) 'Urban design: ecological urban design', *Architects' Journal*, 192, pp. 69–71.

Bentley, I. *et al.* (1985) *Responsive Environments: a manual for designers* (London, Architectural Press).

Costello, A. (1994) Community-based charrettes. *Urban Design Quarterly*, 49, January, pp. 18–19.

Elkin, T. & McClaren, D. (1991) *Reviving the City—towards sustainable urban development* (London, Friends of the Earth).

Engwicht, D. (1992) *Towards an Eco-City: calming the traffic* (Sydney, Envirobook).

Gibson, T. (1991) *Taking the Neighbourhood Initiative—a facilitators guide* (London, Estate Action, DoE).

Hayward, R. & McGlynn, S. (Eds) (1993) *Making Better Places: urban design now* (Oxford, Butterworth Heinemann).

Lennertz, W. (1991) Town making fundamentals, in: A. Kreiger & W. Lennertz (Eds) *Town and Town Making Principles* (New York, Rizzoli).

McGlynn, S. (1993) Reviewing the rhetoric, in: R. Hayward & S. McGlynn (Eds) *Making Better Places: urban design now* (Oxford, Butterworth Heinemann).

Murrain, P. (1993) Urban expansion: look back and learn, in: R. Hayward & S. McGlynn (Eds) *Making Better Places: urban design now* (Oxford, Butterworth Heinemann).

Ravetz, A. (1980) *Remaking Cities: contradictions of the recent urban environment* (London, Croom Helm).

Reade, E. (1982) Section 52 and corporatism in planning. *Journal of Planning and Environment Law*, January, pp. 8–16.

Source and copyright

This chapter was published in its original form as:

McGlynn, S. and Murrain, P. (1994), 'The Politics of Urban Design', *Planning Practice & Research*, 9, 311–320.

Reprinted with permission of Taylor & Francis Ltd (http://www.tandf.co.uk/journals).

34

Heroes and servants, markets and battlefields

Ian Bentley
[1999]

To understand the form-production process, we need an approach which takes account of real people doing practical things. In this chapter, we shall review a range of problematics which might offer what we need here, since they all stress the role of individual action in the form-generation process.

The simplest of these 'problematics of action' is that of the 'heroic form-giver', which is based on the idea that built form is generated through the creative efforts of particular individuals. These heroes propose forms, whilst others merely implement them. More complex is the view that there are many actors involved in the form-production process, and that the outcome is determined by power-plays between them. The most basic version of this approach claims that those actors with the most power simply issue orders to those with less. More complex is the 'market signals' perspective – a more action-orientated conception than the basic market problematic – which sees resource-poor actors such as designers responding to market signals which indicate the kinds of schemes which those with the necessary resources are willing to fund. An alternative, more sophisticated version is the 'battlefield' problematic, in which the various actors are seen not merely as ordering each other around, or as responding to market signals, but rather as plotting and scheming to use their power in the best ways they can devise, in attempts to achieve the built forms they want. In this chapter, we shall review each of these problematics in turn. As our starting point we shall take as 'hero' the architect: in the current complex division of labour, architects are highly visible at the sharp end of the form-production process as a whole.

Both in popular and in professional culture, it is certainly the architect who is most often cast in the leading role. In popular culture, this position is most famously celebrated in Ayn Rand's best-selling novel *The Fountainhead*.[1]

Throughout, the novel celebrates the idea that the prime generator of built form is the creative power of the individual architect. Of course, it is admitted, many other people are in various ways involved in the making of a building; but it is only the individual architect who breathes form into the process. In the words of the architect hero:

> *Every creative job is achieved under the guidance of a single individual thought. An architect requires a great many men to erect his building. But he does not ask them to vote on his design . . . An architect uses steel, glass, concrete, produced by others. But the materials remain just so much steel, glass and concrete until he touches them.*[2]

This view, in more measured guise, is deeply embedded in professional design culture too. It is expressed, for example, every time an architect refers to 'my building'. And it is reinforced, and disseminated to a wider public, through all those coffee-table books with titles like *The Buildings of Joe Bloggs*.

This idea that the individual architect has a crucially important influence on built form seems to be supported by a great deal of evidence. It is clear, for example, that certain architects do have remarkably distinctive and consistent personal styles, which mark their designs out from those of other people. Buildings by Le Corbusier, say, at a given stage in the development of his complex career, do have an obvious family resemblance between them; and they do all look different from those by (say) Daniel Libeskind or Aldo Rossi.

In practice, however, relatively few architects seem to play Roark's 'form-giver' role, though many more would probably like to: indeed the rarity of genius is a key message of *The Fountainhead* itself. In some way, a relatively small band of designers seems to mark out a fairly limited range of design paths, which are then followed quite closely by the majority of practitioners. There are so many 'followers' that the similarities between different individuals' designs, at a given historical moment, usually seem far more striking than their differences. It is only this, indeed, which enables us to talk in terms of 'architectural styles' as we do.

One explanation for these similarities puts them down to psychological differences between individual designers, seeing variations in creativity as the factors which distinguish 'leaders' from 'followers'. This may help to explain why most designers follow paths laid down by others, but by itself it cannot explain why those particular leaders are chosen as the ones to be followed along those particular paths at particular historical moments. If creativity alone were the key to architectural leadership, then (for example) the Archigram designers of the 1960s, like Ron Herron who made way-out proposals for cities which walked about, would have been assured of a massive following. In fact, their practical influence on built form was virtually nil. Creativity, it seems, is not enough. There must be other factors at work in deciding who follows whom.

The Fountainhead itself gives us clues about what these factors might be. Though poor Roark works desperately to maintain his heroic vision of his ideal creation, in the end he is driven to blow the building up because it is so botched by others' actions. This is all a matter of power. Roark has the power to destroy, but lacks the resources which he needs to turn his vision into bricks and mortar, whilst those who do have the resources which are necessary to build also have their own agendas about how these resources should be used. In some circumstances (probably rather few, as Roark found out) this agenda might be centred on a desire to support the architect in creating a work of art; but equally it might not. Anyone with any experience of the real-world development process knows very well that usually it is not. In most cases, therefore, the idea that built form flows directly from the architect's individual inspiration has to be understood as a powerful myth, rather than as a statement of fact.

Given the complex division of labour in the modern development process,[3] together with the fact that power is very unequally distributed amongst the various actors involved, it is equally implausible to think that any other actor, alternative to the architect, might be a heroic form-maker either. This raises an interesting question: how could such an implausible concept as the 'heroic form-maker' ever have become so widely accepted? What do any of the actors in the form-production process have to gain from it?

For architects, trying to make a living, the benefits are obvious. If form is believed to be the result of their own creativity – 'my building' – then it is theirs to sell in the market. As Ayn Rand said of Roark 'the materials remain just so much steel, glass and concrete until he touches them. What he does with them is his individual product and his individual property.'[4] At another level, this ideology also supports the interests of other powerful actors in the development process, for it implies that it is only architects who can be blamed for the creation of unloved places – these are *their* creations, after all. This is extremely convenient for everyone else involved, for it draws a veil over their activities, inhibits any deeper criticisms of the form-production process, and thereby enables it to continue unchanged.

In the end, then, the 'hero' problematic has helped us to develop our understanding of how the ideological level of the form-production process works, but it clearly has so many drawbacks in other areas that it can be of no further help to us. To make further progress we have to go beyond it, to explore the range of problematics which comprehend built form as generated through a process of interaction between a range of actors, each with access to different sources and levels of power.

The simplest way of conceiving these interactions is in terms of 'masters and servants', whereby those with the most power simply command the actions of those with the least. This concept is widespread, in both popular and professional cultures. In its commonest formulation, it is those with economic power – those who fund building projects – who are seen as ruling the form-production process, in a built-form version of 'whoever pays the piper calls the tune.'

At first sight, this approach seems very plausible. Buildings are extremely expensive to produce, and it seems likely that those who are able to put resources into developing them would do so for their own purposes. In the context of capitalism, these purposes are usually concerned with making profits: there is no reason, after all, to think that most major property developers are particularly interested in art for its own sake. The example of Lord Peter Palumbo, the commercial property developer who has also served as Chairman of the Arts Council, is surely the exception whose very noteworthiness proves the contrary general rule. And even if this were not the case, most major property developers themselves have shareholders, who invest their money in the expectation of profit, and will stop supporting the developer's very existence as a developer if acceptable profits are not produced.

To an important degree, then, the resources needed to construct buildings are only made available with strings attached. In their hearts, most people – including artist-architects – know this perfectly well. It was these strings which tangled up the efforts even of the heroic Howard Roark in Ayn Rand's novel, causing him such distress that he blew up his botched creation in a rage. But real-life architects have mortgages to pay and children to feed like anyone else. Like most of us, they would probably come round in the end to doing what their patrons dictate, without Howard's heroics.

On the face of it, all this supports the idea of the developer as master of all the actors in the development process; which offers one way of explaining, for example, why so many different architects are involved in producing similar buildings. If all office developers (say) have the same profit-orientated objectives, and if it is mostly these objectives which determine the forms of office blocks, then it is not surprising that so many office buildings are so much alike.

In practice, however, things cannot be so simple, if only because there are other contenders for a 'master' role. For example, the idea of the planner as 'master' seems to be widely held amongst architects.

In the end, though, this 'master and servant' problematic is no more convincing than the idea of the heroic form-giver. This is largely because it ignores the problems which face even the most powerful actors when they try to control the work of all the specialised experts, such as architects, who are involved in the modern development process. The idea that 'whoever pays the piper calls the tune' is unconvincing in this situation, because building projects are not at all like tunes. Tunes, after all, are predictable and are known in advance to those who pay the piper, whilst buildings are often one-offs, and in any case are always on unique sites. Even when buildings themselves are standardised (as, for example, in many speculative housing estates) the overall layout of each 'estate' is unique. Patrons, therefore, cannot know exactly what they will be paying for, in advance of some design process carried out by design experts.

As with the 'heroic form-maker' approach, the widespread nature of the idea that 'those with the most power always win' probably owes a great deal to its ideological role in the form-production process; it absolves those actors who lack access to economic or political power from struggling too hard to achieve whatever they believe to be the best form for the situation in hand. Though sometimes a mite depressing, this makes the working lives of relatively powerless actors a great deal less stressful and, no doubt, more efficient for developers in economic terms.

If patrons cannot know, in advance of the design process, exactly what they will be paying for, they can nevertheless know whom they are paying for, when they buy the services of professional advisers in the marketplace. Clearly, patrons are most likely to buy the services of those whose track records demonstrate a willingness and aptitude for working in the patron's interest. As Phillippo advises, in a guide for developers: 'It is not advisable to try to change the style of an architect; but to find an architect who in the opinion of the market analysts is in demand.'[5]

At this point, then, it begins to look as though the limitations of the 'master and servant' approach might be overcome if we adopt the perspective of the 'market signals' problematic, according to which the various actors in the development process are kept in line not by brute force, but by market signals which indicate the sorts of services and forms which patrons are willing to fund. How far can this can take us?

We can best explore this approach by starting from the position of design professionals setting out their stalls in the marketplace, competing with each other to sell their services. One important way of improving cost effectiveness in professional work is through a process of increasing specialisation, in which broad and complex tasks are split down into ever-narrower parts. For a given cost, this enables a greater degree of specialised expertise to be applied to each given aspect of the development process, to the benefit of whoever is in a position to buy the services concerned. The market process therefore supports the emergence of an ever more complex and specialised division of labour in the production of urban space.

Particular professionals, with their particular specialised skills, build up track records, for which they are hired (or not). Market signals, broadcast through the professional media, enable their competitors to see which sorts of services and forms are bankable, and which are not. In capitalist situations, disciplines of unemployment and bankruptcy ensure that it is only the bankable services and forms, and the ideologies which support them, which are widely replicated. Through their own responses to market signals, therefore, most of the actors in this complex division of labour get themselves into line, with no need for overt shows of force. All this makes sense in the abstract, but it ignores the practical difficulty of controlling all the experts in the development 'team' once they have been hired. Believe me: as an ex-property developer myself, I know how difficult this is.

The difficulty arises, at least in part, because of a mutual ignorance and antipathy between the various members of the development team, a state of affairs which arises through the process of increasing specialisation itself. As each new service is offered as an innovation in the marketplace, it has to be seen by potential buyers as being distinct from the other services which are already on offer: it has to develop its own 'unique selling point'. This means that the promoters of each new service have to emphasise the differences between that service and its possible competitors.

One result of this process is that many of the actors in the development process carry out their work according to different value-systems. The British economist Ralph Morton, for example, points out that, although architects and structural engineers both emphasise the fundamental importance of design in their work, 'they each mean by "design" an almost totally different activity', with architects stressing the art dimension and engineers the scientific. In contrast to both, he argues, surveyors often have 'a primary concern with market efficiency and value for money where value itself is defined in monetary terms'.[6]

Within this general situation, there seems to be a particularly strong conflict between the values of most architects and those of many of their patrons. In the context of capitalism, where most buildings are produced in speculative markets, and many patrons' objectives are primarily financial, we find that many architects nevertheless have non-commercial values. Comparing his own results with those of Anastasi, Mackinnon, for example, showed that US architects were far less motivated by financial considerations than ordinary citizens, let alone (presumably) property developers.[7] Interestingly, the divergence is particularly marked in the case of the prestigious 'leaders' of architectural culture.

Mackinnon carried out his study in 1962, but the situation is probably not changing very fast. In a 1990 review, Ralph Morton shows how limited is the teaching of economic matters in UK schools of architecture, suggesting that this 'seems to stem partly from a belief that the subject is peripheral and there is simply no time for it; but it stems also from a fear that contact with the philistine world of the economist will contaminate the creative imaginative world of the young architect'.[8] This situation is further complicated by a range of studies which clearly show that there are also considerable divergences in the evaluation of urban places between architects and non-architects[9] and between architects and town planners.[10]

At first sight, this situation seems fraught with potential disaster for all concerned. Patrons do not have the knowledge to design buildings themselves, whilst their professional advisers are difficult to control and also – particularly in the case of the architect – are often actively hostile to the sorts of objectives which many patrons have, in so far as they understand them at all. Morton himself certainly sees this as a negative situation, remarking on 'the failure of the built environment professions to use their enormous collective skills and knowledge to a common purpose'.[11]

All this means that it is extremely difficult for patrons to control the experts' work in any detail. Even if the patron and the design professional were to share the same objectives, so that the professional was consciously trying to implement the patron's stated policies, still a degree of autonomous professional action would in principle be unavoidable, because no policy can ever be stated in a form which is detailed enough to be directly applicable, without interpretation, to every individual design situation. In the real-life situation of the development process, where the objectives of the patron and the expert are in conflict, it is even more difficult for the patron to exercise close control, as Dietrich Rueschemeyer reminds us:

> *Where complex knowledge is used in the performance of work . . . it makes control and supervision very costly if not impossible since detailed control of experts requires equally well-qualified controllers. 'Lay' customers – however rich, prestigious or powerful – cannot themselves exercise control because they often do not know enough even to define what their problem is, not to mention monitoring its solution.*[12]

This general point is certainly relevant to the form-generation process in particular, as the architect Vittorio Magnano Lampugnani points out:

> The public client is almost without exception an abstract entity, a vacuous and vague sort of bureaucratic figment. And the private client, who at least puts in an appearance – usually – in flesh and blood, is not capable of expressing precise, concrete and unequivocal demands.[13]

The sociologist Robert Gutman also supports the view that many patrons cannot specify what they want with any certainty:

> I have spoken with architects for several of the universities involved in major building projects here [Britain] and in America, and they are agreed that the task of developing university briefs was difficult but also fascinating and exciting. It was difficult because no one involved in the clients' organization – not the vice-chancellor or president, not the building committee, the department heads and professors – no one was able to articulate for them in any easy fashion their objectives except in the most vague terms.[14]

Admittedly this was written back in the 1970s, but more recent opinion confirms the same view. Bernard Tschumi – who, as an eminent practising architect, should be in a position to know from first-hand experience – tells us that 'in our contemporary society, programs are inherently unstable.'[15] As he sees it, 'Few can decide what a school or a library should be or how electronic it should be, and perhaps fewer can agree on what a park in the twenty first century should consist of.'[16] This inherent vagueness gives any expert actor a degree of autonomy, which can be enhanced by drawing on the power of inner resources such as initiative, determination or moral commitment, rather than merely relying on access to external sources of economic or political power. When we start focusing on such potentials, however, we have moved outside the limits of the market problematic. We now find ourselves in a place which resembles a battlefield rather than the friendly bustle of a marketplace. How far can this 'battlefield' problematic offer us further insights into how form-production works? In particular, how far can it help us understand the scope for using the relative autonomy of particular actors to outwit the big battalions?

A particularly adroit example of how to play a weak hand with consummate skill is given by the architect Zaha Hadid, designing a housing project for the IBA organisation in Berlin. Here, Hadid has been asked to design a three-storey building, but she does not want to do so:

> I always made faces and frowned, so they said mine could be five storeys. So I asked was that an average? I spoke no German, which is a good thing sometimes. I don't speak Japanese or German, so I can always pretend that I don't understand what they are saying. They always say we didn't understand what you asked us so the contract is wrong, and so on. So I played the same game. I asked was it an average of five storeys? And they said yes. After many trials and errors we had two buildings . . . one is eight storeys high and one is three, averaging out five and a half. So I had half a story [sic] to bargain for. Again that was crazy, but I said you did tell me in writing it was an average of five and that was that, as far as I was concerned.[17]

In this situation, Hadid has very little obvious power in the 'master and servant' sense, yet she has achieved more or less what she wanted, through an adroitly handled process of negotiation. If, as relatively powerless people, we want to maximise the impact we can make on urban form, there is much we can learn from this. Let us analyse the situation in more detail, to see if we can get a clearer understanding of how she did it.

First, she has what Shoukry Roweis[18] calls 'knowledge power': she knows things the others do not, and the others need that knowledge. She has something they want, which gives her an initial bargaining position. Second, the strength of this position is enhanced by the fact that Zaha Hadid has a considerable international reputation in the world of avantgarde architecture. This endows her with what the French social anthropologist Pierre Bourdieu calls 'cultural capital';[19] which, no doubt, is amongst the reasons why she was hired in the first place. The logic of their own commissioning decision implies that the people who hired her *must* respect what she says and does. Third, the division of labour in the modern form-production process is organised in such a way that it is usually only 'designers', such as architects, who make proposals for physical designs, except in the most general terms. As an architect, this gives Zaha Hadid a crucial element of initiative, so far as physical form is proposed. It is her proposal, once made, which sets the agenda for the subsequent process of negotiation about form. Taken together, these factors of knowledge power, cultural capital and initiative give Hadid three cards to play in the negotiation game. Clearly she must have played them well, since she gets what she wants. How does her strategy work?

First, we can see that these cards are not played indiscriminately, but are mobilised in support of clear objectives. We can see, for example, that she has a clear conception of the form – or at least, the kind of form – she wants. This conception is set according to her own internal rules. Partly these are rules about what constitutes 'good design' in her terms, but she also has rules about the way architects ought to behave in their relationships with their clients, rules about which potential negotiating ploys would be legitimate in which circumstances. If these internal rules are transgressed, internal psychological sanctions come into force. Beyond a certain point of compromise over the physical form, for example, a sense of guilt – a sense of betraying one's own values – might have become so strong that quitting the job might have been the only way of coping with it. In our example, this point was never reached. We might sense a degree of guilt, however, about working to the letter rather than the evident spirit of the client's brief – a sense of guilt warded off by reference to another, 'higher' internal rule of general fair play. '*They* always say we didn't understand . . . so I played the same game.'[20]

Not all the rules and sanctions within which Hadid has to work are internal ones. There is also a complex envelope of external rules and sanctions which determine the space within which she can operate. For example, too much design compromise – even if she could live with it herself – would run the risk of losing the cultural capital which is bestowed by the acclamation of her peers. This would be a serious matter, for cultural capital brings with it respect, and therefore enhanced negotiating power. Conversely, pushing too hard to get what she wants runs up against the ultimate external sanction of unemployment. Repeated too often, this would lead in turn to the higher order sanction of bankruptcy. Together, these webs of internal and external rules, and the sanctions through which they are enforced, create a 'field of opportunity' within which the designer can work. The success of the negotiation, from her point of view, depends on her ability to get where she wants to within this field. And that, in turn, depends on her ability to mobilise her own resources – resources such as initiative, determination, knowledge and cultural capital – so as to influence the other parties to the negotiation in the most effective way.

The effective targeting of resources depends largely on mobilising them to offer the other actors things they want, or to prevent them from getting these, unless they grant one's own objectives. The practical difficulty here lies in knowing how far the other actors can be pushed before they arrive at the limits of the opportunity field, where they come up against internal or external sanctions on their own actions.

For example, developers working in the private sector have rules about making profits. These are not optional rules, for they are externally enforced through sanctions of bankruptcy; in a capitalist society, private-sector developers have no escape from this, if they want to stay in business. But where does the limit of the field of opportunity lie in this regard? How does the designer (for example) know how far developers can be pushed before they really have to dig in their heels? It is not hard to see that the more the designer (or any other actor) understands the rules and sanctions of the other actors – particularly those with the most power – the more effectively the designer's own resources can be targeted. In this particular case, for example, it would clearly be advantageous for designers to understand how to do developer-type financial feasibility calculations, to prevent the wool being pulled over their eyes too easily.

In the Zaha Hadid example, she is in fact negotiating with a non-profit developer of social housing, so different rules and sanctions apply. Still, even developers like these have rules about how their resources are to be allocated, and targets about how many housing units (for example) they are to build for a given allocation. Sensibly, she accepts these limits; arguing about the form, but proposing a building of the same average height, and therefore the same internal content, as the developers' brief requires. As part of the negotiated deal, the developer is of course getting something else he wants: the 'Zaha Hadid original' for whose production she was hired in the first place. This clearly sets a favourable climate of negotiation from the outset. In turn, this makes it easier for the developer to accept a breach of the 'I pay the piper so I should call the tune' rule which lies somewhere under the surface of all commercial transactions, particularly since this breach is legitimated by the claim of a simple misunderstanding ('I don't understand what they are saying') and enforced by calling on a whole network of legal rules and sanctions too ('you did tell me in writing'). Finally, hanging silently in the air in this negotiation, is the fact that 'I always made faces and frowned.' The fact that she bothers to tell us this suggests that it has some significance. I should like to believe that it shows a woman from an ethnic minority using the issues of gender and ethnicity, which must so often have proved disadvantageous, as positive assets, in a negotiation where the other actors are probably mostly men, bound nowadays by at least some degree of middle-class political correctness.

To summarise, this example has helped us to focus on a number of factors which appear to be important in the form-production battlefield. First there is the question of the power available to the various actors: access to economic or political power, or to valued knowledge or cultural capital. Second, there are the rules according to which the various actors operate in the form-production process. Third, there are the sanctions through which these rules are enforced. And finally there is the issue of initiative: who gets to set the agenda about what?

So far so good: we have developed some ideas which can help us understand what is going on in the negotiations which are central to the form-production process. In the process, however, we have been brought face-to-face with (but rather glossed over) the sheer complexity of these negotiations. Let us now consider the practical implications of this complexity in more depth.

First of all, not only are there many actors, interacting in complex ways, but also they are each addressing issues which are complex in their own right. Each of these issues – even considered separately – comprises a web of loosely-defined considerations, complexly connected into social, political, economic and cultural domains.

Clearly this is a field of work which cannot be carried out by some systematic process of generating and evaluating all the possible options for action. If we try to do so – as some did during the 1960s, for example – we find ourselves in the dilemma identified by the American design theorist John Eberhard, in this amusing (but horribly believable) account from that time:

This has been my experience in Washington when I had money to give away. If I gave a contract to a designer and said, 'The doorknob to my office really doesn't have much imagination, much design content. Will you design me a new doorknob?' He would say 'Yes', and after we establish a price he goes away. A week later he comes back and says 'Mr Eberhard, I've been thinking about that doorknob. First, we ought to ask ourselves whether a doorknob is the best way of opening and closing a door.' I say, 'Fine, I believe in imagination, go to it.' He comes back later and says 'You know, I've been thinking about your problem, and the only reason that we have to worry about doorknobs is that you presume you want a door to your office. Are you sure that a door is best way of controlling egress, exit, and privacy?' 'No, not at all.' 'Well, I want to worry about that problem.' He comes back a week later and says, 'The only reason we have to worry about the aperture problem is that you insist upon having four walls around your office. Are you sure that is the best way of organizing this space for the kind of work you are doing as a bureaucrat?' I say 'No, I'm not sure at all.' Well, this escalates until (and this has literally happened in two contracts, although not through this exact process) our physical designer comes back and he says with a very serious face, 'Mr Eberhard, we have to decide whether capitalistic democracy is the best way to organize our country before I can possibly attack your problem.'[21]

Lest anyone imagines that it might be possible to overcome this problem with the aid of some new generation of supercomputers – admittedly these did not exist when Eberhard wrote his story – let us remember that we should still be faced with the further level of complexity which flows from the difficulties of co-ordinating and controlling the many members of the so-called 'development team', a difficulty which deepens by the day, because the complexity of the form-production process itself appears everywhere to be increasing, though it has advanced further in some countries than in others. At its most complex, in countries like the UK and the USA, the development process involves many professionals influencing the form-generation process alongside the architect.

In discussing how the development process works, Cadman and Austin-Crowe point directly to issues of co-ordination and control:

In order to be really effective, each of these separate roles must be combined within the development team. Indeed one of the most important functions of the developer is to be able to select and bring together a team of advisers who complement each other and work well together.[22]

And yet things somehow get done. And, more surprising still, they seem to get done more or less to the satisfaction of all the mutually ignorant and faintly hostile actors who are involved in the form-production process. We do not always find property developers making spectacularly low profits. Nor are our prisons or psychiatric hospitals full of architects who have blown up their buildings or had nervous breakdowns. Indeed, property developers sometimes make very handsome profits, and it seems that these are not necessarily achieved at the cost of unbearable angst amongst the architects involved. Quite the contrary: the evidence suggests that architects on the whole enjoy their work. In Britain, for example, they are willing to undergo a seven-year period of professional training, in order to join one of the worst-paid and least-respected professions in the country.

The compensation is a high level of job-satisfaction; and when we ask where this comes from, we find that it stems from the 'creative design' aspect of the work. Studying 600 German architects in 1965, for example, Bolte and Richter found that the statement 'my chosen profession should give me the opportunity to do creative work' was chosen as the most important of a number of alternative views by 66 per cent of the architects involved;[23] whilst Salaman – questioning 52 London architects in 1970 – found that for 63 per cent of them 'creativity plus design enjoyment' gave the major part of their work satisfaction.[24] If anything, this orientation may be strengthening. In her 1979 study of over 400 architects in 152 Manhattan firms, for example, the sociologist Judith Blau found that 'of the architects interviewed 98 per cent mentioned creativity as the distinctive feature of architecture when compared to other professions'.[25]

On the face of it, all this is hard to understand. Patrons cannot themselves design, and have difficulty in controlling the efforts of those who can. And yet, in most instances, their complex interests seem to be satisfied, at least to an extent they can live with, through the creative efforts of architects and other professional advisers who, when not actively hostile to those interests, are primarily concerned with other issues altogether. In reaching this point, we have gone as far as the various strands of the 'problematic of action' can take us. We have seen that though human action is central to the form-production process, we cannot understand that process entirely as the outcome of the actions of heroic individuals, nor as the result of orders handed down from masters to servants, nor through the co-ordinating effects of market signals. Far more convincing is the more complex understanding offered by the 'battlefield' problematic, in which actors deploy their resources of economic or political power, valued knowledge or cultural capital, in more or less adroit ways, in attempts to make things happen as they want.

Even this more sophisticated problematic, however, has only taken us so far. Eventually it has left us with an apparent paradox: it seems as though something 'above' all the various actors must be co-ordinating their actions. But . . . it is not plausible to imagine that built form is determined by factors 'outside' human action. How can individual actions be co-ordinated by something which is not outside themselves? If we are to move forward, that is the question which must be addressed.

Notes

1. Rand, A., *The Fountainhead*, Harmondsworth, Penguin, 1943.
2. Rand, A., *The Fountainhead*, Harmondsworth, Penguin, 1994 (1943).
3. For discussion see Cadman, D. and Austin Crowe, L., *Property Development*, London, Spon, 1978.
4. Rand, A. *The Fountainhead*, Harmondsworth, Penguin, 1994 (1943), 714.
5. Phillippo, G., *The Professional Guide to Real Estate Development*, New York, Dow Jones, 1976, 87, cited in Rabinowitz, H., 'The Developer's Vernacular: The Owner's Influence on Building Design', *Journal of Architectural and Planning Research*, Vol. 13, No. 1, 1996, 36.
6. Morton, R., 'Professional Ideologies and the Quality of the British Environment', in *Proceedings of the Bartlett International Summer School*, London, London University, 1992, 10.
7. MacKinnon, D., 'The Nature and Nurture of Creative Talent', *American Psychologist,* 7/171, 1962.
8. Morton, R., *The Teaching of Economics in Schools of Architecture*, London, RIBA, 1990, 73.
9. Hershberger, R.C., 'A study of meaning in architecture', in Sanoff, H. and Cohn, S. (eds), *Proceedings of the First Annual EDRA Conference*, Raleigh, North Carolina State University, 1969; Devlin, K., 'An Examination of Architectural Interpretation: Architects Versus Non-Architects' *Journal of Architectural and Planning Research*, 7 (3), 235–44, 1990; Groat, L., 'Meaning in Post-Modern Architecture: An Examination Using the Methodological Sorting Task', *Journal of Environmental Psychology*, 2 (1), 3–22, 1982.
10. Hubbard, P.J., *Diverging Evaluations of the Built Environment: Planners Versus the Public*, in Neary, S.J., Symes, M.S. and Brown, F.E., *The Urban Experience: A People–Environment Perspective*, London, Spon, 1994.
11. Morton, R., 'Professional Ideologies and the Quality of the British Environment', in *Proceedings of the Bartlett International Summer School*, London, London University, 1992, 11.
12. Rueschemeyer, D., *Power and the Division of Labour*, Cambridge, Polity Press, 1986, 108.

13. Lampugnani, 1992, 114.

14. In Lipman, 1976, 24.

15. Tschumi, B., *Architecture and Disjunction*, Cambridge, Mass., MIT Press, 1996, 20–1.

16. Tschumi, B., *Architecture and Disjunction*, Cambridge, Mass., MIT Press, 1996, 21.

17. Hadid, in Noever, P. (ed.), *Architecture in Transition: Between Deconstruction and New Modernism,* Munich, Prestel, 1991, 51.

18. Roweis, S.T., *Knowledge-Power and Professional Practice*, in Knox, P. L. (ed.), *The Design Professions and the Built Environment,* London, Croom Helm, 1988.

19. Bourdieu, P., *Distinction, A Social Critique of the Judgement of Taste*, trans. Nice, R., London, Routledge and Kegan Paul, 1984.

20. Hadid, in Noever, P. (ed.), *Architecture in Transition: Between Deconstruction and New Modernism,* Munich, Prestel, 1991, 51.

21. Eberhard, J.P., 'We Ought to Know the Difference', in Moore, C.T. (ed.), *Emerging Methods in Environment Design and Planning,* Cambridge, Mass.: MIT Press, 1970, 364–5.

22. Cadman, D. and Austin Crowe, L., *Property Development*, London, Spon, 1978, 208.

23. Bolte, K. M. and Richter, H. J., 'Der Architekt: sein Beruf und seine Arbeit', *Detail*, Vol. 8, No. 5, 1965.

24. Salaman, G., 'Architects and their Work', *Architects' Journal*, Vol. 21, No. 1, 1970.

25. Blau, J. R., *Architects and Firms: A Sociological Perspective on Architectural Practice,* Cambridge, Mass., MIT Press, 1987.

Source and copyright

This chapter was published in its original form as:

Bentley, I. (1999), 'Heroes and Servants, Markets and Battlefields', in Bentley, I. (1999), *Urban Transformations: Power, people and urban design*, Routledge, London, 28–43.

© 1999 Routledge. Reproduced with kind permission of Taylor & Francis Books UK.

35

Private-property decision makers and the quality of urban design

Alan Rowley

[1998]

Urban design needs to be inclusive, rather than exclusive, of sponsors' and users' interests and concerns: . . . it needs to use language that sponsors and users understand. . . . I mean the language of money and the market place—we need to promote the idea that quality sells. (Gummer, 1997, pp. 7–8)

Introduction

Since 1945 the property industry has transformed the character and form of towns and cities across Europe and North America. The total value of property in the UK now exceeds £1 trillion and is approximately equal in value to the equities and gilts markets together. By 1989, immediately before the recession in Britain and elsewhere, approaching 80% of all new construction orders in the UK, by cost, excluding infrastructure, were in the private sector and were for profit-related developments (CSO, 1993). Although the proportion had fallen back to 68% by 1993, it subsequently climbed steadily to reach 75% by 1996 (CSO, 1997). Private-property decision makers— developers, investors and occupiers—exert a power-ful influence on the quality of urban design, yet the role and influence of the property industry on the quality of the built environment and, more specific-ally, the impact on property values of differing urban design approaches, have attracted astonishingly little attention from academics and others in the property industry and the design professions. The resulting vacuum has allowed misconceptions, myths and even prejudices to thrive.

Urban design practitioners and scholars alike have tended to shy away from examining this critical aspect of their work, sometimes in the erroneous belief that it was beyond their field of concern but possibly fearing that it was beyond their compre-hension. Some of Jonathan Barnett's early writings, based on his experience in the Urban Design Group of New York City, represent notable exceptions to urban design's traditional reticence on the subject (Barnett, 1974, 1982) but even Jon Lang's ' " tour de force" of urban design scholarship' (Carmona, 1996, p. 355) only devotes a single chapter, comprising a mere 14 pages, to a discussion of the development process. This said, Lang correctly acknowledges that:

The position that many urban designers take is that understanding the nature of land develop-ment processes is outside their domain of inter-est. . . . This lack of understanding reduces their role in creating the future city and places them at the whim of the development community. (Lang, 1994, p. 371)

In July 1994, the Department of the Environment (DoE) published a discussion document to launch the 'Quality in Town and Country' initiative. The aims of the document and the initiative were to raise awareness of the importance of good design and quality both in individual buildings and in the built environment as a whole; to encourage debate and stimulate ideas about how best to achieve quality in the future; and to challenge others to see what they were prepared to do to help achieve quality.

The Royal Institution of Chartered Surveyors (RICS), Britain's property profession, responded to the DoE's initiative by commissioning research to examine the involvement of private property decision makers in urban design. The DoE supported and actively participated in the study which was undertaken by a team, led by the writer, from the Department of Land Management and Development at The University of Reading, in association with DEGW, planners, architects and designers.

This paper outlines the aims and objectives of the research; it describes the approach adopted; and it summarizes its findings and conclusions.

Aims and objectives of the research

The aim of the study was to assess how closely and in what ways property developers—including housebuilders, investors and occupiers—become involved in the process of urban development and design, and to determine in what ways and to what extent they can and do influence the quality of urban design.

In essence, the research sought to develop a more holistic appreciation of the processes by which quality of urban design may be achieved; how this quality is delivered and subsequently maintained; and who is involved, the extent of their influence and their potential role in securing quality of urban design.

Programme, approach and research methodology

The research was undertaken during the period July–October 1995. It focused on mainstream developments—essentially, offices, shops and housing—and it concentrated exclusively on the processes of private sector profit-seeking development for investment or sale, and on the agencies involved. The research entailed a literature review; the formulation of a checklist of urban design considerations for use as a common vocabulary in the research; the completion of five case studies of contrasting developments; and six focus-group sessions held to obtain the views of retail and office occupiers, investors, commercial developers, housebuilders and designers.

Urban design considerations

Urban design involves people who exercise professional skill as designers as well as those who exercise influence including developers, investors and occupiers. The quality of urban design is the product of the conscious and unconscious design decisions of many different interests and individuals. Urban designers have difficulty defining *urban design* and agreeing what constitutes good urban design amongst themselves; consider, then, the problem of defining and discussing *quality of urban design* with unselfconscious urban designers! To overcome this obstacle, 50 urban design considerations were identified which were grouped into four bundles of concerns. These were functional and social use considerations; natural environment and sustainability considerations; visual considerations; and considerations relating to the quality of the urban experience.

The 50 urban design considerations, and the list was not intended to be exclusive, underpin a range of competing views about what constitutes quality of urban design (Rowley, 1994). One of the research tasks was to establish whether and how far developers, investors and occupiers thought these considerations were relevant to their concerns and priorities. Developers and their designers normally had little difficulty in attaching a weight to individual considerations, but investors and particularly commercial occupiers were usually more comfortable prioritizing groups of broadly related considerations: for example, the visual impact of the development and the 'feel' or 'buzz' of a place.

The five developments were:

- *Arlington Business Park, Theale, Berkshire*: In a lakeside setting, on the edge of Reading, adjacent to the M4.
- *Ealing Broadway Centre, West London*: A mixed-use development comprising 104 000 m^2 of accommodation on a 5 ha site in the town centre.
- *Brindleyplace, Birmingham*: A mixed-use development on a 7 ha inner-city site.
- *Fair Ridge, High Wycombe, Buckinghamshire*: A housing development on a 5 ha, former playing field site, on the outskirts of High Wycombe, close to the M40.

- *Great Notley Garden Village, Braintree, Essex*: A free-standing 'garden village' for 5000 people, on a 186 ha greenfield site south of Braintree.

Table 35.1 is an assessment of the relative urban design qualities of each of the five developments. There are considerable dangers in making such comparisons and the results should be treated with caution. Nevertheless the figures provide an indication of how close each development comes to achieving a 'very good quality' of urban design judged in terms of each of the four groups of urban design considerations as well as in overall terms. The assessment was based on a number of sources comprising comparatively brief visits to each development by the two professionally qualified designers in the research team, each independently scoring the development against every consideration on the checklist and subsequently arriving at an agreed performance rating; reports and comments by other team members; and discussions and interviews with developers, investors, commercial occupiers and residents. In the event, the judgement of the professional designers in the research team was the dominant influence on the results of this assessment process.

The developments were first assessed in respect of each consideration on a scale of 0 (absent quality) up to 4 points (very good quality). An assessment was then made of the urban design quality of a development under each of the four groups of considerations (functional & social use; natural environment & sustainability; visual; and the urban experience). Each consideration was assumed to be of equal significance to all other considerations—a very contentious premise—and the individual ratings were aggregated and expressed as a mean average rating on the scale 0–4 for that bundle of considerations. Finally, an overall assessment was made of the urban design quality of each development. Each of the four groups of considerations was assumed to be of equal significance with the other groups—another questionable assumption—and the mean group averages were aggregated and expressed as an overall mean average rating on the scale 0–4.

Other limitations of the assessment include the fact that three of the five case study developments were incomplete; there are ambiguities, overlaps and contradictions between the urban design considerations; the lack of comments by the users—workers, shoppers and passers-by—of the three commercial developments; the restricted times of visits to developments; the lack of quantitative assessment where

considerations allowed, for example of noise levels; and the biases of the two professionally qualified assessors.

Response to the research objectives

Role and importance of urban design considerations

All of the property people involved in the research incorporated urban design considerations into their decision making in some way. They differed in the range and nature of the considerations; the weight they attached to different considerations; and the importance they attached to the quality of urban design relative to their other priorities. The 50 urban design considerations are not equally relevant to all types of development and location and the size or scale of development is also an important factor. Achieving quality of urban design in a town centre shopping development involves giving different weight to different considerations from those of an office-led development in a similar location; and a housing development on the edge of a town is different again.

Developers attached more importance to urban design than either investors or occupiers and they also took the widest range of considerations into account. It seems likely that with developments of the type considered in the five case studies, commercial property developers attach more importance to urban design quality than housebuilders. Urban design considerations can play a significant part in the decision making of commercial property developers but since some development characteristics attract a greater premium than others, developers emphasize such features and tend to downplay those qualities which are less rewarding financially. There is less consensus between housebuilders about the range and importance of urban design considerations. Most volume housebuilders focus their attention on the dwelling, often at the expense of its setting, but they will look at any angle to get a competitive edge. One angle is something special in terms of the street scene. Housebuilders tend to aim for 'appropriate' or 'good enough' quality[1] and believe they have little incentive to take a longer term view. Relatively few residential developers have experience of developing urban sites, unlike their commercial counterparts.

Investors and occupiers take a similar range of urban design considerations into account but

TABLE 35.1
Assessment of the urban design quality of the case study developments

URBAN DESIGN CONSIDERATIONS	COMMERCIAL LED			RESIDENTIAL LED	
	THEALE	EALING	BRINDLEYPLACE	FAIR RIDGE	GREAT NOTLEY
Functional and social use					
(1) Convenience, safety and comfort in the devt. of:					
• pedestrians	2	4	4	2	3
• car users	4	3	3	4	3
• cyclists	1	3	2	2	4
• public transport users	1	3	3	1	3
(2) Servicing/refuse arrangements	3	4	4	4	4
(3) Special needs	2	2	3	2	3
(4) Community etc. facilities in devt.	0	3	4	0	3
(5) Accessibility of other uses from devt.	2	4	4	1	2
(6) The integration of pedestrians and vehicles	2	3	4	2	3
(7) Accessibility of devt. by car	4	4	4	2	3
Accessibility of devt. by bus/train/cycle/on foot	1	4	4	1	2
(8) Security and crime	3	3	4	3	3
(9) The user-friendly design of spaces	3	3	3	1	3
(10) Freedom of access within the development	2	3	4	3	3
(11) Signing of buildings	2	3	2	2	2
(12) Overlooking and privacy	3	3	3	2	2
Total score (maximum = 64)	35	52	55	32	46
Mean average performance	2.2	3.3	3.4	2.0	2.9
(Modal average)	(2)	(3)	(4)	(2)	(3)
Natural environment and sustainability					
(13) Integration of site features	4	3	4	2	4
(14) Microclimate in spaces	2	3	3	2	2
(15) Noise/air quality in spaces	3	2	2	2	3
(16) Tidiness/cleanliness	4	3	3	2	3
(17) Wildlife	3	0	0	1	3
(18) Trees, vegetation and water	4	1	2	1	3
(19) Energy efficiency	2	2	2	1	2
(20) Adaptability	3	2	3	2	3
(21) Efficient use of land and space	2	3	4	2	2
(22) Durability of materials and finishes	2	3	3	2	3
(23) Costs of maintaining spaces	2	2	3	2	2
Total score (maximum = 44)	31	24	29	19	30
Mean average performance	2.8	2.2	2.6	1.7	2.7
(Modal average)	(2)	(3)	(3)	(2)	(3)

(*Continued*)

Table 35.1 (*Continued*)

URBAN DESIGN CONSIDERATIONS	CASE STUDY DEVELOPMENTS				
	COMMERCIAL LED			RESIDENTIAL LED	
	THEALE	EALING	BRINDLEYPLACE	FAIR RIDGE	GREAT NOTLEY
Visual					
(24) External design and appearance	3	3	3	2	3
(25) Visual relationship with context	3	3	4	2	3
(26) Variety of buildings	2	3	4	2	3
(27) Landscape design	3	3	4	1	3
(28) Visual order and coherence	3	3	3	2	4
(29) Formality or informality	3	3	3	1	3
(30) Definition of space	3	3	4	2	3
(31) Visual grain	2	3	3	1	2
(32) Human scale	2	3	3	2	3
(33) Density of devt.	2	3	3	2	2
(34) Defined entrances	2	2	3	1	3
(35) Design of street furniture, art etc.	2	3	3	1	3
Total score (maximum = 48)	30	35	40	19	35
Mean average performance	2.5	2.9	3.3	1.6	2.9
(Modal average)	(2/3)	(3)	(3)	(2)	(3)
The urban experience					
(36) Area image	3	3	3	2	3
(37) Mix of uses	0	3	3	0	2
(38) Assemblage of buildings, spaces and uses	1	3	4	1	3
(39) Pedestrian flows	1	4	3	1	2
(40) Evening activity	0	2	4	0	1
(41) Opportunities for entertainment	0	2	4	0	1
(42) Opportunities for meeting friends	1	3	4	0	1
(43) Opportunities for people-watching	1	3	4	1	1
(44) Range of sensory experience	2	2	3	1	3
(45) Sense of arrival	2	3	4	2	3
(46) Legibility	2	3	3	2	3
(47) The freedom of experience	2	2	3	3	3
(48) Scope for personalization	1	1	2	4	2
(49) The sense of community	1	2	3	2	3
(50) The sense of history or place	1	2	3	1	3
Total score (maximum = 60)	18	38	50	20	34
Mean average performance	1.2	2.5	3.3	1.3	2.3
(Modal average)	(1)	(3)	(3)	(1)	(3)
Overall mean average performance of the four groups of considerations	2.2	2.7	3.2	1.7	2.7
(overall modal average—all considerations)	(2)	(3)	(3)	(2)	(3)

investors tend to take a longer term view and are, therefore, more inclined to seek 'enduring' or 'sustainable' quality. Occupiers of commercial property see urban design as potentially important but other short-term considerations dominate their thinking and their decisions. Residential owner-occupiers attach most importance to securing value for money from the dwelling itself, at least when purchasing a new property. However, once residents have moved in their priorities may change. It was not part of the brief to consider the importance of urban design considerations to purchasers of second-hand homes but this is certainly an area which merits further research. House-buyers, like the other occupiers, are constrained by considerations of location, price and choice.

Benefits and constraints on taking urban design considerations into account

Developers

Property developers must manage a host of financial, logistical and production tasks and resolve the varied, often conflicting, objectives of all the parties involved in the development process. Developers usually bear the immediate responsibility for the financial success or failure of a project; and for many people, it is the developer who is ultimately responsible for the quality and appearance of a development.

Property development is a challenging task entailing a network of operations including market research, site acquisition, project financing, securing planning permission and other approvals, design and costing, construction, marketing, letting and disposal. Design is only one aspect of a complex process and developers see all aspects of design as essentially a means to a financial end and not as an end in itself. Developers' general design concerns include: investor and occupier requirements, preferences and tastes—in particular the 'price' they will pay for a product that responds to these; flexibility of both building and site layout to meet changing circumstances; buildability; cost efficiency and value for money; visual impact including the 'image' of the completed development as an aid to sale or letting; and the management implications including the 'running costs' of the completed development. One challenge for developers is to influence the design process in a way which maximizes their own goals without stifling their designers' creativity and performance (Buckley, 1990).

Developers see several benefits resulting from paying attention to urban design considerations. These are often interrelated but they include helping to secure sites for development; winning over public opinion in support of a development proposal and promoting a wider sense of involvement and 'ownership' of a development; creating a new location or 'address'; increasing the financial profitability of a development; giving a development a distinct and marketable visual image; ensuring product differentiation; and attracting people to the development, for example, to provide trade for retailers.

Developers acknowledge that in some circumstances, some of these benefits can only be fully realized by adjustments to the 'usual' processes of development and urban design: these include closer collaboration with planning and other authorities; and more active processes of public participation and consultation. With larger, more complex and longer running developments, time spent building mutual respect and understanding may pay dividends later in facilitating approval for the more detailed stages of design and when debating the need for making changes in response to market circumstances. Involving 'the public' may even result in people coming forward to run facilities within a development and is, ultimately, all part of a wider urban design consideration—engendering a sense of community and pride of place.

Developers acknowledge the difficulties of quantifying the benefit they derive from the quality of urban design but this has to be seen in the context of their business and it is clear that urban design considerations do matter to them. Whilst it is easy to cost a development it is much more difficult to place a value on what are often intangible qualities, all the more so if a particular solution is innovative. So developers are frequently driven back onto a 'gut feeling' although a few claim to be able to measure the returns on investment in design quality. For this reason, persuasive architects and masterplanners can have a significant influence on property developers, helping to convince them of the added value better design may realize even if this involves an increased cost initially. Brindleyplace provides several illustrations of this. For example, an office building designed by Porphyrious Associates incorporates a 54-metre high clock tower as a landmark in the locality; this feature is reported to have added £0.5 million to construction costs but it will not increase the rental value of the completed building. Housebuilders are apparently more aware than commercial developers of the relationship between the costs of an improved quality of urban design and market price and this is presumably due to the nature of their product and their business which is more akin to retailing.

The research identified several factors which developers acknowledge influence and sometimes constrain the attention they give to urban design. These are customer—occupiers, investors or housebuyers—requirements, preferences and priorities; the timing of the development related to market conditions and the business cycle; land ownership, costs and values; the size of the project and the timescale for the development; and finally the role, contribution and general attitude of the public authorities towards a particular development.

Investors

Property investment funds tend to adopt an acquisition policy that focuses on properties that are acceptable to a large number of similar institutions. They seek properties that will produce an increasing rental income over a long period of time; be flexible and easily adapted to alternative occupiers; be acceptable to tenants with sound credit ratings; and be acceptable to other investing institutions. So far as urban design is concerned, these considerations lead investors to concentrate on those attributes of a development they judge appropriate for the expected demands of the target or probable occupiers. Sometimes this might involve placing considerable emphasis on the design characteristics of developments that promise to attract occupiers with aspirations about the kind of property and environment their company should occupy. In other cases, investors will place little emphasis on urban design considerations because they do not expect the occupiers to be sensitive to such concerns. If some investors are sceptical about the importance of good design, it reflects their perception of the occupiers' indifference. In the case studies where the viability of the project depended on the creation of a premium or unique image, at Brindleyplace for example, there was a clear recognition that attention to all aspects of design, private or public, would be a worthwhile proposition.

Investors believe that if the quality of urban design has any pay-off it will show up in improving the investment performance of the properties either by enhancing their initial rental value or by lengthening their economic life. One of the surprising features emerging from the research was that several investors envisaged that they or their clients would participate in the investment for a period that would extend only just beyond the first rent review of the property—in practice, between six and eight years.

This expected holding period would appear to be an important factor in constraining the decisions taken by investors. Given this approach to the selling-on of assets, it is not at all surprising that investors have to bear in mind the value that will be placed on their properties by potential buyers, and this consideration will be emphasized in times when the real rate of interest is low. Historically, developers and investors have relied on rental growth to reduce the burden of loan interest over a relatively short period of time. As we move, however, into a period in which it is assumed that the level of inflation will remain low and real rates of interest will reduce, the expected long-term performance of investments will have relatively greater impact on investment values and performance in the short run.

The fact that investors may plan to hold their property investments for a relatively short period does not necessarily make them biased in favour of short-term criteria. If property investors plan to sell investments within a six- to eight-year period, they may be concerned to ensure that the condition of the public realm at the time of sale is well maintained. Thus, they might seek more considered design solutions or approve the use of higher quality materials. Such investors can justify this level of attention to urban design because it should maximize the profitability of the investment over the holding period. In times of economic stability and strong competition, there will be incentives to produce features of the development that create value and distinguish one property development from another. But because the property market is characteristically cyclical, investors sometimes find that their expectations of rising rents and capital values do not materialize. In these circumstances the quality of urban design is seen to be expendable. Cutting costs to make the development viable appears to be a considered response of investors to unanticipated change in the property market and to this extent poor urban design may partly be a consequence of the property cycle.

The perceived benefits associated with urban design considerations at Arlington Business Park are relatively parochial and conservative. The investors—and there are several—emphasize their property's intrinsic qualities to its occupants and little benefit is assumed to stem from the relationship between one building and the next. Privacy and control are stressed and the ability of occupants to alter and personalize their own environment is seen as being of no significance. The image of the business park, for example, is seen to be important in so far as it provides no surprises to investors or clients. The quality of the overall vision of the development can be expressed in terms of a trust in the developer who is known to provide a good standard product that is known to attract good quality occupants. Investors do not see a need to require additional features that could improve its market position: in essence, demand is seen to follow and reflect the location of the scheme and the reputation of its developer.

With Brindleyplace, one benefit of the quality of urban design is the sense of prestige attached to the investment. The reputation of the developer is also seen to provide some justification and confidence to the decision to invest in the project. Both the buildings and the public spaces are seen as being constructed to a high specification which should make properties attractive to other investors if they are sold in a few years' time by which stage the development will have been completed. This is consistent with the argument that quality pays in lengthening the life of the investment.

The requirements of occupiers constrain the contribution investors make to the quality of urban design. Investors must consider the longer term management implications of developments: both the costs of day-to-day management and maintenance and the acceptability of these to occupiers as well as the scope to maintain overall control of the environment ensuring that future changes by one party do not undermine the value of the rest.

Occupiers

The importance and priority given to urban design considerations by commercial occupiers is related to business objectives. The benefits may include the ability to recruit staff which is felt to be especially important when starting a new business; the ability to retain existing staff particularly when major relocation and/or rationalization is being undertaken and there are specific groups of employees which must be retained; improved productivity in terms of staff working longer hours or just greater efficiency; improved turnover or sales especially for retailers but also access to clients for business service organizations; and less distraction especially if moving from a building with poor quality urban design where lack of parking, difficult access, and concerns about personal safety and security may be diverting the energy of staff.

Occupiers feel that it is difficult to measure these benefits either as part of the initial decision-making process or as part of a post-occupancy evaluation. When making occupational decisions occupiers build up a matrix of criteria related to both the general

location and the building itself. Many of these criteria are easy to quantify: rents, rates, communications, usable floor area and so on. Conversely, many urban design considerations are seen as subjective and therefore intrinsically more difficult to quantify.

The benefits of good urban design are related to perceptions of cause and effect rather than a clearly definable benefit. For example, if rents are cheaper or the internal space can be used more intensively, the decision maker can be certain that the cost of occupancy will fall. But if an organization moves to a site with improved access and parking or attractive surroundings, it is much more difficult to quantify the precise increase in productivity, let alone to identify the cause of that increase with any certainty. There are numerous external and internal influences on many of the benefits potentially attributable to the quality of urban design, and only a few organizations attempt to assess whether better design has secured those benefits or whether other influences, such as a change in the local economy or improved information technology, have been the prime causes. Retailers are the exception, especially the large multiples which are able to benchmark shops in their portfolio and so begin to distinguish cause and consequence. As a result they can, for example, measure the impact on sales before and after an improvement to the quality of the local environment such as the pedestrianization of a high street.

The main constraints identified by occupiers to giving urban design considerations more attention and priority in their decision making relate to these kinds of issues. The process by which an organization decides where to locate moves progressively from macro to micro considerations. First, an appropriate location is identified. That location decision is generally driven by questions of access to clients, customers and staff. Once a general location has been identified and accepted, individual buildings or sites which are on the market at the time are identified. Each of these is then assessed in terms of whether it will be 'fit for the purpose' and at what cost. As a consequence there are only a small number of properties which will be considered feasible, possibly as few as two or three. This lack of real choice is a major constraint and under such circumstances quality of urban design is a factor which would be 'nice to have' but, in practice, is usually seen as an optional extra.

Occupational decisions are commonly not made in isolation but with reference to the rest of the organization's portfolio. Organizations can be concerned about offices being seen as 'too good' for the purpose. This view is based on the misapprehension that good urban design is necessarily expensive but the question is asked 'why is that basic administrative centre in such a good (expensive) building or part of such a high quality development?' Such questioning reflects a concern for both staff and shareholders. Organizations are concerned about equity for staff, that is providing a similar quality of environment for staff in the organization at the same level. They are also concerned that their shareholders do not feel that the management are wastefully spending money on a 'glossy headquarters' which could be better invested in the core business. This wider context can be a significant constraint particularly for organizations with large and diverse occupational portfolios.

Another major constraint for organizations relates to a much wider issue affecting British industry—short-termism. Organizations have shorter and shorter planning horizons which are reinforced by the capital market structure in the UK. Most organizations are operating to a three- to five-year planning horizon at most. There appears to be a view amongst occupiers that good urban design is more about long-term rather than short-term benefit. Conversely, this issue can highlight a benefit to be derived from good urban design since the quality of a development and of its setting can enhance its disposability. As part of the risk assessment of a building, the ability to vacate and or dispose of a property has become increasingly important and high-quality urban design may be one of the elements which makes a property and its location more acceptable in the long term. The issue of short-termism is unlikely to diminish as organizations are going through a constant process of refocusing and reorganizing but only those organizations which recognize the role of urban design in risk reduction are likely to appreciate this benefit.

A final question raised by occupiers concerns who is or should ultimately be responsible for the quality of urban design? In general, occupiers do not consider quality of urban design to be their responsibility because it is the wider community and not their enterprise which derives the greater benefit. There are some exceptions, major retailers for example who have a vested business interest in the vitality and viability of town and city centres, but most office occupiers see themselves as one small player who can make only a limited impact. This may be a particularly British attitude based on the high degree of individualism with the emphasis on private rights rather than the public realm.

Residential owner-occupiers

The research was only concerned with the attitudes and decisions of the initial purchasers of new houses: it did not address the crucial issue of the effect quality of environment and design may play in the purchase and long-term value of second-hand homes.

Housing and the home environment is quite unlike any other product and strong personal and emotional considerations colour residents' impressions of their surroundings. Choice affects a person's satisfaction with his or her dwelling but when purchasing a new home, choice can be surprisingly limited when other considerations are taken into account. Previous studies of initial purchasers of new houses of the kind typified in the two residential case studies have identified several factors affecting house-purchasers' decisions. These include the price and value, locality, house, estate, liveability, features, and the quality of construction (Bishop & Davison, 1989; Winter et al., 1993). Initial purchasers are influenced by the design features and qualities of residential developments but they may be willing to trade off better urban design against individual features of their own residence. However, the research findings suggest that where competition provides choice at least some purchasers will respond to good urban design.

The sentiments expressed by the residents of Fair Ridge and Great Notley tend to confirm the findings of the earlier studies. At Fair Ridge considerations of location, price and value for money dominated the decision to buy and this would seem to confirm the developer's decision to build to an 'appropriate quality' and no more. Great Notley, on the other hand, points to the potential value to be derived from designing and developing to a higher standard. The level of housebuilding activity in that part of Essex affords prospective purchasers real choice, and the residents the research team met seem to have made a very conscious choice of location and 'estate' which reflects the importance they attached to the quality of their surroundings as well as to the quality of the dwellings.

A consequence is that the residents at Great Notley appear to have taken a longer-term view and are prepared to take more trouble and effort in nurturing and supporting a communal sense of pride. In contrast, the community feeling at Fair Ridge did not seem so strong and there was a sense that the public spaces are not so jealously preserved. Such an inference would be consistent with the view that sensitivity to the urban design of residential development is a factor in preserving the relative value of the individual properties over time.

Incentives and other measures

Few suggestions were made to the research team but analysis of the case studies highlights some pointers. Decisions affecting the quality of urban design are made initially by commercial and residential developers in the early stages of a scheme. In making these decisions, developers understandably are strongly influenced by what they perceive to be the aspirations of the occupiers and investors.

The three case studies which performed best against the checklist of criteria were the schemes which had several characteristics in common: local authority ambition and action to secure a quality of development that reflected a breadth of urban design considerations; single ownership or control of the site making early masterplanning possible; public/private partnership creating greater planning certainty—Brindleyplace and Ealing; if not partnership, then a strong public/private sector collaboration through the planning process—Great Notley; and public participation, reducing the risks of delays and the increased costs which might result from public confrontation. The two case studies which performed least well against the criteria of urban design quality avoided public/private partnership, collaboration or participation and, in the case of Fair Ridge, incurred considerable costs as a result of a confrontational planning approach.

Some developers, especially housebuilders, who build down to a 'good enough' standard do not allow adequate design time in the early stages of a scheme. If they are also operating in a confrontational environment and/or are developing against market trends, as was the case at Fair Ridge, it is easy to see how scarce resources are siphoned off, possibly to fight planning appeals, leaving little room for imaginative detailed design thereafter.

Incentives to encourage developers and other property decision makers to pay more attention to the quality of urban design could therefore start by seeking to provide greater certainty within the planning process through collaboration. Increased certainty reduces development and investment risk; less risk means a lower return on capital becomes acceptable which, in turn, can release more finance and other resources which can be devoted to design quality.

Nevertheless, there are no quick fixes for achieving quality of urban design. Some of the experience with specifically design-related incentives highlights the limitations of such approaches and the difficulties of isolating the qualities to be promoted.

A more widespread understanding of the nature of the development process and of the challenges, difficulties and risks involved, allied with a more collaborative approach to planning, may well be more successful.

Conclusion

General conclusions

The purpose of the research was to study the involvement of private-property decision makers in urban design. The project was the first in the UK to seek the views of those who directly pay for the majority of the built environment. This is largely unexplored territory and it transcends several established academic and professional disciplines. At the end of the study, it was obvious to the research team that they had only seen the tip of the iceberg and the exercise was best seen as a reconnaissance study. Some organizations and individuals showed a reluctance to become involved in the research but many responded positively and the topic aroused their interest.

Urban design, like most aspects of public policy, is a 'wicked problem' (Rittel & Webber, 1974). We long for a clear definition of what it is and for a simple recipe for achieving good design but this is impossible. Quality cannot be easily measured. The public realm fulfils a variety of requirements and we do not all have the same needs of the same places.

The checklist of design considerations was a research device to define the scope and concerns of urban design. The considerations provide a surrogate measure of quality. Developers, investors and occupiers need to be encouraged to give these considerations a higher priority in their decision making; equally, they need to demand environments which reflect the breadth of urban design concerns and not simply a selection which only satisfies the short-term interests of the immediate client. This will require better urban design; not necessarily more costly design but certainly different design. Adequate time must be allowed for this within the development process.

All design involves making choices and striking compromises between the design characteristics of a product; urban design is no exception. The qualities of an environment are the product of the circumstances, values and times in which it was produced. In some respects, the design of the Ealing Broadway Centre now seems out-dated; in contrast, Brindleyplace clearly reflects contemporary thinking and approaches. The character, performance and our experience of places change through time. This fact is rarely taken into account when schemes are being proposed; when investors (or owner-occupiers usually in the case of housing in Britain) decide to buy a development; or when the first occupier decides to take a lease on a property.

We might like to imagine that places will age gracefully. Few do and in reality all require constant maintenance and they tend to become obsolete. Developers, investors and occupiers increasingly consider the life-cycle costs of buildings. We need to show a similar level of awareness and adopt appropriate responses to the care of the public realm. The essential structure of the public realm should last for decades. Too often in urban design short-term considerations and features become confused with the long-term ones. Yet once a development is completed, its essential features cannot be changed without considerable expense.

Achieving a sustainable quality of urban design demands such insights and understanding. However, the need to adopt a longer term view of quality is counter to one significant trend as the horizons of commercial, financial and political decision makers are getting ever shorter (Gibson *et al.*, 1996). Quality of urban design depends on a horizon longer than most participants hold at present, and a sense of pride of ownership and the principle of stewardship of the public realm need to be reinforced or reintroduced.

The processes that create urban environments are complex and the search for quality of urban design seems to run in a circle. Society seeks improved quality; the developer aspires to meet the customers' needs as does the investor; but the requirements and aspirations of most customers are usually too self-centred to meet society's wishes. The challenge is to find ways of breaking the cycle. Planning policy is important but it is only one piece of the jigsaw. The development process is subject to powerful external influences including the ideas and values people hold about the kind of environments they want to occupy, own and use. Education and debate are two of the keys to changing people's expectations and ways of working. To be effective, education must be underpinned by informed inquiry and research; and it must be supported by example and leadership.

Achievements, trends and outlook

The standards of urban design in Britain appear to be improving, albeit gradually, and there are a number of schemes which demonstrate a real concern for the quality of the public realm. Some of these developments had their roots prior to the recession, but others are apparently responses to the switch to an occupier's or buyer's market and to increased competition generally.

There is a growing awareness of the importance of investing in quality, sometimes for long-term commercial reasons, but also because failure to take a long-term view often results in society as a whole paying, possibly dearly, later on. From a narrow perspective, organizations increasingly recognize the importance people, their knowledge and skills play in ensuring the success of business; and the influential role of brand image and the contribution that quality of environment may play in this. These are important trends and ones which could drive enterprises to look ahead and demand better quality of urban design. Whether they lead to development in more or less urban locations is uncertain: this will be the product of a number of influences, including planning and transport policies and public fiscal policy. These changes and trends should help raise standards of urban design. However, ultimately there has to be a demand for, and a willingness to invest in, quality. With urban design, the sum of the standards people individually set and accept is the standard we collectively enjoy.

One overriding lesson from the research for professional and academic urban designers alike is well summarized by Jonathan Barnett's comment, written over 20 years ago:

To produce significant results . . . urban designers must rid themselves of the notion that their work will be contaminated by an understanding of . . . real estate decisions. It is not always necessary to approve; it is essential to understand. (Barnett, 1974, p. 12)

The interrelationship between urban design and the planning process is well established and comprehended even if, for some people, it is an area of continuing debate and controversy. By comparison, the interrelationships between urban design, the development process and the property industry are poorly understood, underresearched and rarely written about. Until this situation is remedied, urban designers are likely to remain at the whim of the development community; similarly most private-property decision makers will still fail to appreciate the extent to which they can profit from investing in quality of urban design.

Note

1. For many, at least in Britain, the notion that *better buildings mean better business* is new and debatable. The dominant attitude in private-property decision making is still the 'appropriate' quality view: this holds that high-quality development, however defined, is unnecessary so long as there is some sort of market for the development at a lower standard; which may be easier to maintain, at least in the short-term; which may demand less skill and care to produce; and which, it is assumed, can be delivered at a lower initial cost. In short, a bargain-basement philosophy! The opposing attitude is that high quality helps generate long-term commercial success: this is termed the 'sustainable' quality view (Wiggington, 1993).

References

Barnett, J. (1974) *Urban Design as Public Policy* (New York, Architectural Record).

Barnett, J. (1982) *An Introduction to Urban Design* (New York, Harper & Row).

Bishop, J. & Davison, I. (1989) *Good Product: Could The Service Be Better? A Study of Purchasers of New Homes* (London, Housing Research Foundation).

Bookout, L.W., Beyard, M.D. & Fader, S.W. (1994) *Value by Design: Landscape, Site Planning and Amenities* (Washington, DC, Urban Land Institute).

Buckley, M.P. (1990) Creative design management, *Urban Land*, April, May and June.

Carmona, M. (1996) Book review of Lang, J. (1994) Urban design: the American experience, *Journal of Urban Design*, 1(3), pp. 355–356.

Central Statistical Office (CSO) (1993) *Monthly Digest of Statistics*, No. 588, December (London, HMSO).

Central Statistical Office (CSO) (1997) *Monthly Digest of Statistics*, No. 616, April (London, HMSO).

Department of the Environment (DoE) (1994) *Quality in Town and Country* (London, DoE).

Gibson, V.A., Rowley, A. & Ward, C. (1996) Does short-termism affect the quality of urban design?, paper presented at The Royal Institution of Chartered Surveyors' *Cutting Edge* Conference, Bristol, 20–21 September.

Gummer, Rt. Hon. J. (1997) A comment by the Secretary of State for the Environment, *Journal of Urban Design*, 2(1), pp. 5–7.

Lang, J. (1994) *Urban Design: The American Experience* (New York, Van Nostrand Reinhold).

Powe, N.A., Garrod, G.D. & Willis, K.G. (1995) Valuation of urban amenities using an hedonic price model, *Journal of Property Research*, 12(5), pp. 137–147.

Rittel, H.W.J. & Webber, M.M. (1974) Wicked problems, in: *Man-Made Futures: Readings in Society, Technology and Design* (London, Hutchinson Educational/Open University).

Rowley, A. (1994) Definitions of urban design, *Planning Practice and Research*, 9(3), pp. 179–197.

Rowley, A., Gibson, V. & Ward, C. (1996) *Quality of Urban Design: A Study of the Involvement of Private Property Decision-makers in Urban Design* (London, Royal Institution of Chartered Surveyors.)

Vandell, K.D. & Lane, J.S. (1989) The economics of architecture and urban design: some preliminary findings, *American Real Estate and Urban Economics Association Journal*, 17(2), pp. 235–260.

Wiggington, M. (1993) Architecture: the rewards of excellence, in: *Better Buildings Mean Better Business*, Report of Symposium, pp. 4–7 (London, Royal Society of Arts).

Winter, J., Coombes, T. & Farthing, S. (1993) Satisfaction with space around the home on large private sector estates, *Town Planning Review*, 64(1), pp. 65–89.

Source and copyright

This chapter was published in its original form as:

Rowley, A. (1998), 'Private Property Decision Makers and the Quality of Urban Design', *Journal of Urban Design*, 3 (2), 151–73.

Reprinted with permission of Taylor and Francis Ltd (http://www.tandf.co.uk/journals).

36

The debate on design review

Brenda Case Scheer
[1994]

Design review is a procedure, like zoning, used by cities and towns to control the aesthetics and design of development projects. Although it is a new phenomena, its adoption by local jurisdictions is growing at a rate that compares to the rapid adoption of zoning in the 1930s. I have recently completed a national survey of planning agencies in more than 370 cities and towns on the topic of their design review processes; 83 percent of the towns surveyed had some form of design review. My initial assumption—that aesthetic review was primarily restricted to historic districts and structures—proved to be wrong. Only twelve respondents reserved design review exclusively for historic structures or districts. Therefore, we can conclude that more than 85 percent of the cities and towns in this country have moved into the arena of design review of ordinary, nonhistoric development projects. This widespread use of design review is also new: 60 percent of the respondents with design review have introduced it in the last twelve years, 10 percent in the last two years.

Design review is a difficult and controversial process that needs thoroughgoing, professional criticism before it is introduced on a wide scale. In spite of the astonishing growth in the adoption of design review, it was very difficult to find resources about design review that did not paint it as a rosy picture, a no-lose situation for planners, designers, and citizens alike. Most planners who answered my survey are satisfied with their design review process; the fine-tuning of guidelines was seen as the major improvement to be made, along with giving themselves more autonomy to make design decisions without board interference. Citizens appear in favor, too, as they survey the results of thirty years of McDonald wastelands and trash spec office buildings, and hope that design

review will solve the problem. Architects, on the other hand, are curmudgeons of a sort, being somewhat reluctant to throw themselves in with design review fans. Architects who responded to our survey for the AIA consider design review "petty, meddling, and useless" (25 percent), while the largest group said they thought it was a "good concept, but had serious flaws" (50 percent) (Gordon, 1992).

Why is this hard look at design review so important? In the end, what does it really matter if we decide to control signs and parking lot landscaping, and require bricks instead of clapboard? Why does it matter if we take the ultimate decisions about the design of buildings away from architects and their clients and put it in the hands of planners, lay persons, and design review boards? Why should anyone but a few prima-donna architects care about this regulation of aesthetics in the city? The massive adoption of design review seems like a tidal wave of approval of this method of development control. Why should we not happily lay aside the admittedly flawed way in which cities and buildings have been built in recent years and respond to the new call, indeed a new recognition of the importance of physical design in the environment?

Using the data from the planners' survey and from the architects' survey, I would like to outline the scope of design review, who is doing it, what they hope to get out of it, and the broad areas of controversy that are being defined across this country and abroad.

Definition

Design Review refers to the process by which private and public development proposals receive independent criticism under the sponsorship of the local government unit, whether through informal or formalized processes. It is distinguished from traditional (Euclidean) zoning and subdivision controls in that it deals with urban design, architecture, or visual impacts. Thus it includes historic preservation review, but not, in my definition, the control exercised by owners' associations or tenant groups, because these are nongovernmental and at least theoretically voluntary. It also does not include review of a project by an owner or owner's agent. Some processes and guidelines are written into the zoning, while some are separate. A few design review processes are advisory, but the vast majority (82 percent) are mandatory and legislated.

Areas of controversy

Many cities and towns sent me their design guidelines and zoning codes that deal with aesthetic issues. In studying these, one gets a better sense of what planners and their governments are hoping to achieve by instituting design review. Some goals are quite lofty, while others, perhaps not surprisingly, are more economic. Common goals include:

- improving the quality of life
- preserving and enhancing a unique place
- maintaining or upgrading the "vitality" of a place (e.g., commercial viability)
- making a comfortable and safe environment for pedestrians
- improving/protecting property values
- making change more acceptable
- making new development compatible or unified

Two other, less frequently mentioned goals include offering community input to development decisions and creating order. Interestingly, improving the design of buildings or making a beautiful city or urban space are rarely goals.

It is hard to imagine how anyone who cares about the urban environment at all could disagree with most of these goals. Yet it seems that rarely does a planner, a citizen, or, especially, an architect engage in the topic of design review without relating their experiences of woe with a design review process. Is this the result of the raw youthfulness of design review (although design control has a long and colorful history inside and outside this country), or are there are conceptual flaws in the idea, flaws that challenge our fundamental ideas about power, beauty, justice, and freedom?

The easy problems

A whole set of problems in the design review process relates to the fact that it is a new regulatory system. When most people talk about flaws in design review, they do not mention power, beauty, justice, or freedom. Instead, they seem to be closely attuned to the mechanical difficulties that plague any form of regulation: it takes too much time, the people who review projects are unqualified, it costs too much, connected people get away with anything, it is too political, the presentation requirements are too stringent, the process needs streamlining, there are too many agencies involved. While acknowledging these issues in the following questions, I do not consider them overwhelming arguments against design review. It is not that they are trivial, but rather that reasonably obvious solutions exist for them.

Design review is time-consuming and expensive. Architects considered delay to be the number two flaw of design review. (The lack of design experience on the part of the reviewers was cited as the primary flaw.) It definitely costs more in professional fees. Of those surveyed, 66 percent estimated the billable hours spent on design review to be between 5 and 25 percent of their time, a percentage that compares to the time spent on the entire preliminary project design. For the client, design review undoubtedly adds to the time and cost of projects. It adds also to the cost of government, which must administer and maintain design review apparatus in the form of additional professional staff, commissions, printed materials, law suits, hearings, and appeals. The additional cost and time factors make the process of design review even more subject to the vagaries of politics: when times are good, government can easily demand design review; when times are bad, clients can no longer afford design review and government is forced to back down or risk losing important construction projects.

Design review is easy to manipulate through persuasion, pretty pictures, and politics. Since the judgment of design is essentially discretionary and inherently difficult, it is easy to use mumbo jumbo design talk to defend decisions that are patently political (pro or con of the proposal) without letting the public become much the wiser. The political tendency is to use aesthetic control for growth control or growth encouragement, or to extract non-design-related amenities in exchange for design approval. Whatever aesthetic purpose design review may have enjoyed becomes completely subordinate to the political agenda in many cases.

Design review is being performed by overworked and inexperienced staff. In the law, the wisest, most experienced minds are called to judge. In design review, the primary reviewer is far more likely to be a junior planner without design background or an unregistered young designer or a politically appointed committee with the common thread of community prestige and power, not design expertise. The staff planners around the country that I have met are tremendously sincere individuals—they study the issues, they work hard to make the right decisions, and they receive very little guidance or reward. They are often overwhelmed by the complexity of design review, which may be the leading cause in their cry for more and better design guidelines—number one reform of design review suggested by planners who review projects.

Design review is not an efficient mechanism for improving the quality of the built environment. Aside from being time-consuming and unpredictable, design review is usually limited to certain areas, uses, or sizes of projects. It is also limited, obviously, to projects undergoing change or being newly built. It is no more effective than zoning in controlling bulk, height, and setbacks (very important elements of urban design), but it is more complicated than zoning and more subject to interpretation and politics.

The endemic problems

I have separately organized the following sets of issues because they are much more difficult to describe fully and much more difficult to solve than the regulatory issues just mentioned. As it turns out, solving one of them tends to cause problems in another; for example, making design less arbitrary and more objective tends to reduce the flexibility to make discretionary decisions that are a necessary element of aesthetic judgment. I have organized them around the robust topics of power, freedom, justice, and aesthetics.

Power

The fundamental question in the issue of power is *who*—who will judge, whose tastes will matter, whose interest it is to control the aesthetic quality of building. Many people will support design review because they believe that it gives more community control over the environment, and in many places this is true. But does the design of urban buildings belong with the community (or rather, with their appointed planning representatives) or with those who are design experts involved in solving the whole building problem?

Design review is the only field where lay people are allowed to rule over professionals directly in their area of expertise. It seems odd that we as a society believe that the improvement of the physical environment can be made by reducing the influence of architects and increasing the influence of planners and lay appointees. As architects, we owe it to ourselves to investigate how this serious turn of events could occur. Are we being punished for the International Style? Are we seen as lackeys of the greedy developer/builder? Have we lost the respect of the public because we no longer even try to defend design excellence in the face of our clients' wishes? Are we elitist, making projects that only we can understand and interpret, without attempting to educate the public or even reach them?

It is certain that architects—even those who approve of design review—are not willing to concede the judgment of design to lay persons. The number one complaint of architects who answered our survey about design review was that the reviewers were not trained professionals with experience in designing buildings. Nearly every architect who cited an exemplary process told us that what made it exemplary was the presence of knowledgeable professionals as reviewers. Even the city agency planners complained about non-professional members of review boards. Yet about 45 percent of all bodies that review project design do not have even one architect on them. Architects whose experience includes being reviewed by other designers are more likely to accept design review, although they may still find it flawed. Several respondents lamented the lay reviewer by making comparisons to the medical world, where lay people are not permitted to interfere with professional judgments.

Design review is grounded in personal—not public—interest. Perhaps if there were a public realm, a sense of public responsibility about the environment that led to design review, it would be a more legitimate process. For now, it is recognizably not so, being more a matter of protecting private property values from "offending" intrusions rather than a genuine public-spirited activity (Scheer, 1992). When neighbors attend design review sessions, their comments, even the fact of their attendance and concern, have more to do with the desire to stop someone from diminishing the view from their deck or to halt the construction of nearby apartment buildings or shopping centers in their backyards. While these are legitimate concerns, they are essentially self-centered, not public-centered. Neighbors seem to realize the inappropriateness of these self-centered concerns, because their rhetoric (as is the developers' rhetoric) is often disguised as protection of the public. Design review is not even effective at controlling the self-centered problems, since the common result of review will be to put a pretty face on a problem. Zoning is a much more powerful and direct tool to address size, layout, and location, but public officials are reluctant to use it. Reducing the size of buildings or denying a permit does not add to the tax base or economic growth, and promoters of large projects tend to wield political influence.

Community aesthetic input seems most legitimate when a public space is involved. Cincinnati's Fountain Square, for instance, is the subject of much public debate about its design, most of it by people who have a special interest, but at least some of which is genuine concern for the symbolic and public role that it has.

Freedom

The flip side of power is freedom. Unlike some of our international friends, the spirit of community in this country is heavily tempered by the belief in the rights of the individual. A somewhat related concept is the view that diversity—taken to mean varying perspectives, disagreements, and cultural differences—is a strength for society as a whole because it provides a wealth of criticism and a wealth of ideas: it keeps us on our toes. The constitution protects the individual from the power of the collective government and allows diversity to flourish.

Is design review a violation of the First Amendment right to free speech? The answer rests on two questions: 1) Are architecture and other aspects of the built environment protected as "speech" under the Constitution? 2) Can the government show a legitimate interest that would override the protection afforded to free speech in this case?

Although there has not been a single case adjudicated on the specific issue of architecture and the First Amendment, nearly all legal theorists who have approached the subject of aesthetic legislation (notably Williams, 1977; Poole, 1987; and Costonis, 1982) agree that architecture should be given the protection afforded to most forms of symbolic expression. In what appears to be an interesting contradiction, recent cases have expanded First Amendment protection to cover "commercial speech" such as signs and advertising, while at the same time the courts have overwhelmingly supported the increase in the regulation of design.

Although the language of the First Amendment clearly states that "Congress shall make no law . . . abridging the freedom of speech," there are many examples of laws in the United States that make it clear that freedom of speech is limited. In order to demonstrate that regulations and practices of design review are legitimate limits on First Amendment freedoms, theoretically a jurisdiction would need to define a very powerful public interest that would override the protection of free speech. It seems to be a dubious assertion to claim that the public interest is substantially served by controlling the color of awnings or requiring that the style of new construction is compatible with existing buildings. Even if the test requiring a substantial government interest could be met, this interest would have to be justified on grounds (such as public safety) that are not related to the suppression of an aesthetic message. In other words, it seems clear that laws that have *as their primary purpose* the curtailing of aesthetic styles or the forcing of homogeneity (known in architecture as "contextuality") would encounter First Amendment problems.

Why is it important to concern ourselves with extending First Amendment protection to architectural expression? One of the purposes of the First Amendment is to protect the individual from the tyranny of the majority. Design review/design guidelines can be interpreted as a way of reinforcing a majority-based, cultural bias (i.e., historic, white, European), especially in a threateningly pluralistic architectural and cultural milieu. Architecture is like a beacon, announcing the status, values, and interests of its culture, its creators, and its inhabitants. It could even be argued that the communicative message of architecture is so strong that community leaders, in formulating design controls, are simply trying to control the message. By excluding certain culturally diverse architectural languages or unpopular architectural styles, we literally suppress a minority viewpoint and prevent those with a different, even critical, perspective from speaking. Thus, if you believe that cosmetic imitation of quaint New England village architecture is false and damaging to the authenticity of place, you will have to express that belief without utilizing its clearest language—architecture. And the places where meaningful architecture of this nature can be explored are rapidly vanishing.

Design review rewards ordinary performance and discourages extraordinary performance. This has come to be known as the "Dolby" effect: a review that cuts out the highs and the lows. Although it is frequently cited as a criticism, it is probably less an issue in actual practice, where the excellent, exceptional, and original design proposed is often treated pretty well by design reviewers, especially if it has a famous name attached to it, and especially if the reviewers have design training. A much more severe and insidious problem, however, is related to the *perception* of the Dolby effect, because designers begin to anticipate the range of acceptability of particular reviewers and therefore rarely waste their clients' time proposing something original or exceptional. Of 170 architects who answered our survey, 80 percent felt that their proposals were somewhat or strongly influenced by what they knew to be acceptable to a design reviewer. Some architects told us that they liked design review because it brought them more clients who were impressed with their ability to design projects that were approved quickly. When contemplating the cumulative effects of this tendency, one can only become fearful of the mediocre quality of the future built environment and the dwindling potential for truly exceptional works of architecture in this era.

Justice

Some forms of design review are more "fair" than others; that is, the rules are clearer and more objective, and the procedures are more predictable and consistent. It may seem that we should move this issue to the "solvable" side of the column, chalking it up to the newness of design review and the lack of tested processes and model codes. We must keep in mind, however, that the purpose of design review is not to deliver justice to the players, but to deliver the best environment to the community. Because of the slippery nature of design, a less discretionary system may not be flexible enough to work. Therefore, the explicit and fair process might not be the one that delivers the best environment. What follows is a discussion of the issues associated with justice and protection of the individual in design review, but

the foregoing problem must be recalled while we explore these.

Design review is arbitrary and vague. Many areas of the law fall under discretionary ruling; in fact, making orderly discretionary decisions is one of the purposes of the judicial system. A police officer exercises discretion in deciding whether to arrest someone or to let him or her go. When discretion gets out of hand, as it sometimes does with the police, more rules and guidelines are laid down to limit the discretion. Just as there is no way to create a rule for every possible circumstance confronting a police officer, there is no way to formalize every rule about design. Therefore, even the most "objective" design review rests on discretionary judgment. This is not the essential legal objection, however; it is the degree to which these discretionary judgments are made consistent and nonarbitrary. Guidelines help, but many cities don't have them. Even where guidelines exist they may essentially be so vague as to be meaningless, insisting, for example, on "appropriate" scale or "compatible" design. Architects consistently complain of being sabotaged by the unclear language and unclear intentions of design review, which are clarified only in response to a specific proposal.

Design review judgments are not limited. Even though a city or town has guidelines, it is rare that the process of design review is limited to reviewing those items covered by guidelines; rather, the guidelines seem to represent a starting point, after which reviewers are relatively free to critique whatever they like or dislike about a project. There are limits, but these seem to be drawn from a political consensus about how much power the reviewers may exert. In exemplary cases, design reviewers must not only adhere to guidelines explicitly and exclusively, but must also publish "findings" that denote their critique in terms of the guidelines. Unfortunately, the more common pattern is a free-for-all, where the designer can be attacked for any aesthetic or conceptual decision and where no official document records the review criticisms.

Design review lacks due process. Because there are usually no limitations on what is reviewed, the designer is completely at the mercy of the power of the design reviewer. Also, not all projects are subject to the same process, since the process varies from district to district and use to use, and the rules and players are constantly changing. (Only 15 percent of cities have review systems unchanged from ten years ago.) In 12 percent of cities with design review, there is no appeal of a review body's decision. Most important, in most places design review is inconsistently applied. There are no provisions for referencing earlier cases or building up case law that would limit the interpretation of guidelines or judgments and help designers and interested citizens defend their positions.

Design review is difficult to protest on aesthetic grounds. Consider the situation of an architect whose building design is severely altered, but not rejected, by the design review body. He or she has two choices: carry out the alterations and get on with the project (a choice the client is likely to support), or mount a time-consuming and expensive battle, possibly losing the client and commission in the process, as well as alienating a design board that he or she must seek approvals from on a regular basis. Thus the very nature of the design review process (use of "negotiated" coercion, discretionary decisions, uneven power balance, client/architect relationship) works against an individual's ability or desire to try fight for aesthetic decisions.

Unless the developer finds it to his or her monetary advantage, cases about design seldom go to court. So, while "takings" suits, which claim monetary loss, are common, First Amendment suits, which claim the right of free expression, are nonexistent. Coupled with the tendency of clients to select architects on the basis of their ability to make it through the review process quickly, this may mean that an architect with thoughtfulness, creativity, and design integrity is at a distinct disadvantage.

Aesthetics

A design reviewer must sooner or later face up to the difficulty of deciding what is right and what is wrong—in short, making judgments. Some have argued that design review could simply drop the idea of beauty, since it is too slippery to be legal, and focus instead on "shared values" (Costonis, 1987). It is clear that many aesthetic decisions are complicated by moral issues (values). We may share the belief, for example, that mowed lawns are attractive. On the other hand, mowed lawns are not good for the environment because they waste water and provide no shelter for wildlife. Fields of native flowers may not only be better in a moral sense, they may also be more beautiful. Or maybe not. It doesn't help that these decisions are relative: one man's wildflowers are another's weed-infested lawn. Clapboard is fine here, but not there. Sign variety is desired in Times Square but not on Court House Square.

Design review is reluctant to acknowledge that there are no rules to create beauty. Architecture today admits of no reference standards, no abstract principles, no Vitruvius or Alberti or even Le Corbusier to dictate propriety. Principles of good design, for today's architects, are not universal, they are specific to the problem, place-centered, expressive of time and culture. For design review to be consistent, on the other hand, principles must be harder, broader, and applicable across the board. The arbitrariness of design review is a result of the vagueness of the guidelines, and the inconsistency of the reviewers. The solution would seem to be more definite guidelines, more precise rules, judgment tempered by precedent. The tendency to increase the use of objective criteria bears this out. Yet, design excellence is not easily defined by hard and fast principles, beauty is not subject to objective criteria, and judgments are necessarily dependent on the aesthetic response to singular, particular case, not a universal abstraction. A conflict between the increasing objectivity of design review guidelines and the very nature of postmodern architectural thought is inevitable.

Planners do not seem to be morally conflicted at the prospect of making objective criteria, on the other hand. Perhaps it is because that, in the haste to draw up the sign control standards or the contextual controls, the important questions are not being asked. What makes cities well designed or beautiful? Is making a consistent place the same as making a beautiful place? What makes a building beautiful? How can design review take heed of the different aesthetic responses that people have? Shall design review view the building as an object, to be judged without reference to its meaning or use or place in the larger site? Shall design review judge only those surficial aspects of the object such as its style or roof line? Shall design review only concern itself with contextual issues like massing and relationship to streets and leave meaning or style alone? How about the message, the "reading" of buildings—if it contributes to our response to the building, can design review judge that as well? If so, how can we give the architect freedom in his or her message? What can possibly serve as criteria for judgement? No wonder it is such a tangle.

Design review principles tend to be abstract and universal, not specific, site-related, or meaningful at the community scale. Along with the use of contextual patterns as design criteria, my survey of cities and towns with design review revealed nearly universal agreement on the elements that cities review: more than 90 percent of towns review fences and buffers, parking lot location and landscaping, signs, screening of loading and trash areas and building height. The most popular principles of good design (with at least 80 percent of towns agreeing) are directed at simple "neatening up": screening service areas and parking lots, reducing the variety of signs, and re-creation and infill of contextual patterns. Ironically, the least popular or irrelevant, according to the planners who responded, were design principles that were more specifically related to building or urban design, for example, encouraging public spaces or fountains. Other than those popular principles directed at the desire to protect a site's natural environment (a finding that slightly conflicts with the same planners' admission that they do not actually review a project's response to microclimate, sunlight and shadows, the generation of pollution, or energy efficiency), most design principles being used extensively are extremely general and transferable from one place to another.

Design review encourages mimicry and the dilution of the authenticity of place. By simplifying the rules and guidelines, by encouraging banal imitations, by denying originality, creativity, or expression of difference in any way, the design review system eventually creates a dead place, a place without surprises or exigencies of site or landmarks. Fortunately, the city's uncontrollable actors (age, events, change) take care of such superficiality by immediately beginning the process of writing over it. And fortunately, too, design review is usually not that effective and is almost never followed up after a few years. But what of places that are effectively controlled for long periods of time? Some cities that have had stringent design review for long periods of time, like Cincinnati's Mariemont (a village designed in 1921 by John Nolen), *are* completely distinct from their chaotic neighbors, with a serenity that comes only from common architectural expression and homogeneity. It could be argued that the excellent quality of Nolen's original plan for Mariemont, the coherent and consistent design of the original buildings, and the respect that this excellence inspired affected later developments a great deal more than design controls. Nevertheless, Mariemont has resisted any changes through the offices of its design review. It is as if it is frozen in time. The price of its homogeneity is fossilization, an inability to change. In a tiny town like Mariemont, the price is undoubtedly worth it. But in a large, functioning, active city, such rigidity could be functionally, morally, and socially dangerous.

Outside of special historic enclaves like Charleston, South Carolina, Mariemont, or Boston's Beacon Hill,

places where extreme control is exerted have a kinship to theme park perfection or urban fantasy and embody an idea that life lived here is not real life fraught with pain and crisis and emotion, but an artificial one, cleaned up, predictable, and safe. Thus the overcontrolled Battery Park City is the Disneyland equivalent of the real New York City—it is New York rendered as a stage set, spooky and unreal because it lacks the scars of urbanity: street people, vendors, handmade signs, noise, and bustle (Russell, 1992). Sadly, this approach also dilutes the meaning of the real space it imitates or preserves under glass. The camouflage of new "old" buildings resulting from misguided design review makes the authentic old buildings disappear and lose their importance and distinction.

Design review is the poor cousin of urban design. Ideally, design review's purpose would be to serve an urban design vision specifically developed for the place, the processes, and the public will. Of particular focus and importance for urban design implementation would be the public investment: streets, sidewalks, plazas, public buildings, maintenance, parks. The use of design review for this purpose is relatively rare. Of the cities with design review, less than 30 percent subject public buildings to design review and only 18 percent review public infrastructure for design.

Design review generally focuses on single projects rather than working from an urban design program. Sometimes, design review is performed in a vacuum, operating as a studio jury, with judgments and critiques rendered on the design merits of a single project, without a concern for its place in the urban ensemble or its impacts on the nature of the surrounding space. (Of those with design review, 26 percent did not use contextualism in any way as a measure of design quality.) More often, design review is concerned with surroundings, specifically *context*, which has become confused in meaning. At the current time, planners who use context as a measure agree strongly that contextual fit means that 1) new buildings and rehabs should respect the existing pattern of buildings and open space and 2) designs that diverge widely from surroundings should not be allowed. This, too, though, is not an urban design vision or plan, but simply the recognition of an old, existing pattern that in itself constitutes too simplistic a view of urban design. Planners without physical training may find this a comforting and completely adequate approach to urban design but it negates the importance of design to create urban space, connect places, and create hierarchy and meaning. If urban design were simply a matter of the repetition of old patterns, as it seems the practice of design review encourages, there would be no opportunity to design new responses to changes in the world, like the advent of computer communication and shopping malls.

Design review is a superficial process. Of course, the effectiveness of design review is limited by the type of things commonly reviewed: reviewers focus on the surface materials and stylistic quality of buildings, and the concealment of cars and signs. Yet the condition of the urban and suburban environment has more to do with the use of ubiquitous and automobile-scaled typologies—K-Marts, strip shopping centers, gas stations, fast food chains, endless pavement—than whether K-Mart has blue metal or yellow awnings or even tasteful signs. Landscaping, buffers, fences, and other popular design review requests are just ways of hiding the problem, not fixing it. The catalog of what is wrong with our environment is a catalog of what is wrong with our culture: the dominance of greed and consumption, the lack of public responsibility (on the part of both residents and builders), the deterioration of the inner city from poverty and crime, the energy waste of sprawl and automobile domination, and the abuse of the natural setting. To the extent that government is allowed to think that it is "taking care" of the "ugly" problem through the institution of design review, it is a diversion of political energy from environmental, social, and economic problems and, not insignificantly, it is a diversion from the necessity for genuine urban design. The design review solution is in fact reminiscent of the urban renewal solution: urban renewal postulated that the solution to the unsightly and deteriorating inner city was to tear it down and build new office buildings and high-priced housing.

The invitation to debate

This is a fascinating topic because there seems to be no end to the ideas it engages: power, freedom, beauty, morality, justice, discretion, authenticity. After five years of being a design reviewer and five years subsequently of studying it, I have come to be concerned with the enormous effect that widespread design review will have on our cities and towns, on the profession of architecture, and on the public life and freedom of our people. These effects are just beginning to be clear. What is not clear is whether design review, a very powerful government tool, can be directed in a way that answers some of the problems addressed above. Its potential for abuse and misdirection is very strong, and even dangerous. Yet the need for thoughtful urban design in American places grows every day, and the rights of the community to expect local government to contribute to good design is unquestionable.

References

Costonis, John. 1982. "Law and Aesthetic Regulation: A Critique and a Reformation of the Dilemma." *Michigan Law Review* 80:355.

Costonis, John. 1989. *Icons and Aliens: Law, Aesthetics and Environmental Change.* Champaign: University of Illinois.

Gordon, Doug. 1992. "Guiding Light or Backseat Driver" *AIA Memo*, December, p. 28.

Poole, Samuel, III. 1987. "Architectural Appearance Review Regulations and the First Amendment: The Good, the Bad and the Consensus Ugly." *Urban Lawyer* 19 (Winter): 287–344.

Russell, Francis. 1992. "Battery Park City: An American Dream of Urbanism." *Proceedings of the International Symposium on Design Review*, p. 315.

Scheer, David. 1992. "Design Performance." *Proceedings of the International Symposium on Design Review*, p. 133.

Williams, Stephen. 1977. "Subjectivity, Expression, and Privacy: Problems of Aesthetic Regulation." *Minnesota Law Review* 62 (November): 1–58.

Source and copyright

This chapter was published in its original form as:

Case Scheer, B. (1994), "Introduction: The Debate on Design Review", in Case Sheer, B. and Presier, W.F.E. (1994) (editors), *Design Review: Challenging Urban Aesthetic Control*, Chapman & Hall, New York, 3–9.

Reprinted with kind permission of Springer.

37

The inner city

Andres Duany, Elizabeth Plater-Zyberk and Jeff Speck
[2000]

For much of the twentieth century, America's inner cities have suffered from the unanticipated consequences of government policy and urban planning. The availability of the massive interstate system for daily commuting made it easy to abandon the city for houses on the periphery. The widespread construction of parking lots downtown further eased the automotive commute while turning the city into a paved no-man's-land. Racism, redlining, and the concentration of subsidized housing projects destabilized and isolated the poor, while federal home-loan programs, targeting new construction exclusively, encouraged the deterioration and abandonment of urban housing. Worse yet, the application in the city of suburban zoning standards, with their deeper setbacks and higher parking requirements, prevented the renovation of existing buildings, which became illegal under the new code.

Thinking of the city in terms of its suburban competition

The fact that policy and planning can be blamed for our cities' problems is actually encouraging—it implies that better policy and better planning can produce better cities. But that is not enough. To be effective today, urban leaders must stop thinking of their cities strictly from the inside out, only from the point of view of their own citizens. That approach may seem virtuous, but it ignores the reality of regional competition in an open market. Urban leaders must borrow a page from the suburban developers' handbook and look at their communities from the outside in, through the eyes of a customer who is comparison-shopping. A family or company moving to a metropolitan area has a choice between the city and the suburb, both of which are competing for its business. Will it be a house on Maple Street, or one in a gated subdivision? Will it be an office suite downtown, or a glass box in the business park? Often the greatest disadvantage of the city is not its own problems per se but the extreme competence and ingenuity of the suburban developers, who are constantly raising the expectations of consumers.

Suburban development is a well-honed science. New subdivisions outperform the city in category after category—in their amenity package, civic decorum, physical health; in their retail management, marketing techniques, investment security, their permitting process, and so on. Exploring each of these categories in turn helps show how the city can once again become competitive. Of course, the following discussion of what cities can learn from the suburbs should not overshadow the important physical distinctions between suburban and urban places, differences that are to be celebrated and reinforced. The greatest mistake the planners of the sixties and seventies made was to try to save the city by turning it into the suburb. Their approach could not have been worse. The future of the city lies in becoming more citylike, more pedestrian-friendly, more intense, more urban, more urbane.

The amenity package

The new suburbs are known for their private yards, their tennis clubs, their golf courses, and their guardhouses. The city does not offer these amenities in abundance, nor should it attempt to. Perhaps the best-known urban amenities are cultural and sports events. These are indeed an advantage of city life, but they are not the most effective way to renew a downtown, as some suggest. These events may periodically attract suburban visitors, but they are not sufficient to persuade people to live or work in the city. Instead, the most significant amenity that the city can offer potential residents is a *public realm*, with the vibrant street life that phrase implies. Such an environment is the compensation the city offers its customers for forgoing the suburban amenity package. If it exists, it can be enough, as downtowns from Manhattan to Portland show.

The key to active street life is creating a twenty-four-hour city, with neighborhoods so diverse in their use that they are inhabited around the clock. Eating, shopping, working, socializing—no one activity can flourish in the absence of any other, since they are all mutually reinforcing. As Jane Jacobs observed, a business district such as Wall Street normally cannot support fine restaurants, as there are not enough local residents to generate adequate dinner traffic; the restaurants are forced to make all their money between 12 and 2 p.m. The same is true of other businesses, such as health clubs, which rely on both daytime and evening clientele. Urban revitalization must begin, then, by reinstating the balance among the widest range of local uses.

Civic decorum

The first job of city government, as any resident or business owner will tell you, is to "keep it clean and safe." Suburban developers have taught prospective home buyers to expect both scrupulous security and excellent maintenance. When it comes to security, customers demand not just safety but the perception of safety, which means that all potential signs of danger must be eliminated, including graffiti and litter. These are not truly difficult to eliminate, but they must be specifically targeted and assigned a dedicated staff member, since they often slip through the cracks of city bureaucracy.

Suburban maintenance derives much of its effectiveness from providing management in small increments, through homeowners' associations (HOAs). The willingness of tax-averse citizens to pay considerable monthly fees to these associations demonstrates that elective taxation is viable if the revenues are spent in proximity, where residents feel they have some control over the outcome. The same technique can be applied to the city, and has been used with success. There are over one hundred private management districts in New York City alone, the most notorious of them focusing on Times Square. Many have complained about the sanitized, tourist-oriented outcome, but few will suggest that it has not achieved its aim.

Whether or not it implies the creation of private management districts, the success of the suburban HOA has a lot to teach the city regarding the appropriate scale of governance. The faceless bureaucracy of a large city tends to become accessible and responsive if it is broken down into neighborhood-scale increments. Indeed, some issues that seem irresolvable at the citywide level, such as parking policy, are best addressed street by street.

Physical health

Fifty years ago, America's cities provided a pedestrian environment that compared favorably with the world's best cities. What has happened in the intervening decades has been sheer lunacy: in an attempt to lure auto-dependent suburbanites downtown, consultants of every ilk turned our cities into freeways. Interstate highways were welcomed into the city core, streets were widened and made one-way, street trees were cut down, sidewalks were narrowed or eliminated, and on-street parking was replaced by massive parking lots, often on the sites of demolished historic buildings. The result was the evisceration of the public realm.

In some cities, the street was relegated entirely to the poor and the homeless in favor of underground malls and pedestrian bridges, which continue to sap vitality from the street. Cities such as Dallas and Minneapolis built these stratified systems not because of the weather but to allow cars free rein of the terra firma. Dallas justified its system with the following explanation: "One of the chief contributing factors to traffic congestion is crowds of pedestrians interrupting the flow of traffic at intersections." What some cities would now give to regain those pedestrian crowds!

It is difficult to count the number of cities that have been extensively damaged by kowtowing to the demands of the automobile. So many come to mind—Detroit, Hartford, Des Moines, Kansas City, Syracuse, Tampa—that it has to be considered the standard American urban condition. The typical result is a downtown where nobody walks, a no-man's-land brutalized by traffic. In the apotheosis of this condition—in which the mixed-use street has been replaced by an "analogous city" of pedestrian bridges and tunnels, the outcome approaches the condition of a suburban mall. But the city cannot compete with the suburb by becoming more suburban, since it has no hope of providing the same amount of convenient parking and open space.

Designing the city around automobiles has yet to be widely recognized as misguided, and pedestrians are losing the battle against the car on a daily basis. New York City has recently made it an infraction for pedestrians to cross certain midtown streets where vehicles turn onto one-way avenues. Meanwhile, in the name of pedestrian safety, traffic engineers in Los Angeles are erasing the city's crosswalks. They are taking this approach because "more pedestrians are killed in crosswalks than in unmarked intersections," ignoring that the streets with crosswalks are wider and faster. It is troubling that most efforts meant to "improve" pedestrian safety end up limiting pedestrian access.

That said, the solution is not the removal of cars from the city—far from it. The most vital American public spaces are full of cars. But these cars move slowly, due to the appropriate design of the thoroughfares. Just as in residential neighborhoods, city streets must be narrow—lanes should be ten feet wide, not twelve—with on-street parallel parking to protect the pedestrian. To make life easier for both walkers and drivers, streets should be two-way (typically one lane in each direction), since one-way streets contribute to speeding and make it difficult to find one's way around. Traffic lights must have short cycles, to avert both driver and pedestrian frustration.

The taming of the automobile is a necessary but not sufficient precondition to pedestrian life. Sidewalks must be lined with continuous building frontage, with few blank walls, parking lots, or other gaps that undermine the spatial definition of the street. Because there are never enough high-quality frontages for all streets to satisfy these criteria, the city may need to engage in what could be called *urban triage*. In pedestrian crises, as in battle, the worst-off must sometimes be sacrificed for the greater good. In the city, this means designating an "A/B" street grid. "A" streets must maintain a high standard of spatial definition and pedestrian interest, while "B" streets can be assigned to the lower-grade uses—the parking lots, garages, muffler shops, and fast-food drive-throughs. The A streets must be organized in a continuous network so that the pedestrian experience is uninterrupted. A pedestrian will cross unattractive side streets when walking on a street that provides an otherwise continuous urban fabric of buildings fronting the sidewalk with doors and windows.

The need for a clear A/B hierarchy is particularly evident in newer cities such as Dallas. Its downtown has at least a dozen city blocks of excellent pedestrian quality. Unfortunately, no two are adjacent to each other. A person cannot walk more than four hundred feet in any direction without being confronted by automobile-dominated banality. By attempting to be universally excellent, most cities are universally mediocre. The A/B grid is eminently practical because it recognizes that many cities are beggars. Desperate for the twenty-five jobs, they will accept onto their Main Street a McDonald's with an iridescent plastic jungle gym in front and a drive-through at the side. With an A/B grid, a city can give McDonald's a choice: behave in a responsible way—with doors and windows on the sidewalk and the drive-through to the rear—and you get a site on Main Street; behave in your standard boorish suburban way, and it's off to the access road with you.

One of the most compelling reasons for an A/B grid is the demand for parking lots and garages, which must not be allowed to erode the network of A streets. But even well-placed parking, in excess, can be a bad thing. Like automobile use, parking rarely costs the driver as much as it should, and is thus a *free good*. For this reason, there is always an outcry for more parking, just as there is always a demand for more lanes of traffic. Building additional parking lots causes more people to drive downtown, which requires the construction of more roadway, creating demand for yet more parking lots. The question is not how much parking is enough but how many of its buildings a city must level before it gives up trying to meet the demand.

When it comes to parking, every city must eventually answer two questions: Do new buildings have to provide their own parking, and where should that parking go? Most cities answer both of these questions incorrectly. A commitment to suburban standards of parking is a commitment to a second-class transit system used by virtually no one but the poor, since everyone else will drive. Further, most cities require new and renovated buildings to provide their own parking on site. This is probably the single greatest killer of urbanism in the United States today. It prevents the renovation of old buildings, since there is inadequate room on their sites for new parking; it encourages the construction of anti-pedestrian building types in which the building sits behind or hovers above a parking lot; it eliminates street life, since everyone parks immediately adjacent to their destination and has no reason to use the sidewalk; finally, it results in a low density of development that can keep a downtown from achieving critical mass. All told, there is nothing to be said in favor of the on-site parking requirement. Cities that wish to be pedestrian-friendly and fully developed should eliminate this ordinance immediately and provide public parking in carefully located municipal garages and lots. Parking must be considered a part of the public infrastructure, just like streets and sewers.

Consideration of the pedestrian scale must also play a role in the provision of transit. Diesel-belching buses are a poor substitute for benevolent streetcars, trolleys, and jitneys. Where laying track is not affordable, the city should consider small electric trams, which have brought new life to cities such as Chattanooga and Santa Barbara.

The reader will notice that, in discussing the physical form of the city, we have not once advocated the use of brick sidewalks, festive banners, bandstands, decorative bollards, or grassy berms ("the Five B's"). The quick fix of the eighties, the Five B's now decorate many an abandoned downtown, along with the latest-model light poles, trash cans, and decorative tree grates. There is nothing wrong with any of the Five B's, except for the fact that, alone, they can do little to bring a downtown back to life. Actually, some retail consultants argue that decorative streetscapes are counterproductive because they distract shoppers from what they really should be looking at: the store windows. The average shopfront has only eight seconds to catch the attention of a passing pedestrian, so no competition is needed from flashy sidewalks or decorative planters.

Retail management

The sad fact is that the newest, most spectacular suburban shopping center would fail within a few months if it were managed as haphazardly as the typical main street. In order for Main Street to compete against the mall, it must be run with all the expertise lavished on the mall.

Suburban retailers are predatory by definition. Most new malls, big-box outlets, and other shopping centers are built not to satisfy unmet demand but to steal demand from existing retailers. Since malls survive by undermining other malls (and main streets), they have refined the techniques of merchandising to a science. Mall designers know that, upon entering, people tend to turn right, and walk counterclockwise. They know that visitors will most

likely purchase sunglasses if they are near the rest rooms. They know that women's clothing stores will fare badly if placed near the food court. How can Main Street possibly compete? Fortunately, many of the concepts and techniques that mall designers use can be easily adapted for the benefit of the city core:

> *Centralized Management*
> *Joint Advertising and Merchandizing*
> *Anchors*
> *Strategic Relation of Anchors and Parking*
> *Proactive Leasing and Retail Mix*
> *Dimensions*
> *Retail Continuity*
> *Incubators*

All of the above techniques depend to some degree upon managed retail, a concept that causes some to bristle. "Whatever happened to a natural diversity?" they ask. "Are there any *real* places left?" The surprising answer to that question is that a *lack* of management has proven to be the enemy of diversity. It is why Key West has become an emporium of T-shirt shops, and why the only lunch available on Rodeo Drive for under ten dollars consists of potato chips and a soda. When left alone, retailers tend to repeat easy successes and entire sectors become homogeneous. Variety is achieved not through natural selection but through careful programming. Thanks to management, the main street of Disney's Celebration provides not only restaurants for four different price ranges but a bar that is required to stay open until the last movie gets out. Even if there are only two customers, martinis are available at midnight. Does this make Celebration any worse, or any less real?

Marketing

Suburban developers have lapsed into a bigger-is-better, "build it and they will come" mentality. Typically, they direct their efforts at the largest market segments only, providing huge tracts of housing and big-box retail. This approach may make some sense in the urban periphery, where a critical mass is necessary to attract customers, and where homogeneity is considered a virtue. But in the city, where a diversity of form and activity already exits—and is cherished—development must be approached on a smaller scale, and with a thorough understanding of the customer base.

One of the most effective ways to revitalize an underbuilt city core is to subdivide undeveloped superblocks into smaller increments affordable to individual investors. This technique opens the door for local stakeholders to become small-scale developers, lessening the city's dependence on the few national-scale real-estate corporations. The town house lot, usually no more than twenty-four feet wide, is an ideal increment of development, as it can hold a home, a business, or both. Many superblocks now lie fallow, thanks to the unsuccessful mega-projects of the eighties, "quick fix" solutions that failed owing to their reliance on unrealistically large increments of investment.

In addition to operating at the correct scale, renewal efforts must proceed with realistic expectations about who will move downtown, and market accordingly. According to William Kraus, the market segment that pioneers difficult areas is the "risk-oblivious": artists and recent college graduates. These are followed by the "risk-aware": yuppies; and finally by the "risk-averse": the middle class. City developers must anticipate this often inevitable sequence, and provide the appropriate housing at the appropriate time. For example, the risk-oblivious are not well served by finished units with separate bedrooms but by lofts, which are large, tough, inexpensive, yet easily converted to yuppie housing upon the arrival of the risk-aware.

To encourage urban pioneers, cities must be prepared to bend the rules a little. Zoning that prohibits housing in commercial and industrial areas—often largely empty and therefore affordable—must be replaced with a mixed-use classification. The on-site parking requirement can be waived, as pioneers can be expected to park on the street, if they own cars at all. In addition, a number of antiquated laws, introduced to fight the tenement houses of the turn of the century, can make urban pioneering prohibitively expensive. For example, the BYOS (bring your own sheetrock) unit should be legalized, and developers should be able to get certificates of occupancy for apartments that are habitable but as yet unfinished. Otherwise, urban living will be affordable only to those who have no desire to live there.

Any proper urban marketing analysis must also include families with children, the market segment that is hardest for the city to serve. Bringing families downtown is possible only with good schools, and good city schools rarely occur without a consolidated regional school district. Only if city schools are able to share the resources of those in the wealthier suburbs can large numbers of parents be convinced to locate their families downtown. When a consolidated school district is not a realistic possibility, cities should take measures to encourage parochial and charter schools downtown, giving them land and other special incentives. It is important to be realistic: revitalization

efforts should not focus unduly on bringing families back to the inner city. In truth, many urban neighborhoods do quite well in the absence of children. Of course, the long-term health and diversity of a city is ultimately tied closely to the quality of its schools.

A more difficult issue to tackle is gentrification. At the macroscopic level, activists are justified in their fight against gentrification if it is likely to result in the displacement of tenants. But at the microscopic level of the neighborhood, fighting gentrification is tantamount to fighting *improvement*; revitalization will not occur without it. Indeed, the challenge faced by most center cities today is not to provide affordable housing—which they typically supply at alarming ratios, thanks to public subsidies—but to create a market for middle-class housing. Cities, after all, cannot flourish without taxpaying residents. For this reason, city planners charged with the task of revitalizing a downtown have little choice but to encourage gentrification or resign from their job. It is sometimes helpful to investigate the source of the complaint: the cry of "gentrification" is less often sounded by citizens who fear displacement than by politicians who suspect that racial and economic integration will undermine their power base.

One technique that has been used to stop gentrification is to limit the rise in tax assessments. But keeping real estate assessments down can be a real problem, as this can prevent home and business owners from obtaining building improvement loans. Once again, fighting gentrification proves counterproductive to the improvement efforts of existing residents. For this reason, governments and activists must turn their attention from stopping gentrification to mitigating its negative impact. Gentrification became a dirty word because it used to occur in the absence of a safety net, and many a displaced tenant in the sixties had nowhere to go. Nowadays, that need not be the case.

Discussion of urban marketing and development implies something that many might find surprising: a proactive municipal government acting in the role of the developer. Rather than waiting for Gerald Hines or Hyatt to come to town, civic leaders must develop a physical vision for their city which they commit to and then actively promote. Rather than being victimized by the self-interests of the private sector, they must determine the type, scale, and quality of new growth and then act as the lead booster for that growth.

This approach seems inescapable when one considers the greater expense and difficulty that developers face when they try to work downtown. As the developer Henry Turley puts it, "It costs $1.25

to build downtown what it costs $1.00 to build in the suburbs, and that's ignoring all the hassles." For this reason and others, developers operate on an extremely tilted playing field, one that discourages inner-city investment in favor of exurban Greenfield development. Thus, while it is the first rule of regional planning to concentrate growth in existing urban centers, many factors conspire against doing so, including fragmented property ownership, title problems, inappropriate zoning, higher land costs, deteriorating or inadequate infrastructure, environmental contamination, historic preservation limitations, complex regulatory frameworks, unwieldy permitting processes, neighborhood politics, opposition to gentrification, and higher taxes, to name a few. As a result of these disincentives, inner-city development tends to attract only those investors who are either altruistically motivated or efficient manipulators of government subsidies. Until the disincentives are eliminated, the inner city will continue to be outperformed by the outer suburbs.

Investment security

Owing to single-use zoning and deed restrictions, suburbia offers developers and purchasers enormous predictability regarding their investment. If a family buys a single-family house in a new subdivision, it can be certain that it will never be surrounded by anything but single-family houses. Similar assurance can be found in an office park. Whether or not the result is something to celebrate, it is certainly comforting.

In contrast, the risk associated with urban development can be summed up in a single word: *dingbat*. A dingbat is a type of small apartment building, popular throughout the Sun Belt, which sits on stilts over a parking lot—a direct outcome of the ubiquitous American on-site parking requirement. The construction of a single dingbat on a street of row houses is all that is necessary to bring down the real estate value of the entire block. Yet, in many cities, there is nothing to stop this from occurring. Zoning has a history of changing over time with little regard to building compatibility. Moreover, most zoning codes, focused on numbers and ratios rather than on physical form, can't tell the difference between a dingbat and a block of row houses, as they may be statistically identical. For better or worse, the city

will not be able to compete against the suburb for risk-averse investors until it can provide the same level of protection against dingbats and their ilk. Without physical predictability, there can be no investment security.

The best way to ensure predictability in downtown neighborhoods is with an *urban code*. This cannot be a conventional words-and-numbers zoning code, focusing only on uses and square feet, but must instead be a physically based code that visually describes the building's volume, articulation, and relationship to the street—in other words, its *building type*. This code should ensure that all building types are pedestrian-friendly, and that buildings are located near buildings of similar type. It should also specify the building's alignment, in order to shape public spaces. This discipline is especially important in areas of mixed use, as it is a consistent streetscape that makes different uses compatible. Such a code is not difficult to write, but it requires an approach to city planning that has fallen out of use in recent years. Rather than specifying what it doesn't want, this code specifies what it does want, which implies a degree of proactive physical vision that is currently rare among urban planning and zoning boards. One such urban code is the Traditional Neighborhood Development Ordinance, which is currently being used and imitated by municipalities nationwide.

In certain instances, it makes sense to complement the urban code with a second document, an *architectural code*. Cities and neighborhoods hoping to achieve a high degree of harmony in building style—either to protect and enhance their historic character or to develop a new character of their own—can benefit from a code that addresses building materials, proportions, colors, and other surface design issues. Charleston, Santa Barbara, Nantucket, and Santa Fe are well-known places that owe their success in part to architectural coding.

The good news about these codes is that once they are evolved and enacted, processing can be simplified dramatically. Because these codes are prescriptive rather than proscriptive, buildings that correspond to their specific physical criteria can be permitted automatically and allowed to move forward immediately. To assist in this process, city planning and building departments must be encouraged to see themselves as an enabling staff rather than a regulatory staff.* Instead of fighting

---

* Ideally, each developer submittal should be handled by a single contact, and all of the necessary approvals should be integrated into a single process, such that zoning, architectural, historic preservation, public works, environmental, and all other reviews occur simultaneously.

bad development, they can concentrate on supporting good development, which is a much more rewarding job. The implementation of such a process would be an important step in leveling the playing field between suburban and urban development, so that suburban developers could be enticed back into the inner city.

The permitting process

There is a general perception that it is difficult to get projects permitted in the suburbs. This is often true, but only as it refers to *projects:* not to buildings, but to entire office parks and subdivisions, which are often the size of towns. In the suburbs, there are two types of developer: the master developer, who must secure the initial site permits, and the building developer, who then constructs individual buildings within the project. While an office park developer may have to endure a painful permitting process, the builder who subsequently wishes to place an office building within that park faces no hassles whatsoever. He is given a site, a building footprint, and perhaps some rules regarding construction quality, and he's ready to go. Only a routine building permit stands between him and construction.

The problem with developing individual buildings in the inner city is that there are no master developers running interference for the building developers. Instead, the would-be builder must weed through a complicated and confusing zoning code and then prepare for a series of confrontations with permitting authorities, local organizations, and resistant neighbors. If the city is to compete against the suburb, someone must play the role of the master developer, and in most cases this someone can only be the city government itself. As discussed above, the city can best achieve true predictability by replacing its zoning ordinances with a physical plan, one with as much precision as that of a new office park, in which every projected building is given shape. This plan must be created through a public process in which citizens participate with the understanding that the outcome will become the law. Once completed and enacted, this plan will control future growth, such that potential developers know exactly what they can build and when they can start construction. Under such a system—currently active in West Palm Beach, Florida, and Providence, Rhode Island—the city can begin to offer building developers a permitting environment that does not make them flee to the suburbs in frustration.

There are many benefits to creating a physically prescriptive master plan for a city, not the least of which is that it allows government to return to the business of governing. Currently, city commission agendas are overwhelmed by a disproportionate number of contests over individual real estate projects, as if real estate were more important than schooling, public safety, economic development, or quality of life. These battles are fought precisely because there is no master plan in place to guide development. Completing and enacting a new city master plan can often seem like a war, but isn't it better to wage one big war and get it over with, rather than fighting new battles every week?

One wonders why more cities have not completed effective master plans, and why some cities create master plans but fail to enact them. As with the perpetuation of any patently unworkable system, the answer lies in the fact that certain powerful people benefit from the status quo. In the case of real estate permitting, the situation is clear. Most cities currently have on the books a vast collection of land-use ordinances so vague, confusing, and negotiable that few developers even try to follow them. In such an environment, the developers know that the most important design decision they can make is to retain the right attorney or planner. There is no shortage of such experts, who essentially tell developers, "I'll get you the best deal in town."

These consultants thrive in the swamp of unpredictability. A master plan that offers clarity is their mortal enemy, as it immediately diminishes the value of their services. When such a plan is completed, they begin to stir, warning their developer clients, "Watch out—if that plan is passed, you'll lose your flexibility!" Eventually, the master plan is rejected, and the status quo prevails. For this reason, master plans must be enacted in principle as quickly as possible. The record still belongs to our plan for Stuart, Florida, which was presented at 4 p.m. one day and was law four hours later. Any realistic master plan will include an implementation component with a schedule for its passage.

It is natural to be cautious, even pessimistic, when addressing the subject of master plans. So many "shelf plans" have been completed—plans that do nothing but gather dust—that wise municipalities do not jump into the planning process without trepidation. Why spend the time and money, when so many plans have failed? The obvious answer to this question is to study the plans that have been successful and to find out what made them so. While it is dangerous to generalize, most successful plans seem to share two qualities: first, they were completed through a fully open, interactive, public involvement process; and second, they include a physically based urban code that was passed into law. As such, they are not dependent on the future goodwill of individuals who may not even be there in the long term.

Thanks to changing demographics and a strong economy, America's cities have already begun to experience a renaissance. More and more people are finding suburbia poorly suited to their needs, especially the bored young and the non-driving old. It is not unreasonable to expect that the early years of the twenty-first century will be a time of reinvestment in our older downtown cores. As it occurs, it is essential that growth follow traditional neighborhood principles rather than being simply a higher-density version of auto-dependent sprawl. This latter outcome is by no means unlikely, since so many developers are experienced in suburban building and nothing else. It will fall to the cities to protect themselves from a watered-down future of isolated towers and parking lots. If they are successful, not only will their own citizens benefit but so will the many residents of nearby suburbia, who will again be given the opportunity to experience authentic urbanity on a regular basis.

References

Hart, Stanley, and Alvin Spivak. *The Elephant in the Bedroom: Automobile Dependence and Denial; Impacts on the Economy and Environment.* Pasadena, Calif.: New Paradigm Books, 1993.

Howard, Philip K. *The Death of Common Sense: How Law Is Suffocating America.* New York: Random House, 1994.

Kay, Jane Holtz. *Asphalt Nation: How the Automobile Took Over America, and How We Can Take It Back.* New York: Crown, 1997.

Kent, Christopher. *Market Performance: The Town of Seaside.* Report written 1991, updated 1999.

Lasch, Christopher. *The Revolt of the Elites and the Betrayal of Democracy.* New York: W. W. Norton, 1995.

Petersen, David. "Smart Growth for Center Cities." *ULI on the Future: Smart Growth—Economy, Community, Environment.* Washington, D.C.: Urban Land Institute, 1998: 46–56.

Tu, Charles, and Mark Eppli. *Valuing the New Urbanism: The Case of Kentlands.* Report by the George Washington University Department of Finance, 1997.

Source and copyright

This chapter was published in its original form as:

Duany, A., Plater-Zyberk, E. and Speck, J. (2000), 'The Inner City', *Suburban Nation: The Rise of Sprawl and the Decline of the American Dream,* North Point Press, New York, 153–182.

Reprinted by permission of S11/sterling Lord Literistic, Inc. Copyright 1999 Andres Duany.

Bibliography

Alexander, C. (1979), *The Timeless Way of Building*, Oxford University Press, Oxford.

Alexander, C., Ishikawa, S. and Silverstein, M. (1977), *A Pattern Language: Towns, Buildings, Construction,* Oxford University Press, Oxford.

Appleyard, D. (1991), 'Foreward,' from Moudon, A.V. (1991), *Public Streets for Public Use*, Columbia University Press, New York, 5–8.

Ashworth, G.J. (1997), 'Conservation as preservation or as heritage: Two paradigms and two answers', *Built Environment*, **23** (2), 92–102.

Bacon, E. (1992, first published in 1967), *Design of Cities*, Thames & Hudson, London.

Banerjee, T. (2001), 'The future of public space: beyond invented streets and reinvented places', *Journal of the American Planning Association*, **67**, 9–24.

Barnett, J. (1982), *An Introduction to Urban Design*, Harper & Row, New York.

Bentley, I. (1999), *Urban Transformations: Power, people and urban design*, Routledge, London.

Bentley, I., Alcock, A., Murrain, P. McGlynn, S. and Smith G. (1985), *Responsive Environments: A Manual for Designers*, Architectural Press, London.

Bosselmann, P. (1998), *Representations of Places: Reality and Realism in City Design*, University of California Press, Berkeley.

Brand, S. (1994), *How Buildings Age: What happens after they are built*, Penguin Books, Harmondsworth.

Buchanan, P. (1988), 'A report from the front', *Architects Journal*, **188**, 21–7.

Calthorpe, P. (2005), 'New Urbanism: Principles or style?', in Fishman, R. (editor) (2005), *New Urbanism: Peter Calthorpe versus Lars Lerup*, Michigan Debates on Urbanism (Volume II), The University of Michigan, Ann Arbor, 15–38.

Cantacuzino, S. (1994), *What Makes a Good Building? An inquiry by the Royal Fine Art Commission*, RFAC, London.

Carmona, M. (2001), *Housing Design Quality, Through Policy, Guidance and Review*, London, Spon Press.

Carmona, M., de Magalhaes C., Edwards, M., Awuor, B. and Aminossehe, S. (2000), *The Value of Urban Design*, Thomas Telford.

Carmona, M., Heath, T., Oc, T. Tiesdell, T. (2003), *Public Places Urban Spaces, The Dimensions of Urban Design*, Oxford, Architectural Press.

Carr, S., Francis, M., Rivlin, L.G. and Stone, A.M. (1992), *Public Space*, Cambridge University Press, Cambridge.

Conzen, M.P. (1960), 'Alnwick: A study in town plan analysis', *Transactions, Institute of British Geographers*, **27**, 1–122.

Cooper Markus, C. and Sarkissian, W. (1986), *Housing As If People Mattered*, University of California Press, Berkeley, California.

Cowan, R. (2004), *A Dictionary of Urbanism*, Streetwise, London.

Cullen, G. (1971), *The Concise Townscape*, second edition Architectural Press, London. (First edition published 1961.)

Cuthbert, A. (2003), *Designing Cities, Critical Reading in Urban Design*, Blackwell Publishing, Oxford.

Dickens, P.G. (1980), 'Social sciences and design theory', *Environment & Planning B: Planning & Design*, **7**, 353–60.

Duany, A., Plater-Zyberk, E. and Speck, J. (2000), *Suburban Nation: The Rise of Sprawl and the Decline of the American Dream*, North Point Press, New York, 153–82.

Duffy, F. (1990), 'Measuring Building Performance', *Facilities*, May.

Ellis, C. (2004), 'The New Urbanism: Critiques and rebuttals', *Journal of Urban Design*, **7**(3), 261–91.

Gehl, J. (1996), *Life Between Buildings: Using Public Space*, Arkitektens Forlag, Skive.

Gehl, J. (1971, third edition 1996), *Life Between Buildings: Using public space*, Arkitektens Forlag, Skive.

George R.V. (1997), 'A procedural explanation for contemporary urban design', *Journal of Urban Design*, **2**(2), 143–61.

Gibberd, F. (1953), *Town Design*, Architectural Press, London.

Goldberger, P. (1996), 'The Rise of the Private City', in Vitullo-Martin, J. (1996) (Editor), *Breaking Away: The Future of Cities: Essays in Memory of Robert F. Wagner, Jnr*, The Twentieth Century Fund Press, New York, 135–47.

Hannigan, J. (1998), *Fantasy City: Pleasure and profit in the postmodern metropolis*, Routledge, London.

Hillier, B. (1988), 'Against enclosure', in Teymur, N., Markus, T. and Wooley, T. (1988) (editors), *Rehumanising Housing*, Butterworths, London, 63–88.

Hillier, B. (1996a), *Space is the Machine*, Cambridge University Press, Cambridge.

Hillier, B. (1996b), 'Cities as Movement Economies', *Urban Design International*, **1** (1), 41–60.

Hillier, B. (1999), 'The hidden geometry of deformed grids: Or, why space syntax works, when it looks as though it shouldn't', *Environment & Planning B: Planning & Design*, **26**, 169–91.

Hillier, B. and Hanson, J. (1984), *The Social Logic of Space*, Cambridge University Press, Cambridge.

Hillier, B. and Penn, A. (2004), 'Rejoinder to Carlo Ratti, *Environment & Planning B: Planning & Design*, **31** (4), 501–11.

Hillier, B., Penn, A., Hanson, J., Gajewski, T. and Xu, J. (1993), 'Natural Movement: or configuration and attraction in urban pedestrian movement', *Environment & Planning B: Planning & Design*, **20**, 29–66.

Jacobs, J. (1961), *The Death and Life of Great American Cities*, Penguin, Harmondsworth.

Jacobs, J. (1961, 1984 edition), *The Death and Life of Great American Cities: The failure of modern town planning*, Peregrine Books, London.

Jarvis, R. (1980), 'Urban environments as visual art or social setting', *Town Planning Review*, **51**, 50–66.

Kelbaugh, D. (2002), *Repairing the American Metropolis*, University of Washington Press, Seattle, 94–132.

Knox, P. (1987), 'The social production of the built environment: Architects, architecture and the post-modern city', *Progress in Human Geography*, **11**, 354–78.

Knox, P. and Ozolins, P. (2000), 'The built environment', in Knox, P. and Ozolins, P. (2000) (Editors), *Design Professionals and the Built Environment: An Introduction*, Wiley, London, 3–10.

Krier, L. (1990, 'Urban Components', in Papadakis, A. and Watson, H. (eds), *New Classicism: Omnibus Edition*, Academy Editions, London, 196–211.

LaFarge, A. (2000) (editor), *The Essential William H. Whyte*, Fordham University Press, New York.

Lang, J. (1994), *Urban Design: The American Experience*, Van Nostrand Reinhold, New York.

Loukaitou-Sideris, A. (1996), 'Cracks in the City: Addressing the constraints and potentials of urban design', *Journal of Urban Design* **1** (1), 91–103.

Loukaitou-Sideris, A. and Banerjee, T. (1998), 'Postmodern urban form', in Loukaitou-Sideris, A. and Banerjee, T. (1998), *Urban Design Downtown: Poetics and Politics of Form*, University of California Press, Berkeley.

Lynch, K. (1960), *The Image of the City*, MIT Press, Cambridge, Mass.

Lynch, K. (1972), 'The presence of the past', *What Time is This Place?*, MIT Press, Cambridge, Mass.

Lynch, K. (1984), *Reconsidering The Image of the City*, in Banrejee, T. and Southworth, M. (1991) (editors), *City Sense and City Design: Writings and Projects of Kevin Lynch*, MIT Press, Cambridge, Mass., 247–56.

MacCormac, R. (1994), 'Understanding Transactions', *Architectural Review*, **194**, 1165, 70–3.

McGlynn, S. and Murrain, P. (1994), 'The politics of urban design', *Planning Practice & Research*, **9**, 311–20.

McHarg, I. (1969), *Design with Nature*, Doubleday & Company, New York.

Madanipour, A. (1997) 'Ambiguities of urban design', *Town Planning Review*, **68** (3), 363–83.

Martin, L. (1972), 'The grid as generator', in Martin, L. and March, L. (1972) (editors), *Urban Space and Structures*, Cambridge University Press, Cambridge, 6–27.

Maslow, A. (1962), *Towards a Psychology of Being'*, Van Nostrand, New York.

Mitchell, D. (1995), 'The End of Public Space? People's Park, Definitions of the Public and Democracy', *Annals of the Association of American Geographers*, **85**, 108–133.

Norberg-Schulz, C. (1971), *Existence, Space and Architecture*, Studio Vista, London.

Oldenburg, R. (1999), *The Great Good Place: Cafes, coffee shops, bookstores, bars, hair salons and the other great hangouts at the heart of a community*, second edition, Marlowe & Company, New York. (First edition published 1989.)

Project for Public Space (2001), *How to Turn A Place Around: A handbook for creating successful public spaces*, Project for Public Space, Inc, New York.

Punter, J. and Carmona, M. (1997) *The Design Dimension of Planning, Theory, Content and Best Practice for Design Policies*, London, E&FN Spon.

Ratti, C. (2004a), 'Space syntax: Some inconsistencies', *Environment & Planning B: Planning & Design*, **31** (4), 487–99.

Ratti, C. (2004b), 'Rejoinder to Hillier and Penn', *Environment & Planning B: Planning & Design*, **31** (4), 513–16.

Relph, E. (1976), *Place and Placelessness*, Pion, London.

Rowe, C. and Koetter, F. (1978), *Collage City*, MIT Press, Cambridge Mass.

Rowley, A. (1998), 'Private property decision makers and the quality of urban design', *Journal of Urban Design*, **3** (2), 151–73.

Scheer, B.C. (1994), 'Introduction: The debate on design review', in Case Scheer, B. and Presier, W. (1994) (editors), *Design Review: Challenging Urban Aesthetic Control*, Chapman & Hall, New York, 3–9.

Sharp, T. (1946), *The Anatomy of the Village*, Penguin, Harmondsworth.

Sharp, T. (1948), *Oxford Replanned*, Architectural Press, London.

Sircus, J. (2001), 'Invented Places', *Prospect*, **81**, Sept/Oct, 30–35.

Sitte, C. (1889), *City Planning According to Artistic Principles* (translated by Collins, G.R. and Collins, C.C, 1965), Phaidon Press, London.

Steadman, P. (2004), 'Guest editorial: Developments in space syntax', *Environment & Planning B: Planning & Design*, **31** (4), 483–86.

Sternberg, E. (2000), 'An integrative theory of urban design', *Journal of the American Planning Association*, **66** (3), 265–78.

Tibbalds, F. (1992), *Making People-Friendly Towns: Improving the public environment in towns and cities*, Longman, Harlow.

Tiesdell, S. and Adams, D. (2004), 'Design matters: Major house builders and the design challenge of brownfield development contexts', *Journal of Urban Design*, **9** (1), 23–45.

Trancik, R. (1986), *Finding Lost Space: Theories of Urban Design*, Van Nostrand Reinhold, New York.

Tugnutt, A. and Robertson, M. (1987), *Making Townscape: A contextual approach to building in an urban setting*, Batsford, London.

Venturi, R., Scott Brown, D. and Izenour, S. (1972), *Learning from Los Vegas: The Forgotten Symbolism of Architectural Form*, MIT Press, Cambridge, Mass.

White, E. (1999), *Path–Portal–Place, Appreciating Public Space in Urban Environments*, Architectural Media Ltd, Tallahassee.

Whyte, W.H. (1980), *The Social Logic of Small Urban Spaces*, Conservation Foundation, Washington D.C.

Whyte, W.H. (1988), *City: Rediscovering the Centre*, Doubleday, New York.

Worskett, R. (1969), *The Character of Towns: An approach to conservation*, Architectural Press, London.

Zukin, S. (1991), *Landscapes of Power: From Detroit to Disneyland*, Blackwell, Oxford.

Zukin, S. (1995), *The Cultures of Cities*, Blackwell, Oxford, 49–77.

Index

University of Strathclyde
Dept. of Architecture and Building Science
Library